HUMAN DEVELOPMENT 96/97

Twenty-Fourth Edition

Editor

Karen L. Freiberg
University of Maryland, Baltimore

Dr. Karen Freiberg has an interdisciplinary educational and employment background in nursing, education, and developmental psychology. She received her B.S. from the State University of New York at Plattsburgh, her M.S. from Cornell University, and her Ph.D. from Syracuse University. She has worked as a school nurse, a pediatric nurse, a public health nurse for the Navajo Indians, an associate project director for a child development clinic, a researcher in several areas of child development, and a university professor. She is the author of an award-winning textbook, *Human Development: A Life-Span Approach*, which is now in its fourth edition. She is currently on the faculty at the University of Maryland, Baltimore County.

A Library of Information from the Public Press

Cover illustration by Mike Eagle

Dushkin Publishing Group/
Brown & Benchmark Publishers
Sluice Dock, Guilford, Connecticut 06437

The Annual Editions Series

Annual Editions is a series of over 65 volumes designed to provide the reader with convenient, low-cost access to a wide range of current, carefully selected articles from some of the most important magazines, newspapers, and journals published today. Annual Editions are updated on an annual basis through a continuous monitoring of over 300 periodical sources. All Annual Editions have a number of features designed to make them particularly useful, including topic guides, annotated tables of contents, unit overviews, and indexes. For the teacher using Annual Editions in the classroom, an Instructor's Resource Guide with test questions is available for each volume.

VOLUMES AVAILABLE

Abnormal Psychology
Africa
Aging
American Foreign Policy
American Government
American History, Pre-Civil War
American History, Post-Civil War
American Public Policy
Anthropology
Archaeology
Biopsychology
Business Ethics
Child Growth and Development
China
Comparative Politics
Computers in Education
Computers in Society
Criminal Justice
Developing World
Deviant Behavior
Drugs, Society, and Behavior
Dying, Death, and Bereavement
Early Childhood Education
Economics
Educating Exceptional Children
Education
Educational Psychology
Environment
Geography
Global Issues
Health
Human Development
Human Resources
Human Sexuality

India and South Asia
International Business
Japan and the Pacific Rim
Latin America
Life Management
Macroeconomics
Management
Marketing
Marriage and Family
Mass Media
Microeconomics
Middle East and the Islamic World
Multicultural Education
Nutrition
Personal Growth and Behavior
Physical Anthropology
Psychology
Public Administration
Race and Ethnic Relations
Russia, the Eurasian Republics, and Central/Eastern Europe
Social Problems
Sociology
State and Local Government
Urban Society
Western Civilization, Pre-Reformation
Western Civilization, Post-Reformation
Western Europe
World History, Pre-Modern
World History, Modern
World Politics

Cataloging in Publication Data
Main entry under title: Annual Editions: Human development. 1996/97.
    1. Child study—Periodicals. 2. Socialization—Periodicals. 3. Old age—Periodicals. I. Freiberg, Karen L., *comp*. II. Title: Human development.
ISBN 0-697-31666-1   155'.05   72-91973
HQ768.A44

Twenty-Fourth Edition

Printed in the United States of America

Editors/Advisory Board

EDITOR

Karen L. Freiberg
University of Maryland, Baltimore

ADVISORY BOARD

STAFF

To the Reader

In publishing ANNUAL EDITIONS we recognize the enormous role played by the magazines, newspapers, and journals of the *public press* in providing current, first-rate educational information in a broad spectrum of interest areas. Within the articles, the best scientists, practitioners, researchers, and commentators draw issues into new perspective as accepted theories and viewpoints are called into account by new events, recent discoveries change old facts, and fresh debate breaks out over important controversies.

Many of the articles resulting from this enormous editorial effort are appropriate for students, researchers, and professionals seeking accurate, current material to help bridge the gap between principles and theories and the real world. These articles, however, become more useful for study when those of lasting value are carefully *collected, organized, indexed,* and *reproduced* in a *low-cost format,* which provides easy and permanent access when the material is needed.

That is the role played by *Annual Editions.* Under the direction of each volume's *Editor,* who is an expert in the subject area, and with the guidance of an *Advisory Board,* we seek each year to provide in each ANNUAL EDITION a current, well-balanced, carefully selected collection of the best of the public press for your study and enjoyment. We think you'll find this volume useful, and we hope you'll take a moment to let us know what you think.

Annual Editions: Human Development 96/97 articles highlight many of the more important topics being studied by developmentalists today. These articles have been collected to make your exploration of human behavior interesting, even exciting! They have been weighed together thoughtfully, with input from many expert advisors.

The selections in this compendium have been arranged by age, chronologically, beginning before birth and ending with death. This separation is useful for organizational purposes. However, the ages of human development are more like a circle. Each age is inseparable from all others. One's entire life is a convergence of things from the beginning, from the middle, and from the end of life. Likewise, *Annual Editions: Human Development 96/97* is arranged by topic to give an order to your readings. But each topic of human development is embodied in all the others. Life is a junction of things physical, cognitive, social, emotional, anthropological, economic, and spiritual. A linear view of development is too shallow and oversimplistic. As you read these selections, keep in mind the unity and continuity of all life. The whole person is paramount.

Many of the articles in this edition of *Annual Editions: Human Development* ask questions that have no answers. They are intended to make you ponder various alternatives. Life frequently has no right or wrong answers, but relative answers based on environment and extenuating circumstances. Controversy can promote healthy mental exercise. Different viewpoints should be considered. Ultimately, every human being can choose to accept or reject proposals that are advanced based on his or her own careful consideration of alternate perceptions.

No one theoretical perspective has been adapted by all the writers of these collected papers. Several theorists are discussed in various places. Many authors are eclectic; they have employed individual elements from a variety of theories in their literary frameworks.

An ecological view of human development considers the unity and continuity of human groups within their physical and social environments. In keeping with an ecological framework, we have carefully included selections for you to read that deal with: (1) microsystems of the ecology (family, school, work); (2) exosystems of the environment (television, community concerns); (3) macrosystems within which we live (economics, government); (4) mesosystems in the middle of other systems (homes vis-à-vis health organizations, schools vis-à-vis neighborhoods); and (5) the unique individual's own paramount contribution to development (genes, brain organization, maturation).

We hope you will be enriched by the selections in this compendium. Please use the postage-paid article rating form on the last page of this book to express your opinions. We hope to maximize both the usefulness of, and your enjoyment of, each revision of *Annual Editions: Human Development.*

Karen Freiberg

Karen Freiberg
Editor

Unit
1

Genetic and Prenatal Influences on Development

Eight selections discuss genetic influences on development, reproductive technology, and the effects of substance abuse on prenatal development.

The concepts in bold italics are developed in the article. For further expansion please refer to the Topic Guide and the Index.

Unit 2

Development during Infancy and Early Childhood

Seven selections profile the impressive abilities of infants and young children, examine the ways in which children learn, and look at sex differences.

The concepts in bold italics are developed in the article. For further expansion please refer to the Topic Guide and the Index.

Unit 3

Development during Childhood—Cognition and Schooling

Eight selections examine human development during childhood, paying specific attention to social and emotional development, cognitive and language development, and development problems.

The concepts in bold italics are developed in the article. For further expansion please refer to the Topic Guide and the Index.

Unit

4

Development during Childhood—Family and Culture

Twelve selections discuss the impact of home and culture
on childrearing and child development. The topics include
parenting styles, family structure, and cultural influences.

The concepts in bold italics are developed in the article. For further expansion please refer to the Topic Guide and the Index.

Unit 5

Development during Adolescence and Young Adulthood

Seven selections explore a wide range of issues and topics concerning adolescence and early adulthood.

Unit 6

Development during Middle and Late Adulthood

Nine selections review a variety of biological and psychological aspects of aging, questioning the concept of set life stages.

The concepts in bold italics are developed in the article. For further expansion please refer to the Topic Guide and the Index.

The concepts in bold italics are developed in the article. For further expansion please refer to the Topic Guide and the Index.

Topic Guide

This topic guide suggests how the selections in this book relate to topics of traditional concern to students and professionals involved with the study of human development. It is useful for locating articles that relate to each other for reading and research. The guide is arranged alphabetically according to topic. Articles may, of course, treat topics that do not appear in the topic guide. In turn, entries in the topic guide do not necessarily constitute a comprehensive listing of all the contents of each selection.

TOPIC AREA	TREATED IN	TOPIC AREA	TREATED IN
Adolescence	36. Adolescence: Whose Hell Is It? 37. Teenage Turning Point 38. HIV Infected Youth Speaks	Depression	36. Adolescence: Whose Hell Is It? 37. Teenage Turning Point 41. Back Off! 42. When Violence Hits Home 44. New Middle Age
Adoption	24. Lifelong Impact of Adoption 39. Psychotrends	Divorce	27. Yours, Mine, and Ours 33. Miracle of Resiliency 40. Is There Love after Baby? 41. Back Off!
Aggression	12. Mental Health for Babies 15. Assertiveness vs. Aggressiveness 26. Sibling Connections 34. Televised Violence and Kids 42. When Violence Hits Home	Drug Abuse	4. Eugenics Revisited 5. Cocaine-Exposed Infants 7. When a Pregnant Woman Drinks 8. Sperm under Siege 36. Adolescence: Whose Hell Is It? 38. HIV Infected Youth Speaks 42. When Violence Hits Home
AIDS	32. Why Kids Have a Lot to Cry About 38. HIV Infected Youth Speaks 39. Psychotrends		
Attachment	12. Mental Health for Babies 26. Sibling Connections	Early Childhood	13. Home Visiting Programs 14. "I Forget" 15. Assertiveness vs. Aggressiveness
Child Abuse	28. Lasting Effects of Child Maltreatment 32. Why Kids Have a Lot to Cry About 33. Miracle of Resiliency 38. HIV Infected Youth Speaks	Education/School	20. Bell, Book, and Scandal 21. How Schools Shortchange Girls 22. Nurturing Creativity 23. Multicultural Education 28. Lasting Effects of Child Maltreatment 31. Alienation and the Four Worlds of Childhood 34. Televised Violence and Kids 49. Grandparent Development and Influence
Cognitive Development	7. When a Pregnant Woman Drinks 9. New Perspective on Cognitive Development 10. Amazing Minds of Infants 13. Home Visiting Programs 14. "I Forget" 16. It's Magical! It's Malleable! It's . . . Memory 17. DNA-Environment Mix 18. The Good, the Bad, and the Difference 19. Life in Overdrive 36. Adolescence: Whose Hell Is It? 43. Man's World, Woman's World?		
		Emotional Development/ Personality	10. Amazing Minds of Infants 11. Realistic View of Biology and Behavior 12. Mental Health for Babies 15. Assertiveness vs. Aggressiveness 17. DNA-Environment Mix 18. The Good, the Bad, and the Difference 19. Life in Overdrive 23. Multicultural Education 26. Sibling Connections 28. Lasting Effects of Child Maltreatment 29. Your Loving Touch 30. EQ Factor
Creativity	16. It's Magical! It's Malleable! It's . . . Memory 19. Life in Overdrive 22. Nurturing Creativity 41. Back Off! 46. Midlife Myths		
Culture	17. DNA-Environment Mix 20. Bell, Book, and Scandal 21. How Schools Shortchange Girls 23. Multicultural Education 30. EQ Factor 31. Alienation and the Four Worlds of Childhood 32. Why Kids Have a Lot to Cry About 33. Miracle of Resiliency 35. Skin We're In 39. Psychotrends 47. Learning to Love Growing Old 49. Grandparent Development and Influence 50. Ageing with Attitude	Ethics/Morality	2. How Far Should We Push Mother Nature? 3. Choosing a Perfect Child 11. Realistic View of Biology and Behavior 18. The Good, the Bad, and the Difference 37. Teenage Turning Point 48. Unlocking the Secrets of Aging

TOPIC AREA	TREATED IN	TOPIC AREA	TREATED IN
Family/Parenting	12. Mental Health for Babies 13. Home Visiting Programs 15. Assertiveness vs. Aggressiveness 24. Lifelong Impact of Adoption 25. Bringing Up Father 26. Sibling Connections 27. Yours, Mine, and Ours 28. Lasting Effects of Child Maltreatment 29. Your Loving Touch 31. Alienation and the Four Worlds of Childhood 33. Miracle of Resiliency 36. Adolescence: Whose Hell Is It?	**Nutrition**	6. War Babies 44. New Middle Age 45. Estrogen Dilemma 48. Unlocking the Secrets of Aging 50. Ageing with Attitude
		Occupation/Work	21. How Schools Shortchange Girls 28. Lasting Effects of Child Maltreatment 31. Alienation and the Four Worlds of Childhood
Fertility	2. How Far Should We Push Mother Nature? 3. Choosing a Perfect Child 24. Lifelong Impact of Adoption	**Physical Development**	13. Home Visiting Programs 17. DNA-Environment Mix 20. Bell, Book, and Scandal 36. Adolescence: Whose Hell Is It?
Genetics	1. Biologists Find Key Genes 2. How Far Should We Push Mother Nature? 3. Choosing a Perfect Child 4. Eugenics Revisited 11. Realistic View of Biology and Behavior 33. Miracle of Resiliency 35. Skin We're In	**Prenatal Development**	1. Biologists Find Key Genes 2. How Far Should We Push Mother Nature? 5. Cocaine-Exposed Infants 6. War Babies 7. When a Pregnant Woman Drinks 8. Sperm under Siege
Health	13. Home Visiting Programs 25. Bringing Up Father 32. Why Kids Have a Lot to Cry About 33. Miracle of Resiliency 34. Televised Violence and Kids 35. Skin We're In 36. Adolescence: Whose Hell Is It? 38. HIV Infected Youth Speaks 45. Estrogen Dilemma	**Self-Esteem**	13. Home Visiting Programs 21. How Schools Shortchange Girls 22. Nurturing Creativity 35. Skin We're In 37. Teenage Turning Point 42. When Violence Hits Home 49. Grandparent Development and Influence
Infant Development	5. Cocaine-Exposed Infants 9. New Perspective on Cognitive Development 10. Amazing Minds of Infants 11. Realistic View of Biology and Behavior	**Sex Differences**	15. Assertiveness vs. Aggressiveness 21. How Schools Shortchange Girls 37. Teenage Turning Point 39. Psychotrends 43. Man's World, Woman's World?
Language/ Communication	13. Home Visiting Programs 23. Multicultural Education 43. Man's World, Woman's World?	**Stress**	16. It's Magical! It's Malleable! It's . . . Memory 27. Yours, Mine, and Ours 32. Why Kids Have a Lot to Cry About 33. Miracle of Resiliency 44. New Middle Age 50. Ageing with Attitude
Late Adulthood	47. Learning to Love Growing Old 48. Unlocking the Secrets of Aging 49. Grandparent Development and Influence 50. Ageing with Attitude 51. Solace of Patterns	**Television**	32. Why Kids Have a Lot to Cry About 34. Televised Violence and Kids
		Teratogens	5. Cocaine-Exposed Infants 7. When a Pregnant Woman Drinks 8. Sperm under Siege
Marriage	27. Yours, Mine, and Ours 39. Psychotrends 40. Is There Love after Baby? 41. Back Off! 42. When Violence Hits Home 46. Midlife Myths	**Violence/Rape**	4. Eugenics Revisited 28. Lasting Effects of Child Maltreatment 32. Why Kids Have a Lot to Cry About 34. Televised Violence and Kids 36. Adolescence: Whose Hell Is It? 38. HIV Infected Youth Speaks 42. When Violence Hits Home
Middle Adulthood	43. Man's World, Woman's World? 44. New Middle Age 45. Estrogen Dilemma 46. Midlife Myths	**Young Adulthood**	39. Psychotrends 40. Is There Love after Baby? 41. Back Off! 42. When Violence Hits Home

Genetic and Prenatal Influences on Development

- Genetic Influences (Articles 1–4)
- Prenatal Influences (Articles 5–8)

Until very recently, life span was defined as birth to death. Increasingly, life span theorists are encompassing prenatal being. The nine months of prenatal existence are the beginning of things human. This is true not only in the physical and structural realm, but also in the cognitive, social, and emotional realms. A burgeoning field of research documents genetic and prenatal influences on development. Human embryology (the study of the first through eighth weeks after conception) and fetology (the study of the second through ninth months of development during pregnancy) have supported the hypothesis that behavior occurs in the embryo and in the fetus. Genetic researchers have provided evidence for the notion that genes direct not only structural development, but also functional and behavioral changes before birth.

Is human prenatal development more a product of genes or of the mother's uterine environment? For years, developmentalists were involved in the nature-nurture controversy, both before and after birth. Those who argued for nature felt that genes and heredity were preponderant. Those who argued for nurture believed that environment exceeded the influence of genes. Current scientific studies of identical twins raised together or apart have taught us that all behavior is multifactorial. The nature-nurture question is moot. It is of no practical importance, since both genes and environment are relevant to any and every behavior. The simplest or most complex behaviors can be altered by multiple environmental stimuli. Conversely, multiple genes can affect both simple and complex actions (polygenic causation). How will the future of human development be impacted by both changes in genes (for example, mutation, genetic engineering) and changes in environment (for example, radiation, drugs, viruses)?

Years ago, genetic science described and explained cell nuclei, chromosomes, genes, DNA, RNA, mitosis and meiosis, dominance and recessiveness, intermediate and polygenic traits, mutations, and the effects of extra or absent chromosomes. The 1990s have brought a spate of new genetic information about nucleotide sequences associated with specific genes, hedgehog genes, gene maps, and gene markers. As more precise knowledge of the nature and location of idiosyncratic genes becomes known, genetic tests may be able to predict the genetic future of embryos and fetuses. It may become practicable to replace some DNA sequences (bad genes) with altered DNA sequences (good genes) during in vitro fertilization. How will this impact human development?

Human development between fertilization and birth is astronomically rapid! Never again in the human life span will change occur as quickly. Growth spurts in infancy and adolescence pale in comparison to prenatal development. Because growth and change occur so rapidly before birth, disrupting them can have alarming long-term consequences. The developing embryo/fetus can be poisoned with toxins that are relatively harmless after birth. Teratology (the study of malformations of the embryo/fetus) has revealed thousands of possible toxins (teratogens) that can affect the unborn baby.

The more common prenatal dangers are from radiation, drugs, and viruses. Alcohol, tobacco, cocaine, AIDS, herpes, cytomegalovirus, and many other teratogens create problems such as being small for gestational age, prematurity, low birth weight, and at-risk status of neonates. Another common problem is malnutrition of the mother during pregnancy. Extra nutrients, especially protein and folic acid, are necessary for optimal development. The deleterious effects of prenatal malnutrition or teratogen exposure can last a lifetime.

The first article in this unit was selected for the scientific excitement it reports and the accompanying sense of wonder it creates for readers. For years, students have asked: "How can a single cell, which divides by mitosis into hundreds of identical cells, differentiate into a baby?" Teachers could only give incomplete, unsatisfying answers about probable repressor substances that inhibit some gene messages while allowing others to direct action. Where do such repressor substances come from? This article provides a satisfying answer. Morphogens exist. They generate form and make structure.

Selections two through four question the new genetic technologies that are being developed and describe the process of in vitro fertilization. How far should humans go to procreate? Are people ready to embrace eugenics?

The last four articles in this unit explore some of the fragile, rapid, and astonishing growth processes that transform a fertilized ovum into a neonate in nine months. Article five is important because it differentiates each cocaine-exposed baby from each other one. It dispels some of the myths and misunderstandings about these infants. Likewise, the article "War Babies" dispels some myths and misunderstandings about limiting caloric intake during pregnancy. Not every fetus suffers alike from seemingly similar insults (cocaine, malnutrition, al-

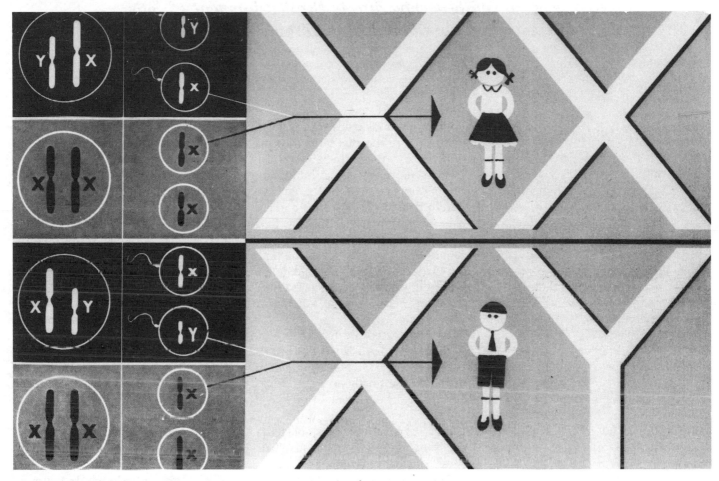

cohol). The next selection of this unit, "When a Pregnant Woman Drinks," presents some of the diverse effects of prenatal alcohol exposure. The essay "Sperm under Siege" is important because it draws male students more personally into the topic of prenatal development. It helps female students appreciate the importance of the biological father.

Looking Ahead: Challenge Questions

How do identical cells, the products of mitotic division of the zygote, differentiate into embryonic structures? What are hedgehogs, and how do they affect cell diversity?

How old is "too old"? When should a woman desist from pregnancy and motherhood? Discuss whether or not it is ageist to limit childbearing to the young.

Discuss whether or not you would elect to have in vitro fertilization and gene replacement therapy to create a perfect child.

Why do some believe that there are real genetic markers for drug abuse, violent behavior, and other societal problems? Would better breeding be useful or do a disservice to humankind?

Discuss whether or not cocaine exposure prenatally creates similar problems in all fetuses. What circumstances contribute to the misunderstandings about cocaine's effects?

How does prenatal malnutrition affect human development, and for how long?

What does alcohol do to the embryo/fetus? How much alcohol is too much during pregnancy?

How do sperm contribute to prenatal development?

Biologists Find Key Genes That Shape Patterning of Embryos

A gene named hedgehog directs the development of cells in the limbs and brain.

Natalie Angier

Rare indeed are the scientific findings that make jaws drop and spirits do cartwheels. But the discovery of a class of genes, given the cheeky name hedgehog, has aroused the passions of developmental biologists so vigorously that their normal reserve and skepticism have dissolved, leaving them groping for ever-stronger ways to express the beauty and consequence of what has been divulged.

Three teams of scientists report in the current issue of the journal Cell that they have finally unearthed what developmental scientists have been seeking for the last 25 years, as they studied the implausibly complex sequence of events that allow a single cell, the fertilized egg, to efflo-resce into a complete animal. They have identified the genes that act on the early embryo to lend it shape and pattern, transforming a nondescript comma of tissue into a vertebrate animal, with limbs and digits, brain and spinal cord, the body shape set from head to heel.

These genes produce so-called morphogens, molecules of celebrated stature that researchers have known must exist but have had tremendous difficulty isolating. The word mor-phogen means "maker of structure," and the hedgehog proteins are just that. Once switched on inside the embryo, the molecules sweep slowly across the primordial buds of tissue and begin generating identifiable form, sculpturing arms, hands and fingers on the sides of the embryo, vertebrae and ribs along its midline, a brain within the skull. The mor-phogen tells the cells it touches where they are situated in the body and what they are destined to become. It gives them their address, their fate, their identity, their purpose in life.

First detected in fruit flies, the hedgehog genes earned their name for their ability, when mutated, to give a fly the bristly appearance of a hedgehog. Their normal function in the fruit fly is to dictate growth, and the latest trio of reports establish that the same genes also dictate struc-tural design in vertebrates.

The papers describe the isolation of hedgehog genes from mice, zebra fish and chickens, three staple organ-isms of laboratory research, widely separated in evolutionary time.

"This new class of signaling mole-cules will probably end up being the most important molecules in verte-brate development," said Dr. Clifford J. Tabin, a developmental biologist at Harvard Medical School and the principle author of one of the three reports. When the results on the hedgehog work first became appar-ent, he said, "I was bouncing off the walls."

Scientists have yet to look for the genes in humans, but they are cer-tain that hedgehog is performing the same role in human embryos as it is in little fish. If this turns out not to be the case, said Dr. Philip W. Ingham, a senior scientist at the Molecular Em-bryology Laboratory at the Imperial Cancer Research Fund in Oxford, England, and the head investigator on another of the new papers, "I'll resign from science."

And with such a big segment of the puzzle of development now snapped into place, researchers said they can begin filling in the rest of the confounding picture of embry-ogenesis. They can start to decipher how the hedgehog molecules interact with other essential players known to participate slightly later in develop-ment, including the famed Hox genes, also assiduous builders of bodies, which themselves are found across the evolutionary scale.

"This is extraordinary work, it's fantastic, and I wish I'd done it," said Dr. Jim Smith, head of the develop-mental biology laboratory at the Na-tional Institute for Medical Research in London. "When I started working on limb development in 1976, we all knew there had to be something like this, but we didn't necessarily think we'd live to see it."

Dr. Smith, who has written a re-view of research on the hedgehog genes that will appear in the next issue of Cell, could not contain his enthusiasm. "It's the sort of thing that brings tears to your eyes," he said.

The work is of an exquisitely basic nature, born more of curiosity about nature than of specific clinical goals. But scientists said the findings may prove useful in the quest for better ways to treat head and spinal cord injuries, as well as degenerative diseases of the brain.

"People these days are very interested in molecules that mediate important decisions in the early development of the central nervous system," said Dr. Andrew P. McMahon, a developmental biologist at Harvard University and the principal researcher on the third of the latest papers. "There are a lot of diseases for which one would like to be able to grow new neurons," and understanding the basic signals of nervous system development is one road toward the shimmering Oz of neurological regeneration.

The protein made by the hedgehog gene organizes the fates of neighboring cells.

The hedgehog morphogens also offer relief to developmental biologists who lately had grown dissatisfied with another proffered candidate for the role of omnipotent morphogen: retinoic acid, or vitamin A. In widely publicized reports a few years ago, scientists suggested that retinoic acid could be the long-sought morphogen that sets up a body plan. However, there were sizable gaps in the data and doubts in the minds of many biologists that retinoic acid worked at such a fundamental level in the embryo.

In the new work, the hedgehog genes pass all the litmus tests that vitamin A had failed, displaying with extraordinary precision the properties that scientific theories about morphogens had predicted. It is turned on, or expressed, at pre-

cisely the right times of development, and in all the right places. And when scientists manipulate embryos and subtly alter the ways in which hedgehog genes are expressed, they get the sort of macabre developmental mutations they are expecting. For example, they can prompt a growing chick to sprout mirror-image sets of wings simply by inserting active hedgehog genes in the tissue abutting that where the genes are normally expressed.

'Exciting Breakthrough'

With the new results, said Dr. Ingham, "we can forget about retinoic acid" as an architect of the body.

For scientists who work on fruit flies, or Drosophila, the new discoveries prove once again how prescient they were to focus on simple animals as a way of comprehending more complex societies.

"It's a very exciting breakthrough and a vindication of the power of model organisms," said Dr. Matthew P. Scott, a professor of developmental biology and genetics at Stanford University School of Medicine. "Here we have a molecule that was found for its role in determining segmentation in insects, and it's turned out to be extremely important in understanding the most interesting properties of vertebrate growth."

Yet with all the enthusiasm surrounding the new finding, scientists admit they have much to learn. For example, they know that in humans, hedgehog in all likelihood switches on sometime around day 15 of pregnancy, to help shape the central nervous system, and is largely finished with that task by day 28. It comes into play shortly afterward in molding the limbs of the body. However, scientists do not yet have a clue as to what activates hedgehog to get morphogenesis rolling.

Nor do they know much about the hedgehog molecules themselves, what sort of proteins they are and how they manage to communicate with embryonic cells to persuade them to

adopt a particular fate. The hedgehog proteins are unlike any detected before, which is both a blessing and a hurdle—a blessing because scientists like novel things and because they knew the molecules they were familiar with were not sufficient to explain the mysteries of development; and a hurdle because they must start from scratch in understanding the molecules. So far, they have found four different hedgehog genes in vertebrate animals, but they suspect there may be more.

The fourth variety, which scientists call Sonic hedgehog, has an illustrious history. Scientists were first inspired to seek morphogens by the seminal research of Dr. John Saunders and others who, in the 1960's and 1970's, painstakingly grafted parts of embryos together to see what resulted. The work yielded a bizarre set of mutant animals with excess or abnormal digits and limbs, but the results were consistent and revealing. Together they indicated that in certain key regions of the primordial embryo, there are what are known as zones of polarizing activity, local headquarters that disseminate essential information about how surrounding cells are supposed to behave.

Scientists' Fantasies Exceeded

"The idea was that these signaling centers sent out a protein that affected neighboring cells and organized their fates," said Dr. Scott.

The signaling protein seems to work in a gradient fashion. By this theory, the protein diffuses from a central zone, getting less concentrated as it spreads. Depending on how much of the informational protein they receive, cells will choose one course of action over another. In the embryonic limb, for example, a heavy dose of the diffusing signal will instruct the cells to prepare to assume the role of a pinkie, while a lighter concentration will inform the cells they are destined to become a thumb.

Neurobiologists also gathered evidence from grafting experiments that a central signaling system helps knead the developing brain into shape. In this case, the zones of information were thought to be located in two embryonic structures, one called the notochord, a stiff rod that serves as the developing creature's temporary backbone, and the other called the floor plate, a bulge of tissue that eventually gives rise to the adult spinal cord. Scientists proposed that the structures jointly secrete a powerful information molecule able to tell surrounding cells whether they are destined to become part of the hind brain, the forebrain, motor nerves or other constituents of the nervous system.

Thus was born the notion of the morphogen, the diffusible conductor of cell fates. Finding it, however, was another matter.

> Scientists suspect that the protein stimulates the response of a master gene inside the cells; this potent gene may in turn set off a string of other genes.

Because recent work in fruit flies indicated that the hedgehog gene helps determine the growth of body segments in the larvae, the three research teams thought it worth the effort to seek the vertebrate equivalents of the gene and check whether hedgehog was somehow involved in animal growth.

The results exceeded their fantasies. The Sonic hedgehog molecule proved to be the desperately sought shaper of bodies. It is expressed in the limb at exactly the site known to be the zone of polarizing activity. It is activated exactly where it should be

A Gene That Signals Direction and Location

Scientists have discovered a class of genes, called hedgehog genes, that lend shape and pattern to the early embryo. Once turned on, these genes make proteins that give neighboring cells signals telling them their position and roles in forming a leg, wing or fin. At other sites, the hedgehog proteins direct development of the the central nervous system.

A fertilized mouse egg grows to be a cluster of 16 cells within three days. In the blastula stage, shown here, there are many more cells, and the inner cells have begun to take on specific roles.

Mouse embryo, 8½ to 9½ days old

At this point, the hedgehog gene switches on in the mouse embryo. The light gray stippled areas of the drawing show the locations of cells that are expressing this gene.

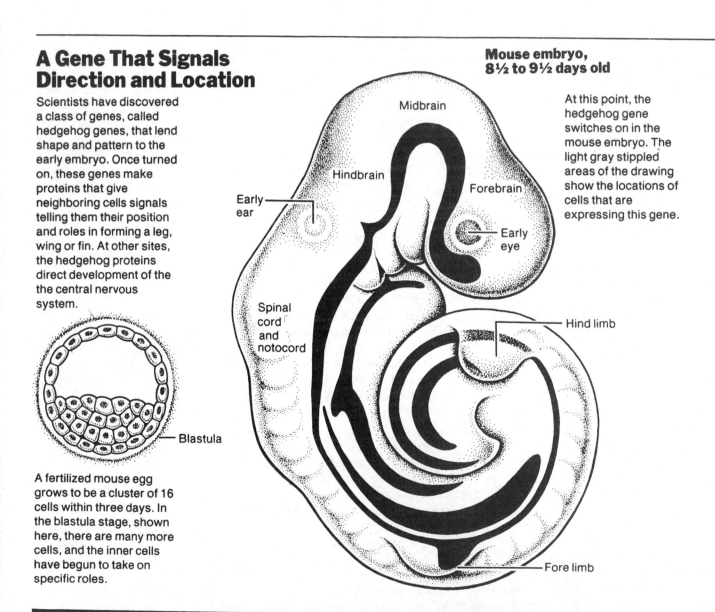

Labels: Midbrain, Hindbrain, Early ear, Spinal cord and notocord, Blastula, Forebrain, Early eye, Hind limb, Fore limb

in the notochord and floor plate in the early central nervous system.

Sonic Hedgehog's Modus Operandi

By manipulating the sonic hedgehog gene alone, the researchers have been able to recapitulate the suite of deformities seen in the older grafting experiments, thus demonstrating they have pinpointed the legendary morphogen.

The scientists have yet to clarify the roles of the three other hedgehog genes they have detected, but these seem more limited in their scope, toiling in specific regions like the sex cells of the body.

The challenge now is to understand the modus operandi of the Sonic hedgehog protein, how it persuades cells to do its bidding as it oozes by them. Scientists suspect that the protein stimulates the response of a master gene inside the cells, perhaps a member of the Hox gene family. That potent gene may in turn set off a string of other genes, which jointly realize the cell's destiny.

Within the early nervous system, the signals arising from the top and from the bottom are involved in formation of specific neurons at specific sites. Neurons at the top are associated with sensory functions, while neurons at the bottom control movement.

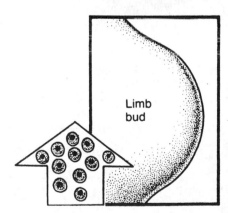
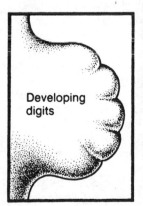

Limb bud

Developing digits

In the limb bud, the positional information from the hedgehog protein makes the cells start defining the arrangement of digits of a future paw.

Mouse embryo, 14 days old

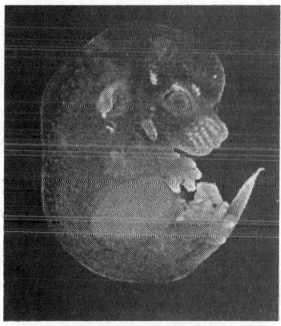

Dr. Bradley R. Smith, Dr. Elwood Lenny, Dr. G. Allan Johnson, Center for In Vivo Microscopy, Duke University Medical Center (N.I.H. National Resource)

Scientists suspect the hedgehog protein stimulates a master gene inside cells that sets off a cascade of other genes. The response to a signal, they think, depends on the local concentration of the hedgehog protein. Biologists expect to find the hedgehog gene in humans, too.

Sources: Dr. Andrew McMahon, Harvard University; "Molecular Biology of the Cell" (Garland)

Nancy Sterngold, The New York Times; Illustration by Michael Reingold

How Far Should We Push

Mother Nature?

*Making Babies: Technology is evolving faster than our ability
to weigh the cost and ethics*

The news came bursting out of Europe and rattled bedrooms around the world. First, a 59-year-old British businesswoman gave birth to twins, using donated eggs implanted in her uterus at a fertility clinic in Rome. Her coup was quickly eclipsed by the news that a 62-year-old Italian woman, who visited the same clinic, will deliver a baby in June. Next came the word that a black woman in Italy had recently given birth to a white baby using donor eggs; she and her Caucasian husband said they wanted to give their child "a better future." Then came an even bigger bombshell: press reports from Scotland said researchers had delivered baby mice using the ovaries of aborted mouse fetuses. There was talk that the process might someday be duplicated in humans, raising the freakish prospect of creating babies whose genetic mothers had never been born.

Things used to be so simple. A father provided sperm, a mother provided the egg and if something went wrong or if either partner was too old, that was just tough luck. But the Brave New World of reproductive technology, and particularly in-vitro fertilization (IVF), has changed all that forever. It is now technologically possible for a single infant to have five contributing parents: sperm donor, egg donor, surrogate mother, in addition to the mom and pop who raise him. The news from Europe showed that once again, technology was pushing the boundaries of the possible, raising questions society isn't prepared to answer or even debate in a cogent way. Is there no upper limit on the age at which women can bear children? (And what's wrong with that, if men can be fathers in their 70s and get ribbed by admiring buddies?) "In the future, people may wait till they retire to have kids—flip the whole life course," mused Arthur Caplan, director of the Center for Biomedical Ethics at the University of Minnesota. Beyond timing when to have their children, should couples be able to select their race? If the Scottish researchers continue their work, could a woman someday abort her daughter and give birth to her own grandchildren? (Talk about skip-generation families.)

To the millions of American couples on the emotional front lines of infertility, the ethical hypotheticals paled against the excitement of new possibilities. "Five years ago, this would have never happened to me," says Charline Pacourek, 45, who subjected herself to seven years of hormone injections, ovulation stimulation, artificial insemination, egg retrieval and embryo transfers. In November she learned that she is finally pregnant, thanks to eggs donated by a friend. Pacourek calls her baby a "miracle—it's fantastic! I would recommend this for anyone."

In Europe, however, government ministers were racing to curtail the high-tech options. French officials proposed banning IVF for women past menopause. Italy announced plans to limit artificial pregnancies at clinics like Dr. Severino Antinori's, where the 59-year-old and 62-year-old women got pregnant. Alarmed that the British woman had gone to Italy after being denied IVF at home, British Health Secretary Virginia Bottomley said she would seek uniform rules across Europe to prevent what some called "procreative tourism." But it's doubtful that the EC could ever agree on such touchy issues. "They have enough problems deciding what sort of cheese should be sold," said Oxford philosophy teacher Jonathan Glover. Germany, still chastened by the legacy of the Nazi experiments, prohibits fertilization by donated sperm or eggs, or any genetic manipulation of embryos.

In the United States, too, there were some calls to stop pushing the frontier of reproductive technology, or at least pause to consider where it is going. "We need to start to define those lines in society that we will not cross," said Dr. Thomas Raffin, codirector of the Stanford University Center for Biomedical Ethics. European-style laws are unlikely here, however. There are no federal rules or guidelines governing the estimated 300 assisted-fertility clinics operating nationwide, which generate some $2 billion in business a year. Starting this fall, a new law sponsored by Rep. Ron Wyden of Oregon will require clinics to report their success rates uniformly, so that consumers can sort out their wildly competing claims. But there are no rules specifying who clinics can or can't treat by age, marital status or any other factor.

'In the future, people may wait till they retire to have kids—flip the whole life course.'

Nor are there rules requiring fertility clinics to match donors and recipients according to characteristics like race and religion. In that sense, the era of "designer babies" is already here. Sperm-bank customers can flip through catalogs listing the height, hair color, eye color, ancestry—sometimes even the IQ—of potential donors. Many donated eggs come from friends or family members; Maryann Fiore's sister provided the eggs for her triplets, born when she was 44. But some programs also have descriptions of potential egg donors from which couples can choose. Debbie Karnell, a nurse at a West Coast fertility clinic, decided to try IVF with donor eggs when she saw the caliber of the women who volunteered. At first, Karnell says she was attracted to the prettiest ones. But in the end, she chose a donor who was young and had already proved her fertility. It worked for Karnell too: she had a baby five months ago, at the age of 46.

Long odds: Biotech gadfly Jeremy Rifkin worries that selecting racial and genetic characteristics is a dangerous step toward eugenics, and thinks that donor eggs should be outlawed. But to many ethicists, the only thing more frightening than unfettered reproductive technology would be Congress playing God and imposing limits. "This is an individual matter, an ethical and moral choice, not the business of government or call-in talk shows," says University of Southern California law professor Susan Estrich. (She also thinks that if society is going to get upset about who's having babies, "we ought to worry more about children having children than a few wealthy middle-aged women with enough resources to do this.") Most couples pursuing IVF technology are indeed affluent; each attempt with donor eggs can cost $10,000 to $20,000, and some women undergo repeated efforts before succeeding or giving up. Only a few states require insurance companies to fund IVF procedures. And because of the expense and long odds, it is one of the few technologies specifically excluded under Bill Clinton's health-reform proposal.

Bluntly put, that leaves rich people free to pursue baby-making technology, and others out of luck. But some ethicists see no problem in that standard: as Caplan views it, society can't stop you from having a child, but it doesn't owe you one by any means. He also says the debate over a double standard for older men and women ignores the simple fact that older men can produce sperm naturally, while older women need help. "No one is talking about devoting a lot of

technology to getting impotent old men to have babies," Caplan says.

Dr. Geoffrey Sher, medical director of the Pacific Fertility Medical Center in San Francisco, says he had misgivings the first time a woman in her 50s came into his office seeking to become pregnant. "I thought, 'Why should we get into this? We don't need this controversy'." But the woman's husband, who was 40 years old, challenged Sher's prejudices by asking if he'd have qualms if their ages were reversed. Sher had to admit he wouldn't, and after that, he decided to resolve every case on an individual basis. His clinic, with one of the largest donor-egg programs in the

---

Rich people can now take extreme measures to make their own babies, but other people can't.

---

country, has treated more than 100 women over 40, and a handful past 50. He claims that 56 percent give birth on the first try, regardless of their age, as long as the donor is under 35 and the recipient has a healthy uterus.

Midnight feedings: Older mothers face some greater risks to their own health from pregnancy. But most IVF programs, like Sher's, carefully screen out candidates who are not in excellent condition. Using donor eggs from younger women eliminates the increased risk of genetic and other problems in an older woman's own eggs. Most doctors are more concerned that fiftysomething mothers won't have the physical stamina to put up with midnight feedings or chase after toddlers. But experts on aging pooh-pooh such fears, noting that scores of grandmothers are energetically raising grandchildren by default these days. "A woman of 59 or 61 on average is pretty healthy today," says Dr. Marcia Ory of the National Institute on Aging. Couples with the financial means to pursue IVF can probably afford a nanny, she notes, and may be better equipped emotionally as well. "Mature mothers make good mothers, especially in contrast to a child-parent of 15."

But isn't it cruel for parents to bear a child when they might not live to see him

or her reach puberty or college? "It's not a very nice prospect for a child of 10 or 12 to go to sleep every night, praying that his or her mother will live as long as he needs her," says Gail Sheehy, author of "Passages" and "The Silent Passage: Menopause." Georgette Bennett thought about that a lot when she decided to try IVF two years ago, when she was 45 and her husband was 21 years older. She got pregnant on the first attempt using her own eggs and sperm her husband had frozen years earlier. The nine months she carried her son was "the world's easiest pregnancy. I never stopped working, never took a single nap." Sadly, her husband died seven weeks before his son was born. Still, Bennett, 47, calls 16-month-old Joshua-Marc "a great monument to my husband." She also says she appointed guardians, and "very consciously set about peopling my son's life with a wide diversity of folk of all ages."

Do the new methods offer real hope, or just more pressure to keep trying at any cost?

For older parents who already have grown kids, the new technology can complicate family relationships. Jonie Mosby Mitchell, a country singer and nightclub owner, had four children with ease in her first marriage: "Boom. Boom. Boom. Boom," she says. She remarried 17 years ago and adopted a baby girl in 1988. She was planning to adopt again when she read an article about postmenopausal pregnancies and decided to try it. She was 52 when she gave birth to Morgan, now 21 months old. One of her older daughters was pregnant the same time she was. Another is pregnant now, and Mitchell has three grandchildren who are older than their uncle. Her new kids call her first husband "grampa." She says her older offspring are a little uncomfortable with all this. (Her oldest daughter said, "Mom, if you've got extra time, spend it with *my* kids.") Having young children in her 50s "is not an easy job," Mitchell admits. "They fight and they argue and they fuss and they want. It poops me out." But overall, she thinks she is a better mother this time than when she was younger and worked on the road.

In truth, IVF clinics see very few 50-something women hoping to start second families. Far more of their patients are women in their 40s who delayed marriage and childbearing, then were surprised to discover how difficult it was to conceive, and how desperately they wanted to. Author Anne Taylor Fleming, now 44, struggled for 10 years to get pregnant before abandoning the attempt, an odyssey she describes in her forthcoming book, "Motherhood Deferred: A Woman's Journey." She says a whole generation of women have been caught in the boomerang of changing attitudes toward motherhood: they were born in the family-focused 1950s, came of age in the '60s era of contraception and free love, and then followed the feminist advice of the '70s to "make money, be equal to men, don't get caught." When they realized that wanting children might be part of feminism too, Fleming says, many were unprepared, as she was. Despite her career, happy marriage and four stepsons, Fleming says, "I was startled by the strong emotion of both wanting a baby and the inability to have one—just knocked sideways."

Like Fleming, many infertile couples eventually have to come to terms with reproductive failure and reconcile themselves to adoption—if they can find an agency that will accept them—or being childless. Does the news that a few 50- and 60-year-old women are having babies really offer more hope—or more long-odds promises to chase? "With so many new techniques at their disposal, it's harder for doctors to say, 'We've gone as far as we can go.' And the couples themselves have an even harder time saying 'Enough is enough'," Ronny Diamond, a New York social worker who counsels infertile couples. Fleming agrees: "It is sort of bitter joy that something else dangles out there." But she says that going through fertility attempts "humbles you about making choices for other women."

For all the startling headlines and new hopes, IVF is "still a horrible, expensive, stressful, emotionally trying crisis in a couple's life and no one would put themselves through it on purpose," says Carole Lieber-Wilkins, a therapist who counsels couples in West Los Angeles. Even if doctors can slow down the biological clock for some women, that doesn't mean that younger women can take late-life pregnancy for granted, or that retirement communities will be setting up day-care centers. Someday scientists may be able to hormonally manipulate men to carry fetuses, or grow human embryos in animal surrogates. (Could your mother, as well as your forefathers, be a chimpanzee?) But marching hand in hand with reproductive breakthroughs is the idea that society has to set priorities, and accept some limits, in an era of scarce medical resources. It will be up to many of these high-tech babies in the future to try to balance all those competing needs.

MELINDA BECK *with* MARY HAGER *and* PAT WINGERT *in Washington,* PATRICIA KING *in San Francisco,* JEANNE GORDON *in Los Angeles,* STANLEY HOLMES *in Chicago and* SUSAN MILLER *in New York*

Choosing a Perfect Child

Brave new technology is allowing us to look at tiny preembryonic 8-cell clusters and decide which ones are healthy enough to be allowed to develop into babies.

Ricki Lewis

Ricki Lewis is the author of Life, *a college biology text, and has written a human genetics text. She is a genetic counselor and an adjunct assistant professor at SUNY Albany and Miami University, where she has taught human genetics and bioethics courses. She has published hundreds of articles for both laymen and scientists.*

Chloe O'Brien, who celebrates her first birthday this month, is a very wanted child, perhaps more so than most. When she was a mere ball of cells, smaller than the smallest speck of sand, a test determined that she would be free of the cystic fibrosis genes that each of her parents carries. Chloe-to-be, along with another ball of cells (a potential twin), was implanted into her mother's uterus. Only one of the two balls of cells, Chloe-to-be, survived the rigors of prenatal development, and Chloe today is a healthy little girl.

The O'Briens had already had a child who suffered from the stiflingly thick mucus clogging the lungs that is a hallmark of cystic fibrosis, the most common genetic disease among Caucasians. They wanted to spare their future children this fate—but they also wanted to avoid having to end a pregnancy that would yield an affected child.

"Previously, couples had to wait from 9 to 15 weeks [after

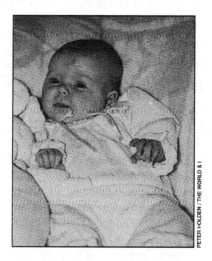

PETER HOLDEN / THE WORLD & I

conception] to find out if their developing baby was affected by a known genetic disease. Now, we can diagnose these inherited diseases within three days after an egg is fertilized in the laboratory, before it is transferred back to the woman," says Mark Hughes of the Baylor College of Medicine in Houston. Hughes, along with John Lesko, also of Baylor, and Alan Handyside, Robert Winston, and Juan Tarin, of Hammersmith Hospital in London, reported the preimplantation diagnosis of cystic fibrosis in September 1992 in the *New England Journal of Medicine.*

The preimplantation genetic diagnosis that confirmed Chloe to be free of the cystic fibrosis gene is built primarily on three existing technologies: in vitro fertil-

ization (IVF); gene amplification, a way to rapidly copy a single gene from a single cell; and gene probing, which detects the gene responsible for the disorder. The latter two interventions are performed on the 8-cell "preembryo."

Few couples have so far had their preembryos examined for genetic problems, and the high costs of the procedure will likely keep the numbers down. However, with the rapid progress being made by the Human Genome Project in identifying genes associated with specific genetic disorders, preembryos in the future may be scrutinized for a wider range of diseases, from rare inherited ailments to the more common heart disease and cancer.

Is a brave new world of mechanized reproduction upon us? To understand how we may someday pick and choose the traits of our children, we must understand the procedures that serve as a backdrop to preimplantation genetic diagnosis.

Prenatal diagnosis—the state of the art

A generation ago, pregnancy was shrouded in secrecy. A woman would discover her expectant state in the second or third month and announce it in the fourth month, when most risk of miscarriage was past. Today, pregnancy is marked by a series of medical tests providing prenatal peeks into the health of the child-to-be.

The most familiar prenatal test is amniocentesis, a procedure in which a needle is inserted into the amniotic sac cushioning a fetus and a small amount of fluid is withdrawn. The fluid contains a few fetal cells, whose nuclei contain the rod-shaped chromosomes, which consist of the genes. If examination reveals missing or extra chromosomes, the fetus is likely to develop into a baby with a serious syndrome.

Today, amniocentesis is a rite of passage for pregnant women over age 35, because at that age the chance of the fetus having a chromosomal problem about equals the risk of amniocentesis causing miscarriage (1 in 200). (The risk of abnormal fetal chromosomes increases with maternal age.)

The major limitation of amniocentesis is that it is performed in the 16th week of pregnancy. By then the fetus is quite well developed. If a chromosome abnormality is detected, the parents are faced with an agonizing choice: either terminate the pregnancy or prepare for the birth of a physically or mentally challenged child.

An alternative to amniocentesis is chorionic villus sampling (CVS), which also examines fetal chromosomes. This procedure can be performed earlier, usually between weeks 8 and 10. The fetus is far smaller and less well developed, about the size and weight of a paper clip, making the decision to end the pregnancy somewhat easier.

CVS was pioneered in China in the 1970s and became available in the United States only in the mid-1980s. Though the World Health Organization endorsed CVS in 1984, it also suggested

The biological basis of preimplantation genetic diagnosis is that all the cells of an individual have the same genes.

that ways be found to diagnose genetic disease earlier, perhaps before the preembryo implants in the uterus. This occurs on the 6th day after sperm meets egg.

The biological basis of preimplantation genetic diagnosis is that all the cells of an individual have the same genes no matter what the stage of development. In principle, the techniques used to examine the genetic material of cells obtained through amniocentesis or CVS should work for cells obtained at other stages of prenatal development, even at the preembryonic stage.

Screening genes

An individual gene in a preembryo's cell can be identified through a technique invented in 1985, the polymerase chain reaction (PCR).

In PCR an enzyme, DNA polymerase, that is essential to the multiplication of DNA in every cell in the body, selectively multiplies only the DNA from the gene of interest. If that gene is present in the original genetic sample being tested it will be rapidly mass-produced in a test tube. If the gene of interest is not present, then it won't be multiplied by the PCR.

If PCR of a single cell from the 8-cell preembryo results in many copies of the target DNA sequence, then the disease-causing gene is there—as happened to a few of Chloe's potential siblings who were not implanted. If the DNA is not amplified, then the sequence of interest is not there. When the cell from 8-cell Chloe-to-be failed its PCR test, it meant that the 7-cell preembryo could develop into a cystic fibrosis-free baby.

The first experiments using PCR to identify preembryos free of a genetic disease took place in 1989 and 1990 in Hammersmith Hospital. Handyside and his team screened preembryos from couples in which the mothers carried a variety of conditions, called X-linked conditions, that occur mostly in males. X-linked conditions are caused by genes on the X chromosome. Since females have two X chromosomes, and males have one X and one Y chromosome, a male preembryo with a Y chromosome and an X chromosome bearing a disease-causing gene would be destined to have the X-linked condition. By using PCR to amplify a DNA sequence unique to the Y chromosome, Handyside's team could choose a female preembryo that could not inherit the disease carried by the mother. The disorders avoided thanks to early attempts at preimplantation genetic diagnosis include adrenoleukodystrophy, a nervous system degeneration that is lethal in early childhood; Lesch-Nyhan syndrome, in which the profoundly retarded child mutilates himself; and other forms of mental retardation.

In August 1992 Jamie Grifo and colleagues at New York Hospital–Cornell Medical Center reported the first child born in the United States after successful blastomere biopsy and genetic testing to avoid X-linked hemophilia.

Candidates for preimplantation genetic diagnosis

Preimplantation genetic diagnosis is a promising option for couples who know that their children are at a high risk for inheriting a certain disease.

According to the laws of inheritance, parents who both carry the same disorder not on the X chromosome, but on one of the other 22 chromosomes, can conceive children who inherit either two normal genes, or two abnormal genes, or, like the parents, one normal and one abnormal gene. The probability of inheriting two of the same gene, either normal or abnormal, is 1 in 4. The probability of being a carrier like the parents with one normal and one abnormal gene is 1 in 2.

Chloe's parents, for example, each have one disease-causing copy of the cystic fibrosis gene, and one normal copy. Thus there

is a 1 in 4 chance that a child conceived by them will suffer with cystic fibrosis.

The mechanics of preimplantation diagnosis

A human preembryo can be obtained in two ways—it can be flushed out of the uterus after being conceived in the normal manner, in which case it is more than 8 cells, or it can be nurtured from an egg fertilized by a sperm in a laboratory dish, the technique of in vitro fertilization (IVF). The first IVF or "test tube baby," Louise Joy Brown, was born in England in 1978, and has since been followed by thousands of other such children.

IVF is now a fairly routine, if difficult and costly, procedure, with hundreds of facilities providing it in the United States alone, and hundreds of others elsewhere. For the IVF procedure, the woman is given pergonal, a drug that causes the ovary to ripen more than one egg at a

time. Eggs, which appear as small bulges in the ovarian lining, are harvested by inserting a laparoscope, a tiny, illuminated telescopelike device, through an incision made near the woman's navel.

The eggs are placed with sperm donated by the man into a laboratory dish, along with other chemicals that simulate the environment in the woman's body. If all goes well, sperm and egg meet and merge. Extra fertilized eggs are frozen and saved in case they are needed later.

On the third day after fertilization comes the blastomere biopsy. The 8-cell, or 8-blastomere, preembryo is immobilized with a holding pipette (a narrow glass tube). Then a single blastomere is removed from the preembryo by exposing the target cell to a stream of acid and gently prodding it with a second, smaller pipette.

The next step is to thoroughly clean the blastomere, because PCR, the gene amplification part

■ In blastomere biopsy, as shown left to right in the sequence below, the 8-cell preembryo is held by one pipette while another narrower one is used to capture a single blastomere, which is used for genetic testing; the remaining seven cells can continue to develop normally. (Magnification 330x)

COURTESY JUAN COTA / BAYLOR COLLEGE OF MEDICINE

Genetic Disease Diagnosis Before Fertilization

The time when we can probe a prenatal human's genes is creeping ever earlier, from the 16-week peek permitted with amniocentesis, to the 8–10-week scrutiny of chorionic villus sampling, to preimplantation genetic diagnosis of an 8-celled, 2–3-day-old preembryo. Yet another technique on the horizon, called polar body removal, may reveal the genetic makeup of an egg before it is fertilized.

In the first step of a two-step cell division that produces an egg with 23 chromosomes, division of the 46-chromosome progenitor germ cell distributes 23 chromosomes to each of the two daughter cells. But one cell, destined to develop into the egg, receives the lion's share of nutrients and other cell components, while the other, called the first polar body, is deprived and scrawny by comparison. The egg and its first polar body are stuck together in the ovary.

If the woman is a carrier for a genetic disease, when the chromosomes are divvied up

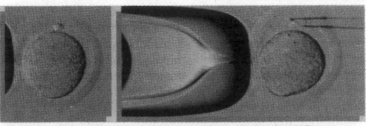

REPRINTED FROM *PREIMPLANTATION DIAGNOSIS OF GENETIC DISEASES*, EDITED BY Y. VERLINSKY AND A.M. KULIEV, COPYRIGHT © 1992, BY PERMISSION OF WILEY-LISS, A DIVISION OF JOHN WILEY AND SONS, INC.

■ *Left:* Diagnosing a genetic disease before fertilization relies on the fact that each egg shares the mother's divided genetic material with a much smaller companion, called the polar body. *Right:* In polar body biopsy, as shown here, the egg is held by the large pipette while the polar body is captured by drawing it into the smaller pipette. (Magnification 188x)

between the polar body and the egg, one normal gene goes to one, and the disease-causing gene to the other. So, if the polar body is examined and found to have the disease-causing gene, then it can be inferred that the corresponding egg does not. That egg can then be fertilized in the lab.

Polar body removal has been tested for more than three years at the Reproductive Genetics Institute of the Illinois Masonic Center in Chicago, yielding one pregnancy that spontaneously aborted due to

incidental chromosomal abnormality. So far a dozen couples have undergone the procedure, for such conditions as cystic fibrosis, hemophilia A, and Duchenne muscular dystrophy, but none has delivered a child.

Researchers are not sure why PBR's track record has so far been so poor. Perhaps the intervention is harming the egg, or perhaps it is just allowing us to see previously unknown ways that development can go awry.

—R.L.

of the process, can give a false genetic diagnosis if even one stray sperm happens to be clinging to the blastomere. When the blastomere is clean, it is broken open by a series of temperature changes to expose and disentangle the DNA. The PCR evaluation is then used to determine if the disease-causing gene is present.

After the blastomere biopsy and PCR, one or two preembryos that have passed the genetic test are implanted into the woman. If pregnancy occurs, human chorionic gonadotropin (hCG), the "pregnancy hormone," appears in the woman's blood and urine by the 14th day. By the fourth week,

an ultrasound exam will show a small, oval area in the uterus. This is the sac containing the embryo.

What we can do versus what we should do

At this time, the two biggest drawbacks to preimplantation genetic diagnosis are the low efficiency and high cost of IVF. In 1990, the American Fertility Society surveyed IVF clinics and found a 14 percent "take-home baby rate." However, Yury Verlinsky, director of the Reproductive Genetics Institute of the Illinois Masonic Medical Center in

Chicago, and Anver Kuliev, director of the research/cell bank at the same facility, point out that the typical couple seeking IVF has fertility problems and tends to be older, whereas couples seeking IVF as a prelude to preimplantation genetic diagnosis would be younger and more fertile.

The cost is out of reach for many. "The average cost of IVF is $7,000-8,000," says James Douglas of the Trinity Medical Center in Carrollton, Texas. Blastomere biopsy plus PCR can add another $2,000—all for a procedure that may have to be repeated.

Although physicians who perform IVF are excited about the value of preimplantation diagnosis for couples whose offspring are at high risk for genetic disease, they are nevertheless pessimistic about the technology's general utility. This is because once the procedure grows beyond its research stage, it will be prohibitively expensive. And even though there are expectations that automating some of the steps could bring the price down, these developments are on the far horizon.

Also, as Margaret Wallace, assistant professor in the genetics division at the University of Florida in Gainesville, points out, there is the problem of the "slippery slope"—who decides that a disorder is awful enough to intervene to prevent a birth? In 1990, she discovered the gene behind neurofibromatosis (NF1), another common inherited illness. NF1 presents a sticky problem—finding the responsible gene does not indicate how severely an individual may be affected. Manifestations of NF1 can range from a few brown spots on the body to thousands of tumors just beneath the skin.

"Blastomere biopsy is being performed only at a few IVF centers that are associated with a major medical teaching facility."

So far, the diseases detected by preimplantation genetic diagnosis cause extreme suffering to very young children, and the goal is prevention. "But for preimplantation diagnosis of some less devastating disorders, some physicians and insurers might not think it is ethical" to choose against implanting a diagnosed preembryo, says Wallace.

Another factor that may stifle development of preimplantation genetic diagnosis is that treatments for some genetic disorders are being developed so rapidly that selecting out affected preembryos may become obsolete before the technology can be perfected. "Cystic fibrosis research is moving so quickly that some may say, who cares who is born with it? We can treat them," says Wallace.

For now, preimplantation genetic diagnosis remains highly experimental. "Blastomere biop-sy is being performed only at a few IVF centers that are associated with a major medical teaching facility," says Douglas.

However, Verlinsky and Kuliev predict that, once the success stories accumulate and the price drops, preimplantation genetic diagnosis will be offered at a few fetal medicine centers, where teams of embryo experts, molecular biologists, geneticists, and obstetricians will perform genetic tests that will grow ever more numerous as the trek through the human genome nears completion.

Although clearly not yet suitable for the general public, preimplantation genetic diagnosis will allow certain couples to avoid what was once their genetic fate—passing on a disease. And so Chloe O'Brien is today what Louise Joy Brown was to the world 15 years ago—a medical pioneer, after whom many will follow.

TRENDS IN BEHAVIORAL GENETICS

EUGENICS REVISITED

Scientists are linking genes to a host of complex human disorders and traits, but just how valid—and useful—are these findings?

John Horgan, *senior writer*

"How to Tell If Your Child's a Serial Killer!" That was the sound bite with which the television show *Donahue* sought to entice listeners February 25. On the program, a psychiatrist from the Rochester, N.Y., area noted that some men are born with not one Y chromosome but two. Double-Y men, the psychiatrist said, are "at special risk for antisocial, violent behavior." In fact, the psychiatrist had recently studied such a man. Although he had grown up in a "Norman Rockwell" setting, as an adult he had strangled at least 11 women and two children.

"It is not hysterical or overstating it," Phil Donahue told his horrified audience, "to say that we are moving toward the time when, quite literally, just as we can anticipate . . . genetic predispositions toward various physical diseases, we will also be able to pinpoint mental disorders which include aggression, antisocial behavior and the possibility of very serious criminal activity later on."

Eugenics is back in fashion. The message that genetics can explain, predict and even modify human behavior for the betterment of society is promulgated not just on sensationalistic talk shows but by our most prominent scientists. James D. Watson, co-discoverer of the double-helix structure of DNA and former head of the Human Genome Project, the massive effort to map our entire genetic endowment, said recently, "We used to think that our fate was in our stars. Now we know, in large part, that our fate is in our genes."

Daniel E. Koshland, Jr., a biologist at the University of California at Berkeley and editor of *Science*, the most influential peer-reviewed journal in the U.S., has declared in an editorial that the nature/nurture debate is "basically over," since scientists have shown that genes influence many aspects of human behavior. He has also contended that genetic research may help eliminate society's most intractable problems, including drug abuse, homelessness and, yes, violent crime.

Some studies cited to back this claim are remarkably similar to those conducted over a century ago by scientists such as Francis Galton, known as the father of eugenics. Just as the British polymath studied identical twins in order to show that "nature prevails enormously over nurture," so do modern researchers. But the primary reason behind the revival of eugenics is the astonishing successes of biologists in mapping and manipulating the human genome. Over the past decade, investigators have identified genes underlying such crippling diseases as cystic fibrosis, muscular dystrophy and, this past spring, Huntington's disease. Given these advances, researchers say, it is only a matter of time before they can lay bare the genetic foundation of much more complex traits and disorders.

The political base for eugenics has also become considerably broader in recent years. Spokespersons for the mentally ill believe demonstrating the genetic basis of disorders such as schizophrenia and manic depression—and even alcoholism and drug addiction—will lead not only to better diagnoses and

treatments but also to more compassion toward sufferers and their families. Some homosexuals believe society will become more tolerant toward them if it can be shown that sexual orientation is an innate, biological condition and not a matter of choice.

But critics contend that no good can come of bad science. Far from moving inexorably closer to its goals, they point out, the field of behavioral genetics is mired in the same problems that have always plagued it. Behavioral traits are extraordinarily difficult to define, and practically every claim of a genetic basis can also be explained as an environmental effect. "This has been a huge enterprise, and for the most part the work has been done shoddily. Even careful people get sucked into misinterpreting data," says Jonathan Beckwith, a geneticist at Harvard University. He adds, "There are social consequences to this."

The skeptics also accuse the media of having created an unrealistically optimistic view of the field. Richard C. Lewontin, a biologist at Harvard and a prominent critic of behavioral genetics, contends that the media generally give much more prominent coverage to dramatic reports—such as the discovery of an "alcoholism gene"—than to contradictory results or retractions. "Skepticism doesn't make the news," Lewontin says. "It only makes the news when you find a gene." The result is that spurious findings often become accepted by the public and even by so-called experts.

The claim that men with an extra Y chromosome are predisposed toward violence is a case in point. It stems from a survey in the 1960s that found more extra-Y men in prison than in the general population. Some researchers hypothesized that since the Y chromo-

gotic twins reared apart are about as similar as are monozygotic twins reared together." (Identical twins are called monozygotic because they stem from a single fertilized egg, or zygote.)

The researchers have buttressed their statistical findings with anecdotes about "eerie," "bewitching" and "remarkable" parallels between reunited twins. One case involved Oskar, who was raised as a Nazi in Czechoslovakia, and Jack, who was raised as a Jew in Trinidad. Both were reportedly wearing shirts with epaulets when they were reunited by the Minnesota group in 1979. They also both flushed the toilet before as well as after using it and enjoyed deliberately sneezing to startle people in elevators.

Some other celebrated cases involved two British women who wore seven rings and named their firstborn sons Richard Andrew and Andrew Richard; two men who both had been named Jim, named their pet dogs Toy, married women named Linda, divorced them and remarried women named Betty; and two men who had become firefighters and drank Budweiser beer.

Other twin researchers say the significance of these coincidences has been greatly exaggerated. Richard J. Rose of Indiana University, who is collaborating on a study of 16,000 pairs of twins in Finland, points out that "if you bring together strangers who were born on the same day in the same country and ask them to find similarities between them, you may find a lot of seemingly astounding coincidences."

Rose's collaborator, Jaakko Kaprio of the University of Helsinki, notes that the Minnesota twin studies may also be biased by their selection method. Whereas he and Rose gather data by combing birth registries and sending questionnaires to those identified as twins, the Minnesota group relies heavily on media coverage to recruit new twins. The twins then come to Minnesota for a week of study—and, often, further publicity. Twins who are "interested in publicity and willing to support it," Kaprio says, may be atypical. This self-selection effect, he adds, may explain why the Bouchard group's estimates of heritability tend to be higher than those of other studies.

One of the most outspoken critics of

---

some confers male attributes, men with an extra Y become hyperaggressive "supermales." Follow-up studies indicated that while extra-Y men tend to be taller than other men and score slightly lower on intelligence tests, they are otherwise normal. The National Academy of Sciences concluded in a report published this year that there is no evidence to support the link between the extra Y chromosome and violent behavior.

Minnesota Twins

No research in behavioral genetics has been more eagerly embraced by the press than the identical-twin studies done at the University of Minnesota. Thomas J. Bouchard, Jr., a psychologist, initiated them in the late 1970s, and since then they have been featured in the *Washington Post, Newsweek,* the *New York Times* and other publications worldwide as well as on television. *Science* has favorably described the Minnesota team's work in several news stories and in 1990 published a major article by the group.

The workers have studied more than 50 pairs of identical twins who were separated shortly after birth and raised in different households. The assump-

tion is that any differences between identical twins, who share all each other's genes, are caused by the environment; similarities are attributed to their shared genes. The group estimates the relative contribution of genes to a given trait in a term called "heritability." A trait that stems entirely from genes, such as eye color, is defined as 100 percent heritable. Height is 90 percent heritable; that is, 90 percent of the variation in height is accounted for by genetic variation, and the other 10 percent is accounted for by diet and other environmental factors.

The Minnesota group has reported finding a strong genetic contribution to practically all the traits it has examined. Whereas most previous studies have estimated the heritability of intelligence (as defined by performance on intelligence tests) as roughly 50 percent, Bouchard and his colleagues arrived at a figure of 70 percent. They have also found a genetic component underlying such culturally defined traits as religiosity, political orientation (conservative versus liberal), job satisfaction, leisure-time interests and proneness to divorce. In fact, the group concluded in *Science,* "On multiple measures of personality and temperament…monozy-

the Minnesota twin studies—and indeed all twin studies indicating high heritability of behavioral traits—is Leon J. Kamin, a psychologist at Northeastern University. In the 1970s Kamin helped to expose inconsistencies and possible fraud in studies of separated identical twins conducted by the British psychologist Cyril Burt during the previous two decades. Burt's conclusion that intelligence was mostly inherited had inspired various observers, notably Arthur R. Jensen, a psychologist at the University of California at Berkeley, to argue that socioeconomic stratification in the U.S. is largely a genetic phenomenon.

In his investigations of other twin studies, Kamin has shown that identical twins supposedly raised apart are often raised by members of their family or by unrelated families in the same neighborhood; some twins had extensive contact with each other while growing up. Kamin suspects the same may be true of some Minnesota twins. He notes, for example, that some news accounts suggested Oskar and Jack (the Nazi and the Jew) and the two British women wearing seven rings were reunited for the first time when they arrived in Minnesota to be studied by Bouchard. Actually, both pairs of twins had met previously. Kamin has repeatedly asked the Minnesota group for detailed case histories of its twins to determine whether it has underestimated contact and similarities in upbringing. "They've never responded," he says.

Kamin proposes that the Minnesota twins have particularly strong motives to downplay previous contacts and to exaggerate their similarities. They might want to please researchers, to attract more attention from the media or even to make money. In fact, some twins acquired agents and were paid for appearances on television. Jack and Oskar recently sold their life story to a film producer in Los Angeles (who says Robert Duvall is interested in the roles).

Even the Minnesota researchers caution against overinterpretation of their work. They agree with their critics that high heritability should not be equated with inevitability, since the environment can still drastically affect the expression of a gene. For example, the genetic disease phenylketonuria, which causes profound retardation, has a heritability of 100 percent. Yet eliminating the amino acid phenylalanine from the diet of affected persons prevents retardation from occurring.

Such warnings tend to be minimized in media coverage, however. Writers often make the same inference that Koshland did in an editorial in *Science:* "Bet-

ter schools, a better environment, better counseling and better rehabilitation will help some individuals but not all." The prime minister of Singapore apparently reached the same conclusion. A decade ago he cited popular accounts of the Minnesota research in defending policies that encouraged middle-class Singaporeans to bear children and discouraged childbearing by the poor.

Smart Genes

Twin studies, of course, do not indicate which specific genes contribute to a trait. Early in the 1980s scientists began developing powerful ways to unearth that information. The techniques stem from the fact that certain stretches of human DNA, called polymorphisms, vary in a predictable way. If a polymorphism is consistently inherited together with a given trait—blue eyes, for example—then geneticists assume it either lies near a gene for that trait or actually is the gene. A polymorphism that merely lies near a gene is known as a marker.

In so-called linkage studies, investigators search for polymorphisms co-inherited with a trait in families unusually prone to the trait. In 1983 researchers used this method to find a marker linked to Huntington's disease, a crippling neurological disorder that usually strikes carriers in middle age and kills them within 10 years. Since then, the same technique has pinpointed genes for cystic fibrosis, muscular dystrophy and other diseases. In association studies, researchers compare the relative frequency of polymorphisms in two unrelated populations, one with the trait and one lacking it.

Workers are already using both methods to search for polymorphisms associated with intelligence, defined as the ability to score well on standardized intelligence tests. In 1991 Shelley D. Smith of the Boys Town National Institute for Communication Disorders in Children, in Omaha, and David W. Fulker of the University of Colorado identified polymorphisms associated with dyslexia in a linkage study of 19 families exhibiting high incidence of the reading disorder.

Behavioral Genetics: A Lack-of-Progress Report

CRIME: Family, twin and adoption studies have suggested a heritability of 0 to more than 50 percent for predisposition to crime. (Heritability represents the degree to which a trait stems from genetic factors.) In the 1960s researchers reported an association between an extra Y chromosome and violent crime in males. Follow-up studies found that association to be spurious.

MANIC DEPRESSION: Twin and family studies indicate heritability of 60 to 80 percent for susceptibility to manic depression. In 1987 two groups reported locating different genes linked to manic depression, one in Amish families and the other in Israeli families. Both reports have been retracted.

SCHIZOPHRENIA: Twin studies show heritability of 40 to 90 percent. In 1988 a group reported finding a gene linked to schizophrenia in British and Icelandic families. Other studies documented no linkage, and the initial claim has now been retracted.

ALCOHOLISM: Twin and adoption studies suggest heritability ranging from 0 to 60 percent. In 1990 a group claimed to link a gene—one that produces a receptor for the neurotransmitter dopamine—with alcoholism. A recent review of the evidence concluded it does not support a link.

INTELLIGENCE: Twin and adoption studies show a heritability of performance on intelligence tests of 20 to 80 percent. One group recently unveiled preliminary evidence for genetic markers for high intelligence (an IQ of 130 or higher). The study is unpublished.

HOMOSEXUALITY: In 1991 a researcher cited anatomic differences between the brains of heterosexual and homosexual males. Two recent twin studies have found a heritability of roughly 50 percent for predisposition to male or female homosexuality. These reports have been disputed. Another group claims to have preliminary evidence of genes linked to male homosexuality. The data have not been published.

Two years ago Robert Plomin, a psychologist at Pennsylvania State University who has long been active in behavioral genetics, received a $600,000 grant from the National Institute of Child Health and Human Development to search for genes linked to high intelligence. Plomin is using the association method, which he says is more suited than the linkage technique to identifying genes whose contribution to a trait is relatively small. Plomin is studying a group of 64 schoolchildren 12 to 13 years old who fall into three groups: those who score approximately 130, 100 and 80 on intelligence tests.

Plomin has examined some 25 polymorphisms in each of these three groups, trying to determine whether any occur with greater frequency in the "bright" children. The polymorphisms have been linked to genes thought to have neurological effects. He has uncovered several markers that seem to occur more often in the highest-scoring children. He is now seeking to replicate his results in another group of 60 children; half score above 142 on intelligence tests, and half score less than 74 (yet have no obvious organic deficiencies). Plomin presented his preliminary findings at a meeting, titled "Origins and Development of High Ability," held in London in January.

At the same meeting, however, other workers offered evidence that intelligence tests are actually poor predictors of success in business, the arts or even advanced academic programs. Indeed, even Plomin seems ambivalent about the value of his research. He suggests that someday genetic information on the cognitive abilities of children might help teachers design lessons that are more suited to students' innate strengths and weaknesses.

But he also calls his approach "a fishing expedition," given that a large number of genes may contribute to intelligence. He thinks the heritability of intelligence is not 70 percent, as the Minnesota twin researchers have claimed, but 50 percent, which is the average finding of other studies, and at best he can only find a gene that accounts for a tiny part of variance in intelligence. "If you wanted to select on the basis of this, it would be of no use whatsoever," he remarks. These cautions did not prevent the *Sunday Telegraph,* a London newspaper, from announcing that Plomin had found "evidence that geniuses are born not made."

Evan S. Balaban, a biologist at Harvard, thinks Plomin's fishing expedition is doomed to fail. He grants that there may well be a significant genetic component to intelligence (while insisting that studies by Bouchard and others have not demonstrated one). But he doubts whether investigators will ever uncover any specific genes related to high intelligence or "genius." "It is very rare to find genes that have a specific effect," he says. "For evolutionary reasons, this just doesn't happen very often."

The history of the search for markers associated with mental illness supports Balaban's view. Over the past few decades, studies of twins, families and adoptees have convinced most investigators that schizophrenia and manic depression are not caused by psychosocial factors—such as the notorious "schizophrenogenic mother" postulated by some Freudian psychiatrists—but by biological and genetic factors. After observing the dramatic success of linkage studies in the early 1980s, researchers immediately began using the technique to isolate polymorphic markers for mental illness. The potential value of such research was enormous, given that schizophrenia and manic depression each affect roughly one percent of the global population.

They seemed to have achieved their first great success in 1987. A group led by Janice A. Egeland of the University of Miami School of Medicine claimed it had linked a genetic marker on chromosome 11 to manic depression in an Amish population. That same year another team, led by Miron Baron of Columbia University, linked a marker on the X chromosome to manic depression in three Israeli families.

The media hailed these announcements as major breakthroughs. Far less attention was paid to the retractions that followed. A more extensive analysis of the Amish in 1989 by a group from the National Institute of Mental Health turned up no link between chromosome 11 and manic depression. This year Baron's team retracted its claim of linkage with the X chromosome after doing a new study of its Israeli families with more sophisticated markers and more extensive diagnoses.

Schizophrenic Results

Studies of schizophrenia have followed a remarkably similar course. In 1988 a group headed by Hugh M. D. Gurling of the University College, London, Medical School announced in *Nature* that it had found linkage in Icelandic and British families between genetic markers on chromosome 5 and schizophrenia. In the same issue, however, researchers led by Kenneth K. Kidd of Yale University reported seeing no such linkage in a Swedish family. Although Gurling defended his result as legitimate for several years, additional research has convinced him that it was probably a false positive. "The new families showed no linkage at all," he says.

These disappointments have highlighted the problems involved in using linkage to study mental illness. Neil Risch, a geneticist at Yale, points out that linkage analysis is ideal for studying diseases, such as Huntington's, that have distinct symptoms and are caused by a single dominant gene. Some researchers had hoped that at least certain subtypes of schizophrenia or manic depression might be single-gene disorders. Single-gene mutations are thought to cause variants of breast cancer and of Alzheimer's disease that run in families and are manifested much earlier than usual. But such diseases are rare, Risch says, because natural selection quickly winnows them out of the population, and no evidence exists for distinct subtypes of manic depression or schizophrenia.

Indeed, all the available evidence suggests that schizophrenia and manic depression are caused by at least several genes—each of which may exert only a tiny influence—acting in concert with environmental influences. Finding such genes with linkage analysis may not be impossible, Risch says, but it will be considerably more difficult than identifying genes that have a one-to-one correspondence to a trait. The difficulty is compounded by the fact that the diagnosis of mental illness is often subjective—all the more so when researchers are relying on family records or recollections.

Some experts now question whether genes play a significant role in mental illness. "Personally, I think we have overestimated the genetic component of schizophrenia," says E. Fuller Torrey, a psychiatrist at St. Elizabeth's Hospital in Washington, D.C. He argues that the evidence supporting genetic models can be explained by other biological factors, such as a virus that strikes in utero. The pattern of incidence of schizophrenia in families often resembles that of other viral diseases, such as polio. "Genes may just create a susceptibility to the virus," Torrey explains.

The Drink Link

Even Kidd, the Yale geneticist who has devoted his career to searching for genes linked to mental illness, acknowledges that "in a rigorous, technical, scientific sense, there is very little proof that schizophrenia, manic depression" and other psychiatric disorders have a genetic origin. "Virtually all the evidence supports a genetic explanation, but there are always other explanations, even if they are convoluted."

The evidence for a genetic basis for alcoholism is even more tentative than that for manic depression and schizophrenia. Although some studies discern a genetic component, especially in males, others have reached the opposite conclusion. Gurling, the University College investigator, found a decade ago that identical twins were slightly *more* likely to be discordant for alcoholism than fraternal twins. The drinking habits of some identical twins were strikingly different. "In some cases, one drank a few bottles a day, and the other didn't drink at all," Gurling says.

Nevertheless, in 1990 a group led by Kenneth Blum of the University of Texas Health Science Center at San Antonio announced it had discovered a genetic marker for alcoholism in an association study comparing 35 alcoholics with a control group of 35 nonalcoholics. A page-one story in the *New York Times* portrayed the research as a potential watershed in the diagnosis and treatment of alcoholism without mentioning the considerable skepticism aroused among other researchers.

The Blum group claimed that its marker, called the A1 allele, was associated with a gene, called the D2 gene, that codes for a receptor for the neurotransmitter dopamine. Skeptics noted that the A1 allele was actually some 10,000 base pairs from the dopamine-receptor gene and was not linked to any detectable variation in its expression.

Since the initial announcement by Blum, three papers, including an additional one by Blum's group, have presented more evidence of an association between the A1 allele and alcoholism. Six groups have found no such evidence (and received virtually no mention in the popular media).

In April, Risch and Joel Gelernter of Yale and David Goldman of the National Institute on Alcohol Abuse and Alcoholism analyzed all these studies on the A1 allele in a paper in the *Journal of the American Medical Association*. They noted that if Blum's two studies are cast aside, the balance of the results shows

BRAIN OF SCHIZOPHRENIC (*right*) appears different from the brain of his identical twin in these magnetic resonance images. Such findings suggest that factors that are biological but not genetic—such as viruses—may play a significant role in mental illness.

The Huntington's Disease Saga: A Cautionary Tale

The identification of the gene for Huntington's disease, which was announced in March, was hailed as one of the great success stories of modern genetics. Yet it provides some rather sobering lessons for researchers seeking genes linked to more complex human disorders and traits.

The story begins in the late 1970s, when workers developed novel techniques for identifying polymorphisms, sections of the human genome that come in two or more forms. Investigators realized that by finding polymorphisms linked—always and exclusively—to diseases, they could determine which chromosome the gene resides in. Researchers decided to test the polymorphism technique on Huntington's disease, a devastating neurological disorder that affects roughly one in 10,000 people. Scientists had known for more than a century that Huntington's was caused by a mutant, dominant gene. If one parent has the disease, his or her offspring have a 50 percent chance of inheriting it.

One of the leaders of the Huntington's effort was Nancy Wexler, a neuropsychologist at Columbia University whose mother had died of the disease and who therefore has a 50 percent chance of developing it herself. She and other researchers focused on a poor Venezuelan village whose inhabitants had an unusually high incidence of the disease. In 1983, through what has now become a legendary stroke of good fortune, they found a linkage with one of the first polymorphisms they tested. The linkage indicated that the gene for Huntington's disease was somewhere on chromosome 4.

The finding led quickly to a test for determining whether offspring of carriers—either in utero or already born—have inherited the gene itself. The test requires an analysis of blood samples from several members of a family known to carry the disease. Wexler herself has declined to say whether she has taken the test.

Researchers assumed that they would quickly identify the actual gene in chromosome 4 that causes Huntington's disease. Yet it took 10 years for six teams of workers from 10 institutions to find the gene. It is a so-called expanding gene, which for unknown reasons gains base pairs (the chemical "rungs" binding two strands of DNA) every time it is transmitted. The greater the expansion of the gene, researchers say, the earlier the onset of the disease. The search was complicated by the fact that workers had no physical clues about the course of the disease to guide them. Indeed, Wexler and others emphasize that they still have no idea how the gene actually causes the disease; treatments or cures may be years or decades away.

The most immediate impact of the new discovery will be the development of a better test for Huntington's, one that requires blood only from the person at risk

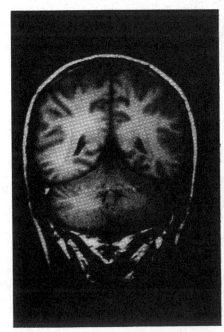
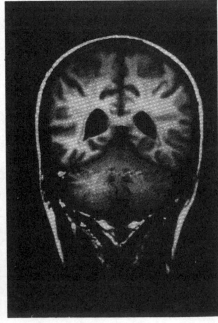

NANCY WEXLER helped to find the gene responsible for Huntington's disease by studying a population in Venezuela that has been ravaged by the disorder.

and not other family members. By measuring the length of the mutant gene, the test might also predict more accurately when carriers will show symptoms.

As difficult as it was to pinpoint the gene for Huntington's, it will be almost infinitely harder to discover genes for behavioral disorders, says Evan S. Balaban, a biologist at Harvard University. Unlike Huntington's disease, he notes, disorders such as schizophrenia and alcoholism cannot be unambiguously diagnosed. Furthermore, they stem not from a single dominant gene but from many genes acting in concert with environmental effects. If researchers do find a statistical association between certain genes and a trait, Balaban says, that knowledge may never be translated into useful therapies or tests. "What does it mean to have a 10 percent increased risk of alcoholism?" he asks.

no association between the D2 receptor and alcoholism, either in the disorder's milder or most severe forms, "We therefore conclude that no physiologically significant association" between the A1 allele and alcoholism has been proved, the group stated. "It's a dead issue," Risch says.

Gelernter and his colleagues point out that association studies are prone to spurious results if not properly controlled. They suggest that the positive findings of Blum and his colleagues may have derived from a failure to control for ethnic variation. The limited surveys done so far have shown that the incidence of the A1 allele varies wildly in different ethnic groups, ranging from 10 percent in certain Jewish groups to about 50 percent in Japanese.

Blum insists that the ethnic data, far from undermining his case, support it,

since those groups with the highest prevalence of the A1 allele also exhibit the highest rates of "addictive behavior." He contends that the only reason the Japanese do not display higher rates of alcoholism is that many also carry a gene that prevents them from metabolizing alcohol. "They're pretty compulsive," explains Blum, who recently obtained a patent for a genetic test for alcoholism.

These arguments have been rejected even by Irving I. Gottesman of the University of Virginia, who is a strong defender of genetic models of human behavior. He considers the papers cited by Blum to support his case to be ambiguous and even contradictory. Some see an association only with alcoholism that leads to medical complications or even death; others discern no association with alcoholism but only with "polysubstance abuse," including cigarette smoking. "I think it is by and large

garbage," Gottesman says of the alleged A1-alcoholism link.

By far the most controversial area of behavioral genetics is research on crime. Last fall complaints by civil-rights leaders and others led the National Institutes of Health to withdraw its funding from a meeting entitled "Genetic Factors in Crime: Findings, Uses and Implications." The conference brochure had noted the "apparent failure of environmental approaches to crime" and suggested that genetic research might yield methods for identifying and treating potential criminals—and particularly those prone to violence—at an early age.

Critics contend that such investigations inevitably suggest that blacks are predisposed to crime, given that blacks in the U.S. are six times more likely than whites to be arrested for a violent crime. In fact, some prominent scientists, notably Richard J. Herrnstein, a psychologist at Harvard, have made this assertion. Others reject this view but insist biological research on attributes linked to violent crime, such as aggression, may still have some value. "People who are unwilling to address genetic and biochemical factors are just putting their heads in the sand," says Goldman, the alcoholism expert. "It is not fair to say that just because there have been geneticists who have had a very narrow view of this in the past, we shouldn't explore this now."

In fact, investigations of the biology of violent crime continue, albeit quietly. Workers at City of Hope Hospital in Duarte, Calif., claim to have found an association between the A1 allele—the alleged alcoholism marker—and "criminal aggression." Last year a group led by Markus J. P. Kruesi of the University of Illinois at Chicago presented evidence of an association between low levels of the neurotransmitter serotonin and disruptive-behavior disorders in children. Kruesi concedes there is no way to determine whether the serotonin levels are genetically influenced. In fact, the serotonin levels might be an effect—a reaction to an environmental trauma—rather than a cause. "This might be a scar marker," he says.

One reason such research persists is that studies of families, twins and adoptees have suggested a genetic component to crime. Glenn D. Walters, a psychologist at the Federal Correctional Institution in Schuylkill, Pa., recently reviewed 38 of these studies, conducted from the 1930s to the present, in the journal *Criminology*. His meta-analysis turned up a small genetic effect, "but nothing to get excited about." He

"Better Breeding"

Fairly or not, modern genetics research is still haunted by the history of eugenics. "It offers a lot of cautionary lessons," says Daniel J. Kevles, a historian at the California Institute of Technology, who wrote the 1985 book *In the Name of Eugenics*. The British scientist Francis Galton, cousin to Charles Darwin, first proposed that human society could be improved "through better breeding" in 1865 in an article entitled "Hereditary Talent and Character." He coined the term "eugenics," from the Greek for "good birth," in 1883.

Galton's proposal had broad appeal. The American sexual libertarian John Humphrey Noyes bent eugenics into an ingenious argument for polygamy. "While the good man will be limited by his conscience to what the law allows," Noyes said, "the bad man, free from moral check, will distribute his seed beyond the legal limit."

A more serious advocate was the biologist Charles B. Davenport, founder of Cold Spring Harbor Laboratory and of the Eugenics Record Office, which gathered information on thousands of American families for genetic research. After demonstrating the heritability of eye, skin and hair color, Davenport went on to "prove" the heritability of traits such as "pauperism," criminality and "feeble-mindedness." In one monograph, published in 1919, he asserted that the ability to be a naval officer is an inherited trait, composed of subtraits for thalassophilia, or love of the sea, and hyperkineticism, or wanderlust. Noting the paucity of female naval officers, Davenport concluded that the trait is unique to males.

Beginning in the 1920s the American Eugenics Society, founded by Davenport and others, sponsored "Fitter Families Contests" at state fairs around the U.S. Just as cows and sheep were appraised by judges at the fairs, so were human entrants (such as the family shown above at the 1925 Texas State Fair). Less amusingly, eugenicists helped to persuade more than 20 U.S. states to authorize sterilization of men and women in prisons and mental hospitals, and they urged the federal government to restrict the immigration of "undesirable" races.

No nation, of course, practiced eugenics as enthusiastically as Nazi Germany, whose program culminated in "euthanasia" ("good death") of the mentally and physically disabled as well as Jews, Gypsies, Catholics and others. As revelations of these atrocities spread after World War II, popular support for eugenics programs waned in the U.S. and elsewhere.

homosexuality is innate, as many homosexuals have long professed. That claim was advanced by a report in *Science* in 1991 by Simon LeVay of the Salk Institute for Biological Studies in San Diego. LeVay has acknowledged both that he is gay and that he believes evidence of biological differences between homosexuals and heterosexuals will encourage tolerance toward gays.

LeVay, who recently left the Salk Institute to found the Institute of Gay and Lesbian Education, focused on a tiny neural structure in the hypothalamus, a region of the brain known to control sexual response. He measured this structure, called the interstitial nucleus, in autopsies of the brains of 19 homosexual males, 16 heterosexual males and six heterosexual women. LeVay found that the interstitial nucleus was almost twice as large in the heterosexual males as in the homosexual males or in the women. He postulated that the interstitial nucleus "is large in individuals oriented toward women"—whether male or female.

Of course, LeVay's finding only addresses anatomic differences, not necessarily genetic ones. Various other researchers have tried to establish that homosexuality is not just biological in its origin—caused, perhaps, by hormonal influences in utero—but also genetic. Some have sought evidence in experiments with rats and other animals. A group headed by Angela Pattatucci of the National Cancer Institute is studying a strain of male fruit flies—which wags have dubbed either "fruity" or "fruitless"—that court other males.

In December 1991 J. Michael Bailey of Northwestern University and Richard C. Pillard of Boston University announced they had uncovered evidence of a genetic basis for male homosexuality in humans. They studied 161 gay men, each of whom had at least one identical or fraternal twin or adopted brother. The researchers determined that 52 percent of the identical twins were both homosexual, as compared with 22 percent of the fraternal twins and 11 percent of the adopted brothers.

Bailey and Pillard derived similar results in a study of lesbians published this year in the *Archives of General Psychiatry*. They compared 147 gay women with identical or fraternal twins or adopted sisters: 48 percent of the identical twins were both gay, versus 16 percent of the fraternal twins (who share only half each other's genes) and 6 percent of the adopted sisters. "Both male and female sexual orientation appeared to be influenced by genetic factors," Bailey and Pillard concluded.

observes that "a lot of the research has not been very good" and that the more recent, better-designed studies tended to turn up less evidence. "I don't think we will find any biological markers for crime," he says. "We should put our resources elsewhere."

Gay Genes

The ostensible purpose of investigations of mental illness, alcoholism and even crime is to reduce their incidence. Scientists studying homosexuality have a different goal: simply to test whether

This conclusion has disturbed some of Bailey and Pillard's own subjects. "I have major questions about the validity of some of the assumptions they are making," says Nina Sossen, a gay woman living in Madison, Wis., whose identical twin is heterosexual. Her doubts are shared by William Byne, a psychiatrist at Columbia University. He notes that in their study of male homosexuality Bailey and Pillard found more concordance between unrelated, adopted brothers than related (but non-twin) brothers. The high concordance of the male and female identical twins, moreover, may stem from the fact that such twins are often dressed alike and treated alike—indeed, they are often mistaken for each other—by family members as well as by others.

"The increased concordance for homosexuality among the identical twins could be entirely accounted for by the increased similarity of their developmental experiences," Byne says. "In my opinion, the major finding of that study is that 48 percent of identical twins who were reared together were discordant for sexual orientation."

Byne also criticizes LeVay's conclusion that homosexuality must be biological—although not necessarily genetic—because the brains of male homosexuals resemble the brains of women. That assumption, Byne points out, rests on still another assumption, that there are significant anatomic differences between heterosexual male and female brains. But to date, there have been no replicable studies showing such sexual dimorphism.

Byne notes that he has been suspected of having an antigay motive. Two reviewers of an article he recently wrote criticizing homosexuality research accused him of having a "right-wing agenda," he says. He has also been contacted by conservative groups hoping he will speak out against the admittance of homosexuals to the military. He emphasizes that he supports gay rights and thinks homosexuality, whatever its

cause, is not a "choice." He adds that genetic models of behavior are just as likely to foment bigotry as to quell it.

"Hierarchy of Worthlessness"

Despite the skepticism of Byne and others, at least one group, led by Dean Hamer of the National Cancer Institute, is searching not merely for anatomic or biochemical differences in homosexuals but for genetic markers. Hamer has done a linkage study of numerous small families, each of which has at least two gay brothers. He says his study has turned up some tentative findings, and he plans to submit his results soon. Hamer's colleague Pattatucci is planning a similar study of lesbians.

What purpose will be served by pinpointing genes linked to homosexuality? In an information sheet for prospective participants in his study, Hamer expresses the hope that his research may "improve understanding between people with different sexual orientations." He adds, "This study is not aimed at developing methods to alter either heterosexual or homosexual orientation, and the results of the study will not allow sexual orientation to be determined by a blood test or amniocentesis."

Yet even Pillard, who is gay and applauds Hamer's work, admits to some concern over the potential uses of a genetic marker for homosexuality. He notes that some parents might choose to abort embryos carrying such a marker. Male and female homosexuals might then retaliate, he says, by conceiving children and aborting fetuses that lacked such a gene.

Balaban, the Harvard biologist, thinks the possible dangers of such research—assuming it is successful—outweigh any benefits. Indeed, he sees behavioral genetics as a "hierarchy of worthlessness," with twin studies at the bottom and linkage studies of mental illness at the top. The best researchers can hope

for is to find, say, a gene associated with a slightly elevated risk of schizophrenia. Such information is more likely to lead to discrimination by insurance companies and employers than to therapeutic benefits, Balaban warns.

His colleague Lewontin agrees. In the 1970s, he recalls, insurance companies began requiring black customers to take tests for sickle cell anemia, a genetic disease that primarily affects blacks. Those who refused to take the test or who tested positive were denied coverage. "I feel that this research is a substitute for what is really hard—finding out how to change social conditions," Lewontin remarks. "I think it's the wrong direction for research, given that we have a finite amount of resources."

Paul R. Billings, a geneticist at the California Pacific Medical Center, shares some of these concerns. He agrees that twin studies seem to be inherently ambiguous, and he urges researchers seeking markers for homosexuality to consider what a conservative government—led by Patrick Buchanan, for example—might allow to be done with such information. But he believes some aspects of behavioral genetics, particularly searches for genes underlying mental illness, are worth pursuing.

In an article published in the British journal *Social Science and Medicine* last year, Billings and two other scientists offered some constructive criticism for the field. Researchers engaged in association and linkage studies should establish "strict criteria as to what would constitute meaningful data." Both scientists and the press should emphasize the limitations of such studies, "especially when the mechanism of how a gene acts on a behavior is not known." Billings and his colleagues strive to end their article on a positive note. "Despite the shortcomings of other studies," they say, "there is relatively good evidence for a site on the X chromosome which is associated with [manic depression] in some families." This finding was retracted earlier this year.

Cocaine-Exposed Infants:
Myths and Misunderstandings

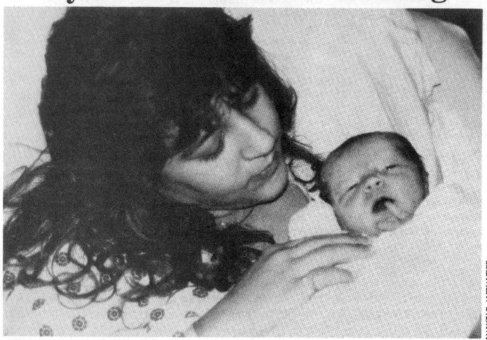

NANCY P. ALEXANDER

Barbara J. Myers
Heather Carmichael Olson
Karol Kaltenbach

Barbara J. Myers, Virginia Commonwealth University, Richmond, VA; Heather Carmichael Olson, University of Seattle, Seattle, WA; Karol Kaltenbach, Jefferson Medical College, Thomas Jefferson University, Philadelphia, PA

Note: All three authors are supported in whole or in part by grants from the National Institute of Drug Abuse which support research and treatment of substance-using mothers and their infants.

What do we really know about cocaine-exposed babies? Are they terribly damaged from birth with disabilities that will affect them all their lives? Is cocaine a teratogen that affects the development of limbs, organs, brains, and emotions? Or is this picture a distortion of the small amount of available research findings? New research findings are emerging almost every day. It is hard to know what to think, for what we knew yesterday is changed in today's press, and what we read today is most likely already out of date. *The simple truth at this point is that we do not yet know what the effects are of prenatal cocaine exposure.*

What does the media publish?

The popular press has covered this emotional topic frequently for a public which is deeply concerned for the welfare of these children. In the effort to spread information widely, the media tend to present a simple, brief, and dramatic picture. This may be an effective way to motivate people into action, but a careful eye is needed to watch for oversimplification, especially since it is common in the media to present individual worst-case stories and then draw broad generalizations.

Most of the media presentations have been decidedly negative in their accounts of drug-exposed infants. Titles of articles sound an alarm before the story begins. Some capitalize on fears about crack cocaine: "Crack Comes to the Nursery" (*Time,* Sept. 19, 1988); "Crack in the Cradle" (*Discover,* Sept. 1989). Others point to an alleged addiction which the babies are born with (a hypothesis no longer supported by most studies of cocaine-exposed infants): "Cocaine Babies: Hooked at Birth" (*Newsweek,* July 28, 1986); "I Gave Birth to an Addicted Baby" (*Good Housekeeping,* April, 1990); "Kids Who Can't Say No" (*Readers's Digest,* February, 1991). Some articles stigmatize these children. *The Washington Post* referred to cocaine-exposed babies as a "bio-underclass," a "potential human plague almost too horrible to imagine" (Sept. 17, 1989).

Magazines and newspapers often begin their articles with heart-wrenching accounts of a single baby who is severely affected, presumably as a result of drug exposure. Those of us who work with infants with disabilities will recognize early signs of trouble and feel a sympathetic connection with the infants and what they face. We should be aware, though, of exaggerations. For example, "Guillermo, a newborn at Broward General Medical Center in Ft. Lauderdale, has spent his whole short life crying. He is jittery and goes into spasms when he is touched. His eyes don't focus. He can't stick out his tongue, or suck. Born a week ago to a cocaine addict, Guillermo is described by his doctors as an addict himself" (*Newsweek,* July 28, 1986). *(A baby who has spent his whole life crying? Does that seem accurate? Is this story really a typical one? Does this account stigmatize Guillermo?)* Or consider the account of an infant named Robert: "Most of the babies at Highland General Hospital in Oakland, California, are asleep at this hour. But little Robert, brought in by his mother, has been awake for days. He cries inconsolably, and his tiny limbs jerk and jitter constantly. Periodically, his hands fly back to the sides of his head and his large, dark eyes freeze wide in startled terror .... At birth, the infant plunged into a nightmarish withdrawal from drugs used by his mother" (*Readers Digest,* February, 1991). *(Is it possible for an infant to be awake for days? Is he seeing nightmares, or are his hands moving up in a simple Moro reflex?)*

In addition to watching out for oversimplification and exaggerations, readers of these articles should remember that study of drug effects is very complex. A first question to ask is how probable it is that disabilities, if and when they are found, are a result of the cocaine exposure. Certainly many babies who are born with disabilities were never exposed to drugs; often, the cause for the problem is never known. When cocaine-exposed infants show disabling conditions, we cannot be certain that prenatal cocaine was responsible. Cocaine-exposed infants, like any other infants, may have parents with previously undetected recessive genetic abnormalities. Their mothers may have avoided prenatal care to escape detection of their drug dependence, and so a variety of obstetrical complications and other health problems might have been left untreated. The mothers may have eaten poorly during the pregnancy and not taken their prenatal vitamins. Most cocaine-using mothers are polydrug users: They drink alcohol, or smoke cigarettes, or use marijuana, or use a variety of prescription or street drugs, cut with a variety of substances. And substance-using women, like any other group of women, can have babies with problems whose cause is unknown. Given this complicated course of prenatal history, it is premature to link every problem shown by a cocaine-exposed infant to the cocaine. Cocaine may indeed have played a role in an infant's problem, but cocaine is just one of the risks, known and unknown, to which these babies were exposed.

Many articles in the media focus on the long-term effects of cocaine exposure. At times it seems that articles are discussing events that have been well documented. Yet studies of cocaine-exposed infants have not followed these children past age three or four, and most studies are of newborn infants. In *The New York Times* (Sept. 17, 1989), for example, we read, "... studies suggest that without help, the children of addicted mothers may be unable to develop into adults with basic employment skills and unable to form close human relationships. " *(Adults without basic employment skills? And unable to form close human relationships? These assertions cannot come from anyone's data, as nobody has followed children that far.)* On the same day, *The Washington Post* noted, "Already, a few [cocaine-exposed children] are turning up in first- and second-grade classrooms around the country, wreaking havoc on themselves and others. Severe emotional damage and even physical deformities not so readily apparent today may mushroom in the near future. The children's irritability and anger—along with their need for love and understanding—will surely grow." *(This article appeared before the group of cocaine-exposed children were old enough to enter school. Why are irritability and anger expected outcomes? Why should there be problems tomorrow—"emotional damage and physical deformities"—which are not apparent today?)* An education journal written for popular use also predicts the future for children exposed to cocaine: "In the typical classroom environment ... cocaine-exposed children tend to react in one of two ways. They withdraw completely, or they become wild and difficult to control" (*The Education Digest,* May, 1990). *(One must read this article carefully to pick up that the author is talking about her own predictions of the future.)* We need to be careful not to create ideas to fill the gaps in our knowledge, especially when we have strong feelings about the topic and want to know the answers now.

What does the research show?

In contrast to these disturbing popular accounts, available research on drug-exposed infants shows a mix of findings: In some studies, especially those published early on, cocaine-exposed infants were found to be different from (and "worse" than) comparison infants. But many studies detect no differences between cocaine-exposed and non-exposed infants, and that is important to know. These "no difference" studies are not readily published in professional journals or noted in the press. Indeed, Koren et al. (1989) documented that research studies which found that substance-exposed infants were *not* different from non-exposed infants were significantly more likely to be rejected for presentation at scientific meetings than were studies which found the substance-exposed infants *to* be different.

Two current research review articles give in-depth and readable examinations of the many research articles published through 1991 (Neuspiel & Hamel, 1991; Myers, Britt, Lodder, Kendall, & Williams-Petersen, in press). Both articles agree that the only finding which seems substantiated across many well-controlled studies is that babies who are prenatally exposed to cocaine are at risk for being younger and smaller at birth: This includes lower birth weight, birth length, head circumference, and gestational age. Cocaine-exposed babies were more likely to have shorter gestation (and thus to be premature); some were also found to be small for gestational age (SGA). Prematurity, SGA, and low birth weight are all risk factors for a variety of poor outcomes, whether or not cocaine has played a role. Thus, when cocaine-exposed children who were born too early or too small have problems, it is difficult to untangle what is the direct, and the indirect, cause. Certainly, cocaine plays at least an indirect causal role in this instance. Even though cocaine exposure places an infant at higher *risk* for prematurity and low birth weight, many exposed infants are born full-term and at appropriate weight. In fact, *the large majority of exposed infants are not premature and not low birth weight,* especially in programs which offer good prenatal care and nutrition education.

For many areas of infant development, one study shows infants exposed to cocaine to be different from comparison infants, while the next study finds no difference. We find this for areas as disparate as incidence of stillbirths, SIDS, anomalies of various organ systems, neurological abnormalities, newborn behavior as measured by the NBAS (Neonatal Behavioral Assessment Scale), social-emotional functioning, and parenting practices.

Why do scientists arrive at such different answers to straightforward questions? As researchers, we point to the methodological problems which accompany this difficult area of study. Although research design questions may seem boring and technical, they are at the heart of our difficulty in answering the complex questions posed by prenatal substance exposure.

Methodological problems in studying prenatal substance exposure

The answers we get about any research question depend in large part on how the research study is structured and conducted. The "ideal" for research is to conduct a true experimental study, with participants randomly assigned to one of several conditions. But random assignment to drug use or nonuse is obviously impossible and unethical. Some "less than perfect" methods are a necessity right from the start. Still, there are steps that can be taken to improve the validity and reliability of research in this area.

A first area of concern is who are the subjects in the study. Consider the following case: A 30-year-old white paralegal started using cocaine in the late 1970's because she thought it wasn't addictive. Concerned about her weight, she wanted to get high on fewer calories than alcohol supplied. Now a successful lawyer, she attends 12-step meetings at lunchtime and is in recovery. Although cocaine is used by people of all social classes and ethnic groups, this middle-class lawyer would not end up as a subject in a typical research project. There are currently *no* published studies of middle- and upper-class cocaine-using mothers and their infants. Rather, low-income women and their infants make up the study populations. This means that conditions of poverty get mixed up with effects of cocaine exposure. In addition, studies often use groups of women who are enrolled in ongoing drug treatment and recovery programs. These mothers are the healthiest, most stable, and most self-aware of low-income drug-using women. Thus we miss out on knowing about both upper-income women and the less motivated of the lower-income women—the

two groups which are probably the "best" and the "worst" of the substance-using population in terms of health, stability, and personal resources. We cannot study babies whose mothers do not want to be studied or for whom no active research study is available.

Researchers have also learned that ascertaining drug use is a very challenging task. Drug users often deny their drug involvement (indeed, "denial" is one of the signs that the individual is in trouble with drugs or alcohol). In some states, admission of drug use is enough to prompt criminal proceedings, so denial may keep a mother out of jail or keep her children from being taken from her. Urine toxicology identifies traces of the drug or its metabolites from use only in the past 2-3 days, and so many users plan ahead and abstain prior to scheduled clinic appointments. Thus, many studies undoubtedly report data from a few drug users mixed in with the non-users. Even when drug use is admitted or discovered, it is difficult to establish the frequency, quantity, quality, type, and timing of substances used. Dose-effect relationships in the human fetus are nearly impossible to establish. Polydrug use, including opiates, marijuana, alcohol, nicotine and prescription drugs, is probably the most common pattern, yet this makes the job of untangling effects even more challenging. We know that smoking significantly reduces birth weight, and that alcohol is a teratogen. It is rare to find a woman who used cocaine during her pregnancy who did not also drink, smoke, or use other drugs; rarer still would be such a woman who also ate well, had good prenatal care, and had a stable and supportive home life. There are a thousand and one individual patterns, which underscores the need to treat each woman and her baby as a unique and individual dyad.

Should the professional who examines a baby know that drug exposure has taken place? While this knowledge may be valuable clinically, it can influence findings in a research study, and so the ideal is to have examiners who are blind to exposure status. Many studies fail to keep examiners blind, and so there is a threat of the examiners' expectations affecting findings. This implies that non-exposed infants are being studied at the same time and in the same setting. Many times there is no comparison group, or the comparison group is different on a number of factors other than cocaine exposure. Comparison groups need to be drawn from the same community as the cocaine-using sample, so that differences which really come from local customs, social class, health practices, and ethnicity are not unknowingly confused with the effects of the cocaine exposure.

After the baby is born and goes home, the caregiving environment becomes critically important. What is a cocaine-user's home environment like? It is no doubt a widely diverse picture, from suburban subdivisions to crowded apartments to shelters for the homeless, but our research at this point offers little information. From a research perspective, it is important not to confound results which stem from prenatal chemical exposure with results which come from how a baby is raised. This area is critical, but we know very little about how the caretaking environment(s) of substance-exposed infants impact their development.

Research with families in which substances are abused is expensive and difficult to do. Even the most well-seasoned and devoted team of researchers can become overwhelmed with both the scientific problems and the personal drain that this work presents. Cocaine-using mothers are a diverse group, and this diversity sometimes includes situations of extreme poverty, unstable lifestyles, and personal danger. Any critical assessment of research in this field should compliment those individuals who are doing the best they know how in a difficult situation.

Continued research in the area of perinatal substance exposure is needed, especially research which is well-designed and carefully conducted. The National Institute of Drug Abuse is currently funding such research. Twenty programs (referred to as the "Perinatal 20") are participating in treatment-research demonstrations involving adult and adolescent pregnant and postpartum women and their children. These sites are working together to share ideas and techniques in an effort to provide sound answers to some of the questions about substance-exposed children and which treatment models are the most effective in producing favorable outcomes for both mother and child.

What is our model of cocaine effects?

With our current state of knowledge, most researchers in this area now view this group of children using a risk model, not a deficit model. That is, we recognize the various risks—biological, environmental, interpersonal—which individuals are subject to, and we also recognize the many strengths and protective factors which individuals may have available. Whether a risk factor such as cocaine exposure shows an impact upon a child's health or behavior depends on the complex interplay of all the risk factors and protective factors. Cocaine exposure is no doubt a biological risk factor, and many prenatally-exposed infants will have other risk factors at work as well. Certainly there are a great many such children whose prenatal care was inadequate, whose lives are chaotic, whose neighborhoods are dangerous, whose diets are terrible, and whose parents are emotionally unavailable to them. But most children also have some protective factors which can soften and relieve the stressors. These might include their general good health, easy temperament, a loving grandparent, a safe and appropriately stimulating home, a mother who loves and cherishes her child, or a community which provides adequate health and intervention services. Whether an individual child shows negative effects of cocaine exposure depends on the complex and ever-changing interactions among all the risk factors and protective factors in the child's life. This model is a graceful one that embraces each of us—every baby, every child, every adult. Not only is it philosophically satisfying, it also is supported by the data. Assessments of children which take into account a great many biological,

environmental, and personal factors, and the ongoing changes in these forces, provide a more accurate prediction of child outcome than do static measures of isolated variables.

What can professionals who work with infants and young children do in the meantime? We cannot wait until all of the research is documented, because large numbers of infants prenatally exposed to drugs are born every day and some may be referred to us for evaluation or services. Here are some suggestions:

(1) Accept that the full picture is not yet known about substance-exposed babies.

(2) Remember the diversity of substance-using families, and be sensitive to the individual mother and her baby.

(3) Resist believing the stereotypes and participating in the stigmatization of drug abusers. Truly accept that it could be you, it could be your sister.

(4) Work from a risk and protective factors model, not a deficit model. Identify the positive factors in infants' and mothers' lives, as well as the problems.

(5) Think in terms of polydrug exposure, not just cocaine exposure. Be especially aware of alcohol effects and cigarette smoking.

(6) From what we know so far, the supports and interventions that substance-exposed infants need are no different from what other babies need. The interventions you offer need to be sensitive to the family's culture, but you will not need a special set of materials and activities for these babies.

(7) Chemical dependence adds new dimensions to what the family needs. As infant interventionists, we need to expand our own training to include knowledge and experience in the course of addiction and recovery. We need to become partners in our communities with agencies that provide substance abuse treatment if we are to be effective advocates for the infants and families we serve

References

Koren, G. Shear, H., Graham, K., & Einarson, T. (1989). Bias against the null hypothesis: The reproductive hazards of cocaine. *The Lancet, 2,* No. 8677, 1440-1442.

Mayes, L. C., Granger, R. H., Bornstein, M. H., & Zuckerman, B. (Jan. 15, 1992). The problem of prenatal cocaine exposure: A rush to judgment. *Journal of the American Medical Association, 267* (No. 3), 406-408.

Myers, B. J., Britt, G. C., Lodder, D. E., Kendall, K. A., & Williams-Petersen, M. G. (In press). Cocaine exposure and infant development: A review of the literature. *Journal of Child and Family Studies.*

Neuspiel, D. R., & Hamel, S. C. (1991). Cocaine and infant behavior. *Journal of Developmental and Behavioral Pediatrics, 12,* 55-64.

Zuckerman, B. , & Frank, D. (1992). "Crack Kids": Not broken. *Pediatrics, 89* (no. 2), 337-339.

WAR
BABIES

What happens when mothers-to-be become the victims of starvation? Now three generations after World War II, we are still learning the disturbing answers.

Jared Diamond

Contributing editor Jared Diamond is a professor of physiology at the UCLA School of Medicine. In June he wrote about the search for eternal youth [for Discover].

It is easy to write now that each person got 400 calories a day. In practice it was quite another thing. . . . People sought food everywhere in the streets and the surrounding countryside. Anything edible was picked up in this way, and they were lucky who found a potato or two or a handful of greens. . . . People dropped from exhaustion in the streets and many died there. Often people were so fatigued that they were unable to return home, before curfew; so they hid in barns or elsewhere to sleep and there died. . . . Older people, who lacked the strength to go searching for food, stayed at home in bed and died.
—Famine and Human Development: The Dutch Hunger Winter of 1944–1945

Among the homey images I recall from my wife's pregnancy are the bigger-than-usual milk cartons in the refrigerator and her vitamin bottles on the kitchen counter. To our generation the value of good nutrition for pregnant women seems obvious. But what makes us so

sure? After all, we can't run experiments on people to prove it. Starving hundreds of pregnant women and then comparing their kids with well-nourished cousins would be absolutely unthinkable.

Yet such an inhuman experiment was indeed once conducted. By imposing a famine on part of the population of the Netherlands during the last seven months of World War II, the Nazis effectively reduced 40,000 pregnant women to starvation. These cruel circumstances resulted in a study of the effects of prenatal nutrition that was grimly well-designed, complete with a control group: while these women were starving, other mothers-to-be in the same society were eating comparatively healthy rations.

Years later, when the babies who survived had grown into adults, epidemiologists could distinguish the different effects of prenatal and postnatal nutrition; they could even discern the effects of malnutrition at different stages of pregnancy, for at the time the famine took hold, some women were further along in their pregnancy than others. Even now we are still learning what toll was exacted by the events of 45 years ago. Only recently have researchers learned that the famine's effects reached far beyond its immediate victims: now that girls born to the starved Dutch women have grown up and had children of their own, it's become apparent that some of these children too are marked by the deprivations suffered years earlier by their grandmothers!

Today we accept without question that proper nutrition is important for maintaining our health as adults and even more important for the development of our children. The evidence seems most persuasive when we look at the malnourished Third World and see shorter life spans, lowered resistance to disease, and high infant mortalities. But even in the industrialized world we can readily see the positive effects of a good diet. For one thing, today's adults tend to be taller than their parents; the difference approaches six inches in Japan. On average, too, people who are poor, with comparatively limited access to food, are shorter and less healthy than their wealthier countrymen. Moreover, it is not just physical health that seems to be at risk. Many tests of mental function suggest that poor nutrition in childhood may affect learning ability throughout life.

One might speculate that if we are so susceptible to the effects of poor nutrition as children, we must be especially sensitive to those effects while we're still in the womb, when our brain and body are forming. And, indeed, many studies have shown an association between poor nutrition, low weight at birth, and poor physical and mental performance later on. Yet it's not easy to prove that inadequate prenatal nutrition itself is the culprit. Sadly, babies poorly nourished in the womb are likely to be poorly nourished after birth as well. Furthermore, diet may not be the only thing influencing their health. Access to medical care, schooling, and stimulation outside school may play a part.

Figuring out just how big a role prenatal malnutrition plays in this miserable chain of events, then, is difficult at best. But the starvation in the Nazi-occupied Netherlands nearly half a century ago offers some thought-provoking answers.

The Dutch tragedy was the result of one of the most controversial decisions of World War II. After the Allied forces invaded Normandy and liberated France in the summer of 1944, our generals debated two strategies for completing Germany's defeat: to advance northeastward from France into Germany's Ruhr industrial region or to push eastward into the Saar. Had all our resources been concentrated on a single strategy, either might have succeeded. In fact both advances were attempted at once, and both ground to a standstill.

The northern advance hinged on the famous Battle of Arnhem, which inspired the film *A Bridge Too Far*. On September 17, 1944, British paratroops were dropped on the Dutch city of Arnhem to take command of a crucial bridge over the Rhine; other Allied forces, meanwhile, tried to join them from the south. Dutch railroad workers courageously called a general strike to impede the Nazis' efforts to bring up reinforcements. But stiff Nazi resistance forced the Allies to retreat, on September 25, after

heavy losses. The Allies then shifted their military effort away from the Netherlands, most of which remained under German occupation until May 1945.

In retaliation for the Dutch strike an embargo on transport in the Netherlands, including transport of food, was ordered by the notorious Nazi Reichskommissar Seyss-Inquart, later tried and hanged at Nuremberg. The predictable result of the embargo, which began in October 1944, was a famine that became progressively worse as stored food supplies were exhausted and that was not lifted until the Netherlands was liberated the following spring. Because an unusually severe winter hampered relief efforts, the famine became known as the Dutch Hunger Winter.

Intake dropped as low as 400 calories a day, down from an already-reduced daily ration of 1,500 calories. Still, some people were better off than others. The hunger was milder in the farming regions of the north and south; it was most severe in the large industrial cities of the west, such as Amsterdam, Rotterdam, and The Hague. Those people with enough strength went to the countryside to seek food, including tulip bulbs, in the fields. The hunger was also somewhat selective by social class: people of higher socioeconomic status were able to use money, property, and influence to obtain additional food.

Altogether 10,000 people starved to death, and malnutrition contributed to the deaths of countless others. Adults in the famine cities who survived lost, on average, 15 to 20 percent of their body weight. Some women weighed less at the end of their pregnancy than at its inception.

When the Allies finally liberated the Netherlands in early May 1945, they rushed in food, and conditions quickly improved. But by then 40,000 fetuses had been subjected to the hardships of famine. Depending on their date of conception, these babies were exposed at various stages of gestation, for periods as long as seven months. For example, babies conceived in April 1944 and born in early January 1945 were exposed to the starvation just in the last trimester of pregnancy; those conceived in February 1945 and born in November 1945 were exposed only in the first trimester. Babies unlucky enough to be conceived in August 1944 and born in May 1945 spent their entire second and third trimesters inside increasingly malnourished mothers.

In the late 1960s four researchers at Columbia University School of Public Health—Zena Stein, Mervyn Susser, Gerhart Saenger, and Francis Marolla, all of whom had studied malnutrition in urban ghettos—realized that much might be learned from the now-grown babies of the Dutch Hunger Winter. The outcomes of pregnancies in the stricken cities of the west could be compared with those in towns to the north or south, outside the worst-hit area. In addition, the results of pregnancies during the famine could be compared with those that occurred before and after it.

Hospital records and birth registries yielded statistics

on the health of the wartime mothers and their newborns. And at least for the boys, follow-up information on those same children as young adults could be extracted from the records of the Dutch military draft system. Virtually all boys at age 19 were called up for an exam that recorded their height and weight, medical history, results of mental-performance tests, level of schooling completed, and father's occupation; the latter served as a rough indicator of socioeconomic status.

A starving mother was forced to unconsciously "choose" whether to devote the few available calories to her own body or to her fetus.

These studies provided some important insights, the first of which concerned the famine's effect on fertility. During the winter of 1944 conceptions quickly declined to one-third the normal level. This suggests that the women's fertility became impaired as their fat reserves, already depleted due to reduced wartime rations, were rapidly used up. The decline was more pronounced for wives of manual workers than of nonmanual workers, presumably because the former had less means to buy their way out of starvation.

The Dutch results agree with other evidence that body weight affects our reproductive physiology. Women in German concentration camps often ceased to menstruate (while low sperm counts and impotence were common among male inmates). Moreover, studies have shown that girls begin menstruating earlier in well-fed industrialized nations than in underfed Third World countries. The same trend applies to the present generation of American women compared with their less well nourished grandmothers. All these pieces of evidence suggest that a woman's fertility is dependent on having sufficient body weight to support conception.

Among the famine babies themselves, the most obvious effects were seen in those who were exposed during the last trimester, which is normally the period when a fetus undergoes its most rapid weight gain: these babies had markedly lower average birth weights (6 pounds 10 ounces) than those born before the famine began (7 pounds 6 ounces). Starvation during the third trimester also resulted in babies who were born slightly shorter and with smaller head circumferences, indicating slightly slower than normal growth of the bones and brain. But the main impact was to retard the growth of muscle and fat.

The prefamine pregnancies had taken place while wartime rations still hovered around 1,500 daily calories—meager for a pregnant woman, who normally requires 2,500 calories a day. Medical records showed that these expectant mothers lost weight themselves but were able to maintain a normal birth weight for their babies. Once rations dropped below 1,500 calories, however, babies began to share the impact. And eventually, as the famine wore on and severe starvation struck, all further weight loss was suffered by the baby rather than the mother. Birth weight recovered quickly when food supplies improved, though: babies born three months after the famine's end had normal weights.

Both during and right after the Hunger Winter there was a sharp rise in infant deaths in the Netherlands' hard-hit cities. For babies exposed to famine only in the first trimester, the rate of stillbirth nearly doubled. Those babies had been conceived just three months before the famine's end, and so they in fact completed most of their gestation inside mothers who were relatively well nourished. Yet malnutrition during those first three months had evidently planted a slow-fuse time bomb that went off at birth.

Still greater, however, was the effect on babies exposed during the second, and especially the third, trimesters. Those babies had a higher-than-normal death rate in their first week of life, and the rate continued to climb until they were at least three months old. Some of these babies died of malnutrition itself, others succumbed to normal childhood infections to which they had lowered resistance. Fortunately, once the famine babies reached the age of one year, their increased risk of death disappeared.

Let's now see how the babies who survived the perils of birth and early infancy were faring 19 years later, when the boys were called up for the draft. In many respects these young men were similar to any others their age. Their height, for example, showed all the usual effects of socioeconomic factors, including family size and diet: sons of manual workers averaged nearly an inch shorter than sons of wealthier fathers, children from families with many mouths to feed were shorter than only children, and later-born sons were shorter than first-born sons. The common thread is that children who have access to less food end up shorter. But postnatal, rather than prenatal, nutrition was the culprit here. If you picked any given group—say, sons of manual workers—the young men whose mothers were starved during pregnancy were no shorter than their peers.

Records from the Dutch draft exams also allowed the Columbia researchers to see if poor nutrition in pregnancy might cause lasting mental deficits as well as physical ones. Experiments with rats had shown that offspring of mothers that are starved in pregnancy end up with fewer-than-normal brain cells and learning disabilities. So when the researchers compared the grown-up famine babies' performance on tests of mental proficiency with the performance of those who had received better prenatal nourishment, they expected to find poorer scores for those who had been starved during gestation.

No such result was forthcoming. The draft exam,

which included tests of verbal, arithmetic, clerical, and mechanical skills, clearly showed the effects of social environment, which were parallel to the physical effects already mentioned—thus, sons of manual laborers, sons from large families, and sons born late into a family of several children tended to score below other young men. But no effect whatsoever could be attributed to prenatal starvation. One possible explanation is that our brain has enough extra cells to preserve mental function even if some of our cells are lost. At any rate, whatever effects can be attributed to nutrition must be due to nutrition after birth, not before it.

The genetic interests of the fetus are served by saving itself. Hence we evolve as fetuses to be parasites commandeering our mother's nutrients.

This, then, was the good news, such as it was. Those starved children who made it to adulthood were no worse off than their better-nourished counterparts. However, the medical records of the male famine babies who never made it to a draft physical did reveal one consequence of prenatal starvation—and it was sobering. Fetuses exposed to famine during their first three months in the womb were twice as likely as others to have defects of the central nervous system, such as spina bifida (in which the spine fails to close properly) and hydrocephalus (a related condition, characterized by fluid accumulating in the brain). The birth defects, it now appears, almost certainly arose from starvation during the first trimester, when the nervous system was being laid down.

Just how did a lack of food have such a dire result? Animal experiments have raised the suspicion that such defects can arise from a deficiency of the B vitamin folic acid early in pregnancy. A year ago this finding was confirmed for humans in a study of 22,776 pregnant women in Boston. Babies born to mothers who took multivitamins including folic acid during the first six weeks of pregnancy had a nearly fourfold lower frequency of central nervous system defects than did babies born to women who did not take such supplements. Brands of multivitamins that lacked folic acid, or multivitamins taken only after the seventh week of pregnancy, offered no protection.

All the results from the Dutch famine studies that I've discussed so far describe the effects of starvation on mothers and their children. But recent findings have raised disturbing questions about the famine's effect on a third generation. By now the famine babies are 45 or 46, and most of the girls have long since had children of their own; the "girls" themselves are women at the end of their reproductive careers. More than 100 of these women happened to have had their babies in the same Amster-

dam hospital in which they themselves were born, which makes for an easy comparison of birth records. An examination of those records has revealed something very odd: it turns out that those women who were themselves fetuses in their first and second trimester during the Dutch Hunger Winter gave birth to underweight babies. That is, the babies were somehow affected by the starvation of their grandmothers many decades earlier.

This result might have been easier to understand if the mothers themselves had been underweight at birth or were small as adults. Neither was true. Recall that starvation in the first or second trimester produced babies with normal birth weights. Only third-trimester starvation led to small babies. Yet, paradoxically, when these small babies later became mothers, they gave birth to normal-size babies. It was the women who were themselves normal size at birth who became mothers of underweight infants.

Somehow the grandmothers' suffering programmed their children in utero so that the grandchildren would be affected. This astonishing result will undoubtedly inspire experiments aimed at identifying the still-unknown cellular mechanism. But what is indisputable is that the Dutch famine left its harsh imprint on at least three generations.

From the perspective of evolutionary biology, the famine posed to the bodies of pregnant mothers an agonizing dilemma. What would you do in a situation threatening both your life and your child's life if anything you did to help one would hurt the other? Think quickly: If you see a car about to crash head-on into your car, do you throw yourself in front of your child sitting strapped in the seat beside you or do you try to protect yourself instead? Now let's make the choice more agonizing: What if your child's subsequent survival hinges on your own? You've all heard the airlines' standard safety announcement that in the event of a loss of cabin pressure, place the oxygen mask on yourself first, *then* place the mask on your child. In that situation, you have to help yourself first, because you'll be in no state to help your child if you are unconscious.

Similarly a mother starving in the Netherlands in 1944 was forced to unconsciously "choose" whether to devote the few available calories to her own body or to her fetus. This is a classic example of a conflict between two genetically related individuals. Natural selection favors the individual who passes on his or her genes to the most descendants. The genetic interests of the fetus are served by saving itself, and hence we evolve as fetuses to be parasites on our mother, commandeering her nutrients as efficiently as possible. But the mother's genetic interests are served by passing her genes to offspring. She gains nothing if her nutritional sacrifices kill not only herself but her child. Perhaps she would be best off, from an evolutionary point of view, if she sacrificed that fetus and tried again later. Yet there is no certainty that she will have another chance later.

The outcome of the Dutch famine indicates that natural selection struck a compromise. When the famine began, a mother's body at first accepted the full brunt, losing weight while preserving the weight of the fetus. In the next stage of famine both the fetus and the mother shared the hardship. In the last stage all weight loss came at the expense of the fetus, because any more weight loss by the mother would have threatened the mother's survival and thereby the survival of her child.

These pregnant women had no say in how their body allocated its precious resources, of course. Natural selection proceeded along its inexorable journey oblivious to any human agony or ethical dilemma. To ask whether the decisions it made were wise, whether they were some-how the "right" decisions, is irrelevant. The choices were arrived at in accordance with the cold logic of evolution and nothing more.

But what about the decisions that created such cruel conditions in the first place? What about the reasoning that even today, in the guise of wartime expediency, can compel one group of people to consciously impose starvation on another and thus scar the lives of unborn generations? For that matter, what about the reduction of social programs in our own society that might subject untold numbers of children, both before and after birth, to the dangers of malnutrition simply by failing to ensure proper nourishment for them and their mothers? The lessons of the Dutch Hunger Winter are there for the learning. We can ignore them only at our children's, and our grandchildren's, expense.

WHEN A PREGNANT WOMAN DRINKS

**ELISABETH
ROSENTHAL**

Elisabeth Rosenthal is an emergency-room physician in New York City.

At the human and behavior genetics Laboratory at Emory University, in Atlanta, a videotape recording shows a smiling 8-year-old girl peering from behind thick glasses at two clear plastic boxes topped by red bows, each containing a chocolate-chip cookie. The game, a psychologist explains, is to open both boxes and remove the cookies—and no eating until both cookies are out. The girl's 35-year-old mother observes.

The child seems to understand and, with the eagerness of a race horse at the gate, lunges at the boxes. For an endless few minutes, she pulls intently at the ribbons and tugs doggedly at the bows, clearly not up to this most elementary task. Fi-

nally, the mother comes to the rescue by untying one box and, with the second still sealed, the grinning child pops a cookie in her mouth.

"Ugh. This is too painful to watch," exclaims Dr. Claire D. Coles, the center's director of Clinical and Developmental Research, as she puts the tape on pause. "Look at that nice little girl. Her face is dysmorphic. She's too small for her age. And her fine motor coordination is awful.

"What's worse, look at the mother. She's also mildly dysmorphic. She spent her childhood in special-ed classes. The whole family suffers from prenatal alcohol exposure. All three kids, the mother, her brother."

In the last decade it has become unquestionably clear that alcohol is a potent teratogen,

which can cause irreversible damage to the body and brain of the developing fetus. Experts like Dr. Coles now believe that women who are pregnant or contemplating pregnancy should not drink—at all.

Fetal alcohol syndrome and its more subtle variant, fetal alcohol effect, are umbrella terms used to describe the condition affecting the scarred offspring of drinking mothers. Victims with the full-blown syndrome, whose mothers generally drank heavily throughout pregnancy, often suffer physical malformations and mental retardation. Even those less fully affected, sometimes the progeny of women who drank only intermittently, may end up with lifelong learning disabilities and behavioral problems.

No one knows exactly how many individuals are afflicted

with fetal alcohol damage, but the estimates are staggering. The Centers for Disease Control estimate that more than 8,000 alcohol-damaged babies are born each year, or 2.7 babies for every 1,000 live births. Others feel that these figures are low. On some Indian reservations, 25 percent of all children are reportedly afflicted.

Although the syndrome was first described in 1973, the broad impact of alcohol-related fetal injury has only recently become apparent to scientists. "The Broken Cord," Michael Dorris's moving memoir about raising a severely alcohol-affected child, brought the syndrome to wider public attention when it was published last summer.

Some experts believe fetal-alcohol exposure is the most

common-known cause of mental retardation in this country. Dr. Robert J. Sokol, dean of the School of Medicine at Wayne State University in Detroit and director of Wayne State's Alcohol Research Center, estimates that 1 out of 10 retarded adults in residential care has fetal alcohol syndrome.

Experts in birth defects see the survivors of drinking pregnancies everywhere. When Dr. Coles recently lectured at a reform school, she recalls, she thought, "My God, half these kids look alcohol affected." And as the syndrome becomes better known, others are beginning to recognize it as well.

"I get a lot of calls saying, 'I've just figured out what's wrong with our 18-year-old adopted son. He's dropped out of school; he's always had learning problems; he's never fit in,' " says Dr. Ann Streissguth of the University of Washington, who has followed a group of children with alcohol-related disabilities for 14 years.

Still, as Dr. Coles says, "the vast majority of kids like this have never been identified or followed. People probably just assumed they were a little stupid or a little funny looking."

As she speaks, I stare sheepishly at the faces of the Atlanta girl and her mother still frozen on the screen: their eyes just slightly too far apart, their thin upper lips, their smallish heads. Although I received my medical training within the last 10 years, without Dr. Cole's coaching I would have missed this diagnosis.

IN SCREENING FOR ALCOhol-related injuries, an expert in birth defects, or dysmorphologist, examines the suspect child for the unusual facial characteristics, small head and body size, poor mental capabilities and abnormal behavior patterns that typify alcohol-related birth defects. In infancy, the evaluation is usually prompted by knowledge of a mother's drinking, or because a newborn develops the shakes or seizures typical of alcohol withdrawal. But at this stage the symptoms are easily overlooked. Only 20 percent of those with the full

syndrome have marked facial abnormalities, and those with the effect look fine.

"Except when a child is grossly dysmorphic," the syndrome is not diagnosed, says Dr. Sterling K. Claren, Aldrich Professor of Pediatrics at the University of Washington School of Medicine in Seattle. As for fetal alcohol effect, he adds, it "really cannot be diagnosed in newborns."

Many children with the full syndrome come to expert attention only after they fail to gain weight and meet developmental landmarks. Sometimes a physician notices an abundance of physical complaints—crossed eyes, heart murmurs or recurrent ear infections—that suggest congenital malformation. Some are not recognized until years later, when they begin having trouble at school. Some are not recognized at all. Dr. José F. Cordero of the Center for Disease Control's Division of Birth Defects and Developmental Disabilities believes that as many as two-thirds of cases of the full syndrome remain undiagnosed, with the figure for those less severely affected even higher.

Dr. Coles and her staff, as part of their study, crisscross Atlanta, turning their trained eyes on the progeny of alcoholic pregnancies to look for signs of damage. On a day in November, she visited a ramshackle housing project to examine a one-month-old boy whose mother is an alcohol and cocaine abuser. She put the baby through a series of tests: shaking rattles near his ear, tweaking a toe with a rubber band, recording his cry.

The boy has no physical signs of fetal alcohol syndrome, she later explains, but his behavior is worrisome. "He is too irritable, too distractable," she said. "Kids at 30 days should be calm and able to focus on a rattle." But, she added, "If you weren't trained you might not recognize this as a substance-abuse baby."

Anne Cutcliffe's adopted daughter had seen various doctors before she was referred to Dr. Coles for an evaluation at age 2. "I guess I recall when I got her at 9 months, she was not

an attractive child," said Mrs. Cutcliffe, who lives in Atlanta and has five older children. "She only weighed 10½ pounds and her eyes were crossed. All she could do was turn from her stomach to her back. I guess it proves love is blind, because I never did see all those things that other people saw." The girl's biological mother was an alcoholic.

AS MANY AS 86 PERCENT of women drink at least once during pregnancy, according to the Public Health Service, and experts estimate that between 20 and 35 percent of pregnant women drink regularly. In a 1989 study of 2,278 highly educated women (39 percent had postgraduate degrees), 30 percent consumed more than one drink a week during pregnancy; only 11 percent smoked.

Alcohol freely crosses the placenta, and the fetus's blood-alcohol level will equal that of the mother's. A recent study in The New England Journal of Medicine showed that women have lower levels than men of the stomach enzyme that neutralizes alcohol, leaving them particularly vulnerable to high levels of alcohol in the bloodstream. The mother's blood alcohol must reach a certain level—the toxic threshold—before the fetus is at risk. Binge drinking seems to be particularly risky. While a drink each night might never push a mother's blood level above the danger threshold, a night of drinking in honor of a birthday might well raise the level enough to endanger the fetus.

The type of damage produced by drinking depends on the fetus's stage of development. The first trimester of pregnancy is devoted to the organization of the fetus's bones and organs, while the second and third trimesters center on growth and maturation. The brain develops throughout the nine-month period. "So we'd predict physical malformations from heavy drinking in the first trimester and growth retardation from drinking in the third," says Dr. Claren. "But brain damage can occur at any time." In addition, the toxic

threshold for brain damage seems to be much lower than for damage to other organs.

There is a rough correlation between the amount a mother imbibes during pregnancy and the severity of the baby's defects, but scientists are struggling to understand the many other factors that come into play. One major mystery is why so many drinking women frequently have apparently normal babies. Even in hopeless alcoholics, the chance of having a baby with the full-blown syndrome is only 35 percent.

The fetus may be more vulnerable on certain days of pregnancy. "Two drinks may be above the threshold on day 33 and on day 39, below," Dr. Claren said.

Women may also differ in their genetic susceptibility to having children with the syndrome, a tendency which some believe may follow ethnic and racial lines. Dr. Sokol has found that black women are seven times more likely to have fetal-alcohol affected children than white women with similar drinking habits. (Pregnant or not, studies have found that black and Hispanic women are more likely to be abstinent than white women. And a woman's alcohol consumption tends to rise with her level of education and income.) The Centers for Disease Control data show that the syndrome is 30 times more commonly reported in Native Americans than it is in whites, and six times more common in blacks.

Dr. Coles believes these figures may be "partly an artifact of reporting. Researchers don't go into nice private hospitals and start looking for alcohol-damaged babies." At least one study found that women of lower socioeconomic status are diagnosed correctly more often.

Although experts stress that there is no evidence in human beings that a rare single drink does damage, most say that with so much still unknown the only prudent course for the pregnant mother is abstinence. "Pregnancy is a time when women should be conservative with their bodies," says Dr. Claren. "Women think three or four times before they take an aspirin. They quit smoking. Then they turn around and have a drink? Some obstetricians advise women not to drink. Many others make up some dose of liquor which they think is O.K. To me that's crazy." Experts recommend that women who are breast-feeding also abstain, because brain maturation continues after birth.

The good news is that those who stop drinking at any time during pregnancy can increase their chances of having a healthy child. In a study conducted by the Boston University Fetal Alcohol Education Program, 85 women who drank heavily stayed with the program until they gave birth. Thirty-three of the women gave up or reduced their drinking before the seventh month of pregnancy; among these women, there was not one baby born with a growth abnormality, according to Dr. Barbara A. Morse, the program's director. Of the 52 women who continued to drink heavily, 21 gave birth to babies with growth retardation, and 5 of these babies had identifiable fetal alcohol syndrome. Moderate drinkers during early pregnancy are advised to quit while they're ahead: "If a woman comes to me three months pregnant and says 'I'm a regular drinker,' " says Dr. Claren, 'I say, 'Whatever you did is probably safe but stop now.' "

The Boston University group has led the way in calling for better counseling and improved drug-treatment opportunities for pregnant women. "Pregnancy is a time of incredible motivation for women," says Dr. Morse, noting that of those heavy-drinking women in the program who received counseling two-thirds were able to cut down considerably or stop altogether. Unfortunately, many in-patient alcohol rehabilitation programs exclude pregnant women, she said. Massachusetts recently opened four residential programs (or 35 beds) to treat pregnant alcoholics and

other substance abusers, making that state the leader nationwide.

RESEARCHERS ARE NOW focusing on moderate drinking during pregnancy in the hopes of learning more about alcohol's most subtle effects. Dr. Nancy Day of the University of Pittsburgh has studied the offspring of close to 700 women since 1988, most of whom reported consuming less than one drink a day during pregnancy. There were no babies with the full syndrome in the group, but there was a correlation between mothers who drank prenatally and the size of the child's head. Many also had an unusual number of "minor physical anomalies"—like crooked toes and funny ears. Most worrisome, the newborns had unusual brainwave patterns, of EEG's, potentially indicative of immature development of the brain.

Animal studies suggest that relatively low-level drinking can lead to damage. Dr. Claren's group at the University of Washington gave monkeys binges of alcohol once a week during pregnancy. The babies were unusually irritable, impulsive and distractable—a familiar triad of symptoms. "The good news is that the mothers had to get enough alcohol to get intoxicated to produce the defects," says Dr. Claren. "The bad news is that even if they only binged during the first three weeks of pregnancy"—equivalent to the first four to six weeks of the human term—"the babies still ended up with behavioral abnormalities."

There were physiological abnormalities as well. Though their brains were the right size and CT scans were totally normal, examination of their brain cells showed abnormal levels of dopamine, an important neurotransmitter. Dr.

Claren sees these findings as a strong physiological correlate of fetal alcohol effect. He hopes PET scans, which can sense chemical abnormalities in the brain, may be helpful in nailing down the often elusive diagnosis.

TWO RESEARCH groups, Dr. Coles's in Atlanta and Dr. Streissguth's in Seattle, have followed alcohol-affected children for 6 and 14 years respectively. They find that some of the traits that are only hinted at in newborns blossom in early childhood, creating potentially disastrous school experiences. In Dr. Coles's group, children at age 6 showed poorer memory, shorter attention spans, lower I.Q.'s, diminished achievement levels and other learning disabilities when compared to normal children. Dr. Streissguth's group also reported attention deficits and other behavior problems at this age.

These shortcomings may add up to a limited ability to learn and to learn from experience. These kids "have a unique flavor among the learning disabled," observes Dr. Claren. "They seem to be really untrainable." Anne Cutcliffe remembers her daughter, at 6, making such slow progress in reading that her teachers decided she should repeat the first grade. When she started first grade a second time, after the four-month summer vacation, she had lost even the small progress she'd made the year before and had to start again at the most basic level.

Most children with the full syndrome will be found, with formal psychological testing, to be "developmentally delayed" and will qualify for special education. But some will limp along in regular classes. Even those who qualify for special education are often

put into classes that don't meet their needs.

Most treatment programs for the mildly mentally handicapped were designed for patients like those with Down's syndrome, who are quiet, good workers and enjoy repetitive tasks. Parents and health professionals describe the alcohol-affected in very different terms: impulsive, unable to learn from mistakes, undisciplined, showing poor judgment, distractable, uninhibited. "We have to shift gears" to meet the needs of alcohol-affected kids, says Dr. Streissguth. He has applied for Federal funding to develop special therapeutic programs designed for them.

The flip side of the alcohol-affected personality is a winning one: outgoing, loving, physical, trusting. But together they lead to trouble. "She'll walk up to anyone on the street and stare at them and make conversation," says Anne Cutcliffe of her daughter. "Immediately she's buddies. It doesn't matter who." And Dr. Streissguth agrees that as young adults those with the syndrome often take sociability and physicality to unwelcome extremes: "They talk too loud and they stand too close. They seem not to pick up on normal social cues."

Paradoxically, researchers in the field say, alcohol-affected children who perform best on standardized tests end up with the toughest existence. Those who are obviously dysmorphic and mentally retarded receive social-service assistance and often end up in group homes. The others "fall into a pit," says Dr. Coles. Many drop out of school in frustration and their disabilities consign them to the margins of society, sometimes involved in prostitution and petty crime. "These are outgoing, trusting, fun-loving people, who are not able to evaluate the risks out there," said Dr. Streissguth.

SPERM UNDER SIEGE

MORE THAN WE EVER GUESSED, HAVING A HEALTHY BABY MAY DEPEND ON DAD

Anne Merewood

IT DIDN'T MAKE SENSE. Kate Malone's* first pregnancy had gone so smoothly. Yet when she and her husband Paul* tried to have a second child, their efforts were plagued by disaster. For two years, Kate couldn't become pregnant. Then she suffered an ectopic pregnancy, in which the embryo began to grow in one of her fallopian tubes and had to be surgically removed. Her next pregnancy heralded more heartache—it ended in miscarriage at four months and tests revealed that the fetus was genetically abnormal. Within months, she became pregnant and miscarried yet again. By this point, some four years after their troubles began, the couple had adopted a son; baffled and demoralized by the string of apparent bad luck, they gave up trying to have another child. "We had been to the top doctors in the country and no one could find a reason for the infertility or the miscarriages," says Kate.

Soon, however, thanks to a newspaper article she read, Kate uncovered what she now considers the likely cause of the couple's reproductive woes. When it all started, Paul had just been hired by a manufacturing company that used a chemical called **paradichlorobenzene, which derives from benzene, a known carcinogen. The article discussed the potential effects of exposure to chemicals, including benzene, on a man's sperm. Kate remembered hearing that two other men in Paul's small office were also suffering from inexplicable infertility. Both of their wives had gone through three miscarriages as well. Kate had always considered their similar misfortunes to be a tragic coincidence. Now she became convinced that the chemical (which has not yet been studied for its effects on reproduction) had blighted the three men's sperm.**

Paul had found a new job in a chemical-free workplace, so the couple decided to try once more to have a baby. Kate conceived immediately—and last August gave birth to a healthy boy. The Malones are now arranging for the National Institute for Occupational Safety and Health (NIOSH), the

*These names have been changed.

federal agency that assesses work-related health hazards for the public, to inspect Paul's former job site. "Our aim isn't to sue the company, but to help people who are still there," says Kate.

The Malones' suspicions about sperm damage echo the concerns of an increasing number of researchers. These scientists are challenging the double standard that leads women to overhaul their lives before a pregnancy—avoiding stress, cigarettes and champagne—while men are left confident that their lifestyle has little bearing on their fertility or their future child's health. Growing evidence suggests that sperm is both more fragile and potentially more dangerous than previously thought. "There seems to have been both a scientific resistance, and a resistance based on cultural preconceptions, to accepting these new ideas," says Gladys Friedler, Ph.D, an associate professor of psychiatry and pharmacology at Boston University School of Medicine.

But as more and more research is completed, sperm may finally be stripped of its macho image. For example, in one startling review of data on nearly 15,000 newborns, scientists at the University of North Carolina in Chapel Hill concluded that a father's drinking and smoking habits, and even his age, can increase his child's risk of birth defects—ranging from cleft palates to *hydrocephalus,* an abnormal accumulation of spinal fluid in the brain. Other new and equally worrisome studies have linked higher-than-normal rates of stillbirth, premature delivery and low birthweight (which predisposes a baby to medical and developmental problems) to fathers who faced on-the-job exposure to certain chemicals. In fact, one study found that a baby was more likely to be harmed if the father rather than the mother worked in an unsafe environment in the months before conception.

The surprising news of sperm's delicate nature may shift the balance of responsibility for a newborn's wellbeing. The research may also have social and economic implications far beyond the concerns of couples planning a family. In recent years a growing number of companies have sought

From *Health*, April 1991, pp. 53-57, 76-77. © 1991 by Anne Merewood. Reprinted by permission.

to ban women of childbearing age from jobs that entail exposure to hazardous substances. The idea is to protect the women's future children from defects—and the companies themselves from lawsuits. Already, the "fetal protection policy" of one Milwaukee-based company has prompted female employees to file a sex discrimination suit that is now before the U.S. Supreme Court. Conversely, if the new research on sperm is borne out, men whose future plans include fatherhood may go to court to *insist* on protection from hazards. Faced with potential lawsuits from so many individuals, companies may be forced to ensure that workplaces are safe for *all* employees.

SPERM UND DRANG

At the center of all this controversy are the microscopic products of the male reproductive system. Sperm (officially, spermatozoa) are manufactured by *spermatagonia,* special cells in the testes that are constantly stimulated by the male hormone testosterone. Once formed, a sperm continues to mature as it travels for some 80 days through the *epididymis* (a microscopic network of tubes behind the testicle) to the "waiting area" around the prostate gland, where it is expelled in the next ejaculation.

A normal sperm contains 23 chromosomes—the threadlike strands that house DNA, the molecular foundation of genetic material. While a woman is born with all the eggs she will ever produce, a man creates millions of sperm every day from puberty onwards. This awesome productivity is also what makes sperm so fragile. If a single sperm's DNA is damaged, the result may be a mutation that distorts the genetic information it carries. "Because of the constant turnover of sperm, mutations caused by the environment can arise more frequently in men than in women," says David A. Savitz, Ph.D., an associate professor of epidemiology and chief researcher of the North Carolina review.

If a damaged sperm fertilizes the egg, the consequences can be devastating. "Such sperm can lead to spontaneous abortions, malformations, and functional or behavioral abnormalities," says Marvin Legator, Ph.D., director of environmental toxicology at the department of preventative medicine at the University of Texas in Galveston. And in some cases, sperm may be too badly harmed even to penetrate an egg, leading to mysterious infertility.

Though the findings on sperm's vulnerability are certainly dramatic, researchers emphasize that they are also preliminary. "We have only a very vague notion of how exposure might affect fetal development, and the whole area of research is at a very early stage of investigation," says Savitz. Indeed, questions still far outnumber answers. For starters, there is no hard evidence that a chemical damages an infant by adversely affecting the father's sperm. A man who comes in contact with dangerous substances might harm the baby by exposing his partner indirectly—for example, through contaminated clothing. Another theory holds that the harmful

pollutants may be carried in the seminal fluid that buoys sperm. But more researchers are becoming convinced that chemicals can inflict their silent damage directly on the sperm itself.

THE CHEMICAL CONNECTION

The most well-known—and most controversial—evidence that chemicals can harm sperm comes from research on U.S. veterans of the Vietnam war who were exposed to the herbicide Agent Orange (dioxin), used by the U.S. military to destroy foliage that hid enemy forces. A number of veterans believe the chemical is responsible for birth defects in their children. The latest study on the issue, published last year by the Harvard School of Public Health, found that Vietnam vets had almost twice the risk of other men of fathering infants with one or more major malformations. But a number of previous studies found conflicting results, and because so little is known about how paternal exposure could translate into birth defects, the veterans have been unsuccessful in their lawsuits against the government.

Scientific uncertainty also dogs investigations into other potentially hazardous chemicals and contaminants. "There seem to be windows of vulnerability for sperm: Certain chemicals may be harmful only at a certain period during sperm production," explains Donald Mattison, M.D., dean of the School of Public Health at the University of Pittsburgh. There isn't enough specific data to make definitive lists of "danger chemicals." Still, a quick scan of the research shows that particular substances often crop up as likely troublemakers. Chief among them: lead, benzene, paint solvents, vinyl chloride, carbon disulphide, the pesticide DBCP, anesthetic gases and radiation. Not surprisingly, occupations that involve contact with these substances also figure heavily in studies of sperm damage. For example, men employed in the paper, wood, chemical, drug and paint industries may have a greater chance of siring stillborn children. And increased leukemia rates have been detected among children whose fathers are medical workers, aircraft or auto mechanics, or who are exposed regularly to paint or radiation. In fact, a study of workers at Britain's Sellafield nuclear power plant in West Cambria found a sixfold leukemia risk among children whose fathers were exposed to the plant's highest radiation levels (about 9 percent of all employees).

Workers in "high-risk" industries should not panic, says Savitz. "The credibility of the studies is limited because we have no firm evidence that certain exposures cause certain birth defects." Yet it makes sense to be watchful for warning signs. For example, if pollution levels are high enough to cause skin irritations, thyroid trouble, or breathing problems, the reproductive system might also be at risk. Another danger signal is a clustered outbreak of male infertility or of a particular disease: It was local concern about high levels of childhood leukemia, for instance, that sparked the investigation at the Sellafield nuclear plant.

The rise in industrial "fetal protection policies" is

adding even more controversy to the issue of occupational hazards to sperm. In 1984, employees brought a class-action suit against Milwaukee-based Johnson Controls, the nation's largest manufacturer of car batteries, after the company restricted women "capable of bearing children" from holding jobs in factory areas where lead exceeded a specific level. The suit—which the Supreme Court is scheduled to rule on this spring—focuses on the obstacles the policy creates for women's career advancement. Johnson Controls defends its regulation by pointing to "overwhelming" evidence that a mother's exposure to lead can harm the fetus.

In effect, the company's rule may be a case of reverse discrimination against men. Males continue to work in areas banned to women despite growing evidence that lead may not be safe for sperm either. In several studies over the past 10 years, paternal exposure to lead (and radiation) has been connected to Wilms' tumor, a type of kidney cancer in children. In another recent study, University of Maryland toxicologist Ellen Silbergeld, Ph.D., exposed male rats to lead amounts equivalent to levels below the current occupational safety standards for humans. The rats were then mated with females who had not been exposed at all. Result: The offspring showed clear defects in brain development.

Johnson Controls claims that evidence linking fetal problems to a father's contact with lead is insufficient. But further research into chemicals' effects on sperm may eventually force companies to reduce pollution levels, since *both* sexes can hardly be banned from the factory floor. Says Mattison: "The workplace should be safe for everyone who wants to work there, men and women alike!"

FATHER TIME
Whatever his occupation, a man's age may play an unexpected role in his reproductive health. When researchers at the University of Calgary and the Alberta Children's Hospital in Canada examined sperm samples taken from 30 healthy men aged 20 to 52, they found that the older men had a higher percentage of sperm with structurally abnormal chromosomes. Specifically, only 2 to 3 percent of the sperm from men between ages 20 and 34 were genetically abnormal, while the figure jumped to 7 percent in men 35 to 44 and to almost 14 percent in those 45 and over. "The findings are logical," says Renée Martin, Ph.D., the professor of pediatrics who led the study. "The cells that create sperm are constantly dividing from puberty onwards, and every time they divide they are subject to error."

Such mistakes are more likely to result in miscarriages than in unhealthy babies. "When part of a chromosome is missing or broken, the embryo is more likely to abort as a miscarriage [than to carry to term]," Martin says. Yet her findings may help explain why Savitz's North Carolina study noted a doubled rate of birth defects like cleft palate and hydrocephalus in children whose fathers were over 35 at the time of conception, no matter what the mothers' age.

Currently, there are no tests available to pre-identify sperm likely to cause genetic defects. "Unfortunately there's nothing offered, because [the research] is all so new," says Martin. But tests such as amniocentesis, alpha fetoprotein (AFP) and chorionic villi sampling (CVS) can ferret out some fetal genetic defects that are linked to Mom *or* Dad. Amniocentesis, for example, is routinely recommended for all pregnant women over 35 because with age a woman increases her risk of producing a Down's syndrome baby, characterized by mental retardation and physical abnormalities.

With respect to Down's syndrome, Martin's study provided some good news for older men: It confirmed previous findings that a man's risk of fathering a child afflicted with the syndrome actually drops with age. Some popular textbooks still warn that men over 55 have a high chance of fathering Down's syndrome babies. "That information is outdated," Martin insists. "We now know that for certain."

THE SINS OF THE FATHERS?
For all the hidden dangers facing a man's reproductive system, the most common hazards may be the ones most under his control.

Smoking. Tobacco addicts take note: Smoke gets in your sperm. Cigarettes can reduce fertility by lowering sperm count—the number of individual sperm released in a single ejaculation. "More than half a pack a day can cause sperm density to drop by 20 percent," says Machelle Seibel, M.D., director of the Faulkner Centre for Reproductive Medicine in Boston. One Danish study found that for each pack of cigarettes a father tended to smoke daily (assuming the mother didn't smoke at all), his infant's birthweight fell 4.2 ounces below average. Savitz has found that male smokers double their chances of fathering infants with abnormalities like hydrocephalus, *Bell's palsy* (paralysis of the facial nerve), and mouth cysts. In Savitz's most recent study, children whose fathers smoked around the time of conception were 20 percent more likely to develop brain cancer, lymphoma and leukemia than were children whose fathers did not smoke (the results still held regardless of whether the mother had a tobacco habit).

This is scary news—and not particularly helpful: Savitz's studies didn't record how frequently the fathers lit up, and no research at all suggests why the links appeared. Researchers can't even say for sure that defective sperm was to blame. The babies may instead have been victims of passive smoking—affected by Dad's tobacco while in the womb or shortly after birth.

Drinking. Mothers-to-be are routinely cautioned against sipping any alcohol while pregnant. Now studies suggest that the father's drinking habits just before conception may also pose a danger. So far, research hasn't discovered why alcohol has an adverse effect on sperm, but it does suggest that further investigation is needed. For starters, one study of laboratory rats linked heavy alcohol use with infertility because the liquor lowered testosterone levels. Another study, from the University of Washington in Seattle, discovered that newborn babies whose fathers drank at least two glasses of wine or two bottles of beer per day weighed an average of 3 ounces less than babies whose fathers were only occasional sippers—even when all other factors were considered.

Illicit Drugs. Many experts believe that a man's frequent use of substances such as marijuana and cocaine may also result in an unhealthy fetus, but studies that could document such findings have yet to be conducted. However, preliminary research has linked marijuana to infertility. And recent tests at the Yale Infertility Clinic found that long-term cocaine use led to both very low sperm counts and a greater number of sperm with motion problems.

WHAT A DAD CAN DO

The best news about sperm troubles is that many of the risk factors can be easily prevented. Because the body overhauls sperm supplies every 90 days, it only takes a season to get a fresh start on creating a healthy baby. Most experts advise that men wait for three months after quitting smoking, cutting out drug use or abstaining from alcohol before trying to sire a child.

Men who fear they are exposed to work chemicals that may compromise the health of future children can contact NIOSH. (Write to the Division of Standards Development and Technology Transfer, Technical Information Branch, 4676 Columbia Parkway, Mailstop C-19, Cincinnati, OH 45226. Or call [800] 356-4674.) NIOSH keeps files on hazardous chemicals and their effects, and can arrange for a local inspection of the workplace. Because it is primarily a research institution, NIOSH is most useful for investigating chemicals that haven't been studied previously for sperm effects (which is why

the Malones approached NIOSH with their concerns about paradichlorobenzene). For better-known pollutants, it's best to ask the federal Occupational Safety and Health Administration (OSHA) to inspect the job site (OSHA has regional offices in most U.S. cities).

There is also advice for men who are concerned over exposure to radiation during medical treatment. Direct radiation to the area around the testes can spur infertility by halting sperm production for more than three years. According to a recent study, it can also triple the number of abnormal sperm the testes produce. Men who know they will be exposed to testicular radiation for medical reasons should consider "banking" sperm before the treatment, for later use in artificial insemination. Most hospitals use lead shields during radiation therapy, but for routine X-rays, even dental X-rays, protection might not be offered automatically. If it's not offered, patients should be sure to request it. "The risks are really, really low, but to be absolutely safe, patients—male or female—should *always* ask for a lead apron to protect their reproductive organs," stresses Martin.

Though the study of sperm health is still in its infancy, it is already clear that a man's reproductive system needs to be treated with respect and caution. Women do not carry the full responsibility for bearing a healthy infant. "The focus should be on both parents—not on 'blaming' either the mother or the father, but on accepting that each plays a role," says Friedler.

Mattison agrees: "Until recently, when a woman had a miscarriage, she would be told it was because she had a 'blighted ovum' [egg]. We never heard anything about a 'blighted sperm.' This new data suggests that both may be responsible. That is not unreasonable," he concludes, "given that it takes both an egg and a sperm to create a baby!"

Development during Infancy and Early Childhood

- Infancy (Articles 9–12)
- Early Childhood (Articles 13–15)

Articles in unit 1 suggested that prenatal existence of an embryo/fetus includes behavior as well as structural development. How much behavior in infancy is instinctive, how much is learned before birth, and how much is acquired after birth?

Jean Piaget, the cognitive developmentalist whose theory triggered the growth of cognitive psychology, felt that behavior of a neonate is all reflexive, based on instincts for survival. New cognitive research is exploring the other possibilities—that fetuses can learn and that newborns can think as well as learn.

Newborns are top-heavy! The head is very large relative to the body, approximately 25 percent of the total length. There is virtually no neck. Within the skull cavity lie all the neurons (impulse-conducting brain cells) the new human will ever have—his or her lifetime supply! Neurons do not divide and replace themselves after birth. They account for approximately 10 percent of the brain, and the other 90 percent of cells are neuroglia. Neuroglia (also known as glial cells) support the neurons. They are almost all completely developed at birth. A few glial cells are added in the first year of life, and then they, too, end their cell division. Neuroglia also last a lifetime. Quite obviously, the newborn's head must be protected!

The infant's brain cells are not well organized at birth. The cells allocated to the lower brain (brain stem, cerebellum) are more well developed than cells allocated to the thinking, reasoning, higher brain (cerebrum). The development of the lower brain allows the infant to live. It directs the vital organ systems. The development of the higher brain requires that neurons already present grow larger, develop cell processes (axon and dendrites), develop myelin sheathing to allow impulses to be conducted, and migrate to their permanent locations in the two cerebral hemispheres. Once neurons are localized, they must also become organized via an intricate system of interconnections among their cell processes. All of this growth and development requires a tremendous supply of nutrients and oxygen and efficient removal of waste products.

Newborns seem to do little besides eat, sleep, and eliminate. This is exactly what they need to do to maximize their potential brain growth and development. Failure to provide an adequate supply of milk or an environment conducive to sleep may prevent brain maturation, sensory and perceptual development, acquisition of motor skills, acquisition of cognitive and language skills, and development of personal and social skills.

As infants grow and develop physically, they need less sleep and more environmental stimulation. As they move from infancy into early childhood, their reliance on milk as the only source of nutrients comes to an end. They require a variety of nutritious foods. As they begin to walk and talk, their physical development must be protected through safety measures and health maintenance. Physical growth, while always vital, seems to be overshadowed by the many exciting cognitive, linguistic, personal, and social growth processes of infancy and early childhood.

Piaget proposed that cognitive development during infancy and early childhood is qualitatively different from the cognitions of older children and adults. Not only do infants know less, but they also comprehend the world through reflexes and simple schemas, then more complex schemas, and finally through mental representations. They do not use cognitions based on sophisticated memory retrieval and logic.

Language develops in children from every culture and language group by proceeding through a series of cries, coos, babbles, holophrases, and telegraphic phrases. Eventually, children use simple, then increasingly more complex, sentences. Stimulation and reinforcement of infant speech do accelerate language development. However, biological readiness and cerebral brain organization are also necessary.

The personal and social skills of neonates include showing distress (crying) and showing delight (cooing). Researchers have noted three basic temperamental styles in early infancy: easy babies, slow-to-warm-up babies, and difficult babies. Each unique baby differs in some personal and social ways from every other infant. However, there is some stability of the three basic temperamental styles through early and late childhood.

Personality and socialization patterns are very susceptible to environmental influences. Behavioral researchers have demonstrated the stimulus-response-reinforcement paradigms that are learned by the developing infant/toddler/preschooler as he or she is shaped by mother, father, other adult caregivers, siblings, and peers. Researchers have also documented the unique

infant's effect on his or her caregivers. Children shape as well as get shaped. Personal and social development is multifactorial and also relies on physical, cognitive, and language development.

Sigmund Freud believed that libidinous (sexual) urges lead infants and young children through oral, anal, and phallic stages of development. Erik Erikson tied social forces into these stages. He believes that when infants are in the oral stage, their central (nuclear) conflict is learning trust vs. mistrust; when toddlers go through the anal stage, their nuclear conflict is learning autonomy vs. shame and doubt; and when preschoolers struggle through the phallic stage, their conflict is learning initiative vs. guilt.

In recent years researchers have focused on attachment as a measure of personal-social development in infancy and early childhood. Most babies become securely attached to all their primary caregivers. Infants in good quality day-care programs often become attached to more primary caregivers than do home-reared infants. Securely attached babies become trusting, autonomous, initiating toddlers and preschoolers. Some babies, however, develop insecure attachments. They may show ambivalent, uncertain, or avoidant patterns of interaction with their caregivers. Efforts need to be made to help these children feel more secure.

The first two unit articles attempt to address the question of infant intelligence. How smart are babies, and how can their intellectual powers be maximized? The next two articles focus on personal and social skills in infancy. Personality may be malleable. If it is, what will promote the healthiest personality development?

The last three articles of this unit are concerned with toddlers and preschoolers moving out into their worlds. What kinds of services will protect their physical development and health? What kinds of questions can adults ask to promote their cognitive processes and memory retrieval systems? The last essay addresses sex-role socialization. Should both boys and girls be helped to be assertive?

Looking Ahead: Challenge Questions

In what ways are infants smarter than Piaget's description of sensorimotor cognition allowed?

What are the intellectual potentials of babies?

How does infant reactivity influence the growth and development of personal and social skills?

How are infants and toddlers changed by day care?

Why should or should not home visiting services be provided to families with young children? What do these services entail?

How can children learn to retrieve memories?

Why should personal and social skills training include lessons on assertiveness as an alternative to aggression or submission in early childhood?

A New Perspective on Cognitive Development in Infancy

Jean M. Mandler

Jean Mandler received her Ph.D. from Harvard in 1956. She is currently professor of psychology and cognitive science at the University of California, San Diego. Her interests are cognition and cognitive development, with emphasis on the representation of knowledge. She has done research on how our knowledge of stories, events, and scenes is organized and the way in which such organization affects remembering. In recent years her research has concentrated on conceptual development in infancy and early childhood. Preparation of this article was supported by an NSF grant. Address: Department of Cognitive Science D-015, University of California, San Diego, La Jolla, CA 92093.

Over the past decade something of a revolution has been taking place in our understanding of cognitive development during infancy. For many years one theory dominated the field—that of the Swiss psychologist Jean Piaget. Piaget's views on infancy were so widely known and respected that to many psychologists at least one aspect of development seemed certain: human infants go through a protracted period during which they cannot yet think. They can learn to recognize things and to smile at them, to crawl and to manipulate objects, but they do not yet have concepts or ideas. This period, which Piaget called the sensorimotor stage of development, was said to last until one-and-a-half to two years of age. Only near the end of this stage do infants learn how to represent the world in a symbolic, conceptual manner, and thus advance from infancy into early childhood.

Piaget formulated this view of infancy primarily by observing the development of his own three children—few laboratory techniques were available at the time. More recently, experimental methods have been devised to study infants, and a large body of research has been accumulating. Much of the new work suggests that the theory of a sensori-motor stage of development will have to be substantially modified or perhaps even abandoned (Fig. 1). The present article provides a brief overview of Piaget's theory of sensorimotor development, a summary of recent data that are difficult to reconcile with that theory, and an outline of an alternative view of early mental development.

In Piaget's (1951, 1952, 1954) theory, the first stage of development is said to consist of sensorimotor (perceptual and motor) functioning in an

Recent research suggests that infants have the ability to conceptualize much earlier than we thought

organism that has not yet acquired a representational (conceptual) capacity. The only knowledge infants have is what things look and sound like and how to move themselves around and manipulate objects. This kind of sensorimotor knowledge is often termed procedural or implicit knowledge, and is contrasted with explicit, factual (conceptual) knowledge (e.g., Cohen and Squire 1980; Schacter 1987; Mandler 1988). Factual knowledge is the kind of knowledge one can think about or recall; it is usually considered to be symbolic and propositional. Some factual information may be stored in the form of images, but these are also symbolic, in the sense that they are constructed from both propositional and spatial knowledge. Sensorimotor knowledge, on the other hand, is subsymbolic knowledge; it is knowing *how* to recognize something or use a motor skill, but it does not require explicitly knowing *that* something is the case. It is the

kind of knowledge we build into robots in order to make them recognize and manipulate objects in their environment, and it is also the kind of knowledge we ascribe to lower organisms, which function quite well without the ability to conceptualize facts. It is the kind of knowledge that tends to remain undisturbed in amnesic patients, even when their memory for facts and their personal past is severely impaired.

In the case of babies, the restriction of functioning to sensorimotor processing implies that they can neither think about absent objects nor recall the past. According to Piaget, they lack the capacity even to form an image of things they have seen before; a fortiori, they have no capacity to imagine what will happen tomorrow. Thus, the absence of a symbolic capacity does not mean just that infants cannot understand language or reason; it means that they cannot remember what they did this morning or imagine their mother if she is not present. It is, in short, a most un-Proustian life, not thought about, only lived (Mandler 1983).

According to Piaget, to be able to think about the world requires first that perceptual-motor schemas of objects and relations among them be formed. Then, symbols must be created to stand for these schemas. Several aspects of Piaget's formulation account for the slow course of both these developments. First, on the basis of his observations Piaget assumed that the sensory modalities are unconnected at birth, each delivering separate types of information. Thus, he thought that one of the major tasks of the first half of the sensorimotor stage is to construct schemas integrating the information from initially disconnected sights, sounds, and touches. Until this integration is

From *American Scientist*, Vol. 78, No. 3, May/June 1990, pp. 236-243. Reprinted by permission of *American Scientist*, journal of Sigma Xi, the Scientific Research Society.

accomplished, stable sensorimotor schemas of three-dimensional, solid, sound-producing, textured objects cannot be formed and hence cannot be thought about.

In addition, babies must learn about the causal interrelatedness of objects and the fact that objects continue to exist when not being perceived. Piaget thought that these notions were among the major accomplishments of the second half of the sensorimotor stage. He suggested that they derive from manual activity—for example, repeated covering and uncovering, poking, pushing, and dropping objects while observing the results. Handling objects leads to understanding them; it allows the integration of perceptual and motor information that gives objects substantiality, permanence, and unique identities separate from the self. Since motor control over the hands is slow to develop, to the extent that conceptual understanding requires physical interaction with objects, it is necessarily a late development. Much of the first year of life, then, is spent accomplishing the coordination of the various sources of perceptual and motor information required to form the sensorimotor object schemas that will then be available to be conceptualized.

According to Piaget, the development of the symbolic function is itself a protracted process. In addition to constructing sensorimotor schemas of objects and relations, which form the basic content or meaning of what is to be thought about, symbols to refer to these meanings must be formed. Piaget assumed that the latter development has its precursors in the expectancies involved in conditioning. For example, the sight of a bottle can serve as a signal that milk will follow, and babies soon learn to make anticipatory sucking movements. This process, essentially the same as that involved in Pavlovian conditioning, does not imply a symbolic function; there is no indication that the baby can use such signals to represent bottles in their absence.

All the anticipatory behavior that Piaget observed throughout the first 18 months was accounted for in similar terms. Signs of anticipation of future events became more wide-ranging and complex but did not seem to require the use of images or other symbols to represent what was about to happen. Rather, Piaget assumed that an established sensorimotor schema set up a kind of imageless expectation of the next event, followed by recognition when the event took place. He used strict criteria for the presence of imagery—for example, verbal recall of the past (which implies the ability to represent absent events to oneself) or rapid problem-solving without trial and error. Neither of these can be ascribed merely to running off a practiced sensorimotor schema, but they require instead some representation of information not perceptually present.

Piaget did not observe recall or covert problem-solving until the end of the sensorimotor period. One might think that the fact that infants begin to acquire language during the latter part of the first year would be difficult to reconcile with a lack of symbolic capacity. However, Piaget characterized early words as imitative schemas, no different in kind from other motor schemas displayed in the presence of familiar situations.

Imitation, in fact, plays an important role in this account, because it provides the source of the development of imagery. Piaget assumed that images are not formed merely from looking at or hearing something, but arise only when what is being perceived is also analyzed. The attempt to imitate the actions of others provides the stimulus for such analysis to take place. Although infants begin to imitate early, it was not until near the end of the first year or beyond that Piaget found his children able to imitate novel actions or actions involving parts of their bodies they could not see themselves, such as blinking or sticking out their

---

William James described the perceptual world of the infant as a "blooming, buzzing confusion"

Figure 1. According to the Swiss psychologist Jean Piaget, babies like the author's 8 month-old grandson shown here have learned to recognize people, and their smile is a sign of that recognition. However, Piaget believed that babies have not yet learned to think at such an early age and thus cannot recall even the most familiar people in their lives when those people are not present. Recent research suggests that this view may be mistaken and that babies such as this one are already forming concepts about people and things in their environment.

tongues. He took this difficulty as evidence that they could not form an image of something complex or unobserved until detailed analysis of it had taken place; it is presumably during this analysis that imagery is constructed. Piaget's study of imitation suggested that such analysis, and therefore the formation of imagery, was a late development in infancy. To complete the process of symbol formation, then, the anticipatory mechanisms of sensorimotor schemas become speeded up and appear as images of what will occur, thus allowing genuine representation. Finally, by some mechanism left unspecified, these newly created images can be used to represent the world independent of ongoing sensorimotor activity.

All these developments—constructing sensorimotor schemas, establishing a coherent world of objects and events suitable to form the content of ideas, learning to imitate and to form images that can be used to stand for things—are completed in the second half of the second year, and result in the child's at last being able to develop a conceptual system of ideas. Images can now be used to recall the past and to imagine the future, and even perceptually present objects can begin to be interpreted conceptually as well as by means of motor interactions with them. With the onset of thought, an infant is well on the way to becoming fully human.

This theory of the sensorimotor foundations of thought has come under attack from two sources. One is experimental work suggesting that a stable and differentiated perceptual world is established much earlier in infancy than Piaget realized. The other is recent work suggesting that recall and other forms of symbolic activity (presumably mediated by imagery) occur by at least the second half of the first year. I will discuss each of these findings in turn.

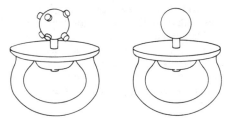

Figure 2. The old idea that the senses are unconnected at birth and are gradually integrated through experience is contradicted by an experiment using bumpy and smooth pacifiers to study the visual recognition of an object that has been experienced only tactilely. A one-month-old infant is habituated to one of the two kinds of pacifiers in its mouth without being allowed to see it. The pacifier is then removed, and the infant is shown both kinds of pacifiers. Infants look longer at the nipple they felt in their mouth. (After Meltzoff and Borton 1979.)

Perceptual development

The notion that the senses are unconnected at birth and that they become integrated only through experience is an old idea that was popularized by William James's (1890) description of the perceptual world of the infant as a "blooming, buzzing confusion." Recent work, however, suggests that either the senses are interrelated at birth or the learning involved in their integration is extremely rapid. There is evidence for integration of auditory and visual information as well as of vision and touch in the first months of life. What follows is a small sample of the research findings.

From birth, infants turn their heads to look at the source of a sound (Wertheimer 1961; Mendelson and Haith 1976). This does not mean that they have any particular expectations of what they will see when they hear a given sound, but it does indicate a mechanism that would enable rapid learning. By four months, if one presents two films of complex events not seen before and accompanied by a single sound track, infants prefer to look at the film that matches the sound (Spelke 1979). Perhaps even more surprising, when infants are presented with two films, each showing only a speaker's face, they will choose the correct film, even when the synchrony between both films and the soundtrack is identical (Kuhl and Meltzoff 1988). In addition, one-month-olds can recognize visually presented objects that they have only felt in their mouths (Fig. 2; Meltzoff and Borton 1979; Walker-Andrews and Gibson 1986). Such data suggest either that the output of each sensory transducer consists in part of the same amodal pattern of information or that some central processing of two similar patterns of information is accomplished. In either case, the data strongly support the view that there is more order and coherence in early perceptual experience than Piaget or James realized.

In addition to sensory coordination, a good deal of information about the nature of objects is provided by the visual system alone, information to which young infants have been shown to be sensitive. For example, it used to be thought that infants have difficulty separating objects from a background, but it appears that such confusion is a rare event, not the norm. Infants may not "see" that a cup is separable from a saucer without picking it up, but in general they do not have difficulty determining the boundaries of objects. They use information from motion to parse objects from the perceptual surround long before they are able to manipulate them manually. At an age as young as three months, they can use the relative motion of objects against both stationary and moving backgrounds to determine the objects' boundaries (Fig. 3; Kellman and Spelke 1983; Spelke 1988). Even stationary objects are seen as separate if they are spatially separated, whether in a plane or in depth. Infants also use motion to determine object identity, treating an object that moves behind a screen and then reappears as one object rather than two (Spelke and Kestenbaum 1986).

Other work by Spelke and by

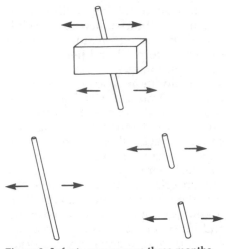

Figure 3. Infants as young as three months can use the perception of relative movement to determine object boundaries. They are habituated to the display shown at the top, which represents a rod moving back and forth behind a block of wood. Then they are tested with the two displays on the bottom: the rod moving as it did before, but with no block in front, or the two pieces of the rod that were visible behind the block, also moving as they did before. Infants tend to continue to habituate to the whole moving rod—that is, they cease to look at it, indicating that it is familiar to them. They prefer to look at the broken rod, indicating that they consider it something new. If the same experiment is done with a stationary rod behind a block, infants exhibit no preference when presented with a whole stationary rod or a broken stationary rod. (After Kellman and Spelke 1983.)

Baillargeon (Baillargeon et al. 1985; Baillargeon 1987a; Spelke 1988) shows that infants as young as four months expect objects to be substantial, in the sense that the objects cannot move through other objects nor other objects through them (Fig. 4), and permanent, in the sense that the objects are assumed to continue to exist when hidden. Finally, there is evidence that by six months infants perceive causal relations among moving objects (Leslie 1988) in a fashion that seems to be qualitatively the same as that of adults (Michotte 1963).

From this extensive research program, we can conclude that objects are seen as bounded, unitary, solid, and separate from the background, perhaps from birth but certainly by three to four months of age. Such young infants obviously still have a great deal to learn about objects, but the world must appear both stable and orderly to them, and thus capable of being conceptualized.

Conceptual development

It is easier to study what infants see than what they are thinking about. Nevertheless, there are a few ways to assess whether or not infants are thinking. One way is to look for symbolic activity, such as using a gesture to refer to something else. Piaget (1952) himself called attention to a phenomenon he called motor recognition. For example, he observed his six-month-old daughter make a gesture on catching sight of a familiar toy in a new location. She was accustomed to kicking at the toy in her crib, and when she saw it across the room she made a brief, abbreviated kicking motion. Piaget did not consider this true symbolic activity, because it was a motor movement, not a purely mental act; nevertheless, he suggested that his daughter was referring to, or classifying, the toy by means of her action. In a similar vein, infants whose parents use sign language have been observed to begin to use conventional signs at around six to seven months (Prinz and Prinz 1979; Bonvillian et al. 1983; see Mandler 1988 for discussion).

Another type of evidence of conceptual functioning is recall of absent objects or events. Indeed, Piaget accepted recall as irrefutable evidence

of conceptual representation, since there is no way to account for recreating information that is not perceptually present by means of sensorimotor schemas alone; imagery or other symbolic means of representation must be involved. Typically we associate recall with verbal recreation of the past, and this, as Piaget observed, is not usually found until 18 months or older. But recall need not be verbal—and indeed is usually not when we think about past events—so that in principle it is possible in preverbal infants.

One needs to see a baby do something like find a hidden object after a delay or imitate a previously observed event. Until recently, only diary studies provided evidence of recall in the second half of the first year—for example, finding an object hidden in an unfamiliar location after

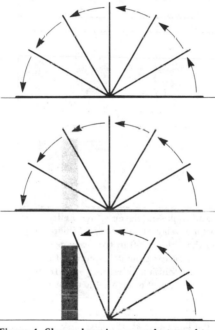

Figure 4. Shown here is a procedure used to demonstrate four- and five-month-olds' memory for the location of a hidden object. At the top is a screen moving through a 180° rotation, to which infants viewing from the right are habituated by repetition. Following habituation, a box is placed behind the screen, and the infants see two test events: an impossible (*middle*) and a possible event (*bottom*). In the impossible event, the screen continues to rotate 180°, moving "magically" through the hidden box (which the experimenter has surreptitiously removed). In the possible event, the screen rotates only to the point where it would hit the box. The infants' surprise at the impossible event demonstrates that they remember an object they cannot see. (After Baillargeon 1987a.)

a 24-hour delay (Ashmead and Perlmutter 1980). Now, however, similar phenomena are beginning to be demonstrated in the laboratory. Meltzoff (1988) showed that nine-month-olds could imitate actions that they had seen performed 24 hours earlier. Each action consisted of an unusual gesture with a novel object—for example, pushing a recessed button in a box (which produced a beeping sound)—and the infants were limited to watching the experimenter carry it out; thus, when they later imitated the action, they could not be merely running off a practiced motor schema in response to seeing the object again. Control subjects, who had been shown the objects but not the actions performed on them, made the correct responses much less frequently. We have replicated this phenomenon with 11-month-olds (McDonough and Mandler 1989).

Because of the difficulties that young infants have manipulating objects, it is not obvious that this technique can be used with infants younger than about eight months. One suspects, however, that if nine-month-olds can recall several novel events after a 24-hour delay, somewhat younger infants can probably recall similar events after shorter delays.

There is a small amount of data from a procedure that does not require a motor response and that, although using quite short delays, suggests recall-like processes. Baillargeon's experiments on object permanence, mentioned earlier, use a technique that requires infants to remember that an object is hidden behind a screen. For example, she has shown that infants are surprised when a screen appears to move backward through an object they have just seen hidden behind it (see Fig. 4). In her experiments with four- and five-month-olds, the infants had to remember for only about 8 to 12 seconds that there was an object behind the screen (Baillargeon et al. 1985; Baillargeon 1987a). However, in more recent work with eight-month-olds, Baillargeon and her colleagues have been successful with a delay of 70 seconds (Fig. 5; Baillargeon et al. 1989). This kind of performance seems to require a representational capacity not attributable to sensorimotor schemas. Not only is an absent

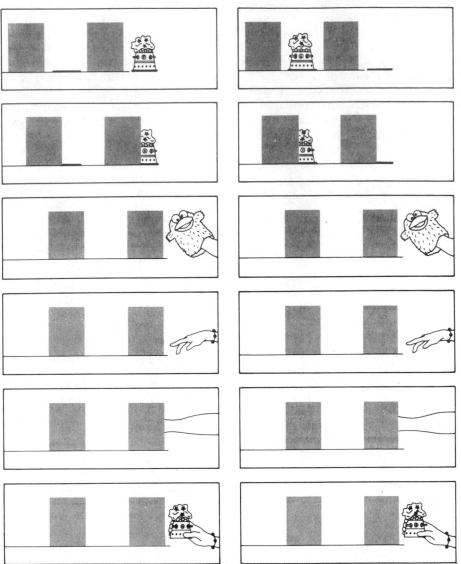

Figure 5. Another procedure involving possible *(left)* and impossible events *(right)* elicits meaningful responses from eight-month-old infants after a delay of 70 seconds. Moving from top to bottom, an object is hidden respectively behind the right or left of two screens; puppets and hand tiptoes are used to keep infants attentive during the delay period; the experimenter reaches behind the right screen and brings the hidden object into view from behind it. (The object was placed there surreptitiously as part of the impossible event.) Surprise at the impossible event indicates memory of the place where the object was hidden. The apparent recall suggests a kind of conceptual functioning that goes beyond the sensorimotor functioning described by Piaget. (After Baillargeon et al. 1989.)

object being represented, but the information is rather precise—for example, Baillargeon (1987b) found that infants remembered not only that an object was hidden but where it was located and how tall it was.

Where do concepts come from?

The data described above indicate that the theory of an exclusively sensorimotor stage of development, in which babies cannot yet represent the world conceptually, is in need of considerable revision. There does not

appear to be a protracted period during which infants have no conception of objects or events and cannot represent them in their absence. A great deal of information is available to and used by infants from an early age, even before they have developed the motor coordination enabling manual exploration that Piaget thought was crucial to conceptual development.

Indeed, a good deal of evidence suggests that we have tended to confuse infants' motor incompetence with conceptual incompetence. Piaget was particularly influenced in his theorizing by the difficulties that

children as old as a year have finding a hidden object, especially when it is hidden in more than one location a number of times in succession. The phenomena he demonstrated have been replicated many times, but it now appears that much of the difficulty infants have in such situations is due not to a lack of understanding of object permanence but to other factors. For example, repeatedly hiding an object in different locations can be confusing and leads to perseverative responding to the same place (see Diamond 1985; Mandler 1988, in press).

If a conceptual system of knowledge has begun to be formed by at least six months and perhaps earlier, where does it come from? Piaget's theory of a transformation of well-developed action schemas into conceptual thought cannot account for conceptual knowledge occurring before the action schemas themselves have developed. On the other hand, perceptual schemas about objects and events develop early. What is needed, then, is some mechanism for transforming these schemas into concepts, or ideas, about what is being perceived, preferably a mechanism that can operate as soon as perceptual schemas are formed.

Little has been written about this problem. One approach is to assume that even young infants are capable of redescribing perceptual information in a conceptual format. I have suggested a mechanism that might accomplish this (Mandler 1988): perceptual analysis, a process by which one perception is actively compared to another and similarities or differences between them are noted. (Such analysis, like other sorts of concept formation, requires some kind of vocabulary; this aspect, still little understood, is discussed below.) The simplest case of perceptual analysis occurs when two simultaneously presented objects are compared, or a single object is compared to an already established representation (i.e., one notes similarities or differences between what one is looking at and what one recalls about it). It is the process by which we discover that sugar bowls have two handles and teacups only one, or that a friend wears glasses. Unless we have engaged in this kind of analysis (or someone has told us), the information will not be accessible for us to think about. Much of the time, of course, we do not make such comparisons, which is why we often can recall few details of even recent experiences.

Although it is analytic, perceptual analysis consists primarily of simplification. Our perceptual system regularly processes vast amounts of information that never become accessible to thought. For example, we make use of a great deal of complex information every time we recognize a face: proportions, contours, subtle shading, relationships among various facial features, and so on. Yet little of this information is available to our thought processes. Few people are aware of the proportions of the human face—it is not something they have ever conceptualized. Even fewer know how they determine whether a face is male or female (this categorization depends on subtle differences in proportions). For the most part we do not even have words to describe the nuances that our perceptual apparatus uses instantly and effortlessly to make such a perceptual categorization.

For us to be able to think about such matters, the information must be reduced and simplified into a conceptual format. One way this redescription is done is via language; someone (perhaps an artist who has already carried out the relevant analytic process) conceptualizes aspects of a face for us. The other way is to look at a face and analyze it ourselves, such as noting that the ears are at the same level as the eyes. The analysis is often couched in linguistic form, but it need not be. Images can be used, but these, in spite of having spatial properties, have a major conceptual component (e.g., Kosslyn 1983).

An infant, of course, does not have the benefit of language, the means by which older people acquire much of their factual knowledge. So if infants are to transform perceptual schemas into thoughts, they must be able to analyze the perceptual information they receive. The perceptual system itself cannot decide that only animate creatures move by themselves or that containers must have bottoms if they are to hold things, and so forth. These are facts visually observed, but they are highly simpli-

fied versions of the information available to be conceptualized.

The notion of perceptual analysis is similar to the process that Piaget theorized as being responsible for the creation of images. He thought that this kind of analysis does not even begin until around eight or nine months and does not result in imagery until later still. However, he had no evidence that image formation is such a late-developing process, and his own description of his children's imitative performance as early as three or four months strongly suggests that the process of perceptual analysis had begun. For example, he observed imitation of clapping hands at that time, a performance that would seem to require a good deal of analysis, considering the difference between what infants see and what they must do. In many places in his account of early imitation, Piaget

noted that the infants watched him carefully, studying both their own and his actions. Other developmental psychologists have commented on the same phenomenon. For example, Werner and Kaplan (1963) noted that infants begin ''contemplating'' objects at between three and five months. Ruff (1986) has documented intense examination of objects at six months (the earliest age she studied).

To investigate contemplation or analysis of objects experimentally is not easy. A possible measure is the number of times an infant looks back and forth between two objects that are presented simultaneously. Janowsky (1985), for example, showed that this measure increased significantly between four and eight months. At four months infants tend to look first at one object and then the other; at eight months they switch back and forth between the two a

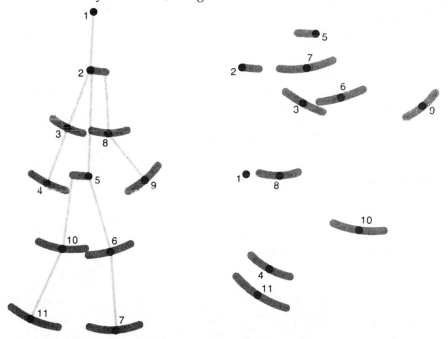

Figure 6. An equally subtle ability is involved in this demonstration of three-month-olds' responses to biological as opposed to nonbiological motion. The infants watch videotapes of computer-generated displays. On the left is a display of 11 point-lights moving as if attached to the head and major joints of a person walking. The motion vectors drawn through each point represent the perceived motions of the display; the lines connecting points, like the numbers and vectors, are not visible to the infants. The display on the right is identical to the normal walker except that the relative locations of the point-lights are scrambled. Correspondingly numbered points in the two displays undergo identical motions. Infants show greater interest in the scrambled display, indicating that they consider it novel. (After Bertenthal et al. 1987.)

good many times. Fox and his colleagues (1979) have reported a similar phenomenon. Interestingly, Janowsky found that the differences in looking back and forth are not associated with differences in total looking time, the rate at which infants habituate to objects (cease to look at them), or accuracy of recognition. So the looking back and forth must serve some other function. I would suggest that it is a comparison process, by which one object is being contrasted with the other.

A vocabulary for concepts

Assuming that perceptual analysis can lead to concept formation, it is still necessary to formulate the vocabulary in which the resulting concepts are couched. But here we face one of the major stumbling blocks in psychological theory: the problem of specifying conceptual primitives (see Smith and Medin 1981). Perhaps because of its difficulty, it has been largely ignored by developmental psychologists, in spite of the fact that any theory of conceptual development must resolve the issue of what the earliest concepts are like, no matter when they may first be formed. Leslie (1988) has offered an analysis of the primitives involved in early causal concepts, and people working on language acquisition have speculated about semantic primitives. For example, Slobin (1985) points out that children must already have concepts of objects and events, as well as relational notions about them, in order for language to be acquired. Since language comprehension begins at around nine to ten months (and perhaps earlier for sign language), some kind of conceptual system must be well established by that time. But we have almost no information as to its character.

Help may come from recent studies by cognitive linguists (e.g., Fauconnier 1985; Johnson 1987; Lakoff 1987). Although the primary goal of these theorists is to understand how language works, their analyses of the root concepts expressed in language may be of use in our search for babies' earliest concepts. For example, Lakoff and Johnson have proposed that image schemas—notions derived from spatial structure, such

as trajectory, up-down, container, part-whole, end-of-path, and link— form the foundation of the conceptualizing capacity. These authors suggest that image schemas are derived from preconceptual perceptual structures, forming the core of many of our concepts of objects and events and of their metaphorical extensions to abstract realms. They demonstrate in great detail how many of our most complex concepts are grounded in such primitive notions. I would characterize image schemas as simplified redescriptions of sensorimotor schemas, noting that they seem to be reasonably within the capacity of infant conceptualization.

The potential usefulness of image schemas as conceptual primitives can be illustrated by the example of the container schema. According to Johnson and Lakoff, the structural elements of this image schema are "interior," "boundary," and "exterior." It has a bodily basis likely to be appreciated by quite young infants, and a perceptual basis that seems to require minimal redescription of the object schemas described earlier. It also has a simple binary logic—either in or not-in; if A is in B and B is in C, then A is in C—that may or may not be the sensorimotor basis of the Boolean logic of classes, as Lakoff suggests, but is certainly a characteristic of concepts as opposed to percepts. (The conceptual system tends to reduce the continuous information delivered by the perceptual system to a small number of discrete values.)

The use of such an image schema might be responsible for the better performance nine-month-old infants show on hiding tasks when a container is used rather than cloths or screens (Freeman et al. 1980). Current work by Baillargeon (pers. com.) suggests that at approximately the same age infants are surprised when containers without bottoms appear to hold things. Of course, these are only fragments of the kind of information needed to document the development of the idea of a container, but

they indicate how we might go about tracking the early establishment of simple concepts.

A more complex concept that may also be acquired relatively early in infancy is that of animacy. Consider some possible sources for such a concept. We know that infants differentiate biological from nonbiological motion as early as three months (Fig. 6; Bertenthal et al. 1987). This perceptual differentiation, although an excellent source of information, does not constitute a concept by itself; it is an accomplishment similar to categorizing male and female faces, which infants have learned to do by six months (Fagan and Singer 1979). As discussed earlier, such perceptual categorization is not accessible for purposes of conceptual thought unless it has been redescribed in conceptual terms. An infant needs to conceptualize some differences between categories of moving objects, such as noting that one type starts up on its own and (sometimes) responds to the infant's signals, whereas the other type does not. An image schema of a notion such as beginning-of-path could be used to redescribe the perceptual information involved in initiation of motion. A link schema (whose elements are two entities and some kind of path between them) could be used to describe the observation of responsivity to self. From such simple foundations might arise a primitive concept of animal, a concept that we have reason to believe is present in some form by at least the end of the first year of life (Golinkoff and Halperin 1983; Mandler and Bauer 1988).

These are some examples of how a conceptual system might emerge from a combination of perceptual input and some relatively simple redescriptions of that input. I have suggested that a mechanism of perceptual analysis could enable such redescription, with the terms of the redescription being derived from spatial structure. The mechanism would not require an extended period of

---

A good deal of evidence suggests that we have tended to confuse infants' motor incompetence with conceptual incompetence

exclusively sensorimotor functioning but would allow conceptualization of the world to begin early in infancy. The data I have summarized indicate that babies do indeed begin to think earlier than we thought. Therefore, it seems safe to assume that they either are born with or acquire early in life the capacity to form concepts, rather than to assume that conceptual functioning can occur only as an outcome of a lengthy sensorimotor stage.

References

Ashmead, D. H., and M. Perlmutter. 1980. Infant memory in everyday life. In *New Directions for Child Development: Children's Memory*, vol. 10, ed. M. Perlmutter, pp. 1–16. Jossey-Bass.

Baillargeon, R. 1987a. Object permanence in 3.5- and 4.5-month-old infants. *Devel. Psychol.* 23:655–64.

———. 1987b. Young infants' reasoning about the physical and spatial properties of a hidden object. *Cognitive Devel.* 2:179–200.

Baillargeon, R., J. De Vos, and M. Graber. 1989. Location memory in 8-month-old infants in a nonsearch AB task: Further evidence. *Cognitive Devel.* 4:345–67.

Baillargeon, R., E. S. Spelke, and S. Wasserman. 1985. Object permanence in five-month-old infants. *Cognition* 20:191–208.

Bertenthal, B. I., D. R. Proffitt, S. J. Kramer, and N. B. Spetner. 1987. Infants' encoding of kinetic displays varying in relative coherence. *Devel. Psychol.* 23:171–78.

Bonvillian, J. D., M. D. Orlansky, and L. L. Novack. 1983. Developmental milestones: Sign language and motor development. *Child Devel.* 54:1435–45.

Cohen, N. J., and L. R. Squire. 1980. Preserved learning and retention of pattern-analyzing skills in amnesia: Dissociation of knowing how and knowing that. *Science* 210:207–10.

Diamond, A. 1985. The development of the ability to use recall to guide action, as indicated by infants' performance on AB. *Child Devel.* 56:868–83.

Fagan, J. F., III, and L. T. Singer. 1979. The role of simple feature differences in infant recognition of faces. *Infant Behav. Devel.* 2:39–46.

Fauconnier, G. 1985. *Mental Spaces*. MIT Press.

Fox, N., J. Kagan, and S. Weiskopf. 1979. The growth of memory during infancy. *Genetic Psychol. Mono.* 99:91–130.

Freeman, N. H., S. Lloyd, and C. G. Sinha. 1980. Infant search tasks reveal early concepts of containment and canonical usage of objects. *Cognition* 8:243–62.

Golinkoff, R. M., and M. S. Halperin. 1983. The concept of animal: One infant's view. *Infant Behav. Devel.* 6:229–33.

James, W. 1890. *The Principles of Psychology*. Holt.

Janowsky, J. S. 1985. Cognitive development and reorganization after early brain injury. Ph.D. diss., Cornell Univ.

Johnson, M. 1987. *The Body in the Mind: The Bodily Basis of Meaning, Imagination, and Reason*. Univ. of Chicago Press.

Kellman, P. J., and E. S. Spelke. 1983. Perception of partly occluded objects in infancy. *Cognitive Psychol.* 15:483–524.

Kosslyn, S. M. 1983. *Ghosts in the Mind's Machine: Creating and Using Images in the Brain*. Norton.

Kuhl, P. K., and A. N. Meltzoff. 1988. Speech as an intermodal object of perception. In *Perceptual Development in Infancy: The Minnesota Symposia on Child Psychology*, vol. 20, ed. A. Yonas, pp. 235–66. Erlbaum.

Lakoff, G. 1987. *Women, Fire, and Dangerous Things: What Categories Reveal about the Mind*. Univ. of Chicago Press.

Leslie, A. 1988. The necessity of illusion. Perception and thought in infancy. In *Thought without Language*, ed. L. Weiskrantz, pp. 185–210. Clarendon Press.

Mandler, J. M. 1983. Representation. In *Cognitive Development*, ed. J. H. Flavell and E. M. Markman, pp. 120–94. Vol. 3 of *Manual of Child Psychology*, ed. P. Mussen. Wiley.

———. 1988. How to build a baby: On the development of an accessible representational system. *Cognitive Devel.* 3:113–36.

———. In press. Recall of events by preverbal children. In *The Development and Neural Bases of Higher Cognitive Functions*, ed. A. Diamond. New York Academy of Sciences Press.

Mandler, J. M., and P. J. Bauer. 1988. The cradle of categorization: Is the basic level basic? *Cognitive Devel.* 3:247–64.

McDonough, L., and J. M. Mandler. 1989. Immediate and deferred imitation with 11-month-olds: A comparison between familiar and novel actions. Poster presented at meeting of the Society for Research in Child Development, Kansas City.

Meltzoff, A. N. 1988. Infant imitation and memory: Nine-month-olds in immediate and deferred tests. *Child Devel.* 59:217–25.

Meltzoff, A. N., and R. W. Borton. 1979. Intermodal matching by human neonates. *Nature* 282:403–04.

Mendelson, M. J., and M. M. Haith. 1976. The relation between audition and vision in the newborn. *Monographs of the Society for Research in Child Development*, no. 41, serial no. 167.

Michotte, A. 1963. *The Perception of Causality*. Methuen.

Piaget, J. 1951. *Play, Dreams and Imitation in Childhood*, trans. C. Gattegno and F. M. Hodgson. Norton.

———. 1952. *The Origins of Intelligence in Children*, trans. M. Cook. International Universities Press.

———. 1954. *The Construction of Reality in the Child*, trans. M. Cook. Basic Books.

Prinz, P. M., and E. A. Prinz. 1979. Simultaneous acquisition of ASL and spoken English (in a hearing child of a deaf mother and hearing father). Phase I: Early lexical development. *Sign Lang. Stud.* 25:283–96.

Ruff, H. A. 1986. Components of attention during infants' manipulative exploration. *Child Devel.* 57:105–14.

Schacter, D. L. 1987. Implicit memory: History and current status. *J. Exper. Psychol.: Learning, Memory, Cognition* 13:501–18.

Slobin, D. I. 1985. Crosslinguistic evidence for the language-making capacity. In *The Crosslinguistic Study of Language Acquisition*, vol. 2, ed. D. I. Slobin, pp. 1157–1256. Erlbaum.

Smith, E. E., and D. L. Medin. 1981. *Categories and Concepts*. Harvard Univ. Press.

Spelke, E. S. 1979. Perceiving bimodally specified events in infancy. *Devel. Psychol.* 15:626–36.

———. 1988. The origins of physical knowledge. In *Thought without Language*, ed. L. Weiskrantz, pp. 168–84. Clarendon Press.

Spelke, E. S., and R. Kestenbaum. 1986. Les origines du concept d'objet. *Psychologie française* 31:67–72.

Walker-Andrews, A. S., and E. J. Gibson. 1986. What develops in bimodal perception? In *Advances in Infancy Research*, vol. 4, ed. L. P. Lipsitt and C. Rovee-Collier, pp. 171–81. Ablex.

Werner, H., and B. Kaplan. 1963. *Symbol Formation*. Wiley.

Wertheimer, M. 1961. Psychomotor coordination of auditory and visual space at birth. *Science* 134:1692.

The Amazing Minds of Infants

Looking here, looking there, babies are like little scientists, constantly exploring the world around them, with innate abilities we're just beginning to understand.

Text by **Lisa Grunwald**
Reporting by **Jeff Goldberg**

Additional reporting: **Stacey Bernstein, Anne Hollister**

A light comes on. Shapes and colors appear. Some of the colors and shapes start moving. Some of the colors and shapes make noise. Some of the noises are voices. One is a mother's. Sometimes she sings. Sometimes she says things. Sometimes she leaves. What can an infant make of the world? In the blur of perception and chaos of feeling, what does a baby know?

Most parents, observing infancy, are like travelers searching for famous sites: first tooth, first step, first word, first illness, first shoes, first full night of sleep. Most subtle, and most profound of all, is the first time the clouds of infancy part to reveal the little light of a human intelligence.

For many parents, that revelation may be the moment when they see

their baby's first smile. For others, it may be the moment when they watch their child show an actual

---

At three months, babies can learn—and remember for weeks—visual sequences and simple mechanical tasks.

---

preference—for a lullaby, perhaps, or a stuffed animal. But new evidence is emerging to show that even before those moments, babies already have wonderfully active minds.

Of course, they're not exactly chatty in their first year of life, so what—and how—babies truly think may always remain a mystery. But using a variety of ingenious techniques that interpret how infants watch and move, students of child development are discovering a host of unsuspected skills. From a rudimentary understanding of math to a

sense of the past and the future, from precocious language ability to an innate understanding of physical laws, children one year and younger know a lot more than they're saying.

MEMORY

Does an infant remember anything? Penelope Leach, that slightly scolding doyenne of the child development field, warns in *Babyhood* that a six- to eight-month-old "cannot hold in his mind a picture of his mother, nor of where she is." And traditionally psychologists have assumed that infants cannot store memories until, like adults, they have the language skills needed to form and retrieve them. But new research suggests that babies as young as three months may be taking quite accurate mental notes.

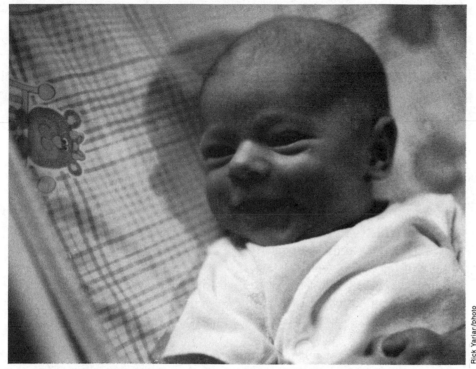

Babies show an unexpected ability to remember surprisingly intricate details.

Rick Yariar/photo

In his lab at the University of Denver, psychologist Marshall Haith has spent much of the past four years putting infants into large black boxes where they lie and look up at TV screens. The program they see is a Haith invention: a sequence of colorful objects appearing on different sides of the monitor. Using an infrared camera linked to a computer, Haith follows the babies' eye movements and has found that after only five tries the babies can anticipate where the next object will appear. With a little more practice, they can foresee a four-step sequence. And up to two weeks later, most can still predict it. Says Haith: "The babies are not just looking. They're analyzing, creating little hypotheses."

Similar findings by Carolyn Rovee-Collier, a psychologist at Rutgers University, suggest that infants can remember surprisingly intricate details. In a typical experiment, she places a baby in a crib beneath an elaborate mobile, ties one of the baby's ankles to it with a satin ribbon, then observes as the baby kicks and—often gleefully—makes it move. When, weeks later, the baby's feet are left untied and the mobile is returned to the crib, the baby will try to kick again, presumably recalling the palmy days of kicking the last time. But if the mobile's elements are changed even slightly, the baby will remain unmoved—and unmoving. "When we change things," explains Rovee-Collier, "it wipes out the memory. But as soon as we bring back what had become familiar and expected, the memory comes right back. What we've learned from this is that even at two and a half months, an infant's memory is very developed, very specific and incredibly detailed."

Rachel Clifton, a psychologist at the University of Massachusetts, says that an infant's experience at six months can be remembered a full two years later. Clifton stumbled upon her findings while researching motor and hearing skills. Three years ago she placed 16 six-month-olds in a pitch-dark room with objects that made different sounds. Using infrared cameras like Haith's, she observed how and when the infants reached for the objects. Later, realizing she had created a unique situation that couldn't have been duplicated in real life, she wondered if the babies would remember their experience. Two years after the original experiment, collaborating with psychologist Nancy Myers, she brought the same 16 children back to the lab, along with a control group of 16 other two-and-a-half-year-olds. Amazingly, the experimental group showed the behavior they had at six months, reaching for objects and showing no fear. Fewer control-group toddlers reached for the objects, and many of them cried.

Says Myers: "For so long, we didn't think that infants could rep-

---

At five months, babies have the raw ability to add.

---

resent in their memories the events that were going on around them, but put them back in a similar situation, as we did, and you can make the memory accessible."

MATH

At least a few parental eyebrows—and undoubtedly some expectations—were raised by this recent headline in *The New York Times:* "Study Finds Babies at 5 Months Grasp Simple Mathematics." The story, which reported on the findings of Karen Wynn, a psychologist at the University of Arizona, explained that infants as young as five months had been found to exhibit "a rudimentary ability to add and subtract."

Wynn, who published her research in the renowned scientific journal *Nature,* had based her experiments on a widely observed phenomenon: Infants look longer at things that are unexpected to them, thereby revealing what they do expect, or know. Wynn enacted addition and subtraction equations for babies using Mickey Mouse dolls. In a typical example, she had the babies watch as she placed a doll on a puppet stage, hid it behind a screen, then placed a second doll behind the screen (to represent one plus one). When she removed the screen to reveal three, not two, Mickey Mouse dolls, the infants stared longer at such incorrect outcomes than they had at correct ones. Wynn believes that babies' numerical understanding is "an innate mechanism, somehow built into the biological structure."

Her findings have been met with enthusiasm in the field—not least from Mark Strauss at the University of Pittsburgh, who a decade ago found that somewhat older babies could distinguish at a glance the difference between one, two, three and four balls—nearly as many objects as adults can decipher without counting. Says Strauss: "Five-month-olds are clearly thinking about quantities and applying numerical concepts to their world."

Wynn's conclusions have also inspired skepticism among some researchers who believe her results may reflect infants' ability to perceive things but not necessarily an ability to know what they're perceiving. Wynn herself warns parents not to leap to any conclu-

sions, and certainly not to start tossing algebra texts into their children's cribs. Still, she insists: "A lot more is happening in infants' minds than we've tended to give them credit for."

LANGUAGE

In an old stand-up routine, Robin Williams used to describe his son's dawning ability as a mimic of words—particularly those of the deeply embarrassing four-letter variety. Most parents decide they can no longer speak with complete freedom when their children start talking. Yet current research on language might prompt some to start censoring themselves even earlier.

At six months, babies recognize their native tongue.

At Seattle's University of Washington, psychologist Patricia Kuhl has shown that long before infants actually begin to learn words, they can sort through a jumble of spoken sounds in search of the ones that have meaning. From birth to four months, according to Kuhl, babies are "universal linguists" capable of distinguishing each of the 150 sounds that make up all human speech. But by just six months, they have begun the metamorphosis into specialists who recognize the speech sounds of their native tongue.

In Kuhl's experiment babies listened as a tape-recorded voice repeated vowel and consonant combinations. Each time the sounds changed—from "ah" to "oooh," for example—a toy bear in a box

was lit up and danced. The babies quickly learned to look at the bear when they heard sounds that were new to them. Studying Swedish and American six-month-olds, Kuhl found they ignored subtle variations in pronunciation of their own language's sounds—for instance, the different ways two people might pronounce "ee"—but they heard similar variations in a foreign language as separate sounds. The implication? Six-month-olds can already discern the sounds they will later need for speech. Says Kuhl: "There's nothing external in these six-month-olds that would provide you with a clue that something like this is going on."

By eight to nine months, comprehension is more visible, with babies looking at a ball when their mothers say "ball," for example. According to psychologist Donna Thal at the University of California, San Diego, it is still impossible to gauge just how many words babies understand at this point, but her recent studies of slightly older children indicate that comprehension may exceed expression by a factor as high as a hundred to one. Thal's studies show that although some babies are slow in starting to talk, comprehension appears to be equal between the late talkers and early ones.

PHYSICS

No, no one is claiming that an eight-month-old can compute the trajectory of a moon around a planet. But at Cornell University, psychologist Elizabeth Spelke is finding that babies as young as four months have a rudimentary knowledge of the way the world works—or should work.

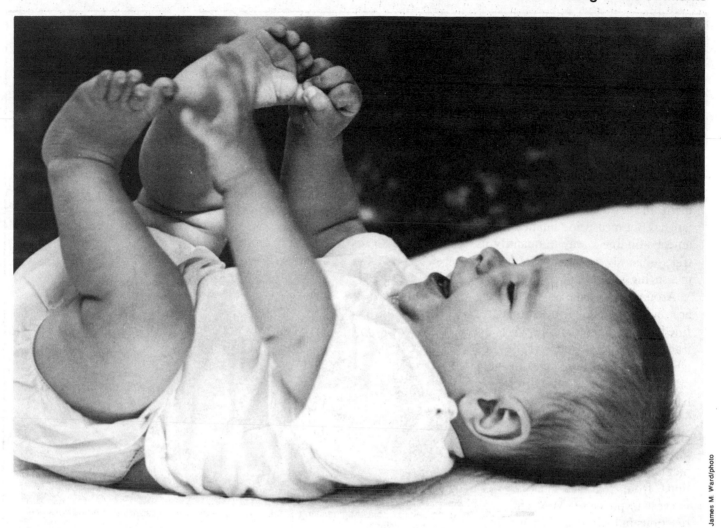

Babies learn how physical objects behave by moving their body parts.

Babies have a built-in sense of how objects behave.

Spelke sets her young subjects up before a puppet stage, where she shows them a series of unexpected actions: a ball seems to roll through a solid barrier, another seems to leap between two platforms, a third seems to hang in midair. Like Karen Wynn with her math experiments, Spelke measures the babies' looking time and has recorded longer intervals for unexpected actions than for expected ones. Again like Wynn, Spelke believes that babies must have some "core" knowledge—in this case, about the way physical objects behave. Says Spelke: "At an age when infants are not able to talk about objects, move around objects, reach for and manipulate objects, or even see objects with high resolution, they appear to recognize where a moving object is when it has left their view and make inferences about where it should be when it comes into sight again."

The notion of an infant's possessing any innate mechanism—other than reflexes like sucking that fade with time—would have shocked the shoes off the pioneers of child development research, who believed, as some still do, that what we know can be learned only through experience. But the belief in biologically programmed core knowledge lies at the heart of the current research—not only with math and physics but with other cognitive skills as well. Indeed, Carnegie Mellon's Mark Johnson believes that the ability of infants to recognize the human face is not learned, as previously thought, but is present at birth. Studying infants, some only 10 minutes old, Johnson has observed a marked preference for pictures of faces to pictures of blank ovals or faces with scrambled features. He believes that we are born with a "template" of the human face that aids our survival by helping us recognize our meal ticket.

EMOTIONS: THE SHY AND THE LIVELY

A growing number of researchers believe early temperament may indicate later troubles.

One thing that infants are *not* good at is hiding what they feel. Fear, glee, rage, affection: Long before babies start talking, emotions tumble out of them in gestures, tears and belly laughs. But measuring infant temperament—finding a way to quantify its traits—has always been harder than measuring skills.

Around the country, researchers are now combining questionnaires filled in by parents, home visits by trained observers, and newly devised lab tests to explore the mystery of temperamenat. Concentrating on babies older than eight months (the age at which the full range of infant emotions has emerged), investigators have designed more than 50 experimental situations to provoke emotions from fear to sadness, from interest to pleasure. Most children's reactions fall within an average range on such tests. But there are babies on either extreme, and psychologist Nathan Fox at the University of Maryland has begun to explore their responses. Putting his babies in electroencephalogram (EEG) helmets, he has found that particularly inhibited babies show a distinctive brain-wave pattern, which others believe may predict later emotional problems, including depression. Although some scientists agree that early behavior can predict later temperament, other researchers argue that enduring character traits are the exception, not the rule. For psychiatrist Stanley Greenspan of Bethesda, Md., the ability of infants to change is an article of faith. Specializing in babies as young as three months, Greenspan says he can treat what he calls the garden-variety problems of sleep disorders, tan-

WHO/photo

Long before babies begin talking, emotions are graphically expressed in their gestures and facial expressions.

trums and anger in a few sessions. (Don't imagine tiny couches for infant patients; although the babies are closely observed, it's the parents who often get treatment.) For more severe problems, such as suspected learning disorders, he recommends more intensive early intervention—often involving a team of therapists—and has found that this can make a huge difference: "Babies who were very scared, shy and inhibited can completely change and become very assertive, outgoing and confident over a number of months."

The University of Washington's Mary Rothbart has compared infants in Japan, the Netherlands and the U.S. and notes that northern European mothers are most prone to ignore their babies' fussiness with

a stiff-upper-lip approach. When tested at one year by having their mothers leave a room, the Dutch babies are the most distressed and ignore their mothers upon their return. Psychologists call this response an "insecure attachment relationship," and some regard it as an early warning of later anxiety disorders. Says Rothbart: "In the process of soothing a baby, you're helping to teach it to shift its attention away from negative sensations. Adults with anxiety disorders may never have learned to do this." Tellingly, when Dutch mothers were instructed to soothe and play with their fussy babies, the follow-up sessions showed positive results. "With intervention," concludes Rothbart, "you can turn things around."

TAKING INFANTS SERIOUSLY

The ultimate question becomes, should education begin at three months?

One question that might leap to the minds of parents newly informed of their infants' skills is a simple one: So what? What does it mean if children really have these unexpected abilities?

Pointing to the findings on memory that she has published with partner Rachel Clifton, Nancy Myers suggests that if memories of the babies' experience allowed them to be unafraid in the pitch-black room, then exposing children to a wide variety of events and places may make them more accepting of similar situations later on. "I don't want to say that mothers should make an extreme effort to stimulate their babies," Myers says, "but taking a baby to different places, allowing him to see and smell different things, is an important means of establishing familiarity. It will allow the baby to feel freer in the future."

But what about other kinds of skills: Should infants' innate abilities with language or math be consciously nurtured and pushed along?

In Philadelphia, instructors at the Institutes for the Achievement of Human Potential have been coaching parents since 1963 to teach their babies to read from birth. Touting "genetic potential," their program recommends that parents write out on cards everything from "nose" to "kiss" to "Mommy." The new findings about infants' skills have hardly gone unnoticed at the Institutes, where director Janet Doman says: "For the past thirty years, we've been saying that children can learn at very early ages. It's nice to know that science is finally validating what we've known all along."

Yet many of the scientists performing the experiments question the value of such intensive efforts. Says Rutgers's Carolyn Rovee-Collier: "Most of us agree that an infant could be taught to recognize letters and numbers. But the problem is that parents who do these kinds of programs start investing a lot in their infants and become very bound up in their success. It puts great strain on the infants and the parents."

University of Denver psychologist Marshall Haith agrees: "Babies are born prepared to take on the world. We've got to get away from the feeling that we've got this wonderful brain sitting there and we've got to keep pumping information into it. Nature wouldn't have done anything so stupid."

To most researchers, the moral of the story seems to be: Respect your baby, but don't go nuts. "Don't waste your child's fun months," says Karen Wynn, who says her findings about math "should be viewed as no more than a new insight for parents who have young children." Says the University of Pittsburgh's Mark Strauss: "Ideally, we can tell parents a lot more about subtle things they can watch happening in their infants, and that will make watching and getting involved more fun."

The Realistic View of Biology and Behavior

Jerome Kagan

Jerome Kagan is professor of psychology at Harvard University. He is the author of Galen's Prophecy: Temperament in Human Nature *(BasicBooks, 1994).*

Although families with more than one child know that each infant brings into the world a distinctive mood and manner, during most of this century Americans have resisted the idea that biology might form at least part of the foundation of some personality traits. The strength of American skepticism is odd, because generations of previous commentators on human nature, beginning with the ancient Greeks, acknowledged that each person's physiology made a small contribution to his or her energy, emotional adaptability, and style of interaction with others.

The source of American resistance, though, is the laudable, egalitarian hope that benevolent home and school experiences can overcome individual biological variations and create a society of relative equals. Because that hope sustains liberal legislation, many people—including scholars—believe that it is dangerous to challenge it, no matter how mildly.

However, the evidence for physiology's influence on some behavior is sufficient to overcome any hesitation to discuss openly the nature of biologically based predispositions. Research in many laboratories, including my own, reveals that many people inherit a physiology that can affect, for example, a proneness to be melancholic or sanguine. At the same time, we must not become so enamored of such discoveries that we forget biology's real limits.

The campaign to suppress discussion of biology grew strong during the opening decades of this century. Politically liberal scholars, joined by journalists of like mind, wished to mute the arguments of conservatives who argued for halting immigration from Eastern Europe on the ground that the immigrants had genetic flaws. The liberals were helped by Ivan Pavlov's discovery of conditioning, in the early 1900's, in a St. Petersburg laboratory. If a dog could be taught to salivate at a sound, surely a child could be taught anything, was the message John Watson, America's first behaviorist, brought to American parents after World War I. That bold claim was congruent with Sigmund Freud's creative hypothesis that family experiences in the early years could create or prevent a future neurosis.

By the late 1920's, the broad acceptance of inherited temperamental traits, which had lasted for two millennia, had been banished, its demise speeded by our society's need to believe in the power of social experience.

As the discipline of psychology—born in Europe during the last quarter of the 19th century—became recognized at American colleges and universities, many faculty members began to emphasize the influence of social experience on behavior. This approach became easier to defend after Hitler proposed the repugnant philosophy that Aryans were superior to other people.

After World War II, social science in America also became more positivistic, demanding objective evidence for all theoretical statements. Neuroscience was still young in the late 1940's and was unable to supply evidence that could explain, for example, how a particular physiological profile might be the foundation of an anxious or an angry mood.

"Hundreds of studies of the way families influence growing children had not produced the powerful generalizations that had been anticipated a half century earlier."

By the 1970's, however, the historical context had again changed. Hundreds of studies of the way families influence growing children had not produced the powerful generalizations that had been anticipated a half century earlier. Equally important,

From *The Chronicle of Higher Education*, October 5, 1994, p. A64. © 1994 by Jerome Kagan. Reprinted by permission of the author.

engineers and scientists had invented ingenious ways to study the brain. Suddenly it became possible to speculate about how a particular neurochemistry could produce excessive anxiety, sadness, or anger. Scientists who put forward such explanations were not treated as intellectual terrorists for suggesting, for example, that a woman with panic attacks might have inherited a neurochemistry that rendered her especially vulnerable to a sudden, inexplicable sharp rise in heart rate, a feeling of suffocation, and a surge of fear.

But I believe that some psychiatrists and neuroscientists are moving too quickly toward a biological determinism that is as extreme as the earlier loyalty of some psychologists to an environmental explanation of behavior. Fortunately, a majority of scientists recognize that no human psychological profile is a product of genes alone. To rephrase a graceful sentence by the philosopher W. V. O. Quine, every behavior can be likened to a pale gray fabric composed of black threads, for biology, and white threads, for experience, but it is not possible to detect any purely black threads nor any white ones.

Support for this more complex, but realistic, view of the relation between brain and behavior is found in the fact that if one member of a pair of identical twins develops schizophrenia, the odds are less than 50 per cent that the other twin will come down with the same psychosis. Because inherited biological propensities do not affect all psychological outcomes equally, the proper strategy is to ask which psychological characteristics are most, and which least, vulnerable to biological forces. Serious depression belongs to the former category, while preference for a seaside holiday belongs to the latter.

At the moment, two psychological categories, which can be observed clearly in children, appear to be heavily influenced by biology. Between 15 per cent and 20 per cent of a large group of healthy infants we studied, who were born into secure homes, were found to have inherited a tendency to be unusually aroused and distressed by new, unexpected events. When they were observed in our laboratory at four months of age, they thrashed their limbs and cried when they saw colorful, moving mobiles or heard tape recordings of human speech. About two-thirds of these easily aroused infants, whom we call "high reactive," became extremely shy, fearful, subdued toddlers. Based on other data, we estimate that about one-half of this group of toddlers will become quiet, introverted adolescents. Not all of the high-reactive infants will become introverted, however, because their life experiences lead them to develop differently.

A second, larger group of infants—about 35 per cent of the children we studied—are the opposite of the high-reactive, shy children. These infants are relaxed and rarely cry when they experience new events. Two-thirds of this group become sociable, relatively fearless young children. Stressful events, however, can produce a fearful or shy manner in such children, even though they began life with a minimally excitable temperament.

Support for a biological contribution to the development of these two types of children comes from the fact that the two groups differ in many aspects of their physiological functioning, as well as in their body build. The fearful children show larger increases in heart rate and blood pressure when they are challenged—signs of a more reactive sympathetic nervous system. They have a higher prevalence of the allergies that produce hay fever and hives (and, surprisingly, possess narrower faces). Studies of identical and fraternal twins support the belief that each of these temperamental types is influenced, in part, by heredity.

Hippocrates and Galen of Pergamon would not have been surprised by these discoveries. Many Americans, however, will be troubled, because they will misinterpret the evidence as implying an exaggerated biological influence on behavior. Some social scientists will also resist acknowledging the contribution of brain chemistry and physiology to behavior because they will worry that, if they let the camel's nose under the tent, the animal will soon be inside, forcing all the residents to leave.

All the more reason that we who study the relationship of biology to behavior must make clear that psychological phenomena, like a fearful or a fearless style of behavior, cannot be reduced completely to a person's biology: The child's life history influences the adult's psychological profile. Because the course of that life history is unknown when children are very young, we cannot at that time select the very small proportion of the 5 per cent to 10 per cent of children whose temperaments dispose them to be fearless, impulsive, and aggressive who will go on to develop an asocial or criminal personality. It would be unethical, for example, to tell parents that their 3-year-old son is at serious risk for delinquent behavior.

Similar arguments can be made about predicting which children will develop panic attacks, depression, or schizophrenia. A small group of children are at risk for each of these disorders because of the physiology they inherit, but we are unable at the present time to say which of the children will eventually develop a particular disorder—because we do not know what vicissitudes life will hold for them.

Perhaps future discoveries will supply the information that will make such predictions accurate enough to warrant benevolent intervention early in the child's life. We will have to wait and see whether that promise can be fulfilled.

A more subtle implication of the research on temperament involves people's willingness to take responsibility for their own actions. I trust that most Americans still believe in the notion of free will—that we can decide what action we will take or not take—and that each of us has a moral obligation to be civil and responsible, even when we wake up feeling blue, angry, or anxious. Our culture still insists that we should pull up our socks and act responsibly, even if that posture comes at some emotional price.

The danger in the new romance with biology is that many people will begin to award temperament too strong a voice, deciding, for example, to be permissive and accepting of friends who lose their tempers too easily. Each of us does inherit a temperamental bias for one or more characteristics, but we also inherit the human capacity for restraint. Most of the time, humans are able to control the behavior that their temperament presses upon them, if they choose to do so. The new research on temperament and biology should not be used to excuse asocial behavior. Rather, the purpose of the inquiry is to help us understand the bases for the extraordinary variation in human motivation, mood, and social behavior.

We would do well to remember that although the poet-philosopher Lucretius believed in temperamental variation he was also convinced that the "lingering traces of inborn temperament that cannot be eliminated by philosophy are so slight that there is nothing to prevent men from leading a life worthy of the gods."

Mental Health for Babies: What Do Theory and Research Teach Us?

Alice Sterling Honig

Alice Sterling Honig, Ph.D., conducts a national infant/ toddler training workshop every June; is a former Research in Review editor for Young Children; *edited* Risk Factors in Infancy; *coauthored (with J.R. Lally)* Infant Caregiving: A Design for Training; *and wrote* Parent Involvement in Early Childhood Education, *which is published by NAEYC.*

Some parents have never thought of how the threats they use in anger might make a baby feel unloved or unlovable. Aside from interaction styles and words, some employed parents need to rethink how they are spending those precious hours between pick-up time and bedtime for the baby. Offer parents specific ideas about how to provide more special attention through activities such as leisurely bath time, picture-book reading with the baby on the parent's lap, dancing to slow music with the baby closely snuggled in the parent's arms, cheek-to-cheek, to encourage infant confidence in adult caring.

As families seek child care for even younger children, more and more infants and toddlers enter nonparental care. Because many early childhood specialists have been prepared predominantly to serve preschool children, there is great urgency for further understanding of the insights of theorists, clinicians, and researchers for providers who wish to extend their competencies to promote the mental health of infants and toddlers.

In the cognitive domain infants and toddlers mostly function in Piaget's sensorimotor and early preoperational period. They are learning about causality (turn the handle and the jack-in-the-box pops up), the permanence and spatial arrangements of objects, and how to use a special activity (such as pulling a string) as a means toward a goal (such as making a pull toy move along). Of course caregivers need to know all about the sensorimotor accomplishments of infants who are learning such a variety of skills, for example, adorning oneself with a pop-it-bead necklace, pretending to walk a toy dog, listening to a music box, learning spatially how to crawl around a detour, or learning to use two hands differentially in play—one to hold a toy and the other to make it work by winding it up.

More serious problems for infants lie in the domain of emotional/social functioning, however. Some caregivers provide the right toys for sensorimotor learning, but they handle infant bodies as objects and focus predominantly on housekeeping chores. They check on wet diapers but forget the *personhood* of each baby. Those who care for infants need, above all, to have as their goal *insuring good infant mental health.*

The earliest research into the outcomes of high-quality university-based infant care found no detrimental emotional effects (Caldwell, Wright, Honig, & Tannenbaum, 1970) and some cognitive advantages, particularly for disadvantaged babies. Yet some recent researchers looking at community infant care have found a disconcerting possibility that full-time infant care begun in the first year of life may be associated with increased cognitive ability but also with increased aggression and noncompliance (Belsky, 1986; Belsky & Rovine, 1988; Egeland, 1991; Park & Honig, 1991); thus, it becomes particularly urgent that caregivers learn as much as possible about the *emotional* dimensions of infant development.

Who are the major theorists clarifying infant/toddler emotional development? Which behavioral warning signals alert and galvanize caregivers toward more specialized efforts to nourish babies' emotional well-being? What specific childrearing practices can boost infant mental health?

Theorists whose ideas help us understand infant mental health

Eric Erikson

In their first year infants struggle with the Eriksonian dialectical problems of acquiring more basic trust (than mistrust) in their own goodness and in their caregivers' benevolence. During their second and third years, toddlers struggle to acquire a secure sense of autonomy and ability to exercise choice. If the sense of will is damaged through adult harshness, emotional indifference, and ridicule/shaming, infants inherit a disturbing legacy. Children may permanently doubt their right to have their own wishes and make their own choices. They may develop a sense of shame or defiance about asserting their will and may express frustration, anger, and rage at being frequently thwarted, misunderstood, and punished for their budding attempts to assert themselves (Erikson, 1963).

Caregivers need to accept with patience rather than exasperation the seesawing, often contradictory behaviors of toddlers. A toddler runs away in defiant and delighted independence when called to lunch or to clean up, but he clings to you and needs to cuddle if he is tired or frightened (Honig, 1990; 1993a). Provide continuity of trust for toddlers. They struggle to assert their wills, but they still need leisurely lap times and reassurance that their tantrums or negativism don't lose them the caregiver's support and nurturance. Perceptive, caring adults bring firmness, clarity of rules, and unconditional commitment, rather than rejection or anger, to confrontations with toddlers. Always be alert. Be especially sure not to get carried away into returning hurt for hurt. Sometimes adults get trapped into *re-creating* negative

struggles for power that may be going on in the home (Wittmer & Honig, 1990). A toddler may be acting with increased stubbornness to family anger and disapproval that he or she does not cooperate yet with demands for more mature behaviors in toileting or neat eating, and that stubbornness—when acted out in child care—can puzzle or upset the unwary caregiver.

Margaret Mahler

Mahlerian theory details stages in infant emotional growth and development in relation to modes of maternal care. Infants move from a close body relationship, during which their inner needs for nursing and bodily contact are paramount; through a "hatching" period, during which they begin to tune in with bright eyes, postural alertness, and genuine interest in the outside world; through a "practicing" subphase, during which they count on the primary loved caregiver as a secure base from which to venture away, using newly developed locomotor skills to explore the environment. From about one and one-half to three years, babies' dawning cognitive abilities permit them to think about and struggle to make sense of separation problems. Baby longs for a return to the closeness originally enjoyed with the primary caregiver; yet, in awesome contradiction, powerful new urges impel the baby in this "rapprochement" period toward new freedom to be a special individual with *separate* wishes and desires (Kaplan, 1978). During this gray, crashing-down, crabby period (Honig, 1991), babies sometimes behave in ways that bewilder and exasperate caregivers. Understanding these emotional struggles of toddlerhood helps. A wise caregiver tunes into the needs of babies to support their growing autonomy while still providing the nurturing responsivity and body-loving care that permit toddlers to develop beyond the rapprochement period into Mahlerian "constancy." The beginning of achieving constancy occurs when the toddler can hold *opposing* emotional feelings (such as loving and yet sometimes feeling angry with the caregiver) in dialectical balance. Constancy helps a child to support lengthy daily separations from parents who are both resented *and* loved. Constancy helps toddlers come to terms with strong differences between their own and adult wishes and preferences. Babies learn to integrate and accept dualities of feeling and still retain clear sense of a loving relationship.

John Bowlby and Mary Ainsworth

Attachment theory is possibly the most powerful new tool that ethological theorists have provided us with in recent decades. Bowlby proposed that infants build nonverbal, internal working models of early relationships with each caregiver (Bretherton & Waters, 1985). These models are unconscious, yet they serve as tenacious templates for expecting other close relationships later in life to be similarly depressed or happy, kind or cruel, orderly or chaotic. Sadly, an abused toddler will often behave in inappropriate ways in child care that can ensnare an unwary caregiver into the punitive, unhappy interactions that the child has already so well internalized and construed as the model for intimate relationships!

Some caregivers provide the right toys for sensorimotor learning, but they handle infant bodies as objects and focus predominantly on housekeeping chores. They check on wet diapers but forget the *personhood* of each baby. Those who care for infants need, above all, to have as their goal *insuring good infant mental health.*

Ethological theory suggests that to ensure survival, nature has equipped babies with the ability to cry loud, cling to the caregiver, call, smile dazzlingly, lift arms to be picked up, creep, and follow after a departing adult. With these fundamental postures and vocalizations, babies enhance their chances of survival through entraining their caregiver into a more caring, close relationship; yet needs for felt security are always in balance with growing needs to explore. When the baby's special person is there emotionally for her, she can explore freely, and the quality of her play will be more focused and creative. When the attachment figure disappears or is rejecting, the quality of play suffers. A baby acts independent in play with peers and toys when he is feeling deeply sure that his special person is readily available to comfort and protect him if fear or tiredness upsets him.

During the last half of the first year of life, infants show a particular strength of *differential* smiling, body molding, approaching, and greeting their special person—usually the parent who has provided most of the intimate bodily care and attention (Honig, 1992); however, babies can and do adopt several different attachment figures. The quality of security or insecurity in the baby's relationship will depend in each case on the *unique* interactions between the baby and that adult (Honig, 1982b). That is why assigning babies to a special caregiver in child care is important. As infants begin to trust the familiar, tender care received daily, they begin to show differential signs of that caregiver becoming a special attachment figure. This is why *stability of provider* and *continuity of care* are so very important. Babies should not be moved like chess pawns to a "younger toddler group" or other such groups! Babies need to feel that they can make sense of and trust sameness in responsive cherishing in their child care facility.

Assessment of security. How is security of attachment assessed? Ainsworth's Strange Situation technique has become the major measure by which infant attachment is determined at 12 and 18 months. A mother and infant enter a toy play room, and during three-minute time periods the baby is first with mother, then with a stranger, then reunited with mother, then alone, then with a stranger, and finally again reunited with mother. From careful analysis of the *reunion* behaviors of the infant when mother enters the room, four kinds of attachment patterns have been noted. *Securely attached* (B) babies actively seek reunion; they sink into and mold onto the body of caregiver. Having "touched base" and relaxed deeply, these babies are then ready to leave the security of the lap to go back to interested play with toys. Their

parents have been identified as promptly responsive to signals of distress and tenderly careful in their holding. The parents of secure babies are sensitive, reciprocal partners rather than intrusive, pushy, resentful, or chaotic in their ministrations.

Babies who begin to seek comfort but then turn away in anger/irritability or struggle to get down from the caregiver's arms are identified as insecure/ambivalent/resistive (C) babies. The parent has shown insensitivity to the C baby's tempos, rhythms, and distress signals. The baby is picked up or attended to more at the parent's convenience or whim rather than when she or he expresses a need.

Two other categories of insecure attachment have been identified. Some babies do not seek the parent upon re-entry. They ignore the adult and continue to play with toys. These avoidant/insecure (A) babies, who look as if they are "mature" in accepting separations, often turn out to be angry at home and hostile and unfeeling with preschool peers. Ainsworth (1982) has reported that mothers of A babies dislike or are impatient with physical caressing. Other babies seem to show intense desires to go to the parent at reunion and equally intense sudden blank looks, anger, or turning away. Main, Kaplan, and Cassidy (1985) label this response "D" for dazed/disorganized/disoriented and report that the mother of a D baby often has a history of early trauma and loss in her own life. Even at six years of age, D children responded to pictured stories of separation between parents and children in ways that reflected extreme discomfort or almost bizarre denial of upset feelings. They were unable to think of ways to cope with separations, such as going to stay with a grandmother. Secure children, in contrast, when presented with separation pictures (such as parents leaving for a night out or for an extended trip), even thought up ingenious solutions such as hiding in the parents' car before they drove off on a two-week vacation!

Attachment research thus has given us subtle tools for discerning from infant responses in daily innumerable,

In their first year infants struggle with problems of acquiring more basic trust (than mistrust) in their own goodness and in their caregivers' benevolence.

small interactions (Stern, 1985) what emotional troubles may be brewing. If a baby is irritable or avoidant, the child care worker may not find this infant pleasurable to play with, to croon to, or to caress. When caregivers are alert to such relationship pitfalls, they are more likely to provide healing opportunities for such infants to become attached securely to their precious person—the caregiver.

Caregivers who wish to meet the needs of under-threes for emotionally supportive care will find perceptive and helpful guidelines in clinicians' unfolding story of the stages of normal emotional/social growth.

Body cues for judging infant mental health

Despite staff attentiveness to prevention of emotional distress, some babies still may not be thriving emotionally in nonparental care or in group care. In such cases perceptive awareness and monitoring of baby behaviors is a caregiver's first line of defense. *Body cues* that the infant or toddler provides to the caregiver are early indicators that mental health may be in jeopardy.

Research and clinical findings specify the following telltale signs that indicate emotional distress and mental health troubles in infants and toddlers:

- dull eyes without sparkle
- back arching and body stiffening as a regular response
- eye gaze avoidance
- pushing away rather than relaxed molding onto the adult
- limp, floppy, listless body (without illness)
- rare smiles despite tender adult elicitation
- diarrhea or very hard stools, without infection present
- difficulties in sinking into deep, refreshing sleep
- compulsive body rocking back and forth
- inconsolable crying for hours
- scattered attention rather than attention flowing freely between caregiver and baby during intimate exchanges
- dysfluency in the older toddler who is already verbal
- head banging against crib persistently
- grimaces of despair
- frozen affect (apathetic look)
- reverse emotions (e.g., giggling hysterically when frightened)

- impassiveness or anger when a peer becomes hurt or distressed
- lack of friendliness to loving adult overtures
- echoic verbalizations (e.g., repeating ends of adult phrases)
- wild, despairing, thrashing tantrums
- constant masturbation daily even when not tired or at naptime
- fearful withdrawal/flinching when caregiver tries to caress
- regular avoidance of/indifference to parent at pick-up time
- anxious "shadowing" of caregiver without letup
- continuous biting/hitting of others with no prior aggressive provocation; strong aversion to "victim-centered discipline" explanations of caregiver
- little if any interest in peers or persons
- banging headlong into furniture or hurting self a lot, without turning to caregiver for comfort
- allowed by other children to aggress strongly, in deference to his "disabled" status, but then mostly avoided by other children in play

Mental health prescriptions

If any of the previously mentioned danger signs appears consistently, then parents and caregivers must mobilize urgently for alleviation of the infant's stress and enhancement of her coping skills (Honig, 1986). Sometimes a family feels isolated and stressed and has little energy left for the baby-holding and attunement that are so necessary to build secure attachment. If a baby does not have at least one secure attachment figure in the family, she or he will be vulnerable to the stress of daily separation from familiar family members. In the child care facility, watch for specific signs of vulnerability. Especially if you observe clusters of such signs, mobilize community and child care resources *and* family members to support the emotionally distressed baby.

Help parents reframe

Some parents have never thought of how the threats they use in anger might make a baby feel unloved or unlovable. Aside from interaction styles and words, some employed parents need to rethink how they are spending

---

During their second and third years, toddlers struggle to acquire a secure sense of autonomy and ability to exercise choice. If the sense of will is damaged through adult harshness, emotional indifference, and ridicule/shaming, infants inherit a disturbing legacy. Children may permanently doubt their right to have their own wishes and make their own choices. They may develop a sense of shame or defiance about asserting their will and may express frustration, anger, and rage at being frequently thwarted, misunderstood, and punished for their budding attempts to assert themselves.

---

those precious hours between pick-up time and bedtime for the baby. Offer parents specific ideas about how to provide more special attention through activities such as leisurely bath time, picture-book reading with the baby on the parent's lap, dancing to slow music with the baby closely snuggled in the parent's arms, cheek-to-cheek, to encourage infant confidence in adult caring (Honig, 1990, 1991).

Professional resources

Professional community mental health resources, especially parent-infant specialists, offer in-center or "kitchen therapy" counseling for parents (Fraiberg, Shapiro, & Adelson, 1984). A staff social worker can alleviate some stresses, such as finding better housing or transportation to medical clinics. A local mental health agency may provide weekly home visitors or trained resource mothers. The Homebuilders model (Kinney, Haapala, & Booth, 1991) provides intensive, daily, in-home casework efforts. Some therapeutic groups specialize in work with parents of very young children with emotional difficulties (Koplow, 1992). Mobilize community network resources to support parents.

Cultural sensitivity

When reaching out therapeutically on behalf of emotionally distressed infants and toddlers, staff will need to be sensitive to *cultural* issues in how families react to child disability or dysfunction. This may entail learning about considerations of shame, of cultural healing practices, or even of family hierarchical status that necessitates talking only with the oldest male, for example, rather than with the mother. Lieberman (1989) advises that the culturally sensitive worker must know about the content of different cultural perceptions and maintain an attitude of openness to find out more about the "values and preconceptions of the other" (p. 197).

Stress prevention: Organizational considerations

Staffing patterns

Caregivers can make changes in the environment and in routines to decrease risk factors that negatively affect optimal infant development. Day care research reveals that variables such as "high caregiver to infant ratios, small group size, stability of caregiving arrangements and adequate staff training" optimize child outcomes (Berger, 1990, p. 371).

Physical health

Child care facilities must ensure the best possible chances for good *physical* health for babies as a basic foundation for mental health. Establish clear, strong guidelines and rules, such as frequent caregiver hand washing and diaper changing.

Space and time arrangements

Caregivers should arrange living spaces thoughtfully to decrease stress, including quiet places that support deep and peaceful sleep times, as well as cubbies and snuggly, soft pillows where a baby can creep for privacy and comfort when group care seems overwhelming. Adults need to plan daily outdoor time with fresh air and safe spaces for toddlers to gallop about. Sometimes stress is reduced by decreasing overstimulation. Conversely, enriching the environment provides grist for exuberant toddlers' safe explorations.

The assigned caregiver will need to provide more one-on-one time for emotionally vulnerable babies. The youngest babies may need to be carried in bodyslings. A caregiver's increasingly sensitive attunement to the infant's needs and more prompt, nurturant responsiveness to distress build basic trust and reassurance. Particularly when such infants are in full-time care early in the first year, well-trained caregivers must develop *personalized,* cherishing relationships and thus try to prevent many of the insecure attachment sequelae—such as increased aggression—that have been reported in the literature. Differences between the parent and the caregiver should be minimized when infant mental health is at stake. Babies need loving and will thrive if they are well "mothered" regardless of the age or sex of the caregiver. The director's role in this special effort is crucial. Some caregivers might begin to feel like possessive "rescuers" of this infant; some may be very upset when the infant graduates from the facility. A director's sensitivity to staff problems is an important consideration as caregivers work hard to build secure mental health for babies who are at risk for emotional distress.

© Subjects & Predicates

Holding infants and toddlers a lot while pleasantly talking, walking, playing, and reading with them strengthens mental health.

Caregiver behaviors that promote infant mental health

In addition to theoretical understanding of infant/toddler development and awareness of stress signs in babies, and in addition to logistical and environmental policies that support infant mental health, the caregiver of under-threes needs practical suggestions for enhancing personal interactions (Honig, 1989). Research findings provide good ideas (1) for positive discipline techniques (Honig & Wittmer, 1990); (2) for ways to ease the adjustment of infants into nonparental care; and (3) for ideas that help caregivers forge a partnership with stressed parents, who occasionally may feel jealous or inadequate and in some cases even resent the trained professional caregiver.

Below are some of the specific *personal interaction patterns* culled from attachment researchers, clinicians, and expert practitioners (Greenberg,1991)—that caregivers can use to promote infant mental health:

- Hold the baby tenderly and cuddle extensively.
- Express verbal joy and bodily pleasure at the baby's being.
- Tempt babies with rich toy variety that permits them to find out how to work toys at their own pace and interest.
- Remember that temperament styles differ—easy, slow-to-warm-up, and triggery/irritable babies need different adult approaches (California State Department of Education, 1990).
- Sensitively interpret infant cues and signals of distress.
- Provide prompt, tuned-in responsiveness to infant cues.
- Be perceptive about a toddler's seesawing needs.
- Reassure with caresses and calm words.
- Offer your body and lap generously for needy babies.
- Send admiring glances baby's way.
- Give babies leisurely chances to explore toys as they wish and at their own tempo without intrusiveness.
- Wait until a toddler shows signs of readiness before insisting on potty training or neat eating.
- Gently rub backs to soothe tired, tense, crabby babies.
- Croon and sing softly, especially in a mode to "speak for the body of the baby" in interpreting his or her needs, as in the following example:

Shoshannah wanted to go home. She could not nap easily and was disconsolate. Her caregiver patted her back soothingly and started a low chanting song to the tune of "The Farmer in the Dell." She sang, "You want your mama to come back. You want your mama to come back. You want your mama to come back soon. You want your mama to come back." Over and over the caregiver slowly sang the simple melody reassuringly, with firm conviction. After about 20 repetitions, during which Shoshannah had quieted and breathed more easily on her cot, the caregiver stopped singing. The toddler stirred restlessly. "Sing more," she asked simply. So Miss Alice sang the song softly several more times until the toddler fell peacefully asleep. Next day at naptime the toddler specifi-cally asked her caregiver, "Sing me the 'I want my mama to come back' song." Satisfied with the simple song sung soothingly several times over, Shoshannah dozed off comfortably. (Honig, 1993b, p. 42)

- Feed babies leisurely and in your arms while regarding them.
- Accept infant attempts to manage self-feeding despite their messiness.
- Massage babies to increase body relaxation and pleasure (Evans, 1990).
- Engage in interactive games like pat-a-cake with baby to further a sense of partnering and intimacy.
- Increase shared meanings by following a baby's pointing finger and commenting on objects pointed to; retrieve an object that the baby asks for; create cognitive "scaffolding" and expand shared meaning through empathetic interpretations (Emde, 1990).
- Use diapering time to enhance a sense of body goodness; caress the rounded tummy; stroke cheeks and hair; tell the baby in delighted tones how delicious and beautiful he or she is.
- Play reciprocal, turn-taking games, such as rolling a ball back and forth while seated on the ground with wide-apart legs, facing each other. Place the seated baby on your knees facing yourself and play a rocking-horse game with slower and then faster motions and rhythms (Honig & Lally, 1981, p. 52).
- Make everyday experiences and routines predictable and reassuring (although not rigidly because special outings or events must become part of a baby's world experiences too) so that the baby gets a secure sense of what to expect and in what sequence.
- Explain your actions even to very young babies. If you are leaving a room to get a supply of new diapers, tell the babies what you are doing, where you are going, and that you will be back soon. Give your babies a sense, not of the absurdity and disconnectedness of life experiences, but of the orderliness and meaningfulness of daily activities. Convince babies that they are important, precious members of the cooperative enterprise called *child care*.
- Be a model of generous and genuine empathetic, but not anxious, comfort when a baby is scared or upset (Honig, 1989).
- Serve as a beacon of security and safety for your babies. Let them know that you are there for them when they need to return for a hug, a pat, a cuddle, or a bodily reassurance.
- Arrange ample floor freedom for play and peer acquaintance.
- Choose the active/calm alert state as the optimal state for engaging tiny babies in cooing turn-taking and other interaction games.
- Send *long-distance* cues to cruising babies that you are their *refueling station* par excellence. Your cheerful words called out, your grin of encouragement from a distance, your smile of pride, and your postures of appreciation confirm for newly creeping-away babies that you are **present** for them and affirming them.

From about one and one-half to three years, babies' dawning cognitive abilities permit them to think about and struggle to make sense of separation problems. Baby longs for a return to the closeness originally enjoyed with the primary caregiver; yet, in awesome contradiction, powerful new urges impel the baby in this "rapprochement" period toward new freedom to be a special individual with *separate* wishes and desires. During this gray, crashing-down, crabby period, babies sometimes behave in ways that bewilder and exasperate caregivers. Understanding these emotional struggles of toddlerhood helps.

• Focus your genuine attention to send each child powerful messages of deeply acceptable selfhood (Briggs, 1975).

• Lure disengaged toddlers who wander and cannot connect with materials or peers into intimate interactions using the Magic Triangle technique of interesting baby in the activity rather than in personal interaction or confrontation (Honig, 1982a).

Caregiver interest and pleasuring engagement teach babies their first lessons of learning *intimacy* (rather than isolation and loneliness) and shared human feelings (rather than callous disregard for others). One of the chilling signs that a toddler has been abused is his indifference or anger, even hitting another toddler who is crying and acting upset. If, by 18 months, a toddler is beginning to show expressions of concern and empathetic attempts to soothe a crying baby or to retrieve for that baby a fallen cracker or toy, then a caregiver knows that baby altruism is emerging positively—a good sign of infant mental health.

The best way for a baby to learn to be a kind and caring person early in life (the critical period for this is before age two) is to have a caregiver who (1) models empathetic nurturance when a baby is distressed, and (2) firmly forbids a baby to hurt another person (Pines, 1979).

Conclusions

Let us work together with families toward more positive practices to prevent any possible disturbing emotional effects of nonparental full-time care early in infancy. Nurturant, body-generous caregivers who talk sincerely and interestedly with babies promote feelings of personal competence. Individualized attention and caresses energize babies to cope well with the world of child care. The challenge is to provide enough supports, education, and respect for child care workers so that they can become skilled new baby-therapists of the future through their attunement with babies and sensitivity to families.

Competent, wise supervisors are invaluable assets for programs that train infant caregivers and infant/parent facilitators. Fenichel (1991) introduces this theme in a special issue of *Zero to Three*. Political, educational, and therapeutic efforts will all be needed to increase training efficacy to achieve the desired goal: tender, tuned-in, responsive caregivers and parents who give the gifts of joy, of intimacy, of courage, and of good mental health to babies.

References

Ainsworth, M.D.S. (1982). Early caregiving and later patterns of attachment. In J.H. Kennell & M.H. Klaus (Eds.), *Birth, interaction and attachment* (pp. 35–43). Skillman, NJ: Johnson & Johnson.

Belsky, J. (1986). Infant day care: A cause for concern? *Zero to Three, 6*(5), 1–7.

Belsky, J., & Rovine, M. (1988). Nonmaternal care in the first year of life and the security of infant/parent attachment. *Child Development, 59,* 157–167.

Berger, S.P. (1990). Infant day care, parent-child attachment, and developmental risk: A reply to Caruso. *Infant Mental Health Journal, 11*(4), 365–373.

Bretherton, I., & Waters, E. (Eds.) (1985). Growing points of attachment theory and research. *Monographs of the Society for Research in Child Development, 50* (1–2, Serial No. 209).

Briggs, D. (1975). *Your child's self esteem.* Garden City, NY: Doubleday.

Caldwell, B.M., Wright, C.M., Honig, A.S., & Tannenbaum, J. (1970). Infant day care and attachment. *American Journal of Orthopsychiatry, 40,* 397–412.

California State Department of Education. (1990). *Flexible, fearful, or feisty: The different temperaments of infants and toddlers* [Video]. Sacramento, CA: Program for Infant/Toddler Caregivers.

Egeland, B. (1991, August). The relation between day care in infancy and outcomes in preschool and the school years. In A. Clarke-Stewart (Chair), *Early child care patterns and later child behavior.* Symposium conducted at the meeting of the American Psychological Association, San Francisco, CA.

Emde, R. (1990). Lessons from infancy: New beginnings in a changing world and a morality for health. *Infant Mental Health Journal, 11*(3), 196–212.

Erikson, E. (1963). *Childhood and society.* New York: Norton.

Evans, L. (1990). Impact of infant massage on the neonate and the parent-infant relationship. In N. Gunzenhauser (Ed.), *Advances in touch: New implications in human development* (pp. 71–79). Skillman, NJ: Johnson & Johnson.

Fenichel, E. (1991). Learning through supervision and mentorship to support the development of infant, toddler and their families. *Zero to Three, 12*(2), 1–9.

Fraiberg, S., Shapiro, V., & Adelson, E. (1984). Ghosts in the nursery: A psychoanalytic approach to the problems of impaired infant-mother relationships. In L. Fraiberg (Ed.), *Clinical studies in infant mental health* (pp. 100–136). Columbus, OH: Ohio University Press.

Greenberg, P. (1991). *Character development: Encouraging self-esteem & self-discipline in infants, toddlers, & two-year-olds.* Washington, DC: NAEYC.

Honig, A.S. (1982a). *Playtime learning games for young children.* Syracuse, NY: Syracuse University Press.

Honig, A.S. (1982b). Research in review. Infant-mother communication. *Young Children, 37*(3), 52–62.

Honig, A.S. (1986). Research in review. Stress and coping in children. In J.B. McCracken (Ed.), *Reducing stress in young children's lives* (pp. 142–167). Washington, DC: NAEYC.

Honig, A.S. (1989). Quality infant/toddler caregiving: Are there magic recipes? *Young Children, 44*(4), 4–10.

Honig, A.S. (1990). Infant-toddler education: Principles, practices, and promises. In C. Seefeldt (Ed.), *Continuing issues in early childhood education* (pp. 61–105). Columbus, OH: Merrill/Macmillan.

Honig, A.S. (1991). For babies to flourish. *Montessori Life, 3*(2), 7–10.

Honig, A.S. (1992). Dancing with your baby means sometimes leading, sometimes following. *Dimensions, 20*(3), 10–13.

Honig, A.S. (1993a). The Eriksonian approach. In J.L. Roopnarine & J.E. Johnson (Eds.), *Approaches to early childhood education* (2nd ed.) (pp. 47–70). New York: Macmillan.

Honig, A.S. (1993b). The power of song. *Pre-K Today, 7*(4), 42–43.

Honig, A.S., & Lally, J.R. (1981). *Infant caregiving: A design for training.* Syracuse, NY: Syracuse University Press.

Honig, A.S., & Wittmer, D.S. (1990). Infants, toddlers and socializa-tion. In R.J. Lally (Ed.), *A caregiver's guide to social emotional growth and socialization* (pp. 62–80). Sacramento, CA: California State Department of Education.

Kaplan, L. (1978). *Oneness and separateness.* New York: Washington Square Press (Simon & Schuster).

Kinney, J., Haapala, D., & Booth, C. (1991). *Keeping families together: The Homebuilders model.* Hawthorne, NY: Aldine De Gruyter.

Koplow, L. (1992). Finding common ground: Facilitating a therapeutic group for diverse parents of young disturbed children. *Zero to Three, 12*(3), 22–26.

Lieberman, A. (1989). What is culturally sensitive intervention? In A.S. Honig (Ed.), Cross-cultural aspects of parenting normal and at-risk children [Special issue]. *Early Child Development and Care, 50,* 197–204.

Main, M., Kaplan, N., & Cassidy, J. (1985). Security in infancy, childhood, and adulthood: A move to the level of representation. In I. Bretherton & E. Waters (Eds.), Growing points of attachment theory and research (pp. 66–104). *Monographs of the Society for Research in Child Development, 50*(1–2, Serial No. 209).

Park, K., & Honig, A.S. (1991). Infant care and later teacher ratings of preschool behaviors. *Early Child Development and Care, 68,* 89–96.

Pines, M. (1979). Good samaritans at age two? *Psychology Today, 13*(1), 66–77.

Stern, D. (1985). *The interpersonal world of the infant: A view from psychoanalysis and developmental psychology.* New York: Basic Books.

Wittmer, D.S., & Honig, A.S. (1990). Teacher re-creation of negative interactions with toddlers. In A.S. Honig (Ed.), *Optimizing early child care and education* (pp. 77–88). London: Gordon & Breach.

Home Visiting Programs and the Health and Development of Young Children

Craig T. Ramey
Sharon Landesman Ramey

Craig T. Ramey, Ph.D., is director of the Civitan International Research Center and professor of psychology, pediatrics, public health science, and sociology at the University of Alabama at Birmingham. He was founder and investigator for a number of prominent early intervention programs, including the Abecedarian Project, Project CARE, and the Infant Health and Development Program.

Sharon Landesman Ramey, Ph.D., is director of the Civitan International Research Center and professor of psychiatry, psychology, public health science, and sociology at the University of Alabama at Birmingham. She is currently co-directing the research and evaluation of the Head Start/Public School Transition Demonstration Project, a randomized trial of early intervention programs.

Abstract

This article presents a conceptual framework for thinking about the health and development of young children. The discussion of theory is followed by a description of how home visiting, as a process, can be used to improve the health and development of young children within their many domains of functioning. The authors . . . conclude that home visiting programs which address only one or a few domains of a child's functioning are not likely to have a robust or lasting effect. Accordingly, to be successful, home visiting programs must be comprehensive in their approach to addressing children's and families' needs in multiple domains of functioning. Finally, an analytical grid is presented to assist in describing and clarifying the relationships among the characteristics of home visiting programs and their desired consequences. The Appendix to this article illustrates application of this grid to describe the Infant Health and Development project.

The preparation of this paper was supported by the David and Lucile Packard Foundation, the Administration for Developmental Disabilities, the Maternal and Child Health Bureau of the Public Health Service, and the Administration for Children, Youth, and Families.

Home visiting appears to be one of the most frequently used early intervention strategies or family support programs in the United States to improve the health and development of children. Although some home visiting programs are conceptualized merely as an efficient or economical means of service delivery, these programs are most often construed as a treatment strategy that contains unique and powerful characteristics relative to improving children's health and development. As one recent review of home visiting programs concluded, however, the diversity among programs providing home visiting and the "incomplete but suggestive empirical support for its usefulness, creates an imperative for a more systematic approach to demonstration and evaluation efforts in this area."[1]

This article outlines one of the next steps in developing such an approach. It offers a conceptual framework for understanding and describing more precisely the modes of operation of home visiting programs and the specific domains of early childhood health and development they intend to address. Thus, the article begins with a discussion of health and development in the first three years of life. Then, the implications of this knowledge for the design of home visiting programs are considered. Finally, an analytical grid is presented as a tool for both describing and evaluating home visiting programs. Although this article focuses on children, programs that improve their health and development are likely also to bring about beneficial changes in their parents and the family as a whole.

Health and Development in the First Three Years of Life

Both health and development involve complex and sophisticated ideas about the human condition. These two terms have many definitions and implications for intervention strategies. For the purpose of conceptualizing home visiting programs and their possible positive effects on children's health and development, definitions should emphasize the multidimensionality of each concept. For example, the World Health Organization has advocated that health be defined as a state of physical, mental, and social well-being.[2] Similarly, we believe that development should be seen as a multidimensional process of simultaneously achieving progressive states of (1) increased differentiation (the ability to make distinctions or to perceive differences in closely related items or ideas), (2) increased ability for self-initiation and self-control, (3) increased interpersonal awareness, and (4) increased social responsibility. The central premise of this article is that, because both health and development are multidimensional and dynamic with each dimension affecting the other, home visiting programs and other early intervention efforts must consider the full range of needs for young children in developing their goals and the strategies to achieve them.

The first three years of life represent the period of most rapid growth and development, especially in terms of central nervous system development and associated

Children's health and development are multidimensional and comprised of distinct, but interdependent, domains of functioning.

physical development and social behavior.[3] It is during the first three years that infants and young children are the most dependent on others for their basic care, including health care, intellectual stimulation, social guidance, and love. Failure to provide for young children's basic needs during this period is likely to result in serious consequences, including impaired health, poor sensory-motor functioning, below average intellectual capacity, and compromised abilities to form positive and lasting social relationships.[4] Therefore, home visiting programs in the first three years of life can and often do have goals of both enrichment and prevention, that is, to enhance health and development by providing services and to prevent the negative consequences of suboptimal care or inadequate family support.

Young children's health and development must be viewed within a conceptual framework that explicitly recognizes that their worlds are fundamentally embedded in and influenced by the specific developmental and ecological contexts of their families and communities.[5] Congruent with the theories of authors such as Bronfenbrenner[6] and Sameroff and Fiese,[7] this perspective emphasizes that the forces which affect young children are dynamic and often are the same ones which directly affect the development and functioning of their families and their communities. Accordingly, to alter the course of children's development, early intervention programs—including those that use home visiting—need to take into account the needs and resources of families and communities, as well as the basic needs of children themselves. . . .

Furthermore, even when focusing only on the children, it is clear that their development is complex. Children's health and development are multidimensional and comprised of distinct, but interdependent, domains of functioning. The eight key developmental domains, based on a content analysis of the developmental literature, are (1) survival, (2) values and goals, (3) a

Figure 1

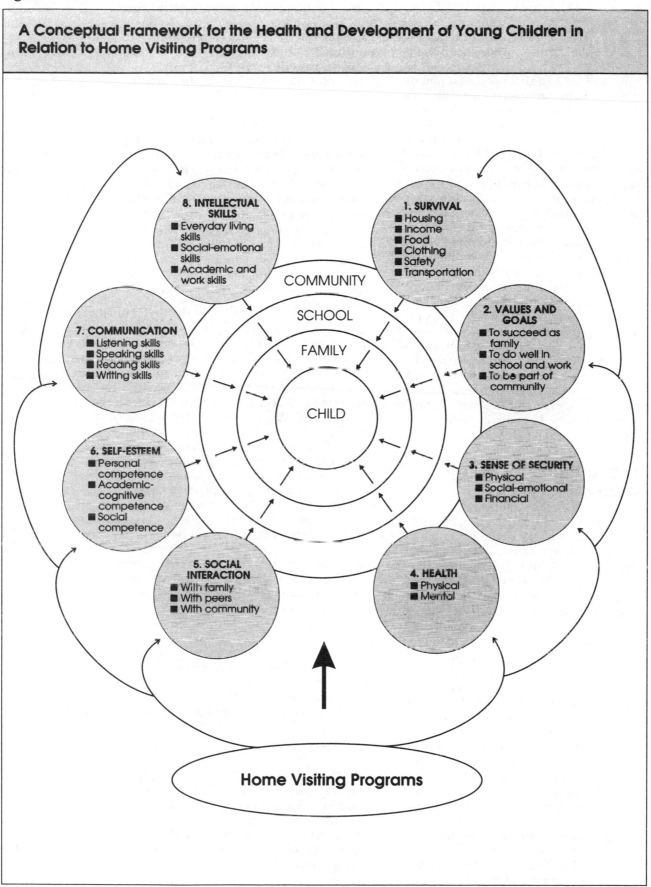

A Conceptual Framework for the Health and Development of Young Children in Relation to Home Visiting Programs

8. INTELLECTUAL SKILLS
- Everyday living skills
- Social-emotional skills
- Academic and work skills

1. SURVIVAL
- Housing
- Income
- Food
- Clothing
- Safety
- Transportation

7. COMMUNICATION
- Listening skills
- Speaking skills
- Reading skills
- Writing skills

2. VALUES AND GOALS
- To succeed as family
- To do well in school and work
- To be part of community

6. SELF-ESTEEM
- Personal competence
- Academic-cognitive competence
- Social competence

3. SENSE OF SECURITY
- Physical
- Social-emotional
- Financial

5. SOCIAL INTERACTION
- With family
- With peers
- With community

4. HEALTH
- Physical
- Mental

COMMUNITY

SCHOOL

FAMILY

CHILD

Home Visiting Programs

sense of security, (4) health, (5) social interaction, (6) self-esteem, (7) communication, and (8) basic intellectual skills. Figure 1 provides examples of functioning within each of these domains.

Within this conceptual framework, the eight domains of functioning comprise the substance of health and development. These domains are intertwined with each other and with the child and family's whole environment. These domains are influenced by the everyday family supports (for example, kinship and friendship networks) and by the community resources (for example, social welfare and health care networks) that form the context within which the young child develops. A central premise of most home visiting programs is that the ecological context of the family can be significantly and positively altered through specific program elements associated with individual home visiting programs. In turn, most programs assume changes in the family environment will mediate changes in the child's everyday experiences. Figure 1 not only presents the eight domains of functioning, but also illustrates the fact that home visiting programs may affect children and families by altering some or all of the major domains of function through strategies directed toward the child, family, school, and/or community.

Implications for Home Visiting Programs

In practice, most home visiting programs place differential and selective emphasis on one or more of the identified eight domains of functioning. Often home visiting programs address first, and with greatest intensity of effort, those needs that appear to home visitors and/or to family members to be the most pressing. For instance, some home visiting programs invest substantial time and resources in helping families to meet needs in the domains of survival (for example, by providing assistance with housing, food, clothing, and transportation) and health (for example, by providing routine checkups and monitoring, encouraging positive health habits, and taking family members to medical appointments). Other home visiting programs emphasize the domains of social interaction and social support for the mother, or systematically seek to change the domains of communication and basic intellectual skills by providing educational programs and direct instruction to mothers and/or their children.

The reasons that programs emphasize different domains of functioning, and may even fail to consider some domains, include the following: (1) the anticipated and most pressing needs of the population with which the program is working, (2) the professional orientation and expertise of the individuals designing and implementing the program, (3) the resources available to the program, and (4) the philosophical orientation of the program (such as whether some domains of functioning are judged to be more or less important or whether home visitors are encouraged not to become involved in some domains for reasons of professional competence or safety). Often, the implicit assumption or hope is that, once the most urgent family issues have been resolved satisfactorily, then there will be time and energy to address other less pressing but important aspects of young children's health and development.

Limiting the focus in home visiting programs to supporting the family first, without special efforts to target the child's early development as well, may be self-defeating. The article by Olds and Kitzman [see *The Future of Children*, Winter 1993, pp. 53–92] reviews the effectiveness of diverse home visiting programs. What is clear from their excellent review of the empirical studies is that there is little evidence that programs which are not intensive and comprehensive, but instead target for change one or a few domains of functioning, are likely to have a lasting beneficial effect, even on the targeted aspects of the lives of children. Those areas may show some improvement; however, in the absence of continuing resource allocation, such changes are unlikely to occur in a robust or lasting manner. In addition, short-term change in one or a few domains will not have a domino, or spillover, effect to other equally important domains of children's functioning. Unfortunately, the nature of developmental processes in young children is such that not one of their needs can wait until other needs are met; children's development does not go on hold while family problems are being solved.

This does not imply that attending to survival and health is less important than focusing on a child's social or intellectual development (or vice versa), but rather that there is a pressing need in the first few years of life to consider simultaneously and to coordinate all of the important needs of a young child. Meeting this need challenges many home visiting programs, especially those in which the amount of time allotted to each home visit is constrained and the frequency of home visits is not sufficient to provide effective assistance in multiple domains. Although a given home visiting program may appear initially to do better at achieving its goals if the scope is narrow and clearly focused, this does not necessarily ensure that the families—and especially the infants and young children—will directly benefit in a lasting way from a narrowly focused program.

A home visiting program does not have to be comprehensive in and of itself. The home visits can be an integral part of a broader early intervention and family support program. . . . In this situation, the issue of coordination across different program components, as well as across the domains of functioning, is highly significant. It is an important challenge in such efforts to minimize fragmentation and duplication.

An Analytical Grid for Describing Home Visiting Programs

The multidimensional and dynamic developmental framework illustrated in Figure 1 and the research suggesting that effectiveness of early intervention similarly requires a multidimensional approach highlight the importance of understanding in detail the goals and scope of home visiting programs when planning or evaluating them. Home visiting programs need to be described in terms of which specific domains of health

There is little evidence that programs which are not intensive and comprehensive, but instead target for change one or a few domains of functioning, are likely to have a lasting beneficial effect.

and development they address directly. In Figure 1, these potential interventions are represented by solid arrows. In essence, this greater specificity can lead to a much

needed and more refined typology of early intervention and home visiting programs based on explicit domains of intended impact and associated strategies and resources.

In addition to considering which domains a given intervention program directly addresses and why (the program's philosophy and strategy), other important dimensions to specify include the timing of the program (including when the home visiting begins in the family's life cycle and its duration), the intensity of the program, (for example, the number of visits per month and the length of each visit), and the coordination of the home visit activities across the various domains of functioning (for example, whether activities for diverse domains are discrete or embedded in larger activities, and whether home visitors and other support personnel communicate with one another frequently and effectively).[5,8] Two additional program features to consider, although difficult to measure well, are (1) cultural sensitivity and adaptation of a program to diverse family ecologies and (2) the quality and degree of implementation of the intended program. These might be determined by the extent to which there is specific documentation verifying program delivery to individual families and children, as well as responses of participants to particular aspects of the program. . . .

Figure 2 summarizes the critical program characteristics that warrant consideration in seeking to better understand home visiting programs and their differential effects. To fully use this model, a home visiting program would be described in detail so that the program's philosophy, implementation strategy, and content would be specified for each domain the program seeks to change.

Appendix Box A1 to this article illustrates use of this grid to describe the Infant Health and Development Program. This analytical grid fosters a comparative analysis of different home visiting programs, recognizing that not all home visiting programs have the same resources or breadth of focus and that they differ in the populations with which they work. For instance, some programs are conceptualized as universal home visiting programs (for example, regularly scheduled home visits to all mothers and newborns within a specific geographic catchment area), whereas many others are targeted for high-risk sub-

Figure 2

An Analytical Grid for Describing Home Visiting Programs

Domains of Functioning

Program Characteristics

	Survival	Values and Goals	Security	Health	Social Interaction	Self-esteem	Communication	Intellectual Skills
Philosophy								
Strategy								
Timing								
Intensity								
Coordination across domains								
Sensitivity to cultural and family context								
Quality and degree of implementation								

populations (for example, substance-abusing women, low birth weight and premature infants, families with multiple preidentified risk factors). On the analytical grid, this would be noted as features of both the program's philosophy and strategy.

This analytical grid is one that is admittedly detailed and potentially quite complex. Yet, all home visiting programs make choices and decisions about each element in this grid, even if sometimes those choices are by default. For instance, when certain functional domains are left out of the planning and conceptualization of a home visiting program or when issues such as timing and intensity are not systematically specified or monitored, these characteristics of the intervention program nonetheless may directly affect its success. Equally important, what is excluded or not addressed in a given home visiting program often reflects unrecognized biases or assumptions that guide the program and its philosophy.

Use of this analytical framework can make both description and evaluation of home visiting programs more precise. Home visiting programs are not monolithic entities, and this grid can help make that clear. In addition, to the extent that future empirical work about home visiting programs can yield more precise information about the nature and format of the programs themselves, as well as a valid and comprehensive description of program participants and their initial and ongoing needs, the conclusions about the effects of home visiting programs will become more useful. A fuller understanding of effectiveness will assist in modifying and replicating promising programs, as well as in guiding public policy about the role of home visiting in improving the health and development of young children.

Conclusion

Home visiting programs are an increasingly important and prominent part of the human service delivery system in the United States to improve the health and development of young children and their families. There is a need to specify in greater detail which aspects of health and development are within the purview of individual home visiting programs. This article offers a conceptual framework and an analytic tool to facilitate the systematic description and evaluation of various home visiting programs. By systematically assessing our expanding knowledge about home visiting, we can direct the use of scarce public resources more precisely and, overall, make home visiting programs more cost-effective.

We gratefully acknowledge the support and the assistance of Zee Hildreth and Leslie Franklin in the preparation of the manuscript.

1. Roberts, R., Casto, G., Wasik, B., and Ramey, C. T. Family support in the home: Programs, policy and social change. *American Psychologist* (1991) 46,2:131–37.

2. World Health Organization. *International classification of impairments, disabilities, and handicaps: A manual of classification relating to the consequences of disease.* Geneva, Switzerland: World Health Organization, 1980.

3. Purpura, D. P. Normal and abnormal development of cerebral cortex in man. *Neuroscience Research Program Bulletin* (1982) 20,4:569–77.

4. Landesman, S. Institutionalization revisited: Expanding views on early and cumulative life experiences. In *Handbook of developmental psychopathology.* M. Lewis and S. Miller, eds. New York: Plenum Press, 1982, pp. 455–62.

5. Ramey, S. L., and Ramey, C. T. Early educational intervention with disadvantaged children—To what effect? *Applied and Preventive Psychology* (1992) 1,3:131–40.

6. Bronfenbrenner, U. *The ecology of human development.* Cambridge, MA: Harvard University Press, 1979.

7. Sameroff, A., and Fiese, B. Family representations of development. In *Parental belief system: The psychological consequences for children* I. Sigel, A. McGillicutty-Delsi, and J. Goodman, eds. Rev. ed. Hillsdale, NJ: Lawrence Erlbaum Associates, Inc., 1992, pp. 347–69.

8. Ramey, C. T., and Ramey, S. L. Effective early intervention. *Mental Retardation* (1992) 30,5:1–9.

9. The Infant Health and Development Program. Enhancing the outcomes of low-birth-weight, premature infants: A multisite randomized trial. *Journal of the American Medical Association* (1990) 263,22:3035–42.

10. Ramey, C. T., Bryant, D. M., Wasik, B. H. et al. The Infant Health and Development Program for low birth weight, premature infants: Program elements, family participation, and child intelligence. *Pediatrics* (1992) 89,3:454–65.

11. Sparling, J., Lewis, I., Ramey, C. T., et al. Partners, a curriculum to help premature, low-birth-weight infants to get off to a good start. *Topics in Early Childhood Special Education* (1991) 11,1:36–55.

(Appendix Box A1 begins on next page.)

The Analytical Home Visiting Grid Applied to the Infant Health and Development Program

The Infant Health and Development Program (IHDP) was an eight-site controlled, randomized trial to test the effectiveness of a multipronged early intervention effort to facilitate the health outcomes and social and intellectual development of the targeted population of low birth weight, premature infants. Many aspects of the program reflect the fact that it was simultaneously a demonstration and research endeavor. The description below refers only to the children and families who received the multipronged intervention of medical services, a center-based child development program, and home visiting services.[9,10,11]

The following narrative illustrates how the analytical home visiting grid would be used to describe this program in greater detail.

Targeted Population

Low birth weight (2,500 g), premature (<37 weeks) infants born in Level III hospitals, with no major congenital anomalies.

Philosophy and Priority for Each Domain

IHDP identified three domains as being of high priority. Home visiting was viewed as one of several methods or strategies for delivering needed supports to families and children. The three targeted domains were: children's health, children's intellectual skills, and children's social interaction. These priorities were selected based on the empirical evidence that this target population is at especially high risk in these three areas during the early years of life. Because the families were expected to be diverse with regard to socioeconomic status as well as cultural and ethnic identity, systematic interventions were not designed in advance regarding many other aspects of family life. Rather, the IHDP's philosophy was to individualize each family intervention largely through the home visiting component of the program. That is, the home visitor was a regularly assigned person who was expected to develop a close working relationship with the families. The home visitors were all college graduates with additional specialized training that focused mostly on the three targeted domains, supplemented by training in how to promote problem-solving skills in parents, so that other family and child needs could be addressed and resolved in a timely and effective manner.

In the three targeted health and developmental domains, the underlying philosophy was as described below.

- **Health.** IHDP's philosophy about health emphasized preventive techniques and regular professional surveillance, consistent with the guidelines recommended by the American Academy of Pediatrics. Because it was assumed that home visiting alone could not ensure adequate health care, this was provided to all participants in either university-based clinics or through private providers. Home visitors facilitated the delivery of health care by explaining the importance of specific procedures, arranging for transportation to offices and clinics, accompanying parents (when useful), and observing the hygiene and health care behaviors in the home. Thus, home visitors were viewed as liaisons in the health domain, but not as the primary providers of health care.

- **Intellectual Skills and Social Interaction.** In contrast, in the area of intellectual skills, the home visitors concentrated on enhancing the parents' decision-making abilities and provided a home education program to promote the children's intellectual development. In the second year of life, the children's home education program closely paralleled that provided to the children in the Child Development Center (on a five-day-a-week, year-round basis). Social interaction was addressed by providing a curriculum that integrated the intellectual and social domains for children. Parents' own interactions with children were observed and discussed during each home visit, problems the parents identified were addressed, and new ideas and materials appropriate to the children's changing developmental needs were introduced on a regular basis (e.g., toys, books, observation sheets).

  Because working with biologically at-risk children, many of whom came from economically and educationally low-resource families, is recognized to be highly demanding, psychological and educational supports were provided to all home visitors on a frequent and regular basis. Home visitors had opportunities for weekly supervision and weekly (or more frequent) contact with other home visitors engaged in similar activities. Excellent benefits were provided to home visitors for health coverage, vacation, and sick leave. If desired, additional psychological counseling was available to home visitors to help with their personal reactions to a potentially highly stressful set of responsibilities.

- **Other Domains.** The IHDP did not specifically intervene in the areas of the family's values and goals for their children (such as the priority the family placed on the child's subsequent school achievement), in large part because of the very young age of the children (infancy to three years) and the more pressing concerns of the children's physical, intellectual, and social well-being based on their premature, low birth weight status.

→

Box A1 (continued)

Survival needs did arise for many low-income, inner-city families, and these were addressed on an individual family basis, often involving referrals to appropriate agencies and the use of the specially developed family problem-solving curriculum. Of necessity, an unanticipated component of some home visiting activities included seeking help for substance abuse and family violence.

- **Overall Philosophy.** The home visiting activities were conceptualized as an important and integral component of an effective early intervention but were not considered sufficient to create the desired positive changes without the other health care and educational components of IHDP. Philosophically, the IHDP endorsed the view that parents are the single most influential people in their children's lives; accordingly, parents must be well supported in this role and must understand and participate (as appropriate) in any supplemental services to enhance their children's developmental outcomes. At the same time, children's early intellectual and social development was considered to be highly important and to depend on the provision of regular and developmentally appropriate stimulation, embedded within the types of everyday activities in which children engage. To ensure this availability to all high-risk children, external supports in the form of the Child Development Centers complemented the home visiting program.

Strategies

The strategies used in the three targeted health and developmental domains are described in the paragraphs that follow.

- **Health.** The strategy for addressing health of the children included (1) regular high-quality health surveillance (following the schedule recommended by the American Academy of Pediatrics for visits and procedures during the first three years of life), including home visitor assistance with scheduling, transportation, referral, and additional care as needed; (2) parent education through home visiting regarding basic nutrition, hygiene, and the need for specialized care of premature and low birth weight children (adapted for each child); (3) in the Child Development Centers, when children were between 12 and 36 months of corrected age (determined as chronological age minus weeks of prematurity), all employees were trained in health care behaviors to meet standards set by the American Academy of Pediatrics and the Centers for Disease Control. Because of the potential vulnerability of these at-risk children, the maintenance of these standards was monitored weekly by project staff, including written documentation, and supplemented by outside professional monitoring. In the domain of health, some children were judged to need specialized therapies, such as physical therapy and speech therapy, and these were provided to all children for whom it was recommended by the primary physician. Transportation and other assistance in receiving these supplemental therapies were facilitated by home visitors and other project staff.

- **Intellectual Skills.** Strategies for promoting intellectual skills included four primary sets of activities:

  1. Enhancing the parents' own intellectual competence, particularly related to everyday problems and decision making, by a specially developed Problem Solving Curriculum. This curriculum was taught by the home visitors and, during each home visit, was implemented and applied to the family's dynamic situation. Data were maintained on parents' progress and use of the problem-solving strategies was promoted.

  2. Enhancing the parents' intellectual skills and their social interactional skills in the service of promoting their child's intellectual development. A home version of the Child Development Center curriculum, known as Partners for Learning,[10] was provided to parents in developmental levels appropriate to their own child's progress. The home visitor helped explain these materials and often demonstrated their use during the home visit.

  3. Promoting children's intellectual development directly, via provision of a high-quality, five-days-a-week, year-round Child Development Center. High standards for the centers were met through the following strategies: the directors hired had advanced degrees in early childhood education or child development; training was provided to the center directors by experienced educators and psychologists (who had previously enacted the curriculum and established other child development centers); teachers had bachelor's degrees or higher and also received in-service orientation, ongoing training, and weekly supervision and feedback on their performance. Teachers and directors, as well as home visitors, maintained daily logs of their activities, including documentation of child-specific encounters and progress. When necessary, staff received supplemental training or were terminated. Full supplies for enacting the curriculum were provided to all centers and home visitors, with adequate budgets for replacing supplies and equipment. Program implementation technical assistance was available from a national center by request from each site. A multidisciplinary team supervising the IHDP program visited external sites at least once a year.

➡️

Box A1 (continued)

The Analytical Home Visiting Grid Applied to the Infant Health and Development Program

Social Development

This domain was addressed within the same curriculum used by parents and by teachers in the Child Development Center. Monthly parent meetings provided another strategy for sharing information with parents which may have helped to promote both social and intellectual development as well as good health care and health outcomes for these children. Monthly parent meetings varied in response to what parents said they were interested in.

Timing

The IHDP home visiting component began at the infant's discharge from the hospital and continued until all infants in the program at a given site reached 36 months corrected age. At 12 months corrected age, each infant entered a specially constructed and staffed Child Development Center. Children attended the center each weekday until all children in the yearly cohort were 36 months corrected age. At that point the children and their families were supported in their transition to other community services as appropriate and available, and the centers were closed and the program terminated or continued under new auspices.

Intensity

Until 12 months of age, home visits were scheduled weekly (although documentation indicates that they were less frequent for some families for a variety of reasons). Between 12 months of age and program termination at 36 months, home visits were scheduled every two weeks. Attempted and completed visits were documented on special forms and entered weekly into a national computer data base as was the specific content of each visit, including both the occurrence of precoded events and extensive clinical notes about particularly noteworthy special conditions or circumstances. Similar documentation occurred for the pediatric and Child Development Center components of the IHDP. These data were summarized monthly by the national program center and shared with project staff at the eight sites. Technical assistance was provided as necessary to increase the likelihood of consistency of program implementation and, therefore, to maximize the probability of close cross-site comparisons.

Coordination Across Domains

The Partners for Learning curriculum[10] that was used in both the home visiting and Child Development Center components contains procedures for internal guidance and documentation and associated forms and charts to coordinate developmental activities for children in the domains of social interaction and intellectual skills. These forms were shared and supplemented by weekly, biweekly, monthly, or as-needed conferences between home visitors and parents; home visitors and teachers at the Child Development Center; and home visitors, parents, pediatricians, and nurses. Each of these conferences was summarized and documented.

Sensitivity to Cultural and Family Context

The IHDP was restricted to families who could receive the program in the English language because of its development and previous experimental testing in that language only. No special programmatic features were designed to tailor the program to particular cultural or linguistic groups. Program personnel were encouraged to consider individual families' preferences. The importance of tailoring services according to individual needs was explicitly recognized in the design and implementation of IHDP.

Quality and Degree of Documentation

Especially because IHDP was a controlled randomized trial to test the effectiveness of a multipronged early intervention program for low birth weight, premature infants, documentation of all program aspects was extensive. Specifically, all contacts with each family were documented in prespecified ways, and all personnel were trained in documentation procedures. To ensure that documentation was maintained with rigor throughout the three years of program implementation, it was reviewed regularly and frequently, and appropriate feedback was provided to program staff so that they knew their notes and forms had been studied by their supervisors. The specificity of documentation for individual families permitted the construction of an individual Family Participation Index, which subsequently was demonstrated to relate clearly to how much benefit the children showed in terms of their intellectual development by ages two and three. Quality was addressed by site visits of professionals not involved in ongoing service delivery at the site at least annually by frequent and systematic review of documentation and phone calls, and by meetings with local site staff. Regular feedback was provided from national program implementation support staff to each local site regarding their performance. ◆

"I Forget"

Kids remember a lot more than they know—or tell us. What are the keys that unlock those precious memories?

David F. Bjorklund, Ph.D., and Barbara R. Bjorklund

David F. Bjorklund, Ph.D., and Barbara R. Bjorklund are the authors of the *Parents Book of Discipline* (Ballantine) and *Looking at Children* (Brooks/Cole).

Our friend Marie laughed when we told her that we were doing a research project on preschoolers' memory abilities. "Preschoolers' memory?" she said with a quizzical look on her face. "Well, if Jonathan is any example, it'll be a very short project."

Marie went on to tell us about her four-year-old son's recent school trip to a fire station. "How was your day?" she asked after school.

"Okay," Jonathan answered.

She tried again: "What did you do at school today?"

"Nothing much," he said.

Thinking she might have been mistaken about the date of the trip, Marie asked, "Wasn't this the day you were going to the fire station?"

"Yeah, we did," Jonathan replied.

"Well, tell me about it!" she prompted.

"We went on a bus and we saw the fire engine and we ate lunch at the park. Lisa gave me her cookies."

For all parents, this exchange has a familiar ring to it. Surely Jonathan remembers more about his field trip to the fire station than the bus ride and lunch in the park. For example, he

probably learned a lot of new things and has many details of the morning tucked away in his memory. But deciding which tidbits to tell his mother first and which words to use to tell them is a difficult task.

How memory works.

There are many aspects of memory that a young child needs to master. First the event must be attended and perceived. Then the child must make some sense of that event so that it can be represented in his mind and recalled later on. If a child doesn't tune in to the important aspects of an event or cannot make sense of what he experienced, there is really nothing for the child to draw on.

Once the youngster has managed to accomplish all of this, the trick is to retrieve the memory, translate the mental picture he has in his head, and bring it to consciousness. The child must then find a way to explain that experience to another person. Broken down into its components, the process of remembering is quite complicated. It is understandable that young children, like Jonathan, often have a hard time doing it.

"Give me a hint!"

One thing that helps jog the memory is a cue. If someone asked you the name of Walter Mondale's running mate in the 1984 election, you might not be able to recall the name immediately. But if that person then told you that the first name of Mondale's running mate was Geraldine, you would no doubt snap your fin-

gers and say, "Ferraro! I knew that all the time."

Children need cues too. According to Wolfgang Schneider, Ph.D.—professor of educational psychology at the University of Wuerzburg, in Germany, and coauthor, with Michael Pressley, of *Memory Development Between Two and Twenty* (Springer-Verlag)—young children have more difficulty retrieving information from their memory than they do storing it. To help them out, we need to use careful questioning techniques, involving a large dose of hints or cues. According to Schneider, the younger children are, the more hints they need to recall information. Robyn Fivush, Ph.D.—associate professor of psychology at Emory University, in Atlanta—and Nina R. Hamond, Ph.D., explain in *Knowing and Remembering in Young Children* (Cambridge University Press) that "younger children recall as much information as older children do, but they need more memory questions in order to do so." In other words, if Marie had asked Jonathan more specific questions when she picked him up, she might have gotten better answers. "Tell me about your trip to the fire station" would have been a good opener. "Did you see the fire fighters' clothes and boots? Did they have a spotted dog like the one we saw on TV? Did you get to see the fire engine? Did the fire chief talk to you?" Any of these questions, with the appropriate follow-up, would have had a better chance of winning detailed answers from a four-year-old than "How was your day?"

What to remember?

Preschoolers also have trouble selecting what to remember. Most adults know to watch the players on the field play ball at a baseball game. We automatically pay less attention to the field-maintenance staff, the players on the bench, and most of the other spectators. Young children do not always tune in to what adults view as the main point of the event. At a baseball game, they may spend more time watching the hot-dog vendors, the bat boys, and the second-base umpire.

We discovered this when we took our five-year-old grandson, Nicholas, to his first play—a community production of *Little Shop of Horrors*. He reported to his mother that the highlight of the afternoon was the punch and cookies that they served at "halftime." After some pointed questioning, she found that he remembered a lot about the play. But the punch and cookies were clearly his strongest recollection.

This reminded us of the family trip we took many years ago to the west coast of Florida, which included a tour of the Ringling Art Museum, in Sarasota. Our son, Derek, a typical five-year-old, wasn't interested in the paintings and sculpture that were featured in the building and gardens. The "art" that captured *his* attention was the pattern on the wood parquet floors. Years later we were amazed that he remembered details of the trip to Sarasota, specifically the patterned floor at "some museum."

Children's perspective of the world is unique, and we respect their sense of wonder at parquet floors and punch and cookies. Life's little details are important to young children. But we need to help them pay attention also to the salient features of events so that their memories of an experience don't exclude the baseball players, the actors on stage, and the art at a museum.

To prepare for an outing, try giving your youngster a child's-eye view of what you expect to happen. Keep it short and simple. Before a recent trip to the Boston Aquarium with our three-year-old grandson, Jeffrey, we told him that we were going to visit a big tank where a lot of fish lived. We told him we would also see some penguins and some other water animals. He would be able to touch some of the water animals if he wanted to, but he didn't have to. This simple summary of the events told him that the fish and water animals were the main topics of interest. No doubt he would also be interested in other children, the vending machines, and so on—which was okay— but the special thing about the trip was the fish and other water animals. A stop at the gift shop for postcards gave us a few more memory aides so that Jeffrey could tell his big brother all about his trip, which he did with reasonable accuracy after a few hints.

Total recall . . . sort of.

One thing that children tend to remember well is recurring events— what typically happens on a day-to-day basis. For example, research by Katherine Nelson, Ph.D.—professor of developmental psychology at the Graduate Center of the City University of New York, in New York City— and her colleagues has shown that preschool children remember novel information in the context of familiar events, such as a special clown cake served at a birthday party. Similarly, in a study by Robyn Fivush and Nina Hamond, two-and-a-half-year-olds— even when questioned about special events, such as a trip to the beach, a camping trip, and a ride on an airplane—tended to recall what adults would consider to be routine information. Take, for instance, the following conversation between an adult and a child about a camping trip, reported by Fivush and Hamond. The child first recalled sleeping outside, which is unusual, but then remembered very routine things:

Interviewer: You slept outside in a tent? Wow, that sounds like fun.
Child: And then we waked up and eat dinner. First we eat dinner, then go to bed, and then wake up and eat breakfast.
Interviewer: What else did you do when you went camping? What did you do . . . after breakfast?
Child: Umm, in the night, and went to sleep.

It seems strange that a child would talk about such routine tasks as waking up, eating, and going to bed when so many new and exciting things must have happened on the trip. But the younger the child, the more she may need to embed novel events in familiar routines. According to Fivush and Hamond's study, everything is new to two-year-olds, and they are constantly learning about their surroundings "so that they can anticipate and predict the world around them. In order to understand novel experience, young children may need to focus on what is familiar about this event, what makes [it] similar to events already known about, rather than what is distinctive or unusual about this event."

Just as strange—or at least surprising—is the accuracy with which children recall long-ago events. For example, two-and-a-half-year-old Katherine, upon seeing an ice cube wrapped in a washcloth, began a detailed account of a bee sting that she had received well over six months earlier, complete with time of day, where she had been when the incident occurred, and what her mother had done to soothe the pain.

This is all the more remarkable because Katherine had begun to talk only six months before, and the accurate account that she was now giving was far more detailed than she could have given at the time of the sting. But this and other impressive acts of long-term memory by young children are always prompted by a very specific cue, in this case the wrapped ice cube. Rarely will a three-year-old who is sitting pensively recount, out of the blue, an event that happened long ago. But with the proper prompt, a flood of information may gush forth.

We're amazed at young children's feats of long-term memory because they're clearly not able to learn as much or as quickly as older children. But learning and remembering are different. According to Charles Brainerd, Ph.D., professor of educational psychology at the University of Arizona, in Tucson, "Despite what our common sense tells us, research shows that learning does not have much to do with what we later remember or forget. A child who can't learn a four-line poem on Tuesday may have a very firm memory of what she had for dinner at Grandma's last month."

Teaching kids to remember.

The ability to remember is not usually thought of as a skill that we need to teach our children. Most of us think that it will simply develop with age: Children grow taller, run faster, and remember more with every birthday. It is true, to a certain extent, that a two-year-old cannot hold in her mind the number of things that a five-year-old can. And much of the trouble that preschoolers get into can be attributed to their forgetting. Young children really do forget to put away their toys, to wash their hands and face, and to return the pretty bracelet to Mommy's bedroom. The best thing that parents can do is to have realistic expectations of what their child can remember, and to be patient. When you're giving instructions, a handy rule of thumb is not to give your child more things to remember than her age. "Go get your shoes and your gloves" is enough for a two-year-old. Three-year-olds can handle three items ("Remember to brush your teeth, comb your hair, and put on your shirt"); most four-year-olds, four related items ("Call your brother for dinner, put away your tricycle, and bring in your jump rope and doll"). In fact, giving children one item less than their age increases the chances that the instructions will be followed.

Parents can play an important role in improving their child's memory. Judith Hudson, Ph.D., an associate professor of psychology at Rutgers University, in New Brunswick, New Jersey, and coeditor of *Knowing and Remembering in Young Children*, believes that children learn how to remember by interacting with their parents. She writes that "remembering can be viewed as an activity that is at first jointly carried out by parent and child and then later performed by the child alone."

In most families, Hudson explains, parents begin talking with young children about things that happened in the past. They ask questions such as, "Where did we go this morning?" "What did we see at the zoo?" "Who went with us?" and "What else did we see?" From these exchanges, children learn that the important facts to remember about events are who, what, when, and where. These conversations help children learn to notice the important details of their experiences and to store their memories in an organized way so that they can easily be recalled.

In studying these exchanges between parents and preschoolers, Hudson found that parents do more than just ask the right questions; they also give the right answers when the child cannot remember. By providing the missing information, Hudson explains, parents help their child learn that if she is having difficulty recalling information, they will help her retrieve it.

A good example of this is a conversation that we overheard while riding on the Metro in Washington, D.C. A young mother and her daughter, who appeared to be around two, were returning home after a trip to the zoo.

Mother: Brittany, what did we see at the zoo?
Brittany: Elephunts.
Mother: That's right! We saw elephants. What else?
Brittany: *(Shrugs and looks at her mother.)*
Mother: Panda bear? Did we see a panda bear?
Brittany: *(Smiles and nods.)*
Mother: Can you say "panda bear"?
Brittany: Panda bear.
Mother: Good! Elephants and panda bears. What else?
Brittany: Elephunts.
Mother: That's right, elephants. And also a gorilla.
Brittany: Gorilla!

The importance of these hand-holding conversations has been shown in research by Hilary Horn Ratner, Ph.D., professor of psychology at Wayne State University, in Detroit. She observed two- and three-year-olds interacting with their mothers at home and recorded the number of times that the mother asked the child about past events. Ratner then tested the children's memories; those whose mothers had asked them many questions about past events showed better memory abilities both at that time and a year later.

Thinking about thinking.
The fact is that preschoolers simply don't think much about their thinking—if at all. They are still in that nice stage of mental life when remembering and learning "just happen." It will be many years before they are able to evaluate their memory ability and to think of how to make it work better.

When parents tell their preschoolers to "think harder" or "remember better," they are wasting their words. But through daily interactions—by not only asking their preschoolers questions that involve memory but also showing them how to answer— parents serve as memory teachers. Their children are then able to use these memory questions later on as they try to recall the details of specific events. Subtly, and almost effortlessly, parents help their children develop the memory, thinking, and learning skills that will be so useful to them throughout their lives.

Assertiveness vs. Aggressiveness

What's the Difference?

Robert H. Deluty

Robert H. Deluty is the Director of the Clinical Psychology Doctoral Program at UMBC. He and his wife of 12 years, Barbara, live in Ellicott City with their children, Laura (7) and David (3).

"Why is my son so aggressive?" "Why won't my daughter stand up for herself?" "Why do my children punch, kick, and scream whenever they are frustrated or angered?" Mental health professionals are routinely asked such questions by concerned parents. Although the questions are simple and straightforward, often the answers are not. Children act aggressively, assertively, or submissively for a wide variety of reasons; generally, a combination of factors underlies how a particular child will behave in any given situation. These factors include how the child sizes up the situation, what response alternatives she can think of, and what she expects will be the consequences of each response alternative.

The assertive child expresses herself openly and directly while respecting the rights and feelings of others. For example, in response to being teased about her new haircut, Sally says calmly, assertively, "Please top teasing me. You wouldn't like it if I made fun of you. I really like the way my hair looks." If assertiveness entails both self-expression and the non-violation of others' rights, then unassertiveness can take one of two forms: aggressiveness or submissiveness. Aggressive children express their thoughts and feelings openly, but they do so coercively and at other people's expense. Submissive children take into account the feelings, power, and authority of others, but deny (or do not stand up for) their own rights and feelings.

For some aggressive children and for some submissive children, the thought of acting assertively simply never occurs to them. These children see their options as limited to "fight" or "flight"; for example, Tommy may think that when he is ridiculed, his only options are to punch, pinch, bite, scream, or spit ("fight" responses), or to run away, cry, hide, or sulk ("flight" responses). In Tommy's world of black and white options, shades of gray (i.e., assertive solutions) are nowhere to be found.

Other aggressive and submissive children, however, can conceive of assertive alternatives, but choose not to exhibit such behavior because they believe that aggressive or submissive acts will yield greater benefits and/or fewer costs than assertive behaviors. For example, James may physically threaten or verbally abuse his classmates because it results in their giving him their lunch money and doing his homework; as far as James is concerned, aggression "pays." In contrast, Patty may exhibit much submissive behavior because she believes submissive acts are kinder and more "ladylike" than aggressive or assertive responses; she may fear that assertive expression will result in unpleasant confrontation and diminished popularity (e.g., "If I let them know how I feel, they may get mad at me and no longer want to play with me"). Clearly, the consequences (real or imagined) that a child associates with particular behaviors have a powerful influence on the actions he/she chooses.

Parents play a critical role in shaping aggressive and prosocial behavior in their children. Boys (who consistently manifest more physical and verbal aggression than girls) tend to be given more freedom that girls to express aggression toward their parents and their peers; in contrast, girls receive relatively more praise for being "good" and are more often threatened with withdrawal of parental love for "bad" behavior. Nonaggressive boys have been shown by psychology researchers to be far more likely than aggressive males to have had parents who placed high demands on them to be "polite" and "responsible."

Although much behavior is shaped into new patterns by direct rewards

Reprinted with permission from *Maryland Family Magazine*, August 1995, pp. 26-27. © 1995 by Maryland Family Publications, Inc., Baltimore, MD.

(e.g., parental compliments) or punishments (e.g., withdrawal of privileges), social behaviors like aggressiveness or assertiveness are acquired largely through the process of imitation or modeling. A crucial determinant of a child's aggressiveness, assertiveness, and submissiveness is the interpersonal behavior exhibited by the parents, teachers, and peers who serve as models in the child's environment. Parents who rant, scream, and slam doors when things don't go their way typically do not have far to look when searching for the principal causes of their children's aggressiveness.

When teaching children how to be assertive, parents must pay careful attention to both the verbal and nonverbal components of assertiveness. Parents need to attend to not only what the child is saying, but how he/she is saying it. An assertive verbalization (e.g., "Please turn down the stereo. It's hurting my ears.") may be undone by a whiny, unsteady voice and poor eye contact. Furthermore, children need to be taught how to be assertive not only in the face of conflict (e.g., in response to frustration, aggression, or ridicule), but also under pleasurable circumstances. Learning how to give or to accept a compliment, or how to express agreement with others' opinions is at least as important as learning how to stand up for oneself in conflictual situations.

It is also important for children to understand that assertive behavior is not always the most adaptive means of handling conflict. Indeed, under certain circumstances, assertiveness would be counter-indicated. If a child is in the process of being physically attacked by a group of older, stronger kids, assertive expression ("Guys, it makes me angry when I'm punched and kicked") would likely be quite unproductive. In some situations, submissively complying with an unreasonable request could strengthen a friendship or advance an important long-range goal. Thus, children need to be advised not only how to express themselves assertively, but also when (and when not) to do so.

Approximately 2000 years ago, the great sage, Hillel, posed the following questions: "If I am not for myself, who will be for me? And if I am only for myself, what am I? And if not now—when?" Some of the most important lessons we can teach our children involve how to balance self-expression and self-interest with concern for others and appreciation of others' rights and feelings. And when should parents teach these lessons? As Hillel asked, "If not now—when?"

Development during Childhood—Cognition and Schooling

- Cognition (Articles 16–19)
- Schooling (Articles 20–23)

Jean Piaget, the founder of cognitive psychology, worked for Thomas Simon and Alfred Binet, the creators of the first standardized intelligence test, when he was young. He was much more intrigued by what children answered incorrectly than by what they knew. This led him to start the now famous Centre for Genetic Epistemology in Geneva, Switzerland. Epistemology is the study of how persons know what they know, the nature of their knowledge, and its extent and validity. Piaget discovered that children know the world qualitatively differently than do adults. Children's biological maturation limits how they organize and store memories. At first, infants only know things from a sensory and a motoric perspective. After language develops, toddlers and preschoolers know things from a language/symbol perspective. By school age, children know things in concrete terms. They can number, seriate, classify, conserve, think backwards and forwards, and think about themselves thinking (metacognition). They are able to use "reason." However, not until after puberty are humans able to know things in an abstract manner and to a more knowledgeable and logical extent.

Contemporary cognitive researchers are refining Piaget's theories. They are discovering that children acquire some abilities earlier than Piaget postulated. Computer simulations of intelligence and information processing are comparing computer neural networks to human neurophysiology and human neuroanatomy. New cognitive theorists are speculating about how the amazingly complex human brain receives, attends to, selects, rehearses, encodes, organizes, stores, and finally retrieves memories.

Can new theories of cognitive development help parents and teachers speed up the rates at which children acquire, store, and retrieve information? Some learning can be accelerated. Is there a price to pay for rapid acquisition of knowledge? Stress is known to impair memory. A slower, relaxed cognitive maturation, like a slower physical maturation, may be more adaptive for humans.

Language development continues as children begin to read, write, and use their memory stores more efficiently. School-age children like to play with language.

They use dialects, coded languages, slang, curse words, and words of other languages. Bilingual or multilingual children may have a more limited use of English in primary school than do monolingual children. However, there are cognitive and psycholinguistic advantages to knowing more than one language. Bilingual, bidialectal, and multilingual children usually have greater long-term flexibility with grammar and syntactical structures.

Children with learning disabilities are very different from children with mental retardation. Some children with learning disabilities are intellectually gifted. Children with learning disabilities receive, attend to, select, rehearse, encode, organize, store, and retrieve information differently. Are these differences in information processing really disabilities or simply alternative ways of knowing? There are many unanswered questions about cognitive differences.

Reading, writing, and arithmetic are basic school subjects. Science and social studies are acceptable school subjects. But should schoolteachers provide students with lessons on ethics and moral behaviors? Who should teach children about AIDS, illegal drugs, and sex? Should cognitive development and schooling be inclusive or exclusive?

Today's schools tend to have overcrowded classrooms, underpaid teachers, and more problems with truancy and delinquency than schools of the past. Parents who can afford it often place their children in private schools. Are public schools able to meet the cognitive needs of today's children? Are they meeting their creative needs as well?

Schools typically test children for academic potential and then track them into sections relative to their high, average, or low ability. Are intelligence tests valid? Would tracking children with different cognitive learning styles be more effective or efficient?

School administrators and teachers often have biased feelings about the educational needs of boys versus girls, or about the needs and motivations of children from different ethnic groups. The quality of life for all people will be enhanced by providing each child with the cognitive and educational stimulation necessary to help him or her reach a maximum level of potential fulfillment.

The first two articles selected for this unit address the biological side of cognitive development. They present up-to-date information about neuronal functioning and genetic potentialities for intelligence. They also remind the reader that environment cannot be disregarded. It is a necessary condition for learning and memory.

"The Good, the Bad, and the Difference" discusses the need for lessons in ethics and morality. It presents theoretical opinions of some leading moral-development scholars.

The report "Life in Overdrive" asks whether children with attention deficits are really disordered, or just different in their cognitive functioning. It offers the reader some intriguing insights into the adaptive skills of persons deemed "hyperactive."

In the subsection on schooling, the reader is challenged to address some controversial issues. "Bell, Book and Scandal" takes a level-headed look at a topic that has inflamed vehement arguments pro and con regarding genetic inheritance of intelligence and the possible racial differences in such inheritance. The article also takes a dispassionate look at intelligence testing. The lay public has been flooded with media presentations about this topic since the publication of *The Bell Curve: Intelligence and Class Structure in American Life* by Charles Murray and Richard Herrnstein (1994).

The American Association of University Women's (AAUW) report on the education of females is a passionate record of present-day sexual inequities in schools. The reader is asked to consider 40 recommendations for changes in the education of males and females.

"Nurturing Creativity in All Your Students" addresses the issue of educating children to memorize by rote and to think in ways convergent with their teachers, versus educating them to think freely and create new and different ideas and products. Methods for enhancing creativity are presented by Julius and Zelda Segal.

The last article in this unit addresses the importance of multicultural education in societies growing in diversity year by year. An acceptance of cultural diversity, it is argued, will enhance the social and emotional maturity, as well as the cognitive maturity, of all children.

Looking Ahead: Challenge Questions

How do billions of neurons, each with thousands of connections to other neurons, make and store memories?

How can children maximize their genetic potential for intelligence? What environments work best?

Who should teach ethics and morality to children?

Why is *The Bell Curve* so controversial? What is "Jensenism" all about?

How do schools shortchange girls? What can be changed?

How can creativity be nurtured in schools?

How do schools shortchange children from diverse ethnic or language backgrounds? What can be changed?

It's Magical! It's Malleable! It's . . . Memory

So complex and evanescent is memory, our best metaphors fall short, bogged down in materialism. Yet through the creative blending and reblending of experience and emotion, memory builds that about us which often seems most solid—our sense of self. We remember, therefore we are.

Jill Neimark

We never know exactly why certain subjects—like certain people—claim us, and do not let us go. Elizabeth Loftus is a research psychologist who has devoted her life to the study of memory, it's mystery and malleability. Of late, she has gained ingenious experiments, which have shown repeatedly that about 25 percent of individuals can be easily induced to remember events that never happened to them—false memories that feel absolutely real.

So it was something of a shock when, at a family gathering, an uncle informed the then 44-year-old Loftus that 30 years earlier, when her mother had drowned, she had been the one to discover the body in the pool. Loftus believed she had never seen her mother's dead body; in fact, she remembered little about the death itself.

Almost immediately after her uncle's revelation, "the memories began to drift back," she recalls in her recent book, *The Myth of Repressed Memory* (St. Martin), "like the crisp, piney smoke from evening camp fires. My mother, dressed in her nightgown, was floating face down. . . . I started screaming. I remembered the police cars, their lights flashing. For three days my memory expanded and swelled.

"Then, early one morning, my brother called to tell me that my uncle had made a mistake. Now he remembered (and other relatives confirmed) that Aunt Pearl found my mother's body." Suddenly Loftus understood firsthand what she had been studying for decades. "My own experiment had inadvertently been performed on me! I was left with a sense of wonder at the inherent credulity of even my skeptical mind."

Memory has become a lightning rod of late. This has been a time of fascinating, grisly stories—of recovered memories of satanic cults, butchered babies, and incest that have spawned

church scandals, lawsuits, suicides, splintered families, murders, and endless fodder for talk shows. Three major books on the fallibility of memory were reviewed on the front page of the *New York Times Book Review* last spring, and three more were published this fall. The essential nature of memory, which ought by rights to be a scientific debate, has so galvanized the culture that laws have actually been revoked and repealed over it; in Illinois, for example, a law that bars people over 30 from filing lawsuits based on remembered abuse was repealed in 1992, and is now being reinstated.

Memory's ambiguities and paradoxes seem to have suddenly claimed us as they have claimed researchers for decades. This fascination cannot be explained away by the human need to memorialize the past—a need that expresses itself beautifully and indelibly in monuments like the Vietnam memorial or the AIDS quilt, and in projects like Steven Spielberg's ongoing documentary of holocaust survivors.

Memory is the likelihood that, among a vast tangle of neurons, the pathway of connections an experience forges in the brain can be reactivated again. It is the ability to repeat a performance—albeit with mistakes.

It's as if we've awakened, at the turn of the millennium, and realized that memory is the bedrock of the self—and that it may be perpetually shifting and terrifically malleable. That image of memory, whose river runs into tabloids and traumas, seems both terrifying and baptismal. If we can repress life-shaping events (such as sexual or physical abuse), or actually invent memories of events that never happened (from UFO abductions to rapes and murders), memory carries a power that promises to utterly reshape the self.

And so it's exciting news that in the past few years, scientists have begun to piece together a picture of memory that is stunning in its specifics:

- Sophisticated PET (positron emission tomography) scans can record the actual firing of the neurons that hold the pictures of our lives, and observe memory move like a current across the brain while it sleeps or wakes.

- How and where the brain lays down and consolidates memory—that is, makes it permanent—is yielding to understanding. As one researcher states, we are seeing "an explosion of knowledge about what parts of the brain are doing what."

- Hormones that help engrave the narrative of our lives into our cells have now been identified.

- Certain drugs block or enhance memory, and they may hold the key to preventing disorders as wide-ranging as Alzheimer's disease and posttraumatic stress disorder (PTSD).

- The well-known "fight-or-flight" response to stress can sear "indelible" memories into the brain.

- Memory is not a single entity residing in a single place. It is the likelihood that the pathway of neurons and connections an experience forges in the brain can be reactivated again. It involves multiple systems in the brain. The emotion associated with a memory, for example, is stored in a different place than the content of the memory itself.

- Some memories occur in a primitive part of the brain, unknown to conscious perception. That part functions "below" the senses, as it were. That is why individuals with brain damage can sometimes learn and remember—without knowing they do so.

- There is a growing understanding that an infant's early experience of emotional attachment can direct the nature and durability of childhood memories and the way they are stored in the brain.

Memory, it turns out, is both far more complex and more primitive than we knew. Ancient parts of the brain can record memory before it even reaches our senses—our sight and hearing, for instance. At the same time, "there are between 200 and 400 billion neurons in the brain and each neuron has about 10,000 connections," notes psychiatrist Daniel Siegel, M.D. "The parallel processing involved in memory is so complex we can't even begin to think how it works."

The one thing that we can say for certain is this: If memory is the bedrock of the self, then even though that self may seem coherent and unchanging, it is built on shifting sands.

13 WAYS OF LOOKING AT THE BRAIN

Moments after being removed from the skull, the brain begins to collapse into a jellylike mass. And yet this wet aspic of tissue contains a fantastic archeology of glands, organs, and lobes, all of which have their own specialized jobs. Much of this archeology is devoted to the complex tasks of memory.

But just what is memory? According to Nobel Prize-winning neuroscientist Gerald Edelman, Ph.D., author of *Bright Air, Brilliant Fire* (Basic Books), memory is the ability to repeat a performance—with mistakes. Without memory, life itself would never have evolved. The genetic code must be able to repeat itself in DNA and RNA; an immune cell must be able to remember an antigen and repeat a highly specific defense next time they meet; a neuron in the brain must be able to send the same signal each time you encounter (for example) a lion escaped from the local zoo. Every living system must be able to remember; but what is most dangerous and wonderful about memory is that it must occasionally make errors. It must be wrong. Mere repetition might explain the way a crystal grows but not the way a brain works. Memory classifies and adapts to our environment. That adaptation requires flexibility. The very ability to make mistakes is precious.

Now you can bravely step into the hall of mirrors that is memory. And though our words to describe this evanescent process are still crude and oversimplistic, here are a few tools to travel with:

Memory can be implicit or explicit. Implicit memory is involved in learning habits—such as riding a bicycle or driving a car. It does not require "conscious" awareness, which is why you can sometimes be lost in thought as you drive and find you've driven home without realizing it. Explicit memory is conscious, and is sometimes called declarative. One form of declarative memory is autobiographical memory—our ability to tell the story of our life in the context of time.

We often talk of memory storage and retrieval, as if memory were filed in a honeycomb of compartments, but these words are really only metaphors. If memory is the reactivation of a weblike network of neurons that were first activated when an event occurred, each time that network is stimulated the memory is strengthened, or consolidated. Storage, retrieval, consolidation—how comforting and solid they sound; but in fact they consist of electrical charges leaping among a vast tangle of neurons.

In truth, even the simplest memory stimulates complex neural networks at several different sites in the brain. The content (what happened) and meaning (how it felt) of an event are laid down in separate parts of the brain. In fact, research at Yale University by Patricia Goldman-Rakic, Ph.D., has shown that neurons themselves are specialized for different types of memories—features, patterns, location, direction. "The coding is so specific that it can be mapped to different areas . . . in the prefrontal region."

What is activating these myriad connections? We still don't know. Gerald Edelman calls this mystery "the homunculus crisis." Who is thinking? Is memory remembering us? "The intricacy and numerosity of brain connections are extraordinary," writes Edelman. "The layers and loops between them are dynamic, they continually change."

Yet the center holds. The master regulator of memory, the hub at the center of the wheel, is a little seahorse-shaped organ called the hippocampus. Like the rest of the brain, it is lateralized; it exists in both the right and left hemispheres. Without it, we learn and remember nothing—in fact, we are lost to ourselves.

THE SEAHORSE AND THE SELF

"He's 33 years old, and he never remembers that his father is dead. Every time he rediscovers this fact he goes through the whole grieving process again," Mark Gluck, Ph.D., a professor at the Center for Molecular and Behavioral Neuroscience at Rutgers University, says of M.P., a young man who lost his memory after a stroke six years ago. Gluck has been studying M.P. for several years. After his stroke, M.P. forgot that on that very morning he had proposed marriage to his girlfriend. "He can store no new information in his long-term memory. If you tell him a phone number and ask him to repeat it, he will; but if you change the subject and then ask him the number, he can't remember. M.P. is going to be living in the present for the rest of his life. He has lost the essential ability of the self to evolve."

M.P. is uncannily similar to one of the most remarkable and intensively studied patients of all time, a man called H.M., who lost his memory after undergoing brain surgery to treat epilepsy. This type of memory loss, called anterograde amnesia, stops time. It usually results from damage to the hippocampus, which normally processes, discards, or dispatches information by sending signals to other parts of the brain.

"The hippocampus is critical for learning," says Gluck, "and it's also one of the most volatile, unstable parts of the brain— one of the first parts damaged if oxygen is cut off. Think of it as a highly maneuverable kayak; it has to immediately capture a whole range of information about an event and needs the ability to go rapidly through many changes. We think the hippocampus serves as a filter, learning new associations and deciding what is important and what to ignore or compress. That's why it's critical for learning." The hippocampus is, in a sense, a collating machine, sorting and then sending various packets of information to other parts of the brain.

One of the most exciting advances in neuroscience may lie ahead as researchers begin to actually model the living brain on the computer—creating a new era of artificial intelligence called neural networks. Gluck and researchers at New York University have begun to model the hippocampus, creating "lesions" and watching what happens—in the hope that they can develop specialized tests that will identify Alzheimer's in its early stages, as well as develop machinery that can learn the way a brain does. Thus far their predictions about its role have been borne out—in fact, Gluck is developing applications for the military so that hippocampal-like computers can learn the early signals of engine malfunctions and sound the alarm long before a breakdown.

The hippocampus does not store memories permanently. It is a way station, though a supremely important one. Like a football player in the heat of the game, it passes the ball to other parts of the brain. This takes minutes, or maybe even hours, according to James McGaugh, Ph.D., of the University of California at Irvine. At that point, memories can still be lost.

They need to be consolidated; the network of neurons responsible for a memory needs to be strengthened through repeated stimuli, until the memory exists independent of the hippocampus, a process known as long-term potentiation (LTP).

Once again, a word picture of this process is extremely crude. In actuality, Edelman points out, "the circuits of the brain look like no others we have seen before. The neurons have treelike arbors that overlap in myriad ways. Their signaling is like the vast aggregate of interactive events in a jungle."

No one is certain how long it takes to fully consolidate a memory. Days? Weeks? Perhaps it takes even years until the linkages of networks are so deeply engraved that the memory becomes almost crystallized—easy to recall, detailed and clear. Individuals like M.P. seem to lose several years of memory just prior to hippocampal damage; so do Alzheimer's patients, who usually suffer hippocampal damage as their brains begin to malfunction, and who recall their childhood days with fine-etched clarity but find the present blurred.

A MAGIC RHYTHM OF MEMORY?

Just how and when do memories become permanent? Scientists now have direct evidence of what they have long suspected— that consolidation of memories, or LTP, takes place during sleep or during deeply relaxed states. It is then that brain waves slow to a rhythm known as "theta," and perhaps, according to McGaugh, the brain releases chemicals that enhance storage.

In an ingenious experiment reported in the journal *Science* last July, researchers planted electrodes in different cells in rats' hippocampi, and watched each cell fire as the animals explored different parts of a box. After returning to their cages, the rats slept. And during sleep the very same cells fired.

There seems to be a specific brain rhythm dedicated to LTP. "It's the magic rhythm of theta! The theta rhythm is the natural, indigenous rhythm of the hippocampus," exclaims neuroscientist Gary Lynch, Ph.D., of the University of California at Irvine. Lynch is known for his inspiring, if slightly mad, brilliance. His laboratory found that LTP is strongest when stimulation is delivered to the hippocampus in a frequency that corresponds to the slow rhythms of theta, of deep relaxation. Research by James McGaugh seems to confirm this: the more theta waves that appear in an animal's EEG (electroencephalogram), the more it remembers.

No wonder, then, that recent experiments show sleep improves memory in humans—and specifically, the sleep associated with dreaming, REM (rapid eye movement) sleep. In Canada, students who slept after cramming for an exam retained more information than those who pulled an all-nighter. In Israel, researchers Avi Karni and Dov Sagi at the Weizmann Institute found that interrupting REM sleep 60 times in a night completely blocked learning; interrupting non-REM sleep just as often did not. These findings give scientific punch to "superlearning" methods like that of Bulgarian psychiatrist Georgi Lozanov, which utilizes deep relaxation through diaphragmatic breathing and music, combined with rhythmic bursts of information.

THE HAUNTED BRAIN

What happens when memory goes awry? It seems that some memories are so deeply engraved in the brain that they haunt an individual as if he were a character in an Edgar Allen Poe story. How, asks Roger Pittman, M.D., coordinator of research and development at the Manchester (New Hampshire) Veterans Administration Medical Center and associate professor at Harvard Medical School, does the traumatic event "carve its canyons and basins of memory into the living brain?"

'We believe that the brain takes advantage of hormones and chemicals, released during stress and powerful emotions, to regulate the strength of memory.' We owe our very lives to this; a dangerous event needs to be recalled.

In any kind of emotionally arousing experience, the brain takes advantage of the fight-or-flight reaction, which floods cells with two powerful stress hormones, adrenaline and noradrenaline. "We believe that the brain takes advantage of the chemicals released during stress and powerful emotions," says James McGaugh, "to regulate the strength of storage of the memory." These stress hormones stimulate the heart to pump faster and the muscles to tense; they also act on neurons in the brain. A memory associated with emotionally charged information gets seared into the brain. We owe our very lives to this: a dangerous, threatening, or exciting event needs to be recalled well so that we may take precautions when meeting similar danger again.

Scientists are now beginning to understand just how emotional memory works and why it is so powerful. According to Joseph Ledoux, Ph.D., of the Center for Neural Science at New York University, the hormones associated with strong emotion stimulate the amygdala, an almond-shaped organ in the brain's cortex.

It's long been known that when rats are subjected to the sound of a tone and a shock, they soon learn to respond fearfully to the tone alone. The shocker is that when the auditory cortex—the part of the brain that receives sound—is completely destroyed, the rats are still able to learn the exact same fear response. How can a rat learn to be afraid of a sound it cannot hear?

The tone, it appears, is carried directly back to the amygdala, as well as to the auditory cortex. Destroy the amygdala, and even a rat with perfect hearing will never learn to be afraid of the sound. As neurologist Richard Restak, M.D., notes, this "implies that much of our brain's emotional processing occurs unconsciously. The amygdala may process many of our unconscious fear responses." This explains in part why phobias are so difficult to treat by psychotherapy. The brain's memory for emotional experiences is an enduring one.

But the ability of the brain to utilize stress hormones can go badly awry—and a memory can become not simply permanent but intrusive and relentless. "Suppose somebody shoots you and years later you're still waking up in a cold sweat with nightmares," says McGaugh. "The hormonal regulation of memory, when pushed to an extreme in a traumatic situation, may make memories virtually indelible."

Such memories seem so powerful that even an innocuous stimulus can arouse them. Roger Pittman compares the inescapable memories of PTSD, where flashbacks to a nightmarish trauma intrude relentlessly on daily life, to a black hole, "a place in space-time that has such high gravity that even light cannot pass by without being drawn into it."

So with ordinary associations and memories in PTSD: "As all roads lead to Rome, all the patient's thoughts lead to the trauma. A war veteran can't look at his wife's nude body without recalling with revulsion the naked bodies he saw in a burial pit in Vietnam, can't stand the sight of children's dolls because their eyes remind him of the staring eyes of the war dead."

The tragic twist is that, Pittman believes, each time a memory floods in again, the same stress hormones are released, running the same neural paths of that particular memory and binding the victim ever tighter in the noose of the past. Yet in response to the stress of recalling trauma, the body releases a flood of calming opiates. These neurochemicals, which help us meet the immediate demands of stress and trauma, might create a kind of unfortunate biochemical reward for the traumatic memory. "This whole question of an appetitive component to trauma is really fascinating and as yet unexplored," notes Pittman. "It may explain the intrusive, repeating nature of these memories. Maybe, however horrible the trauma, there's something rewarding in the brain chemicals released."

A solution, then, to treating the kind of PTSD we see in war veterans and victims of rape and child abuse, might lie in blocking the action of some of these stress hormones. And perhaps a key to enhancing ordinary learning is to create a judicious amount of stress—excitement, surprise, even a healthy dose of fear (like the kind one may feel before cramming for a demanding final exam).

A landmark study recently reported by James McGaugh and Larry Cahill, in *Nature,* indicates that any emotion, even ordinary emotion, is linked to learning. They gave two groups of college students a drug that blocks the effects of adrenaline and noradrenaline, then showed the students a series of 12 slides that depicted scenes such as a boy crossing the street with his mother or visiting a man at a hospital. A control group was told an ordinary story (son and mother visit the boy's surgeon father) that corresponded to some of the slides. The experimental group heard a story of disaster (boy is hit by car; a surgeon attempts to reattach his severed feet).

Two weeks later, the volunteers were given a surprise memory test. Students who heard the ordinary story recalled all 12 slides poorly. The second group, however, recalled significantly better the slides associated with the story of disaster.

Then, in an ingenious twist, McGaugh and Cahill repeated the experiment with new volunteers. Just before the slide show, the experimental group was given a beta blocker—a drug that acts on nerve cells to block the effect of stress hormones. Two weeks later they could not be distinguished from the control group. They similarly remembered all 12 slides poorly.

The implications of this elegant experiment are far reaching. "Let's suppose," postulates McGaugh, "that a plane crashes near Pittsburgh and you're hired to pick out the body parts. If we give you a beta blocker, we impair your 'emotional' memory, the memory for the trauma, without impairing your normal memory."

Pittman looks forward in the next decade to drugs that not only block PTSD but help ameliorate it. "There seems to be a window of opportunity, up to six hours or so in rats in any case, before memories are consolidated." During that time effective drugs, such as beta blockers, might be administered.

MEMORY LOST AND REGAINED

The stories are legendary. Elizabeth Loftus has found ordinary memory to be so malleable that she can prompt volunteers to "remember nonexistent broken glass and tape recorders; to think of a clean-shaven man as having a mustache, of straight hair as curly, of hammers as screwdrivers, to place a barn in a bucolic scene that contained no buildings at all, to believe in characters who never existed and events that never happened."

Sometimes the memories become so seemingly fantastical that they lead to court cases and ruined lives. "I testified in a case recently in a small town in the state of Washington," Loftus recalls, "where the memories went from, 'Daddy made me play with his penis in the shower' to 'Daddy made me stick my fist up the anus of a horse,' and they were bringing in a veterinarian to talk about just what a horse would do in that circumstance. The father is ill and will be spending close to $100,000 to defend himself."

Nobody is quite sure how memories might be lost to us and then later retrieved—so-called repression. Whatever it is, it is a different process than traumatic amnesia, a well-known phenomenon where a particular horrendous event is forgotten because it was never consolidated in long-term memory in the first place. Such is the amnesia of an accident victim who loses consciousness after injury. Repressed memory, on the other hand, is alleged to involve repeated traumas.

According to UCLA's Daniel Siegel, both amnesia and repression may be due to a malfunction of the hippocampus. In order to recall an explicit memory, and to be able to depict it in words and pictures, the hippocampus must process it first. Perhaps, postulates Siegel, the work of the hippocampus is disrupted during trauma—while other components of memory carry on. We know, for example, that primitive responses like fear or excitement stimulate the amygdala directly; learning can occur without our "knowing" it.

If explicit memory is impaired—you forget what happened to you—but implicit memory is intact, you may still be profoundly influenced by an experience. Siegel thinks that some individuals remove conscious attention during repeated trauma, say from an unbearable event like repeated rapes. In the parlance of the mind trade, they "dissociate."

While his theory may explain repressed memory plausibly, it doesn't suggest how the memory emerges decades later, explicit and intrusive. And it doesn't answer the contention of many researchers that such repression is probably rare, and that the wave of repressed memories we are hearing about today may be due to invention.

It turns out that it's relatively easy to confuse imagery with perception. The work of Stephen Kossyln, Ph.D., a psychologist at Harvard University and author of *Image and Brain* (MIT press), has shown that the exact same centers in the brain are activated by both imagination and perception. "PET studies have shown that, when subjects close their eyes and form visual images, the same areas are activated as if they were actually seeing." The strength of the imagined "signal" (or image) is about half that of a real one. Other research shows that the source of a memory—the time, place, or way the memory began—is the first part to fade. After all, the source of a memory is fragile.

If we concentrate on generating images that then get recorded in the web of neurons as if they were real, we might actually convince ourselves that confabulations are true. (This might also explain how some individuals who lie about an event eventually convince themselves, through repeated lying, that the lie is true.)

The fragility of source memory explains why, in a famous experiment by psychologist John Neisser, John Dean's testimony about Richard Nixon was shown to be both incredibly accurate and hugely inaccurate. "His initial testimony was so impressive that people called him a human tape recorder," recalls psychologist Charles Thompson, Ph.D. "Neisser then compared the actual tapes to his testimony, and found that if you really looked at the specifics, who said what and when, Dean was wrong all over the place. But if you just looked at his general sense of what was going on in the meetings he was right on target. His confusion was about the source." In general, supposes Thompson, this is how memory works. We have an accurate sense of the core truth of an event, but we can easily get the details wrong.

'It's easy to confuse memory with experience. The exact same brain centers are activated by imagination and perception.'

"Memory is more reconstructive than reproductive. As time passes, details are lost. We did a study where we asked people to keep a daily diary for up to a year and a half, and later asked them questions about recorded events. The memory of the core event and its content stayed at a high level of about 70 percent, while the peripheral details dropped quickly."

CAN MEMORY CREATE THE SELF?

From Freud on down, it was believed that memories from infancy or early childhood were repressed and somehow inaccessible—but that their clues, like the bits of bread dropped by Hansel and Gretel in the forest, could be found in dreams or in the pathology of waking life. Now we know better. It's that the brain systems that support declarative memory develop late—two or three years into life.

If we don't actually lay down any memories of our first few years, how can they shape our later life? An intriguing answer can be pieced together from findings by far-flung researchers.

Daniel Siegel plows the field of childhood memory and attachment theory. He finds that memory is profoundly affected in children whose mothers had rejected or avoided them. "We don't know why this happens, but at 10 years old, these children have a unique paucity in the content of their spontaneous autobiographical narratives." As adults, they do not recall childhood family experiences.

It may be that memory storage is impaired in the case of childhood trauma. Or it may be, Siegel suggests, that avoidant parents don't "talk to children about their experiences and memories. Those children don't have much practice in autobiographical narrative. Not only are their memories weak or nonexistent, the sense of self is not as rich. As a psychotherapist, I try to teach people to tell stories about their lives. It helps them develop a richer sense of self."

As far as the biology of the brain goes, this may be no different than training an 18-year-old boy to distinguish between whales and submarines; if the hippocampus is continually fed a stimulus, it will allocate more of the brain's capacities to recording and recognizing that stimulus. In the case of autobiographical narrative, however, what emerges is magical and necessary: the self.

That is almost like saying memory creates the self, and in a sense it does. But memory is also created and recreated by the self. The synergy between the two is like two sticks rubbed together in a forest, creating fire. "We now have a new paradigm of memory," notes Loftus, "where memories are understood as creative blendings of fact and fiction, where images are alchemized by experience and emotion into memories."

"I think it's safe to say we make meaning out of life, and the meaning-making process is shaped by who we are as self," says Siegel. Yet that self is shaped by the nature of memory. "It's this endless feedback loop which maintains itself and allows us to come alive."

When we think of our lives, we become storytellers—heroes of our own narrative, a tale that illumines that precious and mysterious "self" at the center. That "I am" cannot be quantified or conveyed precisely and yet it feels absolute. As Christopher Isherwood wrote long ago in *The Berlin Stories*, "I am a camera." Yet, as the science is showing us, there is no single camera—or if there is, it is more like the impressionist, constantly shifting camera of *Last Year at Marienbad*. Memory is malleable—and so are we.

DNA-environment mix forms intellectual fate

People may not be able to exceed their genetic potential, but environmental factors may determine whether that potential is reached.

Beth Azar

Monitor *staff*

Those who believe in destiny think each person's lot in life is determined at conception: Whatever happens is programmed from the start. With so much discussion in the media of genetics and "nature" as opposed to nurture, is "destiny" just an antiquated word for DNA?

Most researchers agree that a combination of biology and environment contribute to behavioral traits. But just what proportion of each is vigorously debated, especially in the area of intelligence.

Some psychologists believe heredity is the dominant influence on intelligence. They base that view on research that concentrates on variations among people in general cognitive ability, or IQ. Others believe such research overemphasizes the concept of IQ and gives too much credit to genetics.

Twins and IQ scores

Most agree that an inadequate environment will decrease an individual's or a population's intelligence, said intelligence researcher Thomas Bouchard, PhD, of the University of Minnesota. However, "when individuals are under reasonably good circumstances . . . much of the variation [in IQ] among them is genetic," said Bouchard, who directs the Minnesota Center for Twin and Adoption Research. As with variations in height—which are considered close to 95 percent genetic—once envi-

ronment is equalized, the only reason for differences in IQ can be biology, said Bouchard.

Researchers estimate that from 40 percent to 80 percent of differences in IQ score are due to inheritance. The higher estimate comes from large studies of identical twins separated at birth. Because identical twins share all the same genes, any truly inherited trait should correlate perfectly. Any trait due to environment should have no more than chance correlation.

Therefore, correlations for identical twins reared in separate environments should give a good estimate of heritability of that trait. In Bouchard's sample of between 42 and 48 pairs of identical twins reared apart (numbers varied between studies), he found very

high rates of correlation for IQ. From his results, he estimates that IQ is between 75 percent and 80 percent heritable. Such data suggest that environment accounts for as little as 20 percent of scores on intelligence tests.

Environmental influences

Certainly "part of the functioning of

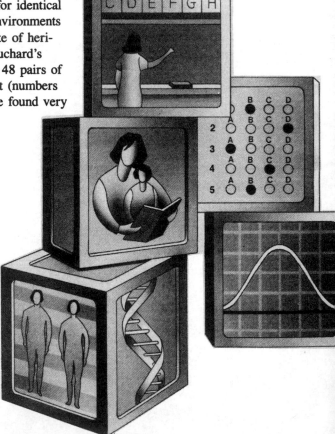

the brain is determined by environmental factors," said Douglas Detterman, PhD, an intelligence researcher at Case Western Reserve University. However it's difficult to say which factors and how big of an effect they have. Few environmental variables have been found that account for a substantial portion of the variation in intelligence, he said.

Factors such as poor nutrition, lead poisoning, poor health care and head injuries have been linked to low IQ scores. But none has been found to account for more than a few percent of the variation in scores, agree researchers.

"Understanding how the environment affects intelligence is the most difficult of all to study," though it's important, said Detterman. He thinks the effect of environment is multifaceted, and it will be extremely complex to find out how all the variables relate, he said.

Socioeconomic status is the one factor that has been strongly linked to IQ. Poverty predicts low IQ in study after study, but it's difficult to determine causation. Most researchers presume that poverty—associated with risk factors such as poor home environment, poor schools and lack of access to special programs—causes a drop in intellectual attainment. But some, such as Richard Herrnstein, PhD, and Charles Murray, PhD, in their recent book, *The Bell Curve*, propose that low IQ may be responsible for low socioeconomic status.

A loaded concept

Researchers shouldn't overestimate the role of inheritance, according to Stephen Ceci, PhD, of Cornell University.

"Every important aspect [of behavior] has a role for biology and a role for ecology," he said. The two are "inextricably intertwined," he added.

Heritability is "an extremely environmentally loaded concept," he said. People may have a certain genetic potential that can't be exceeded, but a conducive environment is what makes an organism "much more able to bring [that potential] to fruition," he said.

Indeed, IQ measures the level of intelligence that the environment has allowed a person to reach, believes Edward Zigler, PhD, director of the Bush Center for Child Development and Social Policy at Yale University and one of the founders of the national Head Start program.

His research on intelligence and learning shows that IQ measures three things: cognitive ability, achievement (accumulated knowledge based on personal experience, such as a definition for the word regatta) and motivational factors, he said. The more traditional view of IQ tests posits that they measure cognitive ability alone.

Cognitive ability, he admits, is "probably the least open to changes," Zigler said. He estimates that approximately 50 percent of cognitive ability is influenced by genetics, which leaves at least 50 percent up to environment, he said. Achievement is somewhat related to cognitive ability, said Zigler, but it is even more affected by environment.

Motivation is almost totally influenced by one's environment, said Zigler. Children learn to be unmotivated; children growing up in poor environments have little incentive to answer test questions, let alone to perform well, he said.

So environment has a larger influ-

ence than genetics in the three combined aspects of IQ, said Zigler. Getting children to use their genetically determined intelligence optimally is the way to improve achievement, he said.

Zigler's research points out what he calls reaction range. Any one person has a maximum and a minimum IQ score that he or she can reach. Environment predicts how optimally one reaches that maximum or how close to the minimum one scores. Environment can account for as many as 25 IQ points, said Zigler.

Preschool programs such as Head Start apply this premise by trying to improve children's overall environments through educational day-care, family programming, nutritional programming and health care.

Contrary to claims of some researchers and the media, the goal of Head Start was never to raise IQ, said Zigler. That became the perceived goal because the first evaluations of the program focused on IQ scores, he said.

Over the past 30 years Zigler has tried to change that perception to one of social competence, he said. This includes producing children who remain in the correct grade for their age, who stay out of special education, who graduate from high school and who don't become pregnant in their teens.

Such programs capitalize on abilities that are underutilized by tapping "a child's motivational system," Zigler said.

IQ aside, "the environment has to be good enough to provide the resources to nurture individual strengths," said Ceci.

The Good, The Bad And The DIFFERENCE

BARBARA KANTROWITZ

Like many children, Sara Newland loves animals. But unlike most youngsters, she has turned that love into activism. Five years ago, during a trip to the zoo, the New York City girl learned about the plight of endangered species, and decided to help. With the aid of her mother, Sara—then about 4 years old—baked cakes and cookies and sold them on the sidewalk near her apartment building. She felt triumphant when she raised $35, which she promptly sent in to the World Wildlife Fund.

A few weeks later, triumph turned into tears when the fund wrote Sara asking for more money. "She was devastated because she thought she had taken care of that problem," says Polly Newland, who then patiently told her daughter that there are lots of big problems that require continual help from lots of people. That explanation worked. Sara, now 9, has expanded her causes. Through her school, she helps out at an inner-city child-care center; she also regularly brings meals to homeless people in her neighborhood.

A sensitive parent can make all the difference in encouraging—or discouraging—a child's developing sense of morality and values. Psychologists say that not only are parents important as role models, they also have to be aware of a child's perception of the world at different ages and respond appropriately to children's concerns. "I think the capacity for goodness is there from the start," says Thomas Lickona, a professor of education at the State University of New York at Cortland and author of "Raising Good Children." But, he says, parents must nurture those instincts just as they help their children become good readers or athletes or musicians.

That's not an easy task these days. In the past, schools and churches played a key role in fostering moral development. Now, with religious influence in decline and schools wavering over

> **A sensitive parent is crucial in encouraging a child's sense of morality and values**
> **—**

the way to teach values, parents are pretty much on their own. Other recent social trends have complicated the transmission of values. "We're raising a generation that is still groping for a good future direction," says psychologist William Damon, head of Brown University's education department. Many of today's parents were raised in the '60s, the age of permissiveness. Their children were born in the age of affluence, the '80s, when materialism was rampant. "It's an unholy combination," says Damon.

These problems may make parents feel they have no effect on how their children turn out. But many studies show that parents are still the single most important influence on their children. Lickona says that the adolescents most likely to follow their consciences rather than give in to peer pressure are those who grew up in "authoritative" homes, where rules are firm but clearly explained and justified—as opposed to "authoritarian" homes (where rules are laid down without explanation) or "permissive" homes.

The way a parent explains rules depends, of course, on the age of the child. Many adults assume that kids see right and wrong in grown-up terms. But what may be seen as "bad" behavior by an adult may not be bad in the child's eyes. For example, a young child may not know the difference between a fanciful tale and a lie, while older kids—past the age of 5—do know.

Many psychologists think that in children, the seeds of moral values are emotional, not intellectual. Such traits as empathy and guilt—observable in the very young—represent the beginning of what will later be a conscience. Even newborns respond to signs of distress in others. In a hospital nursery, for example, a bout of crying by one infant will trigger wailing all around. Research on children's attachment to their mothers shows that babies who are most secure (and those whose mothers are most responsive to their needs) later turn out to be leaders in school: self-directed and eager to learn. They are also most likely to absorb parental values.

The first modern researcher to describe the stages of a child's moral development was Swiss psychologist Jean Piaget. In his groundbreaking 1932 book, "The Moral Judgment of the Child," he described three overlapping phases of childhood, from 5 to 12. The first is the "morality of constraint" stage: children accept adult rules as absolutes. Then comes the "morality of cooperation," in which youngsters think of morality as equal treatment. Parents of siblings will recognize this as the "If he got a new Ninja Turtle, I want one, too," stage. In the third, kids can see complexity in moral situations. They can understand extenuating circumstances in which strict equality might not necessarily mean fairness ("He got a new Ninja Turtle, but I got to go to the ball game, so it's OK.")

Although Piaget's conclusions have been expanded by subsequent researchers, his work forms the basis for most current theories of moral development. In a study begun in the 1950s, Lawrence Kohlberg, a Harvard professor, used "moral dilemmas" to define six phases. He began with 50 boys who were 10, 13 and 16. Over the next 20 years, he asked them their reactions to carefully constructed dilemmas. The most famous concerns a man named Heinz, whose wife was dying of cancer. The boys were told, in part, that a drug that might save her was a form of radium discovered by the town pharmacist. But the pharmacist was charging 10 times the cost of manufacture for the drug and Heinz could not afford it—although he tried to borrow money from everyone he knew. Heinz begged the pharmacist to sell it more cheaply, but he refused. So Heinz, in desperation, broke into the store and stole the drug. Kohlberg asked his subjects: Did Heinz do the right thing? Why?

Kohlberg and others found that at the first stage, children base their answers simply on the likelihood of getting caught. As they get older, their reasons for doing the right thing become more complex. For example, Lickona says typical 5-year-olds want to stay out of trouble. Kids from 6 to 9 characteristically act out of self-interest; most 10- to 13-year-olds crave social approval. Many 15- to 19-year-olds have moved on to thinking about maintaining the social system and being responsible.

Over the years, educators have used these theories to establish new curricula at schools around the country that emphasize moral development. The Lab School, a private preschool in Houston, was designed by Rheta DeVries, a student of Kohlberg's. The teacher is a "companion/guide," not an absolute authority figure. The object of the curriculum is to get kids to think about why they take certain actions and to think about consequences. For example, if two children are playing a game and one wants to change the rules, the teacher would ask the other child if that was all right. "Moral development occurs best when children live in an environment where fairness and justice is a way of life," says DeVries.

Not everyone agrees with the concept of moral development as a series of definable stages. Other researchers say that the stage theories downplay the role of emotion, empathy and faith. In "The Moral Life of Children," Harvard child psychiatrist Robert Coles tells the story of a 6-year-old black girl named Ruby, who braved vicious racist crowds to integrate her New Orleans school—and then prayed for her tormentors each night before she went to bed. Clearly, Coles says, she did not easily fall into any of Kohlberg's or Piaget's stages. Another criticism of stage theorists comes from feminist psychologists, including Carol Gilligan, author of "In a Different Voice." Gilligan says that the stages represent only *male* development with the emphasis on the concepts of justice and rights, not female development, which, she says, is more concerned with responsibility and caring.

But many psychologists say parents can use the stage theories to gain insight into their children's development. At each phase, parents should help their children make the right decisions about their behavior. In his book, Lickona describes a typical situation involving a 5-year-old who has hit a friend over the head with a toy while playing at the friend's house. Lickona suggests that the parents, instead of simply punishing their son, talk to him about why he hit his friend (the boy played with a toy instead of with him) and about what he could do next time instead of hitting. The parents, Lickona says, should also discuss how the friend might have felt about being hit. By the end of the discussion, the child should realize that there are consequences to his behavior. In Lickona's example, the child decides to call his friend and apologize—a positive ending.

For older children, Lickona suggests family "fairness meetings" to alleviate tension. If, for example, a brother and sister are constantly fighting, the parents could talk to both of them about what seem to be persistent sources of irritation. Then, youngsters can think of ways to bring about a truce—or at least a cease-fire.

Children who learn these lessons can become role models for other youngsters—and for adults as well. Sara Newland tells her friends not to be scared of homeless people (most of them rush by without even a quick glance, she says). "Some people think, 'Why should I give to them?' " she says. "But I feel that you should give. If everyone gave food, they would all have decent meals." One recent evening, she and her mother fixed up three plates of beef stew to give out. They handed the first to the homeless man who's always on their corner. Then, Sara says, they noticed two "rough-looking guys" down the block. Sara's mother, a little scared, walked quickly past them. Then, she changed her mind and asked them if they'd like some dinner. "They said, 'Yes, God bless you'," Sara recalls. "At that moment, they weren't the same people who were looking through a garbage can for beer bottles a little while before. It brought out a part of them that they didn't know they had."

With TESSA NAMUTH *in New York and*
KAREN SPRINGEN *in Chicago*

LIFE IN OVERDRIVE

Doctors say huge numbers of kids and adults have attention deficit disorder. Is it for real?

CLAUDIA WALLIS

DUSTY NASH, AN ANGELIC-looking blond child of seven, awoke at 5 one recent morning in his Chicago home and proceeded to throw a fit. He wailed. He kicked. Every muscle in his 50-lb. body flew in furious motion. Finally, after about 30 minutes, Dusty pulled himself together sufficiently to head downstairs for breakfast. While his mother bustled about the kitchen, the hyperkinetic child pulled a box of Kix cereal from the cupboard and sat on a chair.

But sitting still was not in the cards this morning. After grabbing some cereal with his hands, he began kicking the box, scattering little round corn puffs across the room. Next he turned his attention to the TV set, or rather, the table supporting it. The table was covered with a checkerboard Con-Tact paper, and Dusty began peeling it off. Then he became intrigued with the spilled cereal and started stomping it to bits. At this point his mother interceded. In a firm but calm voice she told her son to get the stand-up dust pan and broom and clean up the mess. Dusty got out the dust pan but forgot the rest of the order. Within seconds he was dismantling the plastic dust pan, piece by piece. His next project: grabbing three rolls

of toilet paper from the bathroom and unraveling them around the house.

It was only 7:30, and his mother Kyle Nash, who teaches a medical-school course on death and dying, was already feeling half dead from exhaustion. Dusty was to see his doctors that day at 4, and they had asked her not to give the boy the drug he usually takes to control his hyperactivity and attention problems, a condition known as attention deficit hyperactivity disorder (ADHD). It was going to be a very long day without help from Ritalin.

Karenne Bloomgarden remembers such days all too well. The peppy, 43-year-old entrepreneur and gym teacher was a disaster as a child growing up in New Jersey. "I did very poorly in school," she recalls. Her teachers and parents were constantly on her case for rowdy behavior. "They just felt I was being bad—too loud, too physical, too everything." A rebellious tomboy with few friends, she saw a psychologist at age 10, "but nobody came up with a diagnosis." As a teenager she began prescribing her own medication: marijuana, Valium and, later, cocaine.

The athletic Bloomgarden managed to get into college, but she admits that she cheated her way to a diploma. "I would study and study, and I wouldn't remember

a thing. I really felt it was my fault." After graduating, she did fine in physically active jobs but was flustered with administrative work. Then, four years ago, a doctor put a label on her troubles: ADHD. "It's been such a weight off my shoulders," says Bloomgarden, who takes both the stimulant Ritalin and the antidepressant Zoloft to improve her concentration. "I had 38 years of thinking I was a bad person. Now I'm rewriting the tapes of who I thought I was to who I really am."

Fifteen years ago, no one had ever heard of attention deficit hyperactivity disorder. Today it is the most common behavioral disorder in American children, the subject of thousands of studies and symposiums and no small degree of controversy. Experts on ADHD say it afflicts as many as 3½ million American youngsters, or up to 5% of those under 18. It is two to three times as likely to be diagnosed in boys as in girls. The disorder has replaced what used to be popularly called "hyperactivity," and it includes a broader collection of symptoms. ADHD has three main hallmarks: extreme distractibility, an almost reckless impulsiveness and, in some but not all cases, a knee-jiggling, toe-tapping hyperactivity that makes sitting still all but impossible.

(Without hyperactivity, the disorder is called attention deficit disorder, or ADD.)

For children with ADHD, a ticking clock or sounds and sights caught through a window can drown out a teacher's voice, although an intriguing project can absorb them for hours. Such children act before thinking; they blurt out answers in class. They enrage peers with an inability to wait their turn or play by the rules. These are the kids no one wants at a birthday party.

Ten years ago, doctors believed that the symptoms of ADHD faded with maturity. Now it is one of the fastest-growing diagnostic categories for adults. One-third to

Many adults respond to the diagnosis with relief—a sense that "at last my problem has a name and it's not my fault."

two-thirds of ADHD kids continue to have symptoms as adults, says psychiatrist Paul Wender, director of the adult ADHD clinic at the University of Utah School of Medicine. Many adults respond to the diagnosis with relief—a sense that "at last my problem has a name and it's not my fault." As more people are diagnosed, the use of Ritalin (or its generic equivalent, methylphenidate), the drug of choice for ADHD, has surged: prescriptions are up more than 390% in just four years.

As the numbers have grown, ADHD awareness has become an industry, a passion, an almost messianic movement. An advocacy and support group called CHADD (Children and Adults with Attention Deficit Disorders) has exploded from its founding in 1987 to 28,000 members in 48 states. Information bulletin boards and support groups for adults have sprung up on CompuServe, Prodigy and America Online. Numerous popular books have been published on the subject. There are summer camps designed to help ADHD kids, videos and children's books with titles like *Jumpin' Johnny Get Back to Work!* and, of course, therapists, tutors and workshops offering their services to the increasingly self-aware ADHD community.

T IS A COMMUNITY THAT VIEWS ITSELF with some pride. Popular books and lectures about ADHD often point out positive aspects of the condition. Adults see themselves as creative; their impulsiveness can be viewed as spontaneity; hyperactivity gives them enormous energy and drive; even their distractibility has the virtue of making them alert to changes in the environment. "Kids with ADHD are wild, funny, effervescent. They have a love of life. The rest of us sometimes envy them," says psychologist Russell Barkley of the University of Massachusetts Medical Center. "ADHD adults," he notes, "can be incredibly successful. Sometimes being impulsive means being decisive." Many ADHD adults gravitate into creative fields or work that provides an outlet for emotions, says Barkley. "In our clinic we saw an adult poet who couldn't write poetry when she was on Ritalin. ADHD people make good salespeople. They're lousy at desk jobs."

In an attempt to promote the positive side of ADHD, some CHADD chapters circulate lists of illustrious figures who, they contend, probably suffered from the disorder: the messy and disorganized Ben Franklin, the wildly impulsive and distractible Winston Churchill. For reasons that are less clear, these lists also include folks like Socrates, Isaac Newton, Leonardo da Vinci—almost any genius of note. (At least two doctors interviewed for this story suggested that the sometimes scattered Bill Clinton belongs on the list.)

However creative they may be, people with ADHD don't function particularly well in standard schools and typical office jobs. Increasingly, parents and lobby groups are demanding that accommodations be made. About half the kids diagnosed with ADHD receive help from special-education teachers in their schools, in some cases because they also have other learning disabilities. Where schools have failed to provide services, parents have sometimes sued. In one notable case that went to the U.S. Supreme Court last year, parents argued—successfully—that since the public school denied their child special education, the district must pay for her to attend private school. Another accommodation requested with increasing frequency: permission to take college-entrance exams without a time limit. Part of what motivates parents to fight for special services is frightening research showing that without proper care, kids with ADHD have an extremely high risk not only of failing at school but also of becoming drug abusers, alcoholics and lawbreakers.

Adults with ADHD are beginning to seek special treatment. Under the 1990 Americans with Disabilities Act, they can insist upon help in the workplace. Usually the interventions are quite modest: an office door or white-noise machine to reduce distractions, or longer deadlines on assignments. Another legal trend that concerns even ADHD advocates: the disorder is being raised as a defense in criminal cases. Psychologist Barkley says he knows of 55 such instances in the U.S., all in the past 10 years. ADHD was cited as a mitigating factor by the attorney for Michael Fay, the 19-year-old American who was charged with vandalism and caned in Singapore.

Many of those who treat ADHD see the recognition of the problem as a humane breakthrough: finally we will stop blaming kids for behavior they cannot control. But some are worried that the disorder is being embraced with too much gusto. "A lot of people are jumping on the bandwagon," complains psychologist Mark Stein, director of a special ADHD clinic at the University of Chicago. "Parents are putting pressure on health professionals to make the diagnosis." The allure of ADHD is that it is "a label of forgiveness," says Robert Reid, an assistant professor in the department of special education at the University of Nebraska in Lincoln. "The kid's problems are not his parents' fault, not the teacher's fault, not the kid's fault. It's better to say this kid has ADHD than to say this kid drives everybody up the wall." For adults, the diagnosis may provide an excuse for personal or professional failures, observes Richard Bromfield, a psychologist at Harvard Medical School. "Some people like to say, 'The biological devil made me do it.'"

A DISORDER WITH A PAST Other than the name itself, there is nothing new about this suddenly ubiquitous disorder. The world has always had its share of obstreperous kids, and it has generally treated them as behavior problems rather than patients. Most of the world still does so: European nations like France and England report one-tenth the U.S. rate of ADHD. In Japan the disorder has barely been studied.

The medical record on ADHD is said to have begun in 1902, when British pediatrician George Still published an account of 20 children in his practice who were "passionate," defiant, spiteful and lacking "inhibitory volition." Still made the then radical suggestion that bad parenting was not to blame; instead he suspected a subtle brain injury. This theory gained greater credence in the years following the 1917-18 epidemic of viral encephalitis, when doctors observed that the infection left some children with impaired attention, memory and control over their impulses. In the 1940s and '50s, the same constellation of symptoms was called minimal brain damage and, later, minimal brain dysfunction. In 1937 a Rhode Island pediatrician reported that giving stimulants called amphetamines to children with these symptoms had the unexpected effect of calming them down. By the mid-1970s, Ritalin had become the most prescribed drug for what was eventually termed, in 1987, attention deficit hyperactivity disorder.

Nobody fully understands how Ritalin and other stimulants work, nor do doctors have a very precise picture of the physiology of ADHD. Researchers generally suspect a defect in the frontal lobes of the brain, which regulate behavior. This region is rich in the neurotransmitters dopamine and norepinephrine, which are influenced by drugs like Ritalin. But the lack of a more specific explanation has led some psychologists to question whether ADHD is truly a disorder at all or merely a set of characteristics that tend to cluster together. Just because something responds to a drug doesn't mean it is a sickness.

ADHD researchers counter the skeptics by pointing to a growing body of biological clues. For instance, several studies have found that people with ADHD have decreased blood flow and lower levels of electrical activity in the frontal lobes than normal adults and children. In 1990 Dr. Alan Zametkin at the National Institute of Mental Health found that in PET scans, adults with ADD showed slightly lower rates of metabolism in areas of the brain's cortex known to be involved in the control of attention, impulses and motor activity.

Zametkin's study was hailed as the long-awaited proof of the biological basis of ADD, though Zametkin himself is quite cautious. A newer study used another tool—magnetic resonance imaging—to compare the brains of 18 ADHD boys with those of other children and found several "very subtle" but "striking" anatomical differences, says co-author Judith Rapoport, chief of the child psychiatry branch at NIMH. Says Zametkin: "I'm absolutely convinced that this disorder has a biological basis, but just what it is we cannot yet say."

WHAT RESEARCHERS DO say with great certainty is that the condition is inherited. External factors such as birth injuries and maternal alcohol or tobacco consumption may play a role in less than 10% of cases. Suspicions that a diet high in sugar might cause hyperactivity have been discounted. But the influence of genes is unmistakable. Barkley estimates that 40% of adhd kids have a parent who has the trait and 35% have a sibling with the problem; if the sibling is an identical twin, the chances rise to between 80% and 92%.

Interest in the genetics of ADHD is enormous. In Australia a vast trial involving 3,400 pairs of twins between the ages of 4 and 12 is examining the incidence of ADHD and other behavioral difficulties. At NIMH, Zametkin's group is recruiting 200 families who have at least two members with ADHD. The hope: to identify genes for the disorder. It is worth noting, though, that even if such genes are found, this may not settle the debate about ADHD. After all, it is just as likely that researchers will someday discover a gene for a hot temper, which also runs in families. But that doesn't mean that having a short fuse is a disease requiring medical intervention.

TRICKY DIAGNOSIS In the absence of any biological test, diagnosing ADHD is a rather inexact proposition. In most cases, it is a teacher who initiates the process by informing parents that their child is daydreaming in class, failing to complete assignments or driving everyone crazy with thoughtless behavior. "The problem is that the parent then goes to the family doctor, who writes a prescription for Ritalin and doesn't stop to think of the other possibilities," says child psychiatrist Larry Silver of

Is ADD truly a disorder? Just because something responds to a drug doesn't mean it is a sickness.

Georgetown University Medical Center. To make a careful diagnosis, Silver argues, one must eliminate other explanations for the symptoms.

The most common cause, he points out, is anxiety. A child who is worried about a problem at home or some other matter "can look hyperactive and distractible." Depression can also cause ADHD-like behavior. "A third cause is another form of neurological dysfunction, like a learning disorder," says Silver. "The child starts doodling because he didn't understand the teacher's instructions." All this is made more complicated by the fact that some kids—and adults—with ADHD also suffer from depression and other problems. To distinguish these symptoms from ADHD, doctors usually rely on interviews with parents and teachers, behavior-ratings scales and psychological tests, which can cost from $500 to $3,000, depending on the thoroughness of the testing. Insurance coverage is spotty.

Among the most important clues doctors look for is whether the child's problems can be linked to some specific experience or time or whether they have been present almost from birth. "You don't suddenly get ADD," says Wade Horn, a child psychologist and former executive director of CHADD. Taking a careful history is therefore vital.

For kids who are hyperactive, the pattern is unmistakable, says Dr. Bruce Roseman, a pediatric neurologist with several offices in the New York City area, who has ADHD himself. "You say to the mother, 'What kind of personality did the child have as a baby? Was he active, alert? Was he colicky?' She'll say, 'He wouldn't stop— waaah, waaah, waaah!' You ask, 'When did he start to walk?' One mother said to me, 'Walk? My son didn't walk. He got his pilot's license at one year of age. His feet haven't touched the ground since.' You ask, 'Mrs.

Smith, how about the terrible twos?' She'll start to cry, 'You mean the terrible twos, threes, fours, the awful fives, the horrendous sixes, the God-awful eights, the divorced nines, the I-want-to-die tens!' "

Diagnosing those with ADD without hyperactivity can be trickier. Such kids are often described as daydreamers, space cases. They are not disruptive or antsy. But, says Roseman, "they sit in front of a book and for 45 minutes, nothing happens." Many girls with ADD fit this model; they are often misunderstood or overlooked.

Christy Rade, who will be entering the ninth grade in West Des Moines, Iowa, is fairly typical. Before she was diagnosed with ADD in the third grade, Christy's teacher described her to her parents as a "dizzy blond and a space cadet." "Teachers used to get fed up with me," recalls Christy, who now takes Ritalin and gets some extra support from her teachers. "Everyone thought I was purposely not paying attention." According to her mother Julie Doy, people at Christy's school were familiar with hyperactivity but not ADD. "She didn't have behavior problems. She was the kind of kid who could fall through the cracks, and did."

Most experts say ADHD is a lifelong condition but by late adolescence many people can compensate for their impulsiveness and disorganization. They may channel hyperactivity into sports. In other cases, the symptoms still wreak havoc, says UCLA psychiatrist Walid Shekim. "Patients cannot settle on a career. They cannot keep a job. They procrastinate a lot. They are the kind of people who would tell their boss to take this job and shove it before they've found another job."

Doctors diagnose adults with methods similar to those used with children. Patients are sometimes asked to dig up old report cards for clues to their childhood behavior—an essential indicator. Many adults seek help only after one of their children is diagnosed. Such was the case with Chuck Pearson of Birmingham, Michigan, who was diagnosed three years ago, at 54. Pearson had struggled for decades in what might be the worst possible career for someone with ADD: accounting. In the first 12 years of his marriage, he was fired from 15 jobs. "I was frightened," says Zoe, his wife of 35 years. "We had two small children, a mortgage. Bill collectors were calling perpetually. We almost lost the house." Chuck admits he had trouble focusing on details, completing tasks and judging how long an assignment would take. He was so distracted behind the wheel that he lost his license for a year after getting 14 traffic tickets. Unwittingly, Pearson began medicating himself: "In my mid-30s, I would drink 30 to 40 cups of coffee a day. The caffeine helped." After he was diagnosed, the Pearsons founded the Adult Attention

HAIL TO THE HYPERACTIVE HUNTER

Why is attention deficit hyperactivity disorder so common? Is there an evolutionary reason why these traits are found in as many as 1 in 20 American youngsters? Such questions have prompted intriguing speculation. Harvard psychiatrist John Ratey finds no mystery in the prevalence of ADHD in the U.S. It is a nation of immigrants who, he notes, "risked it all and left their homelands." Characteristics like impulsiveness, high energy and risk taking are therefore highly represented in the U.S. gene pool. "We have more Nobel laureates and more criminals than anywhere else in the world. We have more people who absolutely push the envelope."

But why would ADHD have evolved in the first place? perhaps, like the sickle-cell trait, which can help thwart malaria, attention deficit confers an advantage in certain circumstances. In *Attention Deficit Disorder: A Different Perception,* author Thom Hartmann has laid out a controversial but appealing theory that the characteristics known today as ADHD were vitally important in early hunting societies. They became a mixed blessing only when human societies turned agrarian, Hartmann suggests. "If you are walking in the night and see a little flash, distractibility would be a tremendous asset. Snap decision making, which we call impulsiveness, is a survival skill if you are a hunter." For a farmer, however, such traits can be disastrous. "If this is the perfect day to plant the crops, you can't suddenly decided to wander off into the woods."

Modern society, Hartmann contends, generally favors the farmer mentality, rewarding those who develop plans, meet deadlines and plod through schedules. But there's still a place for hunters, says the author, who counts himself as one: they can be found in large numbers among entrepreneurs, police detectives, emergency-room personnel, race-care drivers and, of course, those who stalk the high-stakes jungle known as Wall Street.

Where is the boundary between personality and pathology? Even an expert in the field like the University of Chicago's Mark Stein admits, "We need to find more precise ways of diagnosing it than just saying you have these symptoms." Barkley also concedes the vagueness. The traits that constitute ADHD "are personality characteristics," he agrees. But it becomes pathology, he says, when the traits are so extreme that they interfere with people's lives.

THE RISKS There is no question that ADHD can disrupt lives. Kids with the disorder frequently have few friends. Their parents may be ostracized by neighbors and relatives, who blame them for failing to control the child. "I've got criticism of my parenting skills from strangers," says the mother of a hyperactive boy in New Jersey. "When you're out in public, you're always on guard. Whenever I'd hear a child cry, I'd turn to see if it was because of Jeremy."

School can be a shattering experience for such kids. Frequently reprimanded and tuned out, they lose any sense of self-worth and fall ever further behind in their work. More than a quarter are held back a grade; about a third fail to graduate from high school. ADHD kids are also prone to accidents, says neurologist Roseman. "These are the kids I'm going to see in the emergency room this summer. They rode their bicycle right into the street and didn't look. They jumped off the deck and forgot it was high."

But the psychological injuries are often greater. By ages five to seven, says Barkley, half to two-thirds are hostile and defiant. By ages 10 to 12, they run the risk of developing what psychologists call "conduct disorder"—lying, stealing, running away from home and ultimately getting into trouble with the law. As adults, says Barkley, 25% to 30% will experience substance-abuse problems, mostly with depressants like marijuana and alcohol. One study of hyperactive boys found that 40% had been arrested at least once by age 18—and these were kids who had been treated with stimulant medication; among those who had

Deficit Foundation, a clearinghouse for information about ADD; he hopes to spare others some of his own regret: "I had a deep and abiding sadness over the life I could have given my family if I had been treated effectively."

PERSONALITY OR PATHOLOGY? While Chuck Pearson's problems were extreme, many if not all adults have trouble at times sticking with boring tasks, setting priorities and keeping their minds on what they are doing. The furious pace of society, the strain on families, the lack of community support can make anyone feel beset by ADD. "I personally think we are living in a society that is so out of control that we say, 'Give me a stimulant so I can cope.' " says Charlotte Tomaino, a clinical neuropsychologist in White Plains, New York. As word of ADHD spreads, swarms of adults are seeking the diagnosis as an explanation for their troubles. "So many really have symptoms that began in adulthood and reflected depression or other problems," says psychiatrist Silver. In their best-selling new book, *Driven to Distraction,* Edward Hallowell and John Ratey suggest that American life is "ADD-ogenic": "American society tends to create ADD-like symptoms in us all. The fast pace. The sound bite. The quick cuts. The TV remote-control clicker. It is important to keep this in mind, or you may start thinking that everybody you know has ADD."

And that is the conundrum. How do you draw the line between a spontaneous, high-energy person who is feeling overwhelmed by the details of life and someone afflicted with a neurological disorder?

DO YOU HAVE ATTENTION DEFICIT?

If eight or more of the following statements accurately describe your child or yourself as a child, particularly before age 7, there may be reason to suspect ADHD. A definitive diagnosis requires further examination.

1. **Often fidgets or squirms in seat.**

2. **Has difficulty remaining seated.**

3. **Is easily distracted.**

4. **Has difficulty awaiting turn in groups.**

5. **Often blurts out answers to questions.**

6. **Has difficulty following instructions.**

7. **Has difficulty sustaining attention to tasks.**

8. **Often shifts from one** uncompleted activity to another.

9. **Has difficulty playing quietly.**

10. **Often talks excessively.**

11. **Often interrupts or intrudes on others.**

12. **Often does not seem to listen.**

13. **Often loses things necessary for tasks.**

14. **Often engages in physically dangerous activities without considering consequences.**

Source: *The ADHD Rating Scale: Normative Data, Reliability, and Validity.*

been treated with the drug plus other measures, the rate was 20%—still very high.

It is an article of faith among ADHD researchers that the right interventions can prevent such dreadful outcomes. "If you can have an impact with these kids, you can change whether they go to jail or to Harvard Law School," says psychologist James Swanson at the University of California at Irvine, who co-authored the study of arrest histories. And yet, despite decades of research, no one is certain exactly what the optimal intervention should be.

TREATMENT The best-known therapy for ADHD remains stimulant drugs. Though Ritalin is the most popular choice, some patients do better with Dexedrine or Cylert or even certain antidepressants. About 70% of kids respond to stimulants. In the correct dosage, these uppers surprisingly "make people slow down," says Swanson. "They make you focus your attention and apply more effort to whatever you're supposed to do." Ritalin kicks in within 30 minutes to an hour after being taken, but its effects last only about three hours. Most kids take a dose at breakfast and another at lunchtime to get them through a school day.

When drug therapy works, says Utah's Wender, "it is one of the most dramatic effects in psychiatry." Roseman tells how one first-grader came into his office after trying Ritalin and announced, "I know how it works." "You do?" asked the doctor. "Yes," the child replied. "It cleaned out my ears. Now I can hear the teacher." A third-grader told Roseman that Ritalin had enabled him to play basketball. "Now when I get the ball, I turn around, I go down to the end of the room, and if I look up, there's a net there. I never used to see the net, because there was too much screaming."

For adults, the results can be just as striking. "Helen," a 43-year-old mother of three in northern Virginia, began taking the drug after being diagnosed with ADD in 1983. "The very first day, I noticed a difference," she marvels. For the first time ever, "I was able to sit down and listen to what my husband had done at work. Shortly after, I was able to sit in bed and read while my husband watched TV."

Given such outcomes, doctors can be tempted to throw a little Ritalin at any problem. Some even use it as a diagnostic tool, believing—wrongly—that if the child's concentration improves with Ritalin, then he or she must have ADD. In fact, you don't have to have an attention problem to get a boost from Ritalin. By the late 1980s, overprescription became a big issue, raised in large measure by the Church of Scientology, which opposes psychiatry in general and launched a vigorous campaign against Ritalin. After a brief decline fostered by the scare, the drug is now hot once again.

Swanson has heard of some classrooms where 20% to 30% of the boys are on Ritalin. "That's just ridiculous!'" he says.

Ritalin use varies from state to state, town to town, depending largely on the attitude of the doctors and local schools. Idaho is the No. 1 consumer of the drug. A study of Ritalin consumption in Michigan, which ranks just behind Idaho, found that use ranged from less than 1% of boys in one county to as high as 10% in another, with no correlation to affluence.

Patients who are taking Ritalin must be closely monitored, since the drug can cause loss of appetite, insomnia and occasionally tics. Doctors often recommend "drug holidays" during school vacations. Medication is frequently combined with other treatments, including psychotherapy, special education and cognitive training, although the benefits of such expensive measures are unclear. "We really haven't known which treatment to use for which child and how to combine treatments," says Dr. Peter Jensen, chief of NIMH's Child and Adolescent Disorders Research Branch. His group has embarked on a study involving 600 children in six cities. By 1998 they hope to have learned how medication alone compares to medication with psychological intervention and other approaches.

BEYOND DRUGS A rough consensus has emerged among ADHD specialists that whether or not drugs are used, it is best to teach kids—often through behavior modification—how to gain more control over their impulses and restless energy. Also recommended is training in the fine art of being organized: establishing a predictable schedule of activities, learning to use a date book, assigning a location for possessions at school and at home. This takes considerable effort on the part of teachers and parents as well as the kids themselves. Praise, most agree, is vitally important.

Within the classroom "some simple, practical things work well," says Reid. Let hyperactive kids move around. Give them stand-up desks, for instance. "I've seen kids who from the chest up were very diligently working on a math problem, but from the chest down, they're dancing like Fred Astaire." To minimize distractions, ADHD kids should sit very close to the teacher and be permitted to take important tests in a quiet area. "Unfortunately," Reid observes, "not many teachers are trained in behavior management. It is a historic shortfall in American education."

In Irvine, California, James Swanson has tried to create the ideal setting for teaching kids with ADHD. The Child Development Center, an elementary school that serves 45 kids with the disorder, is a kind of experiment in progress. The emphasis is on behavior modification: throughout the day students earn points—and are relentlessly

cheered on—for good behavior. High scorers are rewarded with special privileges at the end of the day, but each morning kids start afresh with another shot at the rewards. Special classes also drill in social skills: sharing, being a good sport, ignoring annoyances rather than striking out in anger. Only 35% of the kids at the center are on stimulant drugs, less than half the national rate for ADHD kids.

Elsewhere around the country, enterprising parents have struggled to find their own answers to attention deficit. Bonnie and Neil Fell of Skokie, Illinois, have three sons, all of whom have been diagnosed with ADD. They have "required more structure and consistency than other kids," says Bonnie. "We had to break down activities into clear time slots." To help their sons, who take Ritalin, the Fells have employed tutors, psychotherapists and a speech and language specialist. None of this comes cheap: they estimate their current annual ADD-related expenses at $15,000. "Our goal is to get them through school with their self-esteem intact," says Bonnie.

The efforts seem to be paying off. Dan, the eldest at 15, has become an outgoing A student, a wrestling star and a writer for the school paper. "ADD gives you energy and creativity," he says. "I've learned to cope. I've become strong." On the other hand, he is acutely aware of his disability. "What people don't realize is that I have to work harder than everyone else. I start studying for finals a month before other people do."

COPING Adults can also train themselves to compensate for ADHD. Therapists working with them typically emphasize organizational skills, time management, stress reduction and ways to monitor their own distractibility and stay focused.

IN HER OFFICE IN WHITE PLAINS, Tomaino has a miniature Zen garden, a meditative sculpture and all sorts of other items to help tense patients relax. Since many people with ADHD also have learning disabilities, she tests each patient and then often uses computer programs to strengthen weak areas. But most important is helping people define their goals and take orderly steps to reach them. Whether working with a stockbroker or a homemaker, she says, "I teach adults basic rewards and goals. For instance, you can't go out to lunch until you've cleaned the kitchen."

Tomaino tells of one very hyperactive and articulate young man who got all the way through college without incident, thanks in good measure to a large and tolerant extended family. Then he flunked out of law school three times. Diagnosed with ADHD, the patient took stock of his goals and decided to enter the family restaurant business, where, Tomaino says, he is a raging success. "ADHD was a deficit if he wanted to be a lawyer, but it's an advantage in the restaurant business. He gets to go around to meet and greet."

For neurologist Roseman, the same thing is true. With 11 offices in four states, he is perpetually on the go. "I'm at rest in motion," says the doctor. "I surround myself with partners who provide the structure. My practice allows me to be creative." Roseman has accountants to do the bookkeeping. He starts his day at 6:30 with a hike and doesn't slow down until midnight. "Thank God for my ADD," he says. But, he admits, "had I listened to all the negative things that people said when I was growing up, I'd probably be digging ditches in Idaho."

LESSONS Whether ADHD is a brain disor-der or simply a personality type, the degree to which it is a handicap depends not only on the severity of the traits but also on one's environment. The right school, job or home situation can make all the difference. The lessons of ADHD are truisms. All kids do not learn in the same way. Nor are all adults suitable for the same line of work.

Unfortunately, American society seems to have evolved into a one-size-fits-all system. Schools can resemble factories: put the kids on the assembly line, plug in the right components and send 'em out the door. Everyone is supposed to go to college; there is virtually no other route to success. In other times and in other places, there have been alternatives: apprentice-ships, settling a new land, starting a business out of the garage, going to sea. In a conformist society, it becomes necessary to medicate some people to make them fit in.

This is not to deny that some people genuinely need Ritalin, just as others need tranquilizers or insulin. But surely an epidemic of attention deficit disorder is a warning to us all. Children need individual supervision. Many of them need more structure than the average helter-skelter household provides. They need a more consistent approach to discipline and schools that tailor teaching to their individual learning styles. Adults too could use a society that's more flexible in its expectations, more accommodating to differences. Most of all, we all need to slow down. And pay attention. **—With reporting by Hannah Bloch/New York, Wendy Cole/Chicago and James Willwerth/Irvine**

Bell, book and scandal

For more than a century intelligence testing has been a field rich in disputed evidence and questionable conclusions. "The Bell Curve", by Charles Murray and Richard Herrnstein, has ensured it will remain so

THERE is plenty of room for debate about which was the most amusing book of 1994, or which the best written. But nobody can seriously quibble about which was the most controversial. "The Bell Curve: Intelligence and Class Structure in American Life", an 845-page tome by Charles Murray and Richard Herrnstein*, has reignited a debate that is likely to rage on for years yet, consuming reputations and research grants as it goes.

"The Bell Curve" is an ambitious attempt to resuscitate IQ ("intelligence quotient") testing, one of the most controversial ideas in recent intellectual history; and to use that idea to explain some of the more unpalatable features of modern America. Mr Murray, a sociologist, and Herrnstein, a psychologist who died shortly before the book's publication, argue that individuals differ substantially in their "cognitive abilities"; that these differences are inherited as much as acquired; and that intelligence is distributed in the population along a normal distribution curve—the bell curve of the book's title—with a few geniuses at the top, a mass of ordinary Joes in the middle and a minority of dullards at the bottom (see chart).

Then, into this relatively innocuous cocktail, Messrs Murray and Herrnstein mix two explosive arguments. The first is that different races do not perform equally in the IQ stakes—that, in America, Asians score, on average, slightly above the norm, and blacks, on average, substantially below it. The second is that America is calcifying into impermeable castes. The bright are inter-marrying, spawning bright offspring and bagging well-paid jobs; and the dull are doomed to teenage pregnancy, welfare dependency, drugs and crime.

For the past three months it has been almost impossible to pick up an American newspaper or tune into an American television station without learning more about Mr Murray's views. Dozens of academics are hard at work rebutting (they would say refuting) his arguments. Thanks to the controversy, "The Bell Curve" has sold more than a quarter of a million copies.

Undoubtedly, Mr Murray has been lucky in his timing. Left-wingers point out that Americans have seldom been so disillu-

_____
* The Free Press. New York, 1994

sioned with welfare policy: the voters are turning not just to Republicans, but to Republicans who are arguing seriously about the merits of state orphanages and of compulsory adoption. Mr Murray's arguments answer to a feeling that social policies may have failed not because they were incompetently designed or inadequately funded, but because they are incompatible with certain "facts" of human nature.

Right-wingers retort that it is liberals' addiction to "affirmative action" that has supplied Mr Murray with much of his material. Affirmative action has institutionalised the idea that different ethnic groups have different cognitive abilities: "race norming", now de rigueur in academia, means that a black can perform significantly less well than, say, an Asian, and still beat him into a university. It has also resulted in America's having a compilation of statistics about race unequalled outside South Africa.

Differently weird

The regularity with which discussion of IQ testing turns into an argument that ethnic groups differ in their innate abilities, with blacks at the bottom of the cognitive pile, has done more than anything else to make theorists and practitioners of IQ testing into figures of academic notoriety reviled everywhere from Haight-Ashbury to Holland Park. The early 1970s saw a furious argument about "Jensenism", named after Arthur Jensen, a psychologist at the University of California, Berkeley, who published an article arguing, among other things, that the average black had a lower IQ than the average white. William Shockley, also known as a co-inventor of the transistor, drew the anti-Jensenists' fire by saying that blacks' and whites' brains were "differently wired".

But, even if it could be extricated from arguments about ethnic differences, IQ testing would remain controversial. One reason is that few people like the idea that inequality might be inevitable, the result of natural laws rather than particular circumstances (and the more so, perhaps, when economic inequalities seem likely to widen as labour markets put an ever-higher premium on intelligence). The implication is that egalitarian policies are self-defeating: the more inherited prejudices are broken down, the more society resolves into intellectual castes.

A second reason for controversy is that IQ testers are all too prone to the fatal conceit of thinking that their discipline equips them to know what is best for their fellow men. To most parents the idea that a man with a book of tests and a clipboard can divine what is best for their children is an intolerable presumption (who can know a child as well as its parents?) and an insupportable invasion of liberty (surely people should be free to choose the best school for their children?). Nor has the IQ testers' image been helped by their having often been asked—as in England in the days of the 11-plus school entry examination—to help make already contentious decisions.

A third reason IQ testers excite concern is that they seem to make a fetish of intelligence. Many people feel instinctively that intelligence is only one of the qualities that make for success in life—that looks, luck and charm also play their part; they also like to feel that intelligence is less important than what they call "character", which can turn even a dull person into a useful citizen.

But the thing which, in the end, really frightens people about IQ testing is its message of genetic Calvinism: that IQ both determines one's destiny, and is dictated by one's genes. This flies in the face of the liberal notion that we are each responsible for fashioning our own fate. It also upsets two beliefs held particularly firmly in America: that anybody can win out, provided they have "the right stuff"; and that everybody should be given as many educational chances as possible, rather than sorted out and classified at the earliest possible opportunity. (Thus "Forrest Gump", a film that appeared shortly before publication of "The Bell Curve", enjoyed great popularity and critical acclaim for its portrayal of a well-meaning simpleton who won all America's glittering prizes.)

Hunting down Sir Humphrey

How, then, did so widely distrusted a discipline originate? To answer that question means a trip to a rather unexpected place, the Whitehall of the mid-19th century. Traditionally, jobs in the British civil service had been handed out on the basis of family connections, in a sort of affirmative-action programme for upper-class twits. But as Britain developed a world-beating economy and a world-spanning empire, reformers argued that preferment should go to the most intelligent candidates, their identity to be discovered by competitive examinations.

This innovation proved so successful that policy-makers applied the same principle to the universities and schools. Their aim was to construct an educational system capable of discovering real ability wherever it occurred, and of matching that ability with the appropriate opportunities.

Ironically, it was children at the other end of the ability scale who inspired the first IQ tests as such. The introduction of compulsory schooling for the masses confronted teachers with the full variety of human abilities, and obliged them to distinguish between the lazy and the congenitally dull. Most investigators contented themselves

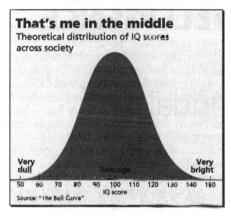

That's me in the middle
Theoretical distribution of IQ scores across society

Very dull — Average — Very bright

50 60 70 80 90 100 110 120 130 140 150
IQ score
Source: "The Bell Curve"

with measuring children's heads. But in 1905 Alfred Binet, a French psychologist, came up with the idea of assigning an age level to a variety of simple intellectual operations, determined by the earliest age at which the average child could perform them, and ranking children both against their peers and against a normal development curve. Binet's idea was refined soon afterwards by introducing the arithmetical device of dividing mental age by chronological age and multiplying by 100.

Two English psychologists turned intelligence testing into a sort of scientific movement. The first was Francis Galton, a rich and well connected man (Charles Darwin was a cousin) who devoted his life to the nascent sciences of statistics and genetics. His motto was "wherever you can, count", and he measured everything from the distended buttocks of Hottentot women (with a theodolite) to the distribution of "pulchritude" in the British Isles. He compiled family trees of everybody from Cambridge wranglers to West Country wrestlers to prove his belief that "characteristics cling to families" and "ability goes by descent."

Combining his two passions, Galton speculated that abilities in the British population were distributed along a "bell curve", with the upper classes at the top and an underclass at the bottom. He was so worried

that those at the bottom of the curve were outbreeding those at the top that he spent most of his fortune bankrolling another "science", eugenics.

Galton's mission was completed by a retired soldier, Charles Spearman. Deciding that the results of certain tests correlated with each other to a remarkable degree, Spearman concluded, in a seminal article published in 1904, that all mental abilities were manifestations of a single general ability, which he called "g": all individuals inherited a fixed quantity of mental energy, which infused every intellectual act they performed and determined what they were capable of in life. The right tests could capture how much "g" each individual possessed and express it as a single number.

Intelligence testing went on to enjoy decades of growing popularity. The American army used it on recruits in the first world war, employing more than 300 psychologists, and other armies followed. Schools used tests to help in streaming or selecting their pupils. Bureaucrats and businessmen used them to identify talented recruits. Tests were thought indispensable for discovering and diagnosing learning problems.

Only in the 1960s did opinion turn sharply against the IQ testers. Educationalists accused them of allowing an obsession with classification to blind them to the full range of human abilities. Sociologists (and sociologically minded psychologists) argued that intellectual differences owed more to social circumstances than to genes. In Britain, disillusionment with IQ tests hastened the introduction of comprehensive schools. In the United States, schools abandoned the use of IQ tests to classify children. In 1978 a district court in San Francisco even ruled unconstitutional the use of IQ tests to place children in classes for the backward if the use of such tests meant that the classes contained a "grossly disproportionate" number of black children.

Dropping clangers

"The Bell Curve" thus represents an attempt to rehabilitate an idea that had fallen into two or three decades of disfavour. But have Messrs Murray and Herrnstein got their science right?

So far, the debate on "The Bell Curve" has been billed as if it were psychometrists (mind-measurers) versus the rest. In fact, IQ testers divide among themselves on all sorts of key issues, from the structure of the mind to the reliability of tests; moreover, Messrs Murray and Herrnstein occupy a rather eccentric position among psychometrists. They are unabashed supporters of Charles Spearman, believing that intelligence is a unitary quality expressible in a single number, such that people who are good at one thing will also be good at others. Yet this is one of the most hotly disputed topics within psychometry. A British pioneer, Godfrey

Thomson, argued that the correlations which so excited Spearman might be explained by the laws of chance. He concluded that the mind had no fixed structure and that intelligence tests gave little more than a hint of a person's mental powers.

Among other psychologists, L.L. Thurstone argued for the existence of dozens of different types of mental abilities, such as mathematical, verbal and visio-spatial abilities. Liam Hudson has found IQ tests to reward a particular type of "convergent" thinker. Howard Gardner thinks there are many sorts of "intelligence".

Synaptitude

IQ testers have clashed and go on clashing over less arcane issues too. They endorse widely different estimates of the heritability of IQ, ranging from 40% to 80%. They squabble about the accuracy of IQ tests: some argue that such tests are nothing more than estimates that need to be repeated frequently and to be supplemented by personal interviews (and indeed, observably, children can learn, or be taught, to raise their IQ scores). Some of the most illustrious psychometrists are even starting to argue that IQ tests should be replaced by physical tests to measure the speed of reactions, the production of glucose in the brain, the speed of neural transmission and even the size of the brain.

Psychometrists disagree, too, about the validity of generalising about groups in the way that Murray and Herrnstein do. It is widely accepted that differences within groups may reflect hereditary factors; but differences between groups are susceptible to other explanations (just as people in one place may be taller on average than people in another place, for example, but for reasons of nutrition, not genetics).

Oddly, Messrs Murray and Herrnstein have chosen to dispute (or ignore) one of the few arguments on which all psychometrists agree: that children do not necessarily have the same IQ as their parents. "The Bell Curve" argues that society is fixing itself into impermeable castes. But psychometry is a theory of social mobility, not social stasis. It tries to explain why bright people often have dull children and dull people often have bright children. Sex ensures that genes are re-sorted in each generation.

In fact, it is hereditarianism's sworn enemy, environmentalism, which is really a theory of social stasis: if the rich and educated can pass on their advantages to their children undisturbed by the dance of the chromosomes, then social mobility will always be something of a freak. Messrs Murray and Herrnstein are, perhaps, environmentalists in hereditarian clothing.

Politically, "The Bell Curve" has reinforced the impression that IQ testers are anti-welfare conservatives. Some are. But IQ tests have been invoked in defence of a wide variety of political positions, respectable and otherwise. American psychologists have popped up to support abominations such as compulsory sterilisation and ethnically sensitive immigration laws. Others have been socialists, keen on upward mobility, child-centred education and generous provision for the backward. In Britain between the wars Labour Party intellectuals such as R.H. Tawney argued for IQ testing as a way to ensure educational opportunities were allocated on the basis of innate ability rather than family connections; psychologists such as Cyril Burt have been passionate supporters of nursery-school education and better treatment of backward children. (The fusty T.S. Eliot, on the other hand, thought IQ tests were a plot to promote social mobility and debase education. A particularly crusty Cambridge don, Edward Welbourne, denounced them as "devices invented by Jews for the advancement of Jews.")

Too clever by half

What makes the IQ debate particularly frustrating is that both sides have long been addicted to exaggeration. The earliest IQ testers were guilty of hubris when they argued that they had invented an infallible technique for measuring mental abilities and distributing educational and occupational opportunities. As if that was not bad enough, they exacerbated their error by claiming that their method contributed to economic efficiency (by making the best use of human resources) and personal happiness (by ensuring that people were given jobs suited to their abilities).

The enemies of IQ testing were also guilty of terrible exaggeration when they accused testers of shoring up capitalism, perpetuating inequality, and justifying sexism, racism, even fascism. In fact, the IQ testers were never anywhere near as influential as they, or their opponents, imagined.

IQ theory played no part in persuading the American Congress to pass the Immigration Restriction Act of 1924; British grammar schools used IQ tests only to supplement other, more traditional selection procedures, such as scholastic examinations and interviews; Hitler and Mussolini had no time for IQ tests that were liable to contradict their own racial prejudices.

What the IQ debate needs now is a dash of cold water. Opponents of testing should forget their over-heated rhetoric about legitimising capitalism and racism. Supporters should fold up their more grandiose blueprints for building the meritocracy, and limit themselves to helping with practical problems. They should point out that IQ tests are useful ways of identifying and diagnosing mental deficiency, just so long as they are administered along with other diagnostic tools by a trained psychologist. They should add that IQ tests can also be useful in helping to allocate places in over-subscribed schools; that, indeed, they are less class-biased than scholastic tests (which favour the well-taught) or personal interviews (which favour the well-brought up). It is a pity that Charles Murray and Richard Herrnstein have chosen to douse the debate not with cold water but with petrol.

The AAUW Report: How Schools Shortchange Girls
— Overview —

— Why a Report on Girls? —

The invisibility of girls in the current education debate suggests that girls and boys have identical educational experiences in school. Nothing could be further from the truth. Whether one looks at achievement scores, curriculum design, or teacher-student interaction, it is clear that sex and gender make a difference in the nation's public elementary and secondary schools.

The educational system is not meeting girls' needs. Girls and boys enter school roughly equal in measured ability. Twelve years later, girls have fallen behind their male classmates in key areas such as higher-level mathematics and measures of self-esteem. Yet gender equity is still not a part of the national debate on educational reform.

Research shows that policies developed to foster the equitable treatment of students and the creation of gender-equitable educational environments can make a difference. They can make a difference, that is, if they are strongly worded and vigorously enforced.

V. Lee, H. Marks and T. Knowles, "Sexism in Single-Sex and Coeducational Secondary School Classrooms," paper presented at the American Sociological Association annual meeting, Cincinnati, OH, August 1991; S. Bailey and R. Smith, *Policies for the Future*, Council of Chief State School Officers, Washington, DC, 1982.

Neither the *National Education Goals* issued by the National Governors Association in 1990 nor *America 2000*, the 1991 plan of the President and the U.S. Department of Education to "move every community in America toward these goals" makes any mention of providing girls equitable opportunities in the nation's public schools. Girls continue to be left out of the debate—despite the fact that for more than two decades researchers have identified gender bias as a major problem at all levels of schooling.

Schools must prepare both girls and boys for full and active roles in the family, the community, and the work force. Whether we look at the issues from an economic, political, or social perspective, girls are one-half of our future. We must move them from the sidelines to the center of the education-reform debate.

A critical step in correcting educational inequities is identifying them publicly. The *AAUW Report: How Schools Shortchange Girls* provides a comprehensive assessment of the status of girls in public education today. It exposes myths about girls and learning, and it supports the work of the many teachers who have struggled to define and combat gender bias in their schools. The report challenges us all—policymakers, educators, administrators, parents, and citizens—to rethink old assumptions and act now to stop schools from shortchanging girls.

Our public education system is plagued by numerous failings that affect boys as negatively as girls. But in many respects girls are put at a disadvantage simply because they are girls. *The AAUW Report* documents this in hundreds of cited studies.

When our schools become more gender-fair, education will improve for all our students—boys as well as girls—because excellence in education cannot be achieved without equity in education. By studying what happens to girls in school, we can gain valuable insights about what has to change in order for each student, every girl and every boy, to do as well as she or he can.

What Do We Teach Our Students?

• The contributions and experiences of girls and women are still marginalized or ignored in many of the textbooks used in our nation's schools.

• Schools, for the most part, provide inadequate education on sexuality and healthy development despite national concern about teen pregnancy, the AIDS crisis, and the increase of sexually transmitted diseases among adolescents.

• Incest, rape, and other physical violence severely compromise the lives of girls and women all across the country. These realities are rarely, if ever, discussed in schools.

Curriculum delivers the central messages of education. It can strengthen or decrease student motivation for engagement, effort, growth, and development through the images it gives to students about themselves and the world. When the curriculum does not reflect the diversity of students' lives and cultures, it delivers an incomplete message.

Studies have shown that multicultural readings produced markedly more favorable attitudes toward nondominant groups than did the traditional reading lists, that academic achievement for all students was linked to use of nonsexist and multicultural materials, and that sex-role stereotyping was reduced in students whose curriculum portrayed males and females in non-stereotypical roles. Yet during the 1980s, federal support for reform regarding sex and race equity dropped, and a 1989 study showed that of the ten books most frequently assigned in public high school English courses only one was written by a woman and none by members of minority groups.

The "evaded" curriculum is a term coined in this report to refer to matters central to the lives of students that are touched on only briefly, if at all, in most schools. The United States has the highest rate of teenage childbearing in the Western indus-trialized world. Syphilis rates are now equal for girls and boys, and more teenage girls than boys contract gonorrhea. Although in the adult population AIDS is nine times more prevalent in men than in women, the same is not true for young people. In a District of Columbia study, the rate of HIV infection for girls was almost three times that for boys. Despite all of this, adequate sex and health education is the exception rather than the rule.

Adolescence is a difficult period for all young people, but it is particularly difficult for girls, who are far more likely to develop eating disorders and experience depression. Adolescent girls attempt suicide four to five times as often as boys (although boys, who choose more lethal methods, are more likely to be successful in their attempts).

Despite medical studies indicating that roughly equal proportions of girls and boys suffer from learning disabilities, more than twice as many boys are identified by school personnel as in need of special-education services for learning-disabled students.

U.S. Department of Education, Office for Civil Rights, 1988.

Perhaps the most evaded of all topics in schools is the issue of gender and power. As girls mature they confront a culture that both idealizes and exploits the sexuality of young women while assigning them roles that are clearly less valued than male roles. If we do not begin to discuss more openly the ways in which

ascribed power—whether on the basis of race, sex, class, sexual orientation, or religion—affects individual lives, we cannot truly prepare our students for responsible citizenship.

These issues are discussed in detail and the research fully annotated in Part 4/Chapters 1 and 3 of The AAUW Report.

How Do Race/Ethnicity and Socioeconomic Status Affect Achievement in School?

• Girls from low-income families face particularly severe obstacles. Socioeconomic status, more than any other variable, affects access to school resources and educational outcomes.
• Test scores of low-socioeconomic-status girls are somewhat better than for boys from the same background in the lower grades, but by high school these differences disappear. Among high-socioeconomic-status students, boys generally outperform girls regardless of race/ethnicity.
• Girls and boys with the same Math SAT scores do not do equally well in college—girls do better.

In most cases tests reflect rather than cause inequities in American education. The fact that groups score differently on a test does not necessarily mean that the test is biased. If, however, the score differences are related to the validity of the test—for example, if girls and boys know about the same amount of math but boys' test scores are consistently and significantly higher—then the test is biased.

A number of aspects of a test—beyond that which is being tested—can affect the score. For example, girls tend to score better than boys on essay tests, boys better than girls on multiple-choice items. Even today many girls and boys come to a testing situation with different interests and experiences. Thus a reading-comprehension passage that focuses on baseball scores will tend to favor boys, while a question testing the same skills that focuses on child care will tend to favor girls.

These issues are discussed in detail and the research fully annotated in Part 3 of The AAUW Report.

Why Do Girls Drop Out and What Are the Consequences?

• Pregnancy is not the only reason girls drop out of school. In fact, less than half the girls who leave school give pregnancy as the reason.
• Dropout rates for Hispanic girls vary considerably by national origin: Puerto Rican and Cuban American girls are more likely to drop out than are boys from the same cultures or other Hispanic girls.
• Childhood poverty is almost inescapable in single-parent families headed by women without a high school diploma: 77 percent for whites and 87 percent for African Americans.

In a recent study, 37 percent of the female drop-outs com-pared to only 5 percent of the male drop-outs cited "family-related problems" as the reason they left high school. Tradi-tional gender roles place greater family responsibilities on adolescent girls than on their brothers. Girls are often expected to "help out" with caretaking responsibilities; boys rarely encounter this expectation.

There has been little change in sex-segregated enrollment patterns in vocational education: girls are enrolled primarily in office and business-training programs, boys in programs leading to higher-paying jobs in the trades.

U.S. Department of Education, 1989.

However, girls as well as boys also drop out of school simply because they do not consider school pleasant or worthwhile. Asked what a worthwhile school experience would be, a group of teenage girls responded, "School would be fun. Our teachers would be excited and lively, not bored. They would act caring and take time to understand how students feel. . . . Boys would treat us with respect. If they run by and grab your tits, they would get into trouble."*

Women and children are the most impoverished members of our society. Inadequate education not only limits opportunities for women but jeopardizes their children's—and the nation's—future.

These issues are discussed in detail and the research fully annotated in Part 2/Chapters 4 and 6 of The AAUW Report.

The research reviewed in this report challenges traditional assumptions about the egalitarian nature of American schools. Young women in the United States today are still not participating equally in our educational system. Research documents that girls do not receive equitable amounts of teacher attention, that they are less apt than boys to see themselves reflected in the materials they study, and that they often are not expected or encouraged to pursue higher level mathematics and science courses. The implications are clear; the system must change.

We now have a window of opportunity that must not be missed. Efforts to improve public education are under way around the nation. We must move girls from the sidelines to the center of educational planning. The nation can no longer afford to ignore the potential of girls and young women. Whether one looks at the issues from an economic, political, or social perspective, girls are one-half of our future.

Significant improvements in the educational opportunities available to girls have occurred in the past two decades. However, twenty years after the passage of Title IX, the achievement of sex- and gender-equitable education remains an elusive dream. The time to turn dreams to reality is now. The

---

*As quoted in *In Their Own Voices: Young Women Talk About Dropping Out,* Project on Equal Education Rights (New York, National Organization for Women Legal Defense and Education Fund, 1988), p. 12.

current education-reform movement cannot succeed if it continues to ignore half of its constituents. The issues are urgent; our actions must be swift and effective.

— The Recommendations —

Strengthened Reinforcement of Title IX Is Essential.

1. Require school districts to assess and report on a regular basis to the Office for Civil Rights in the U.S. Department of Education on their own Title IX compliance measures.
2. Fund the Office for Civil Rights at a level that permits increased compliance reviews and full and prompt investigation of Title IX complaints.
3. In assessing the status of Title IX compliance, school districts must include a review of the treatment of pregnant teens and teen parents. Evidence indicates that these students are still the victims of discriminatory treatment in many schools.

Teachers, Administrators and Counselors Must Be Prepared and Encouraged to Bring Gender Equity and Awareness to Every Aspect of Schooling.

4. State certification standards for teachers and administrators should require course work on gender issues, including new research on women, bias in classroom-interaction patterns, and the ways in which schools can develop and implement gender-fair multicultural curricula.
5. If a national teacher examination is developed, it should include items on methods for achieving gender equity in the classroom and in curricula.
6. Teachers, administrators, and counselors should be evaluated on the degree to which they promote and encourage gender-equitable and multicultural education.
7. Support and released time must be provided by school districts for teacher-initiated research on curricula and classroom variables that affect student learning. Gender equity should be a focus of this research and a criterion for awarding funds.
8. School-improvement efforts must include a focus on the ongoing professional development of teachers and administrators, including those working in specialized areas such as bilingual, compensatory, special, and vocational education.
9. Teacher-training courses must not perpetuate assumptions about the superiority of traits and activities traditionally ascribed to males in our society. Assertive and affiliative skills as well as verbal and mathematical skills must be fostered in both girls and boys.
10. Teachers must help girls develop positive views of themselves and their futures, as well as an understanding of the obstacles women must overcome in a society where their options and opportunities are still limited by gender stereotypes and assumptions.

The Formal School Curriculum Must Include the Experiences of Women and Men From All Walks of Life. Girls and Boys Must See Women and Girls Reflected and Valued in the Materials They Study.

11. Federal and state funding must be used to support research, development, and follow-up study of gender-fair multicultural curricular models.

12. The Women's Educational Equity Act Program (WEEAP) in the U.S. Department of Education must receive increased funding in order to continue the development of curricular materials and models, and to assist school districts in Title IX compliance.

13. School curricula should deal directly with issues of power, gender politics, and violence against women. Better-informed girls are better equipped to make decisions about their futures. Girls and young women who have a strong sense of themselves are better able to confront violence and abuse in their lives.

14. Educational organizations must support, via conferences, meetings, budget deliberations, and policy decisions, the development of gender-fair multicultural curricula in all areas of instruction.

15. Curricula for young children must not perpetuate gender stereotypes and should reflect sensitivity to different learning styles.

Girls Must Be Educated and Encouraged to Understand That Mathematics and the Sciences Are Important and Relevant to Their Lives. Girls Must Be Actively Supported in Pursuing Education and Employment in These Areas.

16. Existing equity guidelines should be effectively implemented in all programs supported by local, state, and federal governments. Specific attention must be directed toward including women on planning committees and focusing on girls and women in the goals, instructional strategies, teacher training, and research components of these programs.

17. The federal government must fund and encourage research on the effect on girls and boys of new curricula in the sciences and mathematics. Research is needed particularly in science areas where boys appear to be improving their performance while girls are not.

18. Educational institutions, professional organizations, and the business community must work together to dispel myths about math and science as "inappropriate" fields for women.

19. Local schools and communities must encourage and support girls studying science and mathematics by showcasing women role models in scientific and technological fields, disseminating career information, and offering "hands-on" experiences and work groups in science and math classes.

20. Local schools should seek strong links with youth-serving organizations that have developed successful out-of-school programs for girls in mathematics and science and with those girls' schools that have developed effective programs in these areas.

Continued Attention to Gender Equity in Vocational Education Programs Must Be a High Priority at Every Level of Educational Governance and Administration.

21. Linkages must be developed with the private sector to help ensure that girls with training in nontraditional areas find appropriate employment.

22. The use of a discretionary process for awarding vocational-education funds should be encouraged to prompt innovative efforts.

23. All states should be required to make support services (such as child care and transportation) available to both vocational and prevocational students.

24. There must be continuing research on the effectiveness of vocational education for girls and the extent to which the 1990 Vocational Education Amendments benefit girls.

Testing and Assessment Must Serve as Stepping Stones Not Stop Signs. New Tests and Testing Techniques Must Accurately Reflect the Abilities of Both Girls and Boys.

25. Test scores should not be the only factor considered in admissions or the awarding of scholarships.

26. General aptitude and achievement tests should balance sex differences in item types and contexts. Tests should favor neither females nor males.

27. Tests that relate to "real life situations" should reflect the experiences of both girls and boys.

Girls and Women Must Play a Central Role in Educational Reform. The Experiences, Strengths, and Needs of Girls From Every Race and Social Class Must Be Considered in Order to Provide Excellence and Equity for All Our Nation's Students.

28. National, state, and local governing bodies should ensure that women of diverse backgrounds are equitably represented on committees and commissions on educational reform.

29. Receipt of government funding for in-service and professional development programs should be conditioned upon evidence of efforts to increase the number of women in positions in which they are underrepresented. All levels of government have a role to play in increasing the numbers of women, especially women of color, in education-management and policy positions.

30. The U.S. Department of Education's Office of Educational Research and Improvement (OERI) should establish an advisory panel of gender-equity experts to work with OERI to develop a research and dissemination agenda to foster gender-equitable education in the nation's classrooms.

31. Federal and state agencies must collect, analyze, and report data broken down by race/ethnicity, sex, and some measure of socioeconomic status, such as parental income or education. National standards for use by all school districts should be developed so that data are comparable across district and state lines.

32. National standards for computing dropout rates should be developed for use by all school districts.

33. Professional organizations should ensure that women serve on education-focused committees. Organizations should utilize the expertise of their female membership when developing educational initiatives.

34. Local schools must call on the expertise of teachers, a majority of whom are women, in their restructuring efforts.

35. Women teachers must be encouraged and supported to seek administrative positions and elected office, where they can bring the insights gained in the classroom to the formulation of education policies.

A Critical Goal of Education Reform Must Be to Enable Students to Deal Effectively with the Realities of Their Lives, Particularly in Areas Such as Sexuality and Health.

36. Strong policies against sexual harassment must be developed. All school personnel must take responsibility for enforcing these policies.

37. Federal and state funding should be used to promote partnerships between schools and community groups, including social service agencies, youth-serving organizations, medical facilities, and local businesses. The needs of students, partic-ularly as highlighted by pregnant teens and teen mothers, require a multi-institutional response.

38. Comprehensive school-based health- and sex-education programs must begin in the early grades and continue sequentially through twelfth grade. These courses must address the topics of reproduction and reproductive health, sexual abuse, drug and alcohol use, and general mental and physical health issues. There must be a special focus on the prevention of AIDS.

39. State and local school board policies should enable and encourage young mothers to complete school, without compromising the quality of education these students receive.

40. Child care for the children of teen mothers must be an integral part of all programs designed to encourage young women to pursue or complete educational programs.

The AAUW Report: How Schools Shortchange Girls

A startling examination of how girls are disadvantaged in America's schools, grades K–12. Prepared by the Wellesley College Center for Research on Women, the book includes recommendations for educators and policymakers, as well as concrete strategies for change. 128 pages/1992. $14.95 AAUW members/$16.95 nonmembers. Bulk prices available.

NURTURING CREATIVITY IN *ALL* YOUR STUDENTS

JULIUS SEGAL AND ZELDA SEGAL

The late Julius Segal, PhD, was a psychologist, author, and lecturer. Zelda Segal is a school psychologist and educational consultant in private practice.

Laura's always asking "why?" For her, no rule goes unchallenged and no fact remains unquestioned. Offer her a toy, and instead of playing with it, she takes it apart to find out how it works. Then she tries to put it together in a completely different way.

Laura's curiosity, contrariness, and adventuresomeness are typical of creative children. Kids like this are willing to test new ideas and dream up possibilities that depart from the norm. They're inquisitive, sometimes exasperatingly so, and always eager to search out the atypical or unusual. They may be known for having "wild and silly" ideas—and they are often targets of ridicule, especially from their peers.

Understandably, many of the traits that characterize creative children may inspire more irritation than admiration. At times, you may have to remind yourself that these are the children who are most likely to grow up to become gifted scientists, inventors, designers, artists, or architects.

But keep in mind that all children—not just those who are obviously innovative thinkers—have the potential to be creative in some facet of their lives. That's why it's important to help foster their creative streak. Be tolerant of students who can't seem to focus on anything in particular. Many children need time to dabble in a variety of areas. Ultimately, most discover an arena in which their interests and skills overlap—and in which they delight in generating novel ideas.

To nurture the creative impulse in every student, do the following:

1. Promote novel ways of thinking. Children can't show much originality if you define their efforts for them. Whenever feasible, offer suggestions and guidance, rather than exacting directions. Provide materials and encouragement for your students, then step back and let them develop their own notions. For example, give the kindergartner an opportunity to be messy with finger paints, allow the 3rd grader to act silly by spewing out meaningless rhymes, or let the 8th grader waste time developing a new and seemingly improbable system for doing long division.

Just as important, suppress the impulse to accomplish a task for a student. Taking over may seem expedient, but it's likely to diminish the child's willingness to pursue a creative effort.

Help your students feel comfortable about sharing or testing out crazy ideas—as long as these fall within acceptable standards of behavior. Show the kids that you value their creative thinking by offering encouragement and respect. Then cheer their innovative approaches. At all costs, avoid censuring or showing disapproval of children who express themselves in ways that may seem odd or even foolish.

2. Encourage resilience to criticism. Prepare your students to expect mixed—or even downright negative—reviews of their seemingly offbeat efforts. For example, explain that a rhyming version of the Pledge of Allegiance might seem "crazy" to classmates or that a new variation of baseball is likely to be viewed as "off-the-wall" by the Little League coach.

When your students do get negative feedback, help them understand that their efforts are intrinsically worthwhile—no matter what others may think. To emphasize the importance of a risk-taking mind-set, you might tell them about biologist Barbara McClintock, whose groundbreaking genetic studies were discounted and even derided for three decades. In 1983, McClintock won the Nobel Prize for her contributions to medicine. She later revealed that she hadn't really worried about the perceptions of others. She always knew she was on the right track.

3. Guide students toward meaningful creative pursuits. To help your students discover new areas of interest—and possible creative outlets—expose them to a variety of options. Then give them a chance to explore as many of these options as is feasible.

Remember that creativity can be displayed not only through the arts and academic areas, but also through hobbies such as photography, cooking, mechanics, or gardening. Encourage students to write about their interests and hobbies. You might even plan a "hobby day" once a month to give the kids a chance to show off their outside interests and expertise. And, when possible, integrate areas of student interest into your curriculum. Such techniques will show your students that you value creativity in all areas.

4. Inspire perseverance. Help your students understand that their first efforts will rarely be their best, then praise their repeated tries. Also, encourage them to appreciate the importance of seeing a project through to completion—no matter what the outcome of their early endeavors. You might even tell them that inventor Thomas Edison is said to have assessed his progress by recognizing that he already knew a hundred reasons why his ideas *wouldn't* work.

5. Communicate your enthusiasm. Make sure you encourage creativity for the love of it, not for tangible rewards. Avoid advertising payoffs in advance. Instead, give bonuses after students have completed projects. When children are motivated to pursue an activity because it's inherently compelling, enjoyable, and satisfying, creativity shines in the results. In contrast, when children's work is motivated by extrinsic factors—such as wanting to impress others or to receive a promised prize—the quality of the product usually suffers.

And remember that children don't always need tangible rewards or bonuses to bring zest to their creative endeavors. Enthusiasm for the project, along with something as simple as an encouraging smile, a pat on the back, or a word of praise, can keep them going.

In communicating your own enthusiasm for the joys of creative pursuits, you're increasing the chances of a creative life for your students. There are seeds of creativity in every child, and who's to say which of those seeds may one day flower to beautify our world?

Multicultural Education

A Challenge for Special Educators

Ann V. Dean

Spencer J. Salend

Lorraine Taylor

Ann V. Dean, *Assistant Professor of Educational Studies*, **Spencer J. Salend** *(CEC Chapter #615) Professor of Educational Studies, and* **Lorraine Taylor** *(CEC Chapter #615) Associate Professor of Educational Studies, State University of New York at New Paltz.*

Multicultural education is an ambiguous concept encompassing the many ways in which educators attempt to acknowledge and understand the increasing diversity in society and in the classroom. The term means widely different things to different interest groups. For example, some humanistic education discourses define multicultural education primarily as the promotion of harmonious relations among students in the classroom (Sleeter & Grant, 1987). At the other end of the spectrum are critical education discourses that define multicultural education as "emancipatory teaching" requiring a critical examination of the relationship between diversity and equality in the classroom (Freire, 1985; Shor, 1992). Critical education theories offer teachers and students a means to disrupt the power relations that exist in the classroom by, for example, asking questions about who is given the authority to talk in the classroom. Teachers cán evaluate their own "teacher talk" and begin to create a classroom atmosphere of shared authority in which *all* students are encouraged to find and express their voices.

Because the definition of multicultural education is so controversial, espe-

Students learn about biases against various cultural groups by studying newspapers.

Photograph by Mark A. Regan.

cially when viewed as a social, political, and cultural construct, it is important to be clear about its goals. Multicultural education seeks to make schools examine and address their role in either empowering or disabling students. It serves as a solid platform from which advocacy groups and educators can promote goals of equal opportunity; racial, ethnic, and religious tolerance; and gender and sexual orientation awareness, and it allows them to openly challenge the content and values of the traditional school curriculum.

Whereas students from culturally and linguistically diverse backgrounds are often viewed as the sole focus of the multicultural education movement, we believe that it should target *all* students. For the purposes of this article, culturally and linguistically diverse students are defined as "those whose native or primary language is not English, and/or who are not native members of the Euro-Caucasian cultural base currently dominant in the United States" (Salend, 1994, p. 22).

Critical Elements of Multicultural Education

To achieve the goals of multicultural education, educators, students, parents, and community members need to work collaboratively to restructure schools so that they incorporate the following critical elements of multicultural education.

Employing Student-Centered Assessment Strategies

While the traditional norm-referenced testing model focuses on labeling students and documenting their failure, in a multicultural education approach assessment data serve as the basis for advocating for students and their families (Cummins, 1986). This approach to assessment examines how the educational system and the curriculum contribute to the problems students are experiencing in school (Hamayan & Perlman, 1992).

Proponents of multicultural education view assessment as an ongoing process dealing with real learning experiences that provide a clear and direct relationship between assessment and instruction. Effective assessment also involves collaboration among students, parents, professionals, and administrators and seeks to empower students in the learning process by making them the center of all assessment activities. Student-centered assessment strategies include self-evaluation questionnaires and interviews, student entries in journals or learning logs, think-alouds, and portfolio assessment. For example, Davison and Pearce (1992) assessed and improved the math performance of a group of Native American students by having them maintain journals describing their reactions to lessons and the problems they were experiencing in learning the material.

Using Culturally Responsive Instruction

An important component of multicultural education is the use of culturally responsive instruction, in which educators employ instructional strategies and curriculum adaptations that are consistent with students' experiences, cultural perspectives, and developmental ages (Collier & Kalk, 1989; Irvine, 1990). For many students, culturally relevant instruction also means a movement away from traditional teaching models that promote the transmission of information through task analysis, structured drills, teacher-directed activities, and independent seatwork. Figueroa, Fradd, and Correa (1989) and Ortiz and Yates (1989) have suggested that educators consider using reciprocal interaction teaching models such as cooperative learning and whole language, which promote empowerment and learning via verbal and written dialogues between students, as well as between students and teachers.

Culturally responsive instruction also involves use of multicultural instructional materials that reflect and validate students' experiences and aspirations. Educators should carefully evaluate instructional materials in terms of the following questions:
• To what extent do the materials include the various social groups that make up society?
• How are various groups depicted in the materials?
• Are the viewpoints, attitudes, reactions, experiences, and feelings of various groups presented accurately?
• Does the material incorporate the history, heritage, language, and traditions of various groups?
• Are the experiences of and issues important to various groups presented in a realistic manner that allows students to recognize and understand their complexities?
• Are the materials factually correct?
• Are the graphics accurate as well as inclusive of and sensitive to various groups?
• Do the materials avoid stereotypes and generalizations about groups?
• Is the language of the materials inclusive and reflective of various groups? (Banks, 1991; Franklin, 1992; Gollnick & Chinn, 1990).

Transforming the Curriculum

One means of making learning relevant for all students is to create a multicultural curriculum that acknowledges the voices, histories, experiences, and contributions of all groups, rather than focusing solely on the needs of students from racial minority groups and students who speak languages other than English (Banks, 1991). A transformative approach to revising the multicultural education curriculum changes the basic structure of the curriculum by encouraging the examination and exploration of concepts, issues, problems, and concerns from a variety of cultural perspectives (Banks, 1991). Students learn to think critically and reflect upon the viewpoints of a variety of cultural, gender, religious, and social class groups. For example, Banks and Sebesta (1982)

developed a lesson that allows students to examine and compare the traditional textbook representation of Christopher Columbus and the Arawak Indians from two different perspectives, thereby allowing students to envision the arrival of European explorers in the New World from the viewpoint of both the explorer and the indigenous peoples.

Teaching Students to Accept and Appreciate Individual Differences

An integral part of a multicultural education curriculum is teaching students to accept and appreciate diversity. An appreciation of and respect for individual differences helps students understand and empathize with the experiences and feelings of their classmates, which can enhance the learning and socialization of all students (Schniedewind, 1992).

Teachers should offer students learning activities that help them understand, accept, and appreciate individual differences related to culture, language, disability, gender, religion, sexual orientation, and socioeconomic status (Salend, 1994). For example, Derman-Sparks (1989) has developed an anti-bias curriculum that deals with the issues of color, language, gender, and disability. The curriculum includes a variety of activities to teach students to be sensitive to the needs of others, think critically, interact with others, and develop a positive self-identity based on their own strengths rather than on the weaknesses of others. Teachers also should help students understand that "difference exists in the context of inequality when some groups of people have more power and resources than those labeled 'different,' and when the dominant group's culture, values, and practices, being the norm, tend to maintain that inequality" (Schniedewind, 1992, p. 4).

The following guidelines can assist teachers in helping students overcome misunderstandings and negative attitudes toward other cultures by teaching them about different cultures and the value of cultural diversity:

• Examine cultural diversity from the standpoint that all individuals have a culture that is to be valued and affirmed.

• Help students view the similarities among groups through their differences.

• Make cultural diversity activities an ongoing and integral part of the curriculum rather than a 1-day "visit" to a culture during holidays or other special occasions.

• Relate cultural diversity experiences to real-life and hands-on experiences that address the students' interests.

• Teach students about the variance of individual behavior within all cultures and emphasize the notion that families and individuals experience their cultures in personal ways (Derman-Sparks, 1989; Martin, 1987).

Teaching Social Responsibility

A common goal of educators committed to multicultural education is to open up possibilities of social change, which can be accomplished by "affirming plurality and difference and…working to create community (Greene, 1993, p. 17). To accomplish this, educators must recognize the need to raise all students' cultural consciousness and teach them to analyze critically the ways in which the culture perpetuates inequality and maintains the status quo (Adams, Pardo, & Schniedewind, 1992). For example, Reissman (1992) used group discussions and projects to help students learn about the biased ways newspapers cover various cultural and linguistic groups and to investigate ways of challenging various forms of discrimination. This approach to teaching involves challenging the assumptions educators, parents, and students hold about traditional school practices and the cultural norms of schools and encouraging an enhanced awareness of social responsibility.

Promoting Family/Community Involvement and Empowerment

Multicultural education also targets the school's interactions with family and community as an important area in need of change and seeks to promote active involvement and empowerment of families and communities in the educational process. This requires schools to examine the historical, economic, social, and political variables that have shaped their interactions with parents and communities and establish coalitions of mutuality and support with the communities they serve (Roberts, Bell, & Salend, 1991).

Rather than viewing parents and communities as disinterested, ineffective, and deficient, a multicultural education approach promotes a collaborative, equal-status dialogue among professionals, parents, and community members (Harry, 1992). Parents are empowered to perform a variety of roles that provide them with a voice in the decision-making process (Cheng, 1992). Salend and Taylor (in press) have identified a variety of strategies and programs that educators can employ to empower parents and establish a reciprocal connection among the family, school, and community.

Understanding Behavior in a Social/Cultural Context

Schools, and therefore the behavioral expectations of teachers, are rooted in the mainstream, middle-class culture. It is important that educators be aware of this potential cultural bias and assess the impact of cultural and class perspectives and language background on student behavior. For example, Boykin (1986) noted that African-American students may engage in a variety of passive and active behaviors to cope with social institutions primarily based on mainstream perspectives. Therefore, educators need to increase their understanding of the ways in which behavior and communication work within a specific social/cultural context, expand their acceptance of individual differences, and promote competence in all students, regardless of cultural, class, or language backgrounds.

Countering Resistance to Change

Educators who hope to create classrooms that affirm diversity and promote a sense of community must be prepared to face many challenges (Greene, 1993). The first challenge is the resistance to change they may encounter from peers, administrators, school board members, parents, students, and other groups who have a vested interest in what goes on in schools. These groups will work to protect their own interests through control of the existing curricula and everyday school practices. As educators begin to recognize and respond to the needs of an increasingly diverse group of students, these changes may be perceived by some individuals and groups as an attempt to usurp their power and upset the status quo.

The second, less obvious challenge is the resistance to change educators might experience within themselves. They must be willing to examine subtle forms of personal resistance. For example, it is not easy for teachers to take a frank look at the power they wield and examine how they use that authority to disable or empower students. It is easier to resist acknowledging the social and political aspects of teaching. Through a thoughtful examination of their assumptions and pedagogical practices, it is possible for teachers to confront their resistance to change and create possibilities for inclusive, multicultural classrooms by asking questions such as the following:

• Am I willing to reflect on the way I use power in the classroom?

• Am I defensive when the assumptions of multicultural education are discussed?

• Is it possible for me to accept that the knowledge made legitimate in schools may not be meeting the needs of my students?

• Am I willing to try to understand the racial, ethnic, linguistic, gender, and class dimensions of teaching?

• Will my authority as a teacher be threatened if I look at how my teaching supports or does not support concepts such as acceptance of individual differences, equality, and justice?

Conclusion

Many of the challenges encountered in advocating for multicultural education are also faced by those who support inclusion. As proponents of educational reform, the multicultural and inclusion movements share mutual goals and seek to provide equality, equity, and excellence for all students. The movements also share common affective goals for students, including developing positive attitudes toward their cultures and the cultures of others, understanding and accepting individual differences, and appreciating the interdependence among diverse groups and individuals.

Many of the critical elements of multicultural education also coincide with those identified for inclusion. Best practices in terms of assessment, culturally responsive instruction, curriculum reform, and an appreciation of individual differences are common to both movements. The empowerment and support of families and communities is another important component that is shared by advocates of both philosophies. By recognizing their commonalities, proponents of these philosophies can create a unified school system in which *all* students are welcomed and affirmed in classrooms that are based on acceptance, belonging, and community. . . .

References

Adams, B. S., Pardo, W. E., & Schniedewind, N. (1992). Changing the ways things are done around here. *Educational Leadership, 49*(4), 37-42.

Banks, J. A. (1991). *Teaching strategies for ethnic studies* (5th ed.). Boston: Allyn & Bacon.

Banks, J. A., & Sebesta, S. L. (1982). *We Americans: Our history and people* (Vols. 1 & 2). Boston: Allyn & Bacon.

Boykin, A. W. (1986). The triple quandary and the schooling of Afro-American children. In U. Neisser (Ed.), *The school achievement of minority children* (pp. 57-92). Hillsdale, NJ: Lawrence Erlbaum.

Cheng, L. L. (1992, November). *Difficult discourse: Making home-school-student connections.* Paper presented at The Council for Exceptional Children's Topical Conference on Culturally and Linguistically Diverse Exceptional Children, Minneapolis.

Collier, C., & Kalk, M. (1989). Bilingual special education curriculum development. In L. M. Baca & H. T. Cervantes (Eds.), *The bilingual special education interface* (2nd ed.) (pp. 205-229). Columbus, OH: Merrill.

Cummins, J. (1986). Empowering minority students: A framework for intervention. *Harvard Education Review, 56*, 18-36.

Davison, D. M., & Pearce, D. L. (1992). The influence of writing activities on mathematics learning of American Indian students. *The Journal of Educational Issues of Language Minority Students, 10*, 147-157.

Derman-Sparks, L. (1989). *Anti-bias curriculum.* Washington, DC: National Association for the Education of Young Children.

Figueroa, R. A., Fradd, S. H., & Correa, V. I. (1989). Bilingual special education and this special issue. *Exceptional Children, 56*, 174-178.

Franklin, M. E. (1992). Culturally sensitive instructional practices for African-American learners with disabilities. *Exceptional Children, 59*, 115-122.

Freire, P. (1985). *The politics of education: Culture, power and liberation.* South Hadley, MA: Bergin & Garvey.

Gollnick, D. M., & Chinn, P. C. (1990). *Multicultural education in a pluralistic society.* Columbus, OH: Merrill.

Greene, M. (1993). The passions of pluralism: Multiculturalism and the expanding community. *Educational Researcher, 22*(1), 13-18.

Hamayan, E., & Perlman, R. (1992). Assessment of language competencies. In Illinois State Board of Education (Eds.), *Recommended practices in the identification, assessment, and provision of special education for culturally and linguistically diverse students* (pp. 46-60). Springfield: Illinois State Board of Education.

Harry, B. (1992). *Culturally diverse families and the special education system.* New York: Teachers College Press.

Irvine, J. J. (1990). *Black students and school failure: Policies, practices and prescriptions.* New York: Praeger.

Martin, D. S. (1987). Reducing ethnocentrism. *TEACHING Exceptional Children, 20*(1), 5-8.

Ortiz, A. A., & Yates, J. R. (1989). Staffing and the development of individualized educational programs for the bilingual exceptional student. In L. M. Baca & H. T. Cervantes (Eds.), *The bilingual special education interface* (2nd ed.) (pp. 183-203). Columbus, OH: Merrill.

Reissman, R. (1992). Multicultural awareness collages. *Educational Leadership, 49*(4), 51-52.

Roberts, G. W., Bell, L. A., & Salend, S. J. (1991). Negotiating change for multicultural education: A consultation model. *Journal of Educational and Psychological Consultation, 2*(4), 323-342.

Salend, S. J. (1994). *Effective mainstreaming: Creating inclusive classrooms.* New York: Macmillan.

Salend, S. J., & Taylor, L. (In press). Working with families: A cross-cultural perspective. *Remedial and Special Education.*

Schniedewind, N. (1992). Appreciating diversity: Promoting equality. *Cooperative Learning, 12*(3), 4-7.

Shor, I. (1992). *Empowering education: Critical teaching for social change.* Chicago: University of Chicago Press.

Sleeter, C. E., & Grant, C. A. (1987). An analysis of multicultural education in the U. S. *Harvard Education Review, 57*, 421-444.

Development during Childhood—Family and Culture

- Family (Articles 24–29)
- Culture (Articles 30–35)

The world expands for bigger, stronger, cognitively more mature school-age children. While family is still vitally important, peers, schoolmates, teachers, neighbors, extracurricular activity leaders, and several significant others play increasingly important roles. The culture, especially as seen through the eyes of peers, siblings, and close friends, becomes very meaningful. Cultural influences include multiple factors that interact with each other, such as religion, styles of dress, music, television, movies, slang language, games played, parents' jobs, and exposure to sex, drugs, and violence.

Psychosocial theorist Erik Erikson emphasized both family and cultural influences on personal and social development in childhood. He was especially concerned with how family and culture impact a school-age child's conflict between becoming industrious and productive versus feeling inferior.

Family responsiveness and family demandingness are both essential to the healthy social and emotional development of school-age children. A working mother, a working father, a single, adoptive, poor, divorced, or even homeless parent can be a good parent when he or she attends to the child's needs for loving support and discipline. Many oversimplistic generalizations have been made about families "at risk" of being poor parents. A school-age child is not necessarily in danger of becoming socially or emotionally disturbed if the mother is employed, or if the father is absent, or if the parents divorce, or if the family lives below the poverty line. Nor is the child necessarily at risk of becoming wretched if he or she is exposed to too much sex, violence, illegal drug use, or delinquent behavior among peers. Some children (called dandelion children) seem to thrive despite multiple stressors and family and cultural adversities. Other children seem to wilt with only a minimal amount of stress. Research has suggested that hardiness in children is enhanced by adequate health, safety, and nutritional care combined with parental affection, discipline, democracy, and togetherness. Resilient children can develop in any economic, political, racial, religious, or social group.

Laurence Kohlberg combined cognitive propositions with social data to develop a social-cognitive theory of moral development. Initially, young children are amoral.

They base right and wrong on simple criteria such as avoiding punishment, pleasing others, and especially pleasing themselves. By school age, their cognitive styles give them a conventional morality. They base right and wrong on criteria such as the approval of others, relationship maintenance, social order maintenance, and respect for authority. When adult role models condone an environment that includes violence, drugs, and sexual promiscuity, children view these behaviors as morally acceptable. Some children experience a great deal of stress trying to figure out why what they hear is wrong is not deemed really wrong by large numbers of people in the culture. The rapidly changing world order and social climate can confuse children cognitively, socially, and emotionally.

Peer pressures, including sibling pressures, increase as children grow older. Peers and siblings can have positive, neutral, or negative impacts on each other. In general, children prefer same-sex siblings and friends during the middle-school years. Friendships are based first on shared activities. Later they become more intimate. Siblings and friends provide a forum for self-disclosure and self-discovery. Parental pressures are usually paramount for decisions about self in school, religious community, and other major activities. Peer and sibling pressures may be paramount for decisions about self in dress, slang usage, television viewing, choice of music, and other minor activities.

The articles in this unit on family and cultural impacts on childhood cover a wide array of concerns from adoption to the new zeal for melanin.

The first subsection on family impact begins by addressing the issue of adoption. An adoptive parent can be everything a biological parent can be to a child, except a blood relative. Lack of genetic links creates experiences of loss among all members of the adoption triad. Loving support and discipline can ameliorate the long-term effects of absent biological ties.

The report "Bringing Up Father" concerns the changing roles of fathers in the family unit. It presents a positive image of the new father assisting with all aspects of child rearing.

Next, two articles in the family subsection speak about sibling relationships. One calls for more research on ten-

Emotional intelligence (EQ) is believed to promote the human ability to successfully cope with challenges. "Alienation and the Four Worlds of Childhood" discusses children's need to identify with family, peers, school, and work. Next, David Elkind's article discusses children's needs to cope with threats to family, peer, school, and work stability. Child pornography, violence, AIDS, unemployment, and other maledictions can create culture shock and contribute to feelings of insecurity and anxiety in children. "The Miracle of Resiliency" discusses the impact of divorce on children. Children can be helped to cope with this event and emerge relatively unscathed. The next selection, "Televised Violence and Kids: A Public Health Problem?" calls for a reduction in the violence being programmed on television. It is difficult for children to cope with such a day-after-day, pervasive, and unrelenting influence. The final unit article clarifies what melanin (dark pigments in skin, hair, and brain) contributes to human anatomy and physiology. Skin and brain melanin differ. Both have positive physiological effects, but skin melanin can have negative psychological effects if a cultural group denigrates it.

sion-free kinship with siblings. "Sibling Connections" points out the profound social and emotional influence brothers and sisters can have on each other. The other article addresses the relationships of stepsiblings to each other. Bebe Moore Campbell, in her report "Yours, Mine, and Ours," gives a dozen ways to help blended families (stepparents, stepchildren, stepsiblings) interact more positively.

The next two articles in the family section present the opposite dimensions of touch: abusive touch and tender, loving touch. While child maltreatment has long-lasting negative effects, the ameliorative effects of cuddling, hugging, kissing, gentle patting, and squeezing are legion. The tender touch needs to be encouraged within family units. The difference between good touching (comfortable) and bad touching (uncomfortable) needs to be clearly distinguished.

Six articles have been included in this unit to clarify the changing cultural climates of children's worlds. Nancy Gibbs, in "The EQ Factor," presents recent brain research that suggests that emotions, not the traditional IQ rating, may be the truest measure of intelligence.

Looking Ahead: Challenge Questions

What is the effect of adoption on biological parents, the adopted child, and adoptive parents?

What description is emerging of fathers in the 1990s?

What description is emerging of siblings in the 1990s?

How can blended families with stepparents, stepchildren, and stepsiblings create a healthy, happy home atmosphere?

In what ways does child maltreatment impact development throughout the life span?

In what ways does tender, loving touch impact on development throughout the life span?

What are the four "worlds" of childhood, and how do they relate to alienation?

Why do today's children cry?

How can parents ameliorate the effects of divorce on children?

How much television violence is too much?

What are the physiological and psychological effects of skin melanin and of brain melanin? Are they related?

The Lifelong Impact of ADOPTION

In many cases, birthparents have trouble dealing with giving up their offspring; adoptees want to know more about their biological roots and genetic history; and adoptive parents are being confronted with issues concerning the raising of their adopted children that no one had warned them about.

Marlou Russell

Dr. Russell is a clinical psychologist in private practice in Santa Monica, Calif., specializing in adoption. She is an adoptee who has been reunited with her birthmother and two brothers.

IMAGINE BEING an adoptive parent who has gone through years of infertility treatment. You recently have adopted an infant and are at a party with it. Someone exclaims, "What a cute baby. Why, I didn't even know you were pregnant!" You wonder if you need to explain.

Now, try to imagine being a birthmother who relinquished a child 25 years ago. You since have married and had two more offspring. You strike up a conversation with someone you've just met. She asks, "How many children do you have?" You hesitate for a moment, then answer, "Two."

Finally, imagine that you were adopted as an infant. You have an appointment to see a new physician for the first time. When you arrive at the office, you are given a two-page form asking for your medical history. When you meet the doctor, he asks, "Does cancer run in your family?" You respond, "I don't know."

The adoption triad has three elements: the adoptive parent or parents, the birthparents, and the adoptee. All members are necessary and all depend on each other, as in any triangle.

There have been many changes in adoption over the years. The basic premise of adoption in the past was that it was a viable solution to certain problem situations. The infertile parents wanted a child; a birthparent was pregnant and unable to raise her offspring; and the infant needed available parents. It was thought that all the triad members would get their needs met by adoption. The records were amended, sealed, and closed through legal proceedings, and the triad members were expected never to see each other again.

It was discovered, however, that there were problems with closed adoption. Some birthparents began having trouble "forgetting" that they had had a child and were finding it hard "getting on with their lives," as suggested by those around them. There were adoptees who wanted to know more about their biological roots and had questions about their genetic history. Some adoptive parents were having difficulties raising their adopted children and were being confronted with parenting issues that no one had told them about.

Clinicians and psychotherapists became involved because more and more adopted children were being brought in for psychotherapy and being seen in juvenile detention facilities, inpatient treatment centers, and special schools. Questions began to be raised about the impact and process of closed adoption.

From these questions, it became clear that there are new basic tenets in adoption. One is that adoption usually is a second choice for all the triad members. For example, most people don't imagine that they will grow up, get married, and adopt children. They expect that they will grow up, get married, and have kids of their own. Girls and/or women also don't expect to get pregnant and give their child to strangers to raise.

Coping with loss

A second basic tenet of adoption is that it involves loss for all involved. A birthparent loses a child; the adoptee loses biological connections; and infertile adoptive parents lose the hope for biological children. Those indirectly involved in adoption also experience loss. The birthparents' parents lose a grandchild, while the siblings of the birthparent lose a niece or nephew.

Since loss is such a major part of adoption, grieving is a necessary and important process. The five stages of normal grief and mourning, as set forth by psychologist

Elisabeth Kübler-Ross, are denial—feeling shocked, numbed, and detached; anger—maintaining that the situation is unfair; bargaining—wanting to make a deal or trade-off; depression—feeling helpless and hopeless; and acceptance—integrating and resolving the loss enough to function.

For triad members, grief holds a special significance. They may not even be aware that they are grieving or mourning their loss. Adoption can create a situation where grieving is delayed or denied. Because adoption has been seen as such a positive solution, it may be difficult for a triad member to feel that it is okay to grieve when everything is "working out for the best."

There are no rituals or ceremonies for the loss of adoption. In the case of death, society provides the rituals of funerals and the gathering of people to support the person who is mourning. If the adoption process is secret, as was the case in many adoptions of the past, there is even less opportunity for mourning. In addition, with adoption, much attention is given to the next step of raising the child or getting on with one's life.

Some triad members resolve their grief by trying to find the person they are grieving for. Search and reunion offers the opportunity to address the basic and natural curiosity that all people have in their inheritance and roots. The missing pieces can be put in the puzzle, and lifelong questions can be answered. In addition, there is an empowering aspect to search and reunion and an internal sense of timing that brings with it a feeling of being in control and trusting one's own judgment. For most people who search, knowing—even if they find uncomfortable information—is better than not knowing.

Whether someone actively searches or not, there usually is some part of the person that is searching internally. A common experience among adoptees and birthparents is scanning crowds, looking for someone who could be their parent or their child. Even triad members who say they aren't interested in seeking will express curiosity and react to the idea of search and reunion.

What holds many triad members back from searching or admitting they are doing so is the fear of causing pain to one of the other triad members. Adoptees may worry about hurting their adoptive parents' feelings and appearing to be ungrateful, while birthparents may be concerned that their child wasn't told of the adoption or that he or she will reject them.

Reunion between triad members is the beginning of a previous relationship. It is where fantasy meets reality. Reunions impact all triad members and those close to them. As with other relationships, there has to be nurturing, attention, and a respect for people's boundaries and needs. Reunions and the interactions within them show that adoption was not just a simple solution, but a process that has lifelong impact.

BRINGING UP FATHER

The message dads get is that they are not up to the job. And a record number don't stick around—even as fathers are needed more than ever.

NANCY R. GIBBS

"I don't have a dad," says Megan, 8, a tiny blond child with a pixie nose who gazes up at a visitor and talks of her hunger. "Well, I do have a dad, but I don't know his name. I only know his first name, Bill."

Just what is it that fathers do?

"Love you. They kiss you and hug you when you need them. I had my mom's boyfriend for a while, but they broke up." Now Megan lives with just her mother and older brother in Culver City, California.

What would you like to do with your dad?

"I'd want him to talk to me." She's hurting now. "I wish I had somebody to talk to. It's not fair. If two people made you, then you should still be with those two people." And she's sad. "I'm not so special," she says, looking down at the floor. "I don't have two people."

She imagines what it would be like for him to come home from work at night.

"It would be just like that commercial where the kids say, 'Daddy, are you all right?' " She smiles, dreaming. "The kids show the daddy that they care for him. They put a thermometer in his mouth. They think he's sick because he came home early. They are sitting on the couch watching TV, and it's like, wow, we can play with Dad!".

Megan thinks her father is in the Navy now. "One day when I get older, I'm gonna go back to Alabama and try to find him."

More children will go to sleep tonight in a fatherless home than ever in the nation's history. Talk to the experts in crime, drug abuse, depression, school failure, and they can point to some study somewhere blaming those problems on the disappearance of fathers from the American family. But talk to the fathers who do stay with their families, and the story grows more complicated. What they are hearing, from their bosses, from institutions, from the culture around them, even from their own wives, very often comes down to a devastating message: We don't really trust men to be parents, and we don't really need them to be. And so every day, everywhere, their children are growing up without them.

Corporate America, for a start, may praise family life but does virtually nothing to ease it. Managers still take male workers aside and warn them not to take a paternity leave if they want to be taken seriously. On TV and in movies and magazine ads, the image of fathers over the past generation evolved from the stern, sturdy father who knew best to a helpless Homer Simpson, or some ham-handed galoot confounded by the prospect of changing a diaper. Teachers call parent conferences but only talk to the mothers. When father arrives at the doctor's office with little Betsy, the pediatrician offers instructions to pass along to his wife, the caregiver presumptive. The Census Bureau can document the 70 million mothers age 15 or older in the U.S. but has scant idea how many fathers there are. "There's no interest in fathers at all," says sociologist Vaughn Call, who directs the National Survey of Families and Households at the University of Wisconsin. "It's a nonexistent category. It's the ignored half of the family."

Mothers themselves can be unwitting accomplices. Even women whose own progress in public life depends on sharing the workload in private life act as "gatekeepers" in the home, to use Harvard pediatrician T. Berry Brazelton's description. Dig deeply into household dynamics, and the tensions emerge. Women say they need and want their husbands to be more active parents but fear that they aren't always reliable. Men say they might like to be more involved, but their wives will not make room for them, and jealously guard their domestic power.

Most troubling of all to some social scientists is the message men get that being a good father means learning how to mother. Among child-rearing experts, the debate rages over whether men and women parent differently, whether there is some unique contribution that each makes to the emotional health of their children. "Society sends men two messages," says psychologist Jerrold Lee Shapiro, father of two and the author of *A Measure of the Man,* his third book on fatherhood. "The first is, We want you to be involved, but you'll be an inadequate mother. The second is, You're invited into the birthing room and into the nurturing process—but we don't want all of you. We only want your support. We're not really ready as a culture to accept men's fears, their anger or their sadness. This is the stuff that makes men crazy. We want men to be the protectors and providers, but we are scared they won't be if they become soft."

So now America finds its stereotypes crushed in the collision between private needs and public pressures. While some commend the nurturing nature of the idealized New Father, others cringe at the idea

From *Time,* June 28, 1993, pp. 52-56, 58, 61. © 1993 by Time Inc. Magazine Company. Reprinted by permission.

of genderless parenting and defend the importance of men being more than pale imitations of mothers. "If you become Mr. Mom," says Shapiro, "the family has a mother and an assistant mother. That isn't what good fathers are doing today." And fathers themselves wrestle with memories of their own fathers, vowing to do it differently, and struggling to figure out how.

THE DISAPPEARING DAD

Well into the 18th century, child-rearing manuals in America were generally addressed to fathers, not mothers. But as industrialization began to separate home and work, fathers could not be in both places at once. Family life of the 19th century was defined by what historians call the feminization of the domestic sphere and the marginalization of the father as a parent. By the 1830s, child-rearing manuals, increasingly addressed to mothers, deplored the father's absence from the home. In 1900 one worried observer could describe "the suburban husband and father" as "almost entirely a Sunday institution."

What alarms modern social scientists is that in the latter part of this century the father has been sidelined in a new, more disturbing way. Today he's often just plain absent. Rising divorce rates and out-of-wedlock births mean that more than 40% of all children born between 1970 and 1984 are likely to spend much of their childhood living in single-parent homes. In 1990, 25% were living with only their mothers, compared with 5% in 1960. Says David Blankenhorn, the founder of the Institute for American Values in New York City: "This trend of fatherlessness is the most socially consequential family trend of our generation."

Credit Dan Quayle for enduring the ridicule that opened the mainstream debate over whether fathers matter in families. In the year since his famous Murphy Brown speech, social scientists have produced mounting evidence that, at the very least, he had a point. Apart from the personal politics of parenting, there are larger social costs to reckon in a society that dismisses fathers as luxuries.

Studies of young criminals have found that more than 70% of all juveniles in state reform institutions come from fatherless homes. Children from broken families are nearly twice as likely as those in two-parent families to drop out of high school. After assessing the studies, economist Sylvia Hewlett suggested that "school failure may well have as much to do with disintegration of families as with the quality of schools."

Then there is the emotional price that children pay. In her 15 years tracking the lives of children of divorced families, Judith Wallerstein found that five years af-

ter the split, more than a third experienced moderate or severe depression. After 10 years a significant number of the young men and women appeared to be troubled, drifting and underachieving. At 15 years many of the thirtyish adults were struggling to create strong love relationships of their own. Daughters of divorce, she found, "often experience great difficulty establishing a realistic view of men in general, developing realistic expectations and exercising good judgment in their choice of partners."

For boys, the crucial issue is role modeling. There are psychologists who suggest that boys without fathers risk growing up with low self-esteem, becoming overly dependent on women and emotionally rigid. "Kids without fathers are forced to find their own ways of doing things," observes Melissa Manning, a social worker at the Boys and Girls Club of Venice, Cali-

It Takes Two

WOMEN'S VOICES ARE MORE SOOTHING. THEY CAN READ THE SIGNALS A CHILD SENDS BEFORE HE OR SHE CAN TALK. BUT AS TIME PASSES, THE STRENGTHS THAT FATHERS MAY BRING TO CHILD REARING BECOME MORE IMPORTANT.

fornia. "So they come up with their own ideas, from friends and from the gangs. Nobody is showing them what to do except to be drunk, deal drugs or go to jail." Then there are the subtler lessons that dads impart. Attorney Charles Firestone, for instance, recently decided it was time to teach his 11-year-old son how to play poker. "Maybe it will help if he knows when to hold 'em, when to fold 'em," he says.

THE ANTI-FATHER MESSAGE

Given the evidence that men are so vital to a healthy home, the anti-father messages that creep into the culture and its institutions are all the more troubling. Some scholars suggest that fatherhood is by its very biological nature more fragile than motherhood, and needs to be encouraged by the society around it. And yet for all the focus on the New Father (the kind who skips the corporate awards dinner to attend the school play), the messages men receive about how

they should act as parents are at best mixed and often explicitly hostile.

Employers that have been slow to accommodate the needs of mothers in their midst are often even more unforgiving of fathers. It is a powerful taboo that prevents men from acknowledging their commitment to their children at work. A 1989 survey of medium and large private employers found that only 1% of employees had access to paid paternity leave and just 18% could take unpaid leave. Even in companies like Eastman Kodak, only 7% of men, vs. 93% of women, have taken advantage of the six-year-old family-leave plan.

Those who do soon discover the cost. "My boss made me pay a price for it emotionally," says a prominent Washington executive who took leaves for both his children. "He was very generous with the time, but he never let me forget it. Every six seconds he reminded me what a great guy he was and that I owed him really, really big. You don't get a lot of points at the office for wanting to have a healthy family life." Men, like women, are increasingly troubled by the struggle to balance home and work; in 1989, asked if they experienced stress while doing so, 72% of men answered yes, compared with 12% a decade earlier, according to James Levine of the Fatherhood Project at the Families and Work Institute of New York City.

Many men will freely admit that they sometimes lie to employers about their commitments. "I announced that I was going to a meeting," shrugged a Washington journalist as he left the office in midafternoon one day recently. "I just neglected to mention that the 'meeting' was to watch my daughter play tennis." Now it is the fathers who are beginning to ask themselves whether their careers will stall and their incomes stagnate, whether the glass ceiling will press down on them once they make public their commitment as parents, whether today's productivity pressures will force them to work even harder with that much less time to be with their kids. In the higher reaches of management, there are not only few women, there are also few men in dual-income families who take an active part in raising their children. "Those who get to the top today," says Charles Rodgers, owner of a 10-year-old family-research organization in Brookline, Massachusetts, called Work/Family Directions, "are almost always men from what used to be the traditional family, men with wives who don't work outside the home."

Many men insist that they long to veer off onto a "daddy track." In a 1990 poll by the Los Angeles *Times,* 39% of the fathers said they would quit their jobs to have more time with their kids, while another survey found that 74% of men said they would rather have a daddy-track job than a fast-track job. But in real life, when they are not talking to pollsters, some fathers recognize the power of their atavistic impulses to earn bread and compete, both of which often leave them ambivalent about their obligations as fathers.

George Ingram, 48, lives on Capitol Hill with his sons Mason, 15, and Andrew, 10. He is the first to admit that single fatherhood has not helped his career as a political economist. "We're torn between working hard to become Secretary of State and nurturing our kids," he says. "You make the choice to nurture your kids, and people think it's great. But does it put a crimp on your career? Yes, very definitely. When I finish this process, I will have spent 15 years on a professional plateau." Ingram finds that his colleagues accept his dual commitments, his leaving every night before 6, or by 5 if he has a soccer practice to coach. In fact they are more accepting of his choices than those of his female colleagues. "I get more psychic support than women do," he says. "And I feel great about spending more time with my kids than my father did."

MATERNAL GATEKEEPERS

The more surprising obstacle men say, arises in their own homes. Every household may be different, every division of labor unique, but sociologists do find certain patterns emerging when they interview groups of men and women about how they view one another's parenting roles. Men talk about their wife's unrealistic expectations, her perfectionism, the insistence on dressing, feeding, soothing the children in a certain way. "Fathers, except in rare circumstances, have not yet become equal partners in parenthood," says Frank Furstenberg, professor of sociology at the University of Pennsylvania. "The restructuring of the father role requires support and encouragement from wives. Presumably, it is not abnormal for wives to be reluctant to give up maternal prerogatives."

Many men describe in frustration their wife's attitude that her way of doing things is the only way. "Dad is putting the baby to bed," says Levine. "He's holding his seven-month-old on his shoulders and walking around in circles. Mom comes in and says, 'She likes it better when you just lay her down on her stomach and rub her back.' Dad gets mad that Mom is undermining his way of doing things, which he thinks works perfectly well."

In most cases, it is still the mother who carries her child's life around in her head, keeping the mental daybook on who needs a lift to piano practice and who needs to get the poetry folder in on time. After examining much of the research on men's housework and child care, Sylvia Hewlett concluded that married men's average time in household tasks had increased only 6% in 20 years, even as women have flooded the workplace. Psychologists Rosalind Barnett and Grace Baruch found that fathers were often willing to perform the jobs they were assigned but were not responsible for remembering, planning or scheduling them.

Women often respond that until men prove themselves dependable as parents, they can't expect to be trusted. A haphazard approach to family responsibilities does nothing to relieve the burdens women carry. "Men haven't been socialized to think about family appointments and how the household runs for kids," notes Marie Wilson of the Ms. Foundation for Women, who constantly hears of the hunger women feel for their husbands to participate more fully at home. "They don't really get in there and pay attention. Mothers often aren't sure they can trust them—not just to do it as they do it, but to do it at a level that you can get away with without feeling guilty."

Some women admit that their own feelings are mixed when it comes to relinquishing power within the family. "I can probably be overbearing at times as far as wanting to have it my way," says the 35-year-old wife of a St. Louis, Missouri, physician. "But I would be willing to relax my standards if he would be more involved. It would be a good trade-off." Here again the attitude is changing with each generation. Women under 35, researchers find, seem more willing than older women, whose own fathers were probably less engaged, to trust men as parents. Also, as younger women become more successful professionally, they are less fearful of relinquishing power at home because their identity and satisfaction come from many sources.

THE NEW FATHER

The redefinition of fatherhood has been going on in virtually every arena of American life for well over 20 years. As women worked to broaden their choices at home and work, the implicit invitation was for men to do likewise. As Levine has observed, Dr. Spock had carefully revised his advice on fathers by 1974. The earlier version suggested that fathers change the occasional diaper and cautioned mothers about "trying to force the participation of fathers who get gooseflesh at the very idea of helping to take care of a baby." The new version of *Baby and Child Care*, by contrast, offered a prescription for the New Fatherhood: "The father—any father—should be sharing with the mother the day-to-day care of their child from birth onward . . . This is the natural way for the father to start the relationship, just as it is for the mother."

By the '80s, bookstores were growing fat with titles aimed at men: *How to Father,* *Expectant Father, Pregnant Fathers, The Birth of a Father, Fathers Almanac* and *Father Power.* There were books about child-and-father relations, like *How to Father a Successful Daughter,* and then specific texts for part-time fathers, single fathers, stepfathers and homosexual fathers. Bill Cosby's *Fatherhood* was one of the best-selling books in publishing history, and *Good Morning, Merry Sunshine,* by Chicago *Tribune* columnist Bob Greene, a journal about his first year of fatherhood, was on the New York *Times* best-seller list for almost a year. Parents can now pick up *Parents' Sports,* a new magazine dedicated to reaching the dad market with stories on the joys of soccer practice.

Institutions were changing too. In his book *Fatherhood in America,* published this month, Robert L. Griswold has traced the history of a fast-changing role that today not only allows men in the birthing room (90% of fathers are in attendance at their child's birth) but also offers them

Mixed Emotions

"WE'RE NOT READY TO ACCEPT MEN'S FEARS . . . OR THEIR SADNESS. WE WANT MEN TO BE THE PROTECTORS . . . BUT WE ARE SCARED THEY WON'T BE IF THEY BECOME SOFT."

postpartum courses in which new fathers learn how to change, feed, hold and generally take care of their infant. Some fathers may even get in on the pregnancy part by wearing the "empathy belly," a bulge the size and weight of a third-trimester fetus. Suddenly available to men hoping to solidify the father-child bond are "Saturday with Daddy Outings," special songfests, field trips and potlucks with dads. Even men behind bars could get help: one program allows an inmate father to read children's stories onto cassette tapes that are then sent, along with the book and a Polaroid picture of Dad, to his child.

"It's become cool to be a dad," says Wyatt Andrews, a correspondent for CBS News who has three children: Rachel, 8, Averil, 7, and Conrad, 5. "Even at dinner parties, disciplinary techniques are discussed. Fathers with teenagers give advice about strategies to fathers with younger kids. My father was career Navy. I don't think he ever spent two seconds thinking about strategies of child rearing. If he said anything, it was 'They listen to me.' "

BRING BACK DAD

These perceptual and behavioral shifts have achieved enough momentum to trigger a backlash of their own. Critics of the New Fatherhood are concerned that something precious is being lost in the revolution in parenting—some uniquely male contribution that is essential for raising healthy kids. In a clinical argument that sends off political steam, these researchers argue that fathers should be more than substitute mothers, that men parent differently than women and in ways that matter enormously. They say a mother's love is unconditional, a father's love is more qualified, more tied to performance; mothers are worried about the infant's survival, fathers about future success. "In other words, a father produces not just children but socially viable children," says Blankenhorn. "Fathers, more than mothers, are haunted by the fear that their children will turn out to be bums, largely because a father understands that his child's character is, in some sense, a measure of his character as well."

When it comes to discipline, according to this school of thought, it is the combination of mother and father that yields justice tempered by mercy. "Mothers discipline children on a moment-by-moment basis," says Shapiro. "They have this emotional umbilical cord that lets them read the child. Fathers discipline by rules. Kids learn from their moms how to be aware of their emotional side. From dad, they learn how to live in society."

As parents, some psychologists argue, men and women are suited for different roles at different times. The image of the New Fatherhood is Jack Nicholson surrounded by babies on the cover of *Vanity Fair,* the businessman changing a diaper on the newly installed changing tables in an airport men's room. But to focus only on infant care misses the larger point. "Parenting of young infants is not a natural activity for males," says David Popenoe, an associate dean of social studies at Rutgers University who specializes in the family. He and others argue that women's voices are more soothing; they are better able to read the signals a child sends before he or she can talk. But as time passes, the strengths that fathers may bring to child rearing become more important.

"At a time when fatherhood is collapsing in our society," warns Blankenhorn, "when more children than ever in history are being voluntarily abandoned by their fathers, the only thing we can think of talking about is infant care? It's an anemic, adult-centered way of looking at the problem." Why not let mothers, he says, do more of the heavy lifting in the early years and let fathers do more of the heavy lifting after infancy when their special skills have more relevance? As children get older, notes William Maddox, director of research and policy at the Washington-based Family Research Council, fathers become crucial in their physical and psychological development. "Go to a park and watch father and mother next to a child on a jungle gym," he said. "The father encourages the kid to challenge himself by climbing to the top; the mother tells him to be careful. What's most important is to have the balance of encouragement along with a warning."

This notion that men and women are genetically, or even culturally, predisposed to different parenting roles strikes other researchers as misguided. They are quick to reject the idea that there is some link between X or Y chromosomes and, say, conditional or unconditional love. "To take something that is only a statistical tendency," says historian E. Anthony Rotundo, "and turn it into a cultural imperative—fathers must do it this way and mothers must do it that way—only creates problems for the vast number of people who don't fit those tendencies, without benefiting the children at all." While researchers have found that children whose fathers are involved in their early rearing tend to have higher IQs, perform better in school and even have a better sense of humor, psychologists are quick to say this is not necessarily a gender issue. "It has to do with the fact that there are two people passionately in love with a child," says Harvard's Brazelton.

The very fact that psychologists are arguing about the nature of fatherhood, that filmmakers are making movies based entirely on fatherlove, that bookstores see a growth market in father guides speaks not only to children's well-being but to men's as well. As much as families need fathers, men need their children in ways they are finally allowed to acknowledge, to learn from them all the secrets that children, with their untidy minds and unflagging hearts, have mastered and that grownups, having grown up, long to retrieve.

—Reported by Ann Blackman/Washington, Priscilla Painton/New York and James Willwerth/Los Angeles

Sibling connections

That most vital but overlooked of relationships

Laura M. Markowitz

The Family Therapy Networker

We agonize over ups and downs with our parents, spouses, and children, but mostly ignore one of our first and most primal bonds—our relationships with our brothers and sisters.

Whether as adults we find those relationships harmonious, acrimonious, or somewhere in between, we discount them at our peril. For the sibling bond is powerful, providing us with connection, validation, and belonging like no other.

Brothers and sisters push buttons you'd forgotten you had, never forget old humiliations and painful nicknames, never let you grow up. They share your obscure, ancient memories of car trips and long-dead pets, know just what you mean about Mom and Dad, and can make you laugh so hard you cry.

To understand the potent cocktail of anger, love, competitiveness, and protectiveness that is the sibling bond is ultimately to come closer to understanding ourselves. Not that understanding always leads to trouble-free friendship. Indeed, achieving tension-free kinship with a sibling is probably impossible, since ambivalence seems to be the most natural state of the relationship. But coming

to know why no one else can make you feel more empathy, anger, or delight than those earliest companions provides a useful insight. May it also lead to a closer bond.

At first, the case appeared to have nothing at all to do with siblings. Alice, a 40-year-old journalist and single mother, came in with her only child, 18-year-old Becky, who had threatened to run away form home because "my mom is like a prison warden." Becky told the therapist, Syracuse University doctoral student Tracy Laszloffy, that she would go live with her Aunt Tess, who had told her she was always welcome. This was her trump card, and it had the desired effect: Her mother's eyes narrowed in anger. "I always knew she'd do something like this to get even with me," said Alice.

"Why do you think Becky wants to get even with you?" the therapist asked.

"Not Becky," explained Alice. "Tess! My older sister always hated me and has never let me forget that when I was born, she had to take care of me.

For there is no friend like a sister In calm or stormy weather; To cheer one on the tedious way, To fetch one if one goes astray, To lift one if one totters down, To strengthen whilst one stands.
—Christina Rossetti

From *Utne Reader,* May/June 1994, pp. 50-62. Excerpted from *Family Therapy Networker,* January/February 1994. © 1994 by Laura M. Markowitz. Reprinted by permission.

She's always making me pay for that. Now she wants to steal my daughter away!"

Laszloffy helped Alice and Becky find a compromise for their most pressing problems—Becky's demand to be allowed to go to unsupervised parties and Alice's insistence that Becky get better grades. Despite Becky's description of her mother as harsh, it became evident that Alice vacillated between the conflicting roles of parent and peer. Laszloffy felt that the real work for this family needed to happen elsewhere. She decided that including Tess in a session might be the key, and her hunch was confirmed when Alice flinched at the suggestion. "Why her? She already knows I'm a screwup." She agreed, however, for Becky's sake.

From the first moment the sisters walked in—Tess a matronly 50-year-old woman in sensible shoes, and Alice looking fashionable in a mini-skirt—it was clear their relationship organized the way they thought about themselves. The sisters immediately began to compare themselves to each other: "She was always the creative one," said Tess. "I never had any real talent, except for making pot roast."

"Yeah, but you were also the good daughter, the one everyone approved of," countered Alice. Tess bristled. Was Alice mocking her for being a stay-at-home mom and housewife?

"I feel judged by Alice constantly," Tess said. "I have arguments with her in my head while I'm vacuuming about who has it better, me or her." She admitted that she did sometimes have regrets about her life, but said she never felt comfortable letting down her guard with her sister.

"I guess I feel threatened when Tess isn't her usual confident and bossy self," Alice said. "It's like a balance we have. One of us is the caretaker, one of us is the. . . . Well, I'm used to being the one who needs taking care of. I'm not sure I'd know what to do if she needed my advice, or help."

The next session began with the sisters reporting on a lunch that week that had ended with a big fight over their memories of their mother. Tess had recalled her as a cold, disengaged woman wrapped up in her own problems; Alice remembered her as being affectionate to the point of being stifling. Laszloffy explained that no siblings grow up in the same family—the emotional, economic, and even physical circumstances of the family are distinct for each child, and the parents often respond differently to each. Tess looked irritated, unused to relinquishing her right, as eldest, to define the way things were. Alice said she felt guilty that she had gotten the "nice" mother while Tess had gotten the "mean" one.

"So why did you run away from home, if Mom was so loving and caring?" Tess asked her sister, referring to the year when 18-year-old Alice dropped out of high school three weeks before graduation and moved to California.

"To get away from her! She was *too* loving; it was suffocating me!" Alice said, frustrated that her sister needed to be told the obvious.

Tess's mouth dropped open. "I thought you ran away because you were mad at me for leaving you at home with Mom when I got married and had kids of my own."

"No! In fact, I was trying to get out of your hair so you wouldn't have to keep taking care of me, because I knew you hated that—and hated me because of it," Alice choked on the last words, tears welling up.

"I never hated you," Tess said softly. "What ever gave you that idea?"

Alice blew her nose. "I'll never forget the time when I was 5, you were 15, and you were supposed to take me to the playground. You

The parent-child bond has been under the microscope, yet sibling connections have been largely ignored.

yelled at Mom that you hated me and wanted to go out with your friends. Then you left." Alice, with her tear-streaked face and forlorn expression, looked like the abandoned little girl she was describing.

Tess had no memory of the incident Alice was talking about. Of course there had been moments she resented having to take care of her baby sister, but most of the time she loved and cherished Alice. "Why do you think I rushed ahead to have babies of my own?" Tess asked her. "Because you had been the best thing in my life, and I wanted to have kids just like you." For the first time in 35 years, Alice could hear the love in her sister's voice.

"I've wanted to be close to you for a long time, but you kept pushing me away," said Tess. "I could never figure out what I had done to make you hate me—hate me so much that you don't even want Becky to visit me." Now Tess was crying too.

"Why didn't we ever talk about this stuff before?" Alice wondered. "We've wasted so much time being mad at things that never really happened the way we thought they did."

They also had spent a lot of time frozen in roles that no longer fit them as adults. In therapy, Alice learned that she could be more of an adult with and parent to Becky without turning into her sister. Tess began to accept that she wasn't as stuck in her life as she imagined. As if they were unfolding a map and seeing a multitude of possible roads to take, each of the sisters could now see herself as more than simply the other's road not taken.

Clearly, the sibling relationship was the pivotal factor in this case, yet there was little in her training to lead Laszloffy—or most family therapists—to consider siblings as a point of leverage. Mental health practitioners have spent a century putting the parent-child bond and marital relationship under the microscope, yet sibling connections have been largely ignored. "My pet peeve with the field is that when we say

'family of origin,' most of us really mean parent-child relationships, which is a very limited and linear view of family that derives from our rigidly hierarchical way of seeing the world," says Ken Hardy, professor of family therapy at Syracuse University.

Laszloffy's case is striking because the intensity between the siblings lay close to the surface. Most of us respond to our brothers and sisters with subtler rumblings, having long ago learned to bury powerful emotions in order to survive years of living with them—resentment at having been an easy target of a sibling's anger; longing for closeness masked by habitual guardedness; hidden desires for attention, approval, vindication. As adults, we still may wish our siblings would apologize for past hurts, abandonments, humiliations; we still may feel responsible for them, afraid for them, stuck with them.

Normally articulate and insightful people grow tongue-tied when it comes to describing their relationships with their siblings. Writers of books about siblings struggle to manufacture encompass-

Only children

Is it really so bad to grow up without sibs?

AT 14 I LEARNED A LESSON THAT MOST KIDS master well before their age hits double digits. When a boy who'd taunted me all through junior high asked me to sign his yearbook, I thought it was a trick—I knew he hated me; he'd been my tormentor for years. So of course I refused. To my surprise, his genuinely quizzical look told me that the request had been sincere.

It was an understandable mistake on my part, though. Most of the kids I knew had learned how to tease and be teased much earlier in life than I finally did. That's because they all had something I lacked: siblings.

As the only child in my family, I grew up with no one to make faces at me, slam me against the wall, steal my hair ribbon, or frighten me with rubber bugs. My parents may have had a bad day now and then, but hey, they never hid

my math book or called me "bunnyface." How was I to know that most kids deal with such treatment every day of their lives?

This lack of sibling savvy made me more sensitive than most of my peers, and maybe I didn't roll with the punches as easily as they did. But those appear to be about the worst effects the absence of brothers and sisters had on me. Otherwise, I grew up happy, made friends, did well in college, and married a great guy (who also happens to be an only child).

So what about the pervasive idea that all children without siblings are selfish, lonely, and spoiled? Well, according to nearly everyone who studies these things, the stereotypical attention-grabbing, foot-stamping, tantrum-throwing only child resides mainly in our collective imagination.

"Being an only child accounts

for no more than about 2 percent of the variants affecting personality and behavior," says Toni Falbo, a professor of sociology and educational psychology at the University of Texas at Austin. "The other 98 percent are determined by a host of more important factors: social class, gender, education, quality of parenting, and family members' physical and psychological health."

After reviewing almost 150 published studies and conducting her own research on the subject, Falbo—who's the country's leading authority on only children—has concluded that onlies are generally just as happy and well-adjusted as kids with siblings. What's more, the differences that do exist are frequently to the onlies' advantage. Only children tend to get slightly better grades, be more ambitious, earn more advanced acing theories about our connection to these people after we no longer have to wear their hand-me-downs, share a bedroom, or put up with their teasing. But there are no givens for what kind of relationships emerge between adult siblings. Some grow up to be one another's closest friends; others become like distant acquaintances, sharing nothing of their adult lives. Some continue to use their siblings as a compass point for measuring who they have become. Some consider each other ancient enemies to avoid, while others casually drift apart without concern. For every "truth" about siblings, the exact opposite also may be correct. Most of us are still trying to figure out who these familiar strangers are to us.

I n the beginning we orbit our parents like planets vying for the position closest to the sun. They are the primary source of light, warmth, and love, but we have to compete with omnipresent siblings who at times eclipse us, collide with us, and even, at odd moments,

awkwardly love us. In myth and literature, the bond between siblings is portrayed as far more ambivalent than the attachment between parents and children, dramatized in extremes of enmity and loyalty. In the Bible, the relationship between the first brothers, Cain and Abel, ended in fratricide. Joseph's brothers sold him into slavery in Egypt. In *King Lear,* Cordelia's older sisters outmaneuvered her to get their father's kingdom and delighted in her banishment. Still, Hansel took hold of Gretel's hand in the forest and promised to protect her; Joseph forgave his brothers and saved them during a deadly famine.

The seeds of enmity between siblings may be planted early: The introduction of a new child into the family is often experienced as an irretrievable loss by the older child. The trauma of being displaced by a younger sibling can turn into rage, envy, even hatred of the usurper. The earliest impulses to commit murder are felt in the young child who has been dethroned as centerpiece of the family. Therapists report cases in which older siblings tried to drown their younger

---

ademic degrees, and display greater self-esteem.

Then why the negative stereotype? Perhaps it's because most people don't have much firsthand experience with only children, who have traditionally been in short supply. A decade ago, just 10 percent of American women had had a single child by the end of their childbearing years. These days, however, that number has jumped to an all-time high of 17 percent—which means that one in six women will be the mother of an only child.

Despite their increasing numbers, Falbo notes that typecasting of only children persists. "The truth," she says, laughing, "is that last-born kids often act more spoiled than onlies do."

Perhaps the sharpest concern many one-child parents feel is that their kids will be lonely. "I did worry at first," admits Anita Daucunas of

Boulder, Colorado, who has a 5-year-old daugher. "But Jennifer is in school all day with other kids, and when she gets home she goes right out to play with the neighborhood children."

At the same time, onlies are often more comfortable playing by themselves. Sandra Lee Steadham of Dallas says that her daughter, 9-year-old Zoe, is outgoing but also enjoys spending time on her own. "For Zoe," she explains, "being alone isn't the same as being lonely."

Like any other type of family, single-child households do have trouble spots. For one thing, the parents of an only child have a tendency to be overly attentive, says Murray Kappelman, a professor of pediatrics and psychiatry at the University of Maryland. Too much concern about the child's health, for example, can encourage hypochondria. Performance

expectations that are too rigorous can create a heightened need for approval, and an overabundance of material rewards can give the child a bad case of the I wants.

"But those tendencies exist with most firstborns," Kappelman emphasizes, "not just with onlies." The fact is that *any* family size creates its own set of problems. There is no perfect number of children.

—*Katy Koontz*
Special Report

Excerpted with permission from Special Report *(March/April 1993). Subscriptions: $15/yr. (6 issues) from Special Report, Box 2191, Knoxville, TN 37901.*

brothers and sisters, or "helped" them have accidents near sharp objects or open windows.

Freud codified the notion of sibling rivalry, which was already widely accepted, saying it was natural that the introduction of a new sibling into a family would stir up envy, aggression, and competitiveness in the other siblings. But normalizing sibling rivalry created an expectation that brothers and sisters were destined to feel lifelong antagonism, resent one another's accomplishments, and envy one another's talents and privileges. Until recently, the phenomenon was believed to be so self-evident that no one bothered to challenge it. But are aggression and envy really the overarching emotions siblings have for one another? Recent feminist theorists suggest that Freud's theory was tainted by male bias. Siblings may not always be locked in mortal combat; interdependence and companionship are as much a part of siblinghood as competition and antagonism, says Laura Roberto, family therapy professor at Eastern Virginia Medical School. "Until we began to see how female development is also forged in affiliation and relationship, we tended to ignore these facets of the sibling bond." Feminists point to the lifelong friendship between many sisters who, increasingly outliving their male relations, may spend the last years of their lives together. This feminist challenge has given us a new lens for regarding both female and male sibling relationships, suggests family therapist Michael Kahn, co-author of *The Sibling Bond.* "Women are more interested in horizontal ties," says Kahn, "and are asking new kinds of questions like, 'What is lost when one sibling wins at another's expense?' "

Other critics point out that sibling rivalry isn't a primary force among siblings in other cultures; in some African societies, for example, one's greatest support, both material and emotional, comes not from one's parents but from one's siblings. Not all families in our society operate exclusively from Eurocentric values of individualism, points out Ken Hardy. For example, as a response to racism, African-American parents, brothers, and sisters often pour all their resources and energy into one child, who carries the family torch like a bright beacon into the institutions of mainstream success. "It is not uncommon to see an African-American family in which one brother is a surgeon or lawyer while the other siblings are locked into menial jobs or struggling with unemployment," he says. "The one who made it sends back money and helps the others, repays the debt."

To look only at the negative feelings of siblinghood is to forget how important we are to one another, how in a sense our siblings are as responsible for creating us as our parents are. All planets, though drawn to the sun, exert a pull on one another, shaping one another's course. "I

was the coddled one; he the witness of coddling," wrote novelist Vladimir Nabokov about his older brother, describing the natural complementarity that exists among siblings.

Our siblings are peers who share not only the same family, but also the same history and culture, not to mention a sizable chunk of our genetic material. Even among those with a significant age difference, siblings' personal histories intertwine so that there is no escaping a mutual influence. During a family therapy session, two adult sisters and their brother talk about how they were influenced by one another. "I learned to be the family entertainer because you and Mom were always fighting," says the brother to his older sister. "I hated the yelling, so I would try to make you both laugh. I still do that whenever I'm around conflict—try to defuse it."

"I think I wouldn't have been such a rebel if you two hadn't been such goody-goodies," says the younger sister. "You still compete with each other, like who's more successful or whose kids are the smartest. Since I was never in the running, I tried to do things neither of you did. Using a lot of drugs was a way to feel like I had something over both of you, like I was more mature or cool."

"I always felt so responsible for you two," says the older sister. "Mom would yell at me if you guys made a mess or got in a fight. I grew up believing that everyone else's problems come first, because other people are younger, smaller, more needy, or whatever. In my marriage, I kept on doing the same thing, putting his needs first because it was what I knew. And having kids just replicated what it was like to be the oldest sister. Since the divorce, I've been trying to figure out who takes care of me."

W hat exactly does it mean to be the product not only of one's parents, but also of one's siblings? How does it happen? The most elaborate theory of siblinghood concerns birth order. Although Freud said that "a child's position in the sequence of brothers and sisters is of very great significance for the course of his later life," the main work in the area of birth order has been done by Austrian-born family therapist Walter Toman, author of *Family Constellation: Its Effects on Personality and Social Behaviour.* Toman's basic assertion is that the order of one's birth determines certain personality characteristics that shape the choices we make and the likelihood of our success and even how we think about ourselves. Toman developed profiles of sibling positions, including only children, saying, for example, that older siblings tend to take on more responsibility and to be somewhat overcontrolling while only children are inclined to be loners, and women who are not fond of children tend to be youngest siblings.

I was the older brother. And when I was growing up I didn't like all those brothers and sisters. No kid likes to be the oldest.... But when they turn to you for help—what can you do? They kept me so busy caring for them that I had no time to become a junkie or an alcoholic.
—James Baldwin

The younger brother hath the more wit.
—English proverb

All happy families resemble one another, but each unhappy family is unhappy in its own way.
—Leo Tolstoy

But even without a highly schematized birth order theory about siblings, practitioners have described siblinghood as the first social laboratory, where we learn how to be a peer. Even when the fights make us cry, we are growing a thicker skin, which we need later on as adults; we learn that life doesn't always seem fair; we learn how to forgive. "After listening to my brother and sister hurl insults at each other one day, I was surprised to see them playing together the next morning as if nothing had happened," says a 40-year-old man. "It was a revelation to me that you could hate someone one day and forget about it the next."

It is possible that in siblinghood we experience more intensity of emotion than in any other relationship that follows. Our worlds are shoulder to shoulder, and our vulnerabilities are laid bare. "I've never loved or hated as intensely as I love and hate my brothers," says a 36-year-old youngest brother of six boys. With our siblings, we test the limits of tolerance and forgiveness more than we do in any other relationship. As long as the family provides an appropriate container for the intensity, siblings can benefit from the lessons.

Unless something goes dramatically wrong, as in sibling incest or sibling illness or death, our relationships with our brothers and sisters rarely take center stage in the therapy room. But increasingly, family therapists are discovering what a gold mine of information and support siblings can be. As inheritors of the same multigenerational legacy, albeit with different views of the family stories, they can often make a unique contribution to therapy. One family therapist was having a hard time with an 8-year-old boy who had set himself on fire twice because he believed his father hated him. The father was a large, impassive man who never looked at his son and spoke to him only when he had to. Hoping for some clue about why the father was so inaccessible, the therapist invited the father's younger brother to a session.

After the therapist outlined the situation, the younger brother turned to his nephew and asked him to wait in the next room. Then he said to his brother, the boy's father, "I remember right before Mom left him, Dad used to tell everyone you were someone else's bastard." The older brother looked numb, but the therapist sighed with relief. He finally understood what was going on under the surface of this family. His own father's rejection of him had left this father feeling confused about what fathers were supposed to say to sons. "He loved his child, but regarded his own silence as a way of protecting his son from the possibly abusive things that might come out of his mouth in anger," says the therapist. What the man was only dimly aware

of himself, his brother had been able to put his finger on immediately.

Family therapy also can help people get out of constraining roles with their siblings. Family-of-origin specialist Murray Bowen years ago described how he dramatically disentangled himself from a lifetime of emotional triangles with his siblings. He believed the family's ongoing emotional process was responsible for the legacy that Walter Toman attributed to birth order. Accordingly, Bowen reasoned that one ought to be able to go back and change the family's emotional process, which created and sustained sibling roles.

One Bowen-trained therapist treated a couple who were fighting about the husband's intrusive family. Lisa was fed up with hearing about her in-laws' problems and wanted Henry to separate himself from their incessant dramas. She was upset that he had loaned his irresponsible younger sister money and had become caught up in the ongoing fight between his older brother and their father. The constant phone calls from Henry's family were driving her crazy. When she drew their family diagram, the therapist says, "a million things seemed to jump out at me," particularly the multigenerational patterns of enmeshment in Henry's family and cutoffs in Lisa's, but the overwhelming fact was the contrast in the couple's birth positions: Henry was a middle child, Lisa an only child.

As an only child, Lisa was used to being the center of attention and didn't like competing with her brother- and sister-in-law. As a middle child, Henry was the family caretaker and peacekeeper, but he wasn't sure he wanted to keep the role. "If I wasn't in the middle of their lives, maybe I'd have more of a life of my own," he said.

The therapist coached Henry on how to develop more independence from his family. "The next time my brother called to complain about Dad, I told him I was sure he could work it out and changed the subject to football," says Henry. His sister called to cry over her latest investment flop, hinting that she needed another loan. "I told her she had a lot of experience pulling herself out of holes, and I was sure she would find a way to do it again," Henry recalls.

The therapist suggested that Lisa could help Henry remember that he was entitled to be the center of attention sometimes, too. During the next family gathering, Henry and Lisa both deliberately steered the conversation to Henry's latest project at work. "It was a surprise to realize that no one in my family knew much about me," says Henry. Changing his behavior shifted his relationship with his siblings, who became "much more respectful of my boundaries," almost timidly asking if it was all right to call, spending more time listening to Henry instead of talking at him.

> Our word *cad* originally meant a younger brother.
> —Bergen Evans

> A brother is born for adversity.
> —Proverbs 17:17

> Some uninformed newspapers printed: "Mrs. C.L. Lane, Sister of the Famous Comedian Will Rogers." They were greatly misinformed. It's the other way around. I am the brother of Mrs. C.L. Lane, the friend of humanity. . . . It was the proudest moment of my life that I was her brother.
> —Will Rogers, after the funeral of his sister Maud

One of the most wrenching issues that brings siblings to family therapy occurs at midlife, when they face the failing health of parents and need to make long-term decisions about their

In siblinghood we may experience more intense emotions than in any other relationship that follows.

care. It's extremely difficult for a family to have to acknowledge the demise of its elders, evoking buried fears of death and abandonment. Often, the grown children don't feel ready for the changing of the guard. "I look in the mirror and see an older, white-haired man, but inside I still feel 25 and way too young to become the older generation," says one therapist, whose elderly father recently came to live with him. "I look at his shrunken body and I can't help feeling repulsed. He used to be a strapping, handsome guy. Now the chronic pain from arthritis doesn't let him sleep. I have to feed him by hand as if he were a baby. It's very sad, and very surreal." Is this what will happen to us, siblings wonder?

Not only does the individual's relationship with the parent change dramatically as the older generation loses its authority, but the need to collaborate closely with a sibling, sometimes after 40 years of mutual alienation, can revive feelings of insecurity, competitiveness, and resentment. In the face of huge existential issues like death, some adult siblings find it is easier to fall back on picking on one another, feeding the illusion that they will be children forever instead of accepting terminal adulthood.

Boston family therapist David Treadway worked with three siblings in their 60s—an eminent jurist, a history professor, and a successful businesswoman. They were not interested in talking about the past, but needed a facilitator to help them come to an agreement about their aging mother.

"They didn't acknowledge that their struggle had anything to do with their childhood roles, but the roots of the conflict surfaced within the first 10 minutes," says Treadway. They found that they could not come to any agreement without first understanding the curse of each one's sibling position. After this exercise, they could begin the hard work of real negotiation and compromise.

In some families, a parent's death removes the force that holds siblings in their habitual orbits. The question then becomes, Will the brothers and sisters drift apart, finally dissolving the tenuous threads of connection? Most of the time siblings find the pull among them is strong enough to draw them into a new configuration. In a family of two brothers and two sisters, after the parents died no one came forward at first to organize family gatherings during the holidays. After spending the first Thanksgiving of their lives apart, they set up a rotation so they would each plan one holiday a year.

When adult siblings maintain their connection in later life, the relationship takes on a special importance because, as veterans of multiple losses—deaths, divorce, children moving away—they realize that no one else alive can remember the way it was when they were children. The parents' deaths may even open up a space for siblings to know each other for the first time without competitive friction. "I never really thought, 'Would I like this person if he were not my brother?'" says a 56-year-old therapist. "After our parents were gone, I found myself calling him up, and he'd call me. We enjoy each other's company now. It's comfortable in a way I don't feel with anyone else because we've known each other forever." It can be a sweet and unexpected discovery to realize that the people with whom one feels the most affinity and closeness after a lifetime of struggle or emotional distance are our own siblings.

Many of us take our siblings for granted. They simply are, as unavoidable as gravity. Even as adults, we may not have devoted much thought to figuring out how they fit into our lives and how they shaped us. There's something in us that resists giving our sibling relationships the credence and attention they deserve. Cherishing our adult autonomy and freedom, we strive to bury our childish vulnerabilities and reinvent ourselves, but our sibs get in the way.

The boy who was teased by the neighborhood kids and grows up to be a confident, successful businessman doesn't want to remember those days of hot tears and humiliation. He may feel uneasy in the presence of the older sister who remembers all too clearly a time he'd rather forget. In a sense, our siblings don't let us put the past behind us. "Every time I see you, I try to be open to the idea that you are a different person than the one I used to know," one brother told his sister. "But it's hard, because I know you so well."

In this knowledge is, perhaps, the paradox of the sibling relationship. Siblings are the living remnant of our past, a buffer against the loss of our own history, the deepest, oldest memories of us. But in these memories lies a terrible power:

I worry about people who get born nowadays because they get born into such tiny families— sometimes into no family at all. When you're the only pea in the pod, your parents are likely to get you confused with the Hope Diamond.
—Russell Baker

Relations are simply a tedious pack of people, who haven't got the remotest knowledge of how to live, nor the smallest instinct about when to die.
—Oscar Wilde

Our siblings hold up a mirror before us, forcing us to look at an image of ourselves that may be either comforting or devastating, perhaps evoking self-acceptance and pride, perhaps shame and humiliation.

There is a fateful perpetuity about sibling relationships: Our brothers and sisters will always be our contemporaries; we can't ever quite leave them. However convenient it would be, we can't consign them to irrelevancy. No wonder that when sibling relationships are bad, they leave deep, irreparable scars of bitterness, betrayal, and rage. No wonder that when they are good, they are a source of profound satisfaction, one of the best and most fulfilling of human ties. Whether our siblings are thorns in our side or balm for our wounds, they are fellow travelers who have witnessed our journey, living bridges between who we once were and who we have become.

Yours, Mine and Ours

*When your spouse comes with a ready-made family, here's how
to make stepparenting easier*

Bebe Moore Campbell

*Essence contributing writer Bebe Moore Campbell is the
stepmother of one and the mother of one.*

When Sharon and Wayne decided to get married after a
four-year courtship that included living together, they
thought they knew everything they needed to know
about each other in order to have a successful union. The
fact that each of them had an ex-spouse and children
(Wayne had a teenage son) didn't seem to matter much.
"I think we expected to be one big happy family overnight," Sharon says with a rueful smile. It didn't happen
quite that way.

"Soon after we married," Sharon continues, "whenever Wayne tried to discipline my son, David would
ignore him and act resentful. And when *his* kids came to
spend the weekend, their behavior was unacceptable to
me. They were loud and lacked self-control, but when I
reprimanded them, Wayne would tell me—in front of
them—that I was overreacting. So we'd have arguments."
Sharon pauses. "After a while I began to realize that I
didn't know how to be a stepmother *or* how to be married
for the second time."

Stepfamilies have been around for centuries, but the
circumstances have changed. Once, most remarriages
occurred after the death of a spouse. Today most second
marriages in the United States take place after divorce.
Remarriages that follow a divorce are complicated by the
human and material residue of former lives—children, ex-
spouses, former in-laws—as well as alimony and support
checks. But these unions can work, especially if you know
what to look out for. Here are some things to keep in
mind to help keep your stepfamily strong:

**Accept from the start the fact that if your divorced mate
has children, you are marrying a family.** "A prospective
stepmother must realize that she's marrying into an
important extension of the spouse. She has to put that
into her mental framework when she's judging the marriage's chances of success," says Dr. Frederick B. Phillips,
president and director of the Progressive Life Center in
Washington, D.C., which offers psychological counseling
for individuals and families. "The mate's family does
create issues, but it doesn't have to create problems."

Second wives or husbands often feel they don't come
first with their spouse because of his or her children.
Biological parents can help their mates see the acceptance
of their parental responsibilities as a positive step for the
entire family. "I used to be a little jealous of the time my
husband spent with his daughter from his first marriage," says Janice, 28, "but then he kept telling me, 'She's
part of the family. When we have children, I'll be the
same with ours.' That made me stop and think."

**Don't expect to love or be loved by your stepchildren
immediately.** Relationships have to develop over time.
Stepfamilies are built on the loss that evolves from death
or divorce, and that disruption can be traumatic for
children who are dragged into a parent's new relationship whether they want to be part of it or not. Stepparents should be aware that many children are still
grieving for the past and that their acceptance of the
stepfamily is linked with the emotional growth process of
their age. The younger the child, the easier it is for her to
adapt. Adolescence, which is often a period of emotional
upheaval under normal circumstances, can be a difficult
time to adjust to a new family.

**The biological parent should let her children know she
cares about her spouse.** "Parents must tell their children
'This person is important to me,' " says Phillips. "Then
the parent must let the children know that they should
treat the new mate with respect. The parent can do things

From *Essence*, May 1991, pp. 118, 120. © 1991 by Bebe Moore Campbell. Reprinted by permission of Janklow, Nesbit, and
Associates.

as the relationship unfolds that encourage rather than demand closeness between the children and the stepparent. Give the stepparent and the children things they can do together. Most of the time kids want to relate to the person who makes their parents happy."

Remember, children often fear being disloyal to their biological parents. So, Phillips explains, they may appear to reject the stepparent as a way to resolve their inner conflicts. "Stepparents should try not to feel threatened when a kid says 'You're not my mother or father,' " says Phillips. "The proper response is 'No, I'm not your biological parent, but I *am* someone who cares about you, and I've discussed my position with your biological parent—and he agrees with me.' "

Stepparents go through changes, too. "My second wife used to communicate with my daughters as if she were a kid," says Ted, a father of three. "Now that one of my daughters lives with us, my wife has had to learn to be a parent."

Ellen, his wife, agrees. "Before we were married, his girls didn't take me seriously," she says. "After we got married, I became more insistent that the girls follow my rules. In the beginning, their reaction took the form of mild rebellion—particularly with the daughter who lives with us. She resisted doing things when she was supposed to. Before I might have let it ride. Now I punish by depriving her of things she likes—television or the telephone. She's beginning to see me as an authority figure."

'Stepfamilies are built on loss from death or divorce—disruption that is traumatic for children dragged into a new relationship.'

Trust is a key issue in resolving conflict over disciplining stepchildren. "Some men feel emasculated because they feel unsure whether or not they are allowed to discipline a stepchild," says Phillips. "If mothers are overly protective, this can create tension. Parents change after they develop confidence in their mates, but this takes time. While it may be inappropriate for an adult who has known a kid for one month to spank him, after two years it may be perfectly correct. The key is for parents to keep talking about the issues until the spouse realizes the stepparent has his child's best interest at heart."

Sharon says it took a while, but she and her husband resolved their conflict about her disciplining his children. "I kept telling him how unfair I thought he was being. I

wrote him letters. Gradually he [b]... with his children. Now if he does... handle his kids, he takes me asi[de]...

Open communication about fi[nances]... saying "I do," a second wife ne[eds]... partner's financial and emotiona[l]... children. Sometimes marrying a [man with finan]cial obligations to his children by a previous marriage may mean that the second wife will have to postpone childbirth or even remain childless. In some instances, a second wife's discretionary income will be needed for bills that her husband's salary can't cover. A new wife needs to realize that when she resents her husband's children for receiving what is rightfully theirs, she must deal with her own insecurity and jealousy. Owning up to those emotions instead of blaming stepchildren is important in resolving feelings that can shatter second marriages.

A stepdaddy is not a sugar daddy. Mothers should honestly discuss with their second husbands the implications of the lack of child support from the child's biological father. Phillips believes that most stepfathers are willing to help with the cost of raising stepchildren but don't want to be viewed as money machines. "I approach stepparenting the same way I do parenting," says Howard, whose 12-year-old stepdaughter lives with him and his wife. "My responsibility is in conjunction with my wife's. I knew my wife's ex didn't contribute child support. I told her not to push for it, because I thought that would scar my stepdaughter. We share some of the costs of her child. That's fine with me. If she asked me to pay for everything, I'd feel she was being unfair."

An ex-spouse may be reluctant to let go of her marriage, particularly the ex-wife who hasn't remarried. "When my husband and I got married, his ex-wife began calling him a lot. Every time we turned around she was asking for advice or asking him to come to her house and 'fix' something. She'd always allude to their children whenever she called, and maybe because he felt guilty or maybe because he liked the attention, my husband would give in to her. I let it slide for a while, then I hit the ceiling," recalls Mary, 37. "I told my husband that he was *my* handyman and not hers, and that if she needed house repairs, she could call a carpenter. After that, when she called with her requests, he would say that he was busy."

"When an ex-mate intrudes too much in a new marriage, the new mate should bring up the problem with her spouse," advises Phillips. "A lot of times men withdraw and allow things to happen. Their new wives may need to prod them to act."

Never bad-mouth a biological parent in front of a stepchild. Hearing a parent disparaged will put unnecessary pressure upon a child, who may harbor resentment long after the adult has resolved the issue. "I once called my

mother a bitch without realizing that the
earshot," says Janice, shaking her head.
saw the look she gave me, I wanted to cut out
gue. I apologized a million times, but it was years
re she forgave me."

Stay clear of battles between a spouse and his ex. "When
it comes to issues between my husband and his ex-wife, I
try to stay neutral," says Ellen. "We may discuss the
situations after the fact, but I let them work it out."
Remember that their problems are *their* problems. But
sometimes it may be helpful for a stepmother and a
natural mother to forge a relationship. They don't have to
be friends, but they do need to acknowledge and accept
that the other person has a role in the child's life.

Make time for the two of you. "Establish a regimen,"
says Phillips. "Couples don't have to be rigid, but they
have to have a plan that allows for a combination of
relationships to develop. If the entire family is together all
day Saturday, parents can stipulate that after nine o'clock
is couple time. Be clear with the children that the two of
you want time together."

Find time to discuss problems as they occur. Attending
marital retreats and other activities designed to enhance
communication can help stepfamilies flourish. When husbands and wives are clear about their commitment to
each other, ex-spouses don't seem as threatening and
children are more likely to cooperate. In such a climate,
the ties that bind adult to child begin to blur and overlap,
and it becomes less about titles and more about love.
"The bottom line," says Phillips, "is that you need effective communication in order to have a healthy relationship. All the problems stepfamilies have don't have to be
resolved. They *do* have to be discussed."

THE LASTING EFFECTS OF CHILD MALTREATMENT

Raymond H. Starr, Jr.

Raymond H. Starr, Jr., is a developmental psychologist on the faculty of the University of Maryland, Baltimore County. He has been conducting research with maltreated children and their families for more than sixteen years and was also a founder and first president of the National Down Syndrome Congress.

Every day, the media contain examples of increasingly extreme cases of child abuse and neglect and their consequences. The cases have a blurring sameness. Take, for example, the fourteen-year-old crack addict who lives on the streets by selling his body. A reporter befriends him and writes a vivid account of the beatings the boy received from his father. There is the pedophile who is on death row for mutilating and murdering a four-year-old girl. His record shows a sixth-grade teacher threatened to rape and kill him if he told anyone what the teacher had done to him. There is the fifteen-year-old girl who felt that her parents didn't love her. So she found love on the streets and had a baby she later abandoned in a trash barrel. And there are the prostitutes on a talk show who tell how the men their mothers had trusted sexually abused them as children. These and hundreds more examples assault us and lead us to believe that abused children become problem adolescents and adults.

Are these incidents the whole story? Case examples are dramatic, but have you ever wondered how such maltreatment changes the course of a child's life? In this sound-bite era, most of us rarely stop to think about this important question. We seldom ask why trauma should play such an important role in shaping the course of a child's life.

To examine these questions, we need to understand what psychologists know about the course of lives and how they study them—the subject of the field of life-span developmental psychology.

LIFE-SPAN DEVELOPMENT

Understanding why people behave the way they do is a complex topic that has puzzled philosophers, theologians, and scientists. The course of life is so complex that we tend to focus on critical incidents and key events. Most of us can remember a teacher who played an important role in our own development, but we have to consider that other teachers may have been important. If his seventh-grade civics teacher, Ms. Jones, is the person Bill says showed him the drama of the law, leading him to become a lawyer, does this mean that his sixth-grade English teacher, Ms. Hazelton, played no role in his career choice? An outside observer might say that Ms. Hazelton was the key person because she had a debate club and Bill was the most able debater in his class.

Case descriptions fascinate us, but it is hard to divine the reasons for life courses from such examples. It is for this reason that scientists studying human behavior prefer to use prospective studies. By following people from a certain age, we can obtain direct evidence about the life course and factors that influence it. However, most of our information comes from retrospective studies in which people are asked what has happened to them in the past and how it relates to their present functioning.

Life-span developmental theory seeks to explain the way life events have influenced individual development. Of necessity, such explanations are complex; lives themselves are complex. They are built on a biological foundation, shaped by genetic characteristics, structured by immediate events, and indirectly influenced by happenings that are external to the family. As if this were not complex enough, contemporary theory holds that our interpretation of each event is dependent on the prior interactions of all these factors.

Hank's reaction to the loss of his wife to cancer will differ from George's reaction to his wife's death from a similar cancer. Many factors can contribute to these differing reactions. Hank may have grown up with two parents who were loving and attentive, while George may never have known his father. He may have had a mother who was so depressed that from the time he was two, he had lived in a series of foster homes, never knowing a secure, loving, consistent parent.

MALTREATED CHILDREN AS ADULTS

Research has shown that there is a direct relation between a child's exposure to negative emotional, social, and environmental events and the presence of problems during adulthood. Psychiatrist Michael Rutter compared young women who were removed from strife-filled homes and who later came back to live with their parents to women from more harmonious homes.[1] The women from discordant homes were more likely to become pregnant as teens, were less skilled in parenting their children, and had unhappy marriages to men who also had psychological and social problems. Adversity begat adversity.

Do the above examples and theoretical views mean that abused and neglected children will, with great certainty, become adults with problems? Research on this issue has focused on three questions: First, do maltreated children grow up to

tween 25 percent and 35 percent.[2] Thus, it is far from certain that an abused child will grow up to be an abusive parent. Physical abuse should be seen as a risk factor for becoming an abusive adult, not as a certainty. Many abusive adults were never abused when they were children.

Researchers have also taken a broader approach by examining the cycle of family violence. Sociologist Murray Straus surveyed a randomly selected national sample of families about the extent of violence between family members.[3] Members of the

as a training ground for later child abuse.

To summarize, this evidence suggests that maltreatment during childhood is but one of many factors that lead to a person's becoming an abusive parent. Being abused as a child is a risk marker for later parenting problems and not a cause of such difficulties. It accounts for, at most, less than a third of all cases of physical abuse. Research suggests that a number of other factors, such as stress and social isolation, also play a role as causes of child abuse.[4]

Research has shown that there is a direct relation between a child's exposure to negative emotional, social, and environmental events and the presence of problems during adulthood.

---

maltreat their children? Second, are yesterday's maltreated children today's criminals? Third, are there more general effects of abuse and neglect on later psychological and social functioning? A number of research studies have examined these questions.

The cycle of maltreatment. It makes logical sense that we tend to raise our own children as we ourselves were raised. Different theoretical views of personality development suggest that this should be the case. Psychoanalytic theorists think that intergenerational transmission of parenting styles is unconscious. Others, such as learning theorists, agree that transmission occurs but differ about the mechanism. Learning parenting skills from our parents is the key mode by which child-rearing practices are transmitted from one generation to the next, according to members of the latter group of theorists.

Research suggests that the correspondence between being maltreated as a child and becoming a maltreating adult is far from the one-to-one relationship that has been proposed. Studies have focused on physical abuse; data are not available for either sexual abuse or neglect. In one recent review, the authors conclude that the rate of intergenerational transmission of physical abuse is be-

surveyed families were asked about experiences of violence when they were children and how much husband-wife and parent-child violence there had been in the family in the prior year.

Straus concluded that slightly fewer than 20 percent of parents whose mothers had been violent toward them more than once a year during childhood were abusive toward their own child. The child abuse rate for parents with less violent mothers was less than 12 percent. Having or not having a violent father was less strongly related to whether or not fathers grew up to be abusive toward their own children. Interestingly, the amount of intergenerational transmission was higher if a parent was physically punished by his or her opposite-sex parent.

Straus also found that the abusive adults in his study did not have to have been abused in childhood to become abusive adults. A violent home environment can lead a nonabused child to become an abusive adult. Boys who saw their fathers hit their mothers were 38 percent more likely to grow up to be abusive than were boys who never saw their father hit their mother (13.3 vs. 9.7 percent). Similarly, mothers who saw their mothers hit their fathers were 42 percent more likely to become abusive mothers (24.4 vs. 17.2 percent). Straus views seeing parents fight

Maltreatment and later criminality. Later criminal behavior is one of the most commonly discussed consequences of child abuse. Research on this subject has examined the consequences of both physical abuse and sexual abuse. Maltreatment has been linked to both juvenile delinquency and adult criminality.

It is difficult to do research on this topic. Furthermore, the results of studies must be carefully interpreted to avoid overstating the connection between maltreatment and criminality. For example, researchers often combine samples of abused and neglected children, making it hard to determine the exact effects of specific forms of maltreatment.

Two types of study have typically been done. Retrospective studies examine the family backgrounds of criminals and find the extent to which they were maltreated as children. It is obvious that the validity of the results of such studies may be compromised by the criminals' distortion of or lack of memory concerning childhood experiences. Prospective studies, in which a sample of children is selected and followed through childhood and into adolescence or adulthood, are generally seen as a more valid research strategy. Such studies are expensive and time-consuming to do.

One review of nine studies concluded that from 8 to 26 percent of delinquent youths studied retrospectively had been abused as children.[5] The rate for prospective studies was always found to be less than 20 percent. In one of the best studies, Joan McCord analyzed case records for more than 250 boys, almost 50 percent of whom had been abused by a parent.[6] Data were also collected when the men were in middle age. McCord found that 39 percent of the abused boys had been convicted of a crime as juveniles, adults, or at both ages, compared to 23 percent of a sample of 101 men who, as boys, had been classified as loved by their parents. The crime rate for both sets of boys is higher than would be expected because McCord's sample lived in deteriorated, urban areas where both crime and abuse are common.

Researchers have also examined the relationship between abuse and later violent criminality. Research results suggest that there is a weak relationship between abuse and later violence. For example, in one study, 16 percent of a group of abused children were later arrested —but not necessarily convicted—as suspects in violent criminal cases.[7] This was twice the arrest rate for nonabused adolescents and adults. Neglected children were also more likely to experience such arrests. These data are higher than would be the case in the general population because the samples contained a disproportionately high percentage of subjects from low-income backgrounds.

The connection between childhood sexual abuse and the commission of sex crimes in adolescence and adulthood is less clear. Most of the small number of studies that have been done have relied upon self-reports of childhood molestation made by convicted perpetrators. Their results show considerable variation in the frequency with which childhood victimization is reported. Incidence figures range from a low of 19 percent to a high of 57 percent. However, we should look at such data with suspicion. In an interesting study, perpetrators of sex crimes against children were much less likely to report that they had been sexually abused during their own childhood when they knew that the truthfulness of their answers would be validated by a polygraph examination and that lies were likely to result in being sent to jail.[8] Thus, people arrested for child sexual abuse commonly lie, claiming that they were abusing children because they themselves had been victims of sexual abuse as children.

To summarize, there is a link between childhood abuse and later criminality. Although some studies lead to a conclusion that this relationship is simple, others suggest that it is really quite complex. The latter view is probably correct.

The case of neglect is an example of this complexity. Widom, in her study discussed above, found that 12 percent of adolescents and adults arrested for violent offenses were neglected as children and 7 percent experienced both abuse and neglect (compared to 8 percent of her nonmaltreated control adolescents and adults).

These data raise an interesting question: Why is neglect, typically considered to be a nonviolent offense, linked to later criminality? Poverty seems to be the mediating factor. Neglect is more common among impoverished families. Poor families experience high levels of frustration, known to be a common cause of aggression. Similarly, we know that lower-class families are, in general, more violent.[9] For these reasons, all the forms of maltreatment we have considered make it somewhat more likely that a maltreated child will grow up to commit criminal acts.

Maltreatment in context. Research suggests that maltreatment during childhood has far-reaching consequences. These are best seen as the results of a failure to meet the emotional needs of the developing child. Indeed, in many cases, the trust the child places in the parent is betrayed by the parent.

This betrayal has been linked to many and varied consequences. The greatest amount of research has focused on the long-term effects of sexual abuse. Studies have looked at samples that are representative of the normal population and also at groups of adults who are seeking psychotherapy because of emotional problems. The most valid findings come from the former type of study. One review of research concluded that almost 90 percent of studies found some lasting effect of sexual abuse.[10]

Sexual abuse has been linked to

a wide variety of psychological disturbances. These include depression, low self-esteem, psychosis, anxiety, sleep problems, alcohol and drug abuse, and sexual dysfunction (including a predisposition to revictimization during adulthood). As was true for the research reviewed in the preceding two sections of this article, any particular problem is present in only a

---

Psychoanalytic theorists think that intergenerational transmission of parenting styles is unconscious.

---

minority of adult survivors of childhood sexual victimization.

We know less about the long-term effects of physical abuse. Most of the limited amount of available research has used data obtained from clinical samples. Such studies have two problems. First, they rely on retrospective adult reports concerning events that happened during childhood. Second, the use of such samples results in an overestimate of the extent to which physical abuse has long-term consequences. Compared with a random sample of the general population, clinical samples contain individuals who are already identified as having emotional difficulties, regardless of whether or not they have been abused.

Researchers in one study found that more than 40 percent of inpatients being treated in a psychiatric hospital had been sexually or physically abused as children, usually by a family member.[11] Also, the abuse was typically chronic rather than a onetime occurrence. The abused patients were almost 50 percent more likely to have tried to commit suicide, were 25 percent more likely to have been violent toward others, and were 15 percent more likely to have had some involvement with the criminal justice system than were other patients at the same hospital who had not experienced childhood maltreatment.

Much research remains to be done in this area. We know little about the long-term consequences of particular forms of abuse. The best that we can say is that many victims of physical and sexual abuse experience psychological trauma lasting into adulthood.

The lack of universal consequences. The above analysis suggests that many victims of childhood maltreatment do *not* have significant problems functioning as adults. Researchers are only beginning to ask why many adult victims apparently have escaped unsullied. Factors that mediate and soften the influence of abuse and neglect are called buffers.

The search for buffers is a difficult one. Many of the negative outcomes that have been discussed in the preceding sections may be the result of a number of factors other than maltreatment itself. For example, abused children commonly have behavior problems that are similar to those that have been reported in children raised by drug addicts or adults suffering from major psychological disturbances. Abused children do not exhibit any problems that can be attributed only to abuse. A given behavior problem can have many causes.

One view of the way in which buffers act to limit the extent to which physical abuse is perpetuated across succeeding generations has been proposed by David Wolfe.[12] He believes that there is a three-part process involving the parent, the child, and the relationships between the two. In the first stage, factors predisposing a parent to child abuse (including stress and a willingness to be aggressive toward the child) are buffered by such factors as social support and an income adequate for the purchase of child-care services. Next, Wolfe notes that children often do things that annoy parents and create crises that may lead to abuse because the parent is unprepared to handle the child's provocative behavior. Amelior-

ating factors that work at this level include normal developmental changes in child behavior, parental attendance at child management classes, and the development of parental ability to cope with the child's escalating annoying actions. Finally, additional compensatory factors work to limit the ongoing use of aggression as a solution to parenting problems.

The amount of intergenerational transmission was higher if a parent was physically punished by his or her opposite-sex parent.

Parents may realize that researchers are indeed correct when they say that physical punishment is an ineffective way of changing child behavior. In addition, children may respond positively to parental use of nonaggressive disciplinary procedures and, at a broader level, society or individuals in the parents' circle of friends may inhibit the use of physical punishment by making their disapproval known. Parents who were abused as children are therefore less likely to abuse their own children if any or all of these mediating factors are present.

Research suggests that the factors mentioned by Wolfe and other influences all can work to buffer the adult effects of childhood maltreatment. These include knowing a nurturing, loving adult who provides social support, intellectually restructuring the maltreatment so that it is not seen so negatively, being altruistic and giving to others what one did not get as a child, having good skills for coping with stressful events, and getting psychotherapy.

One study compared parents who broke the cycle of abuse to those who did not.[13] Mothers who were not abusive had larger, more supportive social networks. Support included help with child care and financial assistance during times of crisis. Mothers who did not continue the abusive cycle also were more in touch with their own abuse as children and expressed doubts about their parenting ability. This awareness made them more able to relive and discuss their own negative childhood experiences.

To summarize, investigators have gone beyond just looking at the negative consequences of childhood maltreatment. They are devoting increasing attention to determining what factors in a child's environment may inoculate the child against the effects of maltreatment. While research is starting to provide us with information concerning some of these mediating influences, much more work needs to be done before we can specify the most important mediators and know how they exert their influences.

Physical abuse should be seen as a risk factor for becoming an abusive adult, not as a certainty.

CONCLUSIONS

We know much about the intergenerational transmission of childhood physical and sexual abuse. Research suggests that abused children are (1) at an increased risk of either repeating the acts they experienced with their own children or, in the case of sexual abuse, with both their own and with unrelated children; (2) more likely to be involved with the criminal justice system as adolescents or adults; and (3) likely to suffer long-lasting emotional effects of abuse even if they do not abuse their own children or commit criminal acts.

This does not mean that abused chil-

People arrested for child sexual abuse commonly lie, claiming that they were abusing children because they themselves had been victims of sexual abuse as children.

dren invariably grow up to be adults with problems. Many adults escape the negative legacy of abuse. They grow up to be normal, contributing members of society. Their escape from maltreatment is usually related to the presence of factors that buffer the effects of the physical blows and verbal barbs.

The knowledge base underlying these conclusions is of varied quality. We know more about the relationship of physical and sexual abuse to adult abusiveness and criminality, less about long-term psychological problems and buffering factors, and almost nothing about the relationship of neglect to any of these outcomes. Almost no research has been done on neglect, a situation leading to a discussion of the reasons behind our "neglect of neglect."[14] Our ignorance is all the more surprising when we consider that neglect is the most common form of reported maltreatment.

The issues involved are complex. We can no longer see the development of children from a view examining such simple cause-effect relationships as exemplified by the proposal that abused children grow up to be abusive adults. Contemporary de-

velopmental psychology recognizes that many interacting forces work together to shape development. Children exist in a context that contains their own status as biological beings, their parents and the background they bring to the task of child-rearing, the many and varied environments such as work and school that exert both direct and indirect influences on family members, and the overall societal acceptance of violence.

Advances in research methods allow us to evaluate the interrelationships of all the above factors to arrive at a coherent view of the course of development. Appropriate studies are difficult to plan and expensive to conduct. Without such research, the best that we can do is to continue performing small studies that give us glimpses of particular elements of the picture that we call the life course.

Research is necessary if we are to develop and evaluate the effectiveness of child maltreatment prevention and treatment programs. Our existing knowledge base provides hints that are used by program planners and psychotherapists to find families where there is a high risk of

maltreatment and to intervene early. But when such hints are all we have to guide us in working to break the cycle of maltreatment, there continues to be risk of intergenerational perpetuation.

1. Michael Rutter, "Intergenerational Continuities and Discontinuities in Serious Parenting Difficulties," in *Child Maltreatment: Theory and Research on the Causes and Consequences of Child Abuse and Neglect*, ed., Dante Cicchetti and Vicki Carlson (New York: Cambridge University Press, 1989), 317–348.

2. Joan Kaufman and Edward Zigler, "Do Abused Children Become Abusive Adults?" *American Journal of Orthopsychiatry* 57 (April 1987): 186–192.

3. Murray A. Straus, "Family Patterns and Child Abuse in a Nationally Representative American Sample," *Child Abuse and Neglect* 3 (1979): 213–225.

4. Raymond H. Starr, Jr., "Physical Abuse of Children," in *Handbook of Family Violence* ed. Vincent B. Van Hasselt, et al. (New York: Plenum Press, 1988): 119–155.

5. Cathy Spatz Widom, "Does Violence Beget Violence? A Critical Examination of the Literature," *Psychological Bulletin* 106 (1989): 3–28.

6. Joan McCord, "A Forty-year Perspective on Effects of Child Abuse and Neglect," *Child Abuse and Neglect* 7 (1983): 265–270. Joan McCord, "Parental Aggressiveness and Physical Punishment in Long-term Perspective," in *Family Abuse and Its Consequences*, ed. Gerald T. Hotaling, et al. (Newbury Park, Calif.: Sage Publishing, 1988): 91–98.

7. Cathy Spatz Widom, "The Cycle of Violence," *Science*, 14 April 1989.

8. Jan Hindman, "Research Disputes Assumptions about Child Molesters," *National District Attorneys' Association Bulletin* 7 (July/August 1988): 1.

9. Murray A. Straus, Richard J. Gelles, and Suzanne K. Steinmetz, *Behind Closed Doors: Violence in the American Family* (New York: Anchor Press, 1980).

10. David Finkelhor and Angela Browne, "Assessing the Long-term Impact of Child Sexual Abuse: A Review and Conceptualization," in *Family Abuse and Its Consequences*, ed. Gerald T. Hotaling, et al.: 270–284.

11. Elaine (Hilberman) Carmen, Patricia Perri Rieker, and Trudy Mills, "Victims of Violence and Psychiatric Illness," *American Journal of Psychiatry* 141 (March 1984): 378–383.

12. David A. Wolfe, *Child Abuse: Implications for Child Development and Psychopathology* (Newbury Park, Calif.: Sage Publishing, 1987).

13. Rosemary S. Hunter and Nancy Kilstrom, "Breaking the Cycle in Abusive Families," 136 (1979): 1320–22.

14. Isabel Wolock and Bernard Horowitz, "Child Maltreatment as a Social Problem: The Neglect of Neglect," *American Journal of Orthopsychiatry* 54 (1984); 530–543.

Your Loving Touch

The hugs, cuddles, and kisses you give your children will benefit
them throughout their lives.

Janice T. Gibson, Ed.D.

Janice T. Gibson, Ed.D., is a contributing
editor of *Parents* Magazine.

Like most mothers, I remember vividly the births of my two children, Robin and Mark. Each time I cuddled my newborn children in my arms—snuggling them gently against my skin and caressing them with my hands and lips—I felt peace and an extraordinarily personal happiness. For each child, born four years apart, it took only an instant for me to fall in love! My joy made me want to continue cuddling and, in the process, strengthened a learned need to hug. Years later, when Mark was in fourth grade, I would hide behind the kitchen door and nab him for a hug when he came home from school. (He always put up with me, except in front of his friends.) And when Robin dressed for the prom, I zipped her gown, patted her on the shoulders, and wrapped my arms around her before she left with her date.

The power of touch.

Affectionate physical contact is meaningful at all age levels. Everyone needs affection, especially when frightened, insecure, or overtired. But particularly for children who cannot yet talk or understand words, cuddling and other forms of affectionate touch convey strong nonverbal messages and serve as important means of communication. When your baby is tired and snuggles in your arms, the gentle body-to-body contact relaxes him and communicates, "You're special. I love you."

Cuddling teaches infants about their environment and the people in it. They explore by touching with their fingers and tongue. Since touching is a reciprocal act, by cuddling your child you teach him to cuddle back. And by responding to his actions, you teach your baby to feel good about himself.

As your child grows older and snuggles with you after a frightening experience, a gentle hug that says "You are safe" will relieve him of his anxiety and help him to feel secure. If during a tantrum he lets you pick him up and hold him on your lap, he will be able to calm down and gain control of his emotions. Furthermore, your affectionate touch can help if your child misbehaves. If he hits his baby brother, for example, you can hold him on your lap as you tell him, "Hitting your brother is not okay." These words, together with the affectionate actions, tell him that although his behavior is not acceptable, you still love him. And when your child exhibits positive behavior, by praising him with a hug and a kiss or an enthusiastic high five, you will convey the message "I'm proud of you."

Why touch is so important.

Physical affection is crucial to a child's development. First of all, parents form strong affectional ties to their children by cuddling and touching them. Gary Johnson, of Delavan, Wisconsin, recalls how he felt after the birth of his first child, Jake: "I got to hold him in my arms for the first twenty minutes of his life. From those first moments together, I never felt strange with him. He was this little helpless creature who needed to be held, cuddled, and protected."

Whether an attachment such as the one Gary describes occurs immediately or over time, it increases the probability that parents will respond to their children's needs. Later, this strong attachment increases the child's psychological well-being.

For babies whose parents don't respond to their signals for close bodily contact, the result is what Mary Ainsworth, Ph.D., professor of psychology emeritus at the University of Virginia, in Charlottesville, has termed "anxious avoidance attachment." She and her colleagues found that babies whose mothers seldom pick them up to comfort them, and who rebuff their attempts to snuggle and cuddle, eventually learn to mask their emotions. When these babies are anxious and upset and most want their mother, they will avoid her so as not to risk being rejected again. "These babies often become adults who don't trust people and find it difficult to form close attachments," remarks Ainsworth. Thus the cycle becomes vicious and self-perpetuating.

The results of a recently completed 36-year study further demonstrate that the effects of parental affection are lifelong. In 1951 a team of psychologists from Harvard University, in Cambridge, Massachusetts, studied 379 five-year-olds in Boston. They asked the children's mothers about their own and their husband's child-rearing practices, including how the mothers responded when their child cried and whether they played with him; whether the father hugged and kissed the child when he came home from work; and whether he spent free time with the child. The researchers found that kindergartners whose parents were warm and affectionate and cuddled them frequently were happier, played better, and had fewer feeding, behavior, and bed-wetting problems than did their peers raised by colder and more reserved parents.

In a 1987 follow-up study involving 76 of the original subjects, researchers found that as adults, those who were raised by warm, nurturing parents tended to have longer, happier marriages and better relationships with close friends than did adult peers whose early child rearing was not so warm. According to psychologist Carol Franz, Ph.D., one of the study's researchers, "Affectionate touching was always associated with a lot of warmth. The more warmth parents exhibited, the more socially adjusted their child was at midlife."

Cuddling barriers.

Most parents provide what their babies need and want. Holding, carrying, rocking, and caressing are part of child rearing in most societies. Infant massage, in which babies are systematically touched and stroked in caring ways, is practiced throughout the world. In some countries, such as India, mothers massage with scented oils. And in China, moms not only massage their youngsters but also use acupuncture to relax them.

But in contrast with people from other countries, Americans, in general, aren't "touchy." In my own cross-cultural studies of child rearing, I've found that although mothers and fathers in the United States are basically as affectionate as other parents, they tend to refrain from physical expressions of love. Although a baby's need for constant physical attention is obvious, the need is less obvious for older children and adults. Consequently, as U.S. children grow older, touching becomes less a part of parent-child interaction.

Some parents are uncomfortable behaving affectionately because they are afraid that it will spoil their children. Far from spoiling children, however, it teaches them to trust you and to view the world as a safe place to explore. Youngsters whose parents pick them up and hug them when they are hurt, frightened, or insecure develop feelings of security that make it easier for them to do things on their own.

Although there has been a lot of talk about how much more involved dads are today, many fathers still have a problem touching their children affectionately. Ronald Levant, Ed.D., former director of Boston University's Fatherhood Project and coauthor of *Between Father and Child* (Penguin), explains that today's generation of men have been raised to be like their fathers, who were the family breadwinners, and as a result they have grown up to be stoic. "As boys, they did not learn the basic psychological skills that girls did—such as self-awareness and empathy—which are necessary to nurture and care for children."

Furthermore, when dads do give their children affection, they tend to give more hugs and kisses to their daughters than to their sons. Why? Some fathers think that cuddling is not masculine and that too much physical affection will turn boys into "sissies." One dad admitted that when his wife was pregnant with their first child, he secretly hoped for a girl. "My father was not a very tactile person. We mostly shook hands. So I was concerned that if I had a son, I'd be too reserved. I was afraid to touch a son." Levant assures, however, that boys who are cuddled by their dads will not become "sissies" but will learn to be nurturing themselves. And more good news: The fathers of this generation are recognizing that they missed affection from their dads and, says Levant, are "breaking the old molds" of masculine reserve.

Some women also feel uncomfortable kissing and hugging their children because their parents weren't comfortable showing affection. One mother says that on the surface, her parents were warm and loving and she was well taken care of, "but I was rarely touched, hugged, or kissed." She wasn't comfortable cuddling with her children until she went into therapy and talked about her feelings. Now, she says, "I don't even think about it anymore. Hugging comes very naturally."

The high rate of divorce today, and the large number of single-parent homes in which the head of the household must work outside the home, also make it more difficult for some parents to provide the physical affection that their children may want or need at any given time. The recent concern raised by the specter of child abuse hasn't made it easier either. Highly publicized cases of purported sexual abuse of children by caregivers or estranged parents make some adults afraid that cuddling and touching may be construed as sexual and harmful. So what can be done? Although it is critical to protect children from sexual abuse, it is equally important to show all children that they are loved and needed. Children need healthy affection, and parents need to find ways to provide it.

● ● ●

Some parents are uncomfortable behaving affectionately with their children because they are afraid it will spoil them. On the contrary, it will help them develop feelings of security.

● ● ●

There are 1,001 ways to demonstrate affection, and not everyone needs to do it the same way. Parents who aren't comfortable giving their children big hugs and kisses shouldn't feel obliged to do so. Patting on the hand or back—or giving a squeeze—plus some loving words, can convey affection if it is done in a meaningful way.

Cuddling comfort.

Like some parents, some children are uncomfortable about being held closely, not because they don't want affection, but because they are uncomfortable feeling physically constrained. For such children, you can stroke their shoulders or back gently, give them lots of kisses, or tickle them gently so that they don't feel entrapped. Eventually they may even like to be cuddled. Gary Johnson's four-year-old daughter, Hallie, and one-year-old son, Nate, weren't as cuddly from the beginning with their father as was their older brother, Jake. But now Hallie is "Daddy's little girl and a permanent fixture on my lap." And Nate has just recently started to want Gary to cuddle him. "It's a real thrill to me to have him reach out for a hug from Dad," he says.

If you work outside the home and are away for most of the day, be sure that your caregiver supplies all the physical love your child needs. The Johnsons were concerned about leaving their kids in somebody else's care. "Becky and I believe that kids need plenty of physical love and affection, and we were afraid that someone else might not give them enough," says Gary. So they searched carefully. "We were fortunate to find a warm, loving, and wonderful caregiver. We can tell the kids are happy."

When peers become important to your child, he may start to shun your affections, particularly if his friends are present. Statements of rejection, such as "Yuck, Mom, don't kiss me" and "Leave my hair alone," do sting, but they signal that your child is growing up and striving for independence. Because he still needs your affection, you might try hugging him at bedtime when his friends aren't around.

As boys and girls reach puberty, touching becomes charged with sexual meaning, making it hard for many adolescents even to acknowledge the desire to touch or be touched in nonsexual ways. Parents should respect their teens' discomfort. When a hug may be too threatening, you can still express your love with a squeeze of the hand or a pat on the back.

If you are divorced, your child needs love from both you and your ex-spouse, even more than before the separation. So, if possible, work together with your ex-spouse to help your child to understand that both of you care. Sometimes boys raised in fatherless households, interpreting the loss of their father as making them the "man of the house," decide that permitting their mother to hug or kiss them makes them less manly. Mothers should respect these feelings but should not stop showing affection: A hug at bedtime or a lingering pat on the arm while going over homework will do wonders.

A recent experience underscored the message for me that even in adulthood, we still need, and benefit from, touch. It was while my now adult children and I were mourning their father's death. We stood silently for some minutes in a circle, our arms around one another, holding on tightly. The feel of our bodies touching consoled us and gave us strength. It convinced us, in a very concrete way, that we would be able to get on with our lives.

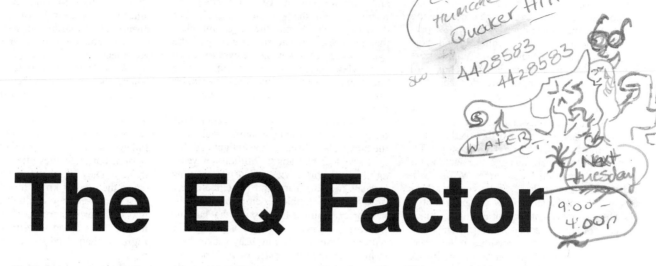

The EQ Factor

New brain research suggests that emotions, not IQ, may be the true measure of human intelligence

NANCY GIBBS

IT TURNS OUT THAT A SCIENTIST can see the future by watching four-year-olds interact with a marshmallow. The researcher invites the children, one by one, into a plain room and begins the gentle torment. You can have this marshmallow right now, he says. But if you wait while I run an errand, you can have two marshmallows when I get back. And then he leaves.

Some children grab for the treat the minute he's out the door. Some last a few minutes before they give in. But others are determined to wait. They cover their eyes; they put their heads down; they sing to themselves; they try to play games or even fall asleep. When the researcher returns, he gives these children their hard-earned marshmallows. And then, science waits for them to grow up.

By the time the children reach high school, something remarkable has happened. A survey of the children's parents and teachers found that those who as four-year-olds had the fortitude to hold out for the second marshmallow generally grew up to be better adjusted, more popular, adventurous, confident and dependable teenagers. The children who gave in to temptation early on were more likely to be lonely, easily frustrated and stubborn. They buckled under stress and shied away from challenges. And when some of the students in the two groups took the Scholastic Aptitude Test, the kids who had held out longer scored an average of 210 points higher.

When we think of brilliance we see Einstein, deep-eyed, woolly haired, a thinking machine with skin and mismatched socks. High achievers, we imagine, were wired for greatness from birth. But then you have to wonder why, over time, natural talent seems to ignite in some people and dim in others. This is where the marshmallows come in. It seems that the ability to delay gratification is a master skill, a triumph of the reasoning brain over the impulsive one. It is a sign, in short, of emotional intelligence. And it doesn't show up on an IQ test.

For most of this century, scientists have worshipped the hardware of the brain and the software of the mind; the messy powers of the heart were left to the poets. But cognitive theory could simply not explain the questions we wonder about most: why some people just seem to have a gift for living well; why the smartest kid in the class will probably not end up the richest; why we like some people virtually on sight and distrust others; why some people remain buoyant in the face of troubles that would sink a less resilient soul. What qualities of the mind or spirit, in short, determine who succeeds?

The phrase "emotional intelligence" was coined by Yale psychologist Peter Salovey and the University of New Hampshire's John Mayer five years ago to describe qualities like understanding one's own feelings, empathy for the feelings of others and "the regulation of emotion in a way that enhances living." Their notion is about to bound into the national conversation, handily shortened to EQ, thanks to a new book, *Emotional Intelligence* (Bantam; $23.95) by Daniel Goleman. Goleman, a Harvard psychology Ph.D. and a New York *Times* science writer with a gift for making even the chewiest scientific theories digestible to lay readers, has brought together a decade's worth of behavioral research into how the mind processes feelings. His goal, he announces on the cover, is to redefine what it means to be smart. His thesis: when it comes to predicting people's success, brainpower as measured by IQ and standardized achievement tests may actually matter less than the qualities of mind once thought of as "character" before the word began to sound quaint.

At first glance, there would seem to be little that's new here to any close reader of fortune cookies. There may be no less original idea than the notion that our hearts hold dominion over our heads. "I was so angry," we say, "I couldn't think straight." Neither is it surprising that "people skills" are useful, which amounts to saying, it's good to be nice. "It's so true it's trivial," says Dr. Paul McHugh, director of psychiatry at Johns Hopkins University School of Medicine. But if it were that simple, the book would not be quite so interesting or its implications so controversial.

This is no abstract investigation. Goleman is looking for antidotes to restore "civility to our streets and caring to our communal life." He sees practical applications everywhere for how companies should decide whom to hire, how couples can increase the odds that their marriages will last, how parents should raise their children and how schools should teach them. When street gangs substitute for families and schoolyard insults end in stabbings, when more than half of marriages end in divorce, when the majority of the children murdered in this country are killed by parents and stepparents, many of whom say they were trying to discipline the child for behavior like blocking the TV or crying too much, it suggests a demand for remedial emotional education. While children are still young, Goleman argues, there is a "neurological window of opportunity" since the brain's prefrontal circuitry, which regulates how we act on what we feel, probably does not mature until mid-adolescence.

And it is here the arguments will break out. Goleman's highly popularized conclusions, says McHugh, "will chill any veteran scholar of psychotherapy and any neuroscientist who worries about how his research may come to be applied." While many researchers in this relatively new field are glad to see emotional issues finally taken seriously, they fear that a notion as handy as EQ invites misuse. Goleman admits the danger of suggesting that you can assign a numerical yardstick to a person's character as well as his intellect; Goleman never even uses the phrase EQ in his book. But he (begrudgingly) approved an "unscientific" EQ test in *USA Today* with choices like "I am aware of even subtle feelings as I have them," and "I can sense the pulse of a group or relationship and state unspoken feelings."

"You don't want to take an average of your emotional skill," argues Harvard psychology professor Jerome Kagan, a pioneer in child-development research. "That's what's wrong with the concept of intelligence for mental skills too. Some people handle anger well but can't handle fear. Some people can't take joy. So each emotion has to be viewed differently."

EQ is not the opposite of IQ. Some people are blessed with a lot of both, some with little of either. What researchers have been trying to understand is how they complement each other; how one's ability to handle stress, for instance, affects the ability to concentrate and put intelligence to use. Among the ingredients for success, researchers now generally agree that IQ counts for about 20%; the rest depends on everything from class to luck to the neural pathways that have developed in the brain over millions of years of human evolution.

It is actually the neuroscientists and evolutionists who do the best job of explaining the reasons behind the most unreasonable behavior. In the past decade or so, scientists have learned enough about the brain to make judgments about where emotion comes from and why we need it. Primitive emotional responses held the keys to survival: fear drives the blood into the large muscles, making it easier to run; surprise triggers the eyebrows to rise, allowing the eyes to widen their view and gather more information about an unexpected event. Disgust wrinkles up the face and closes the nostrils to keep out foul smells.

Emotional life grows out of an area of the brain called the limbic system, specifically the amygdala, whence come delight and disgust and fear and anger. Millions of years ago, the neocortex was added on, enabling humans to plan, learn and remember. Lust grows from the limbic system; love, from the neocortex. Animals like reptiles that have no neocortex cannot experience anything like maternal love; this is why baby snakes have to hide to avoid being eaten by their parents. Humans, with their capacity for love, will protect their offspring, allowing the brains of the young time to develop. The more connections between limbic system and the neocortex, the more emotional responses are possible.

It was scientists like Joseph LeDoux of New York University who uncovered these cerebral pathways. LeDoux's parents owned a meat market. As a boy in Louisiana, he first learned about his future specialty by cutting up cows' brains for sweetbreads. "I found them the most interesting part of the cow's anatomy," he recalls. "They were visually pleasing—lots of folds, convolutions and patterns. The cerebellum was more interesting to look at than steak." The butchers' son became a neuroscientist, and it was he who discovered the short circuit in the brain that lets emotions drive action before the intellect gets a chance to intervene.

A hiker on a mountain path, for example, sees a long, curved shape in the grass out of the corner of his eye. He leaps out of the way before he realizes it is only a stick that looks like a snake. Then he calms down; his cortex gets the message a few milliseconds after his amygdala and "regulates" its primitive response.

Without these emotional reflexes, rarely conscious but often terribly powerful, we would scarcely be able to function. "Most decisions we make have a vast number of possible outcomes, and any attempt to analyze all of them would never end," says University of Iowa neurologist Antonio Damasio, author of *Descartes' Error: Emotion, Reason and the Human Brain.* "I'd ask you to lunch tomorrow, and when the appointed time arrived, you'd still be thinking about whether you should come." What tips the balance, Damasio contends, is our unconscious assigning of emotional values to some of those choices. Whether we experience a somatic response—a gut feeling of dread or a giddy sense of elation—emotions are helping to limit the field in any choice we have to make. If the prospect of lunch with a neurologist is unnerving or distasteful, Damasio suggests, the invitee will conveniently remember a previous engagement.

When Damasio worked with patients in whom the connection between emotional brain and neocortex had been severed because of damage to the brain, he discovered how central that hidden pathway is to how we live our lives. People who had lost that linkage were just as smart and quick to reason, but their lives often fell apart nonetheless. They could not make decisions because they didn't know how they felt about their choices. They couldn't react to warnings or anger in other people. If they made a mistake, like a bad investment, they felt no regret or shame and so were bound to repeat it.

If there is a cornerstone to emotional intelligence on which most other emotional skills depend, it is a sense of self-awareness, of being smart about what we feel. A person whose day starts badly at home may be grouchy all day at work without quite knowing why. Once an emotional response comes into awareness—or, physiologically, is processed through the neocortex—the chances of handling it appropriately improve. Scientists refer to "metamood," the ability to pull back and recognize that "what I'm feeling is anger," or sorrow, or shame.

Metamood is a difficult skill because emotions so often appear in disguise. A person in mourning may know he is sad, but he may not recognize that he is also angry at the person for dying—because this seems somehow inappropriate. A parent who yells at the child who ran into the street is expressing anger at disobedience, but the degree of anger may owe more to the fear the parent feels at what could have happened.

In Goleman's analysis, self-awareness is perhaps the most crucial ability because it allows us to exercise some self-control. The idea is not to repress feeling (the reaction that has made psychoanalysts rich) but rather to do what Aristotle considered the hard work of the will. "Anyone can become angry—that is easy," he wrote in the *Nicomachean Ethics.* "But to be angry with the right person, to the right degree, at the right time, for the right purpose, and in the right way—that is not easy."

Some impulses seem to be easier to control than others. Anger, not surprisingly, is one of the hardest, perhaps because of its evolutionary value in priming people to action. Researchers believe anger usually arises out of a sense of being trespassed against—the belief that one is being robbed of what is rightfully his. The body's first response is a surge of energy, the release of a cascade of neurotransmitters called catecholamines. If a person is already aroused or under stress, the threshold for release is lower, which helps explain why people's tempers shorten during a hard day.

Scientists are not only discovering where anger comes from; they are also exposing myths about how best to handle it. Popular wisdom argues for "letting it all hang out" and having a good cathartic rant. But Goleman cites studies showing that dwelling on anger actually increases its power; the body needs a chance to process the adrenaline through exercise, relaxation techniques, a well-timed intervention or even the old admonition to count to 10.

Anxiety serves a similar useful purpose, so long as it doesn't spin out of control. Worrying is a rehearsal for danger; the act of fretting focuses the mind on a problem so it can search efficiently for solutions. The danger comes when worrying blocks thinking, becoming an end in itself or a path to resignation instead of perseverance. Overworrying about failing increases the likelihood of failure; a salesman so concerned about his falling sales that he can't bring himself to pick up the phone guarantees that his sales will fall even further.

But why are some people better able to "snap out of it" and get on with the task at hand? Again, given sufficient self-awareness, people develop coping mechanisms. Sadness and discouragement, for instance, are "low arousal" states, and the dispirited salesman who goes out for a run is triggering a high arousal state that is incompatible with staying blue. Relaxation works better for high-energy moods like anger or anxiety. Either way, the idea is to shift to a state of arousal that breaks the destructive cycle of the dominant mood.

The idea of being able to predict which salesmen are most likely to prosper was not an abstraction for Metropolitan Life, which in the mid-'80s was hiring 5,000 salespeople a year and training them at a cost of more than $30,000 each. Half quit the first year, and four out of five within four years. The reason: selling life insurance involves having the door slammed in your face over and over again. Was it possible to identify which people would be better at handling frustration and take each refusal as a challenge rather than a setback?

The head of the company approached psychologist Martin Seligman at the University of Pennsylvania and invited him to test some of his theories about the importance of optimism in people's success. When optimists fail, he has found, they attribute the failure to something they can change, not some innate weakness that they are helpless to overcome. And that confidence in their power to effect change is self-reinforcing. Seligman tracked 15,000 new workers who had taken two tests. One was the company's regular screening exam, the other Seligman's test measuring their levels of optimism.

One Way to Test Your EQ

UNLIKE IQ, WHICH IS GAUGED BY THE FAMOUS STANFORD-Binet tests, EQ does not lend itself to any single numerical measure. Nor should it, say experts. Emotional intelligence is by definition a complex, multifaceted quality representing such intangibles as self-awareness, empathy, persistence and social deftness.

Some aspects of emotional intelligence, however, can be quantified. Optimism, for example, is a handy measure of a person's self-worth. According to Martin Seligman, a University of Pennsylvania psychologist, how people respond to setbacks—optimistically or pessimistically—is a fairly accurate indicator of how well they will succeed in school, in sports and in certain kinds of work. To test his theory, Seligman devised a questionnaire to screen insurance salesmen at MetLife.

In Seligman's test, job applicants were asked to imagine a hypothetical event and then choose the response (A or B) that most closely resembled their own. Some samples from his questionnaire:

You forget your spouse's (boyfriend's/girlfriend's) birthday.
A. I'm not good at remembering birthdays.
B. I was preoccupied with other things.

You owe the library $10 for an overdue book.
A. When I am really involved in what I am reading, I often forget when it's due.
B. I was so involved in writing the report, I forgot to return the book.

You lose your temper with a friend.
A. He or she is always nagging me.
B. He or she was in a hostile mood.

You are penalized for returning your income-tax forms late.
A. I always put off doing my taxes.
B. I was lazy about getting my taxes done this year.

You've been feeling run-down.
A. I never get a chance to relax.
B. I was exceptionally busy this week.

A friend says something that hurts your feelings.
A. She always blurts things out without thinking of others.
B. My friend was in a bad mood and took it out on me.

You fall down a great deal while skiing.
A. Skiing is difficult.
B. The trails were icy.

You gain weight over the holidays, and you can't lose it.
A. Diets don't work in the long run.
B. The diet I tried didn't work.

Seligman found that those insurance salesmen who answered with more B's than A's were better able to overcome bad sales days, recovered more easily from rejection and were less likely to quit. People with an optimistic view of life tend to treat obstacles and setbacks as temporary (and therefore surmountable). Pessimists take them personally; what others see as fleeting, localized impediments, they view as pervasive and permanent.

The most dramatic proof of his theory, says Seligman, came at the 1988 Olympic Games in Seoul, South Korea, after U.S. swimmer Matt Biondi turned in two disappointing performances in his first two races. Before the Games, Biondi had been favored to win seven golds—as Mark Spitz had done 16 years earlier. After those first two races, most commentators thought Biondi would be unable to recover from his setback. Not Seligman. He had given some members of the U.S swim team a version of his optimism test before the races; it showed that Biondi possessed an extraordinarily upbeat attitude. Rather than losing heart after turning in a bad time, as others might, Biondi tended to respond by swimming even faster. Sure enough, Biondi bounced right back, winning five gold medals in the next five races.
—By Alice Park

Among the new hires was a group who flunked the screening test but scored as "superoptimists" on Seligman's exam. And sure enough, they did the best of all; they outsold the pessimists in the regular group by 21% in the first year and 57% in the second. For years after that, passing Seligman's test was one way to get hired as a MetLife salesperson.

Perhaps the most visible emotional skills, the ones we recognize most readily, are the "people skills" like empathy, graciousness, the ability to read a social situation. Researchers believe that about 90% of emotional communication is nonverbal. Harvard psychologist Robert Rosenthal developed the PONS test (Profile of Nonverbal Sensitivity) to measure people's ability to read emotional cues. He shows subjects a film of a young woman expressing feelings—anger, love, jealousy, gratitude, seduction—edited so that one or another nonverbal cue is blanked out. In some instances the face is visible but not the body, or the woman's eyes are hidden, so that viewers have to judge the feeling by subtle cues. Once again, people with higher PONS scores tend to be more successful in their work and relationships; children who score well are more popular and successful in school, even then their IQs are quite average.

Like other emotional skills, empathy is an innate quality that can be shaped by experience. Infants as young as three months old exhibit empathy when they get upset at the sound of another baby crying. Even very young children learn by imitation; by watching how others act when they see someone in distress, these children acquire a repertoire of sensitive responses. If, on the other hand, the feelings they begin to express are not recognized and reinforced by the adults around them, they not only cease to express those feelings but they also become less able to recognize them in themselves or others.

Empathy too can be seen as a survival skill. Bert Cohler, a University of Chicago psychologist, and Fran Stott, dean of the Erikson Institute for Advanced Study in Child Development in Chicago, have found that children from psychically damaged families frequently become hypervigilant, developing an intense attunement to their parents' moods. One child they studied, Nicholas, had a horrible habit of approaching other kids in his nursery-school class as if he were going to kiss them, then would bite them instead. The scientists went back to study videos of Nicholas at 20 months interacting with his psychotic mother and found that she had responded to his every expression of anger or independence with compulsive kisses. The researchers dubbed them "kisses of death," and their true significance was obvious to Nicholas, who arched his back in horror at

Square Pegs in the Oval Office?

IF A HIGH DEGREE OF EMOTIONAL INTELLIGENCE IS A PREREQUISITE FOR OUTstanding achievement, there ought to be no better place to find it than in the White House. It turns out, however, that not every man who reached the pinnacle of American leadership was a gleaming example of self-awareness, empathy, impulse control and all the other qualities that mark an elevated EQ.

Oliver Wendell Holmes, who knew intelligence when he saw it, judged Franklin Roosevelt "a second-class intellect, but a first-class temperament." Born and educated as an aristocrat, F.D.R. had polio and needed a wheelchair for most of his adult life. Yet, far from becoming a self-pitying wretch, he developed an unbridled optimism that served him and the country well during the Depression and World War II—this despite, or because of, what Princeton professor Fred Greenstein calls Roosevelt's "tendency toward deviousness and duplicity."

Even a first-class temperament, however, is not a sure predictor of a successful presidency. According to Duke University political scientist James David Barber, the most perfect blend of intellect and warmth of personality in a Chief Executive was the brilliant Thomas Jefferson, who "knew the importance of communication and empathy. He never lost the common touch." Richard Ellis, a professor of politics at Oregon's Willamette University who is skeptical of the whole EQ theory, cites two 19th century Presidents who did not fit the mold. "Martin Van Buren was well adjusted, balanced, empathetic and persuasive, but he was not very successful," says Ellis. "Andrew Jackson was less well adjusted, less balanced, less empathetic and was terrible at controlling his own impulses, but he transformed the presidency."

Lyndon Johnson as Senate majority leader was a brilliant practitioner of the art of political persuasion, yet failed utterly to transfer that gift to the White House. In fact, says Princeton's Greenstein, L. B. J. and Richard Nixon would be labeled "worst cases" on any EQ scale of Presidents. Each was touched with political genius, yet each met with disaster. "To some extent," says Greenstein, "this is a function of the extreme aspects of their psyches; they are the political versions of Van Gogh, who does unbelievable paintings and then cuts off his ear."

History professor William Leuchtenburg of the University of North Carolina at Chapel Hill suggests that the 20th century Presidents with perhaps the highest IQs—Wilson, Hoover and Carter—also had the most trouble connecting with their constituents. Woodrow Wilson, he says, "was very high strung [and] arrogant; he was not willing to strike any middle ground. Herbert Hoover was so locked into certain ideas that you could never convince him otherwise. Jimmy Carter is probably the most puzzling of the three. He didn't have a deficiency of temperament; in fact, he was too temperate. There was an excessive rationalization about Carter's approach."

That was never a problem for John Kennedy and Ronald Reagan. Nobody ever accused them of intellectual genius, yet both radiated qualities of leadership with an infectious confidence and openheartedness that endeared them to the nation. Whether President Clinton will be so endeared remains a puzzle. That he is a Rhodes scholar makes him certifiably brainy, but his emotional intelligence is shaky. He obviously has the knack for establishing rapport with people, but he often appears so eager to please that he looks weak. "As for controlling his impulses," says Willamette's Ellis, "Clinton is terrible." —*By Jesse Birnbaum.*
Reported by James Carney/Washington and Lisa H. Towle/Raleigh

her approaching lips—and passed his own rage on to his classmates years later.

Empathy also acts as a buffer to cruelty, and it is a quality conspicuously lacking in child molesters and psychopaths. Goleman cites some chilling research into brutality by Robert Hare, a psychologist at the University of British Columbia. Hare found that psychopaths, when hooked up to

electrodes and told they are going to receive a shock, show none of the visceral responses that fear of pain typically triggers: rapid heartbeat, sweating and so on. How could the threat of punishment deter such people from committing crimes?

It is easy to draw the obvious lesson from these test results. How much happier would we be, how much more successful as individuals and civil as a society, if we were more alert to the importance of emotional intelligence and more adept at teaching it? From kindergartens to business schools to corporations across the country, people are taking seriously the idea that a little more time spent on the "touchy-feely" skills so often derided may in fact pay rich dividends.

In the corporate world, according to personnel executives, IQ gets you hired, but EQ gets you promoted. Goleman likes to tell of a manager at AT&T's Bell Labs, a think tank for brilliant engineers in New Jersey, who was asked to rank his top performers. They weren't the ones with the highest IQs; they were the ones whose E-mail got answered. Those workers who were good collaborators and networkers and popular with colleagues were more likely to get the cooperation they needed to reach their goals than the socially awkward, lone-wolf geniuses.

When David Campbell and others at the Center for Creative Leadership studied "derailed executives," the rising stars who flamed out, the researchers found that these executives failed most often because of "an interpersonal flaw" rather than a technical inability. Interviews with top executives in the U.S. and Europe turned up nine so-called fatal flaws, many of them classic emotional failings, such as "poor working relations," being "authoritarian" or "too ambitious" and having "conflict with upper management."

At the center's executive-leadership seminars across the country, managers come to get emotionally retooled. "This isn't sensitivity training or Sunday-supplement stuff," says Campbell. "One thing they know when they get through is what other people think of them." And the executives have an incentive to listen. Says Karen Boylston, director of the center's team-leadership group: "Customers are telling businesses, 'I don't care if every member of your staff graduated with honors from Harvard, Stanford and Wharton. I will take my business and go where I am understood and treated with respect.'"

Nowhere is the discussion of emotional intelligence more pressing than in schools, where both the stakes and the opportunities seem greatest. Instead of con-

stant crisis intervention, or declarations of war on drug abuse or teen pregnancy or violence, it is time, Goleman argues, for preventive medicine. "Five years ago, teachers didn't want to think about this," says principal Roberta Kirshbaum of P.S. 75 in New York City. "But when kids are getting killed in high school, we have to deal with it." Five years ago, Kirshbaum's school adopted an emotional literacy program, designed to help children learn to manage anger, frustration, loneliness. Since then, fights at lunchtime have decreased from two or three a day to almost none.

Educators can point to all sorts of data to support this new direction. Students who are depressed or angry literally cannot learn. Children who have trouble being accepted by their classmates are 2 to 8 times as likely to drop out. An inability to distinguish distressing feelings or handle frustration has been linked to eating disorders in girls.

Many school administrators are completely rethinking the weight they have been giving to traditional lessons and standardized tests. Peter Relic, president of the National Association of Independent Schools, would like to junk the SAT completely. "Yes, it may cost a heck of a lot more money to assess someone's EQ rather than using a machine-scored test to measure IQ," he says. "But if we don't, then we're saying that a test score is more important to us than who a child is as a human being. That means an immense loss in terms of human potential because we've defined success too narrowly."

This warm embrace by educators has left some scientists in a bind. On one hand, says Yale psychologist Salovey, "I love the idea that we want to teach people a richer understanding of their emotional life, to help them achieve their goals." But, he adds, "what I would oppose is training conformity to social expectations." The danger is that any campaign to hone emotional skills in children will end up teaching that there is a "right" emotional response for any given situation—laugh at parades, cry at funerals, sit still at church. "You can teach self-control," says Dr. Alvin Poussaint, professor of psychiatry at Harvard Medical School. "You can teach that it's better to talk out your anger and not use violence. But is it good emotional intelligence not to challenge authority?"

SOME PSYCHOLOGISTS GO further and challenge the very idea that emotional skills can or should be taught in any kind of formal, classroom way. Goleman's premise that children can be trained to analyze their feelings strikes Johns Hopkins' McHugh as an effort to reinvent the encounter group: "I consider that an abominable idea, an idea we have seen with adults. That failed, and now he wants to try it with children? Good grief!" He cites the description in Goleman's book of an experimental program at the Nueva Learning Center in San Francisco. In one scene, two fifth-grade boys start to argue over the rules of an exercise, and the teacher breaks in to ask them to talk about what they're feeling. "I appreciate the way you're being assertive in talking with Tucker," she says to one student. "You're not attacking." This strikes McHugh as pure folly. "The author is presuming that someone has the key to the right emotions to be taught to children. We don't even know the right emotions to be taught to adults. Do you really think a child of eight or nine really understands the difference between aggressiveness and assertiveness?"

The problem may be that there is an ingredient missing. Emotional skills, like intellectual ones, are morally neutral. Just as a genius could use his intellect either to cure cancer or engineer a deadly virus, someone with great empathic insight could use it to inspire colleagues or exploit them. Without a moral compass to guide people in how to employ their gifts, emotional intelligence can be used for good or evil. Columbia University psychologist Walter Mischel, who invented the marshmallow test and others like it, observes that the knack for delaying gratification that makes a child one marshmallow richer can help him become a better citizen or—just as easily—an even more brilliant criminal.

Given the passionate arguments that are raging over the state of moral instruction in this country, it is no wonder Goleman chose to focus more on neutral emotional skills than on the values that should govern their use. That's another book—and another debate. —*Reported by Sharon E. Epperson and Lawrence Mondi/New York, James L. Graff/Chicago and Lisa H. Towle/Raleigh*

ALIENATION

AND THE FOUR WORLDS OF CHILDHOOD

The forces that produce youthful alienation are growing in strength and scope, says Mr. Bronfenbrenner. And the best way to counteract alienation is through the creation of connections or links throughout our culture. The schools can build such links.

Urie Bronfenbrenner

Urie Bronfenbrenner is Jacob Gould Shurman Professor of Human Development and Family Studies and of Psychology at Cornell University, Ithaca, N.Y.

To be alienated is to lack a sense of belonging, to feel cut off from family, friends, school, or work—the four worlds of childhood.

At some point in the process of growing up, many of us have probably felt cut off from one or another of these worlds, but usually not for long and not from more than one world at a time. If things weren't going well in school, we usually still had family, friends, or some activity to turn to. But if, over an extended period, a young person feels unwanted or insecure in several of these worlds simultaneously or if the worlds are at war with one another, trouble may lie ahead.

What makes a young person feel that he or she doesn't belong? Individual differences in personality can certainly be one cause, but, especially in recent years, scientists who study human behavior and development have identified an equal (if not even more powerful) factor: the circumstances in which a young person lives.

Many readers may feel that they recognize the families depicted in the vignettes that are to follow. This is so because they reflect the way we tend to look at families today: namely, that we see parents as being good or not-so-good without fully taking into account the circumstances in their lives.

Take Charles and Philip, for example. Both are seventh-graders who live in a middle-class suburb of a large U.S. city. In many ways their surroundings seem similar; yet, in terms of the risk of alienation, they live in rather different worlds. See if you can spot the important differences.

CHARLES

The oldest of three children, Charles is amiable, outgoing, and responsible. Both of his parents have full-time jobs outside the home. They've been able to arrange their working hours, however, so that at least one of them is at home when the children return from school. If for some reason they can't be home, they have an arrangement with a neighbor, an elderly woman who lives alone. They can phone her and ask her to look after the children until they arrive. The children have grown so fond of this woman that she is like another grandparent—a nice situation for them, since their real grandparents live far away.

Homework time is one of the most important parts of the day for Charles and his younger brother and sister. Charles's parents help the children with their homework if they need it, but most of the time they just make sure that the children have a period of peace and quiet—without TV—in which to do their work. The children are allowed to watch television one hour each night—but only after they have completed their homework. Since Charles is doing well in school, homework isn't much of an issue, however.

Sometimes Charles helps his mother or father prepare dinner, a job that everyone in the family shares and enjoys. Those family members who don't cook on a given evening are responsible for cleaning up.

Charles also shares his butterfly collection with his family. He started the collection when he first began learning about butterflies during a fourth-grade science project. The whole family enjoys picnicking and hunting butterflies together, and Charles occasionally asks his father to help him mount and catalogue his trophies.

Charles is a bit of a loner. He's not a very good athlete, and this makes him somewhat self-conscious. But he does have one very close friend, a boy in his class who lives just down the block. The two boys have been good friends for years.

Charles is a good-looking, warm, happy young man. Now that he's beginning to be interested in girls, he's gratified to find that the interest is returned.

PHILIP

Philip is 12 and lives with his mother, father, and 6-year-old brother. Both of his parents work in the city, commuting more than an hour each way. Pandemonium strikes every weekday morning as

From *Phi Delta Kappan*, February 1986, pp. 430-436. © 1986 by Phi Delta Kappa, Inc. Reprinted by permission of the author and *Phi Delta Kappan*.

the entire family prepares to leave for school and work.

Philip is on his own from the time school is dismissed until just before dinner, when his parents return after stopping to pick up his little brother at a nearby day-care home. At one time, Philip took care of his little brother after school, but he resented having to do so. That arrangement ended one day when Philip took his brother out to play and the little boy wandered off and got lost. Philip didn't even notice for several hours that his brother was missing. He felt guilty at first about not having done a better job. But not having to mind his brother freed him to hang out with his friends or to watch television, his two major after-school activities.

The pace of their life is so demanding that Philip's parents spend their weekends just trying to relax. Their favorite weekend schedule calls for watching a ball game on television and then having a cookout in the back yard. Philip's mother resigned herself long ago to a messy house; pizza, TV dinners, or fast foods are all she can manage in the way of meals on most nights. Philip's father has made it clear that she can do whatever she wants in managing the house, as long as she doesn't try to involve him in the effort. After a hard day's work, he's too tired to be interested in housekeeping.

Philip knows that getting a good education is important; his parents have stressed that. But he just can't seem to concentrate in school. He'd much rather fool around with his friends. The thing that he and his friends like to do best is to ride the bus downtown and go to a movie, where they can show off, make noise, and make one another laugh.

Sometimes they smoke a little marijuana during the movie. One young man in Philip's social group was arrested once for having marijuana in his jacket pocket. He was trying to sell it on the street so that he could buy food. Philip thinks his friend was stupid to get caught. If you're smart, he believes, you don't let that happen. He's glad that his parents never found out about the incident.

Once, he brought two of his friends home during the weekend. His parents told him later that they didn't like the kind of people he was hanging around with. Now Philip goes out of his way to keep his friends and his parents apart.

THE FAMILY UNDER PRESSURE

In many ways the worlds of both

Institutions that play important roles in human development are rapidly being eroded, mainly through benign neglect.

---

teenagers are similar, even typical. Both live in families that have been significantly affected by one of the most important developments in American family life in the postwar years: the employment of both parents outside the home. Their mothers share this status with 64% of all married women in the U.S. who have school-age children. Fifty percent of mothers of preschool children and 46% of mothers with infants under the age of 3 work outside the home. For single-parent families, the rates are even higher: 53% of all mothers in single-parent households who have infants under age 3 work outside the home, as do 69% of all single mothers who have school-age children.[1]

These statistics have profound implications for families — sometimes for better, sometimes for worse. The determining factor is how well a given family can cope with the "havoc in the home" that two jobs can create. For, unlike most other industrialized nations, the U.S. has yet to introduce the kinds of policies and practices that make work life and family life compatible.

It is all too easy for family life in the U.S. to become hectic and stressful, as both parents try to coordinate the disparate demands of family and jobs in a world in which everyone has to be transported at least twice a day in a variety of directions. Under these circumstances, meal preparation, child care, shopping, and cleaning — the most basic tasks in a family — become major challenges. Dealing with these challenges may sometimes take precedence over the family's equally important child-rearing, educational, and nurturing roles.

But that is not the main danger. What

---

threatens the well-being of children and young people the most is that the external havoc can become internal, first for parents and then for their children. And that is exactly the sequence in which the psychological havoc of families under stress usually moves.

Recent studies indicate that conditions at work constitute one of the major sources of stress for American families.[2] Stress at work carries over to the home, where it affects first the relationship of parents to each other. Marital conflict then disturbs the parent/child relationship. Indeed, as long as tensions at work do not impair the relationship between the parents, the children are not likely to be affected. In other words, the influence of parental employment on children is indirect, operating through its effect on the parents.

That this influence is indirect does not make it any less potent, however. Once the parent/child relationship is seriously disturbed, children begin to feel insecure — and a door to the world of alienation has been opened. That door can open to children at any age, from preschool to high school and beyond.

My reference to the world of school is not accidental, for it is in that world that the next step toward alienation is likely to be taken. Children who feel rootless or caught in conflict at home find it difficult to pay attention in school. Once they begin to miss out on learning, they feel lost in the classroom, and they begin to seek acceptance elsewhere. Like Philip, they often find acceptance in a group of peers with similar histories who, having no welcoming place to go and nothing challenging to do, look for excitement on the streets.

OTHER INFLUENCES

In contemporary American society the growth of two-wage-earner families is not the only — or even the most serious — social change requiring accommodation through public policy and practice in order to avoid the risks of alienation. Other social changes include lengthy trips to and from work; the loss of the extended family, the close neighborhood, and other support systems previously available to families; and the omnipresent threat of television and other media to the family's traditional role as the primary transmitter of culture and values. Along with most families today, the families of Charles and Philip are experiencing the unraveling and disintegration of social institutions that in the past were central to the health and well-being of children and their parents.

Notice that both Charles and Philip come from two-parent, middle-class families. This is still the norm in the U.S. Thus neither family has to contend with two changes now taking place in U.S. society that have profound implications for the future of American families and the well-being of the next generation. The first of these changes is the increasing number of single-parent families. Although the divorce rate in the U.S. has been leveling off of late, this decrease has been more than compensated for by a rise in the number of unwed mothers, especially teenagers. Studies of the children brought up in single-parent families indicate that they are at greater risk of alienation than their counterparts from two-parent families. However, their vulnerability appears to have its roots not in the single-parent family structure as such, but in the treatment of single parents by U.S. society.[3]

In this nation, single parenthood is almost synonymous with poverty. And the growing gap between poor families and the rest of us is today the most powerful and destructive force producing alienation in the lives of millions of young people in America. In recent years, we have witnessed what the U.S. Census Bureau calls "the largest decline in family income in the post-World War II period." According to the latest Census, 25% of all children under age 6 now live in families whose incomes place them below the poverty line.

COUNTERING THE RISKS

Despite the similar stresses on their families, the risks of alienation for Charles and Philip are not the same. Clearly, Charles's parents have made a deliberate effort to create a variety of arrangements and practices that work against alienation. They have probably not done so as part of a deliberate program of "alienation prevention" — parents don't usually think in those terms. They're just being good parents. They spend time with their children and take an active interest in what their children are thinking, doing, and learning. They control their television set instead of letting it control them. They've found support systems to back them up when they're not available.

Without being aware of it, Charles's parents are employing a principle that the great Russian educator Makarenko employed in his extraordinarily success-

ful programs for the reform of wayward adolescents in the 1920s: "The maximum of support with the maximum of challenge."[4] Families that produce effective, competent children often follow this principle, whether they're aware of it or not. They neither maintain strict control nor allow their children total freedom. They're always opening doors — and then giving their children a gentle but firm shove to encourage them to move on and grow. This combination of support and challenge is essential, if children are to avoid alienation and develop into capable young adults.

From a longitudinal study of youthful alienation and delinquency that is now considered a classic, Finnish psychologist Lea Pulkkinen arrived at a conclusion strikingly similar to Makarenko's. She found "guidance" — a combination of love and direction — to be a critical predictor of healthy development in youngsters.[5]

No such pattern is apparent in Philip's family. Unlike Charles's parents, Philip's parents neither recognize nor respond to the challenges they face. They have dispensed with the simple amenities of family self-discipline in favor of whatever is easiest. They may not be indifferent to their children, but the demands of their jobs leave them with little energy to be actively involved in their children's lives. (Note that Charles's parents have work schedules that are flexible enough to allow one of them to be at home most afternoons. In this regard, Philip's family is much more the norm, however. One of the most constructive steps that employers could take to strengthen families would be to enact clear policies making such flexibility possible.)

But perhaps the clearest danger signal in Philip's life is his dependence on his peer group. Pulkkinen found heavy reliance on peers to be one of the strongest predictors of problem behavior in adolescence and young adulthood. From a developmental viewpoint, adolescence is a time of challenge — a period in which young people seek activities that will serve as outlets for their energy, imagination, and longings. If healthy and constructive challenges are not available to them, they will find their challenges in such peer-group-related behaviors as poor school performance, aggressiveness or social withdrawal (sometimes both), school absenteeism or dropping out, smoking, drinking, early and promiscuous sexual activity, teenage parenthood, drugs, and juvenile delinquency.

This pattern has now been identified in a number of modern industrial societies, including the U.S., England, West Germany, Finland, and Australia. The pattern is both predictable from the circumstances of a child's early family life and predictive of life experiences still to come, e.g., difficulties in establishing relationships with the opposite sex, marital discord, divorce, economic failure, criminality.

If the roots of alienation are to be found in disorganized families living in disorganized environments, its bitter fruits are to be seen in these patterns of disrupted development. This is not a harvest that our nation can easily afford. Is it a price that other modern societies are paying, as well?

A CROSS-NATIONAL PERSPECTIVE

The available answers to that question will not make Americans feel better about what is occurring in the U.S. In our society, the forces that produce youthful alienation are growing in strength and scope. Families, schools, and other institutions that play important roles in human development are rapidly being eroded, *mainly through benign neglect.* Unlike the citizens of other modern nations, we Americans have simply not been willing to make the necessary effort to forestall the alienation of our young people.

As part of a new experiment in higher education at Cornell University, I have been teaching a multidisciplinary course for the past few years titled "Human Development in Post-Industrial Societies." One of the things we have done in that course is to gather comparative data from several nations, including France, Canada, Japan, Australia, Germany, England, and the U.S. One student summarized our findings succinctly: "With respect to families, schools, children, and youth, such countries as France, Japan, Canada, and Australia have more in common with each other than the United States has with any of them." For example:

• The U.S. has by far the highest rate of teenage pregnancy of any industrialized nation — twice the rate of its nearest competitor, England.

• The U.S. divorce rate is the highest in the world — nearly double that of its nearest competitor, Sweden.

• The U.S. is the only industrialized society in which nearly one-fourth of all infants and preschool children live in families whose incomes fall below the poverty line. These children lack such basics as adequate health care.

• The U.S. has fewer support systems for individuals in all age groups, including adolescence. The U.S. also has the highest incidence of alcohol and drug abuse among adolescents of any country in the world.[6]

All these problems are part of the unraveling of the social fabric that has been going on since World War II. These problems are not unique to the U.S., but in many cases they are more pronounced here than elsewhere.

WHAT COMMUNITIES CAN DO

The more we learn about alienation and its effects in contemporary post-industrial societies, the stronger are the imperatives to counteract it. If the essence of alienation is disconnectedness, then the best way to counteract alienation is through the creation of connections or links.

For the well-being of children and adolescents, the most important links must be those between the home, the peer group, and the school. A recent study in West Germany effectively demonstrated how important this basic triangle can be. The study examined student achievement and social behavior in 20 schools. For all the schools, the researchers developed measures of the links between the home, the peer group, and the school. Controlling for social class and other variables, the researchers found that they were able to predict children's behavior from the number of such links they found. Students who had no links were alienated. They were not doing well in school, and they exhibited a variety of behavioral problems. By contrast, students who had such links were doing well and were growing up to be responsible citizens.[7]

In addition to creating links within the basic triangle of home, peer group, and school, we need to consider two other structures in today's society that affect the lives of young people: the world of work (for both parents and children) and the community, which provides an overarching context for all the other worlds of childhood.

Philip's family is one example of how the world of work can contribute to alienation. The U.S. lags far behind other industrialized nations in providing child-care services and other benefits designed to promote the well-being of children and their families. Among the most needed benefits are maternity and paternity leaves, flex-time, job-sharing

> C aring is surely an essential aspect of education in a free society; yet we have almost completely neglected it.

arrangements, and personal leaves for parents when their children are ill. These benefits are a matter of course in many of the nations with which the U.S. is generally compared.

In contemporary American society, however, the parents' world of work is not the only world that both policy and practice ought to be accommodating. There is also the children's world of work. According to the most recent figures available, 50% of all high school students now work part-time — sometimes as much as 40 to 50 hours per week. This fact poses a major problem for the schools. Under such circumstances, how can teachers assign homework with any expectation that it will be completed?

The problem is further complicated by the kind of work that most young people are doing. For many years, a number of social scientists — myself included — advocated more work opportunities for adolescents. We argued that such experiences would provide valuable contact with adult models and thereby further the development of responsibility and general maturity. However, from their studies of U.S. high school students who are employed, Ellen Greenberger and Lawrence Steinberg conclude that most of the jobs held by these youngsters are highly routinized and afford little opportunity for contact with adults. The largest employers of teenagers in the U.S. are fast-food restaurants. Greenberger and Steinberg argue that, instead of providing maturing experiences, such settings give adolescents even greater exposure to the values and lifestyles of their peer group. And the adolescent peer group tends to emphasize immediate gratification and consumerism.[8]

Finally, in order to counteract the

mounting forces of alienation in U.S. society, we must establish a working alliance between the private sector and the public one (at both the local level and the national level) to forge links between the major institutions in U.S. society and to re-create a sense of community. Examples from other countries abound:

• Switzerland has a law that no institution for the care of the elderly can be established unless it is adjacent to and shares facilities with a day-care center, a school, or some other kind of institution serving children.

• In many public places throughout Australia, the Department of Social Security has displayed a poster that states, in 16 languages: "If you need an interpreter, call this number." The department maintains a network of interpreters who are available 16 hours a day, seven days a week. They can help callers get in touch with a doctor, an ambulance, a fire brigade, or the police; they can also help callers with practical or personal problems.

• In the USSR, factories, offices, and places of business customarily "adopt" groups of children, e.g., a day-care center, a class of schoolchildren, or a children's ward in a hospital. The employees visit the children, take them on outings, and invite them to visit their place of work.

We Americans can offer a few good examples of alliances between the public and private sectors, as well. For example, in Flint, Michigan, some years ago, Mildred Smith developed a community program to improve school performance among low-income minority pupils. About a thousand children were involved. The program required no change in the regular school curriculum; its principal focus was on building links between home and school. This was accomplished in a variety of ways.

• A core group of low-income parents went from door to door, telling their neighbors that the school needed their help.

• Parents were asked to keep younger children out of the way so that the older children could complete their homework.

• Schoolchildren were given tags to wear at home that said, "May I read to you?"

• Students in the high school business program typed and duplicated teaching materials, thus freeing teachers to work directly with the children.

• Working parents visited school classrooms to talk about their jobs and about how their own schooling now helped them in their work.

WHAT SCHOOLS CAN DO

As the program in Flint demonstrates, the school is in the best position of all U.S. institutions to initiate and strengthen links that support children and adolescents. This is so for several reasons. First, one of the major — but often unrecognized — responsibilities of the school is to enable young people to move from the secluded and supportive environment of the home into responsible and productive citizenship. Yet, as the studies we conducted at Cornell revealed, most other modern nations are ahead of the U.S. in this area.

In these other nations, schools are not merely — or even primarily — places where the basics are taught. Both in purpose and in practice, they function instead as settings in which young people learn "citizenship": what it means to be a member of the society, how to behave toward others, what one's responsibilities are to the community and to the nation.

I do not mean to imply that such learnings do not occur in American schools. But when they occur, it is mostly by accident and not because of thoughtful planning and careful effort. What form might such an effort take? I will present here some ideas that are too new to have stood the test of time but that may be worth trying.

Creating an American classroom. This is a simple idea. Teachers could encourage their students to learn about schools (and, especially, about individual classrooms) in such modern industrialized societies as France, Japan, Canada, West Germany, the Soviet Union, and Australia. The children could acquire such information in a variety of ways: from reading, from films, from the firsthand reports of children and adults who have attended school abroad, from exchanging letters and materials with students and their teachers in other countries. Through such exposure, American students would become aware of how attending school in other countries is both similar to and different from attending school in the U.S.

But the main learning experience would come from asking students to consider what kinds of things *should* be happening — or not happening — in American classrooms, given our na-

tion's values and ideals. For example, how should children relate to one another and to their teachers, if they are doing things in an *American* way? If a student's idea seems to make sense, the American tradition of pragmatism makes the next step obvious: try the idea to see if it works.

The curriculum for caring. This effort also has roots in our values as a nation. Its goal is to make caring an essential part of the school curriculum. However, students would not simply learn about caring; they would actually engage in it. Children would be asked to spend time with and to care for younger children, the elderly, the sick, and the lonely. Caring institutions, such as daycare centers, could be located adjacent to or even within the schools. But it would be important for young caregivers to learn about the environment in which their charges live and the other people with whom their charges interact each day. For example, older children who took responsibility for younger ones would become acquainted with the younger children's parents and living arrangements by escorting them home from school.

Just as many schools now train superb drum corps, they could also train "caring corps" — groups of young men and women who would be on call to handle a variety of emergencies. If a parent fell suddenly ill, these students could come into the home to care for the children, prepare meals, run errands, and serve as an effective source of support for their fellow human beings. Caring is surely an essential aspect of education in a free society; yet we have almost completely neglected it.

Mentors for the young. A mentor is someone with a skill that he or she wishes to teach to a younger person. To be a true mentor, the older person must be willing to take the time and to make the commitment that such teaching requires.

We don't make much use of mentors in U.S. society, and we don't give much recognition or encouragement to individuals who play this important role. As a result, many U.S. children have few significant and committed adults in their lives. Most often, their mentors are their own parents, perhaps a teacher or two, a coach, or — more rarely — a relative, a neighbor, or an older classmate. However, in a diverse society such as ours, with its strong tradition of volunteerism, potential mentors

abound. The schools need to seek them out and match them with young people who will respond positively to their particular knowledge and skills.

The school is the institution best suited to take the initiative in this task, because the school is the only place in which all children gather every day. It is also the only institution that has the right (and the responsibility) to turn to the community for help in an activity that represents the noblest kind of education: the building of character in the young.

There is yet another reason why schools should take a leading role in rebuilding links among the four worlds of childhood: schools have the most to gain. In the recent reports bemoaning the state of American education, a recurring theme has been the anomie and chaos that pervade many U.S. schools, to the detriment of effective teaching and learning. Clearly, we are in danger of allowing our schools to become academies of alienation.

In taking the initiative to rebuild links among the four worlds of childhood, U.S. schools will be taking necessary action to combat the destructive forces of alienation — first, within their own walls, and thereafter, in the life experience and future development of new generations of Americans.

1. Urie Bronfenbrenner, "New Worlds for Families," paper presented at the Boston Children's Museum, 4 May 1984.
2. Urie Bronfenbrenner, "The Ecology of the Family as a Context for Human Development," *Developmental Psychology*, in press.
3. Mavis Heatherington, "Children of Divorce," in R. Henderson, ed., *Parent-Child Interaction* (New York: Academic Press, 1981).
4. A.S. Makarenko, *The Collective Family: A Handbook for Russian Parents* (New York: Doubleday, 1967).
5. Lea Pulkkinen, "Self-Control and Continuity from Childhood to Adolescence," in Paul Baltes and Orville G. Brim, eds., *Life-Span Development and Behavior*, Vol. 4 (New York: Academic Press, 1982), pp. 64-102.
6. S.B. Kamerman, *Parenting in an Unresponsive Society* (New York: Free Press, 1980); S.B. Kamerman and A.J. Kahn, *Social Services in International Perspective* (Washington, D.C.: U.S. Department of Health, Education, and Welfare, n.d.); and Lloyd Johnston, Jerald Bachman, and Patrick O'Malley, *Use of Licit and Illicit Drugs by America's High School Students — 1975-84* (Washington, D.C.: U.S. Government Printing Office, 1985).
7. Kurt Aurin, personal communication, 1985.
8. Ellen Greenberger and Lawrence Steinberg, *The Work of Growing Up* (New York: Basic Books, forthcoming).

Why kids have a lot to cry about

David Elkind, Ph.D.

David Elkind, Ph.D., professor of child study at Tufts University, is the author of more than 400 articles. He is perhaps best known for his books The Hurried Child; All Grown Up and No Place to Go *and* Ties That Stress: Childrearing in a Postmodern Society. *He is an active consultant to government agencies, private foundations, clinics, and mental-health centers.*

"Mommy," THE FIVE-YEAR-OLD GIRL asked her mother, "why don't you get divorced again?" Her thrice-married mother was taken aback and said in return, "Honey, why in the world should I do that?" To which her daughter replied, "Well, I haven't seen you in love for such a long time."

This young girl perceives family life and the adult world in a very different way than did her counterpart less than half a century ago. Likewise, the mother perceives her daughter quite differently than did a mother raising a child in the 1940s. Although this mother was surprised at her daughter's question, she was not surprised at her understanding of divorce, nor at her familiarity with the symptoms of romance.

As this anecdote suggests, there has been a remarkable transformation over the last 50 years in our children's perceptions of us, and in our perceptions of our children. These altered perceptions are a very small part of a much larger tectonic shift in our society in general and in our families in particular. This shift is nothing less than a transformation of the basic framework, or paradigm, within which we think about and thus perceive our world. To understand the changes in the family, the perceptions of family members, and of parenting that have been brought about, we first have to look at this broader "paradigm shift" and what it has meant for family sentiments, values, and perceptions.

FROM MODERN TO POSTMODERN
Without fully realizing it perhaps, we have been transported into the postmodern era. Although this era has been called "postindustrial" and, alternatively, "information age," neither of these phrases is broad enough to encompass the breadth and depth of the changes that have occurred. The terms modern and postmodern, in contrast, encompass all aspects of society and speak to the changes in science, philosophy, architecture, literature, and the arts—as well as in industry and technology—that have marked our society since mid-century.

THE MODERN AND THE NUCLEAR FAMILY
The modern era, which began with the Renaissance and spanned the Industrial Revolution, was based upon three related assumptions. One was the idea of *human progress*—the notion that the natural direction of human and societal development is toward a more equitable, peaceful, and harmonious world in which every individual would be entitled to life, liberty, and the pursuit of happiness. A

second assumption is *universality*. There were, it was taken as given, universal laws of nature of art, science, economics, and so on that transcended time and culture. The third basic assumption was that of *regularity*—the belief that the world is an orderly place, that animals and plants, geological layers and chemical elements could be classified in an orderly hierarchy. As Einstein put it, "God does not play dice with the universe!"

These assumptions gave a unique character and distinctiveness to modern life. Modern science, literature, architecture, philosophy, and industry all embodied these premises. And they were enshrined in the Modern Family as well. The modern nuclear family, for example, was seen as the end result of a progressive evolution of family forms. Two parents, two or three children, one parent working and one staying home to rear the children and maintain the home was thought to be the ideal family form toward which all prior, "primitive" forms were merely preliminary stages.

SENTIMENTS OF THE NUCLEAR FAMILY

The Modern Family was shaped by three sentiments that also reflected the underlying assumptions of modernity. One of these was Romantic Love. In premodern times, couples married by familial and community dictates. Considerations of property and social position were paramount. This community influence declined in the modern era, and couples increasingly came to choose one another on the basis of mutual attraction. This attraction became idealized into the notion that "Some enchanted evening, you will meet a stranger" for whom you and only you were destined ("You were meant for me, I was meant for you"), and that couples would stay together for the rest of their lives, happily "foreverafter."

A second sentiment of the Modern Family was that of Maternal Love—the idea that women have a maternal "instinct" and a need to care for children, particularly when they are small. The idea of a maternal instinct was a thoroughly modern invention that emerged only after modern medicine and nutrition reduced infant mortality. In premodern times, infant mortality was so high that the young were not even named until they were two years old and stood a good chance of surviving. It was also not uncommon for urban parents to have their infants "wet-nursed" in the country. Often these

infants died because the wet-nurse fed her own child before she fed the stranger, and there was little nourishment left. Such practices could hardly be engaged in by a mother with a "maternal instinct."

The third sentiment of the Modern Family was Domesticity, a belief that relationships within the family are always more powerful and binding than are those outside it. The family was, as Christopher Lasch wrote, "a haven in a heartless world." As a haven, the nuclear family shielded and protected its members from the evils and temptations of the outside world. This sentiment also extended to the family's religious, ethnic, and social-class affiliations. Those individuals who shared these affiliations were to be preferred, as friends and spouses, over those with different affiliations.

PARENTING THE INNOCENT

The modern perceptions of parenting, children, and teenagers grew out of these family sentiments. Modern parents, for example, were seen as intuitively or instinctively knowledgeable about child-rearing. Professional help was needed only to encourage parents to do "what comes naturally." In keeping with this view of parenting was the perception of children as innocent and in need of parental nurturance and protection. Teenagers, in turn, were seen as immature and requiring adult guidance and direction. Adolescence, regarded as the age of preparation for adulthood, brought with it the inevitable "storm and stress," as young people broke from the tight nuclear family bonds and became socially and financially independent.

These modern perceptions of parenting and of children and youth were reinforced by the social mirror of the media, the law and the health professions. Motion pictures such as the Andy Hardy series (starring Mickey Rooney) depicted a teenage boy getting into youthful scrapes at school and with friends from which he was extricated by his guardian the judge, played by Harlan Stone. Fiction similarly portrayed teenagers as immature young people struggling to find themselves. Mark Twain's Huck Finn was an early version of the modern immature adolescent, while J. D. Salinger's Holden Caulfield is a modern version.

Modern laws, such as the child-labor laws and compulsory-education statutes were enacted to protect both children and

adolescents. And the health professions attributed the mental-health problems of children and youth to conflicts arising from the tight emotional bonds of the nuclear family.

POSTMODERNITY AND THE POSTMODERN FAMILY

The postmodern view has largely grown out of the failure of modern assumptions about progress, universality, and regularity. Many of the events of this century have made the idea of progress difficult to maintain. Germany, one of the most educationally, scientifically, and culturally advanced countries of the world, engaged in the most heinous genocide. Modern science gave birth to the atomic bomb that was dropped on Hiroshima and Nagasaki. Environmental degradation, pollution, population explosions, and widespread famine can hardly be reconciled with the notion of progress.

Secondly, the belief in universal principles has been challenged as the "grand" theories of the modern era—such as those of Marx, Darwin, and Freud—are now recognized as limited by the social and historical contexts in which they were elaborated. Modern theorists believed that they could transcend social-historical boundaries; the postmodern worker recognizes that he or she is constrained by the particular discourse of narrative in play at the time. Likewise, the search for abiding ethical, moral, and religious universals is giving way to a recognition that there are many different ethics, moralities, and religions, each of which has a claim to legitimacy.

Finally, the belief in regularity has given way to a recognition of the importance of irregularity, indeterminacy, chaos, and fuzzy logic. There is much in nature, such as the weather, that remains unpredictable—not because it is perverse, but only because the weather is affected by non-regular events. Sure regularity appears, but irregularity is now seen as a genuine phenomenon in its own right. It is no longer seen, as it was in the modern era, as the result of some failure to discover an underlying regularity.

In place of these modern assumptions, a new, postmodern paradigm with its own basic premises has been invented. The assumption of progress, to illustrate, has given way to the presumption of *difference*. There are many different forms and types of progress, and not all progressions are necessarily for the better. Likewise, the belief in universals has moved aside for the belief in *particulars*. Different phenomena may have different rules and principles that are not necessarily generalizable. For example, a particular family or a particular class of children is a non-replicable event that can never be exactly duplicated and to which universal principles do not apply. Finally, the assumption of regularity moved aside to make room for the principle of *irregularity*. The world is not as orderly and as logically organized as we had imagined.

As the societal paradigm has shifted, so has the structure of the family. The ideal nuclear family, thought to be the product of progressive social evolution, has given way to what might be called the *Permeable Family* of the postmodern era. The Permeable Family encompasses many different family forms: traditional or nuclear, two-parent working, single-parent, blended, adopted child, test-tube, surrogate mother, and co-parent families. Each of these is valuable and a potentially successful family form.

The family is permeable in other ways as well. It is no longer isolated from the larger community. Thanks to personal computers, fax and answering machines, the workplace has moved into the homeplace. The homeplace, in turn, thanks to childcare facilities in office buildings and factories, has moved into the workplace. The home is also permeated by television, which brings the outside world into the living room and bedrooms. And an ever-expanding number of TV shows (*Oprah, Donahue, Geraldo, and Sally Jessy Raphael*), all detailing the variety of family problems, brings the living room and the bedroom into the outside world.

Quite different sentiments animate the postmodern Permeable Family than animated the modern nuclear family. The transformation of family sentiments came about in a variety of ways, from the civil-rights movement, the women's movement, changes in media, and laws that were part of the postmodern revolution. Because there is a constant interaction between the family and the larger society, it is impossible to say whether changes in the family were brought about by changes in society or vice versa. Things moved in both directions.

For a number of reasons, the Modern Family sentiment of Romantic Love has been transformed in the Postmodern era into the sentiment of *Consensual Love*. In contrast to the idealism and perfectionism of Romantic Love, consensual love is re-

alistic and practical. It recognizes the legitimacy of premarital relations and is not premised on long-term commitment. Consensual Love is an agreement or contract between the partners; as an agreement it can be broken. The difference between Romantic Love and Consensual Love is summed up in the prenuptial agreement, which acknowledges the possible rupture of a marriage—before the marriage actually occurs. The current emphasis upon safe sex is likewise a symptom of consensual, not romantic, love.

The Modern Family sentiment of maternal love has yielded to other changes. Today, more than 50 percent of women are in the workforce, and some 60 percent of these women have children under the age of six. These figures make it clear that non-maternal and non-parental figures are now playing a major role in child-rearing. As part of this revision of child-rearing responsibilities, a new sentiment has emerged that might be called *shared parenting*. What this sentiment entails is the understanding that not only mothers, but fathers and professional caregivers are a necessary part of the child-rearing process. Child-rearing and childcare are no longer looked upon as the sole or primary responsibility of the mother.

The permeability of the Postmodern Family has also largely done away with the Modern Family sentiment of domesticity. The family can no longer protect individuals from the pressures of the outside world. Indeed, the impulse of the Permeable Family is to move in the other direction. Permeable Families tend to thrust children and teenagers forward to deal with realities of the outside world at ever earlier ages. This has resulted in what I have called the "hurrying" of children to grow up fast. Much of the hurrying of children and youth is a well-intentioned effort on the part of parents to help prepare children and youth for the onrush of information, challenges, and temptations coming at them through the now-permeable boundaries of family life.

POSTMODERN PARENTS OF KIDS WITHOUT INNOCENCE

These new, postmodern sentiments have given rise to new perceptions of parenting, of children, and of adolescents. Now that parenting is an activity shared with non-parental figures, we no longer regard it as an instinct that emerges once we

have become parents; it is now regarded as a matter of learned *technique*.

Postmodern parents understand that doing "what comes naturally" may not be good for children. There are ways to say things to children that are less stressful than others. There are ways of disciplining that do not damage the child's sense of self esteem. The problem for parents today is to choose from the hundreds of books and other media sources bombarding them with advice on child-rearing. As one mother said to me, "I've read your books and they sound okay, but what if you're wrong?"

With respect to children, the perception of childhood innocence has given way to the perception of childhood competence. Now that children are living in Permeable Families with—thanks to television—a steady diet of overt violence, sexuality, substance abuse, and environmental degradation, we can no longer assume they are innocent. Rather, perhaps to cover our own inability to control what our children are seeing, we perceive them as competent to deal with all of this material. Indeed, we get so caught up in this perception of competence that we teach four- and five-year-olds about AIDS and child abuse and provide "toys" that simulate pregnancy or the dismemberment that accidents can cause unbuckled-up occupants. And the media reinforce this competence perception with films such as *Look Who's Talking* and *Home Alone*.

If children are seen as competent, teenagers can no longer be seen as immature. Rather they are now seen as sophisticated in the ways of the world, knowledgeable about sex, drugs, crime, and much more. This is a convenient fiction for parents suffering a time-famine. Such parents can take the perception of teenage sophistication as a rationale to abrogate their responsibility to provide young people with limits, guidance, and supervision. Increasingly, teenagers are on their own. Even junior and senior high schools no longer provide the social programs and clubs they once did.

This new perception of teenagers is also reflected in the social mirror of media, school and law. Postmodern films like *Risky Business* (in which teenager runs a bordello in the parents' home) and *Angel* (demure high school student by day, avenging hooker by night) are a far cry from the Andy Hardy films. Postmodern TV sitcoms such as *Married with Children* and *Roseanne* present images of teenage sophistication hardly reconcilable with the teenagers portrayed in modern

TV shows such as *My Three Sons* or *Ozzie and Harriet*. Postmodern legal thinking is concerned with protecting the *rights* of children and teenagers, rather than protecting children themselves. Children and teenagers can now sue their parents for divorce, visitation rights, and for remaining in the United States when the family travels overseas.

REALITY IS HERE TO STAY

The postmodern perceptions of children as competent and of teenagers as sophisticated did not grow out of any injustices nor harm visited upon children and youth. Rather they grew out of a golden era for young people that lasted from the end of the last century to the middle of this one. Society as a whole was geared to regard children as innocent and teenagers as immature, and sought to protect children and gradually inculcate teenagers into the ways of the world.

In contrast, the perceptions of childhood competence and teenage sophistication have had detrimental effects upon children and youth. Indeed, these perceptions have placed children and teenagers under inordinate stress. And it shows. On every measure that we have, children and adolescents are doing less well today than they did a quarter century ago, when the new postmodern perceptions were coming into play. While it would be unwise to attribute all of these negative effects to changed perceptions alone—economics and government policy clearly played a role—it is also true that government policy and economics are affected by the way young people are perceived.

The statistics speak for themselves. There has been a 50-percent increase in obesity in children and youth over the past two decades. We lose some ten thousand teenagers a year in substance-related accidents, not including injured and maimed. One in four teenagers drinks to excess every two weeks, and we have two million alcoholic teenagers.

Teenage girls in America get pregnant at the rate of one million per year, twice the rate of the next Western country, England. Suicide has tripled among teenagers in the last 20 years, and between five and six thousand teenagers take their own lives each year. It is estimated that one out of four teenage girls manifests at least one symptom of an eating disorder, most commonly severe dieting. The 14- to 19-year-old age group has the second-highest homicide rate of any age group.

These are frightening statistics. Yet they are not necessarily an indictment of the postmodern world, nor of our changed perceptions of children and youth. We have gone through enormous social changes in a very brief period of time. No other society on Earth changes, or can change, as rapidly as we do. That is both our strength and our weakness. It has made us, and will keep us, the leading industrial nation in the world because we are more flexible than any other society, including Japan.

But rapid social change is a catastrophe for children and youth, who require stability and security for healthy growth and development. Fortunately, we are now moving toward a more stable society. A whole generation of parents was caught in the transition between Modern and Postmodern Family sentiments; among them, divorce, open marriage, and remarriage became at least as commonplace as the permanent nuclear family. The current generation of parents have, however, grown up with the new family sentiments and are not as conflicted as their own parents were.

As a result, we are slowly moving back to a more realistic perception of both children and teenagers, as well as toward a family structure that is supportive of all family members. We are moving towards what might be called the *Vital Family*. In the Vital Family, the modern value of togetherness is given equal weight with the Postmodern Family value of autonomy. Children are seen as *growing into competence* and as still needing the help and support of parents. Likewise, teenagers are increasingly seen as *maturing into sophistication*, and able to benefit from adult guidance, limits, and direction.

These new perceptions pop up in the media. Increasingly, newspapers and magazines feature articles on the negative effects pressures for early achievement have upon children. We are also beginning to see articles about the negative effects the demands for sophistication place upon teenagers. A number of recent TV shows (such as *Beverly Hills 90210*) have begun to portray children and youth as sophisticated, but also as responsible and accepting of adult guidance and supervision. There is still much too much gratuitous sex and violence, but at least there are signs of greater responsibility and recognition that children and adolescents may not really be prepared for everything we would like to throw at them.

After 10 years of traveling and lecturing all over the country, I have an impression that the American family is alive and well. It has changed dramatically, and we are still accommodating to the changes. And, as always happens, children and youths are more harmed by change than are adults. But our basic value system remains intact. We do have a strong Judeo-Christian heritage; we believe in hard work, democracy, and autonomy. But our sense of social and parental responsibility, however, was temporarily deadened by the pace of social change. Now that we are getting comfortable in our new Permeable Family sentiments and perceptions, we are once again becoming concerned with those who are young and those who are less fortunate.

As human beings we all have a need to become the best that we can be. But we also have a need to love and to be loved, to care and to be cared for. The Modern Family spoke to our need to belong at the expense, particularly for women, of the need to become.

The Permeable Family, in contrast, celebrates the need to become at the expense of the need to belong, and this has been particularly hard on children and youth. Now we are moving towards a Vital Family that ensures both our need to become and our need to belong. We are not there yet, but the good news is, we are on our way.

the
MIRACLE
OF RESILIENCY

DAVID GELMAN

There are sharp differences in the way children bear up under stress

A prominent child psychiatrist, E. James Anthony, once proposed this analogy: there are three dolls, one made of glass, the second of plastic, the third of steel. Struck with a hammer, the glass doll shatters; the plastic doll is scarred. But the steel doll proves invulnerable, reacting only with a metallic ping.

In life, no one is unbreakable. But child-health specialists know there are sharp differences in the way children bear up under stress. In the aftermath of divorce or physical abuse, for instance, some are apt to become nervous and withdrawn; some may be illness-prone and slow to develop. But there are also so-called resilient children who shrug off the hammer blows and go on to highly productive lives. The same small miracle of resiliency has been found under even the most harrowing conditions—in Cambodian refugee camps, in crack-ridden Chicago housing projects. Doctors repeatedly encounter the phenomenon: the one child in a large, benighted brood of five or six who seems able to take adversity in stride. "There are kids in families from very adverse situations who really do beautifully, and seem to rise to the top of their potential, even with everything else working against them," says Dr. W. Thomas Boyce, director of the division of behavioral and developmental pediatrics at the University of California, San Francisco. "Nothing touches them; they thrive no matter what."

Something, clearly, has gone right with these children, but what? Researchers habitually have come at the issue the other way around. The preponderance of the literature has to do with why children fail, fall ill, turn delinquent. Only recently, doctors realized they were neglecting the equally important question of why some children *don't* get sick. Instead of working backward from failure, they decided, there might be as much or more to be learned from studying the secrets of success. In the course of looking at such "risk factors" as poverty, physical impairment or abusive parents, they gradually became aware that there were also "protective factors" that served as buffers against the risks. If those could be identified, the reasoning went, they might help develop interventions that could change the destiny of more vulnerable children.

At the same time, the recognition that many children have these built-in defenses has plunged resiliency research into political controversy. "There is a danger among certain groups who advocate nonfederal involvement in assistance to children," says Duke University professor Neil Boothby, a child psychologist who has studied children in war zones. "They use it to blame people who don't move out of poverty. Internationally, the whole notion of resiliency has been used as an excuse not to do anything."

The quest to identify protective factors has produced an eager burst of studies in the past 10 or 15 years, with new publications tumbling off the presses every month. Although the studies so far offer no startling insights, they are providing fresh perspectives on how nature and nurture intertwine in childhood development. One of the prime protective factors, for example, is a matter of genetic luck of the draw: a child born with an easygoing disposition invariably handles stress better than one with a nervous, overreactive temperament. But even highly reactive children can acquire resilience if they have a consistent, stabilizing element in their young lives—something like an attentive parent or mentor.

The most dramatic evidence on that score comes not from humans but from their more researchable cousins, the apes. In one five-year-long study, primate researcher Stephen Suomi has shown that by putting infant monkeys in the care of supportive mothers, he could virtually turn their lives around. Suomi, who heads the Laboratory of Comparative Ethology at the National Institute of Child Health and Human Development, has been comparing "vulnerable" and "invulnerable" monkeys to see if there are useful nurturing approaches to be learned. Differences of temperament can be spotted in monkeys before they're a week old. Like their human counterparts, vulnerable monkey infants show measurable increases in heart rate and stress-hormone production in response to threat situations. "You see a fairly consistent pattern of physiological arousal, and also major behavioral differences," says Suomi. "Parallel patterns have been found in human-developmental labs, so we feel we're looking at the same phenomena."

Left alone in a regular troop, these high-strung infants grow up to be marginal figures in their troops. But by putting them in the care of particularly loving, attentive foster mothers within their first four days of life, Suomi turns the timid monkeys into social lions. Within two months, they become bold and outgoing. Males in the species Suomi has been working with normally leave their native troop at puberty and eventually work their way into a new troop. The nervous, vulnerable individuals usually are the last to leave home. But after being "cross-fostered" to loving mothers, they develop enough confidence so that they're first to leave.

Once on their own, monkeys have complicated (but somehow familiar) patterns of alliances. Their status often depends on whom they know and to whom they're related. In squabbles, they quickly generate support among friends and family members. The cross-fostered monkeys grow very adept at recruiting that kind of support. It's a knack they somehow get through interaction with their foster mothers, in which they evidently pick up coping styles as well as information. "It's essentially a social-learning phenomenon," says Suomi. "I would argue that's what's going on at the human level, too. Evidently, you can learn styles in addition to specific information."

In the long run, the vulnerable infants not only were turned around to normality, they often rose to the top of their hierarchies; they became community leaders. Boyce notes there are significant "commonalities" between Suomi's findings and studies of vulnerable children. "The implications are that vulnerable children, if placed in the right social environment, might become extraordinarily productive and competent adult individuals," he says.

Children, of course, can't be fostered off to new parents or social conditions as readily as monkeys. Most resiliency research is based on children who have not had such interventions in their lives. Nevertheless, some of the findings are revealing. One of the definitive studies was conducted by Emmy E. Werner, a professor of human development at the University of California, Davis, and Ruth S. Smith, a clinical psychologist on the Hawaiian island of Kauai. Together,

they followed 698 children, all descendants of Kauaiian plantation workers, from their birth (in 1955) up to their early 30s. About half the children grew up in poverty; one in six had physical or intellectual handicaps diagnosed between birth and age 2. Of the 225 designated as high risk, two thirds had developed serious learning or behavior problems within their first decade of life. By 18 they had delinquency records, mental-health problems or teenage pregnancies. "Yet one out of three," Werner and Smith noted, "grew into competent young adults who loved well, worked well, played well and expected well."

Some of the protective factors the two psychologists identified underscore the nature-nurture connection. Like other researchers, they found that children who started out with robust, sunny personalities were often twice lucky: not only were they better equipped to cope with life to begin with, but their winning ways made them immediately lovable. In effect, the "nicer" the children, the more readily they won affection—both nature and nurture smiled upon them. There were also other important resiliency factors, including self-esteem and a strong sense of identity. Boyce says he encounters some children who even at 2 or 3 have a sense of "presence" and independence that seem to prefigure success. "It's as if these kids have had the 'Who am I' questions answered for them," he says.

One of the more intriguing findings of the Kauai research was that resilient children were likely to have characteristics of both sexes. Boys and girls in the study tended to be outgoing and autonomous, in the male fashion, but also nurturant and emotionally sensitive, like females. "It's a little similar to what we find in creative children," observes Werner. Some other key factors were inherent in the children's surroundings rather than their personalities. It helped to have a readily available support network of grandparents, neighbors or relatives. Others note that for children anywhere, it doesn't hurt at all to be born to well-off parents. "The advantage of middle-class life is there's a safety net," says Arnold Sameroff, a developmental psychologist at Brown University's Bradley Hospital. "If you screw up, there's someone to bail you out."

In most cases, resilient children have "clusters" of protective factors, not just one or two. But the sine qua non, according to Werner, is a "basic, trusting relationship" with an adult. In all the clusters in the Kauai study, "there is not one that didn't include that one good relationship, whether with a parent, grandparent, older sibling, teacher or mentor—someone consistent enough in that person's life to say, 'You count,' and that sort of begins to radiate other support in their lives." Even children of abusive or schizophrenic parents may prove resilient if they have had at least one caring adult looking out for them—someone, as Tom Boyce says, "who serves as a kind of beacon presence in their lives."

Such relationships do the most good when they are lasting. There is no lasting guarantee for resiliency itself, which is subject to change, de-

Researchers can spot differences of temperament in monkeys before they're a week old

pending on what sort of ups and downs people encounter. Children's ability to cope often improves naturally as they develop and gain experience, although it may decline after a setback in school or at home. Werner notes that around half the vulnerable children in the Kauai study had shaken off their previous problems by the time they reached their late 20s or early 30s. "In the long-term view, more people come through in spite of circumstances. There is an amazing amount of recovery, if you don't focus on one particular time when things are falling apart."

Ironically, this "self-righting" tendency has made the resiliency issue something of a political football. Conservatives have seized on the research to bolster their case against further social spending. "It's the politics of 'It's all within the kid'," says Lisbeth Schorr, a lecturer in social medicine at Harvard Medical School whose book, "Within Our Reach: Breaking the Cycle of Disadvantage," has had a wide impact in the field. "The conservative argument against interventions like Operation Head Start and family-support programs is that if these inner-city kids and families just showed a little grit they would pull themselves up by their own bootstraps. But people working on resilience are aware that when it comes to environments like the inner city, it really doesn't make a lot of sense to talk about what's intrinsic to the kids, because the environment is so overwhelming."

So overwhelming, indeed, that some researchers voice serious doubts over how much change can be brought about in multiple-risk children. Brown's Sameroff, who has been dealing with poor inner-city black and white families in Rochester, N.Y., says the experience has left him "more realistic" about what is possible. "Interventions are important if we can target one or two things wrong with a child. So you provide psychotherapy or extra help in the classroom, then there's a lot better chance." But the children he deals with usually have much more than that going against them—not only poverty but large families, absent fathers, drug-ridden neighborhoods and so on. "We find the more risk factors the worse the outcome," says Sameroff. "With eight or nine, *nobody* does well. For the majority of these children, it's going to involve changing the whole circumstance in which they are raised."

O thers are expressing their own reservations, as the first rush of enthusiasm in resiliency research cools somewhat. "A lot of the early intervention procedures that don't follow through have been oversold," says Emmy Werner. "Not every-

one benefited equally from such programs as Head Start." Yet, according to child-development specialists, only a third of high-risk children are able to pull through relatively unaided by such interventions. Says Werner: "At least the high-risk children should be guaranteed basic health and social programs."

Interestingly, when Suomi separates his vulnerable monkeys from their foster mothers at 7 months—around the same time that mothers in the wild go off to breed, leaving their young behind—the genes reassert themselves, and the monkeys revert to fearful behavior. According to Suomi, they do recover again when the mothers return and their new coping skills seem to stay with them. Yet their experience underscores the frailty of change. Boyce, an admirer of Suomi's work, acknowledges that the question of how lasting the effects of early interventions are remains open. But, he adds, programs like Head Start continue to reverberate as much as 15 years later, with reportedly higher school-completion rates and lower rates of delinquency and teen pregnancies.

Boyce recalls that years ago, when he was at the University of North Carolina, he dealt with an 8-year-old child from an impoverished, rural black family, who had been abandoned by his mother. The boy also had "prune-belly syndrome," an anomaly of the abdominal musculature that left him with significant kidney and urinary problems, requiring extensive surgery. But he also had two doting grandparents who had raised him from infancy. They showered him with love and unfailingly accompanied him on his hospital visits. Despite his physical problems and loss of a mother, the boy managed to perform "superbly" in school. By the age of 10, when Boyce last saw him, he was "thriving."

Children may not be as manageable or resilient as laboratory monkeys. If anything, they are more susceptible in the early years. But with the right help at the right time, they can overcome almost anything. "Extreme adversity can have devastating effects on development," says psychologist Ann Masten, who did some of the groundbreaking work in the resiliency field with her University of Minnesota colleague Norman Garmezy. "But our species has an enormous capacity for recovery. Children living in a hostile caregiving environment have great difficulty, but a lot of ability to recover to better functioning if they're given a chance. That's a very important message from the resiliency literature." Unfortunately, the message may not be getting through to the people who can provide that chance.

There are kids from adverse situations who do beautifully and seem to rise to their potential

Televised Violence and Kids: A Public Health Problem?

When Leonard Eron surveyed every 8-year-old child in Columbia County, New York, in 1960, he found something he wasn't looking for: an astonishing, and unmistakable, correlation between the amount of violence the youngsters saw on television and the aggressiveness of their behavior.

More than three decades and two follow-up studies later, after several related research projects and countless hearings and conferences, the work of Eron and his ISR colleague, L. Rowell Huesmann, has become an "overnight sensation." As leading researchers on the effects of media violence on the young, they have been making the rounds of TV talk and news programs and radio call-in shows, while fielding almost daily calls from reporters.

Their message is ultimately a simple one: Aggression is a learned behavior, it is learned at an early age, and media violence is one of its teachers. But because it is a learned behavior, there is hope that it can be unlearned, or never taught in the first place.

Both Eron and Huesmann are professors of psychology at the University of Michigan and research scientists at ISR's Research Center for Group Dynamics. Huesmann is also a professor of communication and acting chair of the Depart-ment of Communication. Their talents and interests have complemented each other since they met at Yale in the early 1970s. Eron's research interest is aggression, while Huesmann, who minored in mathematics as a U-M undergraduate in the early '60s, brings his prowess in data analysis and expertise in cognitive mechanisms and development to the team.

"I wanted to measure child-rearing practices as they related to aggression" in the 1960 survey, says Eron. "The parents knew what the study was about and, in the interviews, we were asking sensitive questions about how parents punished their children, what their disagreements were, and so forth. So we wanted to buffer those with what we called 'Ladies' Home Journal' questions — Had they read Dr. Spock? How often did their child watch TV? What were his or her favorite shows?

"But the computer was unaware of our humor and analyzed those TV programs," he adds. "And, lo and behold, the more aggressive that kids were in school, the higher the violence content of the shows they watched."

But that still left the chicken-and-egg ambiguity. Did watching violent TV make kids more aggressive, or did more aggressive kids watch violent TV?

That's where time, and Huesmann, came in. In 1970, the U.S. Surgeon General formed a committee on television and social behavior, and asked Eron to re-survey as many of the Columbia County kids as he could find. Eron, in turn, sought the services of Huesmann, then an assistant professor at Yale.

"How can they say their programs have no effect on behavior when they're in the business of selling ads?"

—Leonard Eron

"The analysis of long-term data on children's behavior required some sophisticated mathematical and statistical analysis," says Huesmann, "and that was the area in which I was trained."

The project also struck another responsive chord, he says: "The models that had been advanced to explain the long-terms effects of television violence were lacking an explanation of how the effects of watching television violence could last way into adulthood."

So it was back to the Hudson Valley of upstate New York in 1971. They found about 500 of the now 19-year-olds from the original sample of 875 youngsters. The results were just as powerful, if not more so.

"The correlation between violence-viewing at age 8 and how aggressive the individual was at 19 was higher than the correlation between watching violence at age 8 and behaving aggressively at age 8," says Eron. "There was no correlation between violence-viewing at age 19 and aggressiveness at 19. It seems there was a cumulative effect going on here."

Its persistence was documented once more in 1981, when 400 of the subjects were surveyed again, along with 80 of their offspring. The 30-year-old men who had been the most aggressive when they were 8 had more arrests for drunk

---

"The evidence is overwhelming. The strength of the relationship is the same as cigarettes causing lung cancer. Is there any doubt about that?"

—Leonard Eron

---

driving, more arrests for violent crime, were more abusive to their spouses . . . and had more aggressive children. And of the 600 subjects whose criminal justice records were reviewed, those who watched more violence on TV when they were 8 had been arrested more often for violent crimes, and self-reported more fights when consuming alcohol.

In other words, their viewing choices and behavior as 8-year-olds were better predictors of their behavior at age 30 than either what they watched on TV or how aggressively they behaved later in life.

"Children learn programs for how to behave that I call scripts," says Huesmann. "In a new social situation, how do

you know how to behave? You search for scripts to follow. Where is a likely place for those scripts to come from? From what you've observed others doing in life, films, TV. So, as a child, you see a Dirty Harry movie, where the heroic policeman is shooting people right and left. Even years later, the right kind of scene can trigger that script and suggest a way to behave that follows it. Our studies have come up with a lot of evidence that suggests that's very possible. Moreover, we find that watching TV violence affects the viewer's beliefs and attitudes about how people are going to behave."

The longitudinal data were so compelling that the 1993 report of the American Psychological Association's Commission on Violence and Youth, which Eron chaired, stated unequivocally that there is "absolutely no doubt that higher levels of viewing violence on television are correlated with increased acceptance of aggressive attitudes and increased aggressive behavior."

"The evidence is overwhelming," says Eron. "The strength of the relationship is the same as cigarettes causing lung cancer. Is there any doubt about that?"

Only among those who profit from tobacco, just as TV and movie industry executives have generated most of the criticism of the ISR colleagues' work. While the media in general were fascinated by the damning data, especially after the APA report was released last August, the visual media in particular were equally eager to defend themselves and defuse the evidence.

This is not a message the industry wants to hear. Its position is that the off-on switch is the ultimate defense, and parents wield it. Eron says that's unrealistic.

"Parents can't do it all by themselves, especially in these days

of single-parent families and two parents working," he says. "They can't be with their children all the time."

If the industry can't or won't regulate itself, should the government intervene? It's an obvious question to ask and a difficult one to answer, especially for believers in the First Amendment.

"The scientific evidence clearly shows that long-term exposure to TV violence makes kids behave more aggressively," says Huesmann, "but it doesn't show the same effect on adults. What you watch now won't have nearly the effect of what you saw when you were 8. What we're talking about is regulating what kids see, not adults, and there are reasonable precedents for this — alcohol and tobacco regulations, for example."

"What we're talking about is regulating what kids see, not adults, and there are reasonable precedents for this—alcohol and tobacco regulations, for example."

—L. Rowell Huesmann

In their view, watching TV violence is every bit as dangerous to kids as smoking and drinking. They see it as a matter of public health, not free speech. And they are grimly amused by the industry's protestations of exculpability. "How can they say their programs have no effect on behavior when they're in the business of selling ads?" Eron asks.

Then there are those who wonder how it is that Detroit and Windsor, Ontario, which face each other across the Detroit River and receive the same TV signals, have such disparate crime rates. "If we said TV violence is the only cause, then they'd have an argument," says Eron. "But we don't say that."

They are, in fact, well aware that any number of psychological, physiological and macro-social factors are simmering in the stew of violence. "TV is really a minor part of our research," says Eron, "although it's gotten the most play. We're interested in how children learn aggression. Violence on TV is only one cause, but it's a cause we can do something about."

Two projects they are currently involved in show signs of making progress toward that end. Huesmann is directing the second phase of a study begun in 1977 that looks, he says, at "whether the effects of media violence generalize across different countries and cultures."

Researchers are collecting longitudinal data on subjects in Poland, Australia, Finland and Israel, as well as the United States. Meanwhile, Eron, Huesmann and three researchers at the University of Illinois (where Huesmann spent 20 years before returning to U-M in 1992) are conducting an ambitious study of inner-city schools "in which we are trying to change the whole school atmosphere," says Eron.

In the former study, almost 2,000 children were interviewed and tested in either first or third grade and for two consecutive years thereafter. "In all countries, the children who watched more violence were the more aggressive," says Huesmann. "This was a study showing that this was a real effect across countries and not a special, one-time study of Columbia County."

The only exceptions were found in Australia and Israel. In Australia, there was a correlation between watching violence and behaving aggressively, but it was not as persistent as in other countries. In Israel, the correlation was stronger for city-raised children than for those growing up in kibbutzes. Huesmann suspects that the communal nature of the kibbutz, with its attendant reinforcement of pro-social behaviors, neutralized the effect of televised violence. And Australia? "We have no good explanation," he says.

"As a child, you see a Dirty Harry movie, where the heroic policeman is shooting people right and left. Even years later, the right kind of scene can trigger that script and suggest a way to behave that follows it."

—L. Rowell Huesmann

Perhaps the second phase, revisiting subjects who are now in their early 20s, will provide one. Interviewing is almost complete in the United States and Finland and began in Poland this winter as one of the collaborative projects between ISR and ISS [Institute for Social Studies], its Polish sibling. Work will begin in Israel near the end of 1994.

The project in Illinois attempts to measure the relative influence of multiple contexts, including schools, peers,

families, and neighborhoods, and the cost-effectiveness of targeting each. "This is a public health model," says Eron, "from primary prevention to tertiary prevention."

Both teachers and students will be taught techniques for handling aggression and solving problems. Youngsters who are believed to be at high risk for becoming aggressive will also be seen in groups of six by research staffers. And half of those youngsters will receive family therapy as well, what Eron calls "an increased dosage" of treatment.

"We don't think just working with kids in the schools will help much," Eron says. "Studies show kids change attitudes, but there's no data to show they change behavior. In this program, we're trying to change the whole school atmosphere. We're also trying to see what the cost-effectiveness is. Is it enough to have a school program? Or do you always have to do family therapy, which is the most costly? Does it really add to the effectiveness of the treatment?"

The problem clearly isn't simple, but some of the data are nonetheless clear. "Over the years, Rowell and I have testified at many congressional hearings," says Eron, "and now it's having an effect. The public sentiment is there's too much of this stuff, and we've got the data to show it. I think we are having an impact, finally."

Eron himself estimates that TV is only responsible for perhaps 10% of the violent behavior in this country. "But," he says, "if we could reduce violence by 10%, that would be a great achievement."

the skin we're in

We humans are mesmerized by melanin, the pigment that gives color to our skin, but almost always for quite the wrong reasons.

Christopher Wills

Christopher Wills is a professor of biology at the University of California at San Diego. He is the author of The Wisdom of the Genes *and* Exons, Introns, and Talking Genes. *An excerpt from his most recent book,* The Runaway Brain: The Evolution of Human Uniqueness, *appeared in the August 1993* Discover.

MELANIN IS IN THE NEWS these days. There's a pseudo-scientific idea floating around that says that if you have lots of melanin—the pigment that colors your skin and hair and the irises of your eyes—you will be smart and exquisitely attuned to life's rhythms and have a warm, outgoing personality. In short, you will be nicer and more talented than people with less melanin—that is, white people.

Proponents of this idea, such as Leonard Jeffries, chairman of the Department of Black Studies at the City College of New York, have based their conclusions on the single scientific fact that melanin is found not only in the skin but also in the brain, and they have used the compound's presence there to imbue it with magical properties. Their "melanist" approach has gone beyond promulgation in a few pamphlets and backroom debates; it is now being taught at a number of high schools and colleges in the United States, usually as part of an effort to correct a Eurocentric view of the world. Not surprisingly, such programs have generated a great deal of criticism in the mainstream, white-dominated press—which the melanists claim is in itself an expression of racism. Why, they counter, hasn't an equal amount of disapproval been directed against the pronouncements of white biological superiority?

Two wrongs, of course, do not make a right. As a reaction and antidote to white racism, melanism is understandable. But from a scientific standpoint it is just wrong. There's no evidence for melanist claims of black superiority, just as there's no evidence for the pseudoscientific claims of white superiority that have been made for centuries. That's not to say that melanin isn't a fit subject for scientific inquiry. Indeed, just the opposite: what research has shown us is that the *real* story of melanin is much more interesting, and tells us more about ourselves, than any magical hokum trotted out to support divisions between the races.

We are visually oriented animals, and the color of a stranger's skin, if different from our own, is often the characteristic we notice first. Of all the superficial differences that divide us—the shape of our nose, the texture of our hair, and so on—none seems to mesmerize us as much as skin color. Our hyperawareness of it shapes our perception not only of others but of ourselves as well. As psychologists have shown, among blacks in this country, at least, the darkest-skinned children in a group or family are often treated less well than other children by their teachers, their peers, and even their parents and thus suffer repeated blows to their self-esteem. Obviously, differences in skin color matter greatly to society—but is there any physical basis for all the prejudice and psychological damage that these differences have generated?

TODAY GENETICISTS LIKE MYSELF would say no. We have known for decades that variation in skin color is caused by rather small genetic differences, and it seems *highly* unlikely that these differences have anything to do with intelligence, personality, or ability. Sadly, though, genetics itself has not always been free of the taint of racism. The models that early geneticists used to explain the inheritance of skin color actually had a segregationist bias, reflecting the pervasive prejudice of their time. The white American eugenicist Charles Benedict Davenport set the tone (so to speak) in 1913 with an investigation into the genetics of "Negro-white crosses." Davenport was as racist as most of his contemporaries, and he assumed that blacks were inferior to whites. He did, however, correctly deduce that there were distinct genes that control skin color. But he thought only two genes were involved and that each of them came in two forms, or alleles: a "white" allele and a "black" allele. How dark you were was a function of how many of the four alleles you inherited from your mother and father were "black."

Davenport assumed that the black and white alleles were clearly different from each other, as the black and white races themselves, he thought, were clearly different from each other. We now know that this is not correct and that the differences between the alleles carried by the different races are small. But Davenport was right in his conclusion that a rather small number of genes make substantial contributions to skin color—more than two, it turns out, but fewer than half a dozen. And, as he noticed, skin color is inherited independently of other characteristics used to differentiate between races. Among the grandchildren of interracial marriages, he saw, there were often individuals with light skin and tightly kinked hair, and others with dark skin and straight hair. Skin color and hair texture were thus not indissolubly wedded.

Davenport knew nothing about how genes work and so had no notion of how his black alleles caused pigment to form. Only recently have studies at the molecular level shown how slight the allelic differences between races really are, and how few the steps that separate all of us from being as dark as the Bougainville Islanders of the South Pacific or as pale as Swedes.

What we have learned is that the mechanics of pigment formation are surpassingly subtle. Melanocytes, the cells that form the pigment melanin (and that occasionally run amok, giving rise to the malignant tumors known as melanomas), are closely related to nerve cells. Both types of cell arise in a part of the early embryo called the dorsal ectoderm, but while nerve cells mostly stay put to form the core of the nervous system, melanocytes migrate along with other cells to give rise to the skin. As they mature, melanocytes and nerve cells continue to share some attributes. Like nerve cells, melanocytes develop branching processes that attach to nearby cells. But whereas nerve cells use their branches to send messages, melanocytes use theirs to send packets of pigment to adjacent skin cells. A single melanocyte can color quite a large bit of the skin by pumping pigment into the cells that adjoin it.

WE NOW KNOW THAT IN MICE more than 50 different genes influence how melanin forms and when and where it's deposited. So it's likely that a similar number of genes will turn up in humans as well, although perhaps only half a dozen will be shown to have really substantial effects. The pigments they produce, though they're all lumped together under the melanin label, can actually be black, brown, yellow, or red. They all have a common starting point in tyrosine, an amino acid made in large amounts in the melanocytes and converted by the enzyme tyrosinase into a compound called dopaquinone. At first, biochemists thought that dopaquinone then underwent spontaneous chemical changes to form the long polymer molecules that make up melanin. But the truth was much more complex—it takes a bewildering mixture of reactions, some spontaneous and some catalyzed by enzymes, to get from dopaquinone to melanin. To cut a very long story short, dopaquinone follows two different routes, one leading to black and brown pigments, and the other to red and yellow pigments.

The master enzyme in all this is tyrosinase. If the gene for this enzyme is defective, the result is a person with albinism, someone who makes no melanin at all. But the most remarkable discovery made by molecular biologists has been that most of us, regardless of skin color, have quite enough tyrosinase in our melanocytes to make us very black. In those of us with light skin, something is preventing the enzyme from functioning at full capacity—and that seems to be a combination of two genetic mechanisms: a switch that causes the cell to make most of the tyrosinase in an inactive form, and a tendency to make a lot of inhibitors of the enzyme. In the body, the effects of either or both of these mechanisms can be modified by such environmental factors as exposure to ultraviolet light. People with albinism are highly sensitive to ultraviolet, which can easily damage skin and eyes, but most of us, regardless of which alleles we have for skin color, can protect ourselves by darkening our skin through tanning.

So it turns out that what separates blacks and whites is not different numbers of clearly different black and white alleles, but rather a collection of tiny genetic differences in the way the genes possessed by all of us are regulated—how much tyrosinase is made in an active form, how much and how many of the various tyrosinase inhibitors are made, and so on. Mutations with dramatic effect do contribute to color variation in the human population—for example, people with albinism don't make functional tyrosinase, and redheads make only small amounts—but these mutations affect only a relatively small number of people. Other mutations that lighten or darken skin color occasionally happen. Children with piebaldism, for instance, are born with a white forelock and colorless patches on their forehead and trunk. Another, more dramatic example is melasma, a skin condition that sometimes runs in families. A child with this condition is born with large patches of darker-than-normal pigmentation, which spread as the child grows older. In the late 1970s an even more unusual condition was described, in Mexico: a child was born with light skin that turned a deep, uniform black by the age of 21 months. (It is not yet known whether this condition is inherited.)

SUCH MUTATIONS ARE PROBABLY the tip of the iceberg. Richard King, a molecular geneticist at the University of Minnesota who has examined color variation in mice, suspects that much milder mutations must also happen in humans but that they tend to go unnoticed because they fall within the range of normal pigmentation. He is convinced that we are not exempt from the mutation-and-selection process that has repeatedly resulted in lighter and darker strains of animals over the course of evolution. The most famous example of such evolution is industrial melanism in moths, in which dark forms that arise by mutation are selected for in polluted areas and selected against when the pollution goes away.

In animals, melanin comes and goes at the dictates of evolutionary pressures. It is reasonable to assume, then, that we humans have this molecule not because it makes us smarter but primarily because it helps us survive a variety of environmental conditions. Clearly melanin protects us from the ravages of ultraviolet light. Some of the most darkly pigmented people in the world, natives of the North Solomon Islands, almost never get basal cell carcinoma or melanoma, and if they do have melanomas, these tumors arise on the light-skinned soles of their feet. Caucasians living in Hawaii, on the other hand, have the highest documented skin cancer rate in the United States.

But while the protective effect of having a lot of melanin is clear, it is rather less clear why many groups of humans living far from the equator have lost much of their pigment. One popular theory is based on the fact that exposure of our skin cells to ultraviolet light is necessary for the formation of a precursor of vitamin D, which in turn is required for proper bone formation. Thus, the theory goes, people who live at high latitudes—where the sun hangs low in the sky and where people are forced to keep their skin covered during much of the year—can still make enough of this precursor if they have little ultraviolet-blocking pigmentation in their skin. Conversely, the large quantities of pigment in the skins of people in the tropics should prevent them from producing too *much* vitamin D, which can be as harmful as too little and can cause inappropriate calcium deposits in tissues.

In evolutionary terms, of course, it makes sense that most of us have all the machinery in place to make us black or white or anything in between. Darker and lighter "races" of animals are quite common, and probably arose as a response to the dangers of predation. Dark and light *Sceloporus* lizards from Colorado will even move about in a laboratory setting to match themselves to the appropriate background, an instinctive attempt to protect themselves against sharp-eyed predators. My guess is that over a span of hundreds of millions of years our remote animal ancestors had to change color repeatedly, for a great variety of reasons ranging from protective camouflage to sexual attractiveness. Much of this must have taken place long before they had acquired enough brains to be prejudiced about it.

Even in *Homo sapiens* there are many examples of groups that have evolved toward a lighter or darker skin color than that of their close relatives. The Negritos of the islands of Luzon and Mindanao in the Philippines, for instance, superficially resemble other dark-skinned groups in Africa and Australia. Yet their overall genetic affinities turn out to be far stronger to the lighter-skinned Asian peoples who surround them. This suggests that the Negritos' ancestors may once have been lighter and that they independently evolved features that are somewhat reminiscent of black Africans, or that the Asian peoples surrounding them were also once much darker and evolved toward lighter skin—or possibly both. Another example is the Ainu of northern Japan, who have light skin but overall are very similar genetically to the darker-skinned groups that surround them. The evolution of skin color was apparently not a onetime event; it has occurred repeatedly during the history of our species.

WHAT ABOUT NEUROMELANIN, that other melanin, found in our brains, that Jeffries and his fellow melanists have made so much of? More skin melanin, they imply, must mean more brain melanin—which is, in some undefined fashion, good. As we have seen, melanocytes and nerve cells *do* have a common origin in the fetus, and indeed it's likely that nerve cells once evolved from primitive melanocytes. But this evolutionary connection does not mean that the pigment of the skin is somehow connected with the function of the brain. People with albinism, who have no melanin in their skin, hair, or eyes, have normal amounts of melanin in their brain cells. And even though the ultimate source of both types of melanin is tyrosine, the processing pathways leading to neuromelanin are quite different from those leading to skin melanin—in the brain, tyrosine is converted into dopamine, a neurotransmitter, which in turn gives rise to neuromelanin. Finally, it should be pointed out that while neuromelanin is by its very nature highly visible in brain tissues, it is only one of thousands of compounds unique to the brain and is unlikely to be freighted with mystic significance.

As for the real significance of brain melanin, the jury is still out—we have no idea what it does. We do know that a lot of it is found in the substantia nigra (the "black substance"), a darkly colored structure buried deep in the brain that makes dopamine. We also know that melanin-rich cells in the substantia nigra are the ones most likely to be destroyed in people who have Parkinson's disease, resulting in tremors and rigidity. But whether this preferential destruction is due to some property of the neuromelanin or is the result of some other process that just happens to destroy neuromelanin-rich cells is not yet clear. What *is* clear is that neuromelanin isn't obviously related to skin pigment, much less to a warm, outgoing personality.

Still, melanin may confer some benefits we have yet to learn about. Intriguingly, there are hints that people with lots of skin melanin are less prone to hearing damage than the more lightly pigmented among us. And as it turns out, melanin of the skin variety is indeed found in certain cells of the cochlea of the inner ear. But whether it is melanin or something else in these cells that confers the protection is unknown. Melanin has also been connected with an odd benefit of smoking. Tobacco smoke stimulates production of skin melanin, particularly in the cells lining the mouth and possibly in other tissues as well. One study has actually suggested that smokers have less noise-induced hearing loss than nonsmokers (other studies, however, have shown the reverse). The benefit, if any, is hardly enough to justify taking up the habit, though smokers will be comforted to know that if increased melanin production does protect their hearing, they may be able to go on listening to every wheeze and rattle of their abused lungs.

Clearly melanin is a handy and fascinating compound, with an intriguing evolutionary history. But because its effects are so visible in our skin, it has for centuries been made to bear an utterly undeserved burden of sociological and political significance. As is detailed elsewhere in this issue, there are far more genetic differences *among* the people who make up these arbitrary constructs we call races than there are differences *between* races. It is time to move away from simplistic efforts to explain all our differences in terms of just one molecule and to pay attention to the tens of thousands of other molecules that make up our wondrously complex cells—and selves.

Development during Adolescence and Young Adulthood

- Adolescence (Articles 36–38)
- Young Adulthood (Articles 39–42)

North American culture has seen a prolongation of adolescence in recent years. G. Stanley Hall, at the turn of the last century, described adolescence as a holding pattern between childhood and adulthood. He saw adolescence as roughly equivalent to the teenage years, beginning with puberty and ending with maturity, or adulthood. Today many youth find reasons to postpone permanent jobs, independence from the family of origin, marriage, and creation of a family of procreation. They postpone maturity, or adulthood, well into their twenties.

North American culture has also seen a prolongation of young adulthood in recent years. The boundary between adolescence and adulthood is vague. Theoretically, adolescence ends when one is independent. In actuality, many youth claim young adulthood status while still maintaining financial and social dependence on their family of origin. The end of young adulthood and the commencement of middle age is obscure. Most adults view themselves as young adults while they are navigating the complicated course of rearing children and/or climbing their career ladders. Middle adulthood arrives when they launch their offspring and/or achieve some measure of success in their careers. This may occur for some persons while in their 30s and for others while in their 40s or 50s. Defining oneself as middle-aged is a personal and idiosyncratic event.

The biological changes of adolescence are profound. Every organ system matures. Skeleton, skin, muscles, brain, spine, heart, blood vessels, glands, hormones, lymph nodes, white and red blood cells, lungs, bronchi, digestive structures, urinary structures, sensory systems: all are affected by changes in the reproductive system. Adolescents and young adults who exercise, sleep, follow nutritional guidelines, and practice health and safety maintenance usually achieve near their potential development in all these areas. If they continue healthful living and stress management, they can retain the vim and vigor of these organ systems for many years.

The cognitive and personal-social aspects of adolescence and young adulthood are radically altered by increased sexual libido and reproductive system maturation. Sex urges and procreative urges are powerful. So, too, are social pressures to postpone bonding, marriage, and childbearing. Adolescents today have more socially accepted sexual options than did their parents or grandparents. They also have more complicated sexual decisions and concerns: rape, date rape, sexually transmitted diseases, AIDS, pornography, phone sex, computer sex, virtual reality sex. Development in personal and social realms and choices of education and career often depend on their decisions about sexual behavior.

The cognitive style of adolescents and young adults usually moves from concrete operational thought to formal operational thought. The mature brain can deal with abstractions, unlimited possibilities, and many combinations of logic. Not every adult reaches the same degree of formal operational thought. Some full-potential achievers may experience postformal operational thought, practical operational thought, or dialectical thought.

K. Warner Schaie proposed that different life experiences trigger different cognitive operations. Childhood and early adolescence initiate cognitive acquisition. Late adolescence and early adulthood open the door to cognitive achievement. Early and middle adulthood usher in concern for cognitive responsibility and cognitive executive functioning. Late adulthood inaugurates integrative and reintegrative cognitive functioning.

Lawrence Kohlberg, a Harvard professor, proposed that cognitive maturity is a necessary but not a sufficient condition for moral and ethical reasoning. Personal and social factors also influence moral behaviors.

Erik Erikson, the psychosocial theorist, stressed environmental and cultural influences on adolescents as they struggle to resolve their conflict between achieving a firm sense of their own autonomous identity versus living with

a wavering sense of identity confusion and role diffusion. Sex urges, societal views of adolescent sexuality; cognitive changes, societal acceptance of altered cognitive abilities, and moral/ethical life decisions all play a forceful role in identity achievement. Closely aligned with the identify vs. role-confusion conflict is the intimacy vs. isolation conflict of young adulthood. In Erik Erikson's view, some females resolve the intimacy conflict first and then acquire a firmer sense of identity by living vicariously within their husband's role. Although Erikson did not state it, the same might be true of some males achieving a firmer sense of identity vicariously through their wife's role. Erikson felt that both identity and intimacy are difficult to achieve unless earlier needs for trust, autonomy, initiative, and industry have been met.

Role confusion and a sense of isolation often lead adolescents to try to escape life through drugs, alcohol, suicide, irresponsible sex, and violence.

The articles selected for this unit on adolescence and young adulthood reflect the turbulence associated with this phase of the life span. The first unit article takes a look at a circle of influence: adolescents on middle-aged

parents, and middle-aged parents on adolescents. The next article, "Teenage Turning Point," focuses on sex differences through the adolescent period. Do we do a better job of preparing males or females for adulthood roles? The essay "HIV Infected Youth Speaks about Needs for Support and Health Care" was selected for the emotional impact it will have on all readers. It deals with many topics: child abuse, rape, drug abuse, and AIDS. It depicts a slice of the all-too-real life of one adolescent turned young adult today.

The four selections about young adulthood address concerns that have their advent in adolescence: procreative urges, the effects of children on parental relationships, the effects of too much intimacy on couples' relationships, and problems associated with increased aggression and violence in society. What kind of people are young adults becoming? What interventions could help them become happier, healthier people? The articles not only present problems, but also suggest solutions for a happier state of affairs for young adults in the late 1990s.

Looking Ahead: Challenge Questions

How can parents and adolescents mutually approach each other and provide reciprocal support, rather than becoming alienated from one another?

Why do so many female adolescents suffer from low self-esteem?

What is important in supportive health care for adolescents who are HIV positive?

Where are psychotrends taking tomorrow's families?

How can marriages remain happy after the birth of babies?

How much intimacy is good for a relationship? How important is separateness?

Why is domestic violence so common? How can both batterers and their victims be helped?

Adolescence
Whose Hell Is It?

The image of teenagers as menacing and rebellious is a big fiction that's boomeranging on kids. We've mythologized adolescence to conceal a startling fact: It is indeed a difficult and turbulent time—for parents. The trouble is, kids look like adults much sooner than ever before. Kids wind up feeling abandoned—and angry at the loss of their safety net. If we haven't got adolescence exactly figured out yet, there's some consolation in the fact that it's a brand-new phenomenon in human history.

Virginia Rutter

I recently spent the weekend with a friend's 13-year-old son. In contrast to the tiny tots most of my friends have, Matthew seemed much more like an adult. The time spent with him wasn't so much like baby-sitting; it was like having company. It was impressive to see how self-sufficient he was. Simple matters struck me: he didn't need someone to go to the bathroom with him at the movies; he could help himself to ice cream; he was actually interested in following the O. J. Simpson story, and we discussed it.

He was polite, thoughtful, and interesting. While the intensive caretaking necessary for smaller children has its own rewards (I suppose), Matthew's contrasting autonomy was pleasant to me. And so I imagined it would be for parents of adolescents. But then, I am not a parent. And most parents report not feeling pleasant about their adolescents.

The weekend reminded me of how easy it is to think of these youngsters as adults. Compared to an eight-year-old, an adolescent is a lot like an adult. Can't reason like an adult, but doesn't think like a child anymore, either. Some parents are tempted to cut 'em loose rather than adjust to the new status of their teenager. Others fail to observe their

adolescent's new adultlike status, and continue monitoring them as closely as a child. But it's obvious that adolescents aren't miniature adults. They are individuals on their way to adulthood; their brains and bodies—to say nothing of their sexuality—stretching uneasily toward maturity.

A couple of teachers are my heroes. My history teacher is great because he listens to what everybody has to say and never judges.
—Chelsea, 14, Bakersfield, California

Yet the sight of kids reaching for some form of adult status commonly evokes contempt rather than curiosity. Negative feelings about teenagers have a strong grip on American culture in general, and on surprising numbers of parents in particular. It's not uncommon for parents to anticipate their child's adolescence with fear and trepidation even before they've gotten out of diapers. They expect a war at home.

"It becomes a self-fulfilling prophesy that adolescence is seen as this bizarre, otherworldly period of development, complete with a battleground set for World War III," says Tina Wagers, Psy.D., a psychologist who treats teens and their families at Kaiser Permanente Medical Center in Denver.

We were all once 13, but it seems we can no longer imagine what kind of parenting a 13-year-old needs. Perhaps it's gotten worse with all the outside opportunities for trouble kids have—gangs, guns, drugs. Families used to extend their turf into their children's schools, friends, and athletic activities. But kids now inhabit unknown territory, and it is scary for parents. "I think this fear and lack of understanding makes some parents more likely to back off and neglect teenagers," reports Wagers. "There is an expectation that you can't influence them anyhow."

This skeptical, sometimes hostile view of teens, however, was countered by my experience with Matthew. I found him hardly a "teenager from hell." Like most teens, Matthew prefers to be with his own friends more than with family or other grown-ups. He's not good with time, and music, basketball, and girls are more central to him than achievement, responsibility, and family. (Despite his tastes, he does very well in school.) At home there is more conflict than there has been in the past, though not less love and commitment to his mom, with whom he lives in eastern Washington.

The story of Matthew falls in line with new research on adolescents, and it's causing psychologists to totally revise conventional wisdom on the subject. According to psychologist Laurence Steinberg, Ph.D., of Temple University, the majority of adolescents are not contentious, unpleasant, heartless creatures. They do not hate their parents—although they do fight with them (but not as much as you might think). "In scrutinizing interviews with adolescents and their families, I reaffirmed that adolescence is a relatively peaceful time in the house." Kids report continued high levels of respect for their parents, whether single, divorced, or together, and regardless of economic background.

When fighting does occur, it's in families with younger teenagers, and it has to do at least in part with their burgeoning cognitive abilities. Newly able to grasp abstract ideas, they can become absorbed in pursuing hypocrisy or questioning authority. In time, they learn to deploy relativistic and critical thinking more selectively.

NOT A DISEASE

If adolescents aren't the incorrigibles we think—then what to make of the endless stream of news reports of teen sexism, harassment, drug abuse, depression, delinquency, gangs, guns, and suicide?

Any way you measure it, teens today are in deep trouble. They face increasing rates of depression (now at 20 percent), suicide (12 percent have considered it, 5 percent attempted), substance abuse (20 percent of high school seniors), delinquency (1.5 million juvenile arrests—about 1 percent of teens—in 1992), early sexual activity (29 percent have had sexual relations by age 15), and even an increased rate of health problems (20 percent have conditions that will hamper their health as adults). And kids' problems appear to be getting worse.

How to reconcile the two parts of the story: adolescents aren't so bad, but a growing number are jeopardizing their future through destructive behavior? Though we look upon teenagers as time bombs set to self-destruct at puberty, in fact the problems teens face are not

encoded in their genes. Their natural development, including a surge of hormonal activity during the first few years of adolescence, may make them a little more depressed or aggressive—but how we treat them has much more to do with teenagers' lives today. From the look of it, we aren't treating them very well.

A CRISIS OF ADULTS

If what goes on in adolescence happens largely in the kids, what goes wrong with adolescence happens primarily in the parents. "It wasn't until I turned to the parents' interviews that I really got a sense that something unusual was going on," reports Steinberg of his ongoing studies of over 200 adolescents and their families. As he details in his recent book, *Crossing Paths: How Your Child's Adolescence Triggers Your Own Crisis* (Simon & Schuster), Steinberg finds that adolescence sets off a crisis for parents.

Teenagers say that parents are not understanding and I don't think it is always that way.
—Gabriel, 16, Albuquerque, New Mexico

Parents do not have positive feelings during the time their kids go through adolescence, and it isn't simply because they expect their kids to be bad (although that's part of it). Scientists have studied the behavior and emotions of parents as well as their adolescent children, and found that when children reach puberty, parents experience tremendous changes in themselves. What's more, they shift their attitudes toward their children. It isn't just the kids who are distressed. Parents are too. Consider the following:

- Marital satisfaction, which typically declines over the course of marriage, reaches its all-time low when the oldest child reaches adolescence. Married parents of adolescents have an average of seven minutes alone with each other every day. For the marriages that don't pass the point of no return during their kids' teen years, there is actually an increase in satisfaction after the kids complete adolescence.

- Happily married parents have more positive interactions with their kids than unhappy parents. In single-parent families, parental happiness also influences their response to adolescence.

- In a surprising finding, the marital satisfaction of fathers is directly affected by how actively their adolescents are dating. Especially when sons are busy dating, fathers report a marked decline in interest in their wives. Dads aren't lusting for the girls Johnny brings home, they just miss what now seem like their own good old days.

Adults want kids to learn to take care of themselves. Kids need guides and advice. That is how you help people mature—not by leaving them alone.
—Michelle, 16, Clackamas, Oregon

- In family discussions, parents become increasingly negative toward their adolescents—there's more criticism, whining, frustration, anger, and defensiveness expressed verbally or in grimaces. While the kids are always more negative than their parents (it comes with increasing cognitive ability, in part), the parents are actually increasing the amount of negativity toward their children at a higher rate.

- Working mothers don't spend less time at home with their teenagers than nonworking moms do, but they do risk higher levels of burnout, because they continue to cover the lioness' share of work at home. On the other hand, a mother's employment makes her less vulnerable to the ups and downs of parenting an adolescent. Maternal employment also benefits kids, especially teen daughters, who report higher levels of self-esteem.

- Despite their fulfillment, mothers' self-esteem is actually lower while they are with their adolescents than when they are not. After all, a mother's authority is constantly being challenged, and she is being shunted to the margins of her child's universe.

- Teenagers turn increasingly to their friends, a distancing maneuver that feels like an emotional divorce to parents. Since mothers are generally more emotionally engaged with their children than are fathers, the separation can feel most painful to them. In fact, mothers typically report looking forward to the departure of their kids after high school. After the kids leave, mothers' emotional state improves.

- Fathers emotional states follow a different course. Fathers have more difficulty launching their adolescents, mostly because they feel regret about the time they didn't spend with them. Fathers have more difficulty dealing with their kids growing into adolescence and adulthood; they can't get used to the idea that they no longer have a little playmate who is going to do what daddy wants to do.

Add it all up and you get a bona fide midlife crisis in some parents, according to Steinberg. All along we've thought that a midlife crisis happens to some adults around the age of 40. But it turns out that midlife crisis has nothing to do with the age of the adult—and everything to do with the age of the oldest child in a family. It is set off by the entry of a family's first-born into adolescence.

Once the oldest child hits adolescence, parents are catapulted into a process of life review. "Where have I been, where am I now, where am I going?" These questions gnaw at parents who observe their children at the brink of adulthood.

It hits hardest the parent who is the same sex as the adolescent. Mothers and daughters actually have more difficulty than fathers and sons. In either case, the children tend to serve as a mirror of their younger lost selves, and bear the brunt of parents' regrets as parents distance themselves.

Steinberg tracks the psychological unrest associated with midlife crisis in parents:

- The onset of puberty is unavoidable evidence that their child is growing up.
- Along with puberty comes a child's burgeoning sexuality. For parents, this can raise doubts about their own attractiveness, their current sex life, as well as regrets or nostalgia for their teenage sexual experiences.
- The kids' new independence can make parents feel powerless. For fathers in particular this can remind them of the powerlessness they feel in the office if their careers have hit a plateau.
- Teens also become less concerned with their parents' approval. Their peer

group approval becomes more important. This hits mothers of daughters quite hard, especially single mothers, whose relationship to their daughters most resembles a friendship.

- Finally, de-idealization—kids' often blunt criticism of their parents—is a strong predictor of decline in parental mental health. Parents who used to be the ultimate expert to their kids are now reduced to debating partner for kids who have developed a new cognitive skill called relativism.

A clear picture begins to emerge: parents of a teenager feel depressed about their own life or their own marriage; feel the loss of their child; feel jealous, rejected, and confused about their child's new sexually mature looks, bad moods, withdrawal into privacy at home, and increasing involvement with friends. The kid is tied up in her (or his) own problems and wonders what planet mom and dad are on.

EMOTIONAL DIVORCE

The sad consequence is that parents who experience a midlife crisis begin avoiding their adolescent. Although a small proportion of parents are holding on to their teens too closely—usually they come from traditional families and have fundamentalist religious beliefs—more parents are backing off. The catch is that these teenagers want their parents' guidance. But more and more they just aren't getting it.

Some parents back away not out of their own inner confusion but because they think it's hip to do so. Either way, letting go causes confusion in the kids, not help in making their way into adulthood. Even if they are irritating or irritable, or just more withdrawn than they used to be, teens are seeking guidance.

Adults need to understand that it is very difficult to be a teenager nowadays. It takes a lot of understanding with so many problems like guns, drugs, AIDS, and gangs.
—Melissa, 14, Dallas, Texas

"I have this image of a kid groping through adolescence, kind of by himself" confides therapist Wagers, who sees a lot of parents out of touch with their kids. "The parents swarm around him, but don't actually talk to him, only to other people about him."

The mantra of therapists who work with adolescents and their families is "balance." Parents have to hold on, but not too tightly. They need to stay involved, even when their kids are ignoring them. Roland Montemayor, Ph.D., professor of psychology at Ohio State, finds it is not so different from learning how to deal with a two-year-old. You must stay within earshot, and be available whenever they falter or get themselves into trouble.

With a two-year-old, trouble means experimenting with mud pies or bopping a playmate; with a 14-year-old, it means experimenting with your car keys or sex. The task is the same—keep track of them and let them know what the rules are. Parents unfortunately taken up with their own midlife concerns may not embrace the task. God knows, it isn't easy. But it is vital.

Among parents who have gone through a real divorce, the emotional divorce that occurs between adolescents and their parents can heighten difficulty. It may reawaken feelings of sadness. Parents who don't have many interests outside the family are also vulnerable. Their kids are telling them to "Get a life!"—and that is exactly what they need to do.

DROPOUT PARENTS

As an adolescent reaches age 13, the time she is spending with parents is typically half that before age 10. "Teens come home and go into their bedrooms. They start to feel more comfortable by themselves than with siblings or parents around. They talk on the phone with friends, and their biggest worry usually has to do with a romantic interest," explains Reed Larson, Ph.D., who studies families and adolescents at the University of Illinois, Champaign-Urbana. Larson, coauthor of the recent book, *Divergent Realities: The Emotional Lives of Mothers, Fathers, and Adolescents*, studied 55 families who recorded their feelings and activities for one week, whenever prompted at random intervals by a beeper. He surveyed another 483 adolescents with the beeper method.

The families' reports revealed that a mutual withdrawal occurs. "When kids withdraw, parents get the message. They even feel intimidated. As a result they don't put in the extra effort to maintain contact with their kids," observes Larson. The kids feel abandoned, even though they're the ones retreating to their bedroom. The parents, in effect, cut their kids loose, just when they dip their toes in the waters of autonomy.

I don't think adults understand how complicated kids' minds are today, how much they think; they don't just accept something but wonder why it is.
—Adam, 14, Bethesda, Maryland

Separation is natural among humans as well as in the animal kingdom, Larson notes. Yet humans also need special care during this life transition—and suffer from reduced contact with parents and other adults. They still need to be taught how to do things, how to think about things, but above all they need to know that there is a safety net, a sense that their parents are paying attention and are going to jump in when things go wrong. The kids don't need the direct supervision they received at age two or eight, but they benefit emotionally and intellectually from positive contact with their parents.

Despite the tensions in family life, studies continue to confirm that the family remains one of the most effective vehicles to promote values, school success, even confidence in peer relationships. When it works, family functions as what Larson calls a "comfort zone," a place or a relationship that serves as a home base out of which to operate. Kids feel more secure, calm, and confident than those without a comfort zone. Similarly, Steinberg finds, the one common link among the many successful adolescents in his studies is that they all have positive relationships with their parents. Without positive relationships, the kids are subject to depression and likely to do poorly in school.

Parental withdrawal is a prime characteristic of families where adolescents get into trouble. It often catapults families into therapy. Wagers tells the story of a single parent who wasn't simply withdrawn, her head was in the sand: "I was seeing a mother and her 12-year-old son, who had depression and behavior problems. The mother called me up one time to say she had found all this marijuana paraphernalia in her son's room, in his pocket. She said she wasn't sure what it means. When I said 'it means that he's smoking pot,' she was very reluctant to agree. She didn't want to talk to her son about why he was getting into trouble or smoking pot. She wanted me to fix him." (Eventually, in therapy, the mother learned how to give her son a curfew and other rules, and to enforce them. He's doing much better.)

Teenagers know what is happening around them in school but adults hide things. Parents should shield their kids from some things but not so much that kids are afraid to go out into the world.
—Sarah, 17, Hanover, NH

Marital problems also enter into the distancing equation. Although the marital decline among teens' parents is part of the normal course of marriage, the adolescent can exacerbate the problem. "Here is a new person challenging you in ways that might make you irritable or insecure," explains Steinberg. "That can spill over into the marriage. The standard scenario involves the adolescent and the mother who have been home squabbling all afternoon. Well, the mom isn't exactly going to be in a terrific mood to greet her husband. It resembles the marital problems that occur when a couple first has a new baby." Trouble is, when the parents' marriage declines, so does the quality of the parenting—at a time when more parental energy is needed.

As if there are not enough psychological forces reducing contact between parents and adolescents today, social trends add to the problem, contends Roland Montemayor. Intensified work sched-

ules, increased divorce and single parenthood, and poverty—often a result of divorce and single parenthood—decrease parent–child contact. A fourth of all teenagers live with one parent, usually their mother. Families have fewer ties to the community, so there are fewer other adults with whom teens have nurturing ties. The negative images of teenagers as violent delinquents may even intimidate parents.

ALONE AND ANGRY

Whatever the source, parental distancing doesn't make for happy kids. "The kids I work with at Ohio State are remarkably independent, yet they are resentful of it," says Montemayor. "There is a sense of not being connected somehow." Kids are angry about being left to themselves, being given independence without the kind of mentoring from their parents to learn how to use their independence.

I am insecure about my future. The main view toward people in my generation is that we are all slackers and it's kind of disturbing. We are actually trying to make something of ourselves.
—Jasmine, 16, Brooklyn, New York

Adult contact seems to be on teenagers' minds more than ever before. Sociologist Dale Blythe, Ph.D., is an adolescence researcher who directs Minneapolis' noted Search Institute, which specializes in studies of youth policy issues. He has surveyed teens in 30 communities across the country, and found that when you ask teens, they say that family is not the most important thing in their lives—peers and social activities are. Nevertheless a large proportion of them say that they want more time with adults—they want their attention and leadership. They want more respect from adults and more cues on how to make it in the adult world. What a shift from 25 years ago, when the watchword was "never trust anyone over 30"!

The Invention of Adolescence

Are Romeo and Juliet the Quintessential adolescents? On the yes side, they were rebelling against family traditions, in the throes of first love, prone to melodrama, and engaged in violent and risky behavior. But the truth is that there was no such thing as adolescence in Shakespeare's time (the 16th century). Young people the ages of Romeo and Juliet (around 13) were adults in the eyes of society—even though they were probably prepubescent.

Paradoxically, puberty came later in eras past while departure from parental supervision came earlier than it does today. Romeo and Juliet carried the weight of the world on their shoulders—although it was a far smaller world than today's teens inhabit.

Another way to look at it is that in centuries past, a sexually mature person was never treated as a "growing child." Today sexually mature folk spend perhaps six years—ages 12 to 18—living under the authority of their parents.

Since the mid-1800s, puberty—the advent of sexual maturation and the starting point of adolescence—has inched back one year for every 25 years elapsed. It now occurs on average six years earlier than it did in 1850—age 11 or 12 for girls; age 12 or 13 for boys. Today adolescents make up 17 percent of the U.S. population and about a third of them belong to racial or ethnic minorities.

It's still not clear exactly what triggers puberty, confides Jeanne Brooks-Gunn, Ph.D., of Columbia University Teachers College, an expert on adolescent development. "The onset of puberty has fallen probably due to better nutrition in the prenatal period as well as throughout childhood. Pubertal age—for girls, when their first period occurs—has been lower in the affluent than the nonaffluent classes throughout recorded history. Differences are still found in countries where starvation and malnutrition are common among the poor. In Western countries, no social-class differences are found." Although adolescence is a new phenomenon in the history of our species, thanks to a stable and abundant food supply, we've already hit its limits—it's not likely puberty onset will drop much below the age of 12.

If kids look like adults sooner than ever before, that doesn't mean they are. The brain begins to change when the body does, but it doesn't become a grown-up thinking organ as quickly as other systems of the body mature. The clash between physical maturity and mental immaturity not only throws parents a curve—they forget how to do their job, or even what it is—it catapults teens into some silly situations. They become intensely interested in romance, for example, only their idea of romance is absurdly simple, culminating in notes passed across the classroom: "Do you like me? Check yes or no."

Puberty isn't the only marker of adolescence. There's a slowly increasing capacity for abstract reasoning and relative thinking. Their new capacity for abstraction allows teens to think about big things—Death, Destruction, Nuclear War—subjects that depress them, especially since they lack the capacity to ameliorate them.

The idea that everything is relative suddenly makes every rule subject to debate. As time passes, teens attain the ability to make finer abstract distinctions. Which is to say, they become better at choosing their fights.

Teens also move toward autonomy. They want to be alone, they say, because they have a lot on their minds. Yet much of the autonomy hinges on the growing importance of social relationships. Evaluating the ups and downs of social situations indeed requires time alone. Family ties, however, remain more important than you might expect as teens increase identification with their peers.

Whatever else turns teens into the moody creatures they are, hormones have been given far too much credit, contends Brooks-Gunn. In fact, she points out, the flow of hormones that eventually shapes their bodies actually starts around age seven or eight. "Certain emotional states and problems increase between ages 11 and 14, at the time puberty takes place. These changes are probably due to the increased social and school demands, the multiple new events that youth confront, their own responses to puberty, and to a much lesser extent hormonal changes themselves."

The nutritional abundance that underlies a long adolescence also prompted the extension of education, which has created a problem entirely novel in the animal kingdom—physically mature creatures living with their parents, and for more years than sexually mature offspring ever have in the past. College-bound kids typically depend on their parents until at least age 21, a decade or more after hitting puberty.

Historically, children never lived at home during the teen years, points out Temple University's Laurence Steinberg. Either they were shipped out to apprenticeships or off to other relatives.

Among lower primates, physically mature beasts simply are not welcome in the family den; sexual competition makes cohabiting untenable. But for animals, physical maturity coincides with mental acuity, so their departure is not a rejection.

The formal study of adolescence began in the 1940s, just before James Dean changed our perception of it forever. There is a long-standing tradition of professional observers looking at adolescence as a pathology—and this one really did start with Freud. It continues still.

A 1988 study reported that although the under-18 population actually declined from 1980 to 1984, adolescent admissions to private psychiatric hospitals increased—450 percent! The study suggests a staggering cultural taste for applying mental health care to any problem life presents. It also hints at the negative feelings Americans have toward adolescence—we consider it a disease.

The study of adolescence has come with a context—a culture of, by, and for youth, arising in the postwar boom of the 1950s and epitomized by James Dean. Once the original badass depressive teenager from hell, Dean seems quaintly tame by today's standards. But the fear and loathing he set in motion among adults is a powerful legacy today's teens are still struggling to live down.—V.R.

SILENCED SEX

Who can talk about teens without talking about sex? The topic of teenage sexuality, however, heightens parents' sense of powerlessness. Adults hesitate to acknowledge their own sexual experience in addressing the issue. They resolve the matter by pretending sex doesn't exist.

Sexuality was conspicuous by its absence in all the family interviews Steinberg, Montemayor, or Larson observed. Calling sex a hidden issue in adolescence verges on an oxymoron. Sprouting pubic hair and expanding busts aren't particularly subtle phenomena. But adolescent sexuality is only heightened by the silence.

So it's up to parents to seek more contact with their kids—despite the conflict they'll encounter. "The role of parents is to socialize children, to help them become responsible adults, to teach them to do the right thing. Conflict is an inevitable part of it" says Montemayor. He notes that one of the biggest sources of conflict between parents and teens is time management. Teens have trouble committing to plans in advance. They want to keep their options wide open all the time. The only surefire way to reduce conflict is to withdraw from teenagers—an equally surefire way to harm them.

"In other countries parents don't shy away from conflict. In the United States we have this idea that things are going to be hunky-dory and that we are going to go bowling and have fun together. Most people in the world would find that a pretty fanciful idea. There is an inevitable tension between parents and adolescents, and there's nothing wrong with that."

A postpubescent child introduces a third sexually mature person into the household, where once sex was a strictly private domain restricted to the older generation. It's difficult for everyone to get used to.

No matter how you slice it, sex can be an awkward topic. For parents, there's not only the feeling of powerlessness, there's discomfort. Most parents of adolescents aren't experiencing much sexual activity—neither the mechanics of sex nor its poetry—in this stage of the marriage (though this eventually improves).

The fact that fathers' marital satisfaction decreases when their kids start to date suggests the power of kids' sexuality, no matter how silenced, to distort parental behavior. Sex and marital therapist David Schnarch, Ph.D., points out that families, and the mythology of the

culture, worship teen sexuality, mistakenly believing adolescence is the peak of human sexuality. Boys have more hard-ons than their dads, while the girls have less cellulite than their moms.

These kids may have the biological equipment, says Schnarch, but they don't yet know how to make love. Sex isn't just about orgasms, it is about intimacy. "All of our sex education is designed to raise kids to be healthy, normal adults. But we are confused about what we believe is sexually normal. Textbooks say that boys reach their sexual peak in late adolescence; girls, five to 10 years later. The adolescent believes it, parents believe it, schools believe it. In the hierarchy dictated by this narrow biological model of sexuality, the person with the best sex is the adolescent. On the one hand we are telling kids, 'we would like you to delay sexual involvement.' But when we teach a biological model of sexuality, we imply

to the kids 'we know you can't delay. We think these are the best years of your life.' "

Parents can help their children by letting them know that they understand sex and have valuable experience about decisions related to sex; that they know it isn't just a mechanical act; that they recognize that teens are going to figure things out on their own with or without guidance from their parents; and that they are willing to talk about it. But often, the experience or meaning of sex gets lost.

I asked a woman whose parents had handed her birth control pills at age 15 how she felt about it now, at age 30. "I wish sex had been a little more taboo than it was. I got into a lot more sexual acting out before I was 20, and that didn't go very well for me. Even though my parents talked about the health consequences of sex, they did not mention other consequences. Like what it does to your self-esteem when you get involved in a series of one-night stands. So I guess I wish they had been more holistic in

> I don't feel any pressure about sex. It's a frequent topic of conversation, but we talk about other things, too—when I'm going to get my history paper done, movies, music. I listen to classical music a lot. I think about my maturity a lot, because I have recently had losses in my immediate family and it feels like I am maturing so fast. But then sometimes I feel so young compared to everything out there. I think adults have always felt that teens were more reckless.—**Amanda, 16, New York City**

their approach to sex. Not just to tell me about the pill when I was 15, but to understand the different issues I was struggling with. In every other aspect of my life, they were my best resource. But it turns out sex is a lot more complicated

> Teenagers, like adults, are all different. One has a job that is hard, another has more money and more education, and one just gets by. It is unfair to look at all teens the same way. You have maturity in you, but you just don't want to show it because it's no fun. We've got problems, but not really big ones like my uncle who came over from China when he was 16, or going to war when you're 18. If teenagers make it through this era, adults will just bash the next generation of teenagers.—**Mike, 14, Brooklyn, New York**

than I thought it was when I was 15. At 30, sex is a lot better than it was when I was a teenager."

The distortions parents create about teen sexuality lead directly to events like the "Spur Posse," the gang of teenage football stars in Southern California who systematically harassed and raped girls, terrorizing the community in the late 80s. The boys' fathers actually appeared on talk shows—to brag about their sons'

Jackie Joyner-Kersee, the Olympic track star, is my hero because she has accomplished so much and she is one of the main female athletes.
—Kristy, 12, Woodbridge, New Jersey

---

conquests. "The fathers were reinforcing the boys' behavior. It was as if it were a reflection on their own sexuality," observes Schnarch.

By closing their eyes to teen sexual behavior, parents don't just disengage from their kids. They leave them high and dry about understanding anything

---

My hero is Queen Latifah. She is herself and doesn't try to be somebody else. My mother is also my hero because she raises me as well as she can and she is a single parent.
—Maria, 15, Bronx, New York

---

more than the cold mechanics of sex. Kids raised this way report feeling very alone when it gets down to making intimate decisions for the first time. They feel like they haven't been given any help in what turns out to be the bigger part of sex—the relationship part of it.

Returning to the authoritarian, insular family of Ward, June, Wally, and the Beaver is not the solution for teenagers any more than it is for their parents. But teenagers do need parents and other responsible adults actively involved in their lives, just as younger children do. Only when it comes to teenagers, the grown-ups have to tolerate a lot more ambiguity—about authority, safety, responsibility, and closeness—to sustain the connection. If they can learn to do that, a lot of young people will be able to avoid a whole lot of trouble.

Teenage Turning Point

Does adolescence herald the twilight of girls' self-esteem?

BRUCE BOWER

Youngsters often experience a decline in self-esteem as they enter their adolescent years, a time marked by the abrupt move from the relatively cloistered confines of elementary school to the more complex social and academic demands of junior high. Social scientists have documented this trend — often more pronounced among girls — over the past 20 years through questionnaires and interviews aimed at gauging how adolescents feel about themselves.

But a new survey of U.S. elementary and secondary students bears the worst news yet about plummeting self-esteem among teenage girls. The controversial findings, released in January by the American Association of University Women (AAUW), have refocused researchers' attention on long-standing questions about the meaning of such studies and their implications, if any, for educational reform and for male and female psychological development.

The concept of self-esteem itself remains vague, contends psychiatrist Philip Robson in the June 1990 HARVARD MEDICAL SCHOOL MENTAL HEALTH LETTER. Some researchers assess a person's "global" self-esteem with questions about general feelings of worth, goodness, health, attractiveness and social competence. Others focus on people's evaluations of themselves in specific situations. Robson, of Oxford University in England, notes that an individual might score high on one type of test but not on another, presumably because the measures reflect different aspects of self-esteem.

Moreover, he argues, high test scores may sometimes indicate conceit, narcissism or rigidity rather than healthy feelings of self-worth.

Despite the complexities involved in determining how people truly regard themselves, the AAUW survey suggests that adolescent girls experience genuine, substantial drops in self-esteem that far outpace those reported by boys. Girls also reported much less enthusiasm for math and science, less confidence in their academic abilities and fewer aspirations to professional careers.

The survey, conducted last fall by a private polling firm commissioned by AAUW, involved 2,400 girls and 600 boys from 36 public schools throughout the United States. Black and Hispanic students made up almost one-quarter of the sample. Participants, whose ages ranged from 9 to 16 (fourth through tenth grades), responded to written statements probing global self-esteem, such as "I like the way I look" and "I'm happy the way I am."

In a typical response pattern, 67 percent of the elementary school boys reported "always" feeling "happy the way I am," and 46 percent still felt that way by tenth grade. For girls, the figures dropped from 60 percent to 29 percent.

For both sexes, the sharpest declines in self-esteem occurred at the beginning of junior high.

Compared with the rest of the study sample, students with higher self-esteem liked math and science more, felt better about their schoolwork and grades, considered themselves more important and felt better about their family relationships, according to the survey.

Boys who reported doing poorly in math and science usually ascribed their performance to the topics' lack of usefulness, whereas girls who reported a lack of success in these areas often attributed the problem to personal failure.

Although the survey included too few boys to allow a racial breakdown for males, race did appear to play an important role in the strength of self-esteem among girls. White and Hispanic girls displayed sharp drops in all the measured areas of self-esteem — appearance, confidence, family relationships, school, talents and personal importance — as they grew older. In contrast, more than half the black girls reported high levels of self-confidence and personal importance in both elementary and high school, and most attributed this to strong family and community support, says psychologist Janie Victoria Ward of the University of Pennsylvania in Philadelphia, an adviser to the study. Their confidence in their academic abilities, however, dropped substantially as they passed through the school system, Ward says.

"Something is going on in the schools that threatens the self-esteem of girls in general," asserts psychologist Nancy Goldberger, another adviser to the survey. "A lot of girls come to doubt their own intelligence in school."

Goldberger, who teaches psychology at the Fielding Institute in Santa Barbara, Calif., calls for intensive, long-term studies to address how schools shortchange female students.

An AAUW pamphlet published last August argues that school-age girls represent the proverbial square peg attempting to fit into the round hole of most educational programs.

Starting early in life, societal pressures urge girls and boys to think and behave in contrasting ways that create gender-specific learning styles, according to the AAUW pamphlet. Schools, however, generally tailor instructional techniques to the learning style of boys, leaving girls with a tattered education and doubts about their academic abilities, the pamphlet contends.

This argument rests heavily on research directed by Harvard University psychologist Carol Gilligan. In her much-praised and much-criticized book, *In a Different Voice* (1982, Harvard University Press), Gilligan asserted that girls and boys generally follow divergent paths of moral development. She based her contention on several studies of Harvard undergraduates, men and women at different points in the life cycle, and women considering abortion.

In Gilligan's view, females respond to an inner moral voice emphasizing human connections and care, and they attempt to solve moral dilemmas by responding to the needs and situations of those affected by the problem. Males, on the other hand, focus on abstract principles such as justice and follow a moral code centered on the impartial application of rules of right and wrong.

Gilligan's most recent research, described in *Making Connections: The Relational Worlds of Adolescent Girls at Emma Willard School* (1990, Harvard University Press), draws on findings collected over a three-year period among 34 students at a private girls' school in Troy, N.Y. Gilligan and her co-workers argue that many girls, at least in this predominantly white, privileged sample, show an aggressive confidence in their identities and ideas around age 11, only to find their self-assurance withering by age 15 or 16.

During this period of increasing separation from parents, marked by a search for an independent identity and future career possibilities, girls feel torn between responding to others and caring for themselves, the Harvard researchers maintain. In addition, they say, adolescent girls encounter more pressure from parents and teachers to keep quiet and not make a fuss than do adolescent boys or younger girls.

The gender gap seen in academic achievement during early adolescence arises largely because a social and educational emphasis on career development and personal advancement clashes with girls' distinctive sense of connection to others, Gilligan's team asserts. The researchers maintain that girls often learn best and gain increased self-confidence through collaboration with other students and faculty, not through competition among individuals as practiced in most schools.

Boys, in contrast, often perform best on competitive tasks or in games with a strict set of prescribed rules, the investigators contend.

Some adolescence researchers argue that Gilligan paints too stark a contrast between the moral development of boys and girls. Others say Gilligan's ideas have an intuitive appeal, but her small studies lack a sound empirical foundation on which to build educational reforms. These researchers see Gilligan's work as a preliminary corrective for previous studies, based largely on male participants, that suggested the ability to reason from abstract principles represented the pinnacle of moral development.

Similarly, social scientists differ over the extent to which self-esteem dips during adolescence and the meaning of the AAUW survey data. In fact, some investigators question whether a significant gender gap in self-esteem exists at all.

Most surveys of teenagers' self-esteem, including the AAUW project, focus on students and neglect school dropouts. This approach may lead to overestimates of self-esteem among boys, argues sociologist Naomi Gerstel of the University of Massachusetts in Amherst. More boys than girls drop out of school, and male dropouts may regard themselves in an especially poor light, Gerstel points out.

Furthermore, she says, since no one has examined the moral "voice" of boys in the intensive way Gilligan studied her group of girls, Gilligan's theory has yet to meet a scientifically rigorous test. Gilligan's ideas prove "problematic" when educators attempt to use them to formulate specific educational reforms, Gerstel writes in the Jan. 4 SCIENCE.

The self-esteem reports gathered in the AAUW survey fail to provide evidence for any particular need to change school instruction, contends psychologist Joseph Adelson of the University of Michigan in Ann Arbor. "It's been known for some time that girls report greater self-esteem declines in adolescence, but the reasons for those declines are unclear," he says. "It's inappropriate to take the correlations in this survey to politicized conclusions about educational reform."

In his view, gender differences in mathematics achievement remain particularly mysterious and probably stem from a number of as-yet-unspecified social or family influences (SN: 12/6/86, p.357). Preliminary studies directed by Carol S. Dweck, a psychologist at Columbia University in New York City, suggest that bright girls show a stronger tendency than bright boys to attribute their difficulty or confusion with a new concept — such as mathematics — to a lack of intelligence. Thus, when bright girls confront mathematics, initial confusion may trigger a feeling of helplessness, Dweck writes in *At The Threshold* (1990, S. Shirley Feldman and Glen R. Elliot, editors, Harvard University Press).

Many girls with considerable potential in mathematics may deal with this sense of helplessness by throwing their energies into already mastered verbal skills, Dweck suggests. Rather than indict their intelligence, both boys and girls who shrink from challenging new subjects may need to learn how to channel initial failures into a redoubled effort to master the material, she says.

Gender differences in reported well-being — an aspect of personal experience closely related to self-esteem — also prove tricky to study, Adelson observes. A statistical comparison of 93 independent studies, directed by psychologist Wendy Wood of Texas A&M University in College Station, serves as a case in point. In examining these studies, which focused on well-being and life satisfaction among adult men and women, Wood and her colleagues found that women reported both greater happiness *and* more dissatisfaction and depression than men. Wood contends that societal influences groom women for an acute emotional responsiveness, especially with regard to intimate relationships, and that this helps explain why women report more intense emotional highs and lows than men.

"No clear advantage can be identified in the adaptiveness and desirability of [men's and women's] styles of emotional life," she and her colleagues write in the March 1989 PSYCHOLOGICAL BULLETIN.

Researchers have yet to conduct a similar statistical comparison of the literature on adolescent self-esteem and well-being. But according to Adelson, a persistent problem plagues the interpretation of all such studies. If females generally show more sensitivity to and awareness of emotions than males, they may more easily offer self-reports about disturbing feelings, creating a misimpression that large sex differences exist in self-esteem, he suggests.

Although this potential "response bias" muddies the research waters, psychologist Daniel Offer of Northwestern University in Evanston, Ill., cites several possible explanations for the tendency among early-adolescent girls to report more self-dissatisfaction than boys.

One theory holds that since girls experience the biological changes of puberty up to 18 months before boys, they may suffer earlier and more pronounced self-esteem problems related to sexual maturity. Several studies have found that early-maturing girls report the most dissatisfaction with their physical appearance, a particularly sensitive indicator of self-esteem among females. Social pressures to begin dating and to disengage emotionally from parents may create additional problems for early-maturing girls, Offer says.

Other research suggests that, unlike their male counterparts, adolescent girls often maintain close emotional ties to their mothers that interfere with the development of a sense of independence and self-confidence, Offer says. In addition, parents may interrupt and ignore girls more than boys as puberty progresses, according to observational studies of families, directed by psychologist John P. Hill of Virginia Commonwealth University in Richmond.

Despite these findings, the director of the most ambitious longitudinal study of adolescent self-esteem to date says her findings provide little support for the substantial gender gap outlined in the AAUW survey, which took a single-point-in-time "snapshot" of self-esteem.

During the 1970s, sociologist Roberta G. Simmons of the University of Pittsburgh and her co-workers charted the trajectory of self-esteem from grades 6 through 10 among more than 1,000 youngsters attending public schools in Milwaukee and Baltimore. Simmons discusses the research in *Moving Into Adolescence* (1987, Aldine de Gruyter).

Overall, adolescents reported a gradual increase in self-esteem as they got older, she says, but many girls entering junior high and high school did experience drops in feelings of confidence and self-satisfaction.

Simmons agrees with Gilligan that adolescent girls increasingly strive for intimacy with others. Large, impersonal junior high schools throw up a barrier to intimacy that initially undermines girls' self-esteem, Simmons asserts. As girls find a circle of friends and a social niche, their self-esteem gradually rebounds, only to drop again when they enter the even larger world of high school.

"We don't know if that last self-esteem drop [in high school] was temporary or permanent," Simmons points out.

As in the AAUW survey, Simmons' team found that black girls, as well as black boys, consistently reported positive and confident self-images.

But given the increased acceptance of women in a wide variety of occupations since the 1970s, Simmons expresses surprise at how much the self-esteem of girls lagged behind that of boys in the AAUW survey.

A new study of 128 youngsters progressing through junior high, described in the February JOURNAL OF YOUTH AND ADOLESCENCE, also contrasts with the AAUW findings. The two-year, longitudinal investigation reveals comparable levels of self-esteem among boys and girls, notes study director Barton J. Hirsch, a psychologist at Northwestern University. Hirsch and his colleagues used a global self-esteem measure much like the one in the AAUW survey.

The researchers gathered self-reports from boys and girls as the students neared the end of sixth grade, then repeated the process with the same youngsters at two points during seventh grade and at the end of eighth grade. Students lived in a midwestern city and came from poor or middle-class families. Black children made up about one-quarter of the sample.

In both sexes, about one in three youngsters reported strong self-esteem throughout junior high school, the researchers report. These individuals also did well in school, maintained rewarding friendships and frequently participated in social activities.

Another third of the sample displayed small increases in self-esteem, but their overall psychological adjustment and academic performance were no better than those of the group with consistently high self-esteem.

Chronically low self-esteem and school achievement dogged 13 percent of the students, who probably suffered from a long history of these problems, Hirsch says.

But the most unsettling findings came from the remaining 21 percent of the youngsters. This group — composed of roughly equal numbers of boys and girls — started out with high self-esteem, good grades and numerous friends, but their scores on these measures plunged dramatically during junior high, eventually reaching the level of the students with chronically low self-esteem.

The data offer no easy explanations for the steep declines seen among one in five study participants, Hirsch says. An examination of family life might uncover traumatic events that influenced the youngsters' confidence and motivation, but this remains speculative, he says.

One of the most comprehensive longitudinal studies of the relation between child development and family life (SN: 8/19/89, p. 117) suggests that particular parenting styles produce the most psycho-logically healthy teenagers. The findings indicate that parents who set clear standards for conduct and allow freedom within limits raise youngsters with the most academic, emotional and social competence.

Directed by psychologist Diana Baumrind of the University of California, Berkeley, the ongoing study has followed children from 124 families, most of them white and middle-class. At three points in the youngsters' lives — ages 3, 10 and 15 — investigators assessed parental styles and the children's behavior at home and school.

Baumrind assumes that self-esteem emerges from competence in various social and academic tasks, not vice versa. For that reason, she and her colleagues track achievement scores and trained observers' ratings of social and emotional adjustment, not children's self-reports of how they feel about themselves.

In fact, Baumrind remains unconvinced that girls experience lower self-esteem than boys upon entering adolescence. Her study finds that girls in elementary grades show a more caring and communal attitude toward others, while boys more often strive for dominance and control in social encounters. But by early adolescence, she maintains, such differences largely disappear.

The gender-gap debate, however, shows no signs of disappearing. In a research field characterized by more questions than answers, most investigators agree on one point. "Most kids come through the years from 10 to 20 without major problems and with an increasing sense of self-esteem," Simmons observes.

Yet that trend, too, remains unexplained. "Perhaps the steady increase in self-esteem noted in late adolescence results more from progressive indoctrination into the values of society than from increasing self-acceptance," says Robson. "We simply do not have the empirical data necessary to resolve this question."

HIV Infected Youth Speaks About Needs for Support and Health Care

Wayne Davis is a 24-year-old, HIV positive youth from Oregon who became infected when he was 17. He currently lives in San Francisco and is the coordinator of the HIV Positive Youth Speakers Bureau, sponsored by Health Initiatives for Youth. He recently shared his personal experiences with the editor of Target 2000, stating that it sounded important to have the opportunity to let adolescent health care providers know about the needs of HIV infected youth. The following is his story.

Early Lessons in Life

I think in order to explain how I got where I am today, I have to go back a little earlier than when I actually tested positive for the virus. Most of my life from birth to the age of 9, I was with my mother and she was very abusive. Everyday she beat me. As she beat me she would say things like "this is your fault" and "if only you were a better child I wouldn't beat you like this. I would be a better mother if you were a better child." That taught me that things were my fault. It taught me guilt. It taught me to really feel bad about myself.

I had an uncle who was sexually abusive. He molested my brother and me. That taught me that my body wasn't mine and that other people had the right to do to me whatever they wanted to do. All of my messages growing up were very unhealthy. When I was 9, my mother left and joined the Hare Krishna's. Mental illness runs in my family, my grandmother was really strange and my mother is unstable mentally. She needed other people to run her life. She went through churches and different places to do this. When she joined the Hare Krishna's, I was in a foster home. She wrote us and said "some day you will understand but I have to leave." You know your mother is supposed to be there no matter what. It's a given. It's a very solid form of support. It's fundamental, regardless of how messed up she is, she is supposed to be there. So, her leaving taught me that I can't trust people, I can't trust my environment, I can't trust people to be there. That made me kind of bitter.

I started running away. I had run away before but I started running away to the streets. This was different because before I was running away from the beatings. When I went to the streets I found a real community. I found people who were willing to take care of me, be my friend, and treat me like I had decisions to make. That was really important to me. So I started to run away "to" things instead of "from" things. I started running away to my family on the streets.

Life on the Streets

There are few things that you can do on the streets to survive and being 9 years old there are even fewer things. You could rob people but I was too little. You could do burglaries but I got caught doing that. I couldn't deal drugs because I didn't have the heart for it. There was only one thing left that I could do. That was to sell myself. It made perfect sense to me because all I had known was hurt and that my body wasn't mine. All I had known was that I should feel bad about myself. That just fit right in. I started doing that and it's hard selling yourself on the streets. It really takes something out of you.

The only way that I could live with myself or the only way that I could deal with the pain that I was putting myself through was to do drugs. So I started shooting up speed when I was about 10, which for the first time in my life, I remember clearly I felt like I was in control. I felt that nobody could hurt me or do anything to me. No matter what anybody did I could deal with it. That was a really good feeling. It took foreign substances to make me feel like that but I didn't care. I felt like it and that's what was important. So, that was pretty much my life.

I would run away to the streets and stay gone from the juvenile system for anywhere from a couple of days to a couple of months. I would get caught and, since I was on probation for stealing, they would hold me for 8 days in juvenile hall and then place me into a foster home or group home. I would be there for all of about

3 hours and I would leave. I did that over and over again. All together I've been in 18 different group homes and 26 different foster homes. Finally they didn't have anywhere to send me. They ran out of places to put me so they committed me to the juvenile jail.

One Foster Home

I met a security guard at the juvenile jail who helped me to run away. He befriended me and treated me nice but while I was a runaway, he abused me. He pedophiled me. I remember at one point we were on the lake shooting at bottles and he turned to me and said, "what would stop me from raping you and killing you right now?" I remember I was thinking really hard about what I could say. I told him that I had called my sister and told her where I was and gave her his license plate number. He said, oh that's a good answer. I turned myself in to him and then went back to juvenile hall. They released me and I was back on the streets for awhile. I was about 14 then.

I was doing drugs for a while and I woke up one morning in a pair of shorts. I was in Portland, Oregon in the middle of winter which was really cold. I had the phone number of this security guard in my pocket so I called him up and he came and got me. I lived with him for about 1 1/2 years. I became a foster child of his and I received some really mixed messages from him. On the one hand, he was a real father figure which I had never had. He taught me how to hunt, how to fish, how to farm, and how to be what I felt was a man. On the other hand, at night time I was going to his room and he was having sex with me. It was really a mixed up time of my life. Then he started getting other foster children and ended up getting 6 or 7 other foster children ranging from the age of 9 to 14. I figured out that he was messing with them too and he kicked me out. So I went back to the streets. I felt so bad about myself because I knew what was going on in his home and I just did my best to block it out of my mind by using a lot of drugs.

Down and Out — With HIV

I had heard about HIV. What I was hearing was that if you get it you die and that older gay men get it. I figured out that there was a lot [of] attention that went along with HIV. I was hanging out with this guy who was HIV positive. He was young. He was 23 and he had access to money and to drugs. I did a pile of coke about the size of my fist for about a period of a day with him one time. At the end of it, I was coming down and feeling really bad. I looked at him and realized that he had my way out. I was hurting so bad that I just realized that he could help me out. He could stop my hurting. So I told him to give me his blood and he came over and he did.

So, October 16, 1988, I infected myself. It was strange because when I took the needle out of my arm, I didn't feel any different. For some reason I thought I would feel better. I thought something would change like some sparks would go off or I would become animated or feel better. I didn't. I was still here. I had been tested before that and I had tested negative. A couple days after this incident, I got really sick and went into the hospital. About 6 months later, I tested positive.

I remember when I tested, it was a confidential test. It was the type of place where you had to give a name. It didn't necessarily have to be yours. For some reason I gave them my real name. They called me back and told me to come in and get my results. So there was this woman from the Salvation Army Greenhouse named Margie who was really supportive of me. She is one of the few solid influences I had in my life. I asked her to go with me and she did. She had been diagnosed with cancer before. She had gone into remission and she knew what it was like to be told that you have a life threatening illness. She told me it was good idea to take somebody to hear what was being said because I wouldn't hear anything if I tested positive. She was right. She went in with me and we sat down and they told me that I tested positive to the HIV virus and all I could hear was mumbling and I was kind of just nodding my head. I think I was doing it at the right time.

For the next four years, all I did was get loaded. I don't really remember a lot about it. The things I do remember were really traumatic. I know I hurt a lot of people and myself a lot. I slept with a lot of people. Most of them I used condoms with and a lot of times I didn't. I didn't care. People were items, commodities, things. I was only a thing and that was as deep as people went.

A Move to San Francisco and to Medical Care

When I was 19, I ended up coming down to San Francisco because I was shot at in Portland. When I got here the drugs were better and so I decided to live here. Somebody from Portland told me to go to the Larkin Street Youth Center (see interview on page 4) and get myself "hooked up." I went to Larkin Street and talked with Mike Kennedy. I dressed up to go there. I was trying to show everybody how together I was. When I first meet people, I am really good at being presentable. Somehow or another they knew that I needed to be there. They hooked me up with medical care.

This was the first point in my whole life that I ever had solid medical care. It was a real strange adjustment.

There was a woman there named Susan Wayne, a nurse practitioner, who is really awesome. Every time she saw me, she was really supportive. She wasn't pushy, just supportive. She found the right balance with me. I started seeing her and developed a trust with her. So I started going in for my medical care. When I first started going I went when I was feeling really sick or when I had crabs or whatever. Slowly I went into this phase where I went every couple of weeks to check in. That was cool too. She gave me a little examination and then just sat down and talked with me a couple of minutes. It made me feel like I could be there and didn't have to have a reason. Then I started going when I needed to or just for regular check ups.

I realized during that time how much I was hurting myself. I was trying to find a way to not be hurting myself anymore. I had taken 175 Elavil to overdose and went into a coma. I just wanted to die. I realized that no matter what I tried I wasn't going to die and that I couldn't live the way I was living. So I decided that I needed to change my life. And that's what I did.

At Larkin Street, I was also hooked up with a case manager who was really helpful. When I went into the coma, the case manager was the first person I saw when I woke up. In a lot of ways I found a family. They all gave me the opportunity to try time and time again to help myself. They didn't try to push it on me. That was the key. It was like I picture myself in this room surrounded by doors. Every time a door opens up, it is an opportunity. I have to be looking at the door and get up. I have to have the motivation to walk over to the door, walk through it, and stay through it for the opportunities to happen. All the time I'm sitting there, all of these doors are opening and closing and people are crawling from the doors. It makes a combination of everything being set up at once for a person to be able to change in any direction. At the clinic, they just kept opening the doors. The opportunities empowered me and got me to the clinic when I was sick. More than once, people from the clinic came and got me and took me to where I needed to go — to the clinic or detox or wherever. There were opportunities for drug and alcohol abuse treatment and getting me to the hospital.

A New Life With Help From a Treatment Program

My case manager helped me check into a program called Walden House. It is a behavior modification program. I started learning the fundamental ways to deal with life that I had missed out on while growing up. Life is a rough thing to live in. If you miss out when you are young on how to deal with life, you have a really hard time. That's what they taught me. They taught me how to deal with life. Because I was leaving the streets, I switched my care from Larkin Street to the Cole Street Clinic. I saw the same nurse practitioner. That was really good because I had established a real trust with her.

Deciding What Is Important in Primary Care

I don't go to the Cole Street Clinic anymore. The nurse practitioner moved away and I was getting to the age anyway, where I decided to change my primary care. I found a nurse practitioner who isn't necessarily the most educated person on HIV but when I asked her about it she said that she was really willing to learn. She is a part of the UCSF hospital and they have special HIV services there. I really trust her so I decided this was the right choice.

When I went searching for health care providers, I decided that I wanted a nurse practitioner instead of a doctor. I have found in general, though this isn't always the case, but my experience is that the doctors think they really know everything. But HIV is something that nobody knows everything about. It is important for me to be in the driver's seat regarding what I'm going to do to take care of myself. There are so many different therapies, if I say I don't want to take AZT, I don't want some doctors telling me that I am going to die if I don't. I do a lot of research and need to be in control of my health. I need to work with the provider and have the provider work with me, instead of being told what to do. My experience has been that nurse practitioners are more education oriented and present me with options.

A Better Life

I've been in a relationship now for about 2 1/2 years. We're moving in together in about a month. She's negative. Sex is really hard to deal with in the relationship. If she isn't afraid, I am. If I'm not afraid, she's afraid. There are a lot of other issues to worry about, like what if I die. What if I get sick? So there is a lot more to deal with in this relationship besides the regular issues of being in a relationship. There are a lot of things that go along with one partner being HIV positive and one being negative.

Since I entered the treatment program I've been working with young people at risk. I've been trying to spread the word where I can. I go to schools to speak. I am the coordinator for the speakers bureau now, which is really a big step for me. My life is about healing people, healing myself, and about teaching people some of the things that I've learned along the way. Today I know that I don't have to hurt myself. I know that I don't have to let anybody touch me that I don't want to. I don't have to lie to somebody or do what it was that I used to do just to survive. Today I know that there is a different way. And that's pretty much my story.

PSYCHOTRENDS

Taking Stock of Tomorrow's Family and Sexuality

Where are we going and what kind of people are we becoming? Herewith, a road map to the defining trends in sexuality, family, and relationships for the coming millenium as charted by the former chair of Harvard's psychiatry department. From the still-rollicking sexual revolution to the painful battle for sexual equality to the reorganization of the family, America is in for some rather interesting times ahead.

Shervert H. Frazier, M.D.

Has the sexual revolution been side-tracked by AIDS, and the return to traditional values we keep hearing about? In a word, no. The forces that originally fueled the revolution are all still in place and, if anything, are intensifying: mobility, democratization, urbanization, women in the workplace, birth control, abortion and other reproductive interventions, and media proliferation of sexual images, ideas, and variation.

Sexuality has moved for many citizens from church- and state-regulated behavior to a medical and self-regulated behavior. Population pressures and other economic factors continue to diminish the size of the American family. Marriage is in sharp decline, cohabitation is growing, traditional families are on the endangered list, and the single-person household is a wave of the future.

AIDS has generated a great deal of heat in the media but appears to have done little, so far, to turn down the heat in the bedroom. It is true that in some surveys people *claimed* to have made drastic changes in behavior—but most telling are the statistics relating to marriage, divorce, cohabitation, teen sex, out-of-wedlock births, sexually transmitted diseases (STDs), contraception,

and adultery. These are far more revealing of what we *do* than what we *say* we do. And those tell a tale of what has been called a "postmarital society" in continued pursuit of sexual individuality and freedom.

Studies reveal women are more sexual now than at any time in the century.

Arguably there are, due to AIDS, fewer visible sexual "excesses" today than there were in the late 1960s and into the 1970s, but those excesses (such as sex clubs, bathhouses, backrooms, swinging singles, group sex, public sex acts, etc.) were never truly reflective of norms and were, in any case, greatly inflated in the media. Meanwhile, quietly and without fanfare, the public, even in the face of the AIDS threat, has continued to expand its interest in sex and in *increased,* rather than decreased, sexual expression.

Numerous studies reveal that women are more sexual now than at any time in the century. Whereas sex counselors used to deal with men's complaints about their wives' lack of "receptivity," it is now more often the women complaining about the men. And women, in this "postfeminist"

era, are doing things they never used to believe were "proper." Fellatio, for example, was seldom practiced (or admitted to) when Kinsey conducted his famous sex research several decades ago. Since that time, according to studies at UCLA and elsewhere, this activity has gained acceptance among women, with some researchers reporting that nearly all young women now practice fellatio.

Women's images of themselves have also changed dramatically in the past two decades, due, in large part, to their movement into the workplace and roles previously filled exclusively by men. As Lilian Rubin, psychologist at the University of California Institute for the Study of Social Change and author of *Intimate Strangers,* puts it, "Women feel empowered sexually in a way they never did in the past."

Meanwhile, the singles scene, far from fading away (the media just lost its fixation on this subject), continues to grow. James Bennett, writing in *The New Republic,* characterizes this growing population of no-reproducers thusly: "Single adults in America display a remarkable tendency to multiply without being fruitful."

Their libidos are the target of million-dollar advertising budgets and entrepreneurial pursuits that seek to put those sex drives on line in the information age. From video dating to computer coupling to erotic faxing, it's now "love at first

From *Psychology Today,* January/February 1994, pp. 32-37, 64, 66. Excerpted from *Psychotrends: What Kind of People Are We Becoming?* by Shervert H. Frazier, M.D. © 1994 by Shervert H. Frazier, M.D. Reprinted by permission of Simon & Schuster, Inc.

byte," as one commentator put it. One thing is certain: the computer is doing as much today to promote the sexual revolution as the automobile did at the dawn of that revolution.

Political ideologies, buttressed by economic adversities, *can* temporarily retard the sexual revolution, as can sexually transmitted diseases. But ultimately the forces propelling this revolution are unstoppable. And ironically, AIDS itself is probably doing more to promote than impede this movement. It has forced the nation to confront a number of sexual issues with greater frankness than ever before. While some conservatives and many religious groups have argued for abstinence as the only moral response to AIDS, others have lobbied for wider dissemination of sexual information, beginning in grade schools. A number of school districts are now making condoms available to students—a development that would have been unthinkable before the outbreak of AIDS.

Despite all these gains (or losses, depending upon your outlook) the revolution is far from over. The openness that it has fostered is healthy, but Americans are still ignorant about many aspects of human sexuality. Sexual research is needed to help us deal with teen sexuality and pregnancies, AIDS, and a number of emotional issues related to sexuality. Suffice it to say for now that there is still plenty of room for the sexual revolution to proceed—and its greatest benefits have yet to be realized.

THE REVOLUTION AND RELATIONSHIPS

The idea that the Sexual Revolution is at odds with romance (not to mention tradition) is one that is widely held, even by some of those who endorse many of the revolution's apparent objectives. But there is nothing in our findings to indicate that romance and the sexual revolution are inimical—unless one's defense of romance disguises an agenda of traditional male dominance and the courtly illusion of intimacy and communication between the sexes.

The trend now, as we shall see, is away from illusion and toward—in transition, at least—a sometimes painful reality in which the sexes are finally making an honest effort to *understand* one another.

But to some, it may seem that the sexes are farther apart today than they ever have been. The real gender gap, they say, is a communications gap so cavernous that only the most intrepid or foolhardy dare try to bridge it. Many look back at the Anita Hill affair and say that was the open declaration of war between the sexes.

The mistake many make, however, is saying that there has been a *recent* breakdown in those communications, hence all this new discontent. This conclusion usually goes unchallenged, but there is nothing in the data we have seen from past decades to indicate that sexual- and gender-related communication were ever better than they are today. On the contrary, a more thoughtful analysis makes it very clear they have always been *worse.*

What has changed is our *consciousness* about this issue. Problems in communication between the sexes have been masked for decades by a rigid social code that strictly prescribes other behavior. Communication between the sexes has long been preprogrammed by this code to produce an exchange that has been as superficial as it is oppressive. As this process begins to be exposed by its own inadequacies in a rapidly changing world, we suddenly discover that we have a problem. But, of course, that problem was there for a long time, and the discovery does not mean a decline in communication between the sexes but, rather, provides us with the potential for better relationships in the long run.

Thus what we call a "breakdown" in communications might more aptly be called a *breakthrough.*

Seymour Parker, of the University of Utah, demonstrated that men who are the most mannerly with women, those who adhere most strictly to the "code" discussed above, are those who most firmly believe, consciously or unconsciously, that women are "both physically and psychologically weaker (i.e., less capable) than men." What has long passed for male "respect" toward women in our society is, arguably, *disrespect.*

Yet what has been learned can be unlearned—especially if women force the issue, which is precisely what is happening now. Women's views of themselves are changing and that, more than anything, is working to eliminate many of the stereotypes that supported the image of women as weak and inferior. Women, far from letting men continue to dictate to them, are making it clear they want more *real* respect from men and will accept

nothing less. They want a genuine dialogue; they want men to recognize that they speak with a distinct and equal voice, not one that is merely ancillary to the male voice.

The sexual revolution made possible a serious inquiry into the ways that men and women are alike and the ways that each is unique. This revolutionary development promises to narrow the gender gap as nothing else can, for only by understanding the differences that make communication so complex do we stand any chance of mastering those complexities.

SUBTRENDS

Greater Equality Between the Sexes

Despite talk in the late 1980s and early 1990s of the decline of feminism and declarations that women, as a social and political force, are waning, equality between the sexes is closer to becoming a reality than ever before. Women command a greater workforce and wield greater political power than they have ever done. They are assuming positions in both public and private sectors that their mothers and grandmothers believed were unattainable (and their fathers and grandfathers thought were inappropriate) for women. Nonetheless, much remains to be achieved before women attain complete equality—but movement in that direction will continue at a pace that will surprise many over the next two decades.

Women voters, for example, who have long outnumbered male voters, are collectively a sleeping giant whose slumber many say was abruptly interrupted during the Clarence Thomas–Anita Hill hearings in 1991. The spectacle of a political "boy's club" raking the dignified Hill over the coals of sexual harassment galvanized the entire nation for days.

On another front, even though women have a long way to go to match men in terms of equal pay for equal work, as well as in equal opportunity, there is a definite *research* trend that shows women can match men in the skills needed to succeed in business. This growing body of data will make it more difficult for businesses to check the rise of women into the upper echelons of management and gradually help to change the corporate consciousness that still heavily favors male employees.

As for feminism, many a conservative wrote its obituary in the 1980s, only to find it risen from the dead in the 1990s. Actually, its demise was always imaginary. Movements make headway only in a context of dissatisfaction. And, clearly, there is still plenty for women to be dissatisfied about, particularly in the wake of a decade that tried to stifle meaningful change.

The "new feminism," as some call it, is less doctrinaire than the old, less extreme in the sense that it no longer has to be outrageous in order to call attention to itself. The movement today is less introspective, more goal oriented and pragmatic. Demands for liberation are superseded—and subsumed—by a well-organized quest for power. Women no longer want to burn bras, they want to manufacture and market them.

The New Masculinity

To say that the men's movement today is confused is to understate mercifully. Many men say they want to be more "sensitive" but also "less emasculated," "more open," yet "less vulnerable." While the early flux of this movement is often so extreme that it cannot but evoke guffaws, there is, nonetheless, something in it that commands some respect—for, in contrast with earlier generations of males, this one is making a real effort to examine and redefine itself. The movement, in a word, is *real*.

Innumerable studies and surveys find men dissatisfied with themselves and their roles in society. Part of this, undoubtedly, is the result of the displacement men are experiencing in a culture where *women* are so successfully transforming themselves. There is evidence, too, that men are dissatisfied because their own fathers were so unsuccessful in their emotional lives and were thus unable to impart to their sons a sense of love, belonging, and security that an increasing number of men say they sorely miss.

The trend has nothing to do with beating drums or becoming a "warrior." It relates to the human desire for connection, and this, in the long run, can only bode well for communications between humans in general and between the sexes in particular. Many psychologists believe men, in the next two decades, will be less emotionally closed than at any time in American history.

More (and Better) Senior Sex

People used to talk about sex after 40 as if it were some kind of novelty. Now it's sex after 60 and it's considered not only commonplace but healthy.

Some fear that expectations among the aged may outrun physiological ability and that exaggerated hopes, in some cases, will lead to new frustrations—or that improved health into old age will put pressure on seniors to remain sexually active beyond any "decent" desire to do so.

But most seem to welcome the trend toward extended sexuality. In fact, the desire for sex in later decades of life is *heightened*, studies suggest, by society's growing awareness and acceptance of sexual activity in later life.

Diversity of Sexual Expression

As sex shifts from its traditional reproductive role to one that is psychological, it increasingly serves the needs of the individual. In this context, forms of sexual expression that were previously proscribed are now tolerated and are, in some cases increasingly viewed as no more nor less healthy than long-accepted forms of sexual behavior. Homosexuality, for example, has attained a level of acceptance unprecedented in our national history.

More Contraception, Less Abortion

Though abortion will remain legal under varying conditions in most, if not all, states, its use will continue to decline over the next two decades as more—and better-contraceptives become available. After a period of more than two decades in which drug companies shied away from contraceptive research, interest in this field is again growing. AIDS, a changed political climate, and renewed fears about the population explosion are all contributing to this change.

Additionally, scientific advances now point the way to safer, more effective, more convenient contraceptives. A male contraceptive that will be relatively side-effect free is finally within reach and should be achieved within the next decade, certainly the next two decades. Even more revolutionary in concept and probable impact is a vaccine, already tested in animals, that some predict will be available within 10 years—a vaccine that safely stops ovum maturation and thus makes conception impossible.

Religion and Sex: A More Forgiving Attitude

Just a couple of decades ago mainstream religion was monolithic in its condemnation of sex outside of marriage. Today the situation is quite different as major denominations across the land struggle with issues they previously wouldn't have touched, issues related to

adultery, premarital sex, homosexuality, and so on.

A Special Committee on Human Sexuality, convened by the General Assembly of the Presbyterian Church (USA), for example, surprised many when it issued a report highly critical of the traditional "patriarchal structure of sexual relations," a structure the committee believes contributes, because of its repressiveness, to the proliferation of pornography and sexual violence.

All this will surely pale alongside the brave new world of virtual reality.

The same sort of thing has been happening in most other major denominations. It is safe to say that major changes are coming. Mainstream religion is beginning to perceive that the sexual revolution must be acknowledged and, to a significant degree, accommodated with new policies if these denominations are to remain in touch with present-day realities.

Expanding Sexual Entertainment

The use of sex to sell products, as well as to entertain, is increasing and can be expected to do so. The concept that "sex sells" is so well established that we need not belabor the point here. The explicitness of sexual advertising, however, may be curbed by recent research finding that highly explicit sexual content is so diverting that the viewer or reader tends to overlook the product entirely.

Sexual stereotyping will also be less prevalent in advertising in years to come. All this means, however, is that women will not be singled out as sex objects; they'll have plenty of male company, as is already the case. The female "bimbo" is now joined by the male "himbo" in ever-increasing numbers. Sexist advertising is still prevalent (e.g., male-oriented beer commercials) but should diminish as women gain in social and political power.

There's no doubt that films and TV have become more sexually permissive in the last two decades and are likely to continue in that direction for some time to come. But all this will surely pale alongside the brave (or brazen) new world of "cybersex" and virtual reality, the first erotic emanations of which may well be experienced by Americans in the coming two decades. Virtual reality aims to be just that—artificial, electronically induced experiences that are virtually indistinguishable from the real thing.

The sexual revolution, far from over, is in for some new, high-tech curves.

FROM BIOLOGY TO PSYCHOLOGY: THE NEW FAMILY OF THE MIND

Despite recent pronouncements that the traditional family is making a comeback, the evidence suggests that over the next two decades the nuclear family will share the same future as nuclear arms: there will be fewer of them, but those that remain will be better cared for.

Our longing for sources of nurturance has led us to redefine the family.

Demographers now believe that the number of families consisting of married couples with children will dwindle by yet another 12 percent by the year 2000. Meanwhile, single-parent households will continue to increase (up 41 percent over the past decade.) And household size will continue to decline (2.63 people in 1990 versus 3.14 in 1970). The number of households maintained by women, with no males present, has increased 300 percent since 1950 and will continue to rise into the 21st century.

Particularly alarming to some is the fact that an increasing number of people are choosing never to marry. And, throughout the developed world, the one-person household is now the fastest growing household category. To the traditionalists, this trend seems insidious—more than 25 percent of all households in the United States now consist of just one person.

There can be no doubt: the nuclear family has been vastly diminished, and it will continue to decline for some years, but at a more gradual pace. Indeed, there is a good chance that it will enjoy more stability in the next two decades than it did in the last two. Many of the very forces that were said to be weakening the traditional family may now make it stronger, though not more prevalent. Developing social changes have made traditional marriage more elective today, so that those who choose it may, increasingly, some psychologists believe, represent a subpopulation better suited to the situation and thus more likely to make a go of it.

As we try to understand new forms of family, we need to realize that the "traditional" family is not particularly traditional. Neither is it necessarily the healthiest form of family. The nuclear family has existed for only a brief moment in human history. Moreover, most people don't realize that no sooner had the nuclear family form peaked around the turn of the last century than erosion set in, which has continued ever since. For the past hundred years, reality has chipped away at this social icon, with increasing divorce and the movement of more women into the labor force. Yet our need for nurturance, security, and connectedness continues and, if anything, grows more acute as our illusions about the traditional family dissipate.

Our longing for more satisfying sources of nurturance has led us to virtually redefine the family, in terms of behavior, language, and law. These dramatic changes will intensify over the next two decades. The politics of family will be entirely transformed in that period. The process will not be without interruptions or setbacks. Some lower-court rulings may be overturned by a conservative U.S. Supreme Court, the traditional family will be revived in the headline from time to time, but the economic and psychological forces that for decades have been shaping these changes toward a more diverse family will continue to do so.

SUBTRENDS

Deceptively Declining Divorce Rate

The "good news" is largely illusory. Our prodigious national divorce rate, which more than doubled in one recent 10-year period, now shows signs of stabilization or even decline. Still, 50 percent of all marriages will break up in the next several years. And the leveling of the divorce rate is not due to stronger marriage but to less marriage. More people are skipping marriage altogether and are cohabiting instead.

The slight dip in the divorce rate in recent years has caused some prognosticators to predict that younger people, particularly those who've experienced the pain of growing up in broken homes, are increasingly committed to making marriage stick. Others, more persuasively, predict the opposite, that the present lull precedes a storm in which the divorce rate will soar to 60 percent or higher.

Increasing Cohabitation

The rate of cohabitation—living together without legal marriage—has been growing since 1970 and will accelerate in the next two decades. There were under half a million cohabiting couples in 1970; today there are more than 2.5. The trend for the postindustrial world is very clear: less marriage, more cohabitation, easier and—if Sweden is any indication—less stressful separation. Those who divorce will be less likely to remarry, more likely to cohabit. And in the United States, cohabitation will increasingly gather about it both the cultural acceptance and the legal protection now afforded marriage.

We need to realize the "traditional family" is not particularly traditional.

More Single-Parent Families and Planned Single Parenthood

The United States has one of the highest proportions of children growing up in single-parent families. More than one in five births in the United States is outside of marriage—and three quarters of those births are to women who are not in consensual unions.

What is significant about the single-parent trend is the finding that many single women with children now prefer to remain single. The rush to the altar of unwed mothers, so much a part of American life in earlier decades, is now, if anything, a slow and grudging shuffle. The stigma of single parenthood is largely a thing of the past—and the economic realities, unsatisfactory though they are, sometimes favor single parenthood. In any case, women have more choices today than they had even 10 years ago; they are choosing the psychological freedom of single parenthood over the financial security (increasingly illusory, in any event) of marriage.

More Couples Childless by Choice

In the topsy-turvy 1990s, with more single people wanting children, it shouldn't surprise us that more married couples don't want children. What the trend really comes down to is increased freedom of choice. One reason for increasing childlessness among couples has to do with the aging of the population, but many of the reasons are more purely psychological.

With a strong trend toward later marriage, many couples feel they are "too old" to have children. Others admit they like the economic advantages and relative freedom of being childless. Often both have careers they do not want to jeopardize by having children. In addition, a growing number of couples cite the need for lower population density, crime rates, and environmental concerns as reasons for not wanting children. The old idea that "there must be something wrong with them" if a couple does not reproduce is fast waning.

The One-Person Household

This is the fastest growing household category in the Western world. It has grown in the United States from about 10 percent in the 1950s to more than 25 percent of all households today. This is a trend that still has a long way to go. In Sweden, nearly *40 percent* of all households are now single person.

"Mr. Mom" a Reality at Last?

When women began pouring into the work force in the late 1970s, expectations were high that a real equality of the sexes was at hand and that men, at last, would begin to shoulder more of the household duties, including spending more time at home taking care of the kids. Many women now regard the concept of "Mr. Mom" as a cruel hoax; but, in fact, Mr. Mom *is* slowly emerging.

Men *are* showing more interest in the home and in parenting. Surveys make clear there is a continuing trend in that direction. Granted, part of the impetus for this is not so much a love of domestic work as it is a distaste for work outside the home. But there is also, among many men, a genuine desire to play a larger role in the lives of their children. These men say they feel "cheated" by having to work outside the home so much, cheated of the experience of seeing their children grow up.

As the trend toward more equal pay for women creeps along, gender roles in the home can be expected to undergo further change. Men will feel less pressure to take on more work and will feel more freedom to spend increased time with their families.

More Interracial Families

There are now about 600,000 interracial marriages annually in the United States, a third of these are black-white, nearly triple the number in 1970, when 40 percent of the white population was of the opinion that such marriages should be illegal. Today 20 percent hold that belief. There is every reason to expect that both the acceptance of and the number of interracial unions will continue to increase into the foreseeable future.

Recognition of Same-Sex Families

Family formation by gay and lesbian couples, with or without children, is often referenced by the media as a leading-edge signifier of just how far society has moved in the direction of diversity and individual choice in the family realm. The number of same-sex couples has steadily increased and now stands at 1.6 million such couples. There are an estimated 2 million gay parents in the United States.

And while most of these children were had in heterosexual relationships or marriages prior to "coming out," a significant number of gay and lesbian couples are having children through adoption, cooperative parenting arrangements, and artificial insemination. Within the next two decades, gays and lesbians will not only win the right to marry but will, like newly arrived immigrants, be some of the strongest proponents of traditional family values.

The Rise of Fictive Kinships

Multiadult households, typically consisting of unrelated singles, have been increasing in number for some years and are expected to continue to do so in coming years. For many, "roommates" are increasingly permanent fixtures in daily life.

In fact housemates are becoming what some sociologists and psychologists call "fictive kin." Whole "fictive families" are being generated in many of these situations, with some housemates even assigning roles ("brother," "sister," "cousin," "aunt," "mom," "dad," and so on) to one another. Fictive families are springing up among young people, old people, disabled people, homeless people, and may well define one of the ultimate evolutions of the family concept, maximizing, as they do, the opportunities for fulfillment of specific social and economic needs outside the constraints of biological relatedness.

THE BREAKUP OF THE NUCLEAR FAMILY

It's hard to tell how many times we've heard even well-informed health professionals blithely opine that "the breakup of the family is at the root of most of our problems." The *facts* disagree with this conclusion. Most of the social problems attributed to the dissolution of the "traditional" family (which, in reality, is *not* so traditional) are the product of other forces. Indeed, as we have seen, the nuclear family has itself created a number of economic, social, and psychological problems. To try to perpetuate a manifestly transient social institution beyond its usefulness is folly.

What *can* we do to save the nuclear family? Very little.

What *should* we do? Very little. Our concern should not be the maintenance of the nuclear family as a *moral* unit (which seems to be one of the priorities of the more ardent conservative "family values" forces), encompassing the special interests and values of a minority, but, rather, the strengthening of those social contracts that ensure the health, well-being, and freedom of individuals.

Is There Love After Baby?

Why the passage to parenthood rocks even the best of couples today: A cautionary tale.

Carolyn Pape Cowan, Ph.D., and Philip A. Cowan, Ph.D.

Carolyn Pape Cowan, Ph.D., and Philip A. Cowan, Ph.D., are co-directors of the Becoming a Family Project at the University of California at Berkeley. Carolyn codirects the Schoolchildren and Their Families Project and is the co-editor of Fatherhood Today: Men's Changing Roles in the Family. *Philip is the author of* Piaget: With Feeling, *and co-editor of* Family Transitions: Advances in Family Research, Vol. 2. *They are the parents of three grown children.*

Babies are getting a lot of bad press these days. Newspapers and magazine articles warn that the cost of raising a child from birth to adulthood is now hundreds of thousands of dollars. Television news recounts tragic stories of mothers who have harmed their babies while suffering from severe postpartum depression. Health professionals caution that child abuse has become a problem throughout our nation. Several books on how to "survive" parenthood suggest that parents must struggle to keep their marriage alive once they become parents. In fact, according to recent demographic studies, more than 40 percent of children born to two parents can expect to live in a single-parent family by the time they are 18. The once-happy endings to family beginnings are clouded with strain, violence, disenchantment, and divorce.

What is so difficult about becoming a family today? What does it mean that some couples are choosing to remain "child-free" because they fear that a child might threaten their well-established careers or disturb the intimacy of their marriage? Is keeping a family together harder than it used to be?

Over the last three decades, sociologists, psychologists, and psychiatrists have begun to search for the answers. Results of the most recent studies, including our own, show that partners who become parents describe:

• an ideology of more equal work and family roles than their mothers and fathers had;

•actual role arrangements in which husbands and wives are sharing family work and care of the baby less than either of them expected;

•more conflict and disagreement after the baby is born than they had reported before;

•and increasing disenchantment with their overall relationship as a couple.

To add to these disquieting trends, studies of emotional distress in new parents suggest that women and possibly men are more vulnerable to depression in the early months after having a child. Finally, in the United States close to 50 percent of couples who marry will ultimately divorce.

We believe that children are getting an unfair share of the blame for their parents' distress. Based on 15 years of research that includes a three-year pilot study, a 10-year study following 72 expectant couples and 24 couples without children, and ongoing work with couples in distress, we are convinced that the seeds of new parents' individual and marital problems are sown long before baby arrives. Becoming parents does not so much raise new problems as bring old unresolved issues to the surface.

Our concern about the high incidence of marital distress and divorce among the parents of young children led us to study systematically what happens to partners when they become parents. Rather than simply add to the mounting documentation of family problems, we created and evaluated a new preventive program, the Becoming a Family Project, in which mental-health professionals worked with couples during their transition to parenthood, trying to help them get off to a healthy start. Then we followed the families as the first children progressed from infancy through the first year of elementary school.

What we have learned is more troubling than surprising. The majority of husbands and wives become more disenchanted with their couple relationship as they make the transition to parenthood. Most new mothers struggle with the question whether and when to return to work. For those who do go back, the impact on their families depends both on what mothers do at work and what fathers do at home. The more unhappy parents feel about their marriage, the more anger and competitiveness and the less warmth and responsiveness we observe in the family during the preschool period—between the parents as a couple and between each parent and the child. The children of parents with more tension during the preschool years have a harder time adjusting to the challenges of kindergarten.

For couples who thought having a baby was going to bring them closer together, the first few months are especially confusing and disappointing.

On the positive side, becoming a family provides a challenge that for some men and women leads to growth—as individuals, as couples, as parents. For couples who work to maintain or improve the quality of their marriage, having a baby can lead to a revitalized relationship. Couples with more satisfying marriages work together more effectively with their children in the preschool period, and their children tend to have an easier time adapting to the academic and social demands of elementary school. What is news is that the relationship *between* the parents seems to act as a crucible in which their relationships with their children take place.

The transition to parenthood is stressful even for well-functioning couples. In addition to distinctive inner changes, men's and women's roles change in very different ways when partners become parents. It seems to come as a great surprise to most of them that changes in some of their major roles affect their feelings about their overall

relationship. Both partners have to make major adjustments of time and energy as individuals at a time when they are getting less sleep and fewer opportunities to be together. They have less patience with things that didn't seem annoying before. Their frustration often focuses on each other. For couples who thought that having a baby was going to bring them closer together, this is especially confusing and disappointing.

Why does becoming a parent have such a powerful impact on a marriage? We have learned that one of the most difficult aspects of becoming a family is that so much of what happens is unexpected. Helping couples anticipate how they might handle the potentially stressful aspects of becoming a family can leave them feeling less vulnerable, less likely to blame each other for the hard parts, and more likely to decide that they can work it out before their distress permeates all of the relationships in the family.

But when things start to feel shaky, few husbands and wives know how to tell anyone, especially each other, that they feel disappointed or frightened. "This is supposed to be the best time of our lives; what's the matter with me?" a wife might say through her tears. They can't see that some of their tension may be attributable to the conflicting demands of the very complex stage of life, not simply to a suddenly stubborn, selfish, or unresponsive spouse.

Becoming a family today is more difficult than it used to be. Small nuclear families live more isolated lives in crowded cities, often feeling cut off from extended family and friends. Mothers of young children are entering the work force earlier; they are caught between traditional and modern conceptions of how they should be living their lives. Men and women are having a difficult time regaining their balance after having babies, in part because radical shifts in the circumstances surrounding family life in America demand new arrangements to accommodate the increasing demands on parents of young children. But new social arrangements and roles have simply not kept pace with the changes, leaving couples on their own to manage the demands of work and family.

News media accounts imply that as mothers have taken on more of a role in the world of paid work, fathers have taken on a comparable load of family work. But this has just not happened. It is not simply that men's and women's

roles are unequal that seems to be causing distress for couples, but rather that they are so clearly discrepant from what both spouses expected them to be. Women's work roles have changed, but their family roles have not. Well-intentioned and confused husbands feel guilty while their overburdened wives feel angry. It does not take much imagination to see how these emotions can fuel the fires of marital conflict.

Separate (Time)Tables

As they bring their first baby home from the hospital, new mothers and fathers find themselves crossing the great divide. After months of anticipation, their transition from couple to family becomes a reality. Entering this unfamiliar territory, men and women find themselves on different timetables and different trails of a journey they envisioned completing together.

Let's focus on the view from the inside, as men and women experience the shifting sense of self that comes with first-time parenthood. In order to understand how parents integrate Mother or Father as central components of their identity, we give couples a simple pie chart and ask them to think about the various aspects of their lives (worker, friend, daughter, father, so on) and mark off how large each portion feels, not how much time they spend "being it." The size of each piece of the pie reflects their psychologic involvement or investment in that aspect of themselves.

Almost all show pieces that represent parent, worker or student, and partner or lover. The most vivid identity changes during the transition to parenthood take place between pregnancy and six months postpartum. The part of the self that women call Mother takes up 10 percent of their pictures of themselves in late pregnancy. It then leaps to 34 percent six months after birth, and stays there through the second year of parenthood. For some women, the psychological investment in motherhood is much greater than the average.

Most of the husbands we interviewed took on the identity of parent more slowly than their wives did. During pregnancy, Father takes half as much of men's pie as their wives' Mother sections do, and when their children are 18 months old, husbands identity as parent is still less than one third as large as their wives'. We find that the larger the difference between husbands and wives in the size of their parent piece of the pie when their babies are six months old, the less satisfied both spouses are with the marriage, and the more their satisfaction declines over the next year.

The Big Squeeze

Men's and women's sense of themselves as parents is certainly expected to increase once they have had a baby. What comes as a surprise is that other central aspects of the self are getting short shrift as their parent piece of the pie expands. The greatest surprise—for us and for the couples—is what gets squeezed as new parents' identities shift. Women apportion 34 percent to the Partner or Lover aspect of themselves in pregnancy, 22 percent at six months after the birth, and 21 percent when their children are 18 months. Men's sense of themselves as Partner or Lover also shows a decline—from 35 percent to 30 percent to 25 percent over the two-year transition period.

The size of the Partner piece of the pie is connected to how new parents feel about themselves: A larger psychological investment in their relationship seems to be good for both of them. Six months after the birth of their first child, both men and women with larger Partner/Lover pieces have higher self-esteem and less parenting stress. This could mean that when parents resist the tendency to ignore their relationship as a couple, they feel better about themselves and less stressed as parents. Or that when they feel better about themselves they are more likely to stay moderately involved in their relationship.

At our 18-month follow-up, Stephanie and Art talk about the consequences for their marriage of trying to balance—within them and between them—the pulls among the Parent, Worker, and Partner aspects.

Stephanie: We're managing Linda really well. But with Art's promotion from teacher to principal and my going back to work and feeling guilty about being away from Linda, we don't get much time for *us*. I try to make time for the two of us at home, but there's no point in making time to be with somebody if he doesn't want to be with you. Sometimes when we finally get everything done and Linda is asleep, I want to sit down and talk, but Art says this is a perfect opportunity to get some preparation done for one of his teachers' meetings. Or he starts to fix one of Linda's toys—things that apparently are more important to him than spending time with me.

Art: That does happen. But Stephanie's wrong when she says that those things are more important to me than she is. The end of the day is just not my best time to start a deep conversation. I keep asking her to get a sitter so we can go out for a quiet dinner, but she always finds a reason not to. It's like being turned down for a date week after week.

Stephanie: Art, you know I'd love to go out with you. I just don't think we can leave Linda so often.

Stephanie and Art are looking at the problem from their separate vantage points. Art is very devoted to fatherhood, but is more psychologically invested in his relationship with Stephanie than with Linda. In his struggle to hold onto himself as Partner, he makes the reasonable request that he and Stephanie spend some time alone so they can nurture their relationship as a couple. Stephanie struggles with other parts of her shifting sense of self. Although Art knows that Stephanie spends a great deal of time with Linda when she gets home from work, he does not understand that juggling her increasing involvement as Mother while trying to maintain her investment as Worker is creating a great deal of internal pressure for her. The Partner/Lover part of Stephanie is getting squeezed not only by time demands but also by the psychological reshuffling that is taking place inside her. Art knows only that Stephanie is not responding to his needs, and to him her behavior seems unreasonable, insensitive, and rejecting.

Stephanie knows that Art's view of himself has changed as he has become a parent, but she is unaware of the fact that it has not changed in the same way or to the same degree as hers. In fact, typical of the men in our study, Art's psychological investment in their relationship as couple has declined slightly since Linda was born, but his Worker identity has not changed much. He is proud and pleased to be a father, but these feelings are not crowding out his sense of himself as a Partner/Lover. All Stephanie knows is that Art is repeatedly asking her to go out to dinner and ignoring her inner turmoil. To her, his behavior seems unreasonable, insensitive, and rejecting.

It might have been tempting to conclude that it is natural for psychological involvement in one's identity as Partner or Lover to wane over time—but the patterns of the childless couples refute that. The internal changes in each of the new parents begin to have an impact on their relationship as a couple. When women add Mother to their identity, *both* Worker and Partner/Lover get squeezed. As some parts of identity grow larger, there is less "room" for others. The challenge, then, is how to allow Parent a central place in one's identity without abandoning or neglecting Partner. We find that couples who manage to do this feel better about themselves as individuals and as couples.

Who Does What?

How do new parents' internal shifts in identity, and their separate timetables, play out in their marriage? We find that "who does what?" issues are central not only in how husbands and wives feel about themselves, but in how they feel about their marriage. Second, there are alternations in the emotional fabric of the couple's relationship; how caring and intimacy get expressed and how couples manage their conflict and disagreement have a direct effect on their marital satisfaction.

Husbands and wives, different to begin with, become even more separate and distinct in their years after their first child is born. An increasing specialization of family roles and emotional distance between partners-become-parents combine to affect their satisfaction with the relationship.

Behind today's ideology of the egalitarian couple lies a much more traditional reality. Although more than half of mothers with children under five have entered the labor force and contemporary fathers have been taking a small but significantly greater role in cooking, cleaning, and looking after their children than fathers used to do, women continue to carry the overwhelming responsibility for managing the household and caring for the children. Women have the primary responsibility for family work even when both partners are employed full time.

Couples whose division of household and family tasks was not equitable when they began our study tended to predict that it would be after the baby was born. They never expected to split baby care 50-50 but to work as a team in rearing their children. Once the babies are born, however, the women do more of the housework than before they became mothers, and the men do much less of the care of the baby than they or their wives predicted they would. After children appear, a couple's role arrangements—and how both husband and wife feel about them—become entwined with their intimacy.

Ideology vs Reality

In both expectant and childless couples, spouses divide up the overall burden of family tasks fairly equitably. But new parents begin to divide up these tasks in more gender-stereotyped ways. Instead of both partners performing some of each task, he tends to take on a few specific household responsibilities and she tends to do most of the others. His and her overall responsibility for maintaining the household may not shift significantly after having a baby, but it feels more traditional because each has become more specialized.

In the last trimester of pregnancy, men and women predict that the mothers will be responsible for more of the baby care tasks than the father. Nine months later, when the babies are six months old, a majority describe their arrangements as even more Mother's and less Father's responsibility than either had predicted. Among parents of six-month-old babies, mothers are shouldering more of the baby care than either parent predicted on eight of 12 items on our questionnaire: deciding about meals, managing mealtime, diapering, bathing, taking the baby out, playing with the baby, arranging for baby sitters, and dealing with the pediatrician. On four items, women and men predicted that mothers would do more and their expectations proved to be on the mark: responding to baby's cries, getting up in the middle of the night, doing the child's laundry, and choosing the baby's toys.

From this we contend that the ideology of the new egalitarian couple is way ahead of the reality. The fallout from their unmet expectations seems to convert both spouses' surprise and disappointment into tension between them.

Jackson and Tanya talked a lot about their commitment to raising Kevin together. Three months later, when the baby was six months old, Tanya explained that Jackson had begun to do more housework than ever before but

that he wasn't available for Kevin nearly as much as she would have liked.

Tanya: He wasn't being a chauvinist or anything, expecting me to do everything and him nothing. He just didn't *volunteer* to do things that obviously needed doing, so I had to put down some ground rules. Like if I'm in a bad mood, I may just yell: "I work eight hours just like you. This is half your house and half your child, too. You've got to do your share!" Jackson never changed the kitty litter box once in four years, but he changes it now, so we've made great progress. I just didn't expect it to take so much work. We planned this child together and we went through Lamaze together, and Jackson stayed home for the first two weeks. But then—wham—the partnership was over.

Tanya underscores a theme we hear over and over: The tension between new parents about the father's involvement in the family threatens the intimacy between them.

The fact that mothers are doing most of the primary child care in the first months of parenthood is hardly news. What we are demonstrating is that the couples' arrangements for taking care of their infants are *less equitable* than they expected them to be. They are amazed they became so traditional so fast.

It's not just that couples are startled by how the division of labor falls along gender lines, but they describe the change as if it were a mysterious virus they picked up while in the hospital having their baby. They don't seem to view their arrangements as *choices* they have made.

Husbands' and wives' descriptions of their division of labor are quite similar but they do shade things differently: Each claims to be doing more than the other gives him or her credit for. The feeling of not being appreciated for the endless amount of work each partner actually does undoubtedly increases the tension between them. Compared with the childless couples, new parents' overall satisfaction with their role arrangements (household tasks plus decision making plus child care) declined significantly—most dramatically between pregnancy and six months after baby's birth.

Parents who had been in one of our couples groups maintained their satisfaction with the division of household and family tasks. This trend is particularly true for women. Since the actual role arrangement in the group and non-

group participants were very similar, we can see that men's and women's satisfactions with who does what is, at least in part, a matter of perspective.

Some men and women are happy with traditional arrangements. Most of the men in our study, however, wanted desperately to have a central role in their child's life.

Is There Sex after Parenthood?

Most new parents feel some disenchantment in their marriage. It is tempting to blame this on two related facts reported by every couple. First, after having a baby, *time* becomes their most precious commodity. Second, even if a couple can eke out a little time together, the effort seems to require a major mobilization of forces. They feel none of the spontaneity that kept their relationship alive when they were a twosome.

We asked husbands and wives what they do to show their partners that they care. It soon became clear that different things feel caring to different people: bringing flowers or special surprises,

The division of workload in the family wins hands down as the issue most likely to cause conflict in the first two years.

being a good listener, touching in certain ways, picking up the cleaning without being asked.

New parents describe fewer examples of caring after having a baby compared to before, but as we keep finding in each domain of family life, men's and women's changes occur at different times. Between the babies' six- and 18-month birthdays, wives and husbands report that the women are doing fewer caring things for their husbands than the year before. In the parents' natural preoccupation with caring for baby, they seem less able to care for each other.

Both husbands and wives also report a negative change in their sexual relationship after having a baby. The frequency of lovemaking declines for almost all couples in the early months of parenthood.

There are both physical and psychological deterrents to pleasurable sex for new parents. Probably the greatest interference with what happens in the bedroom comes from what happens between the partners outside the bedroom. Martin and Sandi, for example, tell us that making love has become problematic since Ellen's birth. To give an example of a recent disappointment, Martin explains that he had had an extremely stressful day at work. Sandi greeted him with a "tirade" about Ellen's fussy day, the plumber failing to come, and the baby-sitter's latest illness. Dinnertime was tense, and they spent the rest of the evening in different rooms. When they got into bed they watched TV for a few minutes, and then Martin reached out to touch Sandi. She pulled away, feeling guilty that she was not ready to make love.

Like so many couples, they were disregarding the tensions that had been building up over the previous hours. They had never had a chance to talk in anything like a collaborative or intimate way. This is the first step of the common scenario for one or both partners to feel "not in the mood."

Ninety-two percent of the men and women in our study who became parents described more conflict after having their baby than before they became parents. The division of workload in the family wins hands down as the issue most likely to cause conflict in the first two years. Women feel the impact of the transition more strongly during the first six months after birth, and their husbands feel it more strongly in the following year.

Why does satisfaction with marriage go down? It begins, we think, with the issue of men's and women's roles. The new ideology of egalitarian relationships between men and women has made some inroads on the work front. Most couples, however, are not prepared for the strain of creating more egalitarian relationships at home, and it is this strain that leads men and women to feel more negatively about their partners and the state of their marriage.

Men's increasing involvement in the preparation for the *day* of the baby's birth leads both spouses to expect that he will be involved in what follows—the ongoing daily care and rearing of the children. How ironic that the recent widespread participation of fathers in the births of their babies has become a source of new parents' disappointment when the men do not stay involved in their babies' early care.

The transition to parenthood heightens the differences between men and women, which leads to more conflict between them. This, in turn, threaten the equilibrium of their marriage.

Needed: Couples Groups

Family making is a joint endeavor, not just during pregnancy, but in the years to come. Men simply have little access to settings in which they can share their experiences about intimate family matters. Given how stressful family life is for so many couples, we feel it is important to help them understand how their increasing differences during this transition may be generating more distance between them. Most couples must rebalance of the relationship.

Our results show that when sensitive group leaders help men and women focus on what is happening to them as individuals and as a couple during their transition to parenthood, it buffers them from turning their strain into dissatisfaction with each other. Why intervene with couples in *groups*? We find that a group setting provides the kind of support that contemporary couples often lack.

Groups of people going through similar life experiences help participants "normalize" some of their strain and adjustment difficulties; they discover that the strain they are experiencing is expectable at this stage of life. This can strengthen the bond between husbands and wives and undercut their tendency to blame each other for their distress.

Group discussions, by encouraging partners to keep a focus on their couple relationship, help the women maintain their identity as Partner/Lover while they are taking on Motherhood and returning to their jobs and careers. Fathers become painfully aware of what it takes to manage a demanding job and the day-to-day care of a household with baby.

The modern journey to parenthood, exciting and fulfilling as it is, is beset with many roadblocks. Most couples experience stress in the early years of family life. Most men and women need to muster all the strength and skills they have to make this journey. Almost all of the parents in our studies say that the joyful parts outweigh the difficult ones. They also say that the lessons they learn along the way are powerful and well worth the effort.

BACK OFF!

*We're putting way too many expectations on our closest relationships. It's time to
retreat a bit. Consider developing same-sex friendships. Or cultivating a garden.
Whatever you do, take a break from the relentless pursuit of intimacy.*

Geraldine K. Piorkowski, Ph.D.

*You can't miss it. It's the favorite topic of Oprah and all the
other talk shows. It's the suds of every soap opera. And I
probably don't have to remind you that it's the subject of an
extraordinary number of self-help books. Intimate relationships. No matter where we tune or turn, we are bombarded with
messages that there is a way to do it right, certainly some way of
doing it better—if only we could find it. There are countless
books simply on the subject of how to communicate better. Or, if
it's not working out, to exit swiftly.*

We are overfocused on intimate relationships, and I
question whether our current preoccupation with
intimacy isn't unnatural, not entirely in keeping with
the essential physical and psychological nature of people. The
evidence suggests that there is a limit to the amount of closeness
people can tolerate and that we need time alone for productivity
and creativity. Time alone is necessary to replenish psychological resources and to solidify the boundaries of the self.

All our cultural focus on relationships ultimately has, I
believe, a negative impact on us. It causes us to look upon
intimate relationships as a solution to all our ills. And that only
sets us up for disappointment, contributing to the remarkable 50
percent divorce rate.

Our overfocus on relationships leads us to demand too much
of intimacy. We put all our emotional eggs in the one basket of
intimate romantic relationships. A romantic partner must be all
things to us—lover, friend, companion, playmate, and parent.

We approach intimate relationships with the expectation that
this new love will make up for past letdowns in life and love.
The expectation that this time around will be better is bound to
disappoint, because present-day lovers feel burdened by demands with roots in old relationships.

We expect unconditional love, unfailing nurturance, and
protection. There is also the expectation that the new partner
will make up for the characteristics we lack in our own
personality—for example, that he or she will be an outgoing soul
to compensate for our shyness or a goal-oriented person to
provide direction in our messy life.

If the personal ads were rewritten to emphasize the emotional
expectations we bring to intimacy, they would sound like this.
"WANTED: Lively humorous man who could bring joy to my
gloomy days and save me from a lifetime of depression." Or,
"WANTED: Woman with self-esteem lower than mine. With
her, I could feel superior and gain temporary boosts of self-
confidence from the comparison."

From my many years as a clinical psychologist, I have come
to recognize that intimacy is not an unmitigated good. It is not
only difficult to achieve, it is treacherous in some fundamental
ways. And it can actually harm people.

The potential for emotional pain and upset is so great in
intimate relationships because we are not cloaked in the protective garb of maturity. We are unprotected, exposed, vulnerable
to hurt; our defenses are down. We are wide open to pain.

Intuitively recognizing the dangers involved, people normally erect elaborate barriers to shield themselves from closeness. We may act superior, comical, mysterious, or super
independent because we fear that intimacy will bring criticism,
humiliation, or betrayal—whatever an earlier relationship sensi-
tized us to. We develop expectations based on what has happened in our lives with parents, with friends, with a first love.
And we often act in anticipation of these expectations, bringing
about the result we most want to avoid.

The closer we get to another person, the greater the risks of
intimacy. It's not just that we are more vulnerable and defense-
less. We are also more emotionally unstable, childish, and less
intelligent than in any other situation. You may be able to run a
large company with skill and judgment, but be immature,
ultrasensitive, and needy at home. Civilized rules of conduct
often get suspended. Intimacy is both unnerving and baffling.

HEALTHY RETREATS

Once our fears are aroused in the context of intimacy, we tend to
go about calming them in unproductive ways. We make exces-

sive demands of our partner, for affection, for unconditional regard. The trouble is, when people feel demands are being made of them, they tend to retreat and hide in ways that hurt their partner. They certainly do not listen.

Fears of intimacy typically limit our vulnerability by calling defensive strategies into play. Without a doubt, the defense of choice against the dangers of intimacy is withdrawal. Partners tune out. One may retreat into work. One walks out of the house, slamming the door. Another doesn't call for days. Whatever the way, we spend a great deal of time avoiding intimacy.

After many years of working with all kinds of couples, I have come to believe that human nature dictates that intimate relationships have to be cyclical.

When one partner unilaterally backs off, it tends to be done in a hurtful manner. The other partner feels rejected, uncared about, and unloved. Typically, absolutely nothing gets worked out.

However, avoidance is not necessarily unhealthy. Partners can pursue a time out, where one or both work through their conflict in a solitary way that is ultimately renewing. What usually happens, however, is that when partners avoid each other, they are avoiding open warfare but doing nothing to resolve the underlying conflicts.

Fears of intimacy can actually be pretty healthy, when they're realistic and protective of the self. And they appear even in good relationships. Take the fears of commitment that are apt to surface in couples just before the wedding. If they can get together and talk through their fears, then they will not scare one another or themselves into backing off permanently.

After many years of working with all kinds of couples, I have come to believe that human nature dictates that intimate relationships have to be cyclical. There are limitations to intimacy and I think it is wise to respect the dangers. Periods of closeness have to be balanced with periods of distance. For every two steps forward, we often need to take one step back.

An occasional retreat from intimacy gives individuals time to recharge. It offers time to strengthen your sense of who you are. Think of it as constructive avoidance. We need to take some emphasis off what partners can do for us and put it on what we can do for ourselves and what we can do with other relationships. Developing and strengthening same-sex friendships, even opposite-sex friendships, has its own rewards and aids the couple by reducing the demands and emotional expectations we place on partners.

In our culture, our obsession with romantic love relationships has led us to confuse all emotional bonds with sexual bonds, just as we confuse infatuation with emotional intimacy. As a result, we seem to avoid strong but deeply rewarding emotional attachments with others of our own sex. But having recently lost a dear friend of several decades, I am personally sensitive to the need for emotionally deep, same-sex relationships. They can be shared as a way of strengthening gender identity and enjoying rewarding companionship. We need to put more energy into nonromantic relationships as well as other activities.

One of the best ways of recharging oneself is to take pleasure in learning and spiritual development. And there's a great deal to be said for spending time solving political, educational, or social ills of the world.

Distance and closeness boundaries need to be calibrated and constantly readjusted in every intimate relationship. Such boundaries not only vary with each couple, they change as the relationship progresses. One couple may maintain their emotional connection by spending one evening together a week, while another couple needs daily coming together of some sort. Problems arise in relationships when partners cannot agree on the boundaries. These boundaries must be jointly negotiated or the ongoing conflict will rob the relationship of its vitality.

S.O.S. SIGNALS

When you're feeling agitated or upset that your partner is not spending enough time with you, consider it a signal to step back and sort out internally what is going on. Whether you feel anxiety or anger, the emotional arousal should serve as a cue to back off and think through where the upset is coming from, and to consider whether it is realistic.

That requires at least a modest retreat from a partner. It could be a half hour, or two hours. Or two days—whenever internal clarity comes. In the grip of emotion, it is often difficult to discriminate exactly which emotion it is and what its source is. "What is it I am concerned about? Is this fear realistic considering Patrick's behavior in the present? He's never done this to me before, and he's been demonstrating his trustworthiness all over the place, so what am I afraid of? Is it coming from my early years of neglect with two distant parents who never had time for me? Or from my experiences with Steve, who dumped me two years ago?"

Introspective and self-aware people already spend their time thinking about how they work, their motives, what their feelings mean. Impulsive people will have a harder time with the sorting-out process. The best way to sort things out is to pay attention to the nature of the upset. Exactly what you are upset about suggests what your unmet need is, whether it's for love, understanding, nurturance, protection, or special status. And once you identify the need, you can figure out its antecedents.

The kinds of things we get upset about in intimacy tend to follow certain themes. Basically, we become hurt or resentful because we're getting "too much" or "too little" of something. Too many demands, too much criticism, too much domination. Or the converse, too little affectional, conversational, or sexual attention (which translates into "you don't feel I'm important" or "you don't love me"). Insufficient empathy is usually voiced as "you don't understand me," and too little responsibility translates into failure to take on one's share of household and/or financial tasks. All these complaints require some attention, action, or retreat.

SHIFTING GEARS

It's not enough to identify the source of personal concern. You have to present your concerns in a way your partner can hear. If I say directly to my partner, "I'm afraid you're going to leave me," he has the opportunity to respond, "Darling, that's not true. What gave you that idea?" I get the reassurance I need. But if I toss it out in an argument, in the form of "you don't care about me," then my partner's emotional arousal keeps him from hearing me. And he is likely to back away—just when I need reassurance most.

If people were aware that intimate relationships are by nature characterized by ambivalence, they would understand the need to negotiate occasional retreats. They wouldn't feel so threatened by the times when one partner says, "I have to be by myself because I need to think about my life and where I'm going." Or "I need to be with my friends and spend time playing." If people did more backing off into constructive activities, including time to meditate or to play, intimate relationships would be in much better shape today.

If couples could be direct about what they need, then the need for retreat would not be subject to the misrepresentation that now is rampant. The trouble is, we don't talk to each other that openly and honestly. What happens is, one partner backs off and doesn't call and the partner left behind doesn't know what the withdrawal means. But he or she draws on a personal history that provides room for all sorts of negative interpretations, the most common being "he doesn't care about me."

No matter how hard a partner tries to be all things to us, gratifying all of another's needs is a herculean task—beyond the human calling. Criticism, disappointment, and momentary rejection are intrinsic parts of intimate life; developing a thicker skin can be healthy. And maintaining a life apart from the relationship is necessary. Energy invested in other people and activities provides a welcome balance.

GOOD-ENOUGH INTIMACY

Since our intimate partner will never be perfect, what is reasonable to expect? The late British psychiatrist D. W. Winnicott put forth the idea of "good-enough mothering." He was convinced that mothering could never be perfect because of the mother's own emotional needs. "Good-enough mothering" refers to imperfect, though adequate provision of emotional care that is not damaging to the children.

In a similar vein, I believe there is a level of imperfect intimacy that is good enough to live and grow on. In good-enough intimacy, painful encounters occasionally occur, but they are balanced by the strength and pleasures of the relationship. There are enough positives to balance the negatives. People who do very well in intimate relationships don't have a perfect relationship, but it is good enough.

The standard of good-enough intimacy is essentially subjective, but there are some objective criteria. A relationship must have enough companionship, affection, autonomy, connectedness, and separateness, along with some activities that partners engage in together and that they both enjoy. The relationship meets the needs of both partners reasonably well enough, both feel reasonably good about the relationship. If one person is unhappy in the relationship, then by definition it is not good enough for them.

People looking for good-enough intimacy are bound to be happier than those seeking perfect intimacy. Their expectations are lower and more realistic. Time and time again, those who examine the intricacies of happiness have found the same thing—realistic expectations are among the prime contributors to happiness.

WHEN VIOLENCE HITS HOME

Suddenly, domestic abuse,
once perniciously silent, is
exposed for its brutality in the
wake of a highly public scandal

JILL SMOLOWE

DANA USED TO HIDE THE BRUISES ON HER neck with her long red hair. On June 18, her husband made sure she could not afford even that strand of camouflage. Ted ambushed Dana (not their real names) as she walked from her car to a crafts store in Denver. Slashing with a knife, Ted, a pharmaceutical scientist, lopped off Dana's ponytail, then grabbed her throat, adding a fresh layer of bruises to her neck.

Dana got off easy that time. Last year she lost most of her hearing after Ted slammed her against the living-room wall of their home and kicked her repeatedly in the head, then stuffed her unconscious body into the fireplace. Later, he was tearfully despondent, and Dana, a former social worker, believed his apologies, believed he needed her, believed him when he whispered, "I love you more than anything in the world." She kept on believing, even when more assaults followed.

Last Tuesday, however, Dana finally came to believe her life was in danger. Her change of mind came as she nursed her latest wounds, mesmerized by the reports about Nicole Simpson's tempestuous marriage to ex–football star O.J. "I grew up idolizing him," she says. "I didn't want to believe it was O.J. It was just like with my husband." Then, she says, "the reality hit me. Her story is the same as mine—except she's dead."

THE HORROR HAS ALWAYS BEEN WITH US, A PERSIStent secret, silent and pernicious, intimate and brutal. Now, however, as a result of the Simpson drama, Americans are confronting the ferocious violence that may erupt when love runs awry. Women who have clung to destructive relationships for years are realizing, like Dana, that they may be in dire jeopardy. Last week phone calls to domestic-violence hot lines surged to record numbers; many battered women suddenly found the strength to quit their homes and seek sanctuary in shelters. Although it has been two years since the American Medical As-

66 Women are at more risk of being killed by their

sociation reported that as many as 1 in 3 women will be assaulted by a domestic partner in her lifetime—4 million in any given year—it has taken the murder of Nicole Simpson to give national resonance to those numbers.

"Everyone is acting as if this is so shocking," says Debbie Tucker, chairman of the national Domestic Violence Coalition on Public Policy. "This happens all the time." In Los Angeles, where calls to abuse hot lines were up 80% overall last week, experts sense a sort of awakening as women relate personally to Simpson's tragedy. "Often a woman who's been battered thinks it's happening only to her. But with this story, women are saying, 'Oh, my God, this is what's happening to me,'" says Lynn Moriarty, director of the Family Violence Project of Jewish Family Services in Los Angeles. "Something as dramatic as this cracks through a lot of the denial."

Time and again, Health and Human Services Secretary Donna Shalala has warned, "Domestic violence is an unacknowledged epidemic in our society." Now, finally, lawmakers are not only listening—they are acting. In New York last week, the state legislature unanimously passed a sweeping bill that mandates arrest for any person who commits a domestic assault. Members of the California legislature are pressing for a computerized registry of restraining orders and the confiscation of guns from men arrested for domestic violence. This week Colorado's package of anti-domestic-violence laws, one of the nation's toughest, will go into effect. It not only compels police to take abusers into custody at the scene of violence but also requires arrest for a first violation of a restraining order. Subsequent violations bring mandatory jail time.

Just as women's groups used the Anita Hill–Clarence Thomas hearings as a springboard to educate the public about sexual harassment, they are now capitalizing on the Simpson controversy to further their campaign against domestic violence. Advocates for women are pressing for passage of the Violence Against Women Act, which is appended to the anticrime bill that legislators hope to have on President Clinton's desk by July 4. Modeled on the Civil Rights Act of 1964, it stipulates that gender-biased crimes violate a woman's civil rights. The victims of such crimes would therefore be eligible for compensatory relief and punitive damages.

Heightened awareness may also help add bite to laws that are on the books but are often underenforced. At present, 25 states require arrest when a reported domestic dispute turns violent. But police often walk away if the victim refuses to press charges. Though they act quickly to separate strangers, law-enforcement officials remain wary of interfering in domestic altercations, convinced that such battles are more private and less serious.

Yet, of the 5,745 women murdered in 1991, 6 out of 10 were killed by someone they knew. Half were murdered by a spouse or someone with whom they had been intimate. And that does not even hint at the level of violence against women by loved ones: while only a tiny percentage of all assaults on women result in death, the violence often involves severe physical or psychological damage. Says psychologist Angela Browne, a pioneering researcher in partner violence: "Women are at more risk of being killed by their current or former male partners than by any other kind of assault."

AFTER DANA DECIDED TO LEAVE TED IN MAY, SHE used all the legal weapons at her disposal to protect herself. She got a restraining order, filed for a divorce and found a new place to live. But none of that gave her a new life. Ted phoned repeatedly and stalked her. The restraining order seemed only to provoke his rage. On Memorial Day, he trailed her to a shopping-mall parking garage and looped a rope around her neck. He dragged her along the cement floor and growled, "If I can't have you, no one will." Bystanders watched in shock. But no one intervened.

After Ted broke into her home while she was away, Dana called the police. When she produced her protective order, she was told, "We don't put people in jail for breaking a restraining order." Dana expected little better after Ted came at her with the knife on June 18. But this time a female cop, herself a battering victim, encouraged Dana to seek shelter. On Tuesday, Dana checked herself into a shelter for battered women. There, she sleeps on a floor with her two closest friends, Sam and Odie—two cats. Odie is a survivor too. Two months ago, Ted tried to flush him down a toilet.

THOUGH DOMESTIC VIOLENCE USUALLY GOES UNDEtected by neighbors, there is a predictable progression to relationships that end in murder. Typically it begins either with a steady diet of battery or isolated incidents of violence that can go on for years. Often the drama is fueled by both parties. A man wages an assault. The woman retaliates by deliberately trying to provoke his jealousy or anger. He strikes again. And the cycle repeats, with the two locked in a sick battle that binds—and reassures—even as it divides.

When the relationship is in risk of permanent rupture, the violence escalates. At that point the abused female may seek help outside the home, but frequently the man will refuse counseling, convinced that she, not he, is at fault. Instead he will reassert his authority by stepping up the assaults. "Battering is about maintaining power and dominance in a relationship," says Dick Bathrick, an instructor at the Atlanta-based Men Stopping Violence, a domestic-violence intervention group. "Men who batter believe that they have the right to do whatever it takes to regain control."

When the woman decides she has had enough, she may move out or demand that her partner leave. But "the men sometimes panic about losing [their women] and will do anything to prevent it from happening," says Deborah Burk, an Atlanta prosecutor.

male partners than by any other kind of assault."

"The men who batter believe that they have the

To combat feelings of helplessness and powerlessness, the man may stalk the woman or harass her by phone.

Women are most in danger when they seek to put a firm end to an abusive relationship. Experts warn that the two actions most likely to trigger deadly assault are moving out of a shared residence and beginning a relationship with another man. "There aren't many issues that arouse greater passion than infidelity and abandonment," says Dr. Park Dietz, a forensic psychiatrist who is a leading expert on homicide.

Disturbingly, the very pieces of paper designed to protect women—divorce decrees, arrest warrants, court orders of protection—are often read by enraged men as a license to kill. "A restraining order is a way of getting killed faster," warns Dietz. "Someone who is truly dangerous will see this as an extreme denial of what he's entitled to, his God-given right." That slip of paper, which documents his loss, may be interpreted by the man as a threat to his own life. "In a last-ditch, nihilistic act," says Roland Maiuro, director of Seattle's Harborview Anger Management and Domestic Violence Program, "he will engage in behavior that destroys the source of that threat." And in the expanding range of rage, victims can include children, a woman's lawyer, the judge who issues the restraining order, the cop who comes between. Anyone in the way.

For that reason, not all battered women's organizations support the proliferating mandatory arrest laws. That puts them into an unlikely alliance with the police organizations that were critical of New York's tough new bill. "There are cases," argues Francis Looney, counsel to the New York State Association of Chiefs of Police, "where discretion may be used to the better interest of the family."

Proponents of mandatory-arrest laws counter that education, not discretion, is required. "I'd like to see better implementation of the laws we have," says Vickie Smith, executive director of the Illinois Coalition Against Domestic Violence. "We work to train police officers, judges and prosecutors about why they need to enforce them."

"I TOOK IT VERY SERIOUSLY, THE MARRIAGE, THE commitment. I wanted more than anything to make it work." Dana's eyes are bright, her smile engaging, as she sips a soda in the shelter and tries to explain what held her in thrall to Ted for so many years. Only the hesitation in her voice betrays her anxiety. "There was a fear of losing him, that he couldn't take care of himself."

Though Dana believed the beatings were unprovoked and often came without warning, she blamed herself. "I used to think, 'Maybe I could have done things better. Maybe if I had bought him one more Mont Blanc pen.'" In the wake of Nicole Simpson's slaying, Dana now says that she was Ted's "prisoner." "I still loved him," she says, trying to explain her servitude. "It didn't go away. I didn't want to face the fact that I was battered."

IT IS IMPOSSIBLE TO CLASSIFY THE WOMEN WHO are at risk of being slain by a partner. Although the men who kill often abuse alcohol or drugs, suffer from personality disorders, have histories of head injuries or witnessed abuse in their childhood homes, such signs are often masterfully cloaked. "For the most part, these are people who are functioning normally in the real world," says Bathrick of Men Stopping Violence. "They're not punching out their bosses or jumping in cops' faces. They're just committing crimes in the home."

The popular tendency is to dismiss or even forgive the act as a "crime of passion." But that rush of so-called passion is months, even years, in the making. "There are few cases where murder comes out of the blue," says Sally Goldfarb, senior staff attorney for the NOW Legal Defense and Education Fund. "What we are talking about is domestic violence left unchecked and carried to its ultimate outcome." Abuse experts also decry the argument that a man's obsessive love can drive him beyond all control. "Men who are violent are rarely completely out of control," psychologist Browne argues. "If they were, many more women would be dead."

Some researchers believe there is a physiological factor in domestic abuse. A study conducted by the University of Massachusetts Medical Center's domestic-violence research and treatment center found, for instance, that 61% of men involved in marital violence have signs of severe head trauma. "The typical injuries involve the frontal lobe," says Al Rosenbaum, the center's director. "The areas we suspect are injured are those involved in impulse control, and reduce an individual's ability to control aggressive impulses."

Researchers say they can also distinguish two types among the men most likely to kill their wives: the "loose cannon" with impulse-control problems, and those who are calculated and focused, whose heart rate drops even as they prepare to do violence to their partners. The latter group may be the more dangerous. Says Neil Jacobson, a psychology professor at the University of Washington: "Our research

right to do whatever it takes to regain control."

"I didn't want to face the fact I was battered."

shows that those men who calm down physiologically when they start arguing with their wives are the most aggressive during arguments."

There may be other psycho-physiological links to violence. It is known, for instance, that alcohol and drug abuse often go hand in hand with spousal abuse. So does mental illness. A 1988 study by Maiuro of Seattle's domestic-violence program documented some level of depression in two-thirds of the men who manifested violent and aggressive behavior. Maiuro is pioneering work with Paxil, an antidepressant that, like Prozac, regulates the brain chemical serotonin. He reports that "it appears to be having some benefits" on his subjects.

Most studies, however, deal not with battering as an aftereffect of biology but of violence as learned behavior. Fully 80% of the male participants in a Minneapolis, Minnesota, violence-control program grew up in homes where they saw or were victims of physical, sexual or other abuse. Women who have witnessed abuse in their childhood homes are also at greater risk of reliving such dramas later in their lives, unless counseling is sought to break the generational cycle. "As a child, if you learn that violence is how you get what you want, you get a dysfunctional view of relationships," says Barbara Schroeder, a domestic-violence counselor in Oak Park, Illinois. "You come to see violence as an O.K. part of a loving relationship."

The cruelest paradox is that when a woman is murdered by a loved one, people are far more inclined to ask, "Why didn't she leave?" than "Why did he do that?" The question of leaving not only reflects an ingrained societal assumption that women bear primary responsibility for halting abuse in a relationship; it also suggests that a battered woman has the power to douse a raging man's anger—and to do it at a moment when her own strength is at an ebb. "It's quite common with women who have been abused that they don't hold themselves in high esteem," says Dr. Allwyn Levine, a Ridgewood, New Jersey, forensic psychiatrist who evaluates abusers for the court system. "Most of these women really feel they deserve it." Furthermore, says Susan Forward, the psychoanalyst who counseled Nicole Simpson on two occasions, "too many therapists will say, 'How did it feel when he was hitting you?' instead of addressing the issue of getting the woman away from the abuser."

Most tragically, a woman may have a self-image that does not allow her to see herself—or those nearby to see her—as a victim. Speaking of her sister Ni-

cole Simpson, Denise Brown told the New York *Times* last week, "She was not a battered woman. My definition of a battered woman is somebody who gets beat up all the time. I don't want people to think it was like that. I know Nicole. She was a very strong-willed person."

Such perceptions are slowly beginning to change, again as a direct result of Simpson's slaying. "Before, women were ashamed," says Peggy Kerns, a Colorado state legislator. "Simpson has almost legitimized the concerns and fears around domestic violence. This case is telling them, 'It's not your fault.' " The women who phoned hot lines last week seemed emboldened to speak openly about the abuse in their lives. "A woman told me right off this week about how she was hit with a bat," says Carole Saylor, a Denver nurse who treats battered women. "Before, there might have been excuses. She would have said that she ran into a wall."

Abusive men are also taking a lesson from the controversy. The hot lines are ringing with calls from men who ask if their own conduct constitutes abusive behavior, or who say that they want to stop battering a loved one but don't know how. Others have been frightened by the charges against O.J. Simpson and voice fears about their own capacity to do harm. "They're worried they could kill," says Rob Gallup, executive director of AMEND, a Denver-based violence prevention and intervention group. "They figure, 'If [O.J.] had this fame and happiness, and chose to kill, then what's to prevent me?' "

EVEN IF DANA IS ABLE TO HOLD TED AT BAY, THE DAMage he has inflicted on her both physically and psychologically will never go away. Doctors have told her that her hearing will never be restored and that she is likely to become totally deaf within the decade. She is now brushing up the sign-language skills she learned years ago while working with deaf youngsters. At the moment, she is making do with a single set of hearing aids. Ted stole her other pair.

Dana reflects on her narrow escape. But she knows that her refuge in the shelter is only temporary. As the days go by, she grows increasingly resentful of her past, fearful of her present, and uncertain about her future. "I don't know when I'll be leaving, or where I'll be going."

And Ted is still out there.

—Reported by
Ann Blackman/Washington, Wendy Cole/Chicago, Scott Norvell/Atlanta, Elizabeth Rudulph and Andrea Sachs/New York and Richard Woodbury/Denver

Development during Middle and Late Adulthood

- Middle Adulthood (Articles 43–46)
- Late Adulthood (Articles 47–51)

The "use it or lose it" theory suggests that people who use their muscles retain more strength; people who do aerobic exercises retain more stamina; people who have sex retain sexual potency. While use equates to retention, there is a gradual slowing of the rate of repair of cells of all the organ systems (except the central nervous system, where no mitosis occurs). Signs of aging are seen in the skin, skeleton, senses, cardiovascular, respiratory, immune, endocrine, digestive, reproductive, and urinary systems. Loss of height occurs because connective tissue and the spinal disks lose materials and settle with the spinal column. Back muscles weaken, and bones lose some of their minerals. Bone demineralization occurs more rapidly in women than men, due in part to the loss of estrogenic hormones after menopause. Calcium supplementation can reduce bone demineralization.

Diets low in sugars and saturated fats are associated with less bone demineralization, retention of more muscle strength, and general increase in stamina and feelings of vitality in aging adults. Persons with adequate intake of vegetables, fruits, and complex carbohydrates (starches) also retain general good health longer.

Healthful aging seems to be, at least in part, genetically preprogrammed. The females of many species, including humans, outlive the males. Men tend to have earlier declines in their cardiovascular systems. Estrogenic hormones may protect women's hearts and blood vessels.

Intellectual abilities do not decline appreciably with age unless there are concurrent disease conditions affecting brain tissue. The brain at birth has a sufficient supply of neurons to last a lifetime. All neurons that a person will ever have are produced prenatally. There is no mitosis (replacement) of neurons after birth. By middle adulthood, a typical human can lose hundreds of neurons each day. However, this is similar to a pruning process. The unnecessary neurons die, while the most used ones continue to grow larger and add materials to their cell processes (axon and dendrites).

Cognitive abilities in healthy aging humans take many forms. Intelligence and creativity are multifactorial. There are fluid (abstract) reasoning abilities and crystallized (accumulated) knowledge. There are metacomponents, contextual components, and experiential components of the intellectual process. Seven important factors of intel-

ligence, found in different degrees in different people, are self-understanding, social understanding, logical-mathematical reasoning, musical abilities, body-kinesthetic abilities, language skills, and spatial reasoning. One's ken (range of knowledge) and practical skills (common sense) also contribute to cognitive processes. Accumulated knowledge and practical skills grow with age and experience. Humans become more expert at the tasks they frequently do.

Psychosocial theorist Erik Erikson suggested that the most important psychological conflict of middle age is generativity vs. stagnation. Humans who feel productive with their skills and abilities and who help guide the next generation into similar skill usage achieve a sense of generativity. The most important psychological conflict of late adulthood is achieving a sense of ego integrity vs. feeling despair. Ego integrity is fostered by love of others, self-esteem, and a sense that one's life has order and meaning. While Erikson proposed that different conflicts come to the forefront at different ages, he believed that all humans work at all of the psychosocial polarities all through their lives. Thus, all people are continually attempting to achieve and retain feelings of trust, autonomy, initiative, industry, identity, intimacy, generativity, and ego integrity.

A midlife crisis associated with middle age may or may not occur. However, most research studies suggest that middle-aged adults experience a transitional period in their lives associated with events such as career doldrums, launching children, menopause, and physical signs of aging. Many people feel that life is sweeter and more enjoyable after the midlife transition. Many persons turn inward and take better care of themselves rather than expending so much energy trying to please the outside world.

The articles in this unit's subsection on middle age stress the positive aspects of the middle years of life. The first article, "Man's World, Woman's World?" presents sex differences in biological and cognitive brain processes. There are adaptive advantages for both men and women related to brain organization and functions. In "The New Middle Age," Melinda Beck extols the joys of middle age. Beck emphasizes the good things that occur with a midlife reevaluation and transition. "The Estrogen Dilemma" presents the most recent research findings about menopause and a woman's healthy passage through the perimenopausal years. It suggests multiple options for making this transitional time of life a peaceful period. The last subsection essay includes a detailed list of common myths about aging. It debunks the idea of decline and advances the proposition that middle age can bring about creative, growth-promoting development.

The articles in the subsection on aging continue with an upbeat motif. "Learning to Love (Gulp!) Growing Old" advocates conscious enjoyment of the aging process, rather than a denial or a desperate clinging to youth. Sheryl Stolberg then presents factors that will need to be addressed as the baby-boomer generation advances into a healthier, more energetic, happier old age.

The next selection describes the challenges of being a grandparent in the computer age. Robert and Shirley Strom suggest many ways for healthy older adults to keep in step with the younger generation. The last two articles of this unit take a kinder, gentler view of some of the problems of old age. In "Ageing with Attitude," the author suggests policy changes that would benefit all senior citizens, including those experiencing job and housing discrimination and poverty. Robert Sapolsky ends the unit with a look at dying, death, and bereavement in a positive light. Sapolsky finds solace in viewing of the human life span as a cycle complete with predictable patterns and stages.

Looking Ahead: Challenge Questions

Why do men's brains and women's brains function differently?

What are the benefits of passing through a midlife transition? Why is life sweeter on the other side of 50?

Is estrogen replacement necessary after menopause?

When does "happy-ever-after" arrive in marriage?

How does the culture's view of aging affect one's passage through old age?

What moral and ethical issues must be addressed with the healthy graying of Americans?

How can grandparents join the computer generation?

How should we prepare for 1999, the International Year of Aging?

Why is there solace to be found in predictable patterns of living and dying?

Man's World, Woman's World? Brain Studies Point to Differences

Gina Kolata

Dr. Ronald Munson, a philosopher of science at the University of Missouri, was elated when Good Housekeeping magazine considered publishing an excerpt from the latest of the novels he writes on the side. The magazine eventually decided not to publish the piece, but Dr. Munson was much consoled by a letter from an editor telling him that she liked the book, which is written from a woman's point of view, and could hardly believe a man had written it.

New scanner finds more evidence of how the sexes differ in brain functions.

It is a popular motion: that men and women are so intrinsically different that they literally live in different worlds, unable to understand each other's perspectives fully. There is a male brain and a female brain, a male way of thinking and a female way. But only now are scientists in a position to address whether the notion is true.

The question of brain differences between the sexes is a sensitive and controversial field of inquiry. It has been smirched by unjustifiable interpretations of data, including claims that women are less intelligent because their brains are smaller than those of men. It has been sullied by overinterpretations of data, like the claims that women are genetically less able to do everyday mathematics because men, on average, are slightly better at mentally rotating three dimensional objects in space.

But over the years, with a large body of animal studies and studies of humans that include psychological tests, anatomical studies, and increasingly, brain scans, researchers are consistently finding that the brains of the two sexes are subtly but significantly different.

Now, researchers have a new noninvasive method, functional magnetic resonance imaging, for studying the live human brain at work. With it, one group recently detected certain apparent differences in the way men's and women's brains function while they are thinking. While stressing extreme caution in drawing conclusions from the data, scientists say nonetheless that the groundwork was being laid for determining what the differences really mean.

"What it means is that we finally have the tools at hand to begin answering these questions," said Dr. Sally Shaywitz, a behavioral scientist at the Yale University School of Medicine. But she cautioned: "We have to be very, very careful. It behooves us to understand that we've just begun."

The most striking evidence that the brains of men and women function differently came from a recent study by Dr. Shaywitz and her husband, Dr. Bennett A. Shaywitz, a neurologist, who is also at the Yale medical school. The Shaywitzes and their colleagues used functional magnetic resonance imaging to watch brains in action as 19 men and 19 women read nonsense words and determined whether they rhymed.

In a paper, published in the Feb. 16 issue of Nature, the Shaywitzes reported that the subjects did equally well at the task, but the men and women used different areas of their brains. The men used just a small area on the left side of the brain, next to Broca's area, which is near the temple. Broca's area has long been thought to be associated with speech. The women used this area as well as an area on the right side of the brain. This was the first clear evidence that men and women can use their brains differently while they are thinking.

Another recent study, by Dr. Ruben C. Gur, the director of the brain behavior laboratory at the University of Pennsylvania School of Medicine, and his colleagues, used magnetic resonance imaging to look at the metabolic activity of the brains of 37 young men and 24 young women when they were at rest, not consciously thinking of anything.

In the study, published in the Jan. 27 issue of the journal Science, the investigators found that for the most part, the brains of men and women at rest were indistinguishable from each other. But there was one difference, found in a brain structure called the limbic system that regulates emotions. Men, on average, had higher brain activity in the more ancient and primitive regions of the limbic system, the parts that are more involved with action. Women, on average, had more activity in the newer and more complex parts of the limbic system, which are involved in symbolic actions.

Men have larger brains; women have more neurons.

Dr. Gur explained the distinction: "If a dog is angry and jumps and bites, that's an action. If he is angry and bares his fangs and growls, that's more symbolic."

Dr. Sandra Witelson, a neuroscientist at McMaster University in Hamilton, Ontario, has focused on brain anatomy, studying people with terminal cancers that do not involve the brain. The patients have agreed to participate in neurological and psychological tests and then to allow Dr. Witelson and her colleagues to examine their brains after they die, to look for relationships between brain structures and functions. So far she has studied 90 brains.

Several years ago, Dr. Witelson reported that women have a larger corpus callosum, the tangle of fibers that run down the center of the brain and enable the two hemispheres to communicate. In addition, she said, she found that a region in the right side of the brain that corresponds to the region women used in the reading study by the Shaywitzes was larger in women than in men.

Most recently, Dr. Witelson discovered, by painstakingly counting brain cells, that although men have larger brains than women, women have about 11 percent more neurons. These extra nerve cells are densely packed in two of the six layers of the cerebral cortex, the outer shell of the brain, in areas at the level of the temple, behind the eye. These are regions used for understanding language and for recognizing melodies and the tones in speech. Although the sample was small, five men and four women, "the results are very, very clear," Dr. Witelson said.

Going along with the studies of brain anatomy and activity are a large body of psychological studies showing that men and women have different mental abilities. Psychologists have consistently shown that men, on average, are slightly better than women at spatial tasks, like visualizing figures rotated in three dimensions, and women, on average, are slightly better at verbal tasks.

Dr. Gur and his colleagues recently looked at how well men and women can distinguish emotions on someone else's face. Both men and women were equally adept at noticing when someone else was happy, Dr. Gur found. And women had no trouble telling if a man or a woman was sad. But men were different. They were as sensitive as women in deciding if a man's face was sad—giving correct responses 90 percent of the time. But they were correct about 70 percent of the time in deciding if women were sad; the women were correct 90 percent of the time.

"A woman's face had to be really sad for men to see it," Dr. Gur said. "The subtle expressions went right by them."

Studies in laboratory animals also find differences between male and female brains. In rats, for example, male brains are three to seven times larger than female brains in a specific area, the preoptic nucleus, and this difference is controlled by sex hormones that bathe rats when they are fetuses.

"The potential existence of structural sex differences in human brains is almost predicted from the work in other animals," said Dr. Roger Gorski, a professor of anatomy and cell biology at the University of California in Los Angeles. "I think it's a really fundamental concept and I'm sure, without proof, that it applies to our brains."

But the question is, if there are these differences, what do they mean?

Dr. Gorski and others are wary about drawing conclusions. "What happens is that people overinterpret these things," Dr. Gorski said. "The brain is very complicated, and even in animals that we've studied for many years, we don't really know the function of many brain areas."

This is exemplified, Dr. Gorski said,

in his own work on differences in rat brains. Fifteen years ago, he and his colleagues discovered that males have a comparatively huge preoptic nucleus and that the area in females is tiny. But Dr. Gorski added: "We've been studying this nucleus for 15 years, and we still don't know what it does. The most likely explanation is that it has to do with sexual behavior, but it is very, very difficult to study. These regions are very small and they are interconnected with other things." Moreover, he said, "nothing like it has been shown in humans."

And, with the exception of the work by the Shaywitzes, all other findings of differences in the brains or mental abilities of men and women have also found that there is an amazing degree of overlap. "There is so much overlap that if you take any individual man and woman, they might show differences in the opposite direction" from the statistical findings, Dr. Gorski said.

Dr. Munson, the philosopher of science, said that with the findings so far, "we still can't tell whether the experiences are different" when men and women think. "All we can tell is that the brain processes are different," he said, adding that "there is no Archimedean point on which you can stand, outside of experience, and say the two are the same. It reminds me of the people who show what the world looks like through a multiplicity of lenses and say, 'This is what the fly sees.' " But, Dr. Munson added, "We don't know what the fly sees." All we know, he explained, is what we see looking through those lenses.

Some researchers, however, say that the science is at least showing the way to answering the ancient mind-body problem, as applied to the cognitive worlds of men and women.

Dr. Norman Krasnegor, who directs the human learning and behavior branch at the National Institute of Child Health and Human Development, said the difference that science made was that when philosophers talked about mind, they "always were saying, 'We've got this black box.' " But now, he said, "we don't have a black box; now we are beginning to get to its operations."

Dr. Gur said science was the best hope for discovering whether men and women inhabited different worlds. It is not possible to answer that question simply by asking people to describe what they perceive, Dr. Gur said, because "when you talk and ask questions, you are talking to the very small portion of the brain that is capable of talking." If investigators ask people to tell them what they are thinking, "that may or may not be closely related to what was taking place" in the brain, Dr. Gur said.

On the other hand, he said, scientists have discovered that what primates perceived depends on how their brains function. Some neurons fire only in response to lines that are oriented at particular angles, while others seem to recognize faces. The world may well be what the philosopher Descartes said it was, an embodiment of the workings of the human mind, Dr. Gur said. "Descartes said that we are creating our world," he said. "But there is a world out there that we can't know."

Dr. Gur said that at this point he would hesitate to baldly proclaim that men and women inhabit different worlds. "I'd say that science might be leading us in that direction," he said, but before he commits himself he would like to see more definite differences in the way men's and women's brains function and to know more about what the differences mean.

Dr. Witelson cautioned that "at this point, it is a very big leap to go from any of the structural or organizational differences that were demonstrated to the cognitive differences that were demonstrated." She explained that "all you have is two sets of differences, and whether one is the basis of the other has not been shown." But she added, "One can speculate."

Dr. Witelson emphasized that in speculating she was "making a very big leap," but she noted that "we all live in our different worlds and our worlds depend on our brains.

"And," she said, "if these sex differences in the brain, with 'if' in big capital letters, do have cognitive consequences, and it would be hard to believe there would be none, then it is possible that there is a genuine difference in the kinds of things that men and women perceive and how these things are integrated. To that extent it may be possible that in some respects there is less of an easy cognitive or emotional communication between the sexes as a group because our brains may be wired differently."

The Shaywitzes said they were reluctant even to speculate from the data at hand. But, they said, they think that the deep philosophical questions about the perceptual worlds of men and women can eventually be resolved by science.

"It is a truism that men and women are different," Dr. Bennett Shaywitz said. "What I think we can do now is to take what is essentially folklore and place it in the context of science. There is a real scientific method available to answer some of these questions."

Dr. Sally Shaywitz added: "I think we've taken a qualitative leap forward in our ability to ask questions." But, she said, "the field is simply too young to have provided more than a very intriguing appetizer."

Approaches to Understanding Male-Female Brain Differences

Studies of differences in perception or behavior can suggest how male and female thinking may diverge; studies of structural or metabolic differences can suggest why. But only now are differences in brain organization being studied.

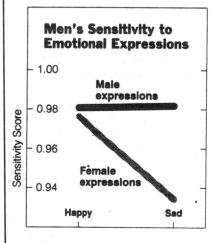

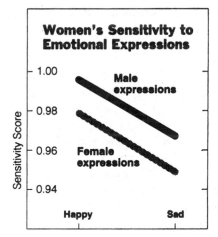

A study compared how well men and women recognized emotions in photos of actors portraying happiness and sadness. Men were equally sensitive to a range of happy and sad faces in men but far less sensitive to sadness in women's faces.

The women in the study were generally more sensitive to happy faces than to sad ones. They were also better able to recognize sadness in a man's face. For both sexes, sensitivity scores reflected the percent of the time the emotion was correctly identified.

the new
MIDDLE AGE

MELINDA BECK

A generation verges toward a mass midlife crisis. But wait: it can be a lot better than you think.

The names are culled from driver's license records, credit-card applications, magazine-subscription forms—any place an unsuspecting consumer might have listed his birth date somewhere along the line. They pour into a data-management firm, where they are standardized, merged and purged of duplications. From there, they are assigned one of several different solicitation packets, then bundled and shipped nationwide. It's a point of great pride with the American Association of Retired Persons that on or about their birthdays, roughly 75 percent of the 2.7 million Americans who turned 50 this year received an offer to partake—for just $8!—in all the benefits of membership in the AARP.

Not since the Selective Service Board sent "greetings" to 18-year-old men during the Vietnam War has a birthday salutation been so dreaded by so many. True, the leading edge of the baby boom won't get the official invitations into the quagmire of the 50s for four more years—but these things are always worse in anticipation than in reality. And the icons of the baby boom are already there. Paul McCartney turned 50 this year; so did Aretha Franklin. Bob Dylan is 51, as are Frank Zappa, Paul Simon and Art Garfunkel. Even the heartthrobs have crossed the great divide: Raquel Welch is pinned up at 51, Robert Redford at 55.

Month by month, individually and collectively, the generation that refused to grow up is growing middle aged. The reminders are everywhere—from the gracefully aging Lauren Hutton (49) in the J. Crew catalog to the now ubiquitous prefix *"aging* baby boomers" to the Oval Office itself. Sure, Bill Clinton and Al Gore will breathe new youth into the presidency that has been held for three decades by the PT-109 crowd. But for many in this competitive cohort, their ascension is just one more reminder of time marching on and leaving accomplishment victims in its wake. *See—the president is 46. You're 49. Weren't you supposed to be CEO by now, or at least know what you want to DO with your life?* To be sure, this is hardly the first generation to hit

or anticipate the Big Five-Oh. The baby boomers' group obsession with aging is already sounding, well, old, to everybody else, and, by conventional definitions at least, most boomers have been "middle aged" since they turned 40. But raised with such outsize expectations of life, they may have a tougher time accepting the age of limitations than other generations. "This group was somehow programmed to never get older—that sets us up for a whole series of disappointments," says psychiatrist Harold Bloomfield in Del Mar, Calif. Rice University sociologist Chad Gordon has another take on the angst that is seizing baby boomers. "Let's face it—aging sucks," he says. "It's filled with all those D words—decay, decrepitude, degeneration, dying . . . Then there's balding, paunchiness, losing sex drives and capabilities, back trouble, headaches, cholesterol and high blood pressure—they all go from the far horizon to close up. Then you worry about worrying about those things."

In truth, authorities on aging and ordinary people who've been there say that middle age isn't so bad. "It's the most powerful and glorious segment of a person's life," says Ken Dychtwald, whose company, Age Wave, counsels businesses on how to serve the needs of the aging population. Dychtwald admits, however, that American culture hasn't universally embraced this idea and that most of the soon-to-be-middle-aged themselves haven't gotten into the swing of it yet.

Instead, they are responding with ever more exaggerated forms of foreboding. Bloomfield says he sees an increase in a once rare condition called *dysmorphophobia*—the intense but unfounded fear of looking ugly. In Hollywood, not only do actresses try desperately to disguise their age, but so do agents, scriptwriters and studio executives. "It's hard to age gracefully out here," says Dr. Mel Bircoll, 52, considered the father of the cosmetic pectoral implant, the calf implant and the fat implant (which he layers into face-lifts to add contour and avoid the "overstretched look"). Bircoll says his clients used to start at 55. Now they come to him at about 45.

All of this might have been grist for a great TV series, but when producer Stan Rogow tried it this season, it flopped. Rogow intended "Middle Ages" to be an upbeat portrayal—"pretty hip, pretty life affirming, not angst-ridden. What we tried to do with the show was to say, 'This is OK. It's better than OK'." Critics liked it but viewers never gave it a chance and, in retrospect, Rogow understands why: "The name was a colossal mistake. 'Middle age' is this horrible-sounding thing you've heard throughout your life and hated." As the low ratings piled up, Rogow said to himself: "We have a problem here, and it's called denial."

But the funny thing about denial is that sometimes it works. In the very act of staving off physical aging through exercise, diet and dye, the StairMaster set has actually succeeded in pushing back the boundaries of "middle age." Boomers will look, act and feel younger at 50 than previous generations did. "Fifty will be like 40," says UCLA gerontologist Fernando Torres-Gil, who predicts that this generation won't confront "old age" until well into their 70s. The broad concept of middle age is starting later and lasting longer—and looking better than ever before. "We're seeing that 50 means all kinds of very vibrant, alive, sexy, dynamic people," says June Reinisch, director of the Kinsey Institute for Research in Sex, Gender and Reproduction at Indiana University. "I'm 49 this year. I wear clothes that my mother never would have thought of wearing when she was this age. When skirts went up, my skirts went up." Rogow, 44, says: "I'd really be shocked if I'm wearing plaid golf pants at 60. I suspect I'll be wearing the same ripped jeans I've been wearing for 20 years. They'll be much cooler then."

The new middle age also features more children than ever before, since this generation has delayed marriage and childbearing. Many men are having second families, with even younger children, well into their 50s. Some may be pushing strollers *and* paying college tuition just when psychologists say they should be busting loose and fulfilling themselves. At the same time, today's middle-agers have aging parents who are starting to need care. "For many people, 50 will be just like 20, 30 and 40—tied to providing basic subsistence needs," says University of Texas psychologist David Drum. "They won't see a chance to change, to repattern their lives."

Yet even as they postponed family responsibilities, many people in this fast-track generation reached the peaks of their careers much earlier than their parents did—and are wondering, "Is that all there is?" even in their 30s and 40s. Many of them will top out earlier, too, as record numbers of middle managers chase fewer and fewer promotions. While previous generations worried about sex and marriage, "career crashes are the baby boom's version of midlife crisis," says Barry Glassner, a University of Southern California sociologist. Women, having forged careers of their own in record numbers, may face the same kind of professional crisis traditionally reserved for men—and their incomes will still be needed to make ends meet. "Lose a job—have any piece of the puzzle taken out—and the whole thing falls apart," says Andrea Saveri, a research fellow at the Institute for the Future in Menlo Park, Calif.

The cruel demographic joke is that just as this generation is hitting middle age with unprecedented family responsibilities, corporate America is mustering legions of fiftysomethings out of the work force through early-retirement plans and less compassionate methods. "There is tremendous doubt about the future," says Saveri. "People see their friends getting pink slips. Their M.B.A.s aren't doing them any good now." Retiring earlier—and living longer—will bring a host of financial, emotional and psychological problems in the years ahead. Today's 50-year-olds still have 20 or 30 more years to live. What are they going to do—and how are they going to pay for it? "The 50s are not the beginning of the end—you have an awful long way to go," says University of Chicago gerontologist Bernice Neugarten, now 76. And that may be the most frightening thought of all.

Midway life's journey I was made aware
  That I had strayed into a dark forest,
And the right path appeared not anywhere.

Dante was 35 years old and frustrated in his quest for political position in 1300 when he wrote the first lines of "The Inferno"—describing perhaps the first midlife crisis in Western literature. Shakespeare charted similar midlife muddles in "King Lear," "Macbeth," "Hamlet" and "Othello" in the early 1600s, though he barely used the phrase "middle age." Sigmund Freud and Carl Jung studied midlife transitions around the turn of the 20th century. But then "midlife" came much earlier in time. In 1900, average life expectancy in the United States was 47 and only 3 percent of the population lived past 65. Today average life expectancy is 75—and 12 percent of the U.S. population is older than 65.

The longer life gets, the harder it is to plot the midpoint and define when middle age begins and ends. "We've broken the evolutionary code," says Gail Sheehy, author of "Passages" and "The Silent Passage." "In only a century, we've added 30 years to the life cycle." Statistically, the middle of life is now about 37, but what we think of as middle age comes later—anywhere from 40 to 70. As chronological age has less and less meaning, experts are groping for other definitions. When the American Board of Family Practice asked a random sampling of 1,200 Americans when middle age begins, 41 percent said it was when you worry about having enough money for health-care concerns, 42 percent said it was when your last child moves out and 46 percent said it was when you don't recognize the names of music groups on the radio anymore.

However it is defined, middle age remains one of the least studied phases in life. "It's the last uncharted territory in human development," said MacArthur Foundation president Adele Simmons in 1989, announcing a $10 million grant to fund the largest scholarly look ever at the period. Team leader Gilbert Brim and his colleagues at the Research Network on Successful Midlife Development are now partway through their eight-year effort, trying to answer, among other things, why some people hit their

How do I know if what I achieve in life should be called serenity and not surrender?

—JUDITH VIORST, 61

■ Percentage of baby boomers who say they have been through midlife crisis: 27
■ Average age of men who marry for second time: 39.2
■ Average age of women who marry for second time: 34.8

SOURCE: GALLUP, NATIONAL CENTER FOR HEALTH STATISTICS

strides at midlife and others hit the wall. To date, they have concluded that there are no set stages or transition points—that what happens to people is more the result of accident, personal experiences and the historical period in which they live. "Midlife is full of changes, of twists and turns; the path is not fixed," says Brim. "People move in and out of states of success."

In particular, Brim's group debunks the notion of a "midlife crisis." "It's such a mushy concept—not like a clinical diagnosis in the medical field," he says. But, Brim adds, "what a wonderful idea! You could load everything on that—letting people blame something external for what they're feeling." Other scholars agree that very few people suffer full-blown crackups—and that dumping the spouse for a bimbo is more the stuff of fiction—or fantasy— than reality. So is the Gauguin syndrome: running off to Tahiti at 43. People do have affairs and end up with different mates—but that is often after marriages have failed for reasons other than midlife malaise.

Still, the mythology persists. "You ask people if they've had a midlife crisis and some say they have," says sociologist Ronald Kessler at the University of Michigan's Institute for Social Research. "Then you ask them what it was and they'll say that they didn't get to be vice president. So what did they do—try to kill themselves? Buy a sports car? Well no, people come to terms with getting older in a most gradual way." The idea of a crisis sometimes provides an excuse for wild and outrageous behavior, says psychologist Susan Krauss Whitbourne at the University of Massachusetts at Amherst: "It sounds romantic and fun—certainly better than complete boredom." She also suspects it's a class phenomenon: well-educated people with money "have the luxury to reflect on these things."

What does commonly happen, experts say, is a more subtle acceptance of life's limitations. One key task may be to change your self-image. "A lot of the more tangible rewards come in the first half of life, such as good grades, first jobs, early promotions, marriage, first children," says psychologist Robert E. Simmons in Alexandria, Va. After that, "it's harder and harder to rely on external gratifications because there aren't as many. So one is thrown back more on one's internal self-esteem system." That can mean finding new forms of satisfaction—from coaching Little League to taking up the saxophone to tutoring kids in school.

The sooner you accept the idea that life may not turn out as you planned, the easier the transition will be. "It's the person who has just been driving himself and getting burnt out, who is starting to turn 50 and who feels like, 'My God, my life is over'," says Bloomfield. Gail Sheehy agrees: "For those who deny, postpone, elude or fantasize to escape coming to terms with [reality], it comes up again around 50 with a double whammy." Sheehy can see this now, at 54. She barely mentioned life past 50 in "Passages" because she was only 35 at the time and couldn't visualize herself at an older age. Now she says she knows that "you have to work your way up to saying 'I'm not going to go backward. I'm not going to try to stay in the same place. That way lies self-torture and eventually

foolishness. I'm going to have the courage to go forward'."

Contrary to conventional wisdom, many people find that the 50s is actually a period of reduced stress and anxiety. "In terms of mental health, midlife is the best time," says Ronald Kessler. One tantalizing bit of biomedical research has found that between 40 and 60, people actually lose cells in the locus coeruleus, the part of the brain that registers anxiety, which may help explain the "mellowing" many people feel in middle age. Depression does tend to peak in this period, however, which may also be linked to biochemical changes in the aging brain.

Not all mood shifts are biochemical. There are definite life events that can bring about profound changes of heart and direction. The list includes divorce; illness; losing a job; the kids leaving home (or returning); the death of parents, spouses and friends. Those can happen at any point in life, but they begin to mount up in the 50s. Any kind of change is stressful and simply fearing these things can bring tension. "It also happens when mentors retire," says University of North Carolina sociologist Glen Elder. "You have to think about yourself playing that role. It's a major transition, one that is hard to come to terms with."

Professional disappointments weigh especially heavily on men, and they are inevitable even for the most successful, from George Bush to laid-off steelworkers. Being forced out of a job in midlife can be devastating—or liberating, if it brings about a rethinking of what's most important. Men (and increasingly, women) who sacrificed time with their families for their careers in their younger years may be particularly regretful when success proves as empty as the nest. "Men our age have lived such a macho fake life," says Rogers Brackmann, 61, a former advertising executive in Chicago. "When I was in the agency business, I was up at 5 o'clock, home at 7:30. For the first 15 years I worked every Saturday. I didn't make it to my kid's Little League games. When I left that environment I realized how hard and unproductive the work was." Rogers packed it in five years ago and says, "I was so happy to get out I can't describe it." Since then he has turned to other new businesses, including inventing, and now holds five patents—including one for a golf-ball washer that doesn't get your hands wet.

Can I ask you a question? Why do men chase women? . . . I think it's because they fear death.
    —Rose (Olympia Dukakis) in "Moonstruck"

Typically, men and women cross paths, psychologically, in middle age. Men become more nurturing and family-oriented. Women become more independent and aggressive. Jung described this as the "contrasexual transition." Northwestern University psychologist David Gutmann found the phenomenon not only in American culture, but also in Navajo, Mayan and Middle Eastern Druze societies he studied for his book "Reclaimed Powers: Toward a New Psychology of Men and Women in Later Life"—suggesting that it is more biological than cultural. Much

---

I live like a monk, almost. A monk with red lips, short dresses and big hair.

—TINA TURNER, 53

■ Percentage of men aged 40 to 49 who say their lives are exciting: 52.4
■ Percentage aged 50 to 59: 43.3
■ Percentage of women aged 40 to 49 who find their lives exciting: 45.6
■ Percentage aged 50 to 59: 40.7

SOURCE: NATIONAL OPINION RESEARCH CENTER

of it has to do with the demands of child rearing, Gutmann explains, in which men provide for the family's physical needs and women do the emotional work, each suppressing the other parts of their personalities. When the children leave home, those submerged forces tend to reassert themselves, Gutmann says.

Ideally, that crossing should be liberating for both halves of the couple and bring them closer together. But often the transition is rocky. "It can be very threatening for men to see their women soar," says counselor Sirah Vettese, Bloomfield's wife. Some men are so unnerved that they do seek out younger, more compliant women, Gutmann says. He thinks Ernest Hemingway is a prime example: devastated after his third wife left him to pursue her own career, the author became increasingly alcoholic. He took another younger wife and killed himself at 61.

It doesn't help that many men wrestling with self-image adjustments in midlife must also accept declining sexual performance. Testosterone levels gradually drop, which can diminish their libido. Erections are less full, less frequent and require more stimulation to achieve. Researchers once attributed that to psychological factors, but increasingly they find that 75 percent of erection dysfunctions stem from physiological problems. "Smoking, diabetes, hypertension, elevated cholesterol—without a doubt, those are the four erection busters," says University of Chicago urologist Laurence A. Levine. Still, psychology does play a role. "If you think you're going to have a problem, suddenly you're going to begin having a problem," says psychologist Jan Sinnott at Towson State University in Baltimore, Md.

Inevitably, pharmaceutical manufacturers have sensed that there's money to be made in the fear of flaccidity. Gynex Pharmaceuticals is researching a daily under-the-tongue testosterone-replacement product called Androtest-SL and already markets an injectable version that is used every two weeks. But there may be considerable side effects. Excessive use of testosterone may lead to testicular atrophy and infertility and spur the growth of some cancers. Too much testosterone can cause some men to grow small breasts, too.

A better remedy for men who find their potency declining is to change the way they think about sex—to take things slower, more romantically and not mourn the seemingly instant erections of their youth. "The midlife male has to finally get the idea that his primary sex organ is not his penis. It's his heart and his brain," says Bloomfield, author of "Love Secrets for a Lasting Relationship." Talking helps, too, though most men are not accustomed to such openness. "It's really important that men and women sit down and say to each other, 'Our lives are changing'," says Vettese.

In many ways, women have it easier in midlife. For all the new willingness to discuss the hot flashes and mood swings some feel during menopause, many women feel a surge of sexual and psychological freedom once their shifting hormones rebalance and they are no longer concerned about getting pregnant. "With each pass-

ing generation, women feel sexier and more desire after menopause," says June Reinisch at the Kinsey Institute. Sheehy says that based on studies she has seen, about one third of women have some noticeable diminution of desire after menopause. That can be rectified with hormone supplements or accepted as it is, if the woman doesn't mind.

What many women *do* mind is finding themselves alone and lost in the discouraging midlife singles scene. Zella Case, co-owner of the Someone Special dating service in Dallas, says, "We have hundreds of women who want in, but so few men." The numbers are right there in the census statistics: there are 14 million single women older than 55, and only 4 million single men. Just ask Victoria Anderson, a Dallas private investigator who turned 50 last month. Divorced 13 years, she's been losing confidence and gaining weight and she frets that she'll never fit into the size 3s in her closet again. She despairs of meeting a new mate on the job—"I deal with criminals and jerks," she says. And as far as the bar scene goes, Anderson says ruefully, the typical question now is not "what's your sign, but what's your cholesterol level?"

Women with stable marriages may find other tensions mounting in midlife. With delayed childbirth, kids may be hitting adolescence just when their mothers are in menopause—a volatile combination. Some women desperately fear losing their faces and their figures—especially if those have been the focus of their self-esteem. But the new burst of postmenopausal independence some feel may help to compensate.

Bobbi Altman literally took flight at midlife. "Turning 50 was the best thing that ever happened to me. I could do anything I wanted to," she says. After suffering through a divorce in her early 40s and raising three children, Altman took up aviation, bought an airplane and, at 59, went to aircraft-mechanic school. Last April she graduated and in June she flew cross-country solo. Now 61, she lives in Laguna Beach, Calif., and is involved with a man who finished law school at 70. Altman flies to work every day at the Santa Monica Museum of Flying, where she is helping to restore a World War II P-39. "Aging is not a loss of youth—it's another stage," she says.

I remember now that the toughest birthday I ever faced was my fortieth. It was a big symbol because it said goodbye, goodbye, goodbye to youth. But I think that when one has passed through that age it's like breaking the sound barrier.
—Writer and director NORMAN CORWIN, 82
quoted in the 1992 book "The Ageless Spirit"

Baby boomers who dread what will happen to them beyond the age of 50 have only to look at what older people are doing with their lives today. The generation preceding them—the first to enjoy the longevity revolution—are going back to school in record numbers, forging new careers and still making great strides in their old ones. Lydia Bronte, a research fellow at the Phelps Stokes Institute in New York, recently com-

> **I feel exactly the same as I've always felt: a lightly reined-in voracious beast.**
>
> —JACK NICHOLSON, 55

■ Percentage of married men aged 40 to 49 who admit to infidelity: 28.4
■ Percentage aged 50 to 59: 24.3
■ Percentage of married women aged 40 to 49 who admit to infidelity: 15.21
■ Percentage aged 50 to 59: 3.3

SOURCE: NATIONAL OPINION RESEARCH CENTER

pleted a five-year study of the work lives of 150 people 65 to 102, and concludes that "many people are as active as they've ever been during those years . . . The single most important thing was that they found work that they loved." Some of Bronte's subjects switched jobs many times over in their lives. Some found their true calling only in their later years. Julia Child, now 80, learned French cooking after her husband took a job in France and started her TV career in her 50s. The late Millicent Fenwick won her first race for Congress at 65.

Still, the image of elderly people as desperate, frail and unproductive prevails, and that brings an unrealistic fear of growing middle aged and older. "People need to profoundly rethink what aging means, not only for themselves as individuals, but for the whole society," says Harry Moody, deputy director of the Brookdale Center on Aging at Hunter College in New York. By 2030, when the oldest boomers are 84 and the youngest have turned 65, thee will be an estimated 65 million Americans 65 and older—more than twice as many as today.

To find more satisfaction and hope in that future, aging baby boomers need to bust out of the rigid "three boxes of life" mentality that has governed the pattern of American lives for so long. Confining education to youth, work and child rearing to the middle years, and retirement to old age makes less and less sense—and it simply won't fly in an economy that is dismissing people from the work world in their 50s, with an ever-longer stretch of life ahead. "We desperately need some real, contributing roles for people in the third third of life," says New York management consultant Bill Stanley. He argues that the whole concept of "retirement" should be retired.

Some change in the image of aging will come about naturally in the decades ahead. Baby boomers, by sheer force of numbers, have always made their stage in life the hip stage to be in. The generation that thought it could change the world overnight has only a few years left before its members become elders themselves. While some of their frantic efforts to stave off aging may constitute denial, some go hand in hand with forging a healthier, more constructive vision of old age that could last even longer than we now suspect. The boomers will go there, riding Stair-Masters to heaven, and that may be their most lasting legacy of all.

With GINNY CARROLL *in Houston,*
PATRICIA KING *in San Francisco,*
KAREN SPRINGEN *and* TODD BARRETT *in Chicago,*
LUCILLE BEACHY *in New York,* JEANNE GORDON
in Los Angeles and CAROLYN FRIDAY *in Boston*

■ **Total face–lifts in U.S., 1990: 48,743 (91% women) percentage aged 35 to 50: 27 percentage aged 51 to 64: 58**
■ **Total tummy tucks in U.S., 1990: 20,213 (93% women) percentage aged 35 to 50: 64 percentage aged 51 to 64: 15**
■ **Total hair transplants in U.S., 1990: 3,188 (100% men) percentage aged 35 to 50: 57 percentage aged 51 to 64: 10**
■ **Median age of an American using hair–color product: women: 43.14, men: 43.02**

SOURCE: AMERICAN SOCIETY OF PLASTIC & RECONSTRUCTIVE SURGEONS, SIMMONS 1992

The Estrogen Dilemma

America's No. 1 drug is an elixir of youth, but women must decide if it's worth the risk of cancer

Claudia Wallis

On Feb. 13, 1963, a new patient strode into the office of the New York City gynecologist Robert A. Wilson. To Wilson, she was nothing less than a revelation or, to be more precise, a walking, talking confirmation of his most deeply held medical convictions. Wilson was a leading proponent of treating menopausal women with the female hormone estrogen. He was convinced that, given early enough and continued throughout life, hormone treatment could actually prevent what he called the "staggering catastrophe" of menopause and the "fast and painful aging process" that attended it.

Wilson's new patient, "Mrs. P.G.," as he later called her, said she was 52 years old, but her body told another story. "Her breasts were supple and firm, her carriage erect; she had good general muscle tone, no dryness of the mucous membranes and no visible genital atrophy. Above all," Wilson noted, "her skin was smooth and pliant as a girl's." When asked about menopause, she laughed and replied, "I assure you, Dr. Wilson, I have never yet missed a period. I'm so regular, astronomers could use me for timing the moon."

Pressed for her secret, the youthful matron eventually revealed she had been taking birth-control pills, containing estrogen and a second female hormone, progesterone. That was the very formula Wilson had developed as a means not only to treat menopausal complaints but also to forestall the aging process. Mrs. P.G. was a lush exemplar of his notion that "menopause is unnecessary. It can be prevented entirely."

Three years later, in a hugely successful book, *Feminine Forever*, Wilson announced the good news to all womankind. "For the first time in history," he wrote, "women may share the promise of tomorrow as biological equals of men. . . . Thanks to hormone therapy, they may look forward to prolonged well-being and extended youth."

Estrogen is indeed the closest thing in modern medicine to an elixir of youth—a drug that slows the ravages of time for women. It is already the No. 1 prescription drug in America, and it is about to hit its demographic sweet spot: the millions of baby boomers now experiencing their first hot flashes. What Wilson didn't appreciate, but what today's women should know, is that, like every other magic potion, this one has a dark side. To gain the full benefits of estrogen, a woman must take it not only at menopause but also for decades afterward.

It means a lifetime of drug taking and possible side effects that include an increased risk of several forms of cancer. That danger was underscored last week by a report in the *New England Journal of Medicine* reaffirming the long-suspected link between estrogen-replacement therapy and breast cancer. Weighing such risks against the truly marvelous benefits of estrogen may be the most difficult health decision a woman can make. And there's no avoiding it.

As research reveals the pros and cons of estrogen, the therapy's popularity has flowed and ebbed like some sort of national hormonal cycle. Wilson's book did wonders for the sale of Premarin (a form of estrogen made from—and named for—a *pregnant mare's urine*). But estrogen use plummeted after 1975, when studies revealed that women taking the hormone had up to a 14-fold increased risk of uterine cancer. Reports of a 30% increased risk of breast cancer scared away many others.

Today estrogen in its various forms—pills, patches and creams—is flowing as never before. Cancer risks have been diminished, doctors believe, by lowering the dosages used in hormone-replacement therapy (HRT). The risk of uterine cancer, in particular, can be virtually eliminated, experts say, by adding synthetic progesterone (progestin) to the estrogen prescription, either combined in one capsule or as a separate pill. Meanwhile a raft of studies showing new and unexpected benefits has propelled medical enthusiasm for the treatment to huge, if not quite Wilsonian, proportions. Estrogen, it seems, can prevent or slow many of the ravages of aging, including:

Menopausal miseries. The oldest and most familiar use of HRT is to relieve the hot flashes, night sweats, vaginal dryness and other symptoms of estrogen "withdrawal" that occur around menopause, when the ovaries produce less and less estrogen.

Heart disease. Several studies, including the famous Nurses Health Study that followed 120,000 nurses for more than 10 years, have found that postmenopausal women on estrogen have about half the incidence of heart disease of those who don't take hormones. HRT seems to improve a woman's ratio of good cholesterol (HDL) to bad cholesterol (LDL) and also maintains the pliability of the blood vessels, lessening the risk of blockage.

Osteoporosis. Estrogen is the most effective means of preventing the thinning of bones that makes older women so vulnerable to fractures. Studies have shown that it cuts the risk of hip fractures up to 50% if treatment begins at menopause. And new evidence suggests that it could help prevent devastating fractures even when treatment begins at 70 or older.

Mental deterioration. Several small trials have indicated that estrogen improves memory for postmenopausal women. And a tantalizing study, reported in 1993, found that HRT enhanced the mental function of women with mild to moderate symptoms of Alzheimer's disease.

Colon cancer. A large study released in April found that estrogen users had a 29% lower risk of dying from colon cancer than nonusers. For those on estrogen more than 10 years, the risk was 55% lower.

Aging skin. HRT seems to help preserve skin elasticity, much as Wilson boasted. It helps maintain the collagen that keeps skin looking plumped up and moist.

Given all this, it's no wonder doctors are handing out estrogen prescriptions with almost gleeful enthusiasm. According to researchers at the Food and Drug Administration, estrogen prescriptions in the U.S. more than doubled between 1982 and 1992. About a quarter of U.S. women at or past menopause—roughly 10 million—take the hormone, making estrogen a billion-dollar business. As baby boomers approach menopause, those numbers will skyrocket.

While gynecologists acknowledge that there are risks to estrogen therapy, they tend to emphasize the pluses. "The benefits of HRT will outweigh the risks for most women," says Dr. William Andrews, former president of the American College of Obstetrics and Gynecology. "Eight times as many women die of heart attacks as die of breast cancer."

Still, the specter of cancer continues to haunt HRT. With last week's *New England Journal* report, hope faded that progestin would offer estrogen users protection against breast cancer, as it does against uterine cancer. In fact, it appears that the combined hormones may put women at a higher risk for breast cancer than estrogen alone. This bad news came in the wake of an alarming report in May suggesting that long-term use of estrogen heightens the risk of fatal ovarian cancer.

"Menopause is unnecessary. Thanks to hormone therapy, [women] may look forward to prolonged well-being and extended youth."

Even before these disturbing reports appeared, American women were distinctly less exuberant about estrogen than their doctors. A 1987 survey showed that 20% of women given a prescription for estrogen never even fill it. Of those who do begin taking the hormone, a third stop within nine months, and more than half quit within one year. Many others go on and off HRT. Some do it because they don't feel quite right on the medication, some because they hate taking drugs, many because they worry about cancer. "I feel like a guinea pig," complains a 52-year-old woman attending a women's discussion group in Minnesota. "In 10 years we'll all be saying 'We should have been on hormones!' or 'Damn it, why did we take those things?'"

For many women there is something fundamentally disturbing about turning a natural event like menopause into a disease that demands decades of medication. And there's something spooky about continuing to have monthly bleeding at age 60, a fairly common consequence of some types of hormone therapy. "Why fight vainly to remain in a stage of life you can't be in anymore, instead of enjoying the stage you are in?" asks Dr. Nada Stotland, 51, an HRT dropout. Stotland, a psychiatrist at the University of Chicago, says she is "extra skeptical, because there are powerful forces that aim one toward prescribed hormones, but there is no profit motive in not prescribing something."

Breast-cancer specialist Dr. Susan Love shares her skepticism: "Many gynecologists are handing out these hormones like M&M's," she says. No matter how beneficial estrogen may seem, no drug treatment comes without drawbacks. In biology as in business, notes the Los Angeles oncologist, "there's no free lunch."

The Power Hormone

To understand the risks and wonders of estrogen therapy, it helps to know something about the hormone's natural role in the body. Estrogen is powerful stuff. Receptors for the hormone are found in some 300 different tissues, from brain to bone to liver. This means that in one way or another, all these tissues respond to the presence of estrogen. Some, including tissues in the urinogenital tract, the blood vessels, the skin and the breasts, require estrogen to maintain their tone and flexibility.

Estrogen levels begin to rise in girls as early as age 8 in response to a symphony of signals that stir sexual development. The hypothalamus, in the brain, acts as the maestro, spurring the pituitary to release hormones, which in turn prompt the ovaries to churn out estrogen. By age 11 or 12, production of estrogen and other hormones by the ovaries is sufficient to trigger the development of the breasts, growth of underarm and pubic hair, and the beginning of menstruation. But because these hormones influence so many tissues, they incite all sorts of adolescent mayhem: oilier hair and blemished skin, lurching moodiness, a growing interest in sex, and sometimes severe menstrual cramps.

In many ways, menopause is a mirror image of this process. Just as estrogen rises gradually in childhood, so it begins to wane some 25 years later, starting in the early 30s. The effects of the decline are rarely noticeable—except in decreasing fertility—until the early 40s, when women enter the transitional period known as perimenopause. Menstruation becomes less regular, the skin becomes dryer, hair turns more brittle and sparser under the arms and between the legs. Some women feel a loss of libido, and many suffer fluctuations in mood analogous to those that afflict adolescents.

Is It Hot in Here?

As estrogen levels drop during perimenopause, the hypothalamus sends out more and more hormonal signals in a desperate attempt to get the ovaries to make more estrogen. But the aging eggs in ovaries respond erratically, explains endocrinologist Lila Nachtigall of New York University. As a result, "estrogen levels can fluctuate from low to high, day by day, and that can drive you crazy."

Since the hypothalamus is also the body's thermostat, its overactivity triggers the famous hot flashes of menopause, described by one sufferer as "a blowtorch aimed right at your face." According to cur-

Weighing the pros and cons

Proven benefits	Benefits very likely	Proven risks	Risks very likely
• Relieves hot flashes, night sweats and other menopausal symptoms	• Reduces risk of heart disease (improves cholesterol profile and makes blood vessels more resilient)	• Increases incidence of cancer of the endometrium (the uterine lining)	• Higher rate of breast cancer
• Reduces bone loss (osteoporosis)	• Reduces risk of colon cancer	• Possible return of menstrual bleeding, if taken with progesterone	• Abnormal blood clots
• Relieves vaginal dryness and atrophy	• Reduces mood swings, mental fogginess and memory lapses	• Premenstrual-type symptoms (fluid retention, tender breasts, irritability)	• Weight gain
	• Keeps skin thicker, moister and more youthful	• May increase growth of benign fibroid tumors in the uterus	• Increases risk of gallstones
			• Headaches

The Big Pro: Estrogen and Sex

FOR MANY WOMEN THE NO. 1 REASON TO TAKE ESTROGEN AFTER MENOPAUSE is to improve their sex lives. "Without it, you may soon have no sex life at all," contends Dr. Lila Nachtigall, co-author of the popular handbook *Estrogen: The Facts Can Change Your Life!* (HarperCollins; $11). The natural waning of estrogen in the middle years often brings physical changes that can ruin a woman's pleasure in sex. The vagina basically reverts to its prepubescent shape: narrower, shorter, dryer, less elastic, with thin walls that tear easily and are prone to infection. The libido may also dry up, if only because sex becomes painful. While many women are spared these problems in their 50s, the odds are they will strike to some degree within a decade of menopause.

Nachtigall is a fervent believer in the healing power of estrogen. "Even for women who are already in deep sexual difficulty, the therapy usually reverses the damage in only a few weeks," she writes. Estrogen creams, applied topically, are very effective at rejuvenating vaginal tissues and are probably safer than pills or patches because they put less hormone into circulation. For those whose sex drive remains stuck in low gear despite HRT, the male hormone testosterone may help, though unless dosages are watched carefully, it can cause deepening voice, growth of facial hair and other unwanted effects.

For the hormone wary there are other measures. Over-the-counter lubricants can make sex more comfortable, and nonprescription moisturizers like Replens or Gyne-Moistrin can help rehydrate dry tissues. One of the best things to keep the machinery humming is sex itself, says Dr. Wulf Utian, co-founder of the North American Menopause Society. As with aging muscles, bones and brain cells, it's a matter of use it or lose it.

rent theory, this may be caused by the hypothalamus' release of an adrenaline-like substance that revs up the metabolism. The same mechanism may cause heart palpitations and nighttime sweating so intense that it can soak through the sheets.

About 85% of women experience some symptoms around menopause, lasting up to five years. At a round-table discussion sponsored by the pharmaceutical company Ciba-Geigy, a group of eight women described their tribulations with an extraordinary mix of candor, desperation and hu-

mor. (The women, most of whom do not take estrogen, agreed to be identified by their first names only.)

Sonia, 48, has "terrible" headaches and wakes up in the middle of the night with hot flashes: "I have to keep a cold washcloth on my night table; I put it on the back of my neck." Marguerite, 43, said she is so irritable before her period that she has taken to warning her officemates, "Next week's the week." For Susan, 48, "vaginal dryness is the worst," and beginning at 41, she was bothered by the unpredictability of

her menstrual cycle: "My period would last 10 days, 12 days, 14 days. Then it would be six weeks, three weeks, two weeks."

More alarming is the gushing bleeding some of the women have experienced, the result, in many cases, of missed hormonal signals and a loss of uterine muscle tone. "Sometimes when I'm at the office and I stand up, the blood is dripping down my leg," said Marian, 45. "What the hell is going on? Am I hemorrhaging?" And a few women complained about bladder-control problems. Joked Marian: "Don't tell me I'm going to replace tampons with Depends!"

Not every woman will feel the symptoms so intensely. Heavy women tend to have an advantage at menopause, since fat cells manufacture a form of estrogen called estrone. Some lucky women, regardless of weight, simply churn out more estrone once estrogen from the ovaries shuts off.

Personal circumstances may matter as much as chemistry. The decline in estrogen often coincides with many life changes. "Your children grow up and move away. You don't look as gorgeous as you used to, and your husband leaves you for a younger woman. These things may leave you vulnerable to depression," says Dr. Stotland of the University of Chicago. "The more a woman feels valued in her life, the less likely she is to have emotional symptoms at menopause. Working women tend to do better than women who stay home."

Women are often shocked when menopausal symptoms strike in the early 40s. The average age of menopause, after all, is 51. Most know little about perimenopause, and their doctors aren't much help. A Gallup poll of women ages 45 to 60 conducted last year found that only 44% were satisfied with the information they received from their doctors about menopause. Until recently, doctors "simply weren't aware of perimenopause," admits endocrinologist Howard Zacur of Johns Hopkins Hospital in Baltimore. "Changes in the cycle at this time of life were misinterpreted and misdiagnosed."

Even now, the odd bleeding patterns of perimenopause are often attributed to fibroid tumors (which may or may not be a factor). Because their symptoms have been poorly understood, many women have undergone unnecessary hysterectomies and D&Cs (dilatation and curettage), a procedure that scrapes away the uterine lining. Roughly 1 out of 4 U.S. women is thrown into "surgical menopause" by the removal of her uterus and ovaries instead of hitting menopause naturally.

Here, Have Some Hormones

The best therapy for perimenopause is "knowing what it is," says Harvard gynecologist

Alan Altman. Exercise, a proper diet and not smoking can also help. (Women who smoke reach menopause an average of two years earlier than nonsmokers.) For 85% of women, the symptoms will stop within one year of their final period. But for those who are in too much misery to wait it out, estrogen can do wonders.

Patricia Thomas, 56, of Baltimore suffered nearly five years with hot flashes, night sweats and sleeplessness. Estrogen completely halted her symptoms and made her feel "wonderful." Barbara Williams, 47, of Chicago was so irritable, she says, that "my family would hate to see me coming home from work." An estrogen patch (plus progesterone pills) evened out her moods. HRT can sometimes alleviate vaguer woes—the generalized achiness that some women feel and a sense of mental fogging. There is a "euphoric effect or general improvement in mental state," says Cleveland endocrinologist Wulf Utian, co-founder of the North American Menopause Society.

But Utian is quick to point out that not every woman should take estrogen. It is not advisable for those with a history or a high risk of breast or uterine cancer. Nor is it recommended for women with clotting problems.

Besides, some women feel lousy on hormones. And many are distressed to find they gain weight (though it's unclear that estrogen is really to blame). When Lynn Schleeter, 44, of New Brighton, Minnesota, was taking estrogen and progesterone, "I was so lethargic, I couldn't walk around the block." She feels more energetic now that she has thrown away her estrogen patch and switched to a regimen of exercise, vitamins and calcium supplements (to fight osteoporosis).

Progesterone pills can be particularly hard to tolerate. Progestin is always prescribed along with estrogen for women with an intact uterus. While estrogen prompts the uterine lining to thicken, progestin signals it to stop growing and slough off; this artificial menstrual cycle seems to prevent endometrial cancer. But progestin often causes cramps, irritability and other PMS like problems. In her 1991 book on menopause, *The Silent Passage*, Gail Sheehy tells how estrogen highs and progestin lows made her feel as though her body was "at war with itself for half of every month."

Estrogen Forever?

Once the storms of perimenopause have cleared, many women see little reason to remain on estrogen. Some enter a period of well-being, famously dubbed "post-menopausal zest" by anthropologist Margaret Mead. In her latest book, *New Passages,* Sheehy calls this the "pits to peak phenomenon": Women emerge from the

A Tonic for the Mind

LONG BEFORE IT WORKS ITS TURBULENT MAGIC AT PUBERTY, LONG BEFORE WE are even born, estrogen leaves its indelible mark on our mental functions. Not only does it help sculpt the brain during the earliest stages of development; it also continues to play a role in learning and memory throughout life. Subtle differences between the male and female brain can be traced to the influences of estrogen and testosterone in the womb. (While all fetuses are exposed to their mother's estrogen, male fetuses produce testosterone in their testes by the 12th week of gestation.) Particularly affected is the hypothalamus, a walnut-size structure located near the top of the brainstem that governs sexual development and sexual behavior and regulates temperature and water balance. Many scientists believe that such gender differences as the male facility with math, the female facility with language, girls' slightly superior hearing and skill at interpreting facial expressions are hardwired prenatally through the influence of the sex hormones.

Certain differences between female and male sexual behavior are programmed prenatally by the influence of estrogen or testosterone on the **hypothalamus,** a brain structure that also regulates temperature.

Estrogen increases the number of connections between nerve cells in the region called the **hippocampus,** which helps govern memory.

TIME Diagram by Joe Lertola

Later these hormones play a housekeeping role in the growth and maintenance of brain cells in both sexes. (In boys some testosterone is converted to estrogen in the brain.) When estrogen is in short supply, memory and thought processes can suffer. Psychologist Barbara Sherwin at Montreal's McGill University has studied the effects of estrogen therapy on women who have had their ovaries removed and thus produce very little estrogen of their own. She found that women who were given injections of estrogen were better at learning and recalling pairs of words than those given a placebo. The effect is intriguingly specific; it involves verbal tasks (at which women tend to excel) but not visual memory.

Even the normal rise and fall of estrogen during a woman's menstrual cycle can affect mental performance. Young women do better on Sherwin's word-pair memory tests during the luteal phase of their cycle, when estrogen and progesterone levels are high, than during menstruation, when hormone levels are low. This doesn't mean women are less competent late in their cycles, says Sherwin; the changes are too minor "to have any real effect in the real world." Still, there is little doubt that the foggy forgetfulness that envelops some women as they approach menopause is a direct result of low estrogen. The fog generally lifts on its own, but hormone therapy can bring an almost instant break in the clouds.

Just how estrogen works in the brain remains obscure, though research by Bruce McEwen at Rockefeller University has shown that the hormone increases the number of connections between nerve cells in the hippocampus, a region that helps govern memory. Estrogen also increases the production of acetylcholine, a brain chemical that is abnormally low in Alzheimer's patients.

Dr. Howard Fillit, a geriatrician at New York City's Mount Sinai Medical Center, has conducted small-scale tests of estrogen with women who have mild to moderate Alzheimer's. Patients who did not know the month or year could recall them after just three weeks on daily doses of hormones. The women became more alert, ate and slept better, and showed improved social behavior. Fillit believes testosterone therapy may prove equally useful for male patients. Estrogen is not yet an approved therapy for Alzheimer's, but as the evidence builds, it is fast becoming one of the brightest hopes in a so far bleak field. —*By Claudia Wallis.*
Reported by Alice Park/New York

morass of menopause with "a greater sense of well-being than any other stage of their lives."

Yet, no matter how marvelous such women may feel, the prevailing medical view is that most should stay on estrogen for a long haul. Unnatural as that sounds, doctors argue that life after menopause is itself somewhat unnatural. "As women have lived increasingly longer lives, they are facing problems their grandmothers never faced," says Dr. Charles Hammond, chairman of obstetrics and gynecology at Duke University Medical Center. "At the turn of the century, women died soon after their ovaries quit." Now they live to face heart disease, osteoporosis, increased fractures—problems that may be prevented in part by taking estrogen.

Unfortunately, estrogen works its preventive wonders only if taken for many years—the longer, the better. To prevent osteoporosis, for instance, a woman must use estrogen continuously for at least seven years, according to recent data from the Framingham study in Boston. Currently, 95% of women on HRT take it for three years or less—"not long enough to get any positive effects on their bones," says Dr. John Gallagher, an endocrinologist at Creighton University in Omaha, Nebraska.

Similarly, researchers studying estrogen and heart disease see the greatest benefits in long-term use. Estrogen helps keep levels of LDL cholesterol low and HDL cholesterol high, which is one reason premenopausal women have a much lower rate of heart disease than their male peers. Without HRT, a woman's risk of a heart attack rises to match that of men within 15 years of menopause. Estrogen also acts directly on blood vessels, causing them to dilate slightly so that blood flow improves, says Dr. Roger Blumenthal of Johns Hopkins Hospital. But these benefits disappear as soon as the patient stops taking hormones.

Given all this, it seems logical to recommend HRT for postmenopausal women with high cholesterol levels or other warning signs of heart disease. Indeed, Blumenthal considers HRT "a first-line therapy" for such women. Likewise, it is now standard practice to give estrogen to women with a high risk of osteoporosis—approximately 1 in 3 U.S. women. Gallagher recommends routine bone-density tests to assess bone condition and at least 10 years of estrogen, beginning at menopause, for those with fragile bones.

While such recommendations are based on the best available research, experts, if pressed, will admit that the research is woefully inadequate. Most of the controlled studies on estrogen therapy have been short-term and can shed no light on long-term risks. "I think the currently available data

are extrapolated to excess with respect to heart disease," complains cardiologist David Herrington of Bowman Gray School of Medicine in Winston-Salem, North Carolina.

What does emerge from the longer-term data is that prolonged use of estrogen appears to increase the risk of breast cancer and other malignancies. And the longer estrogen is taken, the greater the risks. For instance, a study of 240,000 women sponsored by the American Cancer Society found that those who took estrogen for at least six years had a 40% increased risk of fatal ovarian cancer. For those taking estrogen for 11 or more years, the increase jumped to 70%.

"Many gynecologists are handing out these hormones like M&M's. We all know there's no free lunch."

There may be other risks and other advantages of HRT, but what doctors know is limited by the type of research that has been done. Instead of setting up a group of women on HRT and a carefully matched control group that does not take hormones, studies like the Nurses trial simply look at populations of women who make their own choice whether to take estrogen. "The problem with this," explains Dr. Susan Love, "is that women who take hormones go to doctors more, eat well, exercise and are in better health generally than women who don't take hormones." Thus it is hard to tell whether their lower rates of heart disease or colon cancer or fractures reflect HRT or these other healthy habits.

The good news is that a well-designed, long-term study of HRT is finally under way. Last year, in an attempt to redress a historic shortfall in research on women's health, the National Institutes of Health launched the $628 million Women's Health Initiative. In the HRT portion of the study, which will involve 27,500 women, half will be randomly assigned to HRT, half to a placebo. Researchers will follow the women for at least eight years and compare rates of heart disease, osteoporosis, breast cancer and other ailments. When the results are reported, doctors and patients may finally have some clear picture of the risks and benefits of long-term HRT. Alas, that won't be until 2005.

In the meantime, women are faced with a tough choice. Dr. Isaac Schiff,

chief of obstetrics and gynecology at Massachusetts General Hospital, puts it with refreshing bluntness: "Basically, you're presenting women with the possibility of increasing the risk of getting breast cancer at age 60 in order to prevent a heart attack at age 70 and a hip fracture at age 80. How can you make that decision for a patient?"

Those who don't like that choice may want to examine the alternatives. There are other ways to fight osteoporosis and heart disease: don't smoke; get regular exercise that is both weight bearing (to prevent bone loss) and aerobic (to condition the cardiovascular system); eat a diet rich in calcium and low in fat. And, of course, there are other drugs for heart disease and several promising new ones in the pipeline for osteoporosis.

Many of the "alternative" practitioners around the country are suggesting that women seek estrogen from dietary sources. In Los Angeles and Boston, Mexican yams have become all the rage among women of a certain age. Yams contain a weak form of estrogen. San Francisco nutritionist Linda Ojeda, author of *Menopause Without Medicine*, advocates soybeans, which contain a natural progesterone as well as estrogen. The low rate of menopausal complaints among Japanese women may be due in part to their consumption of tofu, she suggests. To relieve hot flashes, Ojeda recommends 6 oz. of tofu four times a week, 800 units of vitamin E daily, plus a few other herbs and vitamins. "Why not start with the least invasive products first? If you have a cold, you start with chicken soup and garlic."

In the final analysis, the decision about estrogen is a highly individual one. It should depend on a woman's assessment of her own health; her family history of cancer, heart disease and osteoporosis; and even on personal philosophy. "I have a hunch that I'll remain on HRT for the rest of my life," says Frida, a Chicago-area college instructor in her early 70s, who feels that estrogen gives her "more energy" and a more youthful appearance. But for Joan Israel, 64, a clinical social worker in Franklin, Michigan, fear of cancer was a deciding factor against estrogen. "So what if you get wrinkles or a little flabby, as long as you are basically healthy?"

As is so often the case in modern medicine, the most a patient can ask of her doctor is to lay out the risks, the benefits and the honest fact that the data are inadequate, and then let her make the choice.

—Reported by
Wendy Cole/Chicago, Alice Park/New York and Martha Smilgis/Los Angeles

*Far from being the slough of despond it is considered, middle age
may be the very best time of life, researchers say—the "it" we work toward*

MIDLIFE MYTHS

WINIFRED GALLAGHER

Winifred Gallagher ("Midlife Myths") is a senior editor of
American Health. *Her latest book [is]* The Power of Place:
How Our Surroundings Shape Our Thoughts, Emotions, and
Actions.

According to the picture of human development drawn by traditional scientific literature, after a busy childhood and adolescence young adults launch their careers and social lives and then stride into a black box, from which they hobble some forty years later to face a darkly eventful senescence. According to popular literature, what takes place inside the box is an anticlimactic, unsatisfying, and even traumatic march over the hill and toward the grave—or, worse, the nursing home. This scenario complements the anecdotes that often figure in conversations about middle age: that friend of a friend whose lifetime investment in career and family went up in the flames of a passion for the au pair, or that second cousin rumored to have gone off the deep end during the "change of life" when the kids left for college.

So entrenched is the idea that middle age is bad or boring or both that the almost 80 million members of the graying Baby Boom generation won't use the term except in referring to Ozzie and Harriet Nelson or Ward and June Cleaver. "We have a problem here, and it's called denial," the television producer Stan Rogow, whose 1992 series *Middle Ages* was a critical success, recently told *Newsweek*. He blames the show's title for its commercial failure: "'Middle age' is this horrible-sounding thing you've heard throughout your life and hated." The denial he describes frustrates the efforts of researchers who are conducting the first comprehensive, multidisciplinary studies of middle age. They are finding that it is not just an aging process but life's peak experience.

The study of development concentrates mostly on life's early stages, when behavioral and physiological growth and change are simultaneous. In the 1960s the new discipline of gerontology revealed that as people lived much further into old age, a reverse synchrony obtained toward life's end. Looking back from studies of the elderly and, to a lesser extent, forward from studies of the young, researchers began to suspect that middle age might be not simply a long interval during which things are worse than they are in youth and better than they are

in old age but a developmental process in its own right—albeit one not particularly tied to changes in the body. Common perceptions of middle age are that it occurs from roughly forty to sixty; in the future, increased longevity and better health may push back the period of middle age even further. The scientists and scholars exploring this part of life, which is probably better described experientially than chronologically—the very concept of middle age itself is something of a cultural artifact, with social and economic components—range from the medically, sociologically, and psychologically oriented John D. and Catherine T. MacArthur Foundation Research Network on Successful Midlife Development (MIDMAC), administered from Vero Beach, Florida, to the psychoanalytically and spiritually grounded C. G. Jung Foundation's Center for Midlife Development in New York City.

Although there are plenty of exceptions, "the data show that middle age is the very best time in life," says Ronald Kessler, a sociologist and MIDMAC fellow who is a program director in the survey research center of the University of Michigan's Institute for Social Research. "When looking at the total U.S. population, the best year is fifty. You don't have to deal with the aches and pains of old age or the anxieties of youth: Is anyone going to love me? Will I ever get my career off the ground? Rates of general distress are low—the incidences of depression and anxiety fall at about thirty-five and don't climb again until the late sixties. You're healthy. You're productive. You have enough money to do some of the things you like to do. You've come to terms with your relationships, and the chance of divorce is very low. Midlife is the 'it' you've been working toward. You can turn your attention toward being rather than becoming."

Whereas Kessler's picture of middle age is drawn from facts and figures, the image in most Americans' minds is based on myths, derived not from the ordinary experiences of most people but from the unusual experiences of a few. Although these make for livelier reading and conversation, they generate an unnecessarily gloomy attitude about the middle years which limits people's horizons, according to Margie Lachman, a psychologist, a MIDMAC fellow, and the director of the Life-span Developmental Psychology Laboratory at Brandeis University. When Lachman asked young adults what it means to be middle-aged, they gave such answers as "You think more

The overwhelming majority of people, surveys show, accomplish the task of coming to terms with the realities of middle age through a long, gentle process—not an acute, painful crisis.

about the past than the future" and "You worry about money for health care." They also assumed that the stress experienced in middle age came from the desire to be young again. Older subjects Lachman surveyed, who knew better, attributed stress to coping with the many demands of the busiest time in life. And whereas the older group saw their lives as generally stable, the younger expected to experience a lot of change—and a crisis—in midlife. "The images and beliefs we have about middle age are the guideposts for our planning, evaluation, and goal-setting," Lachman says. "Are they accurate? Or negative self-fulfilling prophesies?"

Gilbert Brim, a pioneer in the study of social development through the life-span and the director of MIDMAC, agrees. "Passed on from generation to generation," he says, "widely shared cultural beliefs and untested theories about middle age put forward in the media continue to be played out in society. But they're likely to be wrong. There are probably as many myths about midlife now as there were about aging thirty years ago, before the advent of gerontology. The time has come to rid ourselves of these obsolete ideas."

The Inexorable Midlife Crisis?

MOST YOUNGER ADULTS ANTICIPATE THAT BEtween their late thirties and their early fifties a day will come when they suddenly realize that they have squandered their lives and betrayed their dreams. They will collapse into a poorly defined state that used to be called a nervous breakdown. Escape from this black hole will mean either embracing an un-American philosophy of eschatological resignation or starting over—jaded stockbrokers off to help Mother Teresa, phlegmatic spouses off to the StairMaster and the singles scene. In short, they will have a midlife crisis.

If youth's theme is potential, midlife's is reality: childhood fantasies are past, the fond remembrances of age are yet to be, and the focus is on coming to terms with the finite resources of the here and now. The overwhelming majority of people, surveys show, accomplish this devel-

opmental task, as psychologists put it, through a long, gentle process—not an acute, painful crisis. Over time the college belle or the high school athlete leans less on physical assets, the middle manager's horizons broaden beyond the corner office, and men and women fortunate enough to have significant others regard the rigors of courtship with indulgent smiles. In relying on brains and skill more than beauty and brawn, diffusing competitive urges to include the tennis court or a community fundraising project, and valuing long-term friendship and domestic pleasures over iffy ecstasies, these people have not betrayed their youthful goals but traded them in for more practical ones that bring previously unsuspected satisfaction. Ronald Kessler says, "The question to ask the middle-aged person isn't just What has happened to you? but also How has your experience changed your thinking?"

The middle-aged tend to be guided not by blinding revelations associated with emotional crisis but by slowly dawning adaptive insights into the self and others, which Kessler calls "psychological turning points." Early in midlife these usually involve a recognition of limitations: the local politician realizes that she'll never make it to the U.S. Senate, and the high school English teacher accepts that he's not going to be a famous man of letters. In the middle period of middle age the transitions usually concern what Kessler calls a redirection of goals: "You say to yourself, 'I'm killing myself at work, but the thing that really satisfies me is my family. I'm not going to change jobs, but from now on I'm going to focus more on home, and career will mean something different to me.'" In later middle age, turning points, especially for women, often involve a recognition of strength—"just the opposite of what you'd suppose," Kessler says. "The shy violet, for example, finds herself chairing a committee." These soundings taken and adjustments made prompt not dramatic departures from one's life course but gentle twists and curves.

"Mastery experiences," the more robust versions of which figure in Outward Bound–type adventure vacations, can be catalysts for middle-aged people in their ordinary settings as well. One of Kessler's subjects finally got his college diploma at fifty-eight, observing that he

"Mastery experiences," the more robust versions of which figure in Outward Bound–type vacations, can be catalysts for middle-aged people in their ordinary settings as well.

had thereby "resolved a lot of things and completed something important"; in almost the same language, a man of fifty said that he had "done something important" when he became proficient enough in his hobby of electronics to tutor others. Overcoming her lifelong fear of water, one woman learned to swim at the age of forty-five. "One day her family went to the pool, and she just jumped in," Kessler says. "This was a very powerful experience for her, not because she wanted to be a lifeguard but because she had mastered her anxiety as well as a new skill."

Even an apparently negative turning point can have benefits. Quite a few of Kessler's subjects, when asked if they had realized a dream in the past year, said yes, "but quite a few said they had given up on one," he says. "When the folks who have dreamed for years about a big summer house where all the kids would flock finally accept that they don't have the money and the kids have other plans, they release a lot of tension. This kind of surrender is very productive, because dreams that run counter to reality waste a lot of energy."

Although all people make psychological transitions and adjustments in the course of middle age, relatively few experience these as catastrophic. In surveys 10 to 12 percent of respondents report that they have had a midlife crisis, Kessler says. "What they often mean is that the kind of disaster that can happen at other times in life—divorce, or being fired, or a serious illness—happened to them during their middle years." An unusual convergence of such unhappy events can push even a hardy middle-aged person into a state of emotional emergency. "First you notice that your hair is falling out," Gilbert Brim says. "Then you go to the office and learn you didn't get that raise, and when you get home, your wife says she's leaving." But most of those who have a true psychological crisis in middle age—according to MIDMAC, about five percent of the population—have in fact experienced internal upheavals throughout their lives. "They see the world in those terms," says David Featherman, a MIDMAC fellow and the president of the Social Science Research Council, in New York City. "They aren't particularly good at absorbing or rebounding from life's shocks."

People prone to midlife crisis score low on tests of introspection, or reflecting on one's self and on life, and high in denial, or coping with trouble by not thinking about it. "Take the guy who still thinks he's a great athlete," Kessler says. "Somehow he hasn't let reality intrude on his boyhood fantasy. But one day something forces him to wake up. Maybe he's at a family reunion playing ball with his twelve-year-old nephew and he can't make his shots. Suddenly he's an old man, a failure." Heading for the same kind of shock are the people banking on the big promotion that their colleagues know will never happen, along with those who believe that hair transplants and breast implants mean eternal youth. "Such individuals have to work hard to maintain their illusions," Kessler says. "They spend a lot of energy on the cogni-

tive effort of self-delusion, until reality finally intervenes." Because most middle-aged people have grown skilled at monitoring changes in reality—the jump shot isn't what it used to be, the figure has changed for good—they are spared the abrupt, traumatic run-ins with reality that result in a psychic emergency.

Midlife crises are an affliction of the relatively affluent: rosy illusions are easier to maintain when a person is already somewhat shielded from reality. Just as childhood is often constricted among the poor, who early in life face adult realities and burdens, so middle age may be eclipsed by a premature old age brought on by poverty and poor health. Among working-class people, for whom strength and stamina mean earning power, middle age may begin at thirty-five rather than the forty-five often cited in studies by respondents drawn from the sedentary middle class. Because any fanciful notions that poor and blue-collar people might have are rigorously tested by daily life, Kessler says, they rarely dwell in fantasy. "In terms of career, factory workers are likelier to be wherever they're going to be at thirty than executives," he says. "In terms of mental health, being disappointed at what *is* is a better kind of problem to have than being anxious about what will be. Once you know the reality, you can say, 'I can't afford to buy a boat, so I'll rent one for vacations.' Being up in the air is the big problem."

Despite the lurid tales of fifty-year-olds who run off with their twenty-five-year-old secretaries, such events are relatively rare in real-life midlife. Most couples who divorce break up in the first six or eight years of matrimony, and by midlife the majority report being more or less content. "The family-demography side of the midlife crisis just isn't there," says Larry Bumpass, a MIDMAC fellow and a professor of sociology at the University of Wisconsin at Madison, who directs the federally funded National Survey of Families and Households, the largest demographic study of its kind. "After ten or fifteen years together, the probability that a couple will split up is low. I've looked at the data every way possible to see if there's even a blip in the divorce rate when the children leave home, but that's just folklore too."

Even the nature of the difficulties most commonly reported suggests that the majority of the middle-aged operate from a position of strength. "The problems mentioned usually concern not the self but someone else—a child or parent," Kessler says. "Part of the reason for this outward focus is that the middle-aged person has secured his or her own situation and can afford to pay attention to others. Compared with the issues that arise in youth and old age, for most people the management-type problems that crop up in midlife aren't nearly as emotionally devastating."

Carl Jung divided life into halves—the first devoted to forming the ego and getting established in the world, the second to finding a larger meaning for all that effort. He then took the unorthodox step of paying more attention to the second. When shifting from one stage to the other, Jung observed, people experience an external loss of some kind—physical prowess or upward mobility or a relationship. When they treat this loss as a signal that it's time to develop new dimensions, Jung thought, transformation is in store. However, he predicted stagnation or even a breakdown if the loss is met with denial, fear, or a sense of defeat. Aryeh Maidenbaum, the executive director of the C. G. Jung Foundation's Center for Midlife Development, offers the Jungian rule of thumb for midlife crises: "The greater the disparity between the outer and inner person, the greater the chance for trouble. The most important inner need people have is to be seen for who they are. If that's what's happening at midlife, there's no crisis."

The Change for the Worse

IF THERE'S ONE ISSUE REGARDING WHICH MISINFORmation feeds mounting hysteria about middle age, it's menopause. After finishing any of a number of recent books and articles, a reader might conclude that for a few years a middle-aged woman might as well choose between sobbing alone and riding around on a broom. One of the few people who have gleaned their own hard data on the subject is Karen Matthews, a professor of psychiatry, epidemiology, and psychology at the University of Pittsburgh School of Medicine, who has conducted a longitudinal survey of the psychological and physical changes experienced by 500 women passing through menopause. "The fact is that most women do very well in the menopausal transition," she says, refuting the popular image of women who are invariably depressed, extremely unpleasant, or both. "There are some common physical symptoms that aren't fun, notably hot flashes, but only a minority of women—about ten percent—have a tough time psychologically."

Matthews has identified the characteristics of those who experience few problems in menopause and those who experience many. "The women who do well respond to the menopause with action," she says. "That may not be their direct intention, but they end up coping with the stressor by making positive changes. Those who, say, step up their exercise regimen don't even show the biological changes, such as the adverse shifts in lipids implicated in coronary disease, that others do. These 'active copers' say, 'Hey, I look a little different, feel a little less energetic. Why don't I . . .'"

Try hormone-replacement therapy? In evaluating its effects on physical health, women and doctors must juggle evidence suggesting that while HRT cuts the number of hot flashes by about half and reduces vulnerability to osteoporosis and perhaps coronary disease, it may raise the risk of breast cancer and, if estrogen is taken without progestin, uterine cancer. The National Institutes of Health is now conducting a badly needed controlled long-term clinical trial of large numbers of women on HRT which should provide some answers. Meanwhile, some doctors, confronted with incomplete data, tell women that the decision is up to them. Considering the threat of os-

teoporosis and of coronary disease, which is the leading cause of death for women over fifty, many other doctors recommend HRT to those whose risk of breast cancer is low. Still others regard its widespread use with dismay. Their concerns range from the fact that only one in three women is vulnerable to osteoporosis to a flaw in the argument that hormones can prevent heart disease. In part because doctors are cautious about prescribing HRT for women with illnesses such as hypertension and diabetes, the population that takes it is healthier to begin with—a built-in selection bias that skews studies of the therapy's effects. Among HRT's vocal critics are the doctors Sonja and John McKinlay, epidemiologists at the New England Research Institute, in Watertown, Massachusetts. "HRT is inappropriate for the vast majority of women, who shouldn't use it," John McKinlay says. "Yet the pharmaceutical industry's goal is to have every post-menopausal woman on it until death." Having surveyed the literature on menopause and HRT, Alice Rossi, a MIDMAC fellow and an emeritus professor of sociology at the University of Massachusetts at Amherst, says, "I wish we had a better scientific foundation for deciding if it's appropriate for women to take hormones for decades. At this point there's no strong evidence for a pro or anti position."

Although the process of weighing HRT's effects on physical health continues, Matthews has determined that as far as behavioral effects are concerned, HRT is "*not* the most important factor in most women's psychological well-being during menopause." For that matter, she says, women who do and don't use HRT may report differing experiences because they are different types of people to begin with. In Matthews's study the typical user was not only better educated and healthier but also likely to be a hard-driving "Type A" person, less content with the status quo. "These women are up on the literature," Matthews says, "more aware of HRT, and more interested in seeking treatment."

If active copers, whether or not they take hormones, fare best during menopause, Matthews says, the women likely to have the worst time have two disparate things in common: HRT and a low regard for themselves. "Women who have poor self-esteem but don't use hormones don't have a hard time," she says. One hypothesis is that reproductive hormones, particularly progesterone, cause some women to become dysphoric, or moody; if a woman who has this adverse reaction to HRT also has a poor self-image, she is likely to be more upset by a stressor such as a menopausal symptom than a woman with a sturdier ego.

"The idea that most women have a hard time psychologically is the major myth our data have dispelled," Matthews says. "Eighty percent of our subjects thought they were going to become depressed and irritable at menopause, but only ten percent did. Those who had a rough time had showed signs long before of being anxious, depressed, or pessimistic. Menopause makes women with that pre-existing set of characteristics, which are not age-related, more emotionally vulnerable."

Much of the dark mythology of menopause derives not from the thing itself but from simultaneous aspects of the aging process. "It's the physical manifestation of aging—and a woman's reaction to it—that's critical in predicting whether the years from forty-five to fifty-five will be difficult or not," Alice Rossi says. "Society's image of an attractive woman is ten years younger than that of an attractive man. Graying at the temples and filling out a bit can be attractive in a man—look at Clinton and Gore. But their wives are still trying to look twenty-eight." Rossi isn't necessarily advocating the grin-and-bear-it attitude toward aging favored by Barbara Bush. Seeming ten years younger than you are can be a good thing, she says, if it means a concern for good health and well-being, rather than an obsession with youth.

Matthews considers a lot of the anxiety expressed by women about menopause to be unnecessary. In response to the often-heard complaint that there has been no good research on the subject, she points to several major long-term investigations—including hers, one by Sonja and John McKinlay, and one conducted in Sweden—that independently show that the majority of women have no serious problems making the transition.

In discussing a recent bestseller on the subject, Gail Sheehy's *The Silent Passage*, she says, "Ms. Sheehy interviewed me at length, but the experience of menopause she describes in her book is not the one that emerges as typical in the three major studies. Some women have a very difficult menopause, and Ms. Sheehy feels there's a message there. We need to figure out why some women do have problems, so that we can help. "There has been no generation of women like this one. They're better educated. They're healthier to the point that they now live half their adult lives after the menopause. For them, the menopausal transition is best characterized as a time of optimism. It's a bridge—an opportunity for women to think about what they want to do next."

Despite persistent rumors, there's probably no such thing as male menopause. Men simply don't experience a midlife biological change equivalent to the one women undergo. Whereas nature is responsible for that inequity, culture is at the bottom of a far more destructive one. For a research project, John McKinlay videotaped visits to doctors' offices made by patients matched for every variable but gender. The films showed that a man and a woman who complained of the same symptoms were often treated very differently: men were twice as likely to be referred to a medical specialist, and women were much likelier to be referred to a psychotherapist; men were urged toward health-enhancing behavior such as dieting and exercise, but women rarely were. ("This is particularly unfortunate where smoking is concerned," McKinlay says, "because the health benefits for women who give it up may be greater than those for men.") He concludes that the gender-related disparities apparent in much medical literature may reflect what doctors see more than actual physiological differences. Accordingly,

Many studies show that satisfaction with the marital relationship climbs again after couples weather the labor-intensive period of launching careers and babies.

he suspects that when middle-aged men complain of bad moods and decreased libido and energy, most doctors see a need for behavioral change. When women report the same symptoms, many doctors attribute them to menopause and prescribe hormones. "Don't forget that most women get their primary health care from a gynecologist," McKinlay says, "which would be like most men getting theirs from a urologist."

Among endocrinologists outside the United States there is more support for the notion of a male climacteric, in which older men's lower testosterone levels cause decreased fertility, increased body fat, bone loss, and skin-tone changes, along with the same behavioral symptoms that are often attributed to female menopause. While allowing that a small percentage of older men suffer from an endocrinological problem and can benefit from hormone-replacement therapy, McKinlay insists that there is no evidence that the majority would benefit. For that matter, he says, testosterone has little effect on the sexuality of those over fifty or fifty-five, and taking it as a supplement may in fact increase the risk of prostate cancer. Having conducted a study of the sex lives of 1,700 men aged forty to seventy which is considered by many to be the best information on the subject, he says, "There's no physiological, endocrinological, psychological, or clinical basis for a male menopause. Whether or not people believe in it has nothing to do with whether it exists, only with whether the pharmaceutical industry can persuade them that it does. In ten years male climacteric clinics will sprout up to treat a condition that may or may not exist—but, of course, they'll make money."

McKinlay's major reservation about most of the existing research on the effects of reproductive hormones is that it has been conducted with "small, atypical" samples of people who are seeking treatment in the health-care system. "What's talked about in the literature—both professional and popular—is the experience of *patients*," he says, "not healthy people, about whom we know very little."

The Best Years of Your Life Are Over

MANY PEOPLE HAVE A MEMORY FROM ADOLEScence of gazing around a gathering of adults, no longer in the green days of their youth yet dressed to kill and living it up, and thinking the equivalent of "How valiant they are to make an effort at their age." Because Hollywood and Madison Avenue project this same juvenile notion, many of the middle-aged are surprised and relieved to find that their lives aren't nearly so dreary as they expected. After analyzing decades of social research for his 1992 book *Ambition*, Gilbert Brim found that a person's zest for and satisfaction with life don't depend on youth—or on status, sexuality, health, money, or any of the other things one might expect. "What people really want out of life are action and challenge—to be in the ballgame," he says. "To feel satisfied, we must be able to tackle a task that's hard enough to test us, but not so difficult that we'll repeatedly fail. We want to work hard, then succeed."

This maxim has a special resonance for today's middle-aged, career-oriented middle class, often portrayed as beleaguered victims of "role strain" or burnt-out cases operating on automatic pilot. In fact, Brim says, most are instinctively seeking the level of "just manageable difficulty"—an optimum degree of effort that taps about 80 percent of a person's capacity and generates that satisfied, job-well-done feeling. Pushing beyond that level for prolonged periods leaves people stressed and anxious; falling below it leaves them bored. Because what is just manageable at forty might not be at sixty, people rearrange their lives, often unconsciously, to balance capacities and challenges. When one does well at something, one ups the ante; when one fails, one lowers the sights a bit or even switches arenas. Brim draws an illustration from a study of AT&T executives: over time the most successful grew more work-oriented; the others began to turn more to their families and social lives—educating the children or lowering the golf handicap—for feelings of accomplishment. The key point, he says, is that neither group was more satisfied than the other. "This intuitive process by which we constantly reset our goals in response to our gains and losses is one of the most overlooked aspects of adult development."

One way in which the middle-aged are particularly skilled in adjusting their goals is in choosing which Joneses to keep up with. "Our mental health is very much affected by our estimation of how we're doing in terms of the people around us," says Carol Ryff, a psychologist and a MIDMAC fellow who is the associate director of the Institute on Aging and Adult Life, at the University of Wisconsin at Madison. "We all make these important measurements, even though we're often barely conscious of doing so." Whereas the young person launching a career might try to outdo Maurizio Pollini or Donna Karan, the savvy middle-aged one knows that holding to this standard beyond a certain point ensures misery—or a genuine

midlife crisis. Particularly when faced with a difficult situation, the mature person makes a "downward comparison" that puts his own problems in a different perspective and helps him soldier on. Thus the executive who has just been laid off compares his finances not with the Rockefellers' but with those of the couple across the street who are both on unemployment, and reminds himself that at least his wife's position is secure. "The better your mental health, the less often you measure yourself against people who make you feel crummy," Ryff says. "In midlife you begin to say, 'Well, so I'm not in the same category as the Nobelists. That's just not an expectation I'm going to drag around anymore.'"

By middle age most people destined for success have achieved it, which erects some special hurdles in the just-manageable course of life. "Winning is not simply the opposite of losing," Brim says. "It creates its own disruptions." If a person becomes psychologically trapped by the need to do better, go higher, and make more, for example, he can end up operating at 90 to 100 percent of his capacity—a level at which stress makes life very uncomfortable. At this level, too, Brim says, he will begin to lose more than he wins. Burdened with more roles than he can handle, or promoted beyond the level of just-manageable difficulty, he may end up "held together by a thin paste of alcohol, saunas, and antibiotics." Brim says that because our society does not supply many ways to step down gracefully, it "pays the price in burnout and incompetence in high places."

Even those who can sustain Hollywood-style success must do some internal retooling in order to maintain the charge of the just-manageable mode. To keep life interesting, Brim says, the people who handle winning best don't merely raise the challenge in the same area but go into a new one—a sport, a hobby, a community project—where they again find a lot of room for moving up. "Certain professional athletes are good examples," he says. "Because they know that their peak will be short-lived, at a certain point they diversify their aspirations to include family, business interests, and volunteer activities."

So skilled are most people at maintaining a just-manageable life through the years that Brim finds no appreciable differences in the sense of well-being reported by different age groups. Indeed, he says, despite the insistent propaganda to the contrary, "except for concerns about health, most research shows that older people are as happy as younger ones."

Midlife Romance:
The Bloom Is Off the Rose

IF MIDDLE AGE IS SEEN AS A DULL BUSINESS, ITS RELAtionships are imagined to be the dreariest part. In the course of studying beliefs about and images of midlife, Margie Lachman compared the experiences of a group of Boston-area people aged eighteen to eighty-five, and found no evidence that the middle-aged are less loving. In fact, steady levels of intimacy and affection were two of the few constants she tracked. Largely because married people make up the majority of the middle-aged—about 75 percent—most of the data about life relationships concern them. Then too, less is known about other bonds because until the mid-seventies studies of midlife focused on the experience of white middle-class heterosexual men. Although there is still very little information about gay midlife, some data are emerging about how single people in general fare socially during middle age.

It's about time, according to Alice Rossi. "Considering the longer life-span, a person may be without a partner at many points in life," she points out. "We not only marry later today but often have intervals between relationships, and perhaps lengthy spells as widows and widowers." She thinks that the stereotype of the aging spinster who is unfulfilled without a man is heading into the realm of midlife mythology. "There's recent evidence that single women have better mental and physical health and social lives than single men," she says. "Rather than being all alone, they have friends and close family ties, not only with parents but also with young nieces and nephews, with whom they may enjoy special relationships."

As for the married, many studies show that satisfaction with the relationship is lower throughout the child-rearing years that it had been, but climbs again after couples weather the labor-intensive period of launching careers and babies. In Lachman's Boston survey, reports of stress related to marriage decreased steadily from youth through old age. Although divorce and death may account for some of that decline, she says, "people may in fact grow more skilled in handling their relationships." Observing that by midlife couples have fewer fights and more closeness, Ron Kessler says, "Once they get the little kids out of their hair, husbands and wives catch their breath, look at each other, and ask, 'What are we going to talk about now? What was it all about twenty years ago?'"

In his study of sexuality John McKinlay found that only two percent of the 1,700 middle aged and older men reported having more than one current sexual partner. This figure, vastly lower than the usual guesstimates, challenges the stereotype of the bored middle-aged philanderer. Moreover, although McKinlay recorded steady declines in the men's sexual activity, from lusty thoughts to erections, he found no decrease in their sexual satisfaction—a phenomenon Gilbert Brim calls "a triumph of the adaptation of aspirations to realities." Equivalent data about women have not been gathered, but McKinlay's findings complement other surveys that show that aging has little impact on people's enjoyment of sex.

People and their doctors, McKinlay says, should distinguish between sexual problems caused by aging and those caused by things that often get lumped with it, such as poor health, weight gain, lack of exercise, and the use of nicotine or too much alcohol. Compared with a healthy nonsmoking peer, for example, a smoker who has heart disease has a sevenfold greater risk of impotence.

Psychological fitness, too, plays a vital role. A man may think his primary problem is impotence caused by age when in fact his sexual trouble is a symptom of a very treatable depression. "We must not resort to biological reductionism, which is what women have been struggling against," McKinlay says.

Widely publicized conclusions drawn from the sex lives of the ill—that a vigorous sex life is not a reasonable expectation in middle age, for instance—may cast their pall on the well. "When I hear a healthy fifty-year-old man say, 'That sexy stuff is for kids,' I feel sorry for him," McKinlay says. "Only five percent of the women in our institute's long-term study of menopause reported suffering from vaginal dryness, but women are told it's a very common problem after a certain age." Contrary to the stereotype of the asexual older woman, he says, some women feel liberated by menopause and the end of birth control. If older women have a problem with their sex lives, according to McKinlay, it may be that their husbands aren't in good health. His prescription for a vital midlife: "If I were feeling troubled about aging, I'd look first at the behavioral modifications I could make—diet, exercise, alcohol-monitoring, and so on. If they didn't work, then I'd think about treatments."

Having edited a book about sexuality through the course of life, Alice Rossi observes that although the mature expression of eroticism remains poorly understood by science, let alone by our youth-oriented culture, middle-aged people are likely to expand their definition of sex to include sensual, not just reproductive, acts. "If the message we get from society is that we have to keep on acting as we did at thirty," she says, "a lot of us are going to feel that we have a sexual disorder at some point." After a certain age, for example, men in particular may require physical stimulation to feel aroused. An awareness of this normal tendency, Rossi says, added to modern women's generally greater assertiveness, lays the groundwork for a new kind of relationship for older couples—one in which women have a more active role. "If the middle-aged don't feel pressured to conform to a youthful stereotype," she says, "I think we can predict some good things for their sex lives."

The Empty Nest and the Sandwich Generation

WHEN THE ROLE OF FAMILY IN THE EXPERIENCE of middle age is mentioned, one of two scenarios usually comes to mind. In the better established, the abandoned mother waves a tearful good-bye to her last chick and dully goes through the motions of life in the "empty nest." According to Larry Bumpass's demographic survey, however, the nest may be anything but empty: expensive housing and a weak economy and job market mean that the young delay their own marriages and are likelier to return home after a brief foray outside.

The more contemporary midlife family myth concerns the plight of the "sandwich generation": in a recent *Doonesbury* cartoon starring a professional couple, the forty-something husband tells his wife, busy juggling the needs of her children and their grandmother, "Don't die. Everyone's counting on you." Women's entry into the job market has focused much attention on a purported host of adults who make the circuit from the day-care center to Gramps's place to the office with nary a moment for themselves. "It's true that there's a lot going on in your life in middle age and you have little time for leisure," Margie Lachman says. "Fortunately, you're also at your peak in terms of competence, control, the ability to handle stress, and sense of responsibility. You're *equipped* for overload." According to Carol Ryff, people busy with both careers and relationships enjoy not only greater financial security and intellectual and social stimulation but also a psychological benefit. The eminent behavioral scientist Bernice Neugarten thinks that the hallmark of healthy middle age is "complexity," or a feeling of being in control of a crowded life and involved in the world at the same time. Ryff found in the course of one of her studies that this quality was most marked among the first generation to combine family and career. "It seems," she says, "that all the role-juggling that middle-aged people complain about actually makes them feel more engaged in life."

Rossi is dubious that the sandwich-generation problem is either new or widespread. "This phenomenon is a lot like the supposed midlife crisis," she says. "There are people who think that spending two hours a week with Mother is a big deal. But the fact is that very few men or women are caring both for little children and for elderly parents." One reason for this is that the "old old" who need considerable care are still a small group, and few of them are a daily drain on their children. Then, too, as Bumpass says, "over the past several decades the elderly have increasingly lived independently. They're economically more able to do so, and both sides prefer things that way." According to research conducted by Glenna Spitze, of the State University of New York at Albany, close involvement by the middle-aged with their parents—usually with a mother who has already cared for and buried her own husband—is likeliest to occur when the middle-aged person's children are older and need less attention. "For that matter," Rossi says, "rather than being a drain, the children are likely to be a comfort and help. It's important to remember that intimacy with children, which bottoms out from ages fifteen to nineteen, climbs steeply through the twenties and thirties. One of the things to look forward to in midlife is the continuity and shared interests that will come as your children in turn become parents."

To the list of underestimated family pleasures Ryff adds the satisfaction that parents take in knowing that grown-up children have turned out all right. She found that adult offspring are a vital if underrecognized element in middle-aged well-being, and that adjusting to how well or poorly they have matured is another of midlife's important developmental tasks. After studying 215 parents, Ryff found that their adult children's level of psychological adjustment was a major predictor for almost all aspects of both fathers' and mothers' mental health—although mothers took more credit for it. "The literature on parenting includes very little on what *parents* get out of it," she says, "or on how it affects their self-image, especially when the kids are older. Parenting never ends."

At Last, the Reward: Wisdom

LONG ON THE PROCESS OF BECOMING, THE LITERature of human development remains short on the business of being. That adults don't grow and change in the predictable, simultaneously physiological and behavioral fashion that children do partly explains why. So tidy is early development by comparison that it's even possible to link certain ages to certain behavioral stages, such as the "terrible twos" and the "temperamental teens." Although Gail Sheehy's bestseller *Passages* (described by Gilbert Brim as focused on "selected case studies that illustrate a theory that has no broad empirical support") advanced an adult model of such "age-stage" development, research continues to show that the ways in which adults evolve are not universal, not likely to occur in clear-cut stages, and not tied to particular ages. So poorly do the middle-aged fit into developmental patterns, in fact, that the huge National Survey of Families and Households revealed that of more than forty projected "typical midlife events," none was likely to happen at a certain, predictable age.

Biologically oriented behavioral scientists argue that at the individual level certain basic tendencies evident at birth or shortly after are the immutable building blocks of personality. The aversion to novel stimuli which becomes shyness, denoted by a low score in extroversion, is one such element. Some claim, moreover, that anyone can be defined even in early childhood in terms of how high or low he or she scores in tests that measure the "big five"

Most middle-aged adults benefit from knocking about in the world. When they go down a blind alley, they soon recognize the mistake, and save themselves much time and energy.

traits: neuroticism, extroversion, openness, agreeableness, and conscientiousness. This largely biological programming, trait theorists believe, means that personality is set in concrete around the time that physical development ceases. Afterward one may grow in terms of changing attitudes, skills, interests, and relationships, but only in ways consistent with one's big-five template.

Environment-minded researchers, including the MID-MAC team, take the influence of things like attitudes, interests, and relationships more seriously. They're working on a different, flexible model of adult development, based not on genes but on experience. Brim and his colleagues don't dispute that someone born shy or dutiful may very well stay that way, but they stress that whether he or she is raised in a sociable or a reclusive family, has a happy or an unhappy marriage, gets an exciting or a dull job, and has good or poor health will have considerable impact on identity. Bringing up reports of "aberrant outcomes"—people who early in life seem destined for success or failure yet somehow turn out the other way—Brim observes that adult change is shaped not just by the characteristics a person brings to bear on life but also by what life brings to bear on him or her, from family feuds to fatal attractions, religious experiences to traffic accidents. Accordingly, the MIDMAC group and others interested in tracking adult development focus on the ways in which, as a result of the depth and variety of their experience, their subjects' goals and values alter over time.

To illustrate experiential midlife development, Ron Kessler points to ways in which people are shaped by the influence of the workplace. "During early life you're socially segregated—all your school companions are also eight- or twelve-year-olds from the same neighborhood," he says. "Then comes adulthood, and suddenly you're working alongside different kinds of people of different ages. You can look around and say to yourself, 'In twenty years, if I act like him, I could have a heart attack, or end up divorced.' Or 'Sure, she makes a lot of money, but do I really want to work sixty hours a week?'"

Most middle-aged adults benefit from knocking about in the world, a process that greatly increases their efficiency in managing life. When they go down a blind alley, they soon recognize the mistake, and save themselves much time and energy. "Because they have all this material to plot trajectories with, the middle-aged are equipped to do an enormous amount of internal reshuffling," Kessler says. "Unlike younger people, they don't have to test everything themselves in the real world. Adults who learn from their mistakes change and grow, and those who don't, don't." Kessler describes a bright corporate lawyer who remains developmentally stalled in the "becoming" phase appropriate to youth: "He goes around saying '*This* is being a lawyer? I'd rather be a kid *wanting* to be a lawyer.'"

Perhaps the best refutation of the myths that adults don't develop and that adults do develop but only in rigid stages is a new body of research on the genesis of a psychological and cognitive capacity that scientists can only call wisdom. As is often the case in science, this inquiry began with the investigation of a mistaken premise. Assuming that the formalistic SAT-type process was the human norm in solving problems, those studying the effects of aging concluded that older people suffer a cognitive deficit, because they do worse than the young on such tests. The more researchers explored this apparently biological decline, however, the more they had to consider another possibility: people of different ages may perceive the same problem differently.

Any adult who has debated with a bright adolescent about, say, the likelihood that the world's nations will erase their boundaries and create a passportless global citizenry knows that there are two types of intelligence: the abstract, objective, Platonic-dualism sort that peaks early, and the practical, subjective type, born of shirtsleeves experience, which comes later. When asked the way to Rome, the young trace the most direct route very quickly, while their elders ponder: "Why Rome? Is this trip really a good idea? At what time of year? For business or pleasure? Alone or with others?"

The pre-eminent wisdom researcher is Paul Baltes, a MIDMAC fellow and a co-director of the Max Planck Institute for Human Development and Education, in Berlin. Baltes conducts studies of "whether living long can produce a higher level of mental functioning." The cognitive mechanics of the brain—the speed and accuracy with which we process information—are biological and subject to decline, he finds. But the brain's pragmatics—our knowledge and skill in using information—are not. When Baltes's subjects take the intellectual equivalent of a medical stress test, the young do in two seconds what the older do, with many more mistakes, in eight. But, Baltes says, unlike other species, ours can compensate for biological deficits. "If people have hearing problems, society develops hearing aids, and if I train an older subject in test-taking skills, he'll outperform an untutored younger person. By providing knowledge and strategies for using it, culture outwits biology. In all the areas of functioning in which age means more access to information, older people may be better off than young ones." In short, the middle-aged may be slower but they're smarter.

Beyond the commonsensical savvy acquired through daily experience lies a rarefied ability to deal with the fundamental problems of the human condition: matters ambiguous and existential, complex and conflicted, which call for the wisdom of Solomon. Using literary analysis, Baltes finds evidence in all cultures of people equipped to deal with these difficult issues, and he has devised several ways to test for the presence of this ability. In one type of study, subjects read vignettes of difficult situations—for example, a person pondering how to respond to a friend who has decided to commit suicide—and then "think aloud" through their decision-making process to a resolution of the problem. In another type, people with many contacts in the world of high achievers are asked to nominate those they consider especially wise; researchers then monitor how these candidates think about difficult problems. Both forms of testing allow Baltes to score subjects on his "wisdom criteria," which include great factual and procedural knowledge, the capacity to cope with uncertainty, and the ability to frame an event in its larger context. "Those who have these attributes are the people we call wise," he says, "and they are easily recognized. People who are said to have this quality do score higher than others."

To sense the difference between the wise and the hoi polloi, one might imagine a successful fifty-year-old urban lawyer who announces that she is going to quit her job, move to the country, and start a mail-order seed and bulb business. Most listeners will think, if not say, something like "What a crazy idea." But there might be someone who says, "Wait. What are the circumstances? Maybe this lawyer feels that her life has grown sterile. Maybe she has some solid plans for this change. Let's talk some more." According to Baltes's statistics, this wise person is probably neither young nor very old but somewhere between the ages of forty and seventy. "The highest grades we record occur somewhere around sixty," he says. "Wisdom peaks in midlife or later."

While intelligence is essential to wisdom, certain personal qualities predict with greater accuracy who will be wise. Thoreau observed, "It is a characteristic of wisdom not to do desperate things," and Baltes agrees. "Modulation and balance are crucial elements," he says, "because wisdom has no extremes. You can't be passionate or dogmatic and wise at the same time." Just as the Lao-tzus and Lincolns among us are likely to be reasonable and open-minded, they are not likely to be motivated by selfish concerns, at least not markedly so: Machiavelli was clever but not wise.

"At some point in middle age," says David Featherman, of the Social Science Research Council, "we're inclined to become more tolerant of the uncertain, the complex, and the impossible, and even to learn to dismiss some problems as unsolvable or not worth our effort. Perhaps most important, we grow more interested in how our solutions affect others. Along with being good at figuring out what to do in real-life situations themselves, the wise are skilled in advising others—in sharing their wisdom. Unfortunately, Americans' Lone Ranger mentality about solving everything on our own means we don't always profit from this resource." The concern for others that is a hallmark of wisdom seems to augur well for those who have it as well as for its beneficiaries. The evolutionary neurobiologist Paul D. MacLean once observed, "We become nicer mammals as we age." Featherman points out that the benignity integral to wisdom seems characteristic of people who enjoy a happy, healthy old age.

In a youth-obsessed culture the suggestion that at least one element of character emerges only in middle age is both appealing and iconoclastic. "Wisdom doesn't happen at the age of six, or eighteen," Featherman says. "It may take a long time for all of its components to be in place. The timing of its emergence means that in maturity we get a new start—a new way of understanding life that's more apt to benefit others. It may turn out that caring about people is the capstone of the process of living."

Learning to *Love* (GULP!) Growing *Old*

Fear of aging speeds the very decline we dread most. And it ultimately robs our life of any meaning. No wonder there's an attitude shift in the making.

Jere Daniel

Jere Daniel is a free-lance writer specializing in health and human behavior. His articles have appeared in publications as diverse as The New York Times Magazine, American Health, and Family Circle. He has pioneered corporate communications on health and produced a newsletter for America's leading companies. He is also the author of numerous television and radio scripts. He resides in Brooklyn Heights, New York.

Technically, they are all still baby boomers. But on the cusp of 50, much to their surprise, having come late into maturity, they can suddenly envision themselves becoming obsolete, just as their fathers, mothers, grandparents, uncles, and aunts did when they crossed the age-65 barrier, the moment society now defines as the border line between maturity and old age.

Although they may be unprepared psychologically, they are certainly fortified demographically to notice the problems their elders now face—isolation, loneliness, lack of respect, and above all, virtual disenfranchisement from the society they built. The number of people reaching the increasingly mythic retirement age of 65 has zoomed from about seven and a half million in the 1930s (when Social Security legislation decreed 65 as the age of obsolescence) to 34 million today. By the turn of the century, that figure will be 61.4 million.

If the boomers' luck holds out, they will be spared what amounts to the psychological torture of uselessness and burdensomeness that every graying generation this century has faced before them. For there is an attitude shift in the wind. In an irony that boomers will no doubt appreciate (as

rebellion is an act usually reserved for the young), a revolution in attitude about age is coming largely from a corner of the population that has traditionally been content to enjoy the status quo—a cultural elite whose median age is surely over 65.

A small but growing gaggle of experts (themselves mostly elders)—a diverse lot of gerontologists, physicians, psychologists, sociologists, anthropologists, philosophers, ethicists, cultural observers, and spiritual leaders—are the vanguard of a movement to change the way society looks at and deals with growing old. They seek to have us stop viewing old age as a problem—as an incurable disease, if you will—to be "solved" by spending billions of dollars on plastic surgery in an attempt to mask visible signs of aging, other billions on medical research to extend the life span itself,

❝We pretend that old age can be turned into an endless middle age, thereby giving people a false road map to the future.❞

and billions more on nursing and retirement homes as a way to isolate those who fail at the quest to deny aging.

Separately and together, this cultural elite is exploring ways to move us and our social institutions toward a new concept of aging, one they call "conscious aging." They want us to be aware of and accept what aging actually is—a notice that life has not only a beginning and a middle but an end—and to eliminate the denial that now prevents us from anticipating, fruitfully using, and even appreciating what are lost to euphemism as "the golden years."

"Conscious aging is a new way of looking at and experiencing aging that moves beyond our cultural obsession with youth toward a respect and need for the wisdom of age," explains Stephan Rechtschaffen, M.D., a holistic physician who directs the Omega Institute, a kind of New Age think tank that is a driving force in this attitude shift. He would have us:

• Recognize and accept the aging process and all that goes with it as a reality, a natural part of the life cycle; it happens to us all. The goal is to change the prevailing view of aging as something to be feared and the aged as worthless.

• Reverse our societal attitude of aging as an affliction, and instead of spending billions on walling off the aging, spend more to improve the quality of life among the aged.

Our denial of aging has its costs. Rechtschaffen is adamant that it is not merely our elders who suffer. Quoting the late psychoanalyst Erik Erikson, he says, "Lacking a culturally viable ideal of old age, our civilization does not really harbor a concept of the whole of life."

We now live, and die, psychologically and spiritually incomplete. It may be a troubling sense of incompleteness that most stirs an appreciation for age among the baby boomers, so unfamiliar is any sense of incompleteness to the generation that invented the possibility of and has prided itself on "having it all."

Next month, a group of these thinkers will gather at an open-to-the-public conference under the auspices of the Omega Institute. Participants range from Sherwin Nuland, M.D., surgeon-author of the surprise best-seller *How We Die*, to Betty Friedan, who has dissected American attitudes toward aging in her latest book, *Fountain of Youth*, to spiritualist Ram Dass, Columbia University gerontologist Renee Solomon, Ph.D., and Dean Ornish, M.D., director of the University of California's Preventive Medicine Research Institute.

Until now, the conventional wisdom has been that only the aged, or those approaching its border, worry about its consequences: rejection, isolation, loneliness, and mandated obsolescence. Only they care about how they can give purpose to this final stage of their lives.

Sherwin Nuland has clear new evidence to the contrary. His book, *How We Die*, paints a shimmeringly lucid and remarkably unsentimental picture of death—the process and its meaning to the dying and to those around them. The biggest group of readers of this best-seller? Not the elderly, as most observers, and even the author himself, had anticipated. It's the baby boomers. Curiosity about age and death is booming among the boomers.

"The baby boomers, who started out rejecting the wisdom and experience of anyone over 30, are buying my book in droves," Nuland told *Psychology Today*. "To young people, death is an abstract concept. But face-to-face with aging parents and illnesses like cancer and strokes among themselves, newly graying baby boomers stare into their own mortality totally unprepared. Now this best-educated of all our generations wants information and doesn't want to turn away from what it's been trying to escape—the effects of getting old."

We fear and deny aging, the Omega experts emphasize, because we fear and deny death. "In our denial of death and the aging of the body, we have rejected the wisdom of the aged, and in doing so have robbed old age of its meaning and youth of its direction," Rechtschaffen asserts. We pretend that old age can be turned into a kind of endless middle age, thereby giving young people a false road map to the future, one that does not show them how to plan for their whole life, gain insight into themselves, or to develop spiritually.

The signs of denial and anxiety over aging permeate every aspect of our lives. We have no role models for growing old gracefully, only for postponing it. For example:

• The vast dependence on plastic surgery specifically to hide the visual signs of aging is arguably the sharpest index of our anxiety. In just two decades, from the 1960s to the 1980s, the number of rhytidectomies, wrinkle-removing face-lifts, rose from 60,000 to an estimated 2 million a year at an annual cost of $10 billion.

• The negative view of aging is disastrously reinforced by the media. Articles and advertising never show a mature model, even in displaying fashions designed for women over 50. A *Newsweek* cover of a sweating, gray-haired young man bears the cover line, "Oh God…I'm really turning 50." Nursing home ads ask: "What shall we do about Mother?" By some sleight of mind, we not only come to accept these images, we come to expect them as truths.

We denigrate aging, Friedan persuasively notes, by universally equating it with second childhood, "so negatively stereotyped that getting old has become something to dread and feel threatened by." A series of studies by psychologists Ellen Langer, Ph.D. of Harvard and University of Pennsylvania President Judith Rodin, Ph.D. (then at Yale) suggests how we grow to revile our aging selves.

Influenced by the fairy tales we hear as children, and what we see on television and hear in everyday life, we develop negative stereotypes about aging by the time we are six years old, the same age we develop negative stereotypes about race and sex. These stereotypes persist as we grow up, completely unaware that we even acquired them or granted them our unconditional acceptance. With our understanding of the subject forever frozen, we grow into old age assuming the stereotypes to be true. And we live down to them.

If there is a single myth about aging that most symbolizes our dread, it is the assumption that our memory will inevitably decline in old age. In a stunning new study, psychologist Langer has demonstrated that it is our own psychology—the near-universal expectation of memory loss—that actually brings that fate upon us. The lesson to be learned is an extraordinary one: Fear of aging is the single most powerful agent creating exactly what we fear.

The negative stereotypes acquired in childhood parade across the adult life span as expectations. As people age, Langer finds, low expectations lead to "decreased effort, less use of adaptive strategies, avoidance of challenging situations, and failure to seek medical attention for disease-related symptoms."

In her newest study, Langer and Harvard colleague Rebecca Levy, Ph.D., confirm the effect of these negative stereotypes on aging Americans. Using standard psychological measurements of memory, the researchers studied two populations of people who hold their elders in high esteem—elderly mainland Chinese and older, deaf Americans—and compared them to a group of elderly mainstream Americans. In addition, the researchers compared memory retention in the elderly with younger people in all three groups.

Not only did the mainland Chinese and American deaf far outperform the mainstream Americans on four psychological memory tests, but the oldest in these two groups, especially the Chinese, performed almost as well as the youngest. Their performance was so strong even the researchers were surprised. They conclude that the results can be explained entirely by the fact that the Chinese have the most positive, active, and "internal" image of aging across the three cultures studied.

What is particularly striking about the Langer–Levy study is that it meticulously tracks how our fears, which are so culturally constructed, become self-fulfilling prophecies. "The social, psychological component of memory retention may be even stronger than we believed."

Just as our fear of memory loss can create actual memory decline, the dread of aging may be taking its toll on many other body systems.

The current collective view of aging is so relentlessly negative that neither our social institutions nor the aging themselves believe what worldwide research points to—that those of us alive today may be aging better than our parents.

A landmark, 15-year longitudinal study of older people, begun in 1970 by Alvar Svanborg in the industrial city of Gothenburg, Sweden, showed no measur-

able decline in many body functions until after age 70, and very little decline by 81. Cognitive abilities were intact to at least age 75, and still intact in almost all who had reached 81, although speed at rote memory declined. "The vitality of old people in Sweden today, among the longest-lived people in the world, seems to be greater than it was only five or 10 years ago," Svanborg asserts.

American studies of healthy people aging in their own communities, as opposed to those shunted off to institutions, failed to show evidence of decline in intelligence, cognitive skills, and even memory that had appeared in all previous cross-sectional studies of aging. The combined thrust of the studies of "normal aging" is inescapable. Physical and mental decline is not inevitable. Belief that it is accelerates whatever decline occurs.

Still, we continue to mythologize and denigrate aging because we devalue death itself. "We refuse even to admit that we die of old age," says Nuland, a retired Yale surgeon, whose book embodies the proposition that death is a normal stage in the life cycle. This refusal is perpetuated by the medical profession and the law. "I cannot write 'Old Age' on a death certificate even though people over 70 die because they're over 70," he says.

"An octogenarian who dies of myocardial infarction is not simply a weather-beaten senior citizen with heart disease—he is the victim of an insidious progression that involves all of him, and that progression is called aging," Nuland says. He deplores the prevailing view of aging as a disease that can be cured and the biomedical search for a fountain of youth.

"Though biomedical science has vastly increased mankind's average life expectancy (78.6 years for American women, 71.6 for men), the maximum (114 years) has not changed in verifiable recorded history. Even the home-cultured yogurt of the Caucasus cannot vanquish nature," Nuland says. "Trying to add a few more years to the human life span is meaningless and wasteful."

The promise of an extended life span simply adds unnecessary stress to the ability to accept aging. "An extended life span without extended awareness of the possibilities of a productive old age means we aren't sure we're living longer. Maybe we're just dying longer," says Rabbi Zalman Schachter-Shalomi, founder of a pioneering Spiritual Eldering Project at Philadelphia's B'nai Or Religious Fellowship. Schachter-Shalomi is the recipient of

the first annual Conscious Aging Award by the Omega Institute. In place of fear of death we'd be better off with a belief in the possibilities of life, as long as it is lived.

"If age itself is defined as a 'problem,' then those over 65 who can no longer 'pass' as young are its carriers and must be quarantined lest they contaminate, in mind or body, the rest of society," Friedan asserts. So we banish the elderly from our midst and wall them off in nursing homes. We encourage them to isolate themselves in retirement homes and communities, in San Diego condos and Miami Beach hotels.

But isolating ourselves into ageist groups only sets the stage for a class warfare that is bound to get louder and more violent. Younger generations grow to resent the older, and vice versa. And so, says Nuland, the elderly grow demanding and greedy for health and custodial care while the rest of the population bemoans the financial drain the aged make on society, all the while feeling guilty for the situation.

With the old now successfully segregated out, Americans are in no position to exploit the benefits of age—or even to recognize or acknowledge that there are any. Which brings us to the special brand of intelligence called wisdom.

Sure, we have our "elder" statesmen, but the titles are honorary, often conferred with an underlying tinge of humor. They signify reverence for past accomplishments more than real respect for the wisdom that only elders have to contribute. Wisdom remains a very special commodity, a great natural resource that is undervalued—and almost totally untapped in doing what it's meant for: guiding the young. And there's only one way to get it.

It is not easy to talk about wisdom without lapsing into platitudes and vagueness, so a team of European researchers—no surprise there—has taken on the challenge to isolate the features of wisdom in clinical detail. From their ongoing studies of the aging mind, psychologists Paul B. Baltes and Ursula M. Staudinger, both of the Max Planck Institute for Human Development in Berlin, define wisdom:

• It's an expertise that wraps information in the human context of life and relates it to generational and historical flow.

• It is factual and procedural knowledge about the world and human affairs.

• It mingles insight and judgment involving complex and uncertain matters of the human condition; there is an appreciation for and understanding of the uncertainties of life.

• It involves a fine-tuned coordination of cognition, motivation, and emotion, knowledge about the self and other people and society.

• It carries knowledge about strategies to manage the peaks and valleys of life.

• It integrates past, present, and future.

A product of cultural and knowledge-based factors, rather than biologically based mechanics of the mind, wisdom accumulates with time—but only among those who remain open to new experiences. If we must insist on outwitting the constraints of biology, then wisdom—and not the scalpel—is our thing.

It may be that we ignore wisdom because, especially over the lifetime of the boomers, we have come to overvalue, say, rocket science. The technological advancement of modern society has bred in us an infatuation with the data we have accumulated. "We've traded information for wisdom," Rechtschaffen offers.

We have confounded the accumulation of data with its application, or even an understanding of it. Wisdom, on the other hand, always puts information back in the context of human life.

Sherwin Nuland is a man forced by the exigencies of his profession to look time squarely in the eye. Old age, he says, is a "time to become contemplative, to recognize our value to people younger than ourselves." Now in his sixties, Nuland stopped operating when "I realized I was no longer as nimble as a 45-year-old. But I expect to continue contributing my knowledge and experience as long as possible." Unfortunately, he says, "the younger generation doesn't always accept it, from me or others. They see their elders as crotchety and selfish, their maturity and wisdom of no use—outdated. Age warfare continues."

Perhaps we don't recognize the wisdom of aging because our anxiety about the future—of the world, of ourselves—has overwhelmed our respect for history. We live, Rechtschaffen says, with only a linear sense of time. We push inexorably toward the future; the past is nothing. In other eras, we lived by a more circular sense of time, which allowed for a father's, even a grandfather's, experience to guide us. There was an intuitive apprehension—wisdom, if you will—that the way to deal with the future rests in an understanding of the past. Even today, many indigenous tribal societies and Eastern cultures live by a circular sense of time.

The baby boomers have made it successfully, albeit noisily, through the first two-thirds of their lives, having rejected—indeed defying—the teachings of their elders. But the prospect of making it through the next third satisfied with their accomplishments and their selves requires they find inner meaning in their lives.

To give their lives purpose, they might turn from what Nuland calls "the hurly-burly of getting and spending" to a more contemplative life. And they might pay more attention to those who have already crossed the border into old age, to value their experience; to embrace their elders is to embrace their future selves. Perhaps, most of all, they might begin to think of their own death. After all, to be fully alive includes being fully aware of dying.

So long as we lock ourselves into an obsession with the youth culture, we can only develop age rage and dehumanize ourselves, says Betty Friedan. Those who give up their denial of age, who age consciously, "grow and become aware of new capacities they develop while aging....[They] become more authentically themselves."

Unlocking the Secrets of Aging

Scientists are deciphering genetic codes they say will lead to keeping people alive much longer. But the social and ethical implications of sharing the Fountain of Youth are impossible to ignore.

Sheryl Stolberg

Times Medical Writer

In his laboratory at the University of Colorado, molecular biologist Thomas Johnson is studying a translucent worm no bigger than a printed comma. In this simple animal, composed of just 959 cells, Johnson believes he may find the answers to complex questions that have eluded scientists for centuries:

What makes us grow old? Can we stop aging, or at least slow it down?

By breeding tens of thousands of these nematodes, Johnson has created a strain that can live for about five weeks—about 70% longer than the worm's average three-week life span. It appears that the difference between the elderly worms and their shorter-lived counterparts lies in a single gene. Now, Johnson is trying to isolate that gene, and he says he is close.

And if genes can be manipulated to extend the lives of worms, the 48-year-old researcher asks, might not the same be true of people?

"Maybe there are major genes in humans that, if we alter [them], we could project a longer human life span," Johnson said. "This would be an absolutely tremendous sociological finding. It would affect . . . every aspect of the way we live our lives if we all of a sudden had average life spans of 120 years instead of 70 years."

Tremendous indeed. Johnson's work is on the cutting edge of a fascinating scientific sojourn, a modern-day quest for the legendary Fountain of Youth. He is among a growing corps of 2,000 molecular biologists, geneticists, immunologists and other researchers across the United States who are trying to unlock the secrets of aging.

They are tinkering with genes, human growth hormones and new drugs, and with strategies of diet, nutrition and exercise. They are studying patterns of survival in worms, fruit flies, mice and people. They are examining the links between aging and illness—cancer, Alzheimer's, Parkinson's, osteoporosis, heart disease, stroke—as well as the effect of environment on aging.

Their strides in recent years have been so significant that a startling new body of thought has emerged, one that says humans may one day live much longer than anyone dreamed possible. Some go so far as to say that the maximum life span, now at 120 years, and average life expectancy, about 75 years in the United States, could double or triple.

"The ideal of all our work is that sometime in the future, we would take pills that would slow or postpone our aging," said UC Irvine biologist Michael Rose, who is breeding fruit flies that can live up to three times as long as the average fly. "That's the ultimate goal, the man on the moon for all this research. We're not going to have that in five years. But someday it will happen."

Michal Jazwinski, a Louisiana State University biologist who has isolated "longevity assurance genes" in yeast, said. "In the next 30 to 50 years, we will in fact have in hand many of the major genes that determine longevity in humans. What we have been able to see with our yeast is a doubling of the life span. So that could be something that we might aim for in the future."

Scientists are pondering the social and ethical implications of their work. They raise a litany of questions: If the research is successful, what would happen to the nation's overburdened health care and Social Security systems? Would the work force be so crowded with elderly people who have postponed retirement that young people will not be able to find jobs? Would a population boom cause a housing crunch? What would be the effect on our fragile environment?

And, perhaps most important, will living longer also mean living healthier?

"If we are able to produce 150-year-old people but those 150-year-old people spend the last 40 years of their life in a nursing home, we would have created a disaster," said Dr. Richard Sprott, a top official at the National Institute on Aging. "The big public worry is that by increasing the number of people who make it [to advanced ages] we will produce this huge increase in the amount of disease."

In some respects, that is occurring. As the population has grown older, the incidence of age-related diseases such as Alzheimer's and osteoporosis has skyrocketed. The Alliance for Aging Research estimates that it costs the nation $90-billion a year to treat people with Alzheimer's, which affects at least 2 million and possibly 4 million Americans. As these costs continue to rise, experts say, society has a vested interest in finding ways to keep older people healthier.

What we have to do as a society is come to the realization of how much money is going into the medical care of the elderly," said Raymond Daynes, a cellular immunologist at the University of Utah. "We are becoming incredibly sophisticated in preventing individuals who have some acute, devastating illnesses from dying. But we are way behind in providing preventive measures so that [illness] doesn't happen in the first place."

Life expectancy in the United States has increased dramatically since 1900, from 47.3 years to 75.4 years. The greatest gains occurred during the first half of this century, largely because of dramatic reductions in infant mortality and infectious diseases. More recently, as

Daynes notes, smaller gains have resulted from progress against major fatal illnesses, such as heart disease, cancer and stroke.

Improvements in sanitation and living conditions have also made a big difference, and are likely to continue to do so, said James R. Carey, a medical demographer at UC Davis whose recent work with fruit flies has been cited as evidence that there is no arbitrary cap on human life span.

"The people that are 100 years old today were born in 1892," Carey said. "Think about all the things they went through, in terms of lack of medicine and nutrition. They were working hard to make it to 100. Now think about a newborn of today, with the emphasis on nutrition and exercise and medical advances. I would bet that we are going to find 125-, 130-year-olds by the 22nd Century just because of these changes in conditions."

Whether the pace proceeds more quickly than Carey suggests will depend on the outcome of the research being conducted in laboratories today—particularly in the area of genetics, scientists say. Few researchers, however, are willing to make predictions about how soon a breakthrough might come.

Yet as demographic shifts create an older society, and as scientific advances continue, the study of gerontology is enjoying an unprecedented boom. Once suspiciously regarded as the province of charlatans and snake-oil salesmen, longevity research is gaining attention and respect. Now, top-flight scientists are flocking to a field that, as little as five years ago, failed to draw the best and the brightest.

"Aging," said Daynes, "is finally coming of age."

This trend is reflected in funding: The federal government's National Institute on Aging is among the fastest-growing branches of the National Institutes of Health, with a budget that has nearly doubled in the past three years—from $222 million in 1989 to $402 million this year.

However, the budget is still small compared to that of some other arms of NIH—the National Cancer Institute has an annual budget of nearly $2 billion.

Much of the growth in aging research has been fueled by intense interest in Alzheimer's and other age-related diseases. The media have lavished much attention on the subject, particularly since a highly publicized 1990 study in which doses of a synthetic form of human growth hormone were reported to restore youthful vigor to elderly people.

Within the past decade new technologies—such as the ability to conduct transgenic experiments, in which a gene can be transferred from one organism into another—have become available to biologists, making possible certain types of gene research that used to be unthinkable.

"For the last 20 years, a lot of the research has been simply trying to characterize aging in a descriptive way," said Huber Warner, deputy associate director of the NIA's Biology of Aging program. "Now people are beginning to find out what the mechanisms of the aging process are so that they can then try to develop interventions that will slow the process down or prevent it altogether."

Judith Campisi is among those whose work is funded by the National Institute on Aging. At UC's Lawrence Berkeley Laboratory she is studying cellular senescence, the process by which cells keep dividing until they grow old and die. When she entered the field five years ago, she said, science had barely begun to examine the basic mechanisms that control aging.

"Before," she said, "nobody quite knew how to ask critical questions about aging. That has changed dramatically in the past five years. The field has now reached a level of maturity where . . . we are beginning to see a path to at least dream about approaching some answers. Until recently, that dream was not a very viable one."

The answers remain elusive. Aging is an extraordinarily complex puzzle—affected by genetics and the environment and individual habits, such as cigarette smoking and diet and exercise—and Campisi said she and her compatriots each hold only one small piece of it. "We all need each other terribly," she said.

Research is proceeding on many different—albeit interwoven—fronts:

At Bemidji State University in Minnesota, biochemist Gary W. Evans recently reported that dietary supplements of the metal chromium can extend the life span of rats by one-third, and may do the same for humans. At USC, noted gerontologist Caleb Finch is exploring new terrain with his studies on how aging affects the brain.

In Irvine, biologist Rose is breeding red-eyed fruit flies that can live 80 days—double the life span of an average fly—by mating selected flies that are able to reproduce late in life. Rose theorizes that these elderly flies, some of which live six months, are passing longevity genes to their offspring. But a key question remains: Which genes are responsible?

At the University of Colorado, Johnson, the biochemist who is breeding round worms, is taking a slightly different tack. He is mating long-lived nematodes with short-lived ones in an effort to follow the worms' DNA trails. Through a process by which he marks the DNA of the elderly worms, Johnson can see which genetic patterns reappear in the offspring. He has narrowed his search for a "longevity assurance gene" down to a 50-gene region of a single, 3,000-gene chromosome.

In Kentucky, pharmacologist John Carney has learned that when a synthetic compound known as PBN—phenyl butyl nitrone—is injected into gerbils, certain proteins in the brain that deteriorate with age are restored, resulting in improved short-term memory for the animals.

PBN works by combatting the effects of "free radicals"—damaging oxygen byproducts that occur natu-

rally in the body, destroying fats and proteins that are crucial to the way cells function. In certain diseases such as Alzheimer's and Parkinson's, researchers believe, these free radicals run amok.

In addition, scientists at the National Institute on Aging say they have evidence that free radicals speed the aging process. The theory is that if free radicals can be controlled, so too can aging. Researchers are also exploring the effects of "dietary antioxidants"—foods and vitamins including Vitamins C and E, and beta-carotene, a compound that turns into Vitamin A in the body—that may help combat free radicals.

Soon, Carney hopes, PBN will be tried in humans. He and his partner, a biochemist at the University of Oklahoma, have set up a pharmaceutical company to manufacture the drug and are hoping to gain government approval for testing within the next two years.

While Carney studies how a synthetic drug might slow the aging of the brain, Dr. Daniel Rudman of the Veterans Administration Medical Center in Milwaukee has spent the past five years examining how human growth hormones, which occur naturally in the body but decline in secretions as people grow older, affect aging.

Rudman has administered a synthetic form of the hormones to 42 men, ages 60 to 90, and the results have been nothing short of dramatic. Some signs of old age—the shrinking of certain organs, such as the spleen and liver, and the increase of fatty tissue in the body—were reversed by the hormones. After a few months of therapy, Rudman said, 70-year-old men looked as though they were 55.

But a growth hormone is not a cure-all. Given in doses that are too large, it can cause carpal tunnel syndrome, a repetitive stress disorder that commonly affects the wrists of computer users, breast enlargement and a rise in blood sugar. Moreover, it failed to curb other factors associated with aging, such as memory loss and softening of bones. "This,"

Rudman said, "is by no means a total reversal of the aging process."

Another promising hormone is DHEA, a steroid whose natural secretions decline with age. At the University of Utah, immunologist Daynes has discovered that when laboratory mice are given small amounts of DHEA-Sulfate—a water-soluble form of the hormone that had been thought to be irrelevant to the functioning of the body—their immune systems work better and their skin looks more youthful.

Over the long term, Daynes hopes that the hormone might be used as a sort of vitamin for the elderly. "I believe that over the next few years, we are going to prove beyond a shadow of a doubt that some of the physiological changes which are used to define old age are totally preventable," he said. "They don't have to happen."

In the Arizona desert, meanwhile, UCLA Prof. Roy Walford is trying to delay the onset of old age through his diet.

Walford and seven other scientists who are living in a glass-enclosed three-acre greenhouse known as Biosphere II are engaged in the first human version of a well-known study in which Walford found that a severely restricted, low-calorie diet could double the life expectancy of rats and mice.

Now, Walford and the other biospherians are subsisting on 1,800 calories per day, compared to the usual 2,500. According to Walford, the group eats only what is grown in the dome—grains, vegetables, fruit and one serving of meat per week.

According to the 68-year-old Walford, who has been following the diet for more than five years, the group is exhibiting the same changes as the rodents. Each has dropped an average of 14% in body weight since the experiment began 13 months ago. Their cholesterol is lower—an average of 130, down from 200—and their blood sugar has declined.

"This is the first well-monitored human application of the idea," Walford said, "and it indicates that humans respond the same as animals."

But be it gene manipulation, hormones, drugs or nutrition, researchers agree that if their work proves anything, it is that there is no Fountain of Youth, no single elixir that has the power to stop or even slow the aging process.

Instead, they say, advances that come in disparate arenas will over time be put together to create a greater understanding of the aging process. And only when the age-old mystery of aging is unraveled will scientists figure out ways to stop it, or slow it down.

"There is no silver bullet," said Edward Schneider, dean of USC's Andrus Center of Gerontology. Instead, Schneider likens the state of aging research to the decades-old search for a cure for cancer.

"Picture cancer research 30 years ago," he said. "People thought it's simple, we'll give one drug and it will cure all cancer. Well, it didn't work. In the next 10 or 20 years we'll have specific therapies for specific cancers, because cancer is a complex process.

"Imagine cancer being a 1,000-piece puzzle and we have a third of the pieces. Aging is a 100,000-piece puzzle, and we maybe have a tenth of the pieces."

Grandparent Development and Influence

Robert Strom and Shirley Strom

Robert Strom is Professor of Lifespan Developmental Psychology, Division of Psychology in Education, Arizona State University, Tempe, Arizona 85287-0611. Shirley Strom is Research Coordinator, Office of Parent Development International Division of Psychology in Education, Arizona State University, Tempe, Arizona 85287-0611.

ABSTRACT

The educational needs of grandparents have been overlooked. They deserve access to a curriculum that can help them adjust to their changing role and illustrates how to build satisfying family relationships. The nation's first educational program developed for grandparents is described in terms of underlying assumptions, measures to assess learning needs, elements of curriculum, and procedures for instruction. Fieldtest evidence regarding the effectiveness of this approach to strengthening families is presented along with implications for the future.

A strong family is one that includes mutually satisfying relationships and the capacity of members to meet each other's needs (Stinnett & DeFrain, 1985). Most efforts to strengthen families involve classes which help parents acquire effective methods of guidance and set reasonable expectations for children. A similar approach could provide greater success for 55 million grandparents in the United States. Observers agree that grandparents have the potential to make a more significant contribution to their families and society should do whatever is necessary to ensure this possibility (Bengston & Robertson, 1985; Elkind, 1990; Kornhaber, 1986). The status of grandparents can be enhanced by (1) better understanding of how family relationships are influenced by technological change, (2) widespread recognition of the need to establish educational expectations for

This paper was presented to the Japan Society for the Promotion of Science in Tokyo, Japan on July 1, 1991.

grandparents, and (3) the development of practical curriculum to help them adjust to their emerging role.

FAMILY RELATIONSHIPS AND TECHNOLOGICAL CHANGE

Learning in a past-oriented society. When the older people of today were children, the world was changing less rapidly. Because there was a slower rate of progress, the past dominated the present. Consequently, youngsters learned mostly from adults. In those days a father might reasonably say to his son, "Let me tell you about life and what to expect. I will give you the benefit of my experience. Now, when I was your age . . ." In this type of society the father's advice would be relevant since he had already confronted most of the situations his son would face. Given the slow pace of change, children could see their future as they observed the day-to-day activities of parents and grandparents.

There are still some past-oriented societies in the world today, places where adults remain the only important source of a child's education. On the island of Bali in Indonesia, parents can be observed passing on their woodcarving and painting skills to sons and daughters who expect to earn a living in much the same way. Similarly, aboriginal tribes in Australia are determined to perpetuate their traditional community. Amish people in the United States maintain a pattern of living that closely resembles the priorities and routine of their forefathers. For children growing up in each of these static environments, the future seems essentially a repetition of the past. When life is so free of uncertainty, so predictable, it appears justified to teach boys and girls that they should adopt the lifestyle of their elders. Therefore, in every slow-changing culture, grandparents are viewed as experts, as authorities, as models for all age groups. The role expected of children is to be listeners and observers, to be seen but not heard (Strom & Strom, 1987).

Learning in a present-oriented society. When technology is introduced and accelerated in a society, there is a corresponding increase in the pace of social change. Long-standing customs and traditions are permanently modified. Successive generations of grandparents, parents and children come to have less in common. Children today have many experiences that were not part of their parents' upbringing. This means there are some things adults are too old to know simply because we are not growing up at the present time. It is a reversal of the traditional comment to children that "You're too young to understand." Boys and girls now encounter certain conditions which are unique in history to their age group. Access to drugs, life in a single parent family, computer involvement and global awareness are common among children. They are exposed to day care, racially integrated schools, and the fear of life-threatening sexually-transmitted diseases. Adults cannot remember most of these situations because we never experienced them.

The memory of childhood as a basis for offering advice ("When I was your age . . .") becomes less credible as the pace of social change quickens. Because of the gap between experiences of adults and children, there is a tendency to seek advice mostly from peers. An increasing number of people feel that the only persons who can understand them are those at the same stage of life as themselves or who share similar challenges. Unfortunately, when people are limited to their peers for extended conversations, they are less inclined to develop the communication skills needed for successful interaction with other generations.

A peer orientation undermines cultural continuity as it divides the population into special interest groups. Because a rapidly changing society assigns greater importance to the present than the past, older people cease to be seen as models for everyone. Each generation chooses to identify with famous people of their own or next higher age group. Therefore, respect for the elderly declines. Older adults are no longer regarded as experts about much of anything except aging (Strom, Bernard & Strom, 1989).

Learning in a future-oriented society. The phase of civilization we are entering is referred to as the Information Age. Within this context schooling for children begins earlier, continues longer, and includes a vast amount of knowledge which was unavailable to previous generations of students. Given these conditions, children are bound to view the world from a different vantage and therefore should be seen by adults as an important source of learning. Certainly intergenerational dialogue is necessary to shape the future in a democratic society. Unless such contacts are sustained and mutually beneficial, the future could bring conflict as low birth rates provide fewer working age taxpayers to meet the needs of a growing elderly population. Some social scientists expect relationships between the young and older populations to replace the relationship between races as the dominant domestic conflict in the next half century (Toffler, 1990).

Intergenerational relationships are valuable because they offer a broader orientation than can be gained from any peer group. Until recently, it was supposed that aging is accompanied by a sense of perspective. This assumption still makes sense in slow-changing cultures. But, in technological societies the attainment of perspective requires something more than getting older. Becoming aware of how age groups other than our own see things and feel about the world is necessary for a broad perspective and responding to the needs of others. Unless the viewpoints of younger generations are taken into account, perspective tends to diminish rather than grow as people age (Strom & Strom, 1985, 1991).

ESTABLISHING EDUCATIONAL EXPECTATIONS FOR GRANDPARENTS

Our efforts to help grandparents began by offering a free course for them at senior citizen centers and churches in metropolitan Phoenix. The 400 people who enrolled in these classes were told they would learn something of what it is like for children to be growing up in the contemporary society and how parents view their task of raising children at the present time. In return, the participants agreed to share their experience as grandparents. This format was chosen because the literature on family relations revealed a patronizing attitude toward grandparents instead of educational programs to help them grow. Previous investigators had not made an effort to identify grandparent learning needs so there were no educational solutions. The following assumptions emerged from our preliminary research and guide the continuing project (Strom & Strom, 1989).

Grandparent responsibilities can be more clearly defined. Mothers and fathers have access to parenting courses that help them maintain competence in their changing role but similar opportunities are unavailable to grandparents. Instead, they are left alone to wonder: What are my rights and my responsibilities as a grandparent? How can I continue to be a favorable influence as my grandchild gets older? How well am I doing as a grandparent? These kinds of questions are likely to persist until there are commonly known guidelines for setting goals and self-evaluation. Many grandparents have difficulty defining their role and understanding how they could make a greater contribution. As a result the responsibility for raising youngsters has become disproportionate in many families with grandparents assuming less obligation than is in everyone's best interest.

Grandparents can learn to improve their influence. Mothers and fathers who can count on grandparents to share the load for caregiving and guidance less often seek support outside the family. The success of grandparents requires being aware of the parenting goals of sons and daughters and acting as a partner in reinforcing these goals. However, even though research indicates that people remain capable of adopting new attitudes and skills during middle and later life, grandparent development has not received priority in adult education. This missing element lessens the possibility of a meaningful life for many grandmothers and grandfathers.

The concept of life-long learning should include a concern for curriculum development. This means society has to reconsider its view that continuous learning is essential only for young people. The myth that aging is accompanied by wisdom has misled many older adults to underestimate their need for further education. When grandparents are mentally active, they remain a source of advice. Everyone at every age has a responsibility to keep growing in order to achieve their potential.

A practical grandparent program should be widely available. Older men and women have been led to believe that learning in later life should consist of whatever topics they find interesting without any societal expectations as there are for younger learners. But as people continue to age, they should also continue to grow—and not just in terms of acquiring leisure-oriented skills. Some of education in later life should emphasize obligations and roles, just as curriculum does for younger age groups. Senior citizens are the only population without any defined educational needs or cooperatively planned curricula. Since the size of this group is expected to grow faster than any other age segment, it seems reasonable to provide them educational opportunities which can help strengthen their families.

Society should set higher expectations for grandparents. By themselves grandparents may be unable to generate the motivation necessary to stimulate educational commitment within their peer group. This is a difficult task because so many people think of retirement as a time when they can withdraw from active community responsibility. Peers reinforce the perception that being carefree and without obligation is an acceptable goal in later life. The problem is compounded by age segregation. When older adults are limited to one another for most of their interaction, they establish standards which may not be in accord with what the society as a whole believes is best.

In order to favorably revise existing norms for older adults in terms of greater learning and more significant contributions to the family, younger age groups must raise their expectations and make these known. The talent and potential contribution of seniors could enrich the lives of everyone. Accordingly, we should expect them to demonstrate a commitment to personal growth, concern themselves about others through volunteering, and support the schools to ensure a better future for children. If educational expectations are not established for older adults, they will experience less influence and lower self-esteem.

The benefits of grandparent education can be assessed. Popular support can be expected for programs that help grandparents enlarge the scope of their influence, improve their ability to communicate with loved ones, become more self confident, and experience greater respect in the family. These benefits would be even more credible if the sources confirming them included other persons than just the participating grandparents. By comparing the results from three generational versions of the authors' Grandparent Strengths and Needs Inventory, the merits of various educational approaches to family development can be determined. This inventory also enables educators to adapt curriculum in a way that honors group and individual differences (Strom & Strom, 1990; Strom, Strom, & Collinsworth, 1991).

GOALS FOR GRANDPARENT DEVELOPMENT

There are six fundamental aspects of the grandparent experience that we try to influence in our program. Each of them have implications for child and adult development. The goals we pursue are to:

Increase the satisfaction of being a grandparent. It would seem that the longer lifespan today gives grandparents more years to influence their grandchildren. But the actual consequence depends on whether or not a relationship is mutually satisfying. When family members avoid sharing their feelings, or they experience insufficient satisfaction with one another, the relationship is in jeopardy. Grandmothers and grandfathers who enjoy their role are more able to cope with difficulties.

Improve how well grandparents perform their role. The efforts of grandparents to guide grandchildren depend on how self-confident they feel in their family role. Those who seek to support the parenting goals of their sons and daughters will continue to teach grandchildren. These persons realize that it is unreasonable to expect parents to be exclusively responsible for the care and guidance of grandchildren. By being active contributors in the family, they are seen as a valuable and long-term source of influence.

Enlarge the scope of guidance expected of grandparents. There is abundant evidence that, by itself, academic learning is an insufficient preparation for success in life. It follows that grandparents should help grandchildren acquire some of the out of school lessons they need. By defining the aspects of growth that should be obtained at home, it is possible to improve a child's total education and establish a helpful role for grandparents.

Decrease the difficulties of being a grandparent. Grandparents encounter some difficulty in getting along with sons, daughters, in-laws, and grandchildren. The manner in which these problems are handled is a sign of personal effectiveness. Every grandmother and grandfather should have access to education which focuses on their changing role. When grandparents are aware of the childrearing strategies of their sons and daughters and they know the predictable difficulties to expect as grandchildren get older, they can prepare themselves by obtaining the skills necessary for continued success.

Reduce the frustrations experienced by grandparents. Some frustration is to be expected. But grandparents vary in the frequency with which they sense frustration. One way to reduce their discontent is by understanding why certain child behaviors occur and why some of them should be allowed to continue. When the expectations of grandparents are consistent with a child's developmental needs, the tendency is to encourage normative behavior and offer support for a favorable self concept.

Reduce the family information needs of grandparents. Grandparents need accurate perceptions about their grandchild's abilities and their social relationships. Besides the information which teachers and parents provide for them, grandparents should listen to grandchildren themselves to learn about their hopes, fears, goals and concerns. If educational programs for grandparents can regularly include access to the views of people who are the same age as grandchildren, it is easier to understand how family members resemble and differ from their peers.

ELEMENTS OF CURRICULUM AND INSTRUCTION

The learning activities that grandparents consider appealing deserve priority in planning educational programs for them. Just as young students need a variety of teaching methods, older men and women can also benefit from a wide range of instructional techniques. The two courses we have developed on "Becoming A Better Grandparent" and "Achieving Grandparent Potential" follow the same format of focusing on all three generations. Some of the lessons concerning grandparents involve keeping up with the times, giving and seeking advice, communicating from a distance, growing as a couple, and learning in later life. Lessons about the middle generation call for recognizing indicators of parental success, helping single and blended families, developing values and morals, building child self-esteem, and watching television together. The lessons on grandchildren emphasize getting along with others, sharing fears and worries, understanding children's thinking, deciding about sex and drugs, and encouraging the college student. All twenty-four lessons consist of the same instructional elements. In turn, each of these elements deserve a brief explanation.

Discussion and brainstorming. Grandparents meet in small groups to consider agenda from their guidebook that encourages their expression of ideas, concerns, mistakes, goals and solutions (Strom & Strom, 1991a, 1991c). During these discussions the participants inform, challenge, and reassure each other. They quickly discover there is much to gain from sharing feelings and thoughts. Conversations with emotionally supportive peers cause men and women to feel less alone, help them organize their thinking, and increase awareness of the possibilities for becoming a better grandparent. Creative thinking is practiced during each discussion when the group shifts to consideration of a brainstorming task.

Problem solving. The next activity invites grandparents to consider how they might handle a particular problem if they had to cope with it. A family incident is described which offers everyone the same information including several possible solutions. Grandparents like to reflect and then discuss pros and cons they see for each of the given choices. It is stimulating to think of additional options and to identify relevant information that may be missing. Everyone has an opportunity to share their reasoning about the advice they consider to be best. This scenario approach broadens the range of solutions individuals see and discourages premature judgment. Later, in their home, grandparents present the scenarios to relatives and find out their viewpoint.

Grandparent principles. Several written principles accompany each unit. Grandparents rely on these practical guidelines for review, reflection, and personal application. Participants benefit from reading the companion volume of viewpoints which match each lesson in the guidebook (Strom & Strom, 1991b, 1991d). These essays, from which the principles are drawn, offer insights, observations and suggestions for making the grandparent experience more satisfying. In addition, local resource persons can enrich the learning by acquainting grandparents with the way problems are handled in their own community. Because each individual represents a unique family, grandparents must decide for themselves which principles are most appropriate in their present situation, the ones to apply immediately, and those that can be deferred until a later time.

Self-evaluation and observation. Personal growth requires self-examination. Grandparents are encouraged to practice this important skill as part of their homework. Each homework assignment consists of several multiple-choice questions that give participants a chance to state their feelings about issues such as family relationships, communication problems, and expectations of children. The anonymous homework is submitted at the beginning of each class. After responses are tallied for each item, the previously unknown norms of perception and behavior are announced to the class. This helps individuals know how their experience as grandparents resemble and differ from peers.

Intergenerational conversations. Grandparents should strive to know each grandchild as an individual. The way to achieve this goal is through interaction with the particular grandchild. However, most grandmothers and grandfathers admit that they sometimes have difficulty keeping a conversation going with youngsters. This is why they appreciate questions focusing on realms of experience that the generations commonly encounter, topics that transcend age. Every lesson includes a set of questions dealing with topics of mutual concern such as music, health, school, money, fears, friends, and careers. These questions facilitate the dialogue that we expect grandparents to initiate face to face or by phone. Most of the inquiries fit all grandchildren while some are more appropriate for teenagers. A portion of each class session is devoted to hearing grandparents comment about the insights they have acquired through intergenerational interviews.

Grandparents also need to know something about the norms of their grandchild's age group. It is unreasonable to suppose that all the information we need about the orientation of relatives will be provided by them alone. In a society where peers have considerable influence it is wise to find out how people in a grandchild's age group think and feel. This improves our understanding of how loved ones resemble and differ from their peers. One approach we use is to videotape interviews with children and parents who express their views on topics like peer pressure, school stress, and family conflict. This method reflects our belief that the broad perspective of life each of us ought to acquire emerges only when the thoughts and feelings of other age groups are taken into account.

EVALUATING GRANDPARENT SUCCESS

The effectiveness of grandparent education has been confirmed by research. In one study 800 people representing three generations evaluated the attitudes and behavior of grandparents before and after their participation in the "Becoming A Better Grandparent" course. At the end of the program grandparents reported that they had made significant improvements. This progress was corroborated by inventory scores of the parents and grandchildren (Strom & Strom, 1990). Specifically, grandparents benefit from the mentally stimulating experience by understanding how their role is changing, acquiring a broader perspective, learning new attitudes, gaining greater confidence and self-esteem, improving communication skills, and strengthening family relationships (Strom & Strom, 1985, 1989; Strom, Strom & Collinsworth, 1990).

These feelings expressed by the grandparents show the importance of the program for them: "I realized that I must keep on growing in order to understand other family members and be seen by them as a positive influence." "Now I understand my privileges as a grandparent as well as the duties I owe my grandchildren." "I found that helping my son and daughter achieve their parenting goals has upgraded my status to that of a valued partner." "I feel so much better about myself as a grandmother and more optimistic about my grandchildren."

Sons and daughters also identified some important benefits of grandparent education: "My parents seem more willing to share their feelings with us and they are more supportive of the way we are bringing up our children." "Taking this class has really helped my mom think about her role in my child's life. She is working hard to get to know my children as individuals." "My Dad has realized that listening and learning from his grandchildren is the key to being respected by them." "My mother has always been kind and loving to all of us but now she is more interesting to be around. It's fun to hear what she is learning."

It would be pleasing to report a balance in the proportion of men and women who seek to improve themselves through grandparent education. However, just as mothers significantly outnumber fathers in parenting classes, grandmothers are over represented in classes for grandparent development. Usually three out of four students in our courses are grandmothers. Does this ratio indicate that grandmothers need more guidance than grandfathers? On the contrary, it suggests grandmothers are more motivated to keep growing in this aspect of life. This conclusion was reached after comparing the influence of 155 grandmothers and 55 grandfathers who had just completed the program. Assessments were made to determine how each gender was perceived by themselves, their sons, daughters and grandchildren. Although the grandmothers reported having less formal education than grandfathers, they were seen as more successful grandparents in the estimate of all three generations (Strom & Strom, 1989).

In this study grandparents, parents and grandchildren portrayed grandmothers as emotionally closer to grandchildren, better informed about family affairs, and more willing to commit themselves to helping others. They were better at seeing the positive side of situations, learning from other family members, and making their feelings known. Grandmothers were credited with knowing more than grandfathers about the fears and concerns of grandchildren and spending more time with them. They were regarded as more effective in teaching grandchildren how to show trust, get along with others, and handle arguments. Grandmothers were viewed as better at passing on family history and cultural traditions, and more willing to accept help from grandchildren.

Strengths of grandfathers were recognized too. They saw themselves as having less difficulty than grandmothers in giving advice to sons and daughters, and were less frustrated by televiewing and listening habits of grandchildren. Parents observed grandfathers as being more satisfied than grandmothers when grandchildren asked for advice. Grandchildren felt their outlook on life was appreciated more by grandfathers.

Perhaps it is unfair to compare grandfathers with grandmothers. Consider the more positive results that emerge when the emphasis is on identifying change in grandfather attitudes and behaviors after instruction. The grandfathers in this study felt they made improvement in terms of satisfaction with their role, success in carrying out their obligations, effectiveness in teaching, overcoming difficulties, coping with frustrations, and

becoming more informed. Parents and grandchildren confirmed these gains had occurred. By joining grandmothers as participants in family-oriented education, grandfathers have proven they can learn to build more successful relationships with their spouse, children and grandchildren. Toward this goal grandfathers are urged to grow along with their partner and be actively involved in strengthening the family (Strom & Strom, 1989).

CONCLUSION

As we contemplate the future it is important to bear in mind that the baby-boomers, those persons born between 1946–1964, will become the largest group of older adults in history. This population of 77 million people is going to be better educated, healthier, and live longer than preceding generations. If the preparation they receive for retirement focuses only on financial and leisure readiness, a lifestyle of strictly recreation could become the norm. On the other hand, if getting ready for leisure activities is joined by an emphasis on continued responsibility as family members, then baby-boomers can make an enormous contribution to society. This possibility is supported by the emerging concept of grandparent education (Strom & Strom, 1991e).

REFERENCES

Bengston, V., & Robertson, J. (1985). *Grandparenthood*. Beverly Hills, CA: Sage Publications.

Elkind, D. (1990). *Grandparenting*. Glenview, IL: Scott, Foresman.

Kornhaber, A. (1986). *Between parents and grandparents*. New York: St Martin's Press.

Stinnet, N., & DeFrain, J. (1985). *Secrets of strong families*. Boston: Little, Brown.

Strom, R., Bernard, H., & Strom, S. (1989). *Human development and learning*. New York: Human Sciences Press.

Strom, R., & Strom, S. (1985). Becoming a better grandparent. In *Growing together: An Intergenerational sourcebook*, K. Struntz & S. Reville (eds.). Washington, DC: American Association of Retired Persons and Elvirita Lewis Foundation, pp. 57–60.

Strom, R., & Strom, S. (1987). Preparing grandparents for a new role. *The Journal of Applied Gerontology*, 6(4), 476–486.

Strom, R., & Strom, S. (1989). *Grandparent development*. Washington, DC: American Association of Retired Persons Andrus Foundation.

Strom, R., & Strom, S. (1990). Raising expectations for grandparents: A three-generational study. *International Journal of Aging and Human Development*, 31(3), 161–167.

Strom, R., & Strom, S. (1991a). *Achieving grandparent potential: A guidebook for building intergenerational relationships*. Newbury Park, CA: Sage Publications.

Strom, R., & Strom, S. (1991b). *Achieving grandparent potential: Viewpoints on building intergenerational relationships*. Newbury Park, CA: Sage Publications.

Strom, R., & Strom, S. (1991c). *Becoming a better grandparent: A guidebook for strengthening the family*. Newbury Park, CA: Sage Publications.

Strom, R., & Strom, S. (1991d). *Becoming a better grandparent: Viewpoints on strengthening the family*. Newbury Park, CA: Sage Publications.

Strom R., & Strom, S. (1991e). *Grandparent education: A guide for leaders*. Newbury Park, CA: Sage Publications.

Strom, R., Strom, S., & Collinsworth, P. (1990). Improving grandparent success. *The Journal of Applied Gerontology*, 9(4), 480–492.

Strom, R., Strom, S., & Collinsworth, P. (1991). The Grandparent Strengths and Needs Inventory: Development and factorial validation. *Educational and Psychological Measurement*, 51(4).

Toffler, A. (1990). *Powershift*. New York: Bantam Books.

Ageing
with attitude

Human beings are living longer and longer. At the same time, prejudice against older people is getting stronger. Where will this lead us? *Nikki van der Gaag* explores the paradox and suggests a way forward.

'Will you still need me, will you still feed me/When I'm 64?' The Beatles' song may be old itself, but it lies at the heart of what most of us fear about ageing—not death, but neglect; not the added years but lack of love, lack of respect.

We wake up on the morning of our 60th or 65th birthdays, and suddenly we are 'old age pensioners' and 'senior citizens'. We don't feel any different from the day or the month or the year before, but we are now officially 'old'. Suddenly we are no longer part of the workforce, no longer 'productive'.

And many people, both young and old, feed this feeling of uselessness by saying, "I've done my bit, I deserve a rest". So they 'rest'. And the myth of old people as 'past it' is perpetuated from generation to generation.

It is a dangerous myth, not just for our own self-respect as we grow older, but also for a world with an ever-growing population and shrinking resources. If the 'old' do not participate in society, it is society's loss as well as their own.

'Ageing,' says Alex Kalache, Head of the Programme on Ageing at the London School of Hygiene and Tropical Medicine, 'is the number one problem in the world. And if it is not addressed *now*, there will be serious consequences.'[1]

It is the 'number one problem' because the numbers of people over 60 – and particularly those over 80 – are growing fast. In 1959 there were 200 million people over 60 in the world, accounting for eight per cent of the total population. By 2025 there will be 1.2 billion – 14 per cent of the total. Contrary to popular myth, by early in the next century three-quarters of these will live in the Third World.[2]

And it is in developing countries that the growth is greatest and the problems are most acute. Their elderly populations are growing at many times the rate of those in the North. For example, over the next 50 years the numbers of those over 60 in

Britain will increase by 23 per cent and by 100 per cent in the US – but by 201 per cent in Bangladesh and 300 per cent in Brazil.[3]

Where Britain and the US, Australia and Canada have had 100 years to deal with increased longevity, China or Brazil have only 20 or 30 years to deal with the same rate of growth – and fewer resources with which to do so. And even countries which have had an older population for longer are struggling for positive ways of responding.

They are not helped by the fact that 'age' is a relative concept. Each one of us will

In Vilcabamba, you may not be considered 'old' until you are 90. In Potosi, you might be 'old' at 30

know people in their sixties who regard themselves as 'old' – and are therefore seen as 'old' by everyone else. We will also know and people in their seventies, eighties or even nineties who remain very much part of society and who are mentally if not physically agile.

'Old' also varies from country to country and place to place. The Vilcabamba Valley in Ecuador, for example, is known locally as the *Valle de la Ancianidad* (Valley of Old Age) or the *Isla de Imunidad* (Island of Immunity). It is one of three places in the world where many people live to be over 100 – the others are in the Georgian Republic and in Pakistan. No-one really knows why, but a number of factors have been suggested, including the altitude, a mainly vegetable diet with little fat, reasonable work conditions, comparatively little stress, the beneficial effects of the *huilco* tree which recycles air – and the relative isolation of the valley.

Further down in South America, in Potosi in Bolivia, life expectancy is at the other extreme – people don't expect to live beyond their 40th birthday. Mining is the main occupation. The miners and their families suffer from harsh conditions, poverty, overwork, accidents, silicosis and other forms of lung poisoning.[4]

In Vilcabamba, you may not be considered 'old' until you are 90. In Potosi, you might be 'old' at 30.

So if we can't even really generalize about the meaning of 'old', can we say that there is an 'ageing crisis'? Under current conditions and in the light of today's population predictions, I think the answer must be 'yes'. As more and more people live longer and their numbers increase both in actual numbers and relative to the general population, there will be fewer people to care for them if and when they need it. The dependency ratio, as it is called, is also affected by the increasing financial pressures put on families, particularly in the Third World. More and more women everywhere are working. Because women form the vast majority of carers, this also affects the numbers of people able to support elderly members of the family. As governments squeeze pensions and health systems in an attempt to keep taxes low or to conform to the 'structural adjustment' policies imposed by the International Monetary Fund, it is old people who are likely to suffer most.

But this need not be. As Simone de Beauvoir said: 'The meaning or lack of meaning that old age takes on in any given society puts that whole society to the test.'

If so, governments and international agencies have failed that test – neither seriously addressing the issue nor seeing the need to invest major resources in it. For example, one of the main reasons that people in Africa or Asia or South America cite for having large numbers of children is to 'provide security' in old age. If people knew that they could remain independent and yet be supported in their old age, then they would not feel the need to have so many children. Nor would they fear the isolation from society that arises from not having children. And yet, time after time, support for old people is ignored in discussions on population.

As it is 'old' people – both in the North and the South – have been increasingly

In almost every culture, financial independence gives older people respect from others and consequently more dignity

isolated from the rest of society in retirement homes which were seen as the model of how to deal with old age. People's need for health care increases as they grow older, and the seriously-disabled minority need special care and attention. But many people who do not have serious physical or mental disabilities have nonetheless been shut away in unsuitable homes, cut off from the rest of the world.

Today a growing number of governments are promoting another model which ostensibly helps people to live more independently: 'care in the community', as it is often known. What it usually means is 'care in the family' and in most cases it does not spring from a philosophical belief that families care best for their own but rather from the need to find a cheap solution to the problem of caring for the old.

In Muslim countries, putting the aged into old people's homes has always been anathema. King Hassan II has said that: 'If an old-age home were built in Morocco, I believe it would mean the country no longer existed. Moreover, I would be the first to burn it, in an act of auto-da-fé.'[5]

This is all very well, but it puts the burden of caring very much back into the family – usually the women. While families can in some cases provide the support needed, the breakdown of the extended family and the squeezing of household resources have often led to neglect of, rather than succour for the elderly. When resources are stretched, the old are likely to be the ones who go without.

It is precisely for this reason that in most of the world, 'old' people continue to work until they die. They have no choice. They need to earn an income – of sorts – or they don't eat. In Malawi, for example, a recent survey showed that 85 per cent of men over 65 were still part of the 'labour force'. In Liberia it was 70 per cent and in Guatemala, 63 per cent.[6] Indeed, people may even have to work harder as they get older, taking on

the manual labour that younger people do not want to do. Many have to uproot themselves – old women who outlive their husbands are forced to leave their villages to seek work in the cities. In most Third World countries, older people figure as part of the huge informal economy, selling vegetables on the streets or recycling garbage.

In almost every culture, financial independence gives older people more respect from others and consequently more dignity. Yet 'old' people are not considered to be officially productive because they are not usually earning an official wage.

All over the world older people, particularly women, are looking after grandchildren so that their daughters or sons can work. In parts of Africa particularly stricken by the AIDS epidemic, the young and sexually active have nearly all died, leaving the oldest generation to care for the youngest. And in Asia migration to the cities produces the same result.

Unpaid childcare, housework and people-maintenance is the work that makes the world go round. But in a world increasingly based on a cash economy this kind of work is not regarded as 'real work' and the size of their pay packet has become the only measure of a person's worth.

This is illustrated in a classic manner by the World Bank's recent report entitled: *Averting the Old Age crisis: policies to protect the old and promote growth.* This report pretty much ignored the informal economy and advocated a 'three-pillar approach' to financing the old which is based entirely on pensions. But even according to the World Bank, an estimated 60 per cent of the world's labour force and 70 per cent of old people, are part of the informal economy – they have no pension plan and are unlikely to be able to save.

Kasturi Sen, a specialist on ageing and policy issues, has quite a different strategy. She calls it the 'life-cycle approach'. The circumstances that people find themselves in when they are older, she says, is simply a continuation of the situation that they have been in throughout their lives. If you are poor, overworked and in ill-health when you are young, these conditions are likely to be the same or worse when you are old.

She argues that in order to improve the quality of peoples' lives – and especially the lives of women, who in most societies live longer – policies should aim at improving education in earlier life, helping people to move in and out of the labour market, and enabling women to take out financial credit and buy land. Better nutrition and access to contraception would improve health. These things, she says, would do more than anything else to 'reduce the possibilities of acute vulnerability in later stages of life'.[7]

In other words, the 'problem' of the elderly is something which concerns us not only in old age but in youth and middle age as well.

This is also one of the key messages of activist groups on ageing issues like the Gray Panthers. Started in the US in 1970 to oppose the war in Vietnam, they have become a worldwide network active on health care, housing, discrimination and work. Maggie Kuhn, one of the founders, is now in her eighties, but as feisty as ever. She spoke to Betty Friedan about the importance of old and young working together: 'Our philosophy was using gray power with the young for issues on the cutting edge of social change. I think we've established the fact that old age is a triumph. What we've done is establish the intergenerational bond necessary for real social change, the continuity of life. The old and the young need each other. We're opposed to the segregation of old people...

'The meaning or lack of meaning that old age takes on in any given society puts that whole society to the test'

Older people have so much to give to society...'[8]

The recognition that older people have valuable contributions to make is slowly permeating the thinking of development activists. Mark Gorman of HelpAge International recognizes that in recent years there has been 'a growing focus on the involvement of older people as active participants in development'.[9]

In Colombia, older people who are part of *Pro Vida* (For Life) have set up the city's first recycling scheme. In Kenya, a group of middle-aged women got together to tackle the problem of earning income in their later years. They set up schemes for clean water and a successful poultry-keeping project. They called themselves *Itambya Yaa Aka Kichakasimba* (women of Kichakasimba take a step ahead).[10]

In Argentina old people have been leading a militant grassroots campaign since the pension cuts of 1992. They held a 24-hour-a-day vigil in the Plaza de Mayo in Buenos Aires, enduring great cold and hardship until they were finally expelled by the police two months later. After that they began a vigil and protest every Thursday outside Parliament. Occasionally they stopped traffic, occupied government buildings and even scuffled with police and government officials in the streets of the capital.

On many occasions protesters were arrested but sometimes armed riot police

withdrew before them, unable to frighten and unwilling to club down these dignified grandmothers. On 2 March 1994 thousands of elderly people converged on the centre of the capital to mark 100 weeks of these dramatic protests.[6]

Finally the Argentinian Government realized that they could not discredit the protesters. They raised pensions for the oldest, agreed to pay some of the money owed to the poorest and promised a reform of the pension system. But they failed to restore the cuts. So the old people took to the law. As of today, 350,000 court cases have been lodged with the High Court. Around 100,000 have already been won and the 'old people's' protest threatens to throw the whole economic policy of the Argentinian Government off course.

We too can push for change in policy and in attitudes – including our own. We can plan for our old age like the women of Kichakasimba. And we can work together, young, middle-aged and old, to ensure that everyone has enough to provide them with a satisfying and dignified life.

1999 will be the International Year of Ageing. Let us use the four years between now and then to take up the challenge of David Pitt, a non-retired 'retired person' who volunteers here at the New Internationalist:

'Let us direct our energies against those responsible for the poverty... and for declining health services. Let us also do what we can to support those living in other countries where care for the aged is a matter of gross neglect. Let us band together and be willful and cantankerous and obstreperous. Above all, let us never apologize for growing old.'

1 Quotes from Alex Kalache taken from an interview by Nikki van der Gaag. 2 MSJ Pathy (Ed.) 'Ageing in Developing Countries' by Alex Kalache in Principles and Practices of Geriatric Medicine, John Wiley 1991. 3 Kasturi Sen Ageing – Debates on demographic transition and social policy, Zed Press 1994. 4 Ken Tout Ageing in Developing Countries, Oxford University Press 1989. 5 Jeannine Jacquemin Elderly Women and the Family Soroptomist International. 6 Suzanne S Paul and James A Paul Humanity Comes of Age, WCC Publications 1994. 7 Kasturi Sen Women in later life: health, security and poverty, International Health Exchange, April 1994. 8 Betty Friedan The Fountain of Age, Vintage 1993. 9 Mark Gorman from a discussion with Nikki van der Gaag 10 United Nations The World Aging Situation 1991.

The Solace of Patterns

The strange attractors that define life's stages give shape even to grief

ROBERT M. SAPOLSKY

Robert M. Sapolsky is a MacArthur Fellow and a professor of biological sciences and neuroscience at Stanford University. His most recent book, Why Zebras Don't Get Ulcers: A Guide to Stress, Stress-Related Diseases, *and Coping, is published by W. H. Freeman and Company.*

A SHORT TIME AGO MY FATHER died, having spent far too many of his last years in pain and degeneration. Although I had expected his death and tried to prepare myself for it, when the time came it naturally turned out that you really can't prepare. A week afterward I found myself back at work, bludgeoned by emotions that swirled around a numb core of unreality—a feeling of disconnection from the events that had just taken place on the other side of the continent, of disbelief that it was really him frozen in that nightmare of stillness. The members of my laboratory were solicitous. One, a medical student, asked me how I was doing, and I replied, "Well, today it seems as if I must have imagined it all." "That makes sense," she said. "Don't forget about DABDA."

DABDA. In 1969 the psychiatrist Elisabeth Kübler-Ross published a landmark book, *On Death and Dying.* Drawing on her research with terminally ill people and their families, she described the process whereby people mourn the death of others and, when impending, of themselves. Most of us, she observed, go through a fairly well defined sequence of stages. First we deny the death is happening. Then we become angry at the unfairness of it all. We pass through a stage of irrational bargaining, with the doctors, with God: *Just let this not be fatal and I will change my ways. Please, just wait until Christmas.* There follows a stage of depression and, if one is fortunate, the final chapter, serene acceptance. The sequence is not ironclad; indi-

viduals may skip certain stages, experience them out of order or regress to earlier ones. DABDA, moreover, is generally thought to give a better description of one's own preparation for dying than of one's mourning the demise of someone else. Nevertheless, there is a broadly recognized consistency in the overall pattern of mourning: denial, anger, bargaining, depression, acceptance. I was stuck at stage one, right on schedule.

Brevity is the soul of DABDA. A few years ago I saw that point brilliantly dramatized on television—on, of all programs, *The Simpsons.* It was the episode in which Homer, the father, accidentally eats a poisonous fish and is told he has twenty-four hours to live. There ensues a thirty-second sequence in which the cartoon character races through the death and dying stages, something like this: "No way! I'm not dying." He ponders a second, then grabs the doctor by the neck. "Why you little. . . ." He trembles in fear, then pleads, "Doc, get me outta this! I'll make it worth your while." Finally he composes himself and says, "Well, we all gotta go sometime." I thought it was hilarious. Homer substituted fear for depression and got it on the other side of anger. Even so, here was a cartoon suitable to be watched happily by children, and the writers had sneaked in a parody of Kübler-Ross.

But for sheer conciseness, of course, Homer Simpson's vignette has nothing on DABDA. That's why medical students, my laboratory colleague included, memorize the acronym along with hundreds of other mnemonic devices in preparation for their national board examinations. What strikes me now is the power of those letters to encapsulate human experience. My father, by dint of having been human, was unique; thus was my relationship to him, and thus must be my grieving. And yet I come up with something reducible to a medical school acronym. Poems, paintings, symphonies by the most creative artists who ever lived have been born out of mourning; yet, on some level, they all sprang from the pattern invoked by two

pedestrian syllables of pseudo-English. We cry, we rage, we demand that the oceans' waves stop, that the planets halt their movements in the sky, all because the earth will no longer be graced by the one who sang lullabies as no one else could; yet that, too, is reducible to DABDA. Why should grief be so stereotypical?

SCIENTISTS WHO STUDY HUMAN THOUGHT and behavior have discerned many stereotyped, structured stages through which all of us move at various times. Some of the sequences are obvious, their logic a quick study. It is no surprise that infants learn to crawl before they take their first tentative steps, and only later learn to run. Other sequences are more subtle. Freudians claim that in normal development the child undergoes the invariant transition from a so-called oral stage to an anal stage to a genital stage, and they attribute various aspects of psychological dysfunction in the adult to an earlier failure to move successfully from one stage to the next.

Similarly, the Swiss psychologist Jean Piaget mapped stages of cognitive development. For example, he noted, there is a stage at which children begin to grasp the concept of object permanence: Before that developmental transition, a toy does not exist once it is removed from the child's sight. Afterward, the toy exists—and the child will look for it—even when it is no longer visible. Only at a reliably later stage do children begin to grasp concepts such as the conservation of volume—that two pitchers of different shapes can hold the same quantity of liquid. The same developmental patterns occur across numerous cultures, and so the sequence seems to describe the universal way that human beings learn to comprehend a cognitively complex world.

The American psychologist Lawrence Kohlberg mapped the stereotyped stages people undergo in developing morally. At one early stage of life, moral decisions are based on rules and on the motivation to avoid punishment: actions considered for their effects on oneself. Only at a later stage are decisions made on the basis of a respect for the community: actions considered for their effects on others. Later still, and far more rarely, some people develop a morality driven by a set of their own internalized standards, derived from a sense of what is right and what is wrong for all possible communities. The pattern is progressive: people who now act out of conscience invariably, at some earlier stage of life, believed that you don't do bad things because you might get caught.

The American psychoanalyst Erik Erikson discerned a sequence of psychosocial development, framing it as crises that a person resolves or fails to resolve at each stage. For infants, the issue is whether one attains a basic attitude of trust toward the world; for adolescents, it is identity versus identity confusion; for young adults, intimacy versus isolation; for adults, generativity versus stagnation; and for the aged, peaceful acceptance and integrity versus despair. Erikson's pioneering insight that one's later years represent a series of transitions that must be successfully negotiated is reflected in a quip by the geriatrician Walter M. Bortz II of Stanford University Medical School. Asked whether he was interested in curing aging, Bortz responded, "No, I'm not interested in arrested development."

Those are some of the patterns we all are reported or theorized to have in common, across many settings and cultures. I think such conceptualizations are often legitimate, not just artificial structures that scientists impose on inchoate reality. Why should we share such patterning? It is certainly not for lack of alternatives. As living beings, we represent complex, organized systems—an eddy in the random entropy of the universe. When all the possibilities are taken into account, it is supremely unlikely for elements to assemble themselves into molecules, for molecules to form cells, for vast assemblages of cells to form us. How much more unlikely, it seems, that such complex organisms conform to such relatively simple patterns of behavior, of development, of thought.

ONE WAY OF COMING TO GRIPS WITH the properties of complex systems is through a field of mathematics devoted to the study of so-called cellular automata. The best way of explaining its style of analysis is by example. Imagine a long row of boxes—some black, some white—arranged to form some initial pattern, a starting stage. The row of boxes is to give rise to a second row, just below the first. The way that takes place in a cellular automaton is that each box in the first row is subjected to a set of reproduction rules. For example, one rule might stipulate that a black box in the first row gives rise to a black box immediately below it in the next row, only if exactly one of its two nearest neighbors is black. Other rules

MOST COMPLEX PATTERNS
collapse into extinction.
Only a few combinations
beat the odds.

might apply to a black box flanked by two white boxes or two black boxes. Once the set of rules is applied to each box in the first row, a second row of black and white boxes is generated; then the rules are applied again to each box in the second row to generate a third row and so on.

Metaphorically, each row represents one generation, one tick of a clock. A properly programmed computer could track any possible combination of colored boxes, following any conceivable set of reproduction rules, down through the generations. In the vast majority of cases, somewhere down the line it would end up with a row of boxes all the same color. After that, the single color would repeat itself forever. In other words, the line would go extinct.

Return now to my earlier question: How can it be, in this entropic world, that we human beings share so many stable patterns—one nose; two eyes; a reliable lag time before we learn object permanence; happier adulthoods if we become confident about our identities as adolescents; a tendency to find it hard to believe in tragedy when it strikes? What keeps us from following an almost infinite number of alternative developmental paths? The studies of cellular automata provide a hint.

Not all complex patterns, it turns out, eventually collapse into extinction. A few combinations of starting states and reproduction rules beat the odds and settle down into mature stable patterns that continue down through the generations forever. In general, it is impossible to predict whether a given starting state will survive, let alone which pattern it will generate after, say, *n* generations. The only way to tell is to crank it through the computer and see. It has been shown, however, that a surprisingly small number of such mature patterns are possible.

A similar tendency in living systems has long been known to evolutionary biologists. They call it convergence. Among the staggering number of species on this planet, there are only a few handfuls of solutions to the problem of how to locomote, how to conserve fluids in a hot environment, how to store and mobilize energy. And among the staggering variety of humans, it may be a convergent feature of our complexity that there are a small number of ways in which we grow through life or mourn its inevitabilities.

IN AN ENTROPIC WORLD, WE CAN TAKE a common comfort from our common patterns, and there is often consolation in

attributing such patterns to forces larger than ourselves. As an atheist, I have long taken an almost religious solace from a story by the Argentine minimalist Jorge Luis Borges. In his famous short story, *The Library of Babel,* Borges describes the world as a library filled with an unimaginably vast number of books, each with the same number of pages and the same number of letters on each page. The library contains a single copy of every possible book, every possible permutation of letters. People spend their lives sorting through this ocean of gibberish for the incalculably rare books whose random arrays of letters form something meaningful, searching above all else for the single book (which must exist) that explains everything. And of course, given the completeness of the library, in addition to that perfect book, there must also be one that convincingly disproves the conclusions put forth in it, and yet another book that refutes the malicious solipsisms of the second book, plus hundreds of thousands of books that differ from any of those three by a single letter or a comma.

The narrator writes in his old age, in an isolation brought about by the suicides of people who have been driven to despair by the futility of wandering through the library. In this parable of the search for meaning amid entropy, Borges concludes:

Those who judge [the library to be finite] postulate that in remote places the corridors and stairways and hexagons can conceivably come to an end—which is absurd. Those who imagine it to be without limit forget that the possible number of books does have such a limit. I venture to suggest this solution to the ancient problem: *The library is unlimited and cyclical.* If an eternal traveler were to cross it in any direction, after centuries he would see that the same volumes were repeated in the same disorder (which, thus repeated, would be an order: the Order). My solitude is gladdened by this elegant hope.

IT APPEARS THAT AMID THE ORDER WITH which we mature and decline, there is an order to our mourning. And my own recent solitude is gladdened by that elegant hope, in at least two ways. One is inward-looking. This stereotypy, this ordering, brings the promise of solace in the predicted final stage: if one is fortunate, DABDA ends in *A.*

Another hope looks outward, to a world whose tragedies are inexorably delivered from its remotest corners to our nightly news. Look at the image of a survivor of some carnage and, knowing nothing of her language, culture, beliefs or circumstances, you can still recognize in the fixed action patterns of her facial muscles the unmistakable lineaments of grief. That instant recognition, the universal predictability of certain aspects of human beings, whether in a facial expression or in the stages of mourning, is an emblem of our kinship and an imperative of empathy.

Credits/ Acknowledgments

Cover design by Charles Vitelli

1. Genetic and Prenatal Influences on Development
Facing overview—WHO photo. 19—© 1995 by Bob Sacha.
22—Photo courtesy of Drs. E. Fuller Torrey and Daniel R.
Weinberger, NIMH Neuroscience Center, Washington, DC.
23—Photo courtesy of Nick Kelsh. 24—Photo courtesy of the
American Philosophical Society.

2. Development during Infancy and Early Childhood
Facing overview—Photo by Elaine M. Ward. 45—Photo courtesy
of Jean M. Mandler.

3. Development during Childhood—Cognition and Schooling
Facing overview—Photo by Pamela Carley. 92—Drawings by
John Michael Yanson.

4. Development during Childhood—Family and Culture
Facing overview—Photo by Pamela Carley.

5. Development during Adolescence and Young Adulthood
Facing overview—United Nations photo by John Isaac.

6. Development during Middle and Late Adulthood
Facing overview—United Nations photo by F. B. Grunzweig.

ANNUAL EDITIONS ARTICLE REVIEW FORM

■ NAME: _____ DATE: _____

■ TITLE AND NUMBER OF ARTICLE: _____

■ BRIEFLY STATE THE MAIN IDEA OF THIS ARTICLE: _____

_____

■ LIST THREE IMPORTANT FACTS THAT THE AUTHOR USES TO SUPPORT THE MAIN IDEA:

_____

_____

_____

_____

_____

■ WHAT INFORMATION OR IDEAS DISCUSSED IN THIS ARTICLE ARE ALSO DISCUSSED IN YOUR TEXTBOOK OR OTHER READING YOU HAVE DONE? LIST THE TEXTBOOK CHAPTERS AND PAGE NUMBERS:

_____

_____

_____

_____

_____

_____

_____

■ LIST ANY EXAMPLES OF BIAS OR FAULTY REASONING THAT YOU FOUND IN THE ARTICLE:

_____

_____

_____

_____

■ LIST ANY NEW TERMS/CONCEPTS THAT WERE DISCUSSED IN THE ARTICLE AND WRITE A SHORT DEFINITION:

_____

_____

_____

_____

*Your instructor may require you to use this Annual Editions Article Review Form in any number of ways: for articles that are assigned, for extra credit, as a tool to assist in developing assigned papers, or simply for your own reference. Even if it is not required, we encourage you to photocopy and use this page; you'll find that reflecting on the articles will greatly enhance the information from your text.

ANNUAL EDITIONS:
HUMAN DEVELOPMENT 96/97
Article Rating Form

Here is an opportunity for you to have direct input into the next revision of this volume. We would like you to rate each of the 51 articles listed below, using the following scale:

1. Excellent: should definitely be retained
2. Above average: should probably be retained
3. Below average: should probably be deleted
4. Poor: should definitely be deleted

Your ratings will play a vital part in the next revision. So please mail this prepaid form to us just as soon as you complete it.
Thanks for your help!

Annual Editions revisions depend on two major opinion sources: one is our Advisory Board, listed in the front of this volume, which works with us in scanning the thousands of articles published in the public press each year; the other is you—the person actually using the book. Please help us and the users of the next edition by completing the prepaid article rating form on this page and returning it to us. Thank you.

Rating

Article

1. Biologists Find Key Genes That Shape Patterning of Embryos
2. How Far Should We Push Mother Nature?
3. Choosing a Perfect Child
4. Eugenics Revisited
5. Cocaine-Exposed Infants: Myths and Misunderstandings
6. War Babies
7. When a Pregnant Woman Drinks
8. Sperm under Siege
9. A New Perspective on Cognitive Development in Infancy
10. The Amazing Minds of Infants
11. The Realistic View of Biology and Behavior
12. Mental Health for Babies: What Do Theory and Research Teach Us?
13. Home Visiting Programs and the Health and Development of Young Children
14. "I Forget"
15. Assertiveness vs. Aggressiveness: What's the Difference?
16. It's Magical! It's Malleable! It's . . . Memory
17. DNA-Environment Mix Forms Intellectual Fate
18. The Good, the Bad, and the Difference
19. Life in Overdrive
20. Bell, Book, and Scandal
21. The AAUW Report: How Schools Shortchange Girls
22. Nurturing Creativity in All Your Students
23. Multicultural Education: A Challenge for Special Educators

Rating

Article

24. The Lifelong Impact of Adoption
25. Bringing Up Father
26. Sibling Connections
27. Yours, Mine, and Ours
28. The Lasting Effects of Child Maltreatment
29. Your Loving Touch
30. The EQ Factor
31. Alienation and the Four Worlds of Childhood
32. Why Kids Have a Lot to Cry About
33. The Miracle of Resiliency
34. Televised Violence and Kids: A Public Health Problem?
35. The Skin We're In
36. Adolescence: Whose Hell Is It?
37. Teenage Turning Point
38. HIV Infected Youth Speaks about Needs for Support and Health Care
39. Psychotrends: Taking Stock of Tomorrow's Family and Sexuality
40. Is There Love after Baby?
41. Back Off!
42. When Violence Hits Home
43. Man's World, Woman's World? Brain Studies Point to Differences
44. The New Middle Age
45. The Estrogen Dilemma
46. Midlife Myths
47. Learning to Love (Gulp!) Growing Old
48. Unlocking the Secrets of Aging
49. Grandparent Development and Influence
50. Aging with Attitude
51. The Solace of Patterns

(Continued on next page)

ABOUT YOU

Name _____ Date _____
Are you a teacher? ❑ Or student? ❑
Your School Name _____
Department _____
Address _____
City _____ State _____ Zip _____
School Telephone # _____

YOUR COMMENTS ARE IMPORTANT TO US!

Please fill in the following information:

For which course did you use this book? _____
Did you use a text with this Annual Edition? ❑ yes ❑ no
The title of the text? _____
What are your general reactions to the Annual Editions concept?

Have you read any particular articles recently that you think should be included in the next edition?

Are there any articles you feel should be replaced in the next edition? Why?

Are there other areas that you feel would utilize an Annual Edition?

May we contact you for editorial input?

May we quote you from above?

ANNUAL EDITIONS: HUMAN DEVELOPMENT 96/97

| **BUSINESS REPLY MAIL** | | |
| First Class | Permit No. 84 | Guilford, CT |

Postage will be paid by addressee

**Dushkin Publishing Group/
Brown & Benchmark Publishers**
Sluice Dock
Guilford, Connecticut 06437

No Postage
Necessary
if Mailed
in the
United States